Kibbutz Utopia and Politics

The Life and Times of Meir Yaari 1897–1987

Israel: Society, Culture and History

Series Editor: Yaacov Yadgar (Bar-Ilan University, Ramat Gan)

Editorial Board

Alan Dowty
(University of Notre Dame, South Bend, Indiana), Political Science and Middle Eastern Studies

Tamar Katriel
(University of Haifa, Haifa), Communication, Ethnography

David N. Myers
(University of California, Los Angeles), Jewish History

Avi Sagi
(Bar-Ilan University, Ramat Gan), Hermeneutics, Cultural studies, and Philosophy

Yael Zerubavel
(Rutgers University, New Brunswick), Jewish Studies and History

Kibbutz
Utopia and Politics

The Life and Times of Meir Yaari 1897–1987

Aviva Halamish

Translated from the Hebrew by **Lenn Schramm**

Boston
2017

This book was originally published in Hebrew by Am Oved Publishers, Tel Aviv:
Meir Yaari, biographiya qibbutzit: Ḥamishim ha-shanim ha-rishonot, 1897–1947
[Meir Yaari, a Collective Biography: The First Fifty Years, 1897–1947], 2009.
Meir Yaari, ha-admor mi-Merḥavya: Shenot ha-medinah [Meir Yaari, the Rebbe from Merḥavia: The State Years], 2013.

The publication of the English edition was made possible in part by a contribution from the veteran members of Mapam branch in Kiryat Chaim.

Library of Congress Cataloging-in-Publication Data

Names: Halamish, Aviva.

Title: Kibbutz, utopia and politics : the life and times of Meir Yaari, 1897-1987 / Aviva Halamish ; translated from the Hebrew by Lenn Schramm.

Other titles: Me'ir Ya'ari, biographiya qibbutzit: hamishim ha-shanim ha-rishonot, 1897–1947; Me'ir Ya'ari ha-'admor mi-Merhavya – shnot ha-medina.

Description: Brighton, MA: Academic Studies Press, 2017.

Series: Israel: society, culture, and history | Includes bibliographical references and index.

Identifiers: LCCN 2017012850 (print) | LCCN 2017013938 (ebook) | ISBN 9781618116253 (e-book) | ISBN 9781618119834

Subjects: LCSH: Yaari, Meir, 1897-1987. | Labor Zionists—Biography. | Halutzim—Biography. | Mifleget ha-po'alim ha-me'uhedet (Israel) | Shomer ha-tsa'ir (Organization: Israel) | Kibuts ha-artsi ha-shomer ha-tsa'ir (Israel) | Labor Zionism—Israel. | BISAC: HISTORY / Jewish. | BIOGRAPHY & AUTOBIOGRAPHY / Political.

Classification: LCC DS151.Y25 (ebook) | LCC DS151.Y25 H3513 2017 (print) | DDC 307.77/6092 [B] —dc23

LC record available at https://lccn.loc.gov/2017012850

©Academic Studies Press, 2017
Book design by Kryon Publishing, www.kryonpublishing.com

Cover illustration: Yuval Danieli, "Tower" (detail), industrial paint on plywood, 80X60cm, 1998. Courtesy of the artist.

Published by Academic Studies Press in 2017
Academic Studies Press
28 Montfern Avenue
Brighton, MA 02135, USA
P: (617)782-6290
F: (857)241-3149
press@academicstudiespress.com
www.academicstudiespress.com

The publication of this book is supported by the Borderlines Foundation for Academic Studies.

In loving memory of my parents,
Mordechai and Hannah Halamish (Flint)

Contents

Introduction		ix
Chapter 1	Reisha	1
Chapter 2	Vienna	11
Chapter 3	Bitaniyya Illit	25
Chapter 4	Founding a Kibbutz Movement	49
Chapter 5	A Wife and Helpmate	71
Chapter 6	Ideological Collectivism	94
Chapter 7	Facing the Catastrophe	120
Chapter 8	Facing the Forces of Tomorrow	140
Chapter 9	A Gaping Abyss	170
Chapter 10	Against the Current	190
Chapter 11	From Military Glory to Marking Time in the Opposition	213
Chapter 12	Unrequited Love	244
Chapter 13	In the Shadow of Big Brother	271
Chapter 14	The Kibbutz during the Transition from Yishuv to State	290
Chapter 15	For Zionism, for Socialism, for the Brotherhood of the Nations—and in That Order	309
Chapter 16	Fractured Beliefs	335

Chapter 17	The Rebellion of the Sons	353
Chapter 18	A Dove with Folded Wings	392
Chapter 19	Twilight	415
Chapter 20	Epilogue	440
Bibliography		459
Index		471

List of illustrations

1. Yaari wearing Austrian army uniform, 1917. — 24
2. Meir Yaari, his wife Anda and their daughter Rachel, 1924. — 70
3. The presidium table at the fourth World Convention of Hashomer Hatza'ir. — 119
4. Yaari with members of Hasomer Hatza'ir youth movement at the Fernwald DP Camp. — 189
5. Yaari with Yaakov Hazan. — 243
6. Yaari at his office, 1950s. — 289
7. Meir and Anda with members of their Kibbutz. — 308
8. Yaari and Arab members of Mapam. — 334
9. Yaari with Jean-Paul Sartre and Simone de Beauvoir. — 352
10. The extended Yaari family, Merḥavia 1960. — 391
11. Meir Yaari with David Ben-Gurion, Yitzhak Tabenkin and Aharon Beker. — 414
12. Yaari's 80th birthday party. — 439

Introduction

The life of Meir Yaari, the leader of Hashomer Hatza'ir, spanned a full nine decades: 1897 to 1987. He headed a movement that encompassed three different, although related, organizations. The first was the *youth movement*, which was founded in Eastern Europe before the First World War. By 1939, it had 70,000 members in hundreds of branches in 22 countries. The second was the *kibbutz movement*, Kibbutz Artzi (KA), established in 1927 as the countrywide framework for the agricultural settlements associated with that movement, which was one of the pillars of collective settlement in Palestine. By the end of the twentieth century, it had 85 affiliated kibbutzim all over Israel. Hashomer Hatza'ir was also a *political party*, known after 1948 as the United Workers' Party or Mapam. In the first national elections (in 1949), it won 19 seats and became the second-largest faction in the Knesset. But by the time of the first general election after Yaari's passing, it won only three seats and was eventually folded into Meretz when the latter was established.

Even though Yaari never stood at the helm of the ship of state, for many years the movement he headed was a partner in fateful and transformative processes. Its disagreements with the central current of the Zionist and Labor movements and its oppositionist positions did not prevent Hashomer Hatza'ir from taking an active part in shaping the history of the people and the land: aliyah, settlement, and defense in mandatory Palestine and then independent Israel, the organization of resistance and revolt in the ghettos of Nazi-occupied Eastern Europe, and the *beriḥah*—the postwar transfer of Holocaust survivors to DP camps in Germany, Austria, and Italy and their subsequent attempts to reach Palestine.

Before the establishment of the State, Hashomer Hatza'ir was firmly in the political opposition. But the truth is that both then and after independence, it was part of the camp of builders and fighters, a full partner in and contributor to the Zionist enterprise. After that, and within a few years, Mapam was reduced to a small and not particularly influential party; Yaari was left to respond to developments rather than shape them. He frequently expressed his opinion on a broad spectrum of political, social, and personal topics—on the kibbutz, the party, Israel, and the world. The written record he left behind is valuable not only for the study of the movement he headed, but also as a reflection of events in Israel and abroad; it offers instructive lessons and traces key lines in the history of the Jewish people from the end of the First World War until shortly before the first Intifada and the collapse of the Soviet Union (Yaari died in February 1987).

The impact of the Hashomer Hatza'ir youth movement and KA on Israeli society transcends their size and far exceeds Mapam's parliamentary strength. Many Israelis see their period of membership in the youth movement or enrollment in KA educational institutions as a formative chapter in their lives. They recall the stirring years of youth and the high hopes of repairing the world on the personal, national, and societal levels with great nostalgia. Yaari was the paramount leader of this movement for half a century.

Leadership was the main axis of Meir Yaari's life and personality. This book's primary goal is to solve the riddle of his leadership. How did he reach the pinnacle of Hashomer Hatza'ir and how did he maintain his position there for so many years? Why did people remain loyal to him and accept, or even create, an identification of leader and movement that bordered on a cult of personality, while the members themselves minimized their own importance? When did the dissonance between the leader and his flock begin? And once it began—how did Yaari retain his status even after he no longer met his followers' expectations?

This biography's point of departure is that the finished product has a meaning beyond the life story of its protagonist, that reconstructing his life story can help us understand broader phenomena and processes, and that his story can teach us not only about the man himself, but also about the broader picture—the movement he led, the society in which he lived and worked, and the history of the Jewish people and the State of Israel. The biography of a leader is also inescapably the story of those he led. The relationship between the hero of a biography and the period and society in which he worked is also related to the eternal dilemma of "personality and history." It is impossible to understand events exclusively through the lens of historical circumstances or only through that of the individual. The story of Hashomer Hatza'ir is incomplete and in fact meaningless without Yaari. The secret of his leadership cannot be unlocked unless we identify which of his followers' needs and passions he satisfied. Just as Yaari's leadership is central to the history of Hashomer Hatza'ir, it is essential to understand the collective he led in order to comprehend the man's own life. This book does not pretend to recount the full story of Hashomer Hatza'ir, but it does propose—albeit indirectly and implicitly—a factual narrative and interpretation that is different from and complementary to the history of Hashomer Hatza'ir.

Writing the biography of a leader requires finding the proper balance between the stories of the subject and of the collective he headed. Further, a balance must be struck between the public sphere—the man as leader—and the private space of his personal life and intimate relationships, while avoiding the trap of slipping into voyeurism. More details of Yaari's personal life and his intimate thoughts and statements on erotic matters are in the public record than those of just about any other Israeli leader; they are crucial to understanding his leadership. His written and oral legacy includes intimate personal details that cannot be ignored because of their importance regarding the big picture, even though, in isolation, they are liable to come off as juicy morsels that the writer could not resist. There is another dilemma with regard to the boundary between the private and the public: Yaari was beset by illness from his twenties, and there is no avoiding the impact of his health on his ability to function and his status as a leader.

Due diligence requires me to state that I come from a family that was wholly Mapam in body and soul. I was a member of the Hashomer Hatza'ir youth movement, of Mapam, and of Kibbutz Lahav, which belongs to Kibbutz Artzi. I believe that my own biography allows me to live in both worlds. On the one hand, I know the movement from the inside, with its ideological, social, and cultural codes. On the other hand, the passage of time has given me enough emotional distance to preclude the suspicion that this is the work of a "court historian" or—perish the thought—just the opposite, someone with accounts to settle. I will not deny, however, that I approached this project with a fond feeling for the movement, along with a curiosity that was not only professional.

Hashomer Hatza'ir is one of the most intensively researched topics in the history of Zionism, the Yishuv, and the State of Israel. There is no shortage of studies, mainly about the youth movement and Kibbutz Artzi—in large measure thanks to the movement's rich archives, with its cordial and highly capable professional staff. Entering a field that has already been plowed many times over has some advantages, but also poses some difficulties. You can draw on previous works, but frequently must also correct inaccuracies and wrestle with presentations and interpretations you cannot accept. This biography breaks new ground in areas that have never been addressed, adds depth and dimensions to familiar topics, and offers previously unknown details and new interpretations. It also expands the prevailing understanding of the kibbutz. Many English-language studies and books on the kibbutz consider its sociological, anthropological, economic, and educational aspects, but there is an unfortunate dearth of works on the kibbutz written with a historical perspective and methodology.

I vacillated about interviewing people who knew Yaari—relatives, members of Kibbutz Merḥavia, coworkers and colleagues—and ultimately decided against it. By the time I began my research, there were no longer any living witnesses to Yaari's childhood, adolescence, and young adulthood—periods from which almost no authentic materials remain. This meant that I had to rely mainly on his memoirs to reconstruct the events of those years. There were only a few survivors from the pre-State years, and I was afraid that biology might dictate history and the content of the biography. The balance was further tipped by the interminable hours that would have been necessary to collect testimonies and conduct interviews, and by my own experience, and that of my colleagues, that the fruits of this effort tend to be meager and problematic, due to the intrinsic weakness of retrospective interviews and memories of times long past. Moreover, I frequently discovered that the testimonies my colleagues relied on contradicted the written record, or that the information elicited in these interviews was already available and more vivid (and, in my opinion, more reliable) in documents contemporary with the events themselves. The other, and most important, reason for my decision was the ample materials already available: documents in archives and texts written and/or printed in real time, including many intended as no more than innocent chatter. This effectively eliminated the need to rely on testimonies dimmed by the distance of time. Yaari himself left behind abundant materials and deserves special thanks for his assistance in the writing of his biography.

The time has come to enrich the impressive scholarly mosaic of the history of Hashomer Hatza'ir with the biography of its most important leader (the life of Yaakov Hazan, Yaari's partner at the head of the movement, has already been written by Zeev Tzahor). Biographies have become an important, perhaps even the primary, source of historical information for the public at large and seem to be enjoying a new vogue on bookshelves around the world.

Like most biographies, this book moves along the time axis, from the early years of the twentieth century in Galicia through the mid-1980s in Israel. In addition to telling the story of Yaari and his movement, this book is also a narrative, one of many, of the history of the Jewish people in the twentieth century. It discusses pivotal issues in the development of the Yishuv and Israeli society, such as the friction between Zionism and socialism, including the successive incarnations of the attitude towards the Soviet Union, the Arab question, foreign and defense policy, the class struggle, the absorption of new immigrants in towns and kibbutzim, generation gaps and conflicts, and the symbiotic and painful relationship between the Diaspora and the Yishuv. Throughout, the biography blends the individual and collective perspectives and never loses sight of the tension between ideology and reality.

✳✳✳

It is a great pleasure for me to express my heartfelt appreciation of all those who assisted me during the long journey of research, writing, and publication of this work, first in Hebrew and now in the English edition.

The long list begins with Dr. Shlomo Shaltiel, who initiated the proposal that I write a biography of Meir Yaari when he served as the director of research and publications at Yad Yaari, and who provided staunch support throughout all stages of the project. Next comes Prof. Matityahu Mintz, of blessed memory, for his learned suggestions and constant encouragement all along the road.

I would like to thank the staff of the Hashomer Hatza'ir Archives at Givat Haviva, whose professionalism, sympathy, and boundless willingness to help are unequaled; the director of the archives at Kibbutz Merhavia, Zvia Reil, the staff of the Pinhas Lavon Labor Archives, and the dedicated and professional librarians of the Open University of Israel—especially their director, Dr. Hava Mustigman. Special thanks to Yuval Danieli for his professional and cordial assistance in selecting the pictures and for the permit to use his illustration on the cover.

I am grateful to the Havatzelet group for its funding of my research and of the publication in Hebrew, and to the Memorial Foundation for Jewish Culture. I owe special thanks to the veterans of the Mapam branch in Kiryat Chaim for their generous contribution to defraying the costs of the translation into English, and to Dudu Amitay and Netta Shapira, the director and research coordinator, respectively, of Yad Yaari, who were instrumental in obtaining that grant.

Most of the first volume of the Hebrew edition was written when I was a visiting scholar at the Taub Center for Israel Studies at New York University, headed by Prof. Ron Zweig. Most of the second volume was produced while I was a visiting professor at the Schusterman Center for Israel Studies at Brandeis University, headed by Prof. Ilan Troen. I thank both of them for their cordial hospitality. So too Prof. Yael Zerubavel, the founding director of the Allen and Joan Bildner Center for the Study of Jewish Life at Rutgers University; the bulk of the revisions of the Hebrew book to serve as the basis for the English edition were made during my sabbatical there.

This is the place to acknowledge the efforts of Prof. Eli Shaltiel, the editor of the Ofakim Library series of Am Oved Publishers, and all those whose labors helped produce the two volumes of the Hebrew edition.

Words cannot express my gratitude to Lenn Schramm (assisted, in the earlier chapters, by Diana File) for his highly professional translation. The ultimate compliment I can pay is that the English version is often superior to the original.

My sincere thanks to the people at Academic Studies Press for their help in publishing the English version of this book, and most of all to Gregg Stern, Sara Libby Robinson, and Kira Nemirovsky.

I must not omit all the friends who showed unremitting interest in my work, and especially Dahlia and Ricky Friedman, who are like my own family and made my months in New York so pleasant; Linda Rubin, the director of the New York office of Givat Haviva; and Prof. Pnina Lahav of Boston University and Dr. Yoel Rappel and his wife, Dorit, for their friendship and assistance while I was in Boston.

My family showered me with support and love throughout the long journey. My thanks and love to you, Raya, Amos, Danny, Anat, Gili, and Keren, and, dearest of all, my children, Ilan and Maya, and grandchildren, Neil and Harel.

I dedicate this book, with boundless gratitude, esteem, and love, to my parents, Hannah (*née* Maass) and Mordechai Halamish (Flint).

CHAPTER 1
Reisha

Meir, the second son of Frieda and Chaim Wald, was born on April 25, 1897 (or perhaps a day or two earlier), in Kańczuga, a small town in western Galicia.¹ Most of its 6,000 residents were Jewish. When he was about six months old, Meir's family moved to Rzeszów, about 35 kilometers west of Kańczuga and closer to Krakow. Rzeszów, known as "Reisha" in Yiddish, had about 7,000 Jews at the time, who made up more than a third of its population.²

Rzeszów lies in the heart of a broad and level valley that surrounds the winding Wisłok River. The distant horizon is marked by the Carpathian Mountains to the south and by gently rolling wooded hills to the north. Many buildings erected before the Second World War survive; some have been extensively renovated. Two impressive synagogues still stand in the center of town, but their interiors have been modified so extensively that their original purpose is no longer evident. Today they house the municipal archives and are used for cultural activities. In the early twenty-first century, there are no Jews in Rzeszów.

Galicia came under Austrian rule in 1772, after the First Partition of Poland. The San River separated its western section, whose metropolis was Krakow and which had a largely Polish population, from the predominantly Ukrainian eastern half, whose capital was Lwów (also known as Lemberg and today referred to as Lviv). Substantial Jewish

---

1 His tombstone at Kibbutz Merḥavia bears the dates 21 Nisan 5657 and April 25, 1897, which actually fell two days apart. On the official Knesset website, his birth date is given as April 24. See http://knesset.gov.il/mk/eng/mk_eng.asp?mk_individual_id_t=433.
2 *Encyclopaedia Judaica*, s.v. "Rzeszow"; Yaari-Wald, *Qehillat Reyshe*, 58.

minorities lived in both parts of Galicia. The Jews enjoyed equal rights in some domains, including the right to vote, after Austria granted Galicia limited autonomy in 1861; public education was open to Jews at all levels. The official language was German, but the local vernaculars—Polish in the west and Ukrainian in the east—enjoyed a similar status.

The Wald family home, a one-story structure with a roof of wooden tiles and tar, comprised living quarters, a kitchen, and a shop. Meir Yaari's earliest memory took place there. He was two years old, lying in his cradle. His brother Moshe, who was four, rocked him so vigorously that the bed arced from wall to wall and the toddler almost died of fright.[3]

The presence of an older brother, with all that this implied in a Jewish family in Eastern Europe, was the single greatest influence on the development of the Wald family's second son. At family meals, both on weekdays and festive Friday night dinners, the food was served in a fixed order. The mother dished out the finest portion to the father and the next to the oldest son; younger siblings had to be satisfied with a smaller and less filling portion.[4] This preference for the firstborn son and Meir's resentment of that favoritism clouded the relations between the two brothers. When they were temporarily forced to share a bed, they did not exchange a single word for more than a year. Their relationship was marked by estrangement, misunderstandings, and poor communications for many years, until they were both old men. Meir always saw Moshe as a rival and never stopped begrudging him the preferential treatment he received from their parents.

Meir had a much closer relationship with his brother Tuvia, ten years his junior. This relationship was characterized by Tuvia's lifelong admiration of his older brother. The Wald family was completed by a daughter, born when Meir was about 15. Somehow the event did not

---

3 This section is based on the memoirs that Yaari wrote or dictated at various times in his life. They are, in chronological order: (1) interview with Meir Yaari, Oct. 18, 1975, HHA, 95-7.3(1); (2) Yaari, "Memoirs" (1980), KMA, MYF, 8(3); (3) Yaari, "Memoirs" (1981), ibid.; (4) Yaari, "Memoirs" (autograph manuscript), ibid.; (5) Natan Shaham interview with Meir Yaari, Sept. 3, 1983 (presumed date), Yad Yaari; (6) Yaari's oral remarks, Feb. 27, 1984, KMA, MYF, 8(2); (7) Zait and Shamir, *Meir Yaari*, 13–26.
4 Conversation with Yaari's daughter, Rachel Grol-Yaari, Merḥavia, Feb. 2, 2000.

leave much of an impression on him. He failed to mention her birth in his memoirs and I have not found a single document in which he refers to her by name. When he did talk about her many years later, and then only as an afterthought, he could not even remember her exact age. This sister, whose name was Esther, joined the Hashomer Hatza'ir youth movement. When Yaari visited Rzeszów in the 1920s, he found her to be a fine and diligent girl with a strong character. After his efforts to help her obtain an *aliyah* certificate proved fruitless, she emigrated to the United States in the early 1930s.[5] Meir and Esther did not remain in close contact. After their mother's death, they waged a fierce quarrel over her estate, leading to a total rift between them.[6]

During Meir's early childhood, only his grandmother showered him with a love that was not dimmed by the shadow of his elder brother. She was an imposing woman, full of self-confidence. Young Meir bonded to her with every fiber of his being. She often took her favorite grandson into bed with her, to help him fall asleep. One night, when he was four, she woke him up. Between her groans she told him to run to the neighbors and tell them that she was dying. The panic-stricken child jumped out of bed, ran as fast as he could, and started banging on the neighbors' doors: "Jews, save us! Grandma is dying!" By the time he returned to her house, it was full of people and she was no longer among the living. Meir cried bitterly for many hours.[7]

This terrifying experience continued to haunt the boy. More than once, while walking down the street, her image suddenly appeared in front of him, and Meir swooned in horror as she approached. Passersby would call his parents, who tried to revive him by slapping his cheeks and patting him on the back. At his mother's initiative (his father was not enthusiastic about the idea), his parents contacted the local Hassidic rebbe, who lived not far from them, to see if he could help their child. Rabbi Eliezr'l, a handsome man who somewhat resembled Tolstoy, with an impressive and carefully trimmed beard and shining blue eyes, took the child on his lap

---

5 Yaari to the central office of Hashomer Hatza'ir in Galicia, Jan. 7, 1932, KMA, MYF, 1(2).
6 Meir to Anda, Nov. 8, 1933, KMA, MYF, 5(2).
7 Yaari, interview in *Al Hamishmar*, undated, in HHA, 95-7.3(2); "Memoirs" [1979], KMA, MYF, 8(3).

and issued a firm decree: "You will never see your grandmother coming towards you again and you will not faint." And so it was! The rebbe of Reisha had never heard of psychoanalysis, hypnosis, or suggestion, but nonetheless—that is how Yaari explained it many years later—his luminous and suggestive personality healed the child's complex.[8]

The Wald family home was situated at the end of a side street, in front of a two-story building that also belonged to the family. The latter was rented out to various tenants, mainly merchants and artisans, some of whom were alcoholics and given to violence. Another source of income was the shop attached to their home, which was patronized by both Jews and Gentiles. All of them trusted "Pan Wald;" according to Yaari's childhood memories, his father's appearance reminded his Christian neighbors of popular illustrations of Jesus. Frieda managed the store, while Chaim saw to the difficult household tasks, such as chopping wood, repairing the roof, and so on.

Chaim Wald had enjoyed the reputation of a Talmudic prodigy. As such he was considered a good match by Rabbi Yankel Holoshitzer, who wanted a scholar for his daughter Frieda. She, in turn, had an impressive lineage, tracing back to Rebbe Elimelech of Lyzhansk (1717–1787), author of the Hassidic classic *Noam Elimelech*. Yaari often mentioned, with pride, that Rabbi Elimelech was his great-great grandfather, a family connection that, being matrilineal, is difficult to trace. In a moment of candor, Yaari admitted that he could neither confirm nor deny the relationship. After his brother Moshe, the family (and town) historian, told him that there was insufficient documentation of their descent from Rabbi Elimelech, Yaari stopped boasting of it.[9]

Chaim was a handsome man, his beautiful eyes soft as velvet and somewhat dreamy.[10] He took meticulous care of his hair and beard and made sure that his shirt collar was always clean and ironed. He was observant, but not a Hassid. Along with a group of high school, university, and yeshiva students, all younger than him, Wald senior

---

8   Zait and Shamir, *Meir Yaari*, 21.
9   Natan Shaham interview with Meir Yaari, Sept. 3, 1983; Yaari to S. Atir, July 9, 1978, HHA, 7-95.1(1); Yaari, *Al Hamishmar*, Aug. 28, 1970.
10 I have been unable to locate a photograph, so the description is based on his son's recollection.

established a prayer hall for "the progressives." They did not hire a professional cantor. Instead, he filled the position and regaled the congregants with his sweet voice.[11] He was a charismatic leader; the local Jews would come listen to him speak in the city square and tell him their troubles. He engaged in dialogue with his Christian neighbors, published a Yiddish newspaper, the *Reisher folks-tzaytung*, and was active in Zionist circles. This involvement began in the time of the Ḥovevei Zion, before Herzl arrived on the scene. In the early years of the twentieth century he aligned himself with the "Zion Zionists" who opposed the Uganda scheme.[12] Yaari admired his father, appreciated his liberal attitude towards his sons, and respected his work as a Jewish civic leader. But all his stories and memories over the years were shadowed by the gnawing and painful complaint that his father had favored the eldest son, Moshe.

Chaim Wald was only 51 when he succumbed to tuberculosis of the throat in 1924. The town paid him impressive last honors.[13] At three in the afternoon, a large crowd gathered in front of the synagogue for the eulogies. At the mayor's orders, the streetlamps along the route of the funeral procession were draped in black crepe and stores were shuttered. Many people walked behind the coffin, led by the widow, the youngest son Tuvia, and the daughter, Esther. Moshe and Meir were both already in Palestine at this time. Chaim was buried next to his father, Rabbi Joseph Wald, who had passed away in 1881. The funeral remained a topic of conversation in the town for weeks. On the first anniversary of his father's death, Meir visited Rzeszów and made his mother happy by leading the services wrapped in a *tallit*.[14]

Meir was enrolled in a *heder* when he turned three. Between ten and fifteen children were crowded into a small room where the educational focus was rote memorization, with no attempt at understanding the text. The teacher maintained discipline with blows from a

---

11 Zait and Shamir, *Meir Yaari*, 22 and 207.
12 The Uganda scheme was a plan to give a portion of British East Africa to the Jewish people as a homeland. The plan was supported by Theodor Herzl, who proposed it to the Zionist Congress as a temporary refuge for European Jews facing antisemitism.
13 Undated letter in Yiddish from Chaim Fish; trans. by Avraham Goren, KMA, MYF, 5(4).
14 Sadan, *Alufi u-meyuda'i*, 204.

stick. One day, gathering his courage, Meir broke the stick and sent it flying. Even though he was expelled from the *heder*, his parents did not scold him for this act. He had fonder memories of his other teachers. Meir's particular favorite was the man who taught him the Torah with Rashi's commentary and the Aramaic translation (Onkelos), as well as Mishnah. The child walked home alone at the end of the school day. In the winter, when it got dark early, he walked slowly, lighting his way with a lantern.

Meir kept his side locks until he was eight, even though they were a source of much grief. He tried tucking them behind his ears as he walked to school, but the non-Jewish bullies discovered the ruse and beat him up. When he attended public school, he faced more trials as a Jew. For example, when his class was taken to visit the estate of Count Potocki, not far from Rzeszów, the pupils were treated to a sumptuous meal, with delicacies that included roast pork. It was the first time Meir had tasted this forbidden food. He was immediately overcome by nausea and ran outside to vomit.

Because Meir was not a brilliant student, his father decided that the boy would continue his education in a vocational setting rather than an academic high school. His mother's words on this occasion were like a dagger in his heart: "One doctor in the family is enough!" she said, referring to her older son, Moshe.[15] Accordingly, when Meir reached bar mitzvah age he was sent off to a technical school in Krakow, where he boarded with a tailor's family. The location had one advantage in his view: it was situated above the Jewish theater. When he could not sleep because of the romances being conducted by the landlord's two daughters and the fleas in the bedclothes, Meir would go downstairs, stand outside the window looking into the theater, and watch the performances. He did not do well in school. A constant tremor in his hands prevented him from sketching or engaging in the various crafts that required manual dexterity. His living conditions made matters worse. After several frustrating months, during which he lost weight, the young boy gathered his things and started walking home, 180 kilometers away. When he passed through the town of Bochnia, an acquaintance of his father recognized him and sent a telegram

---

15 Zait and Shamir, *Meir Yaari*, 25.

to Reisha. His father, moved to tears, wasted no time coming to collect his son. Before his death, Chaim sent Meir a letter in which he apologized for the Krakow episode.[16] Many years later, when Yaari wrote his memoirs, "Why were my parents so wrong about me?" would be the title he affixed to the chapter on his relationship with his parents.[17]

After Yaari returned to Reisha, his brother Moshe helped him study Latin, Greek, and mathematics in preparation for the high-school entrance exams. In that institution, too, he does not seem to have been a great student. In the subjects that he really enjoyed—Polish literature and history—he excelled, but he was not quick to answer questions; in other subjects, such as geometry and drawing, he did poorly, because he could not draw a straight line.

Between home, high school, and the youth movement, Meir mastered Yiddish, German, Polish, and Hebrew—speaking, reading, and writing. Later he also learned to read and write English.[18]

The First World War cut short his high-school career at the end of the third year. Because he did not complete the highest grade, he was not eligible for a matriculation certificate; he received it later, though, thanks to his military service.

Formal education was the most painful subject in Yaari's relationship with his parents and older brother. When he was almost 80, he wrote to Moshe: "Our parents, particularly Father, may he rest in peace, believed not only that you are the oldest son, but also that you were born for greatness. They did not really believe in my abilities or future prospects."[19] In fact, the Wald family's attitude towards educating their children was the norm among Eastern European Jews of that generation. It was customary to provide a higher education for at least one son, typically the oldest. Moshe graduated high school, where, unlike Meir, he shone in every subject. He continued on to university and eventually earned a doctorate.

When and how did Yaari become a Zionist? In his memoirs, he states that as a three-year-old, when he accompanied his father to the branch of the Zionist Association in Reisha, he saw a picture of Herzl

---

16 Yaari, "Memoirs," Feb. 27, 1984, KMA, MYF, 8(2).
17 Yaari, "Memoirs" (1980), KMA, MYF, 8(3), 17.
18 Kibbutz Merhavia membership card, dated Jan. 1 1944, KMA, MYF, 2(14).
19 Yaari to Dr. Moshe Yaari, Aug. 20, 1976, KMA, MYF, 5(4).

on the wall, looked into his deep eyes, fell in love with the image, and became "a Zionist who adored Herzl."[20] More than ten years after this seminal experience, he joined a Zionist youth movement. His first steps in the movement followed the lead of his older brother, who by then was a key member of the Ze'irei Ziyyon association in Reisha.

The first Zionist youth groups in Galicia formed in the late nineteenth century and soon laid the foundations for what later evolved into Ze'irei Ziyyon. By the end of 1911, there were 65 such groups all over the province, including Reisha.[21] Their 1,274 members were young Jewish high-school students, who engaged mainly in activities of an intellectual nature. They studied Hebrew intensively, along with the annals of the Jewish people, Zionist theory and history, the geography of Eretz Israel, Yiddish literature, and topics related to the Jewish festivals. The young people also made excursions to the mountains, played soccer, went ice-skating, did calisthenics, and sang in a choir. Four points should be emphasized: the Ze'irei Ziyyon groups were intended for Jewish students of high-school age and older, they were for boys only, the activities were of an intellectual nature, and the members did not think of taking concrete steps to realize their Zionism.

Not everyone was happy with these aspects of Ze'irei Ziyyon, leaving ample room for spontaneous initiatives by young Jews in Galicia, based on the scouting model. The first of these groups, Dror, coalesced in Lwów, under the leadership of Henrik (Zvi) Sterner.[22] Sterner was directed to his new path by the Polish translation (published in 1911) of Robert Baden-Powell's *Scouting for Boys*. In the wake of the success of Dror in Lwów, Sterner organized groups based on Baden-Powell's ideas in other cities and promulgated rules for them. He and the other founders of the new organization were influenced by the memorial book, *Yizkor*, published by the Hashomer self-defense organization in Palestine, which reached Galicia two years after its original Hebrew

---

20 Yaari, "Memoirs" (autograph manuscript), KMA, MYF, 8(3).
21 The discussion of Ze'irei Ziyyon is based on Mintz, *Hevlei ne'urim*, 19-30.
22 On the early years of the youth movement Hashomer, see ibid. 31-38, Lamm, *Youth Takes the Lead*, 74-83, 106-108.

edition appeared in 1911.²³ Inspired by that volume, the scouting association in Lwów adopted the name Hashomer (in 1913) and was soon followed by the groups in other towns. When the first convention of the local Hashomer groups in Galicia—fourteen in all—met in March 1914, Sterner was chosen to head the organization.

Hashomer developed a new method for educating youth in the spirit of Zionism and promoting immigration to Palestine. The organization opened its ranks to elementary school pupils of both sexes and placed greater emphasis on physical training and character-building than on content. Both girls and boys studied scouting topics, drilled marching in formation, took hikes in nature, went camping in the Carpathian Mountains, and studied Hebrew, the history of the Jewish people, and the Zionist idea. The educational emphasis was on the collective rather than the individual. The regular activities still took place in sex-segregated troops, but they came into contact in the programs for the entire local group. The members' youth, the mixing of the sexes, and the scouting activities created such a deep sense of collective togetherness that the members of Hashomer could not be satisfied with the purely intellectual activities of Ze'irei Ziyyon when they reached late adolescence. To fill their need, Hashomer expanded its scope and developed programs for teenagers as well. Its educational methods and activities imbued individuals with a sense of social solidarity and a strong attachment to the group. It was no wonder that the organization grew quickly.

From the very beginning, there were major differences, friction, and rivalry between Ze'iri Ziyyon and Hashomer. After all, Sterner's initiative to establish a scouting organization was triggered by his discontent with the former's emphasis on ideology. There were three basic differences between the two organizations. First, Ze'iri Ziyyon focused on intellectual programs and study circles, whereas Hashomer believed that the scouting regime—camping out, excursions in the forests and mountains, drills, and calisthenics—would consolidate the social bond among the members and strengthen their loyalty to the organization and its Jewish-national goals.

---

23 On the memorial book, its content, and the responses to it, see Frankel, "The 'Yizkor' Book."

Secondly, Ze'iri Ziyyon was an organization of high-school students, whereas Hashomer began as an organization of younger children before expanding to include adolescents. Finally, Ze'iri Ziyyon was for boys only, whereas Hashomer was open to girls as well, albeit in separate troops. Ze'iri Ziyyon could not ignore the establishment of the first Scouting groups by Sterner; confronted by the steady growth of Hashomer, it reached the conclusion that cooperation was the order of the day. This direction did not bear fruit until after the start of the First World War, however, when Yaari was already serving in the Austrian Army.

The Ze'iri Ziyyon group in Reisha was called "Jordania." Moshe Wald was one of its leaders; his brother Meir, who joined as a high-school student, served as librarian.[24] In 1913, when he was 16, a Hashomer group was established in the town. When did Meir switch his allegiance to it? Our sources do not provide an unambiguous answer; the main problem is that most of them are retrospective testimonies by Yaari himself. He recalled that, as the librarian of Ze'iri Ziyyon in Reisha, he came across the *Yizkor* book, was deeply impressed, and decided to follow its lead. What attracted him to Hashomer seems to have been primarily its military aspects, deterrence of the Arab gangs, and dedication to defending Jewish lives and property.[25]

In his last year in Reisha, Yaari fell in love with Mina Elfenbein, a young woman with black hair and blue eyes, noted for her intelligence and wit. For about a year, they took hikes outside the city together, held hands when no one was looking, and even kissed once—but never again. His parents were not happy with the relationship, because Mina's father was assimilated, ignorant in Jewish matters, and apathetic to Zionism. Meir and Mina did not keep in close touch after that. During the six or so years that he was in the army and lived in Vienna (before and after his military service), until their final goodbye before he left for Palestine, they exchanged a total of three letters and met only once or twice.[26]

---

24 Mintz, *Hevlei ne'urim*, 237.
25 Yaari, "Memoirs" (1981), KMA, MYF, 8(3), 16.
26 I have not found the letters or any references to them in the archives; this information is based on what Yaari recorded in his later memoirs.

CHAPTER 2
Vienna

On July 28, 1914, Austria-Hungary declared war on Serbia. Within a few months, the conflict had become global, sweeping up millions of people into a whirlpool of battles, conquest, slaughter, suffering, displacement, and life as refugees. The Great War, which was like no war before it, transformed the international order, put values and beliefs to the test, redrew the map of Europe, brought down regimes and rulers, and determined the destiny of people, movements, nations, and countries.

About a month after the start of hostilities, the Russian army invaded Galicia. Between 200,000 and 400,000 Jews, fearing Russian antisemitism, fled to Hungary, Moravia, Bohemia, and Vienna, leaving almost all of their property behind them. Some 137,000 refugees streamed to the metropolis at the start of the war, including 77,000 Jews. Later in the war, following the Russian retreat from Galicia, most of the displaced Jews returned home. Nonetheless, there were still 35,000 Jewish refugees in Vienna in late 1918.[1]

The Wald family split into three groups when the war began. Moshe headed for Vienna to enroll in university. Eight-year-old Tuvia, Esther, who was three or four, and their mother Frieda relocated somewhere slightly more distant from the front lines. Meanwhile, Chaim Wald and his son Meir, then 17, stayed in Reisha. The father continued to work, while his son managed the household, did the shopping, and cooked. During the Russian army's advance on Krakow, when some of the troops passed through Reisha, a band of Cossacks broke into the Wald family home. One of the intruders hurled an iron bar at Chaim, who miraculously escaped unharmed.

---

[1] Piotr Wrobel, "The Jews of Galicia under Austrian-Polish Rule, 1867–1918," http://easteurotopo.org/articles/wrobel/wrobel.pdf [accessed Oct. 23, 2014].

The terrifying experience drove the two men to pack a few belongings and leave Reisha. They picked up Frieda, Tuvia, and Esther from their temporary residence and the entire family made its way to Vienna by train.[2]

The five Walds found a place in the working-class quarter of Floridsdorf, where they sublet rooms from a railway worker who drank heavily and beat his wife. They supported themselves by sewing buttons and braids on Austrian army uniforms. Meir would take the finished goods to the military warehouse in a cart and bring home the pittance paid for the work. After a while he found employment in an ammunition plant in Wöllersdorf, about 50 kilometers from Vienna. He took the factory job far from home primarily to increase his contribution to the family's meager income. It was also an attempt to make his own way and a challenge to the favoritism shown his elder brother. Moshe was continuing his university studies despite the family's financial distress and the trials of the war, which had prevented his younger brother from even completing high school.

Even in wartime Vienna, his older brother continued to overshadow Meir in both the family circle and the youth movement. Moshe Wald was numbered in the first rank of the leadership of Ze'irei Ziyyon in Vienna, while Meir was a rank-and-file member of the Nesher circle—one of the first two Ze'irei Ziyyon groups in Vienna—most of whose members came from Reisha. The group was noted for its intellectual vision, acute thinking, and quest for solutions to the problems of the Jewish people and the world, more than for a unique lifestyle. The leader of the other group, Lilith, was the acclaimed Issachar Reiss.[3] Unlike Yaari's group, Lilith's was marked by youthful romanticism and a strong yearning for the new world in Palestine, and bonded through group singing, nocturnal

---

2 This chapter draws on the following sources, in which there is much duplication and some interdependence: (1) interview with Yaari, Merhavia, Oct. 18, 1975 [interviewer's name not specified], HHA, 95-7.3(1); (2) Yaari interview with Yehuda Karni, undated, ibid.; (3) Yaari's memoirs (1981), KMA, MYF, 8(3); (4) "Meir Yaari: My 70 Years in Hashomer Hatza'ir," transcribed by his secretary, Michael Shapira, Apr. 15, 1983, ibid.; (5) Natan Shaham interview with Meir Yaari, Sept. 3, 1983; (6) Zait and Shamir, *Meir Yaari*, 27–38, 42–43; (7) Shadmi, *Meqorot*, No. 2; (8) letters written by Yaari in those years, cited by Mintz, *Hevlei ne'urim*, 353–360; (9) ibid., 39–81.

3 On Issachar Reiss as the charismatic headmaster of the Tarbut *gymnasium* in Rovno, see Amos Oz, *A Tale of Love and Darkness*, trans. Nicholas de Lange (New York: Houghton Mifflin Harcourt, 2005), 193.

excursions, sessions around bonfires, personal confessions, and strong friendships.[4] During the year he belonged to Nesher, Yaari did not make friends with any of the other members; he does not mention any of them in his memoirs, except for Shlomo Horowitz.

About a year after arriving in Vienna, Yaari—now 18—decided to enlist in the Austrian army. It is not clear whether he was drafted or whether he actually enlisted. If the latter, Yaari probably believed that he would have to serve only one year; in fact, he was not discharged until the war was over. His military service entitled him to a high-school diploma even though he had not completed his last year of studies. The start of his military career, at a school for officer candidates in Austrian Silesia, got off on the wrong foot. He was not well served by his lack of self-confidence and psychological blocks—and perhaps also the fact that he was Jewish. Yaari failed the course and qualified only as a non-commissioned officer. Only at the end of the war was he promoted to sublieutenant.

Yaari served on the front lines for about two-and-a half years. Initially, he was sent to the Russian front. After the Bolshevik Revolution and the collapse of the Eastern Front, he was attached to the forces facing the Italian army in Italy, the Balkans, Montenegro, and the Albanian frontier. When the war ended, his battalion was camped in Sarajevo. Yaari spent many days and nights in the damp trenches (which left him with a nagging case of rheumatism for many years thereafter), and had to cope with all the discomfort and fatigue of a soldier's life. But he never saw actual combat. He encountered many instances of antisemitism, such as the desecration of tombs in a Jewish cemetery. Still, even though he was the only Jewish NCO in a battalion whose commander loathed Jews, he was not directly affected by antisemitism. In photographs from his army years, Yaari is seen with a mane of thick black hair, a resolute expression, thick eyebrows, and set lips. By the end of the war, he had reached his full height of 165.5 centimeters (5' 4").

When Poland regained its independence, at the end of the war, almost all of Galicia was included in its territory. As an officer from Galicia who had just completed his service in the Austrian army, Yaari was now

---

4 Horowitz, *Ha-etmol sheli*, 50.

supposed to be mustered into the Polish army. However, tired of war, broken by military life, and suffering from the effects of rheumatism and malaria, he went AWOL from his unit's bivouac and traveled to visit his family, who had returned to Reisha after the Russian retreat. There he met his prewar girlfriend Mina Elfenbein and exchanged pleasantries with her, but did not tell her about his experiences during the war. She, in turn, did not show great interest in what had happened to him. Yaari spent only a few days in the town of his childhood and adolescence before rushing off to Vienna. He felt that his hasty departure from Reisha had led Mina to have her doubts about their future relationship, and rightly so. One of the explanations that he provided—retrospectively—for his swift departure was his desire to break off with her. Was this the end of their relationship? It is unclear. Mina's attitude towards him and the true nature of their bond remains shrouded in fog. Later, Yaari recounted that when he informed her in 1920 of his decision to leave university and go to Palestine as a pioneer she was taken aback and did not join him, because she did not feel she was capable of living there and doing manual labor. Was that really the case? Or had their relationship already fallen apart, never having been that solid? One way or another, he remembered the refusal by Mina, whom he referred to in his memoirs as "my fiancée," to join him and make aliyah as a real tragedy. Mina stayed in Europe, married a physician, and had two children. All four perished in the Holocaust.[5]

Wearing his military uniform, Yaari made his way from Reisha to Vienna for the second time, with only a tiny sum in his pocket. There had been many changes in the movement since he left the capital three years earlier. Hashomer Hatza'ir had coalesced as a youth movement in Vienna during the First World War, when Yaari was far away at the front. Before the war, Ze'irei Ziyyon and Hashomer competed in the cities and towns where they both had cells. During the war, members of the rival movements found themselves living in close proximity in Vienna. New ties grew up among them, those that already existed grew stronger, and the topic of the future relationship between the two movements came up as a matter of course. Ze'irei Ziyyon's opposition to the scouting model as an educational

---

[5] Yaari's memoirs (1981), KMA, MYF, 8(3), 19.

method faded; when it proposed a merger, the members of Hashomer were quick to agree. Moshe Wald was one of the main negotiators and helped draft the merger agreement that was approved in late 1915. This created a new organization, Hashomerim-Ze'irei Ziyyon. The older Wald brother was elected to the leadership of the united organization and was one of the Hashomer representatives on its provisional council.

As the war continued, further steps were taken to fuse the two groups, which soon came to be called Hashomer Hatza'ir. But whereas the unitary organization was already functioning in Vienna, out in the provinces, in Galicia—where the original groups had been born—the merger remained incomplete. The first convention of all the Galician affiliates of Hashomer and Ze'irei Ziyyon did not meet until the summer of 1918, in Tarnawa Wyżna. The Wald brothers were not there. Meir was still in the army; Moshe, who was also unable to attend, submitted his speech in writing, in Polish, and it was read out to the assembled delegates:

> We want to educate a strong and steadfast generation, not a generation inclined to emotionalism and illusions. Our young people must prepare themselves for a life of toil and become familiar with the role that awaits them here as well as there on the ancestral soil. [...] This is our objective as Shomrim, [...] storing up the potential energy that should be transmuted into a life of physical toil. [...]
>
> We must place the emphasis on education that requires men of action, and bind ourselves to the tradition of active and fighting Judaism. [...] Not pen, paper, and ink, not anthems, confessions and emotionalism, but saws, axes, hoes, threshing-forks, and, *first and foremost hands! Give us hands!*[6]

The entire speech was published in the movement's Polish-language newsletter, *Haszomer*, over the signature "Brother Wald," as part of the full report on the convention. His younger brother certainly read it; when Meir returned to movement activities in Vienna after the war, he knew

---

6 Mintz, *Ḥevlei ne'urim*, 88–89.

the direction the movement had chosen to follow: scout training for boys and girls, Hebrew studies, and preparation for manual labor in Palestine.

In early 1919, Meir arrived in Vienna sporting a new surname, Yaar—the Hebrew translation of the German word *wald*, "forest" (he changed it to Yaari later).[7] He was penniless. Here and there he picked up a few *kronen* by giving private Hebrew lessons to the children of immigrants from Galicia. He appeased his hunger in a public kitchen. By a stroke of luck, one of the servers there was the mother of a movement member, and she made sure that he always received a piece of meat or cutlet with his bowl of soup. This, with half a loaf of bread, was his entire daily ration.[8] His poverty kept him from attending the movement's conventions.[9]

He divided his time between movement activities, his coursework as a regular student at the Agricultural College (*Hochschule*), and attendance at lectures on various topics. Despite the prevailing antisemitic atmosphere at the college, and the Gentile students' attempts to force out the few Jewish students by means of false accusations and various forms of harassment, Yaari completed his first year successfully. Then, only a year-and-a-half short of a degree in agronomy, he decided to drop out and devote the bulk of his time and energy to Hashomer Hatza'ir. His failure to complete his degree never ceased to disturb and frustrate him. He broadened his educational horizons in informal settings, where he was exposed to mentors in various fields and rubbed shoulders with their disciples. He was a regular at the classes at the school for Jewish studies (the Jüdisches Pädagogium) headed by Hirsch Perez Chajes (1876-1927), the chief rabbi of Vienna. Here he attended the lectures by the Hebrew philologist Harry Torczyner (later N.H. Tur-Sinai, 1886-1973) and expanded his knowledge of Jewish topics, especially Hebrew grammar and scriptural exegesis. These studies enriched his language, and he began to pepper his speech with biblical verses and expressions drawn from the various layers of the Hebrew language, complementing his use of Yiddish idioms.

At the meetings of the *Jerubaal* group founded by Siegfried Bernfeld (1892-1953), Yaari was exposed to the host's ideas about the youth

---

7 On the "Vienna Period" of Hashomer Hatza'ir, see Nur, *Hashomer Hatza'ir Youth Movement 1918-1924*, 62-182.
8 Yaari, *Al Hamishmar*, Aug. 28, 1970.
9 Yaari to the central office in Lwów, Dec. 9, 1919, in Mintz, *Ḥevlei ne'urim*, 357-358.

movement. Bernfeld maintained that young Jews had a universal and Zionist vocation, as a result of their ability to shatter petrified frameworks; they were duty-bound to serve their people and could not shirk this responsibility. Through Bernfeld, Yaari was exposed to the ideas of the educational reformer Gustav Wyneken (1875-1964), the creator of the concept of *Jugendkultur*. Wyneken assigned meaning and importance to adolescence per se, and not just as the preparation for adult life: an adolescent should not be seen as just the pupa from which the imago, the adult butterfly, will emerge. Adolescence has its own essence, and teenagers should create their own culture in autonomous groups, independent of adults and without coercion and dictates imposed from on high. From Bernfeld, Yaari learned about the role that Wyneken had assigned to the "pedagogical eros," meaning the pupils' attraction to beauty and to the values that make life worth living—an attraction that is supposed to emerge from the teacher's strong influence on the younger men.[10]

Bernfeld introduced Yaari to the world of psychoanalysis. In Vienna, the young man also encountered the ideas of Gustav Landauer and his idealistic approach, as well as those of Martin Buber and his Hassidic symbolism. He attended an informal class in philosophy in which they read classic German texts, from Kant to Schopenhauer, along with the then-fashionable writings of Otto Weininger the antifeminist (Yaari's definition)—and of Hans Blüher (1888-1955), who covertly preached the ideas of Friedrich Nietzsche and was known for his antisemitism. Yaari also read (though it is not certain when) Blüher's *Die Rolle der Erotik in der männlichen Gesellschaft* (*The Role of Eroticism in a Male Society*, 1919), and its second volume, *Familie und Männerbund* (*Family and Male Bonding*, 1920).[11] His conversations and encounters during his time in Vienna produced a farrago of ideas from the aforementioned thinkers and theories.

When he reached Vienna, Yaari found the movement in a sorry state. The glory days of the local chapter, which had attained its zenith during the war years, were a thing of the past. Its educational elite had gone back to Galicia in 1917. The refugees' return to their homes

---

10 Lamm, *Youth Takes the Lead*, 169-176.
11 Mintz, *Ḥevlei ne'urim*, 303

had similarly thinned out the younger generation. In postwar Vienna, the most active group was the "Third Echelon," whose members were enrolled in institutions of higher education. There was no real movement scene or close and cohesive group. As will be recalled, the young Meir Wald had joined the youth movement at a relatively late age and was originally a member of Ze'irei Ziyyon. As a result, most of the movement activities in which he took part were of an intellectual nature and he had scarcely participated in the field trips, camps, and the like, which younger members of a scouting movement had experienced. Nor did he do so in Vienna, as a counselor. His few scouting experiences of spending time in nature with close companions left a strong impression on him, and in later years he recalled them with nostalgia.

About six months after he came to Vienna, Yaari found himself the default choice to head the chapter, and did so from August to early December 1919. At the movement convention in Tarnów, in August 1919, he was elected to the movement's central council in Galicia, almost certainly because he was the head of the chapter in Vienna. Not content with the mere fact of his election, he asked to have it published in the movement's periodical as if to ratify his new role.

As head of the Vienna chapter, Yaari took a dim view of those who joined the movement for social rather than ideological reasons. He was particularly upset with the counselors who did so. For him, the movement's needs outweighed personal aspirations. He stressed the acceptance of movement discipline and made heavy demands of the group leaders, dismissing those he saw as mediocre. In his reports, he took credit for impressive achievements: since he had taken over the chapter, there had been a major improvement in Hebrew and Jewish studies, members were giving serious thought to an occupation that would be useful in Palestine, and they were devoted to him, Yaari, as a counselor and chapter head. By the end of his term, however, the Vienna chapter was in worse shape than the others. The members lacked enthusiasm, did not know much about Judaism, had failed to master Hebrew, and had no ideals.

Why was Yaari unsuccessful as head of the Vienna chapter? Were there objective reasons, or was it because of his tyrannical conduct and stringent educational demands? Or both of these, as well as other reasons? Perhaps it had to do, at least in part, with his personality and his limited capacity to bond with people. He did not look for friends in Vienna, just as he did not stay in touch with his fellow soldiers from the trenches of the Great War.

During the year that Yaari spent in Vienna, a lively discussion of educational issues and the future of the movement was taking place on the pages of its organs and at its conventions, but he did not take part in them. He did not attend the conventions; nor did he publish anything in the movement organs while he was leading the Vienna chapter. The pedagogical credo he consolidated during that time was expressed in the letters and reports he sent to the movement leadership and to Mordechai Shenhavi, who had immigrated to Palestine in early 1919. From these we learn his belief that Hashomer Hatza'ir must educate its young members to be familiar with their people and involved with its traditional culture, including fluency in the Hebrew language as the key to understanding the Bible. Only the Bible in Hebrew could stir the faith whose lack he bemoaned; hence the first subjects to be tackled should be Hebrew language, Jewish history, and settlement-related topics. Hashomer Hatza'ir must train pioneers to be versed in their ancestors' culture and establish a chain of settlements throughout Palestine. It was not an organization for youngsters only, but should prepare them for aliyah and provide them with a framework for the rest of their lives.[12]

Shortly before the movement convention in Lwów in the spring of 1920, Yaari's byline appeared for the first time in its Polish-language periodical, *Haszomer*, with an article entitled "Ourselves and Palestine."[13] It did not influence the deliberations at the convention or stimulate written responses. It is important mainly in retrospect, in that it gives us a picture of Yaari's ideas just before he moved to Palestine and can serve as a basis for comparison with his later views. The article's basic line was nationalist and Zionist, but with a strong societal orientation. It also makes clear that Yaari was aware of the security and political situation in Palestine but did not give much

---

12 Yaari to the central office in Lwów, August to November 1919, in Mintz, *Ḥevlei ne'urim*, 354–356.
13 Yaari, "Ourselves and Palestine," in Mintz, *Ḥevlei ne'urim*, 360–364.

thought to these issues. Nor did he offer ideas about the Zionist project in general, limiting himself to the future course of Hashomer Hatza'ir.

He believed that the tasks awaiting the comrades in Palestine required suitable advance training in Europe and careful selection of the potential immigrants. He expected that, at first, movement veterans would found autonomous settlements in the Upper Galilee, in districts that were not appropriate for settlement by families, where "only young people interested in the life of men, in a free and meaningful life," could function.[14] In their initial stage, these would be frontier outposts that would begin by taking over the security tasks of Hashomer, the self-defense organization; they would consist exclusively of young men, to avoid the complication of families. The bands of watchmen would settle on land owned by the Jewish National Fund and lead a communal life. Only after they had established themselves would it be time for the second stage, a rural colony whose members would engage in farming and home-based crafts, and perhaps later grow into an industrial village or garden city on the shore of the Sea of Galilee. In this second stage the members would be allowed to marry and establish families, but there would be no rights of inheritance and parents would have no influence on the children's education. In Yaari's model, there would be no private property on a settlement of Hashomer Hatza'ir; but neither would it be run in accordance with the official Communist line of that period (1920). In both stages of settlement, there would be no hired labor or wage conflicts, and thus no class struggle. However, Hashomer Hatza'ir members would not cooperate with the exploiting classes, even in pursuit of the ostensible lofty goal of national unity, and must always demonstrate their solidarity with the proletariat.

His attitude towards the state was negative, with an anarchist-syndicalist tendency. Yaari was also strenuously opposed to political parties, but allowed that, for practical reasons, Hashomer Hatza'ir would have to align itself with one of the two labor parties in Palestine, Ahdut Ha'avodah or Hapoel Hatza'ir. He himself preferred a merger with the Socialist Ahdut Ha'avodah. He summarized his view on this front in a single sentence: "Our main task is to mature into a generation

---

14 Ibid., 361.

that knows how to rise above the state and politics, [...] a generation that knows how to move beyond the narrow confines of family life."[15]

On the organizational level, Yaari proposed convening a conference of all veterans of Hashomer Hatza'ir in Palestine to facilitate their interactions with the various settlement agencies and establish their own employment bureau. Finally, after confessing his awareness that some of his proposals might prove impractical, he clarified: "I do not insist on any point, but only wanted to sketch out a plan here."[16] At this very early stage, Yaari recognized the importance of a guiding principle to steer the organization; he was looking for one but was not locked into any particular idea.

Yaari did not attend the Lwów convention. At that time, he was at a training farm with a random group of young people whose members he did not know and whose political and ideological leanings were a mystery to him. He was enchanted by the young man who led the group, Rudy Kleiner (later Amnon Za'ir of Kibbutz Gan Shmuel), who was just his age and the scion of an assimilated and well-connected Jewish family in Vienna. Yaari was impressed by Kleiner's decision to break with his family and make aliyah as a pioneer and by his initiative to organize the training group, which consisted of a number of young men and one girl. The group lived on a Jewish-owned farmstead not far from Vienna. In the piercing cold, the boys dug up sugar beets from the frozen earth with their bare hands and baled straw with a primitive machine. They all lived together in an unheated room. Every night, after a day of backbreaking toil, the exhausted members collapsed on their cots, still in their clothes, and kept warm by lying close together like sardines. The girl was allotted her own place to sleep and was supposed to do the cooking—but it turned out that she didn't even know how to make tea and her meals usually came out burned and insipid. When the training period was over, the members scattered to the winds and did not make aliyah as a group. Yaari did not stay in touch with any of them.[17]

---

15 Ibid., 362.
16 Ibid., 364.
17 On the training farm, see Meir Yaari, "How Hashomer Hatza'ir was Born," in Yaari-Wald, *Qehillat Reyshe*, 172; Zait and Shamir, *Meir Yaari*, 42–43; "Meir Yaari: My 70 Years in Hashomer Hatza'ir," Apr. 15, 1983, KMA, MYF, 8(3); Natan

Soon after Josef Trumpledor's death (March 1, 1920), Yaari decided that the time had come to go to Palestine. Before he set off, in mid-May, there was another movement convention in Lwów; once again, he was elected in absentia to the central council. There had been several conventions of Hashomer Hatza'ir and its predecessors during and after the First World War, but Yaari did not attend any of them. Nevertheless, the delegates to the Tarnów and Lwów conventions (1919 and 1920) selected him as one of the 21 or 23 members of the council, though he was far from the most prominent among them at the time.[18]

In retrospect, Yaari never made peace with his absence from the core group of the movement's founders. With the collusion of several historians of Hashomer Hatza'ir and compilers of its documents and his own writings, Yaari inserted his name into one of its founding events, the Tarnawa Wyżna convention in the summer of 1918, appropriating the speech written by his brother Moshe that had been read aloud at the convention as his own work. At first, during the 1930s, this was done perhaps through inattention. Later, though, it was published as Meir Yaari's debut composition in the first collection of his writings, *Be-Derekh arukah* (*A Long Road*; 1947), which he helped prepare.[19] The speech was also attributed to him in the first volume of the *Book of Hashomer Hatza'ir*, for which Yaari served on the editorial committee.[20] Particularly amazing is the fact that he took credit for it in the Reisha memorial volume whose editor was his brother Moshe, the true author of the piece in question.

In 1970, David Horowitz revealed the truth in his autobiography, *My Yesterday*.[21] Only then, and in the wake of the storm that ensued, did Meir Yaari confess that he had not written the speech.[22] But this belated admission was not the end of the story; even after that he occasionally repeated the assertion that he had coined the slogan, "first and foremost hands!" The overall impression is that his expropriation

---

Shaham interview with Meir Yaari, Sept. 3, 1983; "Rudi" [Amnon Za'ir], *Vienna Gan Shmuel*, 38–39.
18 Mintz, *Ḥevlei ne'urim*, 190–191 and 416.
19 Yaari, *Be-derekh arukah*, 11.
20 *Sefer Ha-shomer Ha-ẓa'ir*, 1:47–48.
21 Horowitz, *Ha-etmol sheli*, 62.
22 "The Lost Possession Is Restored To Its Owner," Sept. 24, 1970, HHA, 95-7.24(1).

of the speech (or at least the slogan) was a product of the Wald brothers' long sibling rivalry rather than Meir's attempt to burnish his own image by adding his name to the roster of the movement's founders. To a member of the movement who insisted on asking again about the copyright on the speech, he wrote that he was unsure about the paternity of the slogan, "first and foremost—hands," and told the stubborn questioner that he would be well advised to let sleeping dogs lie. "No one will lose by this—especially because I am the person who fulfilled this slogan, in its full and true meaning, through my way of life." Whereas his brother Moshe, even if he wrote that line, had not fulfilled the maxim of "practice what you preach."[23]

---

23   Yaari to David Doron, Mar. 9, 1979, KMA, MYF, 3(3).

Yaari wearing Austrian army uniform, 1917. For two and half years he served on various fronts of the First World War, first as non-commissioned officer and by the end of the war as sublieutenant. *Courtesy of Hashomer Hatza'ir Archive, Givat Haviva.*

CHAPTER 3
Bitaniyya Illit

On May 12, 1920, Yaari began his journey to Palestine.[1] He boarded a train in Vienna for Bratislava, where his traveling companions had assembled. The group consisted of about a dozen young men, but no women. They were all about three years his junior and none had been with him at the training farm. En route, they stopped over in Venice for a few days to see the famous sites. Yaari visited the Doges' Palace in the company of a sandy-haired young man with grey eyes—he never mentioned his name. They spent a long time together in front of Tintoretto's unhappy Bacchus. In the port of Fiume, the group boarded a freighter to Bari, where they switched to another cargo vessel to Alexandria. After a few days enjoying the delights of the Mediterranean city, the young men set sail for Jaffa, which was still the main port of entry to Palestine. Because the harbor there is shallow, ships had to anchor a fair distance offshore. Like many travelers before and since, Yaari's first encounter with Palestine was with the Arab porters who threw the passengers from the ship into their boats as if they were packages.

He arrived in Palestine in mid-June 1920, about six months after the arrival in Jaffa port from Odessa of the SS *Ruslan*, the *Mayflower* of the Yishuv and symbolic start of the wave of immigrants between 1919 and 1923, known as the "Third Aliyah." Even though it is customary to refer to these immigrants as "pioneers" (the Hebrew term is *ḥalutzim*), only about twenty percent of the 35,000 newcomers in those years

---

[1] On his journey to Palestine, see: Yaari to the Diaspora, late February or early March 1921, Mintz, *Ḥevlei ne'urim*, 375-402; Yaari, "My Aliya" (1938), *Sefer Ha-shomer Ha-ẓa'ir* 1, 77-78; Yaari, Memoirs (1980), KMA, MYF, 8(1); Zeev Har-On (Reinharz) to the secretary of Kibbutz Merḥavia, Apr. 27, 1980, KMA, MYF, 3(4); Mintz, *Ḥevlei ne'urim*, 263-270.

belonged to pioneer organizations; about 600 were affiliated with Hashomer Hatza'ir. Yaari came to a country that was still under British military rule. The Balfour Declaration still inspired great hope and the belief in the start of the redemption. Many wanted to make aliyah with no delay. This aspiration was especially prevalent among Jews in Eastern Europe where bands of young men, along with a few young women, organized with the intention of going to Palestine.

In light of the strong interest in aliyah, and after the first groups of *olim* had arrived in Palestine, the Zionist Organization dispatched a series of bulletins and letters to Europe, whose essence was, "Patience, Comrades! It still isn't possible to go to Palestine. The paths and options are still blocked."[2] In the spring and summer of 1919, the Zionist Organization sent out letters and bulletins to its chapters, with the unambiguous warning "not to take any hasty steps towards immigration" before the political fate of Palestine had been clarified, because the economic conditions there could not absorb newcomers.[3]

Palestine's economic capacity was indeed quite limited. The agricultural colonies could not provide jobs to new Jewish immigrants, because the independent farmers there preferred to employ Arab workers, who were cheaper and more experienced than the young men and women fresh off the boat. The kibbutz model of cooperative farming was still in its infancy and had room for only a few new recruits. Industry hardly existed, so the leading economic sector was construction. On July 1, 1920, about two weeks after Yaari arrived in Palestine, Herbert Samuel took up his post as High Commissioner. He immediately launched a series of government-funded public works projects, which provided jobs for many Jewish laborers. In late 1920, Yaari wrote to friends in Europe that the High Commissioner was a passionate Zionist; as long as he was in office there would be no shortage of work, so potential

---

2 Bulletin issued by the Palestine Office, December 1918, in Oppenheim, *Tenu'at he-ḥaluẓ be-folin*, vol. 1, 209.
3 (1) Letter dated Apr. 18, 1919, signed by executive member Julius Simon, CZA Z4/106/29; (2) bulletin signed by Nahum Sokolow, Chaim Weizmann, and Julius Simon, *Ha-ẓefirah*, May 22, 1919; (3) bulletin signed by Chaim Weizmann, Menachem Ussishkin, and Julius Simon, *Hapoel Hatza'ir*, Aug. 21, 1919.

olim must not be held back.⁴ Within a short time, however, this optimistic assumption proved wrong. The Palestine government, still under Samuel, stopped funding public works. There were no more road-building projects and unemployment soared. By 1923, the Jewish economy was in crisis.

When Yaari decided to move to Palestine, aliyah was not yet an obligatory precept for Hashomer Hatza'ir and there was no consensus that its young members should be trained for life in Palestine. At the movement convention in Lwów, about two months before Yaari left for Palestine, the senior leaders of the movement—Eliezer Rieger and Issachar Reiss—maintained that members of the older cohort should continue their studies and devote themselves to educational activities in the Diaspora, not only within the movement but also at Hebrew-language schools. Leading members of the younger group, headed by David Horowitz and Mordechai Shenhavi (who was already living in Palestine and returned to Europe for the convention), wanted to emphasize and speed up aliyah instead.⁵ In the end, the convention did not decide to make aliyah the sole order of the day.⁶ Even if it seems, in retrospect, that aliyah and settlement were natural stages in the adult life of members of Hashomer Hatza'ir, a direct outcome of the education they received in the youth movement, the fact is that they began making aliyah as a response to the question that troubled its first graduates: What now? What should we do when we grow up? The first cohort of the movement reached adulthood at the end of the First World War, just in time for the sea change in the political situation in Palestine. It was this coincidental timing that motivated Hashomer Hatza'ir aliyah in the early 1920s.

The members of the various pioneer organizations who moved to Palestine after the First World War were absorbed by the two labor parties that had been founded by the immigrants of the Second Aliyah: Hapoel Hatza'ir and the newer Aḥdut Ha'avodah, just formed

---

4 Yaari to the movement leadership in Vienna, Oct. 28, 1920, Mintz, *Ḥevlei ne'urim*, 368.
5 Zait, *Ha-ḥolem ve-ha-magshim*, 23.
6 Mintz, *Ḥevlei ne'urim*, 180ff.

as a merger of Po'alei Ziyyon and unaffiliated individuals. The two parties competed for the support of the olim and sent representatives to welcome them at dockside. Unlike most graduates of Hashomer Hatza'ir, whose absorption agency was Hapoel Hatza'ir, Yaari and his group were met in Jaffa by a representative of Aḥdut Ha'avodah and sent to Kinneret, the seven-year-old kibbutz on the shores of the Sea of Galilee. The young men just arrived from Europe were set to work digging holes for eucalyptus saplings. Unaccustomed to the blazing heat of mid-summer, they found the job exhausting; the mattocks blistered their hands. Their physical difficulties were amplified by the negative attitude of the stern and gloomy veterans of Kinneret towards the "new intellectuals," which was not devoid of the typical condescension held by Russian Jews towards Galicians.[7]

No sooner had he reached Kinneret than Yaari found himself at the convention of Aḥdut Ha'avodah, which met there on June 15–16, 1920. This was his first meeting, for better or for worse, with the veterans of the Second Aliyah. As he listened to Zalman Rubashov (later Shazar, Israel's third president) speak in his booming voice, accompanying his oratory with vigorous gestures and fancy footwork, he could not restrain himself from whispering to the person next to him that the speaker resembled a clown. Unfortunately, standing behind Yaari was Shlomo Lavi (Levkovitz; 1882–1963), a future leader of the kibbutz movement known for his temper, who loudly castigated the insolent remark. Offsetting this piece of misfortune, however, the writer Joseph Ḥayyim Brenner (1881–1921), who was also there, took pity on the young man who had aroused Lavi's wrath and delivered him from his fury. Brenner expressed interest in Yaari's background and his movement, and the two of them sat down on a rock to continue their conversation.[8]

The group with whom Yaari traveled to Palestine and spent his first days there consisted of members of Hashomer Hatza'ir from Vienna, including several who had been expelled for failing to comply with the

---

7 Yaari, Memoirs (1980), KMA, MYF, 8(1).
8 Yaari to Muki Tsur, Mar. 10, 1983, KMA, MYF, 3(6).

stringent demands he had enforced when he ran the chapter. Some of them were fond of the bottle; their wild and (for that time and place) deviant behavior heightened the tension between the veterans and the tyros. Eventually the young people were ejected from Kinneret and the group broke up. Yaari did not stay in touch with any of those who shared his aliyah and first absorption pangs.

He continued to spend time with the sandy-haired, grey-eyed young man who had been with him in Venice. On Yom Kippur Eve of 1920, while he was stretched out on the roof of a building in Tiberias—the best place to sleep on the sultry nights of late summer—Yaari heard the wailing of the worshipers in the synagogues on every side. Overcome by nostalgia, he came down from the roof. But when he moved a stone so as to have a better view of the services, he was stung by a scorpion. His friend treated him devotedly until he recovered from the resulting fever and delirium.[9]

During the Third Aliyah, affiliation with some group was all but essential for receiving various services and especially for finding work. The unaffiliated were hard pressed to get by. Public works projects were confided to the workers' organizations; Yaari and his unnamed friend joined a group that was building the road from Tiberias to Zemah, for which Ahdut Ha'avodah was responsible. There he was exposed to the formative experience of the laborers of the Third Aliyah:

> You work along the road. You sit on a pile of rocks, the sun is broiling, the hammer falls with a muffled sound on the rocks, shattering them without an end. The sun wrings the sweat out of us, along with curses and rebellion. You feel like an old man. The blows of the hammer bring you closer to the grave, to the end. The hours crawl by, anxious, pale, and empty to the point of horror. Your thoughts grow tangled and twisted like a monster.[10]

The atmosphere in the road-builders' camp was gloomy and depressing. Strangers sat next to each other at the long tables, waiting for mealtime.

---

9 Zait and Shamir, *Meir Yaari*, 58.
10 Yaari to the Diaspora, late February or early March 1921, Mintz, *Ḥevlei ne'urim*, 383–384.

When the food arrived at long last, the portions were paltry. The din that accompanied the meal evoked a roadside inn. When the weekly day of rest arrived, the workers were generally so tired that they had barely enough energy to sink down on their straw beds and eat bread and jam. A melancholia of barrenness, apathy, and emptiness descended upon Yaari. To escape this depression and despair he gave himself over to hallucinations, travelling on the wings of fantasy and memory to Italy, recalling the gondola rides on the Venetian canals. His only nights of grace were when Shabbat arrived and the weekday routine was interrupted.

> One Friday after work, as the sun was setting, when the carts rolled down the road and raised clouds of dust, I took a walk from Tiberias to Yamah [Yavne'el]. [...] It was almost Shabbat. I ran away from work. Darkness fell. From far away I heard the sound of dance music. In the camp, 200 throats were singing at the top of their lungs. Boys and girls went out to dance. Oh, such dancing, and the laborer's songs. You yearn to satisfy all your desires with a girl. Your heart pounds with desire. The young fellow moans, because he has no girl or family; lust boils inside in him and has no outlet. This dance is the madness of repression. This hoarse song is the only orgy where he can find release. The passion evaporates with the sweat. Dancing can serve as an alternative to unrequited love, to masturbation.[11]

After that, Yaari and his young companion kept walking until they lay down on the shore of the Sea of Galilee

> in the moonlit shade of an avenue of aromatic acacias. We were tired and heavy as lead. [...] The revolt began bubbling within me. "Hey, young man. You are 23. It's Shabbat. A crumb of freedom is calling you." I jumped to my feet and tugged on my friend, with his Gentile face, by his shirt-tail. He woke up at once. In the blink of an eye we threw off our clothes. "My young man, let's fish for the moon

---

11 Mintz, *Ḥevlei ne'urim*, 384.

in the water." [...] The revolt and delirium were pulsing within him, too, and a romantic vein was throbbing inside him too. ... We understood each other. We jumped into the water, penetrating its smooth surface, and cavorted till we were out of breath. He walked in front of me. Beads of silver sweat were dripping down his naked bronze arms. They moved at an alarming speed and inspired me with fear and passion. He walked ahead of me, deeper and deeper into the water, up to his shoulders, up to his neck, and up to his head—to fish for the moon. At such a moment you are willing to betroth death. Suddenly we heard the workers' raucous song. They were coming closer. They brought us back to "real" life and we fled in panic back to the shore.[12]

The two did not shut their eyes for the rest of the night. They talked for about two hours and then, towards daybreak, started walking towards Yavne'el and the laborers' mess. A meeting was in progress there, and one of those present was A. D. Gordon. Gordon's fame had reached Yaari back in Europe, but this was apparently the first time he ever saw and heard him. His words "about labor, about the national sentiment, ... about the feeling of cosmic joy from work, the exalted experiences of people who throw off their materialism and become one with their family, with their people, with their land, and with the entire existence, in a cosmic unity" and "about labor as content;" these ideas, and the audience drinking them in, made a strong impression on Yaari.[13] He felt that all these notions were escaping "through the chinks in the hut. Like shadows, like bats, they flew over the heads of the listeners."[14] He wondered how it was possible "to preach to people about cosmic love, if they have never known happiness on earth."[15]

At the time, most of the olim from Hashomer Hatza'ir were concentrated in three places: Umm al-Aleq (Shuni, not far from present-day Binyamina), Beit Gan (near Yavne'el), and along the Haifa-Jida

---

12 Ibid., 384–385.
13 Ibid., 385.
14 Ibid.
15 Ibid.

road (where Ramat Yishai is located today). Yaari had heard of the band at Beit Gan as an elite group of Shomrim from Galicia, including members of its central council. As will be recalled, he too had been elected to that body, but most of those in Beit Gan had never met him face to face. Still, he was not totally anonymous, and his name was familiar to some from his frequent letters to the movement leadership, especially when he was running the Vienna chapter. When the people at Beit Gan learned that Yaari was planning to visit, they were curious to know who he was and what he had to say.[16]

When he showed up, they gathered outside to meet him; his comments made a strong impression on the participants. In his memoirs, David Horowitz described and analyzed Yaari's remarks at his first meeting with the Beit Gan group, including their content, manner of expression, and reception by the company there:

> He spoke in a shaky voice, a voice of anxiety and adjuration, of pleading and rage. He spoke about the solitary man, alone in his suffering, private and gregarious, a man of endurance and toil. He spoke about Joseph Ḥayyim Brenner and his doctrines. He spoke about the emotional spasms of the young men and women of the movement, who must cope with a bitter and harsh reality. He spoke about eternity, about spiritual values, about the divine, about everything that engaged our attention and gnawed at our hearts. He knew how to create an atmosphere of confession, of ritual, of a monastic order, and his words struck us like hammers, even though they were arcane and vague, at least in part.
>
> However, we could feel his desire to mesmerize, to enchant, and to excite. At some points, his words were similar to those of a magician who relies on psychological effects. [...] His preaching did not convey fully formed axioms, and he did not have much new to say, at least as far as the content was concerned. But embodied in the form was a breath of glad tidings, which acted as a spiritual drug that the members of the group were willing to become addicted to.[17]

---

16 Horowitz, *Ha-etmol sheli*, 94–95.
17 Ibid., 95–96.

Following this visit, Yaari joined the group. Soon it moved to a new location, not far away: Bitaniyya Illit. Here 46 young adults, almost all of them male, set up camp on a ridge with an enchanting view of the Jordan Valley. Spread out before them was a large strip of the blue Sea of Galilee; they were stirred by the beauty of the Galilee, the winding Jordan, the white-capped peak of Mt. Hermon in the distance, the moon's reflection in the waves of the lake, the Golan Heights, and the stunning sight of the sun rising over them.[18]

Every day, the young men and the few young women worked long hours to dig out the rocks, uproot the bushes, and carve out holes for planting olive trees and grapevines. Yaari—by his own admission—did not excel at this, no more than at the road building of previous months. At first, the group slept under the open sky; later, when the rainy season came, they pitched a large tent and set up 46 cots inside it, with no privacy whatsoever and very little in the way of comfort. The wind and rain knocked the tent over repeatedly. It was midwinter before they built the wooden hut they had dreamt of, with a side room for the women, while the men slept in the main hall where all the after-work activities took place. They were hired laborers, working for a pittance. The food was poor and there was barely enough water. Some of the group members arrived with ailments and pains contracted previously; in Bitaniyya Illit they came down with malaria. As more and more of them took to their beds, the group's income plummeted.

When the workload decreased their employer, the Jewish Colonization Association (ICA), decided to cut back on the number of laborers. Of the original 46, only 20 or 22 men and 4 women could be kept on; the others would have to leave. This process, which was referred to as "the great selection," was not carried out by expelling some of the members but by forming a new group. The procedure adopted was that the three leaders—Yaari, David Horowitz, and Binyamin Dror—chose another member, the four chose a fifth, and so on. This method was proposed by Horowitz, but the trauma associated

---

[18] Ibid., 111; Yaari to the Diaspora, late February or early March 1921, Mintz, Ḥevlei ne'urim, 382–383.

with the painful and humiliating process—which was worse than being thrown out, because those not chosen felt rejected by their friends each time their name was not called—came to be associated with Yaari.[19] The four young women who were allowed to stay on were selected in a different way. Two were the girlfriends of Dror and Horowitz; the other two were the sisters of members who were not willing to leave them out. Yaari was not happy about the girls staying; he wanted the remaining group to be all male. Thus it was against his will that one of the young women left at Bitaniyya Illit was Anda Karp. Back in her hometown of Lwów, her brother had promised their father, on the eve of their departure for Palestine, that he would watch over and protect her in the dangerous country they were going to. During the selection process in Bitaniyya, he argued that his sister could not manage without him, especially because she had contracted malaria at Umm al-Aleq. It was not long before 19-year-old Anda and Meir, four years her senior, became a couple.[20]

At the end of the workday, the members assembled to eat their evening meal, which never left them feeling full. They engaged in heart-to-heart conversations, soul-baring confessions, and frequently just sat in silence. Yaari called this "a spiritual feast," at which "we grow addicted to the delirium of confessions and the ritual of conversation."[21] There was an atmosphere of togetherness on the hilltop, with all its advantages and disadvantages. A member who was having an emotional crisis would use a rock to ring an improvised bell, summoning his comrades at any hour of the day or night, and open his heart to them. The atmosphere was supportive, but also suffocating, demanding, and critical. More than once the group fell into petty faultfinding. Sometimes an incautious remark led to an outburst of tears. As time passed, there were more and more manifestations of hysteria at Bitaniyya. The group was turned in on itself, looked down on the world, and was detached from life in the rest of the country. Its

---

19 Horowitz, *Ha-etmol sheli*, 100.
20 A. Yaari, *Ha-derekh mi-merhavya*, 294.
21 Yaari to the Diaspora, late February or early March 1921, Mintz, *Hevlei ne'urim*, 382.

members were not interested in the Histadrut, the English authorities, the Arabs, the farmers, new immigrants, or those leaving the country.[22] Hovering over it all was an erotic tension.

Sex was and remains the juiciest part of the image of Bitaniyya Illit; but here the gap between what actually went on (and in fact, what probably did not) from what was said and written about it is probably the greatest of all. The materials available today leave no doubt about the erotic tension that prevailed there. How could it have been otherwise in an isolated group of young people in their early 20s, with such an extreme gender imbalance and two or three regular couples? The rumors about Bitaniyya Illit spoke of free love. They derived from the high-blown ideas about a sexual collective that can be extracted from what some members of the Bitaniyya group wrote in *Qehilliyatenu* (*Our Community*), a compilation of writings by the Hashomer Hatza'ir pioneers in Palestine, published in 1922. Young men who had a steady relationship with young women found it appropriate to share their experiences with the entire group, as if their relationship was a spiritual achievement for the entire band; these statements created a misleading image of sharing sexual partners, when in fact the sharing went no further than talking about it in public.[23]

Yaari himself made a significant contribution to the image of Bitaniyya as a sexual romp. While he was still there, he wrote to members of Hashomer Hatza'ir abroad that "the foundation of the commune is not only economic, but also erotic sharing. The bourgeois family attitude to sex is the enemy of the commune. A commune cannot exist without a deeper relationship among its members."[24] He did not bother to explain what he meant by the various forms of the term "Eros." "Erotic sharing" can be understood as the essence of a confraternity; in that sense, Eros is simply the comradeship among members of the community, an intimacy that transcends their partnership in production and consumption. With our knowledge of Yaari's past difficulties in

---

22 Yaari, letter dated July 1, 1923, Zait and Shamir, *Meir Yaari*, 138; also Horowitz, *Ha-etmol sheli*, 105–108.
23 See Binyamin Dror in *Qehilliyatenu*, 25–31.
24 Yaari, "Letter from Bitaniyya Illit, 1920," Mintz, Ḥevlei ne'urim, 382.

making friends, we can see his thoughts about the importance of open (emotionally and not necessarily sexually) relationships as an expression of a yearning for deep and meaningful interpersonal relationships. The broader public equated this "erotic sharing" with "free love." In 1927, an article in *Hapoel Hatza'ir* (the news organ for the political party of the same name) attacked the spiritual leaders of Hashomer Hatza'ir for the childishness they had shown when they spoke of free love seven years earlier. Yaari responded at once on the pages of *Davar*, the daily published by the Histadrut Labor Federation, but it is hard to understand from his aggressive stance whether there was any substance to the identification of "erotic sharing" with free love, whether as a matter of intent or of practice.[25] As for intent, what did they mean by the term? Binyamin Dror, for example, spoke about "erotic life" and "sexual life" as not necessarily the same thing.[26] In the popular discourse of those years in central Europe, "Eros" was not a synonym for sex, and it was customary to distinguish "sex," a physical experience, from "Eros," a mental phenomenon associated with love and with aesthetic values.[27] On the practical side, there is no way to determine from Yaari's rebuttal in *Davar* in 1927 whether "erotic sharing" in the physical sense of sexual relations was only a matter of theoretical discussion or whether the group in Bitaniyya indeed practiced it.

Yaari wrote about the issue when he was still at Bitaniyya itself and published the article in *Hapoel Hatza'ir*. But what he said there is not totally clear and can be interpreted in more than one way:

> The youth movement as a form of education recognized that natural society is based on three strong foundations: economics, erotic relations, and the spiritual movement. The Hashomer [Hatza'ir] group aspired to combine these three, both knowingly and unknowingly. It put an end to hypocrisy and [to] sexual dishonesty, eliminated the inability to deal with the impulses and the erotic uncertainty that are so typical

---

25 Yaari, "The Philistines Are upon You," *Davar*, May 26–27, 1927. In the article, Yaari also quotes from the attack by Lufban in *Hapoel Hatza'ir*.
26 *Qehilliyatenu*, ed. Tsur, 31.
27 Nur, "Hashomer Hatzair," 70

of the conventional stereotype of the young Jew from the boys' and girls' course of development. We had something of an opportunity to educate a generation that preserved itself and arrived in Palestine pure and open. We healed our people of some of their hysterical neuroses and corrupted drives. We love the naked youth who stays a child when he grows up, who makes his impulses and physical pleasures holy and does not loathe them.[28]

It is not clear how we should understand the words and intent here. There is certainly room to understand "Eros" as referring not only to friendship and companionship within the community, but also to sexual relations among its members—or to a combination of sexual love with friendship and brotherhood.

Yaari does not make it easy for us to determine whether erotic sharing in the sexual sense was only talked about or actually practiced at Bitaniyya. While he was still living there he wrote: "The relations between the boys and girls—although there remains ample room for improvement—have coalesced among us in a fine fashion and natural manner. They express their spiritual inclinations and are not disturbed by social conventions."[29] This is perfectly ambiguous. Some three years after the Bitaniyya interlude, Yaari wrote to Hashomer Hatza'ir members in Europe that "the boys did not give in to their impulses."[30] Fifty years later, he claimed that the young women at Bitaniyya "were puritanical and no one dared touch them."[31]

The chronicle of Bitaniyya, which became a myth almost before it was history, has reached us as a compound of "what really happened" mixed with multiple layers of legend and literary works, along with the appropriation of events that actually took place at other times and places and not in Bitaniyya in 1920–1921. The first layer in the creation of the Bitaniyya myth was *Qehilliyatenu*, published in 1922. This was a collection

---

28 Yaari, "From the Ferment," *Hapoel Hatza'ir* 15–16, January 1921.
29 Yaari to the Diaspora, late February or early March 1921, Mintz, *Ḥevlei ne'urim*, 378.
30 Yaari, letter dated July 1, 1923, Zait and Shamir, *Meir Yaari*, 138.
31 Yaari to Renana Oved, Dec. 10, 1979, HHA, 95-7.23(4).

of musings, uncertainties, aspirations, ruminations, and factual accounts, whose main themes are conversation, work, Yishuv and Zionist politics, symbols and myths, and the attitude towards tradition, love, and family. The volume, which tends to be identified with Bitaniyya Illit, its members, and their experiences there, made waves in the entire Yishuv, more so in the labor movement, and most of all in the kibbutz movement. The idea of collecting and publishing their musings, soul-searching conversations, and ambitions for the future was born in Bitaniyya, but did not take shape until after its members came down from the hilltop in the spring of 1921 and joined the Shomriya camp, and was published about a year later. Fewer than a third of the contributors were at Bitaniyya; the others were members of the Shomriya Battalion of Hashomer Hatza'ir, which was camped along the Haifa–Jida road.[32] It is not easy to assess the extent to which the contributions were printed as submitted. The volume was edited by Nathan Bistritzky (Agmon, 1896–1980), who also produced the Hebrew translations of some of the material submitted to him in Polish (in which many of the conversations had taken place). Excerpts from the diary of one young woman, which she kept in Polish, appear in *Qehilliyatenu*; the diarist said that she did not recognize them as her own when shown Bistritzky's translated and edited version.[33]

The second layer was Bistritzky's novel *Yamim ve-leylot* (*Days and Nights*), published in 1926. Its publication so soon after the events on which it was based, as well as the author's access to authentic materials related to Bitaniyya, gave it the status of a reliable historical source. A later addition to the myth of Bitaniyya was *When the Candle was Burning*, by Yehuda Yaari (1900–1982; no relation to Meir Yaari), published in 1937 (English translation, 1947). It, too, was based on the saga of Bitaniyya Illit and acquired the status of a primary historical document.[34]

The third stratum came later, in 1970, with the publication of David Horowitz's autobiography, *Ha-etmol sheli* (*My Yesterday*). One

---

32 Margalit, *Ha-shomer Ha-ẓa'ir*, 89. For biographical information about the contributors, see the annotations in *Qehilliyatenu*, ed. Tsur.
33 Armoni, "At Bitaniyya," *Kibbutz*, Apr. 20, 1994 [testimony of Rahel Herd].
34 Yehuda Yaari, *When the Candle Was Burning*.

of its chapters bears the title, "Bitaniyya Illit: The Brotherhood of the Spiritual Ascetics." Yaari responded with a series of three long and indignant articles; the topic became the talk of the day in KA circles and elsewhere.³⁵ Horowitz's book and Yaari's articles inspired Yehoshua Sobol's play *The Night of the Twentieth*, which premiered at the Haifa Theater in early 1976. The play returned Bitaniyya and *Qehilliyatenu* to public attention and fanned interest in the events of the early twenties. In Yaari's opinion, and rightly so, there was not an iota of authenticity in the play and no relationship between its plot and what had taken place at Bitaniyya Illit. But even after a meeting between the two, Sobol declined to modify his play.³⁶

It is obvious that the literary works that supposedly tell the story of Bitaniyya are not faithful to the facts; their authors took poetic license, which is perfectly legitimate. The problem is that the books by Bistritzky and Yehuda Yaari have infiltrated the scholarly writing about that period and, like *Qehilliyatenu*, have been cited as valid historical sources about Bitaniyya, failing to recognize the literary character of the novels, or that most of the contributors to the anthology were never at Bitaniyya in the first place. Then came *The Night of the Twentieth*, which is probably the best-known account of Bitaniyya today. Historians who would correct the picture face a Sisyphean task.

Yamim ve-leylot, which is something of a *roman à clef*, immortalized the young Yaari. Despite Bistritzky's later assertion that his character Alexander Tzuri was not Yaari, the two were equated by readers and the identification stuck. The novel recounts the problematic relationship between Michael Hayut, the "old man" (based on A. D. Gordon) and Tzuri/Yaari:

> When he spoke, the old man never took his mischievous eye off the faces around him, never let a single person recede from his circle

---

35 Horowitz, *Ha-etmol sheli*, 97–112; Yaari, *Al Hamishmar*, Aug. 28, Sept. 4, and Sept. 11, 1970.
36 Sobol, *The Night of the Twentieth*; Raphael Bashan interviews Meir Yaari, Oct. 10, 1977, KMA, MYF, 6(5); Yaari to Renana Oved, Dec. 10, 1979, HHA, 95-7.23(4); "Yaari vs. Sobol," *Bamaḥaneh*, Sept. 22, 1988, 34.

of vision. [...] It was only Alexander Tzuri's face that he always skipped over.

All the same, Alexander Tzuri came to the tent every evening. He entered quietly and bent over, sat curled up and silent, listening submissively for hours on end, never removing his hand from his wife's neck. When he left, close to midnight, standing in the doorway he whispered to Binyamin:

"He hates me. ... He too hates me. ... I am hated, everyone hates me."[37]

This short passage, along with the rest of the novel, might leave the impression that there was an ongoing relationship between Yaari and Gordon; but that was not the case. There is no indication in the contemporary sources that the two ever met during the Bitaniyya period. Later, though, and on more than one occasion, Yaari spoke of Gordon's "frequent visits to Bitaniyya Illit" and his "truly intimate contact" with him.[38] It was only more than 60 years after the Bitaniyya episode that Yaari confessed that he had never had an opportunity to speak to Gordon face to face.[39]

From early youth Yaari saw himself as a leader—a shepherd in search of a flock or community to guide. The Bitaniyya group was his first real opportunity to realize this ambition. His leadership flowered there, as he and his comrades shared the crisis of the sharp transition from the euphoria of the national and personal revolution represented by the act of aliyah to the dejection of the morning after, with all its difficulties. In Bitaniyya, Yaari turned out to be the right man in the right place and time, thanks to his ability to respond to the members' spiritual and emotional needs. He knew how to tune himself to the "special atmosphere of those days, the sense of isolation and apprehension about the future, and how to pluck

---

37 Nathan Bistritzky, *Yamim ve-leylot*, 2: 434–435.
38 Yigal Dunitz interviews Meir Yaari, Dec. 22, 1975, HHA, 95-7.3(3); Yariv Ben-Aharon, "Talking with Meir Yaari," *Shedemot* 72 (1979), 27.
39 Yaari to Muki Tsur, 24 February 1983, KMA, MYF, 3 (6).

on his listeners' heartstrings," David Horowitz recalled years later.[40] The group sessions he led were a blend of guidance, dialogue, and confession, which helped the young men overcome their spiritual and physical aches: the grueling labor, the loneliness, the isolation and emptiness, the absence of young women and the uncertainty about the future. He frequently spoke about the more distant future, beyond the gloomy horizon of their daily tribulations, in order to endow their difficult present with meaning and fill them with hope for a better future. The content of his remarks, imbued with spiritual energy, along with his style and rhetoric, provided his comrades with a quasi-religious experience. While he spoke, dripping with sweat, he would look down, his pupils dilated and his nostrils quivering. He kept dropping his head lower and lower, searching for a face to lock on to, and his intense gaze struck fear in the hearts of his audience. His fingers drummed rhythmically on the table, he hunted for words, he would trail off in the middle of a sentence, and his voice grew weak and even dry.[41]

Yaari was the undisputed leader of the Bitaniyya group. All the accounts, both contemporary and retrospective, reflect his charisma. One of the Bitaniyya company wrote of him: "'A leader!' A young heart is taken aback by this word, but quakes even more when it feels its essence, when it stands under the influence of the magic emitted by the leader, who blazes the trail, who expresses the collective sentiments, who expresses the collective emotional shocks. 'A leader'—a support in distress, a refuge in times of emotional depression."[42] Yaari's leadership was bolstered by his intellectual prowess, his vast store of knowledge, most of it acquired by his own efforts, his unusual ability to listen, and the fact that he was slightly older than his comrades. The age disparity of two to four years was roughly the same as that between

---

40 Horowitz, *Ha-etmol sheli*, 95.
41 Yaari to the Diaspora, late February or early March 1921, Mintz, *Ḥevlei ne'urim*, 388-391; Armoni, "At Bitaniyya," *Kibbutz*, Apr. 20, 1994 [testimony of Rahel Herd].
42 Shlomo, "Letter to the Kibbutz," *Qehilliyatenu*, 219-220. Horowitz called Yaari a charismatic leader, but wrote that he himself was immune to his charm (*Ha-etmol sheli*, 105, 108).

counselors and members of the youth movement, where three years was almost a generation.

When Yaari joined the Beit Gan group he found himself in an inferior position vis-à-vis his rival for its leadership, David (Dolek) Horowitz, who had already acquired a reputation and status back in Galicia. Horowitz had another advantage over Yaari: he, like the third prominent figure in the company, Binyamin Dror, had a steady girlfriend. Yaari caught up with them on this score while they were at Bitaniyya. On the hilltop there, Yaari and Horowitz competed in all domains; Yaari generally emerged with the upper hand. This was due largely to his talent for envisioning the future and keeping his sights pointed forward, whereas Horowitz was hesitant and uncertain about where he himself was going, and all the more so the Bitaniyya group and the other graduates of the movement.

Along with making himself the "boss" of Bitaniyya, Yaari achieved the status of the senior leader of Hashomer Hatza'ir in Palestine. In Europe, before his aliyah, he had never had an opportunity to realize his leadership ambitions, despite his public declarations. As we have seen, he was almost unknown to the group that arrived in Palestine about a month after him and settled in Beit Gan. Joining them right before they went to Bitaniyya Illit served Yaari as the springboard for movement activities throughout the country, initially manifested by his dispatch as the Hashomer Hatza'ir representative to various conventions and active participation in them. His public activities across Palestine were so extensive that we may wonder when he managed to work alongside his comrades at Bitaniyya and lead the group sessions there.[43]

One day in December 1920, as Hanukkah was approaching, most of the members of Bitaniyya Illit set out at dawn for the two-day hike to Haifa, where they took part in the founding convention of the General

---

[43] Shalom Worm, one of the veterans of Bitaniyya, interviewed by Michael Shapira, Jan. 18, 1979: "In effect, he [Yaari] himself was not a full partner in the group and for long stretches he wasn't even there, working and suffering with the rest" (HHA, 95-7.5(4)).

Federation of Hebrew Workers in Palestine—the Histadrut.[44] Before the elections for delegates to the convention, Yaari predicted a strong result for Hashomer Hatza'ir and informed the movement abroad that the "New Immigrant" list—comprising Hashomer Hatza'ir and other groups—would either have a majority at the convention or be the largest faction there.[45] In the end, he was proven wrong. Of the 87 delegates, only 16 represented the New Immigrant list, including eight from Hashomer Hatza'ir, whereas Aḥdut Ha'avodah had 37 delegates and Hapoel Hatza'ir 26. Yaari was the only speaker representing his movement at the convention.

In addition to the elected delegates, many Shomrim from all over the country came to Haifa. Here, the graduates of Hashomer Hatza'ir—led by Yaari—had their first exposure to the Yishuv. Between the plenary sessions, they gathered on the steps of the Technion building on Mt. Carmel and engaged in serious conversations and confessions in the style of Bitaniyya, in front of many listeners from both inside and outside the movement. Yaari spoke about the destruction of the "husks" that separate one person from another and expressed his nostalgia for the landscapes and pealing church bells of Poland.[46] This longing for the countryside and sounds of their birthplace was common to many olim, both recent and long-settled. But the fond memories of "the pealing church bells" provoked the derision of Yitzhak Elazari-Volcani (Wilkansky; 1880–1955) of Hapoel Hatza'ir, a member of the Second Aliyah who had already been in the country for more than a dozen years. Writing in *Hapoel Hatza'ir*, he mocked Yaari's statements, with their candor and heavy load of symbolism, denouncing them as "mystical." He was perfectly aware that the Shomrim had their own inner nature and idiosyncratic style, but pointed out that their ideas were not original and were full of secondhand notions. He expressed displeasure with their insularity and warned that this was liable to cause

---

44 Zait and Shamir, *Meir Yaari*, 88; Horowitz, *Ha-etmol sheli*, 102–103.
45 Yaari, "Letter from Jaffa to the Movement Leadership in Vienna, Oct. 28, 1920," Mintz, *Ḥevlei ne'urim*, 366.
46 Zait and Shamir, *Meir Yaari*, 89–91.

them to lose contact with the broader proletariat.[47] Another member of Hapoel Hatza'ir, Itzhak Lufban (1888–1948), saw the behavior of the Shomrim as typical of people their age, as the "childish acts" and "emotional traumas of young people" who are still nourished by internal romantic conflicts, meditation, the deep tragedy of the loneliness of young people who have not yet come into contact with the real world, and their fear of saying goodbye to their youth.[48]

Yaari soon responded to both Volcani and Lufban, also on the pages of *Hapoel Hatza'ir*.[49] He defended the doubts of the young graduates of Hashomer Hatza'ir, expressed his indignation that outsiders were in such a rush to misrepresent them, sang the movement's praises, and attacked the established political parties. He came out against partisan organizations in general, contrasting them with his preferred form of association, the "community" (*Gemeinschaft*). The article showcased Yaari's talent for polemics. He rebutted the attacks on his movement using the terminology of A. D. Gordon—with direct and explicit reference to Gordon and his thoughts—while employing idioms that were familiar to members of the movement that was identified with Gordon. The article was written in a high style and peppered with Aramaic phrases and German words. It introduced Hashomer Hatza'ir to the broader public for the first time, forging an identification between the movement and the author, Yaari, and making him the movement's best-known spokesman in Palestine.

In both arenas, the Bitaniyya group and the Yishuv as a whole, Yaari excelled in his clear vision of the goal: preserving the Shomrim's distinct identity and unity. He was steadfast not only in his pursuit of this goal, but also in devising the mode to achieve it: winning the support of the Zionist Organization and of the Histadrut for the creation of an economic basis for the graduates of Hashomer Hatza'ir on their own agricultural settlements, scattered all over the country.

---

47 The article by Elazari-Volcani was published under the penname E. Ziyyoni in *Hapoel Hatza'ir*, Dec. 24, 1920.
48 Lufban, *Hapoel Hatza'ir*, Jan. 7, 1921.
49 Yaari, "From the Ferment," *Hapoel Hatza'ir*, Jan. 18, 1921.

He devoted himself to obtaining budgets, land, and other resources where the Shomrim could settle and support themselves.

When they finished their work at Bitaniyya, in April 1921, the group left the place; most of its members joined the Shomriya Battalion, which was then encamped at about the tenth kilometer of the Haifa–Jida Road, near where Kibbutz Yagur stands today. Exploratory talks for a merger between the Shomriya Battalion and the Bitaniyya group had begun even before the latter came down from its campsite. Not everyone in Shomriya was enthusiastic about the idea. One of its young women justified her opposition to a merger by stating that "the thoughts and worldviews of Bitaniyya strike me as sickly, whereas everything about us is healthy. I would not want this infection to penetrate here."[50] She preferred that Shomriya continue to develop in its own way and that Bitaniyya follow its own path. With time, her comrades' sympathy for Bitaniyya grew, "and there was a danger," she wrote, "that Bitaniyya would leave its mark on Shomriya" were the two to join forces.[51] In the spring of 1921, the members of Shomriya paid a group visit to Jerusalem. One can imagine their astonishment when, upon their return, they found their camp occupied by the Bitaniyya group. On the first night of Passover, April 22, 1921, the veteran members and newcomers celebrated the founding of their new joint commune with a stormy dance.[52] This was another seminal event that Yaari missed. He and Anda did not reach the Shomriya camp until the beginning of May, after hiking together through much of the Galilee.

Yaari reached Shomriya with the status of a leader, but the members soon distanced themselves from him and rebelled against his ideas and behavior. They were disgusted by the dictatorial aspects of his leadership style and wanted to free themselves of the feeling he gave them—of being controlled by a person who saw them as clay for the potter to shape as he saw fit. His language and ideas were not music for all ears. As early as his preliminary visit to Shomriya, to investigate the prospects for a merger of the two groups, his rhetoric met with a different reception than at Bitaniyya. The young woman quoted

---

50 Hadaya Rosenbaum to Shenhavi, Mar. 21, 1921, Mintz, Ḥevlei ne'urim, 318.
51 Ibid.
52 Yedidya Shoham, "The Beit-Alfa Chapters," part 2, Dec. 31, 1976, KMA, MYF, 6(6).

above also wrote that "Meir Wald spoke a lot and was very emotional," repeating things that the comrades had already heard many times in the past: "suffering, war, a new and different society, a different attitude towards young women," and so forth.[53] Some of the Shomriya group felt that the unique atmosphere that the Bitaniyyites brought with them interfered with the merged group's transition to the practical stage and was liable to impede the group's ability to found a permanent settlement.

Yaari's stance on the issue of women and their inclusion in the group and commune aroused particular dismay among the members of Shomriya. After the Bitaniyya group arrived in Shomriya, a rift emerged between him and his comrades (or perhaps a pre-existing one grew wider). There were already several couples at Shomriya before the merger; after the new faces arrived, romances quickly developed between young men from Bitaniyya and the young women of Shomriya. The group as a whole, and the couples in particular, disassociated themselves from Yaari's notion of erotic sharing and utterly rejected his ideas about the social status of women and the family, on which we will expand in a later chapter.

One member who saw Yaari as a charismatic leader explained to the others, in what was close to a rebuke, that even a respected leader can become a "broken reed when people lean on him *all the time* and with all their weight!" He criticized his comrades who had failed to understand "that a leader, too, is a human being, not a god, and has different periods in his life like everyone else, with frequent ups and downs."[54] If they expect him to assume "the pose of a prophet at every moment," they are leaving him only two options: either to leave the camp or to turn into a charlatan.[55]

Yaari and the group understood that they had to part company. Many of the members blamed Yaari for attempting to force his views and authority on them, launching a sort of "children's revolt against the father figure" in the camp.[56] The straw that broke the camel's back

---

53 Hadaya Rosenbaum, undated letter, Mintz, *Ḥevlei ne'urim*, 316–317.
54 Shlomo, "Letter to the Kibbutz," *Qehilliyatenu*, 219–220.
55 Ibid.
56 Biographical notes by Arthur Ben-Israel (Beit-Alfa), KMA, MYF, 2(14).

seems to have been Yaari's proposal to hold another selection process in anticipation of the move to a permanent settlement.[57] The potential consequences, even beyond the hurt feelings of those booted out and the ugly atmosphere among those allowed to stay, was social isolation and economic hardship, to the point of starvation, for those deemed unworthy of remaining in the group. In light of the worsening relations between Yaari and the others, the obvious question is not why they went their separate ways but why they had not done so earlier. The answer seems to be the absence of an alternative leader who would lead the coup and replace the deposed leader. Yaari was left without a rival after Horowitz went abroad to visit his family in the spring of 1921. But when the latter returned, in late summer, he joined the group of members who were disgusted with Yaari's leadership and placed himself at the head of those who opposed and attacked him.

The thorny and charged relationship between Yaari and the members of Bitaniyya and Shomriya culminated in dramatic fashion in what the movement's chronicles refer to as "the vigil." (Yaari called it "St. Bartholomew's Eve.") One October evening in 1921, the members gathered. Horowitz sat down on the table and let loose with a three-hour harangue against Yaari. He called him "the Grand Inquisitor," "the Antichrist," and "the Black Satan." He blamed him for imposing a spiritual dictatorship at Bitaniyya, which had triggered a mass hysteria that continued in Shomriya. The assembled company seems to have remained silent. It may be that Yaari decided to leave not because of what he saw as Horowitz's unbridled attack on him, but because none of those whom he had considered his good friends stood up for him or came to his defense.[58] Several words have been applied to that night's climax: departure, ouster, ejection, flight—each suiting a different appraisal of the tense climate and the rift between the two sides and how each saw each other as the instigator. What is certain is that Meir and Anda packed up their few belongings and left the Shomriya camp the next morning, never to return.

---

57 Shoham, "The Beit-Alfa Chapters," part 2, Dec. 31, 1976, KMA, MYF, 6(6); Zait, Ha-ḥolem ve-ha-magshim, 40–43.
58 Yaari to Eli Shadmi, Nov. 4, 1983, KMA, MYF, 6(6).

It is plausible that the harsh and traumatic words of that long Saturday night actually made things easier for Yaari, giving him an excuse for a step that was already in the cards. Was his departure an impulsive act, a decision taken on the spur of the moment, or had he already been thinking about leaving the camp? Bistritzky, who at the time was hard at work on editing *Qehilliyatenu*, wrote to A. D. Gordon less than 48 hours before Yaari left Shomriya, informing him of Yaari and Anda's desire to join Degania (the trailblazing kibbutz where Gordon lived). Bistritzky's letter lavished praise on Yaari: "Everyone [including his opponents] acknowledges, without exception, that he is a great force."[59] He told Gordon that Degania should accept Yaari, because he was favorably inclined towards the concept of the small commune. We do not know whether or how Gordon, who was critically ill at the time, replied. In any case, it is doubtful whether his status at Degania was such as allowed him to have such a request approved. One way or another, this was an idea that never came to fruition.[60]

A chapter in Yaari's life and leadership career, composed of two parts, Bitaniyya and Shomriya, was now over. At the former, he had demonstrated his leadership capacity in all its strengths and advantages; at the latter, its weaknesses and disadvantages emerged. The end of the chapter marks the end of the period of the intimate and total community, isolated from the outside world, in which he was the sole and undisputed leader. Now the man and his comrades (or former comrades, it must be said, with regard to at least some of them and for some time) went their separate ways. The latter went off to settle the land and build agricultural communes, while Yaari himself began a period of wandering and soul-searching.

---

59 Bistritzky to Gordon, 12 Tishrei 5682 [Oct. 14, 1921], HHA, 95-7.5(3). There is another copy of the letter in Gordon's correspondence, where Muki Tsur found it while preparing the new edition of *Qehilliyatenu*. See Tsur to Yaari [February 1983], KMA, MYF, 3(6).

60 When the letter was brought to Yaari's attention many years later, his reaction was scribbled in the margin: "There is no factual basis to this letter, which stands in utter contradiction to his [Yaari's] experiences in that period of 5682." The note is undated and the signature is illegible. HHA, 95-7.5(3).

CHAPTER 4
Founding a Kibbutz Movement

Battered, bruised, and bereft, Yaari departed the Shomriya camp for the unknown, for a life of rootlessness and wandering. In one fell swoop, he had plummeted from the lofty heights of leadership to the deep abyss of almost total anonymity. The man who found it so difficult to forge interpersonal relationships was forced, in that autumn of 1921, to bid farewell to the first significant social network to which he had ever belonged. He did not hesitate to broadcast his inner emotions and feelings, candidly admitting to the members of the movement that after he had parted ways with the community, he sometimes felt as if he had been tossed out into the street. He announced to all who would listen that he wanted to find true comrades.[1]

The period from the autumn of 1921 to the spring of 1923 is a sort of "black hole" in Yaari's biography and an interlude in his career as a leader. With his wife Anda (the full story of their wedding will be told in the next chapter), and sometimes alone, he wandered from place to place, looking for a new group to which he could attach himself. During this odyssey, which took them to eight different way stations before they reached Tel Aviv in late 1922, he made no significant mark on the movement. He was not a contributor to *Qehilliyatenu* and was not a member of Beit Alfa, the first Hashomer Hatza'ir commune that

---
[1] The description of the period between Yaari's departure from the Shomriya camp and the publication of "Rootless Symbols" is based on Yaari, "Letter to the Diaspora," July 4, 1923, Zait and Shamir, *Meir Yaari*, 139-140; Yaari "Memoirs," KMA, MYF, 8(3), 29.

established a permanent settlement, in 1922—thanks in no small part to his efforts. His voice fell mute; he stopped sending letters to the Diaspora and did not publish articles in the press. Because he had been the movement's mouthpiece, his silence meant that Hashomer Hatza'ir was not heard of in the Yishuv for about a year, from the appearance of *Qehilliyatenu* until the publication of his article "Rootless Symbols" ("Semalim telushim").[2]

He took advantage of these months of wandering and isolation for some serious soul-searching; he drew conclusions, learned lessons, and crystallized his thoughts about the movement's future and methods. Yaari's time at the Mikveh Yisrael agricultural school was especially fruitful. The director, Eliyahu Krause, liked Yaari, and suggested that he go convalesce in the hot springs at Tiberias (and provided the funds to make that possible). The mineral-rich water did wonders for Yaari's aching body. His rheumatic pains went away and he settled down to write "Rootless Symbols." In late 1922, he took the manuscript with him to Tel Aviv, where he and Anda joined some two dozen graduates of Hashomer Hatza'ir who were organized as a construction crew. They lived in a tent camp on a hill that later became the site of the first Tel Aviv city hall (now Bialik Street). The poet Avraham Shlonsky, who lived in the tent next to the Yaaris, was the go-between with the editors of the nonpartisan literary journal *Hedim* and probably edited the piece before publication.[3]

The appearance of "Rootless Symbols" in *Hedim*, then the leading Hebrew-language literary journal in both Palestine and the world, restored Yaari's status as the chief spokesman of Hashomer Hatza'ir in Palestine. The article made an immediate impression. Readers cannot avoid being amazed by the intellectual powers of the author, not yet 26, the breadth of his knowledge, his mastery of passages from various sources, and his vivid language. It was a seminal document, even though it did not sketch out a clear line for the future path of Hashomer Hatza'ir in Palestine. We may search in vain for a coherent

---

[2] The article was first published under the title "Rootless Symbols (Isolated Thoughts)" in *Hedim* (spring 1923): 93–106.

[3] Mintz, "Rootless Symbols"; Zait, *Ha-utopia ha-shomerit*, 133–136.

message of the sort found in Lenin's 1902 essay, "What Is Be Done?" Rather than offering a prescription for the future, Yaari scrutinized the past and settled accounts with it; the article is notable for its vague ideas and precious style. Its main purpose seems to have been to pave the way for its author's return to a leadership position.

With that in mind, it wrestled with the youth culture. Its rootless symbols, which had emerged in the Diaspora, were outmoded and no longer valid in Palestine. This was the first public sign of his rejection of Wyneken's notion of *Jugendkultur*. Yaari's criticism of the education provided by Hashomer Hatza'ir was not new. Shortly after making aliyah, he complained that the movement's program in Galicia did not groom its graduates for the tasks they would be facing. As a result, they reached Palestine unprepared, not robust enough, and insufficiently masculine.[4] He was also concerned that the social bond and movement tradition the Shomrim brought with them from Europe would not be enough for them to lead a communal life in Palestine.[5] Having blossomed as a leader in Palestine, Yaari had much to find fault with the movement in the Diaspora and what it had produced in the period before he began influencing its development.

But despite his criticism of the youth movement, Yaari also had a fierce desire to sustain it, preserve its heritage, and maintain the solidarity of its graduates, who had been bonded by their shared experiences in the movement. So his censure and rejection were accompanied by praise for the generosity and willingness to assist others, with no expectation of reward, which the movement had instilled in its members. Evident in his remarks is a tension bordering on self-contradiction. On the one hand, there is Yaari's sense that the youth movement experience forged strong ties among its members and inspired them with a desire to stay together, on the other hand is his argument that the movement provided inadequate training and did not prepare the members for life in Palestine. We can see how this coincides with evidence from other places and at other times that membership

---

4 Yaari, letter from Bitaniyya, early 1921, Mintz, *Ḥevlei ne'urim*, 375.
5 Yaari, letter from Jaffa, Oct. 28, 1920, Ibid., 364.

in Hashomer Hatza'ir provided the young men and women with an experience that was more emotional than cognitive, one that stayed with them for many years but did not necessarily dictate their future affiliation and ideology.

One purpose of "Rootless Symbols" was to hone the unique Shomer identity of the movement's graduates in Palestine, which had been somewhat obscured during the years of the Third Aliyah. Recently arrived Shomrim tended to disperse to points all over the country. They had no central leadership and their link with the movement abroad was severed. Yaari was trying to keep the Shomrim from assimilating into the preexisting organizations and parties, which were controlled by members of the Second Aliyah.

"Rootless Symbols" returned both Yaari and Hashomer Hatza'ir to the public eye, more or less as a package deal. The article was the opening shot in its author's return to the leadership of his movement and a sign of the re-ignition, or at least acceleration, of steps towards a national organization of the Shomrim in Palestine. Occasional voices had already been heard about the need for one. Movement graduates had even held a few meetings in 1920, but with no results. Yaari's cessation of Hashomer activity in the fall of 1921 and withdrawal from the public stage for a year and a half—along with David Horowitz's second trip abroad, soon after—left the Shomrim in Palestine without a leader. From mid-1923, following his return to activity, Yaari became a key player, though not the only one, in reconnecting the organizational thread that had been snapped in the autumn of 1921, linking up the Hashomer groups that had scattered all over the country, and rescuing Hashomer Hatza'ir from its identity crisis—leading to the establishment of Kibbutz Artzi in 1927.

Around Rosh Hashanah, in September 1923, representatives of the Hashomer communes and of movement graduates not affiliated with any group convened in Nahalal for discussions aimed at paving the path to the establishment of a countrywide organization of all the Shomrim in Palestine. The gathering was initiated by recent arrivals from abroad, most of them from the Warsaw chapter, led by Yaakov Hazan, Alexander (Sasha) Szczupak, and Chaim Krongold, who presented the European branch's desire that the movement graduates in Palestine coalesce.[6] Another catalyst for the conference in Nahalal was the idea, then in the air, of consolidating all the Shomer settlement cadres at Shata, near the new Kibbutz Beit Alfa. But what inscribed Nahalal in the annals of Hashomer Hatza'ir is not its deliberations but the fact that this was where Yaari and Hazan met. After all the delegates had gone home, the story goes, the two men found themselves walking together at the gate of Nahalal. They started talking and kept up the conversation for hours as they made their way to Haifa, partly by foot and partly on top of a load of hay in a cart. That night and the next day the two bonded, laying the foundations for the historic collective leadership of Hashomer Hatza'ir that lasted for more than fifty years.[7]

The Nahalal gathering resolved to hold another and larger meeting in two months, at Beit Alfa. The preparations stretched out, however, and it was only after great efforts and repeated postponements that the meeting finally took place on Shavuot weekend, June 7-9, 1924.[8] Yaari insisted that it was just a "meeting" and explained that it was not a movement convention, but just an opportunity for people to get together.[9] It is not clear how many showed up at Beit Alfa; estimates range between 200 and 400.[10] Shomrim made their way there from all over the country, some by foot and some by train, greeting one another and catching up on their news. There was lots of joyful laughter in the "human snake" that made its way from the Shata train station to Beit Alfa. The visitors were put up in tents and huts; the kibbutz bell summoned them to meals. On Friday, June 6, they toured the settlement. In the evening they attended a performance of the Hebrew version of

---

6 Tzahor, *Hazan*, 78-81.
7 Ibid., 80-81; 90-91.
8 On the Beit Alfa conference, see: Margalit, *Ha-shomer Ha-ẓa'ir*, 115-119; Tzahor, *Hazan*, 81-85; Zait, *Ha-ḥolem ve-ha-magshim*, 84-86; Shadmi, *Meqorot*, No. 3, 15-63.
9 Zait and Shamir, *Meir Yaari*, 147.
10 There were 200, according to "Report by Chaim Krongold," in Shadmi, *Meqorot*, No. 3, 21; 400, according to Margalit, *Ha-shomer Ha-ẓa'ir*, 104-105.

The Golem, the Yiddish play by H. Leivick (Leivick Halpern), which ran from 8:30 until 2 in the morning.

The deliberations began the next morning. Not many people showed great interest in them; most of those present wanted mainly to socialize. The theoretical elucidations of Marxist theory by Mordechai Bentov attracted no one. At the end of the first day of discussion, after it was decided to adjourn earlier than planned (because people were tired), the delegates went out to dance a wild *hora*.[11]

Yaari delivered the keynote address. It seemed interminable, and went on even longer because he took a number of breaks. The audience felt that he was wearing them out on purpose and trying to influence them through suggestion. Many did not like this and objected to his style. In his report on the conference, Chaim Krongold, who was not a member of a Shomer commune and came to the meeting from Jerusalem, wrote that on the second day of the deliberations, Yaari delivered a speech "full of passion, to the point of posturing, but a fine and rich speech."[12] On the whole, Krongold was impressed by Yaari's style, but not his knowledge. He felt Yaari was strongly under the influence of Marx, having noted several times that he believed in historical materialism and the key role of economics.

Yaari may have peppered his remarks with Marxist themes, but he was not yet a Marxist. In his lectures at Beit Alfa, he did not expound a carefully reasoned ideology; the bulk of his speech was about Hashomer Hatza'ir's unique attributes in Palestine and the need to perpetuate its existence. He emphasized that Hashomer Hatza'ir had to distinguish itself from the other groups in the country; its members must not amalgamate with the existing parties, because it was imperative that it continue to exist as a separate organization. He suggested the creation of a federation of all the communes of Shomrim.

In his keynote address at Beit Alfa, Yaari did not offer any far-reaching proposals of his own and made sure to hew to the golden mean between the perspectives of others. Sometimes he contradicted

---

[11] The description comes from "Report by Chaim Krongold," in Shadmi, *Meqorot*, No. 3, 15–42.
[12] Ibid., 30.

himself. On the second day of the meeting, when the topic was the organizational framework, he was the last speaker. He had listened to what the comrades had said and picked up their mood. So when his turn came to speak he took a line that made it possible to make progress towards a formal organization. In the vote on the future course of action, Yaari emerged victorious over David Horowitz, whose proposal for a federation with Gedud Ha'avodah (the Trumpeldor Labor Legion), was rejected. Instead, the meeting adopted his idea of a "community" (*Gemeinschaft*) of Shomrim in Palestine with which all the communes and groups would be affiliated. The motion was submitted by Yaari and Szczupak, although its main advocate was Hazan. The first test of cooperation between Yaari and Hazan had been passed successfully.

The impetus for the establishment of the Kibbutz Artzi federation (hereafter KA) came from the desire of the movement members abroad to establish a formal body which they could join after aliyah, along with the needs of the Shomrim already in Palestine for an organization that could help them set up and sustain agricultural settlements and stay in contact with the movement abroad, which was the source of their new blood. Thus the twin motives for organizing were aliyah and settlement, and these two topics were the common thread of all the movement debates and assemblies. The Shomrim in Palestine and abroad had a shared interest, but in 1924 there was a wide disparity in their situations. The former had scattered and were making no headway towards founding settlements, whereas the movement abroad was flourishing. Its dozens of chapters and thousands of members, all of them potential olim, augmented Yaari's belief that the unique character and unity of Hashomer Hatza'ir in Palestine needed to be preserved and helped him persuade his fellow members to accept his position. They believed that hundreds or even thousands of newcomers would join them and reinforce the ranks of the Shomrim in Palestine in the near future.

Yaari left Beit Alfa only half satisfied. There had been no resolution to establish a countrywide federation of Hashomer Hatza'ir kibbutzim, but neither had the idea been scuttled. The line that he had championed—safeguarding the unique character and unity of Hashomer

Hatza'ir—had carried the day, while the threat inherent in Horowitz's proposal, which might well have led Shomrim to join Gedud Ha'avodah or some other group, had been averted. So even though the kibbutz federation remained unborn, the blurring of the Shomer identity and the organizational dispersal of Hashomer Hatza'ir graduates in Palestine was arrested. Yaari had not yet amassed sufficient strength, and the conditions were not yet ripe, for the full implementation of his idea, but he had been able to thwart the antithetical process. For Yaari, his achievement at Beit Alfa was that the flock he wanted to lead did not scatter in every direction and leave the fold.

The meeting at Beit Alfa, including its preparations, catalyzed Yaari's rise to the leadership of the Shomrim in Palestine. He was very active in these preparations, arrived with a clear plan for future activity, and played a central role in the deliberations. The tensions and old scores that the participants brought with them and the social dynamics of the gathering provided a golden opportunity for Yaari to stand out; he was one of the organizers and already well known. By the meeting's end, he was the linchpin of the leadership group of Hashomer Hatza'ir in Palestine and well on his way to claiming this status in the global movement as well.

In the summer of 1924, Yaari sailed for Europe with his wife Anda and their daughter Rachel, who was just past a year old. When he reached Poland, he found that his name had preceded him, both within the movement and outside of it. People were familiar with the articles he had published in Palestine as well as the articles and letters that had appeared in the movement periodicals in Poland. Both good and bad reports on him had filtered back from Palestine, and these served to increase the curiosity about him.[13] His first stop was Galicia, where he attended the provincial convention of Hashomer Hatza'ir in Rytro (August 24-26, 1924). He had returned to his personal and movement origins in Galicia, which he had left at the start of the First World War. He met with the members of the movement like a counselor with his scouts, and attempted to instill the educational message that Shomrim

---

13   Sadan, *Alufi u-meyuda'i*, 197-198.

must prepare themselves socially and vocationally for communal life in Palestine.[14]

When the Rytro gathering was over, Yaari proceeded to Danzig, where he took part in the first World Convention of Hashomer Hatza'ir. No contemporary record of his remarks there survives and we have only retrospective accounts. One secondhand report is that at the end of Yaari's speech, Berl Katznelson commented: "I don't understand how all of you—especially you Lithuanian Jews—can tolerate this psychoanalytic-Marxist-hassidic blather. This is what you will build your movement on? This is what you will teach the young people?"[15] The future literary critic Dov Sadan (then known as Berl Stock), who also heard Yaari's remarks, remembered them as "moving but mixed up."[16]

While back in Europe, Yaari became aware of the ebb tide of Zionism and the leftward political drift of young Jews in general and of members of Hashomer Hatza'ir in particular, many of whom were leaving the movement to join the Communists. In his lively debates with members of the movement in Warsaw, Galicia, and Vienna, he employed Marxist terminology to counter members who had been captivated by Communism or identified with the ideology of Po'alei Ziyyon Left. It is unclear to what extent he had adopted and internalized Marxism by then, and to what extent he was using it to immunize his interlocutors against the attraction of the Left. At the same time, he drew on Gordon and other non-Marxist thinkers when he spoke with other audiences. Even when he drew on Marxist terminology so as to dissuade those who were moving to the Left in their own language, Yaari watched his own tongue. He had to be careful not to endanger the Shomrim's settlement enterprise in Palestine, which was dependent on funding from the Zionist Organization. Its leaders took a dim view of Hashomer Hatza'ir's increasing Leftism. It was feared that overt Marxism would augment the organization's preference for noncollective forms of settlement at the expense of the kibbutz.

---

14 On the trip to Galicia, see Zait, *Ha-utopia ha-shomerit*, 198–203.
15 As reported in 1983 by Yaakov Hazan, whose source was Yaakov Amit. See *Berl and Hashomer Hatza'ir*, 19.
16 Sadan, *Alufi u-meyuda'i*, 200–201.

While Yaari was still visiting Poland in 1925, another threat to Hashomer Hatza'ir surfaced from a different direction: the Gordonia youth movement. The two movements' educational doctrines overlapped in several areas, they addressed similar target audiences, and they competed for representation, budgets, and immigration certificates. The desire to differentiate Hashomer Hatza'ir from the nascent Gordonia hastened Yaari's disengagement from Gordon's ideas, which had begun before the Beit Alfa conference. Now he continued the new line in Europe, while moving towards Marxism. The best explanation for the change in Yaari's attitude towards Gordon and the adoption of Marxism is probably the opposite of the standard view. Yaari did not abandon Gordon because he had become a Marxist; rather, Yaari became a Marxist, among other reasons, in order to move away from Gordon and distinguish his movement from Gordon's ideas and from the movement and party identified with him and his thought. For if Hashomer Hatza'ir was Gordonist, why the insistence on a separate organization rather than joining Hapoel Hatza'ir?

When Yaari went abroad, the Fourth Aliyah was in full swing. The Yishuv and the Zionist world in general were swept up by a euphoric optimism that masses of Jews were about to arrive in Palestine and that the demographic mass to consolidate the National Home and even to establish a Jewish state would soon be achieved. Many of the olim of 1924–1925 came as "capitalists," an immigration category that entitled all those with 500 pounds sterling to their name to immigrate to Palestine, along with their wives and minor children. The middle-class bourgeois composition of the aliyah undermined the idea that immigration had to be regulated and gradual, an approach based on the notion that the first step was to develop a solid economic infrastructure in the country, based on farmers and laborers, and only then could additional olim be absorbed. This concept lay behind an unofficial pact that emerged between the Zionist leadership, bourgeois through and through, and the labor movement, under which the Zionist Organization financed the purchase of land, its initial development, and the establishment of agricultural settlements, while the proletarians provided the manpower—young people who were graduates of the pioneer youth movements and had taken upon themselves the burden of the national enterprise. In the early years of the British Mandate, the Zionist Organization invested almost four times as much in agricultural settlements as it allotted to the urban sector, commerce, and industry taken together, even though four-fifths of the of the immigrants settled in the towns.

But the Fourth Aliyah, in its early stages, ostensibly demonstrated the potential of unstructured immigration; it called into question the need for selective immigration, with preference for organized groups of young adults who had been trained for a life of physical exertion in Palestine. The preferential status that the Zionist Organization granted to people affiliated with the labor movement in matters of aliyah and settlement naturally stirred the antagonism of some circles in the Yishuv and the Zionist movement; the immigration of thousands of members of the lower middle class in 1924 and 1925, who paid their own way and settled down without assistance from the Zionist Organization, increased the criticism directed against the workers' parties and of the favoritism shown them by the Zionist leadership. Rightwing circles demanded that the Zionist Organization subsidize the absorption of middle-class immigrants and not only workers, and that it allocate funds to the towns and not only the farming communities. At the Fourteenth Zionist Congress (1925), fierce debates about the appropriate method for building the country took place. The pioneers were attacked by the right, and they were defended not only by their own representatives, but also the senior leaders of the Zionist Organization, notably Chaim Weizmann and Arthur Ruppin, as well as delegates affiliated with the General Zionists.[17] This was the first Zionist Congress that Yaari attended, but he was not an active participant.

The Fourth Aliyah led some of the Labor Zionist leadership to entertain second thoughts and even heretical notions. Earlier still, during the Third Aliyah, the labor parties' hopes that the National Home could be built exclusively through the means available to the Zionist Organization and other public institutions, with no need for

---

17 Giladi, *Ha-yishuv bi-tequfat ha-aliyah ha-revi'it*, 166–170.

private capital, were dashed. Those assumptions rested on the idea that there was a fundamental contradiction between Zionism and Capitalism, inasmuch as capitalists sought quick profits and would rather employ Arab laborers who were willing to accept lower wages. This idea crystallized as a result of the economic frailty of the agricultural colonies of the First Aliyah and the failure of the struggle for Hebrew labor during the Second Aliyah; it was reinforced by the rising optimism in the early years of the Mandate period that the Jewish people would rally to the cause and contribute vast sums to build the national home. But that hope dissipated quickly. As Yaari explained in a letter to his wife: "After the Balfour Declaration, the Zionist Organization took upon itself the mission of organizing the bulk of the Jewish people around building the land. It hoped to raise millions of pounds every year, but actually collected only half a million."[18] In fact, the amount that came in was even less than that. Accordingly, the Twelfth Zionist Congress (1921) decided that it was necessary to invest both national funds and private capital in building the land. Now, in 1924, the Fourth Aliyah threatened to undermine another basic assumption of the labor camp—the belief that the new Jewish society in Palestine should be built from the ground up as a classless proletarian society, skipping over the stages of capitalism, class warfare, and revolution. In this "constructive socialism," as formulated by Berl Katznelson, there was an innate identification between the interests of the working class and those of the nation as a whole.[19]

The boom of the mid-1920s did not continue for long. By 1926, it was clear that the Jewish economy in Palestine was in trouble. Zionist memory recalls this crisis as the cause of a sharp drop in aliyah, to the point of a negative migration balance in 1927 and zero net gain in 1928.[20] The meager balance in the Zionist treasury made the bad

---

18 Yaari to Anda, July 1, 1928, KMA, MYF, 5(2).
19 Ben-Gurion published an article along these lines in 1925, under the title "The National Vocation of the Working Class," *Kuntres* 210 [Mar. 20, 1925].
20 According to the official statistics of the Mandatory authorities, 5,071 Jews left Palestine in 1927—almost double the number of those who arrived (2,713). In 1928, only 10 more persons immigrated than emigrated.

situation worse. The expert committee that visited the country in 1927, in advance of the establishment of the Jewish Agency, recommended that no new settlements be founded until the existing ones were firmly on their feet; it was particularly skeptical about the future of the collective settlements. The committee stated its admiration of the devotion and passion of the members of these communes, but assessed their prospects for success as very low. Hence it recommended that the establishment of new kibbutzim be frozen at once, that recently established kibbutzim be converted into moshavim (smallholders' villages), and that the older kibbutzim continue to be subsidized for the interim, after which their status would be reevaluated. The Zionist Executive, which included no labor representatives between the Fifteenth (1927) and Sixteenth (1929) congresses, heard this message, imposed a regime of consolidation, and stopped allocating funds for the establishment of new rural settlements.

While the future of the Hashomer Hatza'ir communes in Palestine remained shrouded in uncertainty, the youth movement abroad continued to grow, despite the ideological turbulence it experienced, and despite the Leftward trend whose dangers Yaari had noted while in Europe. But the movement's success there was not transmitted to Palestine. Only some graduates of the movement made aliyah, only a few of those joined the communes, and even fewer remained in them. Out of 378 members of Hashomer Hatza'ir who had made aliyah in 1925, only 27 were absorbed into the movement's communes.[21] At the end of that year, a member of the Warsaw chapter lamented that of the 30,000 young people who had belonged to the youth movement during the past six years, only a thousand had been sent to Palestine and only 400 joined the communes.[22] According to another source, which may be somewhat overstated, some 1,500 members of Hashomer Hatza'ir had made aliyah by early 1927, but only 286 of them were numbered among the founders of KA in the spring of that year.[23]

---

21 Margalit, *Ha-shomer Ha-ẓa'ir*, 104.
22 Zait, *Ha-utopia ha-shomerit*, 180.
23 Margalit, *Ha-shomer Ha-ẓa'ir*, 135.

Yaari was concerned by the situation in the Yishuv in general and in his movement's communes in particular. He was especially troubled by the fact that problems of employment and housing on the agricultural colonies caused some members to leave their commune's camps and move to the beckoning city. In a letter to Europe, written in the spring of 1926, he described the situation in Palestine with a delicate and moving human sensitivity, in eloquent prose—then suddenly switched to an unbridled attack on those who "pack up their bag and go off to study" and on the dropouts who spit into the well from which they had drunk.[24] In contrast to the reigning doctrine in Gedud Ha'avodah, that the building of the land would have to depend chiefly on private capital and that the working class could develop alongside privately owned industry, Yaari insisted that Palestine would rise or fall with agriculture; and agriculture could not succeed without assistance from the national treasury. In this arena, the kibbutzim of Hashomer Hatza'ir faced competition on the right—the moshavim; and they too were the target of his shafts. He asserted that only collective settlements and young people could guarantee the future of agriculture, and that the moshavim had not proven their viability. In general, he stated, older men and women are not the best raw material for farming.[25]

The efforts to found KA, frozen while Yaari was abroad, were renewed as soon as he returned. Before his trip to Europe, he was the initiator and the main driving force of the organizational efforts in Nahalal (1923) and Beit Alfa (1924). Now, back in Palestine, Yaari played a central role in launching the process and keeping it going. Hazan did not join him until late 1926, when he returned from his mission abroad.

Even before this, the council of the Hashomer Hatza'ir communes met in the new town of Afula, still only a year old, in the heart of the Jezreel Valley. Before this gathering, Yaari expounded on the essence of the Shomer identity in the pages of *Davar* (July 26, 1926), which can be summarized as follows: Hashomer Hatza'ir is a movement that

---

24 Yaari, "Letter to the Diaspora," *Hashomer Hatza'ir*, Adar-Nisan 5686 [spring 1926].
25 Ibid.

encompasses a person's entire life, from his teenage years in the youth movement and after that in the kibbutz. It pursues a unity of ideology, politics, and personal and collective life. Yaari emphasized and highlighted the essence of his movement and the importance of education for communal life by means of a counter-example—the sad fate of Gedud Ha'avodah. In his opinion, its decline stemmed from the fact that the Gedud consisted of people who had not undergone previous preparation for communal life. He noted another weakness of Gedud Ha'avodah: its utopian idea of forging a broad commune in Palestine, even before the social revolution had been won, compelling it to accept all comers. These two issues—education as the essence of the Shomer identity and selectivity as a necessary condition for the establishment of the commune—were the central pillars of Yaari's thought and action.

At the first session of the council of Hashomer Hatza'ir communes in Palestine (July 30–August 1, 1926), he did not present a clear line.[26] His remarks were so vague that one of those present complained: "We are not interested in history, but in how things stand today."[27] When he took the floor a second time, Yaari defined the meeting as only preparatory and his statements remained untargeted. Later, though, after others had spoken, he announced that the time for a decision had come. The danger that the communes would disintegrate and the situation of the youth movement in Europe required the establishment of KA. At this meeting, Yaari's ability to shape the discussion and dictate the dynamics of decisions came to the fore: all of his proposals were accepted, ranging from technical issues about the conduct of the deliberations—when to take a recess and when to call for a vote—to the wording of the resolutions.

Yaari proposed that the council vote in favor of political collectivism, a principle that was later known as "ideological collectivism." He had explained this notion in an article he published in *Davar* before the conference: "I reject anarchic freedom within the commune, whatever form it may take, because it wrecks solidarity and fragments the

---

26 Shadmi, *Meqorot*, No. 3, 76–110.
27 Ibid., 81.

spiritual partnership. Such anarchism is a bourgeois luxury. It creates a marketplace of opinions that is more appropriate for idle conversations in a coffee house. [...] But the kibbutz [...] cannot waste its energy on internal party squabbles."[28]

The Afula council resolved that "Kibbutz Artzi will be based on the principle of political collectivism" and that political issues on the agenda must be debated and resolved within KA, on the basis of collective discipline.[29] In addition, it was decided that disagreements would not lead to the creation of separate electoral lists, but would be reflected in the composition of a single list, as a function of the balance of power within KA.

Between the meeting at Beit Alfa in June 1924 and the establishment of KA in April 1927, the Marxist threads that Yaari wove into his remarks at Beit Alfa were almost completely absent from his statements. In general, there was minimal talk of Marxism as a doctrine and almost no use of Marxist analytical tools in the deliberations that led to the establishment of KA. Marxist terminology was more or less restricted to letters addressed to the movement abroad; in Palestine, the emphasis was on the Zionist character of Hashomer Hatza'ir.

On the first three days of April 1927, the founding council of Kibbutz Artzi met in Bat Galim (where Rambam Hospital stands today).[30] Present were representatives of six communes, the future cadres of the following kibbutzim: Mishmar Ha'emeq, Merḥavia, Ma'abarot, Ein Shemer, Afiqim, and Sarid. The Afiqim commune, then known as "Kibbutz Hashomer Hatza'ir from the USSR," elected not to affiliate with KA and joined the United Kibbutz movement (Hakibbutz Hame'uḥad) instead. The Sarid cadre (then "Bivracha"), graduates of the Blau-Weiss movement, did not join KA until 1931. Thus the original core of Kibbutz Artzi consisted of four groups: Mishmar Ha'emeq, Merḥavia, Ma'abarot, and Ein Shemer. The absence of Beit Alfa—the first Hashomer Hatza'ir kibbutz and the only one then in a permanent location, was keenly felt. Beit Alfa did not join Kibbutz Artzi until 1940.

---

28 *Davar*, July 26, 1926.
29 Shadmi, *Meqorot*, No. 3, 110.
30 The discussion of the founding council is based on: Zait, *Meqorot*, No. 5, 135-155; Margalit, *Ha-shomer Ha-ẓa'ir*, 127-150; Tzahor, *Hazan*, 110-113; Zait, *Ha-utopia ha-shomerit*, 234-238.

At the founding council of Kibbutz Artzi, Yaari repeated his assertion that there was a consensus in the Histadrut Labor Federation for the negation of the Exile and that the establishment of a socialist society in Palestine was the only possible means for the total rehabilitation of the national and individual lives of the Hebrew nation. The dispute, he insisted, concerned only the path and the speed with which this would be realized. He expanded on the time element:

> Our platform speaks of two stages: the pioneering stage and the revolutionary stage. It may be impossible to erect a barrier between the stages and say that the pioneering stage extends this far, and from there on is the revolutionary stage. It is only a question of the center of gravity, earlier or later, of the main goal and of the means of getting there. Still, we recognize two stages, which come one after another and do not overlap. It is not two agents working together and at the same time, but two stages that come one after the other.[31]

Yaari made it clear that the current period was not one of revolution and class war, but rather of pioneering and laying foundations. Because it was still the pioneering era, and not yet the revolutionary one, "the important thing is 100% [Zionist] fulfillment, and the community is important. [...] We do not oppose a party in principle, but do think that during the pioneering period it is not essential for us, as an educational movement in the Diaspora and a pioneering movement in Palestine. It [a political party] will be relevant for us when the transition from the pioneering period to the revolutionary period draws closer."[32]

Accordingly, Yaari drew a distinction between a party and a community (using the German terms *Partei* and *Gemeinschaft*). The role of a political party is to wage revolution and run a government; its focus is on seizing power. It must launch a war against the current regime and destroy it, after which it can establish a proletarian regime. On the other hand, the community works by going to the people, through

---

31 Zait, *Meqorot*, No. 5, 144.
32 Ibid.

education of the individual, or through grassroots activity to create primordial values—in short, through pioneering activity.

The situation in Palestine and the quest for an escape from the economic crisis of the second half of the 1920s heightened the politicization of the labor movement and forced Hashomer Hatza'ir to take a stand on these issues. Kibbutz Artzi—according to Yaari—could not limit itself to pioneering fulfillment. Its kibbutzim also had a political function: "We are not a party and we don't want to be a party today; that is why we are an independent ideological and political stream" that enforces ideological collectivism.[33]

The platform that was approved by the founding council, under the heading the "Ideological Axioms of Kibbutz Artzi, founded by Hashomer Hatza'ir," was the fruit of the efforts to defuse the tension, on the brink of open conflict, between the nationalist-Zionist aspect, which had always existed in Hashomer Hatza'ir, and the recently acquired revolutionary socialist-Marxist ideas. The solution was the "theory of stages (*étapes*)," as formulated by Yaari, which stated the primacy—in time—of the nationalist-Zionist stage and postponed the socialist revolution until the national goal had been realized.[34] The authors of the Kibbutz Artzi platform engaged in a debate with the then-dominant positions among the workers in Palestine. To counter the Leftists, in Gedud Ha'avodah and elsewhere, they offered a nationalist and Zionist perspective that was embodied in the first stage: the establishment of the National Home in Palestine on a self-sustaining productive economic basis. To counter Aḥdut Ha'avodah and Hapoel Hatza'ir, they outlined a vision of the future revolution, deferred to the second stage. The platform was also a sort of balancing of the parallelogram of forces within the movement itself: it sought to mollify those pulling leftward by presenting Zionism as the order of the day, and it tried to pacify the moderates by presenting the revolution as a future prospect that did not require action now. The platform phrased everything related to the national goal in the present tense, while all the sections regarding the social goal were stated in the future tense and destined for gradual implementation.

---

33 Ibid., 146.
34 Ibid., 156–158.

As for the place and weight of ideology for Yaari during the founding of KA, he worked by trial and error, with a certain pragmatism in adopting ideas, promoting them, and then sometimes dropping them. His guiding principle was always the desire to keep his flock together and never let them go astray. Thus he abandoned the idea of total sharing, including erotic sharing, which he had championed at Bitaniyya, and never revived it. The religious approach of the A. D. Gordon School, which imbued his article "Rootless Symbols," was replaced within a year or so by ideas with a Marxist coloration. In subsequent years Yaari developed them intermittently during his appearances in Palestine and abroad, as a function of the prevailing conditions in the movement and the outside world, as well as of how they could serve the needs of the movement and of himself as its leader. During the gestational period of KA, he frequently expressed his opinion about the link between reality and ideology: "Ideology does not always proceed in tandem with reality. Sometimes it follows reality."[35]

But make no mistake: Yaari assigned cardinal importance to ideology and its role in both consolidating the movement and preserving its unity. He was constantly looking for a creed that could guide the movement, dressing it up in various forms and contexts, as dictated by circumstances. He was not interested in ideology in the abstract, but as a means to guide political action. At the founding council of KA, Yaari tried to avoid dealing with general issues that were not essential for maintaining the movement's unity. While the platform was being drafted and ratified, he evinced a willingness to compromise on ideological matters, even those he deemed substantive, in order to keep the movement together. Thus, not all the articles he drafted were incorporated into the KA platform as approved by the founding conference. A notable omission was the section devoted exclusively to ideology, which was deferred for further deliberations by the kibbutzim and a decision by future councils. Yaari defined the questions on which no agreements were reached as those whose resolution was not urgent. These included the ultimate objective of Zionism, which of the Socialist Internationals Kibbutz Artzi would join, and which method would be

---

35 Yaari, July 31, 1926, in Shadmi, *Meqorot*, No. 3, 91.

used to wage the class war—parliamentary democracy or dictatorship.[36] These were, without a doubt, weighty questions, and they would continue to preoccupy Kibbutz Artzi and Yaari for many years to come.

Kibbutz Artzi, founded in April 1927, was the first countrywide federation of communes and collective settlements. Hakibbutz Hame'uḥad came next, that August, followed by Ḥever ha-kevutzot in 1929. But when Yaari and his colleagues set out to outline their vision of the collective, they faced two models that had been developed in Palestine: the small, intimate, and homogeneous *kevutzah*, a product of the Second Aliyah, and the *kibbutz*, based to some extent on the concept of Gedud Ha'avodah, with a larger membership and willingness to accept all comers, whatever their background and ideology. The kibbutz of the Shomrim was a synthesis of the two older versions, represented by Degania on the one hand and Ein Ḥarod on the other. Yaari managed to fuse the introversion and individualism of Hashomer Hatza'ir in its early years with the revolutionary approach that it adopted later on. Under the older dispensation, movement alumni were expected to establish settlements that were small, homogeneous communes, whose intrinsic fraternity was both the goal and a way of life. But the later concept required the founding of a kibbutz that was a political framework and revolutionary cell intended to achieve the national and class goals. Hashomer Hatza'ir's distinctive synthesis of the two archetypes led to a type of settlement that was both a self-sufficient unit and a part of a larger ideological and political collective. It was not a small and intimate group, a secluded and isolated unit, focused on developing its own internal solidarity—like the *kevutzah*. But neither was it a large kibbutz, aspiring to grow and welcome new blood, seeing itself primarily as an instrument to achieve the national goals—like the kibbutzim of Hakibbutz Hame'uḥad. According to its platform, KA would consist of pioneer cells of the new society, as a constructive tool of the Jewish working class, and a mainstay of the class war. But the platform was careful to stress that every kibbutz

---

36 Yaari to the Senior Leadership of Hashomer Hatza'ir in Warsaw, in Zait, *Meqorot*, No. 5, 173.

affiliated with Kibbutz Artzi was an "organic unit" with intrinsic and not merely instrumental value, not simply a means for realizing the class or national objectives. Each Hashomer Hatza'ir kibbutz developed as a comprehensive framework that embraced all aspects of its members' lives, small enough to preserve its intimate atmosphere, but at the same time large and robust enough to dispatch members to tasks in the outside world—among the working class in particular and the Yishuv and Zionist movement in general.

The KA platform also stated that kibbutz life required the social and individual preparation of its members, assigning this function to the youth movement in the Diaspora. This was a decisive step in the transformation of Hashomer Hatza'ir from a youth movement, founded in Europe in the second decade of the twentieth century as a response to the needs of Jewish youth then and there, into a movement that could provide a reservoir of working hands for the settlement movement in Palestine. This was a victory for the line that Yaari had championed since he first arrived in Palestine. While drafting the Kibbutz Artzi platform, he had an opportunity to translate his ideas about the nature of Hashomer Hatza'ir education into the definition of the youth movement's goal: it must train its members to live on Shomer kibbutzim in Palestine. This also continued the line, sketched out in "Rootless Symbols," that the time for Wyneken's "youth culture," which assigned intrinsic meaning and importance to adolescence *per se*, and not as preparation for the rest of one's life, had passed. As of 1927, Hashomer Hatza'ir stopped being only a movement of young people, by young people, and for young people, who developed independently of adults and without being dictated to from above, and turned into an arm of KA, a movement subordinate to the leadership in Palestine, headed by Yaari.

Even though the founding council of KA designated a six-person secretariat rather than a chairman, Yaari—who stood out as the first among equals—was accorded that status both inside and outside the movement. His kibbutz, which hosted the founding council, was selected as the location of the KA secretariat. By 1927, Yaari was the recognized leader of Hashomer Hatza'ir, and remained such for almost 50 years.

Meir Yaari, his wife Anda and their daughter Rachel, 1924.
Courtesy of Hashomer Hatza'ir Archive, Givat Haviva.

CHAPTER 5
A Wife and Helpmate

When he arrived in Palestine in the summer of 1920, Yaari was still feeling the pain of separation from his supposed fiancée, Mina Elfenbein, and it did not leave hold of him until he met Anda Karp in Bitaniyya Illit. Anda was born on January 4, 1902, in the city of Brody, in eastern Galicia, and grew up in Lwów.[1] Her family was not observant, and she attended a Polish girls' school. Her mother tongue was Polish and she spoke German as well, but was not proficient in Yiddish. Following the lead of her older brothers, she joined Hashomer Hatza'ir when she was 15. The movement conducted its activities in Polish; her Hebrew was at best rudimentary before her aliyah. Her experiences in the youth movement stayed with her for the rest of her life: admiration to the point of passionate love for the young woman who was her counselor, hikes in the bosom of nature accompanied by loud group singing, and—more than anything—the wonderful poems she knew by heart until her dying day.

The Karp family escaped the postwar pogrom in Lwów unscathed, but they felt a change for the worse in the attitude towards Jews, and Anda encountered manifestations of antisemitism. After the pogrom, the members of the movement began their preparations for aliyah. She followed suit by engaging in simple agricultural tasks on a farm not far from the city. Her father had strong reservations about her decision to make aliyah, but her mother extended enthusiastic support. Anda was 18 when, in the company of some 100 members of Hashomer Hatza'ir, she passed through Vienna a month after Yaari had left the city, *en route* to Palestine. The cruise from Trieste to Jaffa was a jaunty excursion for the Shomrim, brimming with joy and full of song and dance.

---

1 The information about Anda comes from Lurie, *Anda*, unless otherwise specified.

July 19, 1920, the date of Anda Karp's arrival in Palestine, was a scorching summer day. In Jaffa, she too was met by the Arab stevedores who "just picked us up and threw us into the boat."[2] At her first stop in Palestine, Umm al-Aleq, she was set to work deepening the channels to drain the swamp. Like her comrades, she suffered from the heat and the swarms of mosquitoes, and like so many others she came down with malaria. It was while she was hospitalized in Zichron Ya'akov that she first saw Yaari, who had come to pay a sick call on members of the group, but there was no spark between them at that time. They met again in Bitaniyya. Yaari—a garrulous young man with black hair and a wild mustache—did not impress her, although he was strongly taken with her beauty. As already noted, had things developed as he wished and Bitaniyya become an all-male brotherhood, Anda would have been forced out of the camp at the time of the great selection. But as fate would have it, her brother's stubborn insistence meant that she was one of the four young women who remained. She was immediately aware that he was sweet on her.

Anda's demand that she be included on the roster for nighttime guard duty at the Bitaniyya Illit camp ran into solid opposition. The only one who supported her was Yaari; when her turn came to stand watch, he hid in a corner and kept an eye on her, just in case. At dawn, she came back inside, tense and shaking, and stopped insisting on equal rights in that roster. Yaari found another way to show his affection for her. While they were working not far apart, digging holes for olive saplings, he noticed her bleeding calluses and how hard the job was for her. He started up a conversation, and by the by suggested that they divide the labor between them: he would break up the soil with the mattock and then she would remove the clods with the hoe. A bond grew up between them and they went out walking at night (nocturnal walks were the only opportunity for people to be alone at Bitaniyya). She felt his strong attachment and was astounded by his wealth of ideas, by the fact that he always had something to say, and that he listened to her attentively. His mind was in the clouds, occupied by lofty matters, while she felt completely detached from the world and everything that

---

2 Ibid, 24.

was going on around her. What was happening to her, to them, filled her entire world.

As will be recalled, when the Bitaniyya job was over, in the spring of 1921, Anda Karp and Meir Yaari did not go straight to the Shomriya camp, as most of the others did, but hiked through the Galilee as a twosome. Their excursion wound up in Haifa, where the local rabbi married them in a proper religious ceremony—a formality rarely observed by the pioneers in those days. When they reached Shomriya, the couple was allotted a tent of their own, but kept their marriage a dark secret.[3]

The story of their wedding, which Yaari recounted on several occasions, is curious in several respects. The first is why Anda and Meir had a religious ceremony, which ran totally counter to the norm among the Shomrim. It seems to have been Meir's initiative, out of respect for his parents, and Anda agreed without hesitation.[4] The second question has to do with the date of the wedding. The members of Bitaniyya reached the Shomriya camp just before Passover. Meir and Anda's trip, and certainly their visit to Haifa towards the end, took place during the seven-week period after that festival, when religious weddings are banned. In fact, their marriage contract is dated 13 Av 5681 (August 17, 1921), which means that the ceremony took place several months after they joined the Shomriya camp.[5] If so, why did he repeatedly tell people that he and Anda were already married when they reached Shomriya?

The third question is why Yaari rushed to formalize their relationship. How should we explain the fact that he established a family at a time when he was vigorously attacking that very institution? It had only been a short while since he had written that "bourgeois family attitude to sex is the enemy of the commune" and preached in favor of an all-male brotherhood.[6]

What is more, not only did Yaari reject marriage, his attitude towards women was negative and condescending. He did not want to include women in the group because they were not ready for a commune, and their presence

---
3 Yaari, *Al Hamishmar*, Sept. 4, 1970.
4 Interview with Yaari [1978], HHA, 95-7.3(4), 95; Yaari, Memoirs [early 1980s], KMA, MYF, 8(3); Lurie, *Anda*, 39.
5 Mintz, *Ḥevlei ne'urim*, 318-319.
6 Ibid., 382.

would disrupt the group due to their desire to lead a bourgeois family life.[7] In those days, when he expressed his views on "erotic relationships," orally and in writing, he intentionally avoided the phrase "family relationships."[8] Even when he seemed to have changed his mind about all-male companies, having resigned himself to accepting women, and making his peace with the centrality of family in individual and social life, he continued to treat women as inferiors.[9] His only positive references to women during the Bitaniyya period were as child-bearers and mothers, marked by a sort of confusion or identification of the woman-mother with the soil.[10]

Did Yaari's negative attitude towards women and his statements in favor of all-male communes and the establishment of a sort of monastic order uncontaminated by women have anything to do with his sexual orientation? Does the account of that nocturnal dip in the Sea of Galilee in the company of the sandy-haired grey-eyed young man, along with other homoerotic passages in his writings, point to homosexual tendencies?[11]

Twenty years later, Yaari was addressing a group at the movement's ideological symposium:

> In Europe we encountered currents of a youth movement in which love was called 'Eros.' Sharing was an erotic phenomenon. We passed through the stages of rationalization and reached psychoanalysis. There were currents that saw Eros as the glue. Blüher wrote about 'the role of Eros in a company of men,' and this influenced us. We also had examples from Hebrew literature about sharing among men. [...] Many fell into the trap then, including myself. Each of us had a period of decadence.[12]

Yaari's writing of the early 1920s is indeed full of ideas that originated with Blüher, who was homosexual. Blüher saw the unisex group of the

---

7 Ibid., 309, 382, and 400.
8 Ibid., 282.
9 Ibid., 413.
10 Ibid., 398–402.
11 As might be inferred from Mintz, *Ḥevlei ne'urim*, as well as Yair Sheleg, "The Bitaniyya Myth," *Bamaḥaneh*, Sept. 22, 1988.
12 Shadmi, *Meqorot*, No. 4, 11. The symposium took place in September 1940.

German *Wandervogel* as a male society bound together by Eros. For Blüher, Eros meant sexual attraction between men, even though it did not necessarily have to be consummated in a physical relationship. In a later interview, Yaari explained that the Hebrew translation of the role of the erotic in male society is homosexuality, "but we had no idea that this was homosexuality. [...] We thought it was something like Buber's *Gemeinschaft*, the *Gemeinschaft* of Landauer and Buber. We were innocent."[13] He added, at the age of 81, that "Eros" meant "brotherhood, the brotherhood of the *ḥavruta*, the brotherhood of the community."[14] Today, instead of "Eros" he would say "love of humanity and fraternal solidarity." The most appropriate interpretation was, "Love your fellow as yourself." The interviewer did not relent. He wanted an explicit statement as to whether the Eros of Kibbutz Artzi was homosexuality. Yaari replied: "I can't remember a single homosexual in the entire movement of Hashomer Hatza'ir, ever. Not one! [...] It never was and never existed, no one. Nu, do you understand?"[15]

Whether we accept this vigorous denial at face value, or allow that it leaves open the possibility that there was something going on there, we must not forget two points. One is that passages that can be read as having a homosexual meaning or taken as reflecting their author's homosexual tendencies were published and widely circulated at the time and included in both Yaari's and the movement's canonical literature. They were issued by the movement's own publishing house, in a society and era in which homosexuality was unmentionable and considered immoral—and from which Yaari himself, as we have just seen, shrank as from fire. Had his writings been understood by contemporaries as showing homosexual tendencies, they would certainly have been censored or toned down before being printed and reprinted.

The second point is that Yaari's statements in favor of a male-only group should be seen against the background of their time and historical context. We know of revolutionary and pioneering bands of settlers and fighters that were all male—Yaari himself mentioned them

---

13 Interview with Yaari [1978], HHA, 95-7.3(4).
14 Ibid.
15 Ibid.

in his article, "Ourselves and Palestine." So it may well be that Yaari's remarks about male solidarity do not indicate a sexual tendency but stem rather from the primacy of the collective in his world. The same article includes lines almost explicitly in this spirit: "We must act so that the group, and not the family, will be the true focus of activity."[16] He was afraid that the heterosexual family would destroy the commune and barred women from the commune because he saw them as the responsible for the family's destructive character. If so, his preference for men and desire for an all-male society was a byproduct of his placing the good of the collective above all else.

One way or another, Yaari's statements that could be interpreted as reflecting an erotic and sexual preference for men soon came to an end. About a year after he set foot on Palestinian soil he was already married. This is one more item in the gap between what he wrote and said and what he actually did. The dissonance seems to have bothered him; in his comment about the man who had once served as his inspiration we may see a degree of insight into himself: "Blüher, when he wrote his books and pamphlets that attack the erotic life of the family and society, already had a family."[17] In 1936, Yaari "repented" of his earlier attitude towards women; he referred to "Ourselves and Palestine" as a sin, and his ideas about all-male self-defense and labor brigades as a "delusion." Those ideas had been influenced by the psychology of Weininger, Freud, and Nietzsche, whose works he saw, in retrospect, as misogynistic. But these theories had fallen on fertile ground when he was younger, as he explained:

> We were a transitional generation. We passed by rapid steps from the milieu of piety and devotion to the Enlightenment and nationalism, and from there to national and social emancipation. No lines had yet been drawn between the periods. Various influences were mixed together. To this may be added the anti-feminist influence of the Talmud and the winds that were blowing in Hebrew literature. This is how it came about that the first generation of Hashomer Hatza'ir

---

16 Mintz, *Ḥevlei ne'urim*, 362.
17 Zait and Shamir, *Meir Yaari*, 213.

arrived in Palestine with an ideology of sharing and an individualist and even anti-feminist psychology. I do not want to attribute these views to the entire generation of the Third Aliyah, but I do not deny that I too shared them.[18]

Yaari's attitude towards female members of the kibbutz, women in society at large, and the role of the family was complex and inconsistent. For him, respect for a woman as a wife and a monogamous and puritanical attitude towards relations between the sexes went hand in hand with a conservative approach to women's place in society and equality between the sexes. He continued to see the female member of the kibbutz as the "Yiddishe Mama," the Jewish mother of the Diaspora.[19]

Writing about the status of women on the kibbutz, in the early 1930s, he admitted that the objective options for female employment were more restricted than those available to men, enumerating the tasks that women could perform as a matter of destiny: pregnancy, nursing, and childcare limited their freedom, despite the collective childraising system of the kibbutz. There were also objective reasons, such as the harsh climate of Palestine.[20]

From the outset, Yaari was aware that the kibbutz could provide only a partial solution to the question of women's (in)equality.[21] At sundry opportunities he spoke and wrote in slogans about the need to better the situation of the female comrades in various spheres and to include them as equal partners in running the movement.[22] If a kibbutz sent a male-only delegation to meet with him, he would scold them for representing only 50% of the membership. He lacked the ability to exert influence and effect changes in all domains, but even when it came to the composition of the movement's institutions and leadership—an issue where his influence was paramount—he did not translate his high-flown

---

18 Yaari, "On the Road to Equality" (1936), *Be-derekh arukah*, 176.
19 Yaari, "On Graves," *Hedim*, November 1943.
20 Yaari, "Women in the Movement" (1930), *Be-derekh arukah*, 173.
21 Zait and Shamir, *Meir Yaari*, 160 (written in 1926).
22 Meeting of the Kibbutz Artzi Executive Committee, Nov. 23, 1929, HHA, 5-10.1(3); Yaari, "Women in the Movement" (1930), *Be-derekh arukah*, 172-174.

statements about the role of female members into action. When it was proposed to reserve 20% of the slots on party electoral slates for women, Yaari said that he would like to increase the number of women on the list and that it was important to encourage them to be involved politically, but this should not be done by setting fixed percentages for them.[23] His opposition to reserved slots and fixed percentages for any sector was expressed in other cases as well, such as the co-opting of members of the younger generation to key positions. In other words, what was involved was not simply a dismissive attitude towards women but a principle—his desire to leave the decision as to who would serve on movement institutions or be placed on electoral lists to the leadership (to himself, effectively) without having his hands tied by any quotas.

As the years passed, various processes on the kibbutzim worked significant changes in Yaari's thoughts. His rejection of the family as the enemy of the commune was replaced by the realization that the family is in fact necessary and even the keystone of kibbutz life. During the 1930s, he drew on what Marx, Engels, and Lenin had written about the family as a socioeconomic unit, the pros and cons of monogamy, and women's equality. In 1930, addressing the youth movement's third convention in the Diaspora, he posed the question, "Does socialism aspire to eliminate the family as a socioeconomic unit only, or does it also seek to eliminate monogamy and permanent ties between men and women, and even to abolish the bond between parents and their children?" The phrasing of the question makes his answer clear. Relying on Lenin, he rejected "the glass of water theory," which holds that the "sexual act is no more important than any other physiological need, like drinking a glass of water; [...] people cohabit when they feel a need and go their separate ways without emotion."[24] He himself defined such behavior as "sexual life detached from its goal: producing the next generation," and, like Lenin, was opposed to sexual anarchy.[25] He was in favor of the stability of family life because he kept his eye on what was good for women, who lose their youth sooner; if the couple bond is broken after

---

23 Mapam Inner Secretariat, July 19, 1973, HHA, 90.79(1).
24 Yaari, "Women in the Movement" (1930), *Be-derekh arukah*, 172.
25 Ibid.

a few years of family life, the female partner will not have as good a chance of finding a new companion as the man will.[26]

These topics concerned him not only as a counselor in a youth movement and leader of a kibbutz movement, but also as a spouse and family man, and he shared his thoughts with his wife. Incidents on several kibbutzim led him to ponder and draw conclusions about the relationship between spouses, free love, infidelity, and the like, and he wrote about this forthrightly to Anda. He was troubled by the fact that some families stuck together only through weakness, codependence, or habit; sometimes it was the children that kept a couple together, and sometimes fear of public opinion. "All these phenomena are normal in a bourgeois environment, but they are the kiss of death for the kibbutz."[27] He thought the negative reasons for staying married should no longer exist on the kibbutz, where there was no issue of the husband's having to support his wife.

He shared his deep thoughts about the bond between married partners with his wife. He did not think it a sin if a couple split up because their relationship had cooled. It would be more problematic if they stayed together while looking for and finding a liaison outside the family. He had tended to look down on those who did this, although later he changed his mind; concluding that this was an overly subjective assessment, and began distinguishing the theoretical approach to these questions from what suited him personally and the two of them as a couple. He did not see it as sinful to have an affair with another woman while maintaining the existing family, as long as the woman did not feel that she was being taken advantage of or humiliated and as long as it did not involve the seduction of an innocent girl. He told Anda about cases on Beit Alfa where extramarital love actually reinforced the family, but added that he did not envy such people. The situation was particularly difficult if a child was born from such a relationship. He was aware and thanked his lucky stars, he wrote to his Anda, that it had fallen to his lot "to find such a dear woman" and proclaimed, in no uncertain terms, "I am monogamous through and through. My love for you is not only sexual and not even what

---

26 Ibid., 174.
27 Meir to Anda, June 18, 1928, KMA, MYF, 5(2). Only the first page of the letter is in this file; the second page, separated and undated, is in KMA, MYF, 3(1).

they call erotic."²⁸ He had come to realize that their case, with its profound companionship, was unusual, and saw it as a stroke of good luck or grace.

The changes in Yaari's position on romantic and family relationships resulted from his own family situation and his experiences as a spouse and father, but his concern for the future of the kibbutz was always predominant in his thoughts. "The bond between fathers and sons is the eternal chain of human civilization. No socialist or kibbutz movement aspires to abolish these relations," he said in the early 1930s.²⁹ He set responsibility for the second generation of kibbutz society as an ethical tenet beyond challenge. Even though the kibbutz and society must bear the main burden of education, severance of the ties between children and their parents was liable to undermine the stability of kibbutz life in general.³⁰

Yaari always kept the collective at the center. In his youth he believed that there was a conflict of interest between the family and the collective and feared that the former would overshadow the latter, obstructing its development. Later, when he and kibbutz society were older and more mature, Yaari no longer saw the family as a force undermining the foundations of the kibbutz, but as a source of its stability. Looking back, he regretted that while his commune was wandering from place to place in the 1920s and its economic future remained uncertain, the members, particularly the women, avoided having children.³¹ In 1935, he warned that budgetary difficulties were preventing couples from having more than two children. If he had to decide between starting a healthy family and physical improvements on the kibbutz, he preferred a healthy family.³² He rejected the "free" approach to family matters and came out against the aversion to permanent relationships and parenthood.³³

During the Second World War, shortly after their third child was born, Yaari looked back critically and regretfully that "we kept dancing the hora and said we had time enough for a second and third

---

28 Ibid.
29 Yaari, "Women in the Movement" (1930), *Be-derekh arukah*, 173.
30 Ibid., 174.
31 Meir to Anda, June 18, 1928, KMA, MYF, 5(2).
32 Margalit, *Ha-shomer Ha-ẓa'ir*, 259–260.
33 Yaari at the 11th Council of Kibbutz Artzi, September 28–30, 1935, HHA, 5-20.1(7).

child. We told the Master of the Universe to wait for us."[34] Just before the end of the war, he presented the demographic war as the most tragic and fateful of all. "In the next period, we will have to fight this campaign, so that the freedom-loving peoples will not decrease but will be victorious in this demographic battle."[35] And whose role was it to establish kibbutzim with large populations? Yaari asked at the Council of Kibbutz Artzi, and then answered: Their female members. "No one can replace them in this." "(Laughter in the hall)" noted the secretary who was keeping the minutes. Yaari hastened to clarify that his ambition was that the female comrades, in addition to being mothers, would also enjoy equality and share in the responsibilities.[36]

His first child, Rachel, was born at Hadassah Hospital in Tel Aviv in May 1923. After Anda gave birth, the malaria she had contracted at Um al-Aleq came back. The baby, too, caught it, and mother and daughter were hospitalized. After their discharge, they were invited to stay in the home of the Rosolio family because the Yaaris were living in a tent, and the hut that was supposed to serve the commune as a nursery had not yet been built.[37] Anda did not recuperate from the birth and malaria. She felt unwell, had no appetite, lost weight, and was unable to work. When Yaari went on his first mission abroad, in 1924, his wife and daughter joined him. This was an opportunity for them to get to know each other's families. Anda's father was skeptical about his son-in-law's ability to make his way in life, but he made his peace with the match after he attended a Zionist meeting where Yaari spoke and saw how much the audience admired him. Anda and Rachel visited Meir's mother and sister in Reisha shortly after his father's death. The visitors did not feel comfortable there and their stay was brief.[38]

The Yaari family returned to Palestine and the Herzliyya commune, which still lacked a permanent home, in late 1925. But Anda had not fully recovered; in 1927 she went back to Europe alone for an extended

---

34 Yaari to Kibbutz Mishmar Ha'emeq, Feb. 19, 1942, HHA, *heh*-3.36(2).
35 Yaari at the 25th Council of Kibbutz Artzi, Apr. 10, 1945, HHA, 5-20.4(3).
36 Ibid.
37 Rachel (Yaari) Groll, "On an Old Historical Debate," *Bamesheq* [Kibbutz Merhavia newsletter], Apr. 13, 1987, KMA, MYF, 7(4); Lurie, *Anda*, 46–47.
38 Lurie, *Anda*, 61.

period of convalescence. In her absence, Yaari divided his time between the commune, then based in Haifa, and caring for his daughter, on the one hand, and the movement-related activities that took him away from home and sometimes out of the country, on the other. In the fall of 1927 he attended the 15th Zionist Congress in Basel as well as the second world convention of Hashomer Hatza'ir. When he came back to Palestine, his first stop was a three-day session of the Histadrut council. Only then did he return home. The reunion with four-year-old Rachel brought tears to his eyes. The girl clung to him with her whole body, hugging him fiercely. On the first night he was back, she asked him to come to the children's house and tell her a story. The girl had been left without either parent for an entire month and had found the experience very difficult. She felt that she had been abandoned, Yaari wrote to Anda; but, he consoled her and himself, no real harm had been done to the girl. After this, an especially close relationship developed between father and daughter. She became his closest friend. Sometimes he even felt that she was getting too attached to him. When he was home, she was not interested in playing with the other children. Instead, she sat in his room all day, swept it, "chattering away like a bubbling brook. [...] There is nothing she won't do if I ask her to."[39] She had a burning desire to win her father's approval and compliments. He was almost never angry with her. When he was sad, she would say, "Come to me today and don't tell a story. You don't even have to sing. Just come, sit down, and read a book."[40]

Little Rachel would not fall asleep without a kiss and a story from her father. Every evening he went to the children's house, where he told animal stories to his daughter and her bunkmates. He bought an illustrated book by Levin Kipnis and placed it in a drawer in the children's house. No one touched it until "Papa Meir" came in the evening to read it to them. He would sit down, look at Rachel and the others, and begin, "Listen children and I'll tell you a story."

---

39 Meir to Anda, June 6, 1928, KMA, MYF, 5(2).
40 Meir to Anda, Jan. 20, 1928, Ibid.

At once their smiling eyes shine like small electric lanterns, sometimes responding with laughter and sometimes curling their lips, close to tears in their excitement. But I am the wizard who can see the future and will soon alter the situation; the tragedy switches to comic motifs or quiet idylls, the faces become serene and clear again, and when I reach the end—she sighs and fall asleep. . . ."[41]

Before Rachel turned five, her father began teaching her to read. In advance of Passover, the proud father told her mother, who was still abroad, that the girls had baked *matzot*. They could tell the story of the Exodus very well; "in the meantime, they have begun to believe in God and they already have a solid world view."[42]

Yaari made sure to bring Rachel presents from his many trips, and later to his son Aviezer, seven years her junior, and their peers in the children's house. He also brought gifts for Anda, which he could afford because of his frugality with other outlays. Sometimes he added individual notes to the children to the letters he sent Anda. To four-year-old Aviezer he sent a picture of a rabbit he had drawn, and wrote to him, "Hello Aviezer, Here is a fine rabbit. When I told him about you he listened and perked up his ears and sat there contentedly. He knows you are a good boy."[43] Yaari repeatedly asked Anda to recharge the children's memory of their father. "The living relationship is very important to me," he wrote, and shared his pangs of conscience that he did not devote enough time to them.[44]

When Rachel was fifteen and Aviezer eight, Yaari shared his parental bliss with Anda: "Rachel is truly an angel and the little one too has a soul of his own."[45] "Oh—those children," he gushed. "They are our happiness!"[46] When Rachel grew up she wrote directly to her father, and her letters, which he thought "amazing" and "tremendous,"

---

41 Ibid.
42 Meir to Anda, March 31, 1928, Ibid.
43 Meir to Anda, Jan. 1, 1934, Ibid.
44 Meir to Anda, Sep. 28, 1938, Ibid.
45 Meir to Anda, Oct. 18, 1938, Ibid.
46 Meir to Anda, Nov. 10, 1938, Ibid.

gave him great joy. The short letters Aviezer sent him when he was abroad also gave him much pleasure.⁴⁷ In his letters home Yaari also sent his regards to Anda's mother, Sophia, who made aliyah in 1932 and divided her time between her children in Merḥavia, Beit Alfa, and Tel Aviv. She died in Merḥavia in 1940 and was buried there.

In the summer of 1928, more than a year after Anda had gone abroad to convalesce, the movement asked Yaari to embark on a protracted mission in Europe. The kibbutz was not sure what to do. The caretakers wanted Rachel to stay there, but expressed their concern that if she were left alone (again) it would affect her badly. Some of the comrades felt that Yaari should take Rachel with him. In the end, it was decided that Rachel would stay at home and that Yaari would go away for no longer than three months. He himself pondered the matter for a long time, caught between a rock and a hard place. The movement needed him both in Palestine and abroad. And family concerns, too, made it hard for him to refuse the assignment, as he wrote Anda, because "I am strongly pulled to you. And when I imagine what I would do if one fine day I suddenly entered your room in Zakopane [the resort town where she was convalescing], quite unexpected, it is difficult for me to suppress my desire."⁴⁸ And then there was Rachel. He leaned towards leaving her behind and in support of this idea reported what she thought: "Rachel herself keeps sending me abroad every day, so I can bring her back her mother. She promises she won't cry, not even once. I want to think that the hope that we will return together is likely to sustain her while I'm away."⁴⁹ In the end he went without Rachel. In his letters back to the commune, he asked to hear everything about her. He instructed Anda to come to Krakow and wait for him in a hotel, whose name and address he specified: "I want to take advantage of every moment I can spend with you."⁵⁰

At this time, the Herzliyya commune was still in a temporary location in Haifa. By the summer of 1928, Yaari was afraid that the group would disintegrate if it were not allowed to move to some existing agricultural settlement (as opposed to starting a new one). Then the possibility arose

---

47 Meir to Anda, Sep. 28, 1938, Ibid.
48 Meir to Anda, May 3, 1928, Ibid.
49 Meir to Anda, July 1, 1928, Ibid.
50 Ibid.

of settling in Merḥavia. Merḥavia, founded in 1910 by members of the watchman's organization Hashomer and laborers of the Second Aliyah, was the first Jewish settlement in the Jezreel Valley. In early 1911, it was organized as a "workers' cooperative"—a type of settlement based on the ideas of the sociologist and economist Franz Oppenheimer. During the First World War, Merḥavia, like the entire Yishuv, experienced many trials and tribulations; when the war ended, it was beset by economic difficulties augmented by an internal crisis. The problem was the fundamental principle of the cooperative, which was that workers were paid as a function of their diligence and skills, with no mechanism for mutual assistance. When couples married and had children, the family's income decreased because the wife stopped working—precisely when their expenses increased. This led to tension between the "rich" singles and the "poor" families, who abandoned the village one after another. The cooperative fell apart in 1918; a few of the singles stayed on for another year before they too went their way. Several new groups occupied the site during the next decade, including one composed of English and American veterans of the Jewish Legion, which Golda Myerson (later Meir) and her husband Morris joined for a while.

Yaari was enthralled by the possibility that the Herzliyya commune would move to Merḥavia, because of the beauty of the location. In fact, after they settled there in 1929 he never stopped exclaiming over how lovely it was. Yaari was very happy in his commune. "I have never felt so well as in this commune," he wrote to Anda in the summer of 1928.[51] His relations with the other members were almost familial. His comrades wrote to him about what was going on at the kibbutz and its divisions—the field crops, the orchards, the dairy barn, and the beehives—how many children were born and how their names were chosen. When he was away they sent him all the kibbutz newsletters and expressed their concern about his welfare and health, as they would for a close relative.[52] The candid letters he sent home were read out to the entire kibbutz and made a great impression on the members.[53] "Fierce nostalgia draws me

---

[51] Meir to Anda, July 1, 1928, KMA, MYF, 5(2).
[52] Letters to Yaari from members of the kibbutz, KMA, MYF, 1(4) and 1(5).
[53] Schutzberg to Yaari, Nov. 1, 1936, KMA, MYF, 1(4); Pra'i (Peri) to Yaari, Nov. 6, 1938, KMA, MYF, 1(4).

back to the kibbutz and my home. I frequently dream about the children and other people, about the cows and about kibbutz events, both happy and sad."[54] He was part of the kibbutz klezmer band, which assembled in the dining hall and played and sang lustily, with his own voice part of the harmony. But during the 1930s it fell apart gradually, much to his chagrin.[55] Yaari took part in the kibbutz assemblies, was a permanent member of the economic affairs committee, and was considered to be the patron of the dairy barn. At one point he knew almost every cow by name as well as her milk production. From time to time he did his share in the campaigns to uproot the thornbushes that grew in the courtyard.[56] But he was never a rank-and-file member of the kibbutz and was never part of the work roster, neither on weekdays nor on Sabbaths and holidays.

Anda and Meir's second child, Aviezer ("Avik"), was born on February 24, 1930. He was the first child born in Merḥavia, about three months after the group had moved there. When Anda went into labor, Meir's younger brother Tuvia took her in the horse-cart to the Jezreel Valley lying-in hospital in Ein Ḥarod.[57] Uncle Tuvia served as Aviezer's surrogate father during Yaari's many absences and frequently came to pick up the boy from the children's house when Anda was late. In general, Yaari was home at Merḥavia only on weekends, but then he spent—or tried to spend—as much time as possible with his children. He would take Aviezer on tours of the various kibbutz facilities and the orchards, carrying the child on his shoulders, talking to him, and singing as he walked. But even on weekends, people would come steal the father from his son. Both generations sensed what they were missing. Yaari was deeply distressed that he played so small a part in raising his son and was sorry that he devoted so little time to being a father. His son responded to him in kind—and rightly so, his father was pained to admit.[58] When Aviezer went off to the boarding school in Mishmar Ha'emeq, Yaari was

---

54 Meir to the kibbutz, Sept. 23, 1930, KMA, MYF, 1(2).
55 Yaari, "On the Threshold" [1941], *Be-derekh arukah*, 198.
56 A. Yaari, *Ba-derekh mi-Merḥavya*, 90.
57 Lurie, *Anda*, 56.
58 A. Yaari, *Ba-derekh mi-Merḥavya*, 89–90; Meir to Anda, Aug. 3, 1932, KMA, MYF, 5(2).

very busy and cut off from his son's daily life and experiences. Even during vacations they almost never saw each other.[59]

As a father, Yaari was quick-tempered, but also frequently full of joy and excitement. In the evening, when the parents put their children to bed, he would tell his son and the others in his room Hassidic tales and the stories of Rabbi Elimelech of Lyzhansk and reminiscences of his own childhood and adolescence, and would sing to them in his clear, ringing voice. In his and Anda's quarters he often paced back and forth looking for the right phrase, and it was forbidden to disturb him then. The tension in the tiny kibbutz apartment was even greater when he was sick. Everyone had to tiptoe around him whenever he came back from the hospital or a convalescent home in Palestine or abroad. Both generations remembered an episode in which Yaari, at the height of a psychosomatic crisis, chased his six-year-old son from the room because he was making noise. Years passed before Aviezer forgave his father for this, until, on a visit to his parents in Nahariyya, when he was eleven, he lost control, reminded his father of the incident, and they made peace. After that their relationship became closer. When Aviezer was older he sometimes accompanied his father on his trips and listened to his lectures.[60]

There were long periods when Meir and Anda maintained a correspondence marriage. In 1927–28 she was in Europe; in subsequent decades he was the one who was often away from home, on movement-related business or for health reasons. His letters to Anda are a treasure trove of information, thoughts, emotions, and meditations and open a window into his innermost life. Once he wrote something so confidential that he instructed her: "Please—hide this letter very well or burn it!"[61] Obviously (and luckily) she chose the first option. The picture provided by their correspondence is one-dimensional, because her letters to him have not survived. Yaari found an advantage to maintaining the relationship through letters, and admitted that "perhaps it is even easier for me to tell you my thoughts and assessments in writing than to speak them face to

---

59 A. Yaari, *Ba-derekh mi-Merḥavya*, 42–43.
60 The stories as seen from the son's perspective are recounted in A. Yaari, *Ba-derekh mi-Merḥavya*.
61 Meir to Anda, Mar. 2, 1928, KMA, MYF, 5(2). This file contains Yaari's letters to his wife in 1927 and 1928, on which the present account is based.

face."⁶² When he wrote to her he felt that he could go on all day long, had had he not been compelled to write a number of official letters as well.

He needed the correspondence with Anda as he needed to breathe air. He promised that he would write her every week and was very disappointed, to the point of anger and irritation, when a letter from her was delayed. In his letters he offered advice and lectured her: "You write in a lazy way, without a date!" he scolded her when she was in Poland.⁶³ She expressed her fear of writing in Hebrew, and he reassured her: "Don't worry: I will correct your mistakes and we will make it a joint effort."⁶⁴

He wrote to her about earthshaking matters as well; to help her understand what he was talking about he would add a background explanation. He wrote his letters to her in a fine Hebrew script, and sometimes added vowel points, to the entire text or only the difficult words, so that she would understand him better. But she complained about his handwriting, and he promised her: "From now on I will try to write slowly, like a student in first grade, so that even a blind person will be able to read and understand."⁶⁵ And all of this with full vowel points! When he made the effort, his penmanship was clear; when he wrote to his children it was perfectly legible. In later years he often used a typewriter for his letters to Anda, scrawling only his signature and a few words at the bottom in a handwriting that was becoming harder and harder to decipher. His handwriting bothered him, and he envied Ben-Gurion's clear, attractive, and always legible script.

While Anda was recovering in Poland in the late 1920s, Yaari understood her feelings and told her to get over her longing for Rachel and not to worry: the girl was healthy, beautiful, and kind-hearted. He instructed her to stay abroad for at least six months and get rid of the malaria once and for all; otherwise, he wrote her jokingly, he would issue "an order to the government of Palestine not to let you

---

62 Meir to Anda, June 18, 1928, Ibid.
63 Meir to Anda, Jan. 20, 1928, Ibid.
64 Meir to Anda, May 28, 1928, Ibid.
65 Meir to Anda, Jan. 20, 1928, Ibid.

off the boat and to send you back where you came from."⁶⁶ He asked her to "eat and drink and be happy," encouraged her to dress well, and advised her to buy or sew herself a "nice frock. If you want to make me happy, make yourself a tastefully tailored dress and not one like a pioneer's sack."⁶⁷ He ordered her to exercise in the mornings, to take many cold baths, to eat strawberries with cream and drink black beer.⁶⁸ He asked her to tell him everything: how much she weighed, whether she was getting iron drops and keeping tabs on her appetite, whether she had a fever, and if they had checked her spleen recently.⁶⁹ Shortly before her return, he warned her: "Don't you dare come home if you weigh less than sixty kilos. That's the minimum. We won't make a fuss about any excess."⁷⁰

He was parsimonious about his expenses when he traveled and sent her what he saved to pay for her time in Zakopane and other convalescent spas. He made a great effort so that she would have money not only for the trip but also to buy herself pretty clothes and various necessities for their room in the kibbutz, like tablecloths, paintings, and an ashtray, because he wanted their room to be neat and comfortable. In one of his letters, he advised her to study something, especially Hebrew and infant care.⁷¹

Without Anda, Yaari felt "like a fish out of water."⁷² Her protracted illness and their long separation were an extremely difficult test for him. The letters he wrote her from so far away were full of desire and suppressed passion. "I am racing towards you as if on a chariot of fire," he wrote from Lwów in anticipation of their reunion, after several months of separation.⁷³ He was consumed with longing for her. "Every line of a face, every walk that looks like yours and creates

---

66 Meir to Anda, May 3, 1928, Ibid.
67 Meir to Anda, Jan. 20, 1928, Ibid.
68 Meir to Anda, May 3, 1928, Ibid.
69 Meir to Anda, March 31, 1928, Ibid.
70 Meir to Anda, July 26, 1928, Ibid.
71 Meir to Anda, March 2, 1928, Ibid.
72 Meir to Anda, June 18, 1928, Ibid.
73 Meir to Anda, Oct. 1, 1927, Ibid.

the illusion of a resemblance to you makes my blood seethe."[74] When he read her letters, he felt like someone who had just discovered that secret called love. Afterwards, when it was he who traveled abroad while Anda stayed in Palestine, he was again beset by longing for her. With a brimming heart he wrote to her: "I am 'dying' from my longing for you. And on top of that, in a large room with two beds. If only the second bed wasn't empty, and if only, if only. ..."[75] After the children grew up, Anda started accompanying her husband on his trips abroad.

Anda was the only person whose criticism Yaari accepted with love. He self-deprecatingly observed that Anda was generally received cordially wherever she went, while he was greeted with suspicion and heightened vigilance.[76] She was his anchor, his home port, his secure nest; the family circle was almost the only corner of peace and serenity he had left.[77] Anda was the glue that held the Yaari family together, standing faithfully alongside her husband and serving as her children's address for their day-to-day issues.[78]

Yaari's poor health was legendary. He never concealed his physical problems at the time or in his memoirs; nor was he shy about mentioning them during debates with his colleagues.[79] He contracted rheumatism in the trenches of the First World War. During his early years in Palestine he came down with both dysentery and typhus. In the later 1920s he began to suffer from hemorrhoids and went through five operations to treat them. Complications from the surgery left him with digestive problems. In the winter of 1928 he had sciatica during the rainy season; his condition worsened because he was living in a room with a clammy mud floor and the dampness penetrated even through his quilt.[80]

---

74 Meir to Anda, May 3, 1928, Ibid.
75 Meir to Anda, Sept. 28, 1938, Ibid.
76 Yaari, Memoirs [1981], 31, KMA, MYF, 8(3).
77 Meir to Anda, Sept. 8, 1938, KMA, MYF, 5(2).
78 A. Yaari, *Ba-derekh mi-Merḥavya*, 89.
79 Yaari to Pra'i, Sept. 23, 1938, KMA, MYF, 1(2).
80 Meir to Anda, Mar. 2, 1928, KMA, MYF, 5(2).

At 31, he complained that his strength was fading; at 35, he felt that he needed a vacation from his regular activities.[81]

In the summer of 1933, he fell ill with meningitis.[82] When the 18th Zionist Congress adjourned he traveled to Warsaw, where he came down with a high fever and lost consciousness. His illness was so severe (this was before the discovery of penicillin) that he feared he was about to return his soul to his Maker. He was admitted to the Jewish hospital in Warsaw and later spent weeks in a convalescent home.[83] During his illness and hospitalization in Warsaw, Ida Wissotzka, a member of Hashomer Hatza'ir, became his guardian angel; her devoted care made a major contribution to his survival and recovery. She stayed by his bedside day and night, to the point that the hospital staff were certain that she was Yaari's fiancée.[84] An especially warm relationship was forged between the two. At a distance of fifty years he recalled that she "knew how to combine her deep fondness for me with her loyalty to her life partner, Yehoshua, to whom she was already engaged."[85] Wissotzka retained her feelings for Yaari until the end of her life and used to stock his apartment in Tel Aviv with all sorts of treats and delicacies. On occasion, he rewarded her with signs of affection and words of encouragement.

The battle with meningitis affected his behavior. He was easily moved to tears. When he misspoke, he apologized to Anda and hoped she would blame it on his mood after the illness.[86] He was left with a temporary partial paralysis on the left side of his body and other symptoms, including a psychosomatic condition manifested in phenomena like a fear of crossing the street and over-excitement when speaking to an audience; for the rest of his life he was wracked by pains that made it difficult for him to sleep.[87]

---

81 Yaari to Myetek [M. Bentov], Apr. 26, 1928, HHA, 95-7.6(5); Yaari to Hazan, Jan. 7, 1932, HHA, 95-7.7(9).
82 Yaari, Memoirs, Mar. 10, 1981, KMA, MYF, 8(2).
83 Meir to Anda, Nov. 8, 1933, KMA, MYF, 5(2).
84 Yaari, Memoirs, Mar. 10, 1981, KMA, MYF, 8(2).
85 Yaari to Aharon Efrat, Sept. 15, 1982, KMA, MYF, 3(2).
86 Meir to Anda, Nov. 8, 1933, KMA, MYF, 5(2).
87 Yaari to Levavi [undated; probably 1941], HHA, ḥeh-3.36(2b); Yaari, Memoirs, Mar. 10, 1981; Jan. 3, 1984, KMA, MYF, 8(2); Yaari to Moshe Yaari, Aug. 20, 1976, KMA, MYF, 5(4).

In 1937 he came down with neuralgia, which interfered with his ability to walk, use his eyes and fingers, and other things. That summer he went abroad to recover and stayed with Anda in a sanatorium in Switzerland. Whenever he spent time alone in a rest home or spa, he provided her with detailed reports on how many hours he had slept at night, how many times he woke up to go to the bathroom, and how much each test and treatment cost. He also wrote her what he ate at every meal and even bought a cookbook with a thousand recipes and menus for the entire year to give to the women who worked in the kibbutz kitchen. In the wake of his illness, he decided to cut meat out of his diet and proposed that Rachel and Aviezer do the same. In his opinion, meat was harmful and should not be eaten more than twice a week.[88]

Kibbutz Artzi covered the costs of his medical care. Hazan told Yaari not to worry about the financial side of his health and to leave the matter to the movement. He urged Yaari to take advantage of every option for convalescence in Europe, even if it delayed his return to Palestine.[89] Nevertheless, Yaari was afraid that people were grumbling behind his back about the heavy outlays and the fact that he was in an expensive sanatorium.[90] He had the feeling that not everyone at Merḥavia understood his condition and why he was spending so much time abroad. Yaari's brother Tuvia had to persuade him and Anda that all the members were anxious about his health and kept asking whether another letter had arrived from him and how he was feeling.[91] His ailment made him more sensitive to what his comrades thought about him and he came to believe that they held his condition against him. He kept track of who wrote to him, who did not, and who took advantage of his illness to settle

---

88 Yaari to Shlomo Talmon, June 27, 1937, KMA, MYF, 1(2); Yaari, Memoirs, Jan. 3, 1984, KMA, MYF, 8(2); Meir to Anda, Oct. 28, 1937, Sept. 8, 1938, Nov. 15, 1938, KMA, MYF, 5(2); medical certificate signed by Dr. Loewenstein, General Health Fund, Tel Aviv district, July 12, 1938, KMA, MYF, 2(13).
89 Hazan to Yaari, Aug. 24, 1937, KMA, MYF, 1(5); Hazan to Yaari, Oct. 18, 1938, HHA, ḥeh-3.27(1).
90 Meir to Anda, Nov. 15, 1938, KMA, MYF, 5(2).
91 Tuvia to Meir, Oct. 26, 1937, KMA, MYF, 1(5).

accounts with him.[92] How the members treated him during his illness determined his attitude towards them for many years to come, for better or for worse.[93]

He watched his tongue and pen even less than in the past. His behavior reached the point that Hazan wrote bluntly to make him aware of what people around him were feeling:

> You sometimes display unbridled anger towards people. Sometimes you vehemently criticize comrades in front of other (and not always appropriate) people. This can hurt people a lot, but they keep quiet. There is nothing personal here. Perhaps you cannot behave differently now, but it has a harsh effect. But your suspicious nature has an even worse effect.[94]

Why did these comrades, those whom he wounded and others, hold their tongues? Did his poor health impair his standing as a leader? Or did it rather create an obligation towards him, one that he consciously cultivated, and his comrades avoided taking steps that might be interpreted as taking advantage of his frailty, steps they would have taken were they dealing with a healthy man? The explanation of the comrades' silence and acquiescence in Yaari's behavior lies, at least to some extent, in their dependence upon him. They needed his counsel and guidance at times of crisis and when decisions had to be made. In the letter of rebuke quoted above, Hazan also provided details of what had happened at the 20th Zionist Congress (which Yaari did not attend), sought his advice, and asked, almost pleaded: *"What is the right way, Meir? I would very much like you to write me with your comments."*[95]

---

92 Meir to Anda, Sept. 28, 1938, Nov. 10, 1938, KMA, MYF, 5(2).
93 Yaari, Memoirs, Mar. 10, 1981; Apr. 3, 1981, KMA, MYF, 8(2).
94 Hazan to Meir, Sept. 5, 1937, KMA, MYF, 1 (5).
95 Ibid. Emphasis in the original.

CHAPTER 6

Ideological Collectivism

Following the establishment of Kibbutz Artzi in April 1927, Yaari assumed executive responsibility for the entire Hashomer Hatza'ir organization, with its settlements scattered throughout Palestine and dozens of chapters abroad. From his makeshift office he kept track of developments in the movement, perusing many letters, and scribbling his initials in the margin of every scrap of paper he read. Once, after reading the periodical published by the movement in Poland, he sent the central office there a letter full of praise: "It makes a wonderful impression. The supplement on the convention, in particular, stands out for its style and content. Please persevere and you will certainly see a blessing from your labors."[1] His compliments were encouraging, just as his criticisms could be harsh and even insulting. He expressed his opinions about the affairs of the youth movement in the Diaspora, mainly ideological matters, but did not leave a real mark on its development. As a rule, those issues fell into the domain of Hazan, who was and remained the Shomer counselor par excellence.

Yaari was first and foremost the paramount leader of KA. He always delivered the opening address at its councils and conventions, right after the delegates sang the "Internationale." Even when the list of speakers had to be trimmed due to time constraints, and those comrades who did gain the floor were limited to a few minutes, Yaari—who had already made a long opening statement—was permitted to both respond and to summarize with no time limit. An external observer

---

[1] Yaari to Hashomer Hatza'ir leadership in Galicia and Lwów, Jan. 26, 1932, HHA, *heh*-3.3(3a).

noted that everyone paid close attention to his remarks, which radiated "the strong authority of spiritual and educational leadership."[2]

Another outside observer, Berl Katznelson, was much more critical: "You have no solid program," he scolded the members of Hashomer Hatza'ir in 1927, "but you do have a psychology of special interests and an ambition to preserve your existence no matter what. [...] I do not understand the meaning you assign to the concept of 'ideological collectivism.' Your dominant concepts are abstract in nature."[3] Yaari replied by praising "political collectivism," inasmuch as it had saved KA from the sorry fate of Gedud Ha'avodah. For a kibbutz to survive, it must have a stable ideological position; otherwise, it would disintegrate. It was also essential for the education of the youth in the Diaspora.[4] He gave ideological collectivism credit for the movement's unity and ability to establish and maintain large projects and create the new human being.[5]

Yaari also tried to impose ideological collectivism on movement cadres even before they made aliyah. In 1930, he informed Hashomer Hatza'ir headquarters in Warsaw that aliyah dates for groups should not be set exclusively by their seniority; they should also take account of its members' ideological maturity, because that was essential for ensuring its survival in the difficult conditions of those years.[6] He was implacable that a group refusing to adopt ideological collectivism must be dismantled and its members expelled from the movement. He argued that the movement was in any case based on selection, so that only hundreds of its tens of thousands of members came to Palestine. A few mavericks could not be allowed to carry the taint of ideological heresy with them.[7]

---

2 *Zeror mikhtavim* 48, Sept. 6, 1935.
3 Tzur, *Meqorot*, No. 6, 70-71.
4 Ibid., 72-73.
5 Yaari at a meeting of the Kibbutz Artzi Executive Committee, Sept. 13-14, 1938, HHA, 5-10.2(4).
6 Yaari to Hashomer Hatza'ir leadership in Warsaw, Nov. 21, 1930, HHA, heh-3.2(3).
7 Yaari to Pra'i, Apr. 6, 1931, HHA, 95-33. 1(5).

Yaari was irked by claims that ideological collectivism was being forced on the movement and its members and was careful to distinguish the ideological collectivism that he championed and defended from totalitarianism, which, he insisted, did not exist in the movement. He saw the identification of ideological collectivism with totalitarianism as a blood libel, the ugliest slander of all those alleged against Hashomer Hatza'ir, including free love, separatism, aristocracy, insularity, serving as a gateway to the Communists, and contamination by the binationalism of Brith Shalom. And these were only a few of the blemishes that others saw in the movement.[8] Totalitarianism, he wrote, "involves the cult of a leader, in which all wait to hear what he has to say; to whose hands everyone's life is entrusted, for reward or punishment; who can destroy worlds on a whim; whose will alone constitutes law, justice, counsel, and reason. Evil is good if it comes from him, and good is evil if it doesn't come from him."[9] He wrote these words a decade before the publication of Orwell's *1984*.

Yaari's concept of ideological collectivism had a double meaning. First, it connoted the loyalty of all members to the movement's ideological line and, until the establishment of the Hashomer Hatza'ir party in 1946, a ban on membership in any political faction (and after that in any other party). Second, all its member kibbutzim were bound by movement discipline, which meant falling in line with the decisions of the majority. Yaari recognized the need to preserve each settlement's internal autonomy and freedom of social development, but was not willing to renounce the influence of the KA institutions on the kibbutzim. "There cannot be a situation," he said in 1936, "in which the free will of an individual or a kibbutz is decisive. There is no autonomy when it comes to political activity."[10] A kibbutz that does not abide by the decisions of the movement's central institutions must be expelled from Kibbutz Artzi—as he actually threatened to do.[11]

---

8 "Response to the Manifesto," May 15, 1938, HHA, 95-7.8(11); Yaari to Yehuda Gotthelf, Mar. 3, 1938, Ibid.
9 "Response to the Manifesto," May 15, 1938, HHA, 95-7.8(11).
10 Yaari at a meeting of the Kibbutz Artzi Executive Committee, Dec. 22, 1936, HHA, 5-10.1(13).
11 Yaari at a meeting of the Kibbutz Artzi Executive Committee, Oct. 25, 1940, HHA, 5-10.2(5); Yaari to Kibbutz Hazore'a, Nov. 21, 1939, HHA, 95-7.8(12).

Yaari, who stubbornly insisted on enforcing ideological collectivism, certainly knew that kibbutz members were not preoccupied by sublime and lofty ideologies but by matters of daily life. He regretted the emergence of a wall between "life itself," and "ideology" and was troubled that instead of attending kibbutz meetings the members preferred to go off and read a novel in a corner, by the light of a small lamp. In the early 1930s, he complained that when the kibbutz meeting discussed politics or ideology, many stayed away; but when the agenda included topics such as the admission of new member, departures, assistance to relatives, or relationships among themselves, the benches in the dining hall were packed.[12] He certainly did not make light of social issues, because he saw the kibbutz as its members' home—a home with some disadvantages, no doubt, but mainly advantages. He was particularly proud of the kibbutz's ability to guarantee its members' social security. When he himself was hospitalized, Yaari realized just how many benefits kibbutz life provided. He observed that unlike the patients from the city, who could not "afford" to be sick, the kibbutz members could lie calmly in their beds, secure and confident that their illness would not have an economic impact on their families.[13]

He was well aware that it was difficult to engage in cultural diversions after a day of physical labor from which the members returned to their rooms exhausted. He wanted cultural life in the kibbutz to focus on social and national objectives, on a vision of going to the people, on love for the homeland, and on public activities by the kibbutzim in their region. He dismissed all the discussions, whether oral or in the movement's periodical, that expressed "longings and doubts without answers."[14] There are echoes of Bitaniyya and *Qehilliyatenu* in his remarks. He called for an effort to help all the members become fluent in Hebrew, but rejected the idea of granting leave to a handful for advanced study, on the grounds that "university intelligence is not for us."[15] His consistent opposition to higher education for kibbutz members lasted many years.

---

12 Yaari, *Be-derekh arukah*, 164 (from 1934).
13 Letter to the seminary for the female comrades, 1937, Ibid., 109-111.
14 Deliberations of the Kibbutz Artzi Council, Hadera, December 1935, in Margalit, *Ha-shomer Ha-ẓa'ir*, 259.
15 Ibid.

He expected the members to use kibbutz life as the basis for developing cultural activities that expressed the movement's needs. He preferred drama circles and other group activities to mechanisms by which KA could encourage painters and sculptors, although he did not oppose the latter.[16] When an exhibition of works by KA artists opened in April 1938, Yaari was asked to deliver the opening speech. He saw this as an important event, because the works on display were "the fruits of toil gathered from work nooks, created at the expense of leisure hours after work. I have seen works of art here that are no less important than a newspaper editorial."[17] But his pleasure was tempered by a vexing question about the purpose: "What does all this do for the community?"[18] And before he expounded his own position he surveyed—as was his custom—the views of other people, both pro and con:

> Some writers and artists are revolted by such a question. They see this as a utilitarian approach and turn up their noses. There are also writers and artists who go to the other extreme and think that it is possible to put the artist into a Procrustean bed of 'socially useful commissions.' I believe that this exhibition expresses the "middle way." It is not the mannerism or brilliant loneliness of individualism that turns its back on the world, but neither is it enslavement to the 'socially useful.'[19]

Nonetheless, he did make demands of the artists: "I require first of all not a 'clenched fist' but an allusion to the human, from the child's world to our entire cycle of life."[20] He recognized that artists were within their rights to ask the movement to support their efforts and help them bring their works to the public, both inside and outside the movement.[21] Writers and poets saw him as someone they could consult

---

16 Ibid.
17 Yaari, "Opening Remarks," the Third Exhibition of Kibbutz Artzi Artists, HHA, 95-7.26(2).
18 Ibid.
19 Ibid.
20 Ibid.
21 Ibid.

about matters of content and ask for help on practical issues.²² For his own part, Yaari expected the artists to be more socially involved.²³

He was greatly troubled by the phenomenon of those who left the kibbutzim. Even though there were relatively fewer such defectors from KA than the other movements, it was impossible to turn a blind eye to them. In the 1930s, Yaari estimated that the main reasons for these departures was disillusionment, the feeling of being forced to sacrifice too much in the name of collective life, and the kibbutz's failure to respond to requests for financial assistance to relatives.²⁴ On the last front, he understood that people were worried about their parents' situation and wanted to help them out, and he felt the humiliation of members whose request was turned down or who were offered an amount they viewed as inadequate.²⁵

When Yaari's sister requested his assistance in obtaining an immigration certificate, he vacillated between his family duty and the fear of being attacked for exploiting his status. He was afraid that his sister would blame him for indifference to her future, but made it clear that he could not invite her to join his kibbutz, precisely because of his position. In his letter to movement headquarters in Galicia, Yaari phrased his request that his sister receive a certificate as an almost private matter, but asked that it be handled with absolute objectivity, taking no account of his standing. We cannot avoid sensing that he preferred to steer clear of the entire issue; if there needed to be a certificate application in the family member category, his brother Moshe, who worked in Tel Aviv, should handle it.²⁶

In 1934, with the number of requests by kibbutz members for assistance to their families increasing, and the anticipation of prosperity on the kibbutzim and in Palestine, he proposed a complex formula:

---

22 Yaari to Binyamin Tennenbaum, June 24, 1941, HHA, *heh*-3.36(2b); Yaari to Binyamin Tennenbaum, Feb. 15, 1944, HHA, *heh*-3.43(1c).
23 Yaari at the 23rd Kibbutz Artzi Council, June 28-29, 1943, HHA, 5-20.4(1).
24 Yaari, *Be-derekh arukah*, 164 (from 1934).
25 Ibid., 165.
26 Yaari to Hashomer Hatza'ir leadership in Galicia, Jan. 7, 1932, KMA, MYF, 1(2).

We are facing a few more difficult years, [...] but the kibbutz economy is advancing from strength to strength. [...] It follows that a program to provide for parents must be gradual and suited to the course of the kibbutz's development. In the name of such a plan we can demand that members show restraint and self-control and justify a ban on individual solutions. But if we ignore the seriousness of the question, both veteran and younger members will leave us, and the belief that the kibbutz is a home will be undermined.[27]

Complex, dialectical formulations like this, which Yaari developed in abundance in matters of ideology and politics, were not strong enough to resolve social and personal questions and to solve the issue at hand. His optimism for the long term was no comfort to those who needed an immediate solution for their parents, and the kibbutz continued to hemorrhage members.

How many left the kibbutzim because they disagreed with elements of KA ideology and the expectation that they comply with the rules of ideological collectivism and fall into step with its official line? Leading scholars who have studied Hashomer Hatza'ir agree that KA's adoption of Marxism, orchestrated by Yaari, produced a contradiction between the kibbutz way of life and the Marxist thought that overlaid on it. Moreover, ideological collectivism by its very nature, and all the more so its Marxist version, could not be squared with the intrinsic values of the youth movement from which KA was born.[28]

Clearly, ideological collectivism and its Marxist content produced an internal and sometimes tragic tension between the founders' human nature and spiritual orientation, on the one hand, and the course followed by the movement, on the other. Starting in the mid-1920s, the movement's ideology, with its Marxist coloration, and its organizational structure, which was meant to serve as the basis for political activities in the Yishuv as a whole, increasingly clashed with the spiritual and social composition of KA and its members' personal and social aspirations.

---

27 Yaari, *Be-derekh arukah*, 165–166.
28 This discussion is based on Landshut, *Ha-qevutzah*, 73–79 and Margalit, *Ha-shomer Ha-ẓa'ir*, 292–293.

This dialectical tension exacted a heavy toll from individuals and the movement. The personal cost involved repressing one's emotions, renouncing them totally or at least compromising, with the inevitable frustration that involved. The price paid by the movement was the loss of members who could not live with this contradiction.

Ideological collectivism was designed to maintain the integrity and unity of each of the kibbutzim of Hashomer Hatza'ir and of the movement as a whole. In pursuit of that goal, Yaari also sought to keep Hashomer Hatza'ir an independent political stream within the labor movement in Palestine. This is why, in the 1920s, he rejected the idea that KA should cooperate with Aḥdut Ha'avodah and Hapoel Hatza'ir and establish a single workers' party. In his view, the merged group would be a run-of-the-mill urban-based social democratic party, focused on the daily interests of the toiling masses and devoid of a revolutionary vision. For KA, by contrast, he envisioned the role of an independent and uncompromising pioneer vanguard. Hashomer Hatza'ir was not strong enough to work changes in the nascent party from the inside, but as an independent force it could exert pressure from the outside on the united party (which was founded in 1930 as Mapai, the Eretz Israel Workers' Party).[29]

Mapai's institutions and senior echelons lavished much time and energy—innumerable meetings, conversations, discussions, get-togethers, and letters—on wooing Hashomer Hatza'ir and persuading its leaders to join the united party. Under Ben-Gurion's leadership in the 1930s, the party adopted the slogan of "from class to nation," which required the entire working class to organize in a single organization. Ben-Gurion could see no good arguments against unity: "I myself do not believe that you believe what is stated in your platform. [...] One does not exist on the basis of formulas, but of actions—and our actions are your actions."[30]

In all the rounds of negotiation and merger attempts, Mapai made revocation of the principle of ideological collectivism a fundamental

---

29 Yaari, "In the Straits," *Hashomer Hatza'ir*, Adar II 5688 [Feb.-Mar. 1928].
30 Zait, *Ziyyonut be-darkhei shalom*, 122.

requirement, while Hashomer Hatza'ir stuck to its insistence on autonomy for education, the kibbutzim, and ideology even within a united party. Ben-Gurion and Katznelson were prepared to allow KA the same measure of autonomy allowed to Hakibbutz Hame'uḥad: namely, that its members could caucus separately and consult about political issues, too, but that each individual member would be bound by party discipline. This format did not satisfy Yaari and Hazan, who wanted collective autonomy, which meant that the positions of their movement, and not of the party as a whole, would continue to obligate its members even after a merger.[31]

Apart from issues of ideology and realpolitik, there were other factors that informed the opposition to the merger. Individual and group psychology also played their part. The negotiators for Hashomer Hatza'ir phrased their reluctance to merge with Mapai in psychological terms as well. Yehuda Gotthelf spoke of "psychological difficulties," Ben-Ami Gordon referred to an "emotional approach," and Hazan said that "aside from the contrasts between us and Mapai there is also psychological alienation that is hard to overcome."[32] At the same time, emotional issues also forged a sense of closeness among the labor Zionist factions, despite their disagreements, and Yaari admitted that he could not free himself from his deep emotional bond to Mapai's members and actions.[33]

Mapai's courtship of Hashomer Hatza'ir continued throughout the 1930s. One round of merger talks, initiated by Mapai's David Remez, took place on the SS *City of Cairo*, on which Yaari and other delegates returned to Palestine after the 21st Zionist Congress adjourned prematurely, in late August 1939, when the Ribbentrop-Molotov Pact was announced. Yaari's statements then were general and noncommittal. Yes, stronger efforts towards merger should be made, but he could not speak on behalf of Hashomer Hatza'ir, because it was a democratic movement and decisions had to be made by the members; so whatever he said on board was of little value. As for the substance

---

31 Margalit, *Ha-shomer Ha-ẓa'ir*, 274–276.
32 Ibid.
33 Yaari to Berl [Katznelson], Apr. 7, 1942, HHA, *heh*-3.36(2c).

of the matter, Yaari believed that the ground was not yet ready for a "programmatic union." In the terminology of Hashomer Hatza'ir, "programmatic union" was as a codeword for rejection of merger, whose import was: there is no focused agreement between us about the program, the ideological platform, and practical plans. His bottom line, as the ship traversed the Mediterranean, was: "We cannot make any decisions here, but only in Palestine."[34] The Second World War began before they reached home.

Mapai did not give up. The two sides met again about a month later. Mapai sent its top leaders, headed by Ben-Gurion and Katznelson. At the very start of the talks on dry land, the Hashomer Hatza'ir representatives made it known that the KA Executive Committee had not held an in-depth discussion of the merger proposal or designated a delegation for talks with Mapai. Katznelson had good reason to doubt the good faith of his interlocutors. In early November 1939, Yaari publicly announced that Hashomer Hatza'ir had decided to end the negotiations.[35] He called on members of the movement to persevere on their long grey path, "and, the main thing, to build and build! Our time will certainly come!"[36]

Katznelson responded to both Yaari's announcement and to the last round of talks (he had not been party to those on the *City of Cairo*) in a series of articles in *Davar*, under the headline, "It Hurts even When I Laugh."[37] In a caustic tone, Katznelson assailed Yaari and his movement without mercy. For many years, Katznelson had been holding up a mirror to Yaari and the members of Hashomer Hatza'ir, as if he had been assigned the task of exposing the frailties and defects that others perhaps saw but did not dare say aloud, much less criticize. Katznelson's sermon to Hashomer Hatza'ir was marked by a patronizing tone and even a bit of jeering, particularly about the central place in its doctrine of the dictatorship of the proletariat, ideological collectivism, and admiration for the Soviet Union. About

---

34 Conversation on the *City of Cairo*, September 1939, HHA, *heh*-3.21(1a).
35 Yaari, "The Plain Truth," *Davar*, Nov. 7, 1939.
36 Yaari, *Be-meri vikkuaḥ*, Merḥavia 1940, 52.
37 Katznelson, "It Hurts Even When I Laugh," *Davar*, Nov. 29, 1939–Dec. 3, 1939.

a month after the publication of these articles, Yaari responded in a 56-page pamphlet published by Kibbutz Artzi, *A Bitter Dispute* (January 1940). To rebut Katznelson's attacks on Hashomer Hatza'ir, Yaari held up for display the 24 kibbutzim that the movement had established in Palestine, its partnership in every constructive effort by the Histadrut, and its members' endeavors in the Russian-occupied territories of Eastern Europe in the months since the start of the Second World War.

Katznelson, as we have already seen, had no great love for Hashomer Hatza'ir, and understood it even less. To cap it all, he feared the power of its youth movement, which he saw as a threatening rival in the area that was both the apple of his eye and which was Hashomer Hatza'ir's greatest strength—educating the younger generation. Despite Katznelson's antipathy for Hashomer Hatza'ir, or at least his lack of sympathy, empathy, and inability to fathom it, he was very much aware of its attraction for young people. On his visits to Europe he had been exposed to the magic spell that Hashomer Hatza'ir cast on youth and perceived the quality and caliber of its members.[38] We may even surmise that he envied Hashomer Hatza'ir for its intellectual forces and superb educational programs. This was certainly one of his many reasons for wanting to annex it to Mapai.

Katznelson and Yaari had never understood each other, going back to their first conversation at Kinneret on a hot summer day in 1920, shortly after the latter's arrival in Palestine. Twenty years afterwards Katznelson still recalled, with resentment, that Yaari and his comrades had twitted him for being ignorant of Blüher's thought. After Katznelson's death, Yaari attributed their strained relations to the hierarchy of *aliyot* that Katznelson had established and promoted, in which the Second Aliyah was the *ne plus ultra* and its members enjoyed the highest status. Yaari was put off by the haughtiness of the Second Aliyah, whose members assumed "that the basic model had already been forged at Kinneret, Degania, and Sejera" and expected the youngsters of the Third Aliyah to be their obedient successors and worshipers.

---

38 See: Shapira, *Berl*, II, 431–442.

For him, this was the key to his relationship with Katznelson, to the rivalry between Hashomer Hatza'ir and Mapai, and to the competition between the Third Aliyah and its predecessor.[39]

Yaari and Katznelson often found themselves in the same place, but over the course of more than two decades never had a real *tête-à-tête*, even though Yaari longed for one. In 1942, he sent Katznelson his just-published *At the Doors of an Epoch*, with a note that "after perusing my book you will 'perhaps' want to meet with me and get to the bottom of my ideas."[40] But the anticipated meeting never took place. Katznelson died suddenly in the summer of 1944.

Because Kibbutz Artzi was an independent political movement, in addition to being a federation of settlements, its institutions discussed general political issues that were not directly or specifically relevant to kibbutz life. At the very same meeting, its executive committee might discuss the nature of fascism and the differences between its Italian and German versions, what would happen should war break out and the Soviet Union and Britain find themselves on the same side of the fence, and what should be done about a kibbutz that had defaulted on a loan of 70 Palestine pounds.[41] The movement and its institutions, with Yaari in the lead, crystallized a position and opinion on issues of international importance that were much too large for KA to influence in any way. But the principle of ideological collectivism required the movement's institutions and leadership to consolidate a stand on every issue, whether great or small, and provide the members with constant guidance in their perplexity.

Yaari drafted slogans about the land, the nation, and the world, which were essentially educational messages intended to serve as unifying and mobilizing myths. When the gap between reality and the ideals that he preached became so large as to be unbridgeable, Yaari relied on quasi-scholastic verbal acrobatics, which revolved around

---

39 For Katznelson's side, see "It Hurts Even When I Laugh," *Davar*, Nov. 29, 1939–Dec. 3, 1939; for Yaari's side, *Be-meri vikkuaḥ*, 8; also his remarks at the conclusion of the week of mourning for Katznelson, *Be-derekh arukah*, 267–270.
40 Yaari to Berl [Katznelson], Apr. 7, 1942, HHA, *ḥeh*-3.36(2c).
41 Kibbutz Artzi Executive Committee, Apr. 14, 1936, HHA, 5-10.1(12).

the distinction between the problematic short term and the promising long term. His fingerprints are all over the statements of Hashomer Hatza'ir's positions, not only in the documents and publications to which he affixed his name but also in the movement's public statements and the decisions of its institutions.

Both Yaari and Hazan, the movement's long-time leaders, adhered to preserving the uniqueness, unity, and integrity of Kibbutz Artzi as a movement and of each of its affiliated kibbutzim. But so far as the immediate future was concerned, the theory of stages that underlay the organization's ideological platform of 1927 became blurred, almost to the point of eliminating the differences between Hashomer Hatza'ir and Aḥdut Ha'avodah, and—after its founding in 1930—Mapai. They were distinguished mainly by their disagreement with regard to long-term issues that were not yet relevant—"laws for the messianic era." It was actually the near-agreement with Mapai with regard to the short term, along with the fundamental principle that guided Yaari and his movement and their fervent desire to maintain their independence, leading him to cultivate and even widen the gap between them. Yaari emphasized the disagreements that required or justified the independence of Hashomer Hatza'ir rather than what they had in common and could have served as the basis for merger.

Two issues assumed increasing prominence in the demarcation of the borders between Hashomer Hatza'ir and its rivals: the Arab question and the attitude towards the Soviet Union. Here Yaari had to walk a fine line. He emphasized the differences but was careful not to be swept too far left towards the Soviet Union or outside of the Zionist consensus with regard to the Arab question. His guiding light was always the priority of Zionism and the aspiration to achieve a Jewish majority in Palestine.

The ideological core of Hashomer Hatza'ir was maximalist Zionism, based on negation of the exile and recognition that emancipation had run its course in the Diaspora. At some point in the 1920s Yaari grafted Marxism onto this base. As the 1930s progressed he accorded increasing weight to Marxism, but always accorded primacy to Zionism.

One of the hybrid formulations he developed was: "we are revolutionary socialists in pursuit of maximal Zionism."[42] He insisted that there was not and must not be any contradiction between the goals of Zionism and those of socialism; it was only a matter of precedence in time. To eliminate any doubt about his priorities, Yaari proclaimed to the members of his movement: "I am not interested in socialism if there are no Jews in it, if we are not part of it."[43]

We have seen that during his first trip back to Poland, in 1924–1925, Yaari noted the leftward drift of members of Hashomer Hatza'ir, which accelerated in the last years of that decade. He admonished the young Shomrim in Poland against adopting concepts that were out of step with the movement's ideology, particularly Communism, and emphasized that Hashomer Hatza'ir must distinguish itself unambiguously from the Communist Party and its anti-Zionism orientation. Because even a verbal echo might be misleading, he rejected the definition of Hashomer Hatza'ir's line as Zionist-Communist and opted instead for Zionist-socialist-revolutionary.[44] At the same time he fiercely rejected the ostensible "tragic contradiction" between Zionism and Socialism.[45] "There is no contradiction and there must not be a contradiction between the Zionist goal and our socialist goal," he wrote in the movement's newspaper abroad in early 1929.[46] He never tired of emphasizing the primacy of Zionism in the Hashomer Hatza'ir ideology and stressed that there was no contradiction between the realization of Zionism and the realization of Socialism.

Yaari was aware of the ideological and organizational risk inherent in the line, propagated by Mordechai Orenstein (later Oren), that called for fuller identification with historical materialism, and was troubled by the leftist influence on the Zionist enterprise. He was afraid that a leftward bent would make problems for Hashomer Hatza'ir among the moneyed classes. In the early 1930s, this prudence was associated with

---

42 Yaari to Avigdor Hame'iri, 19 May [1935?], HHA, 95-7.7(11).
43 The Fifth General Council of Kibbutz Artzi, July 12-17 1935, HHA, 5-20.2(1).
44 *Hashomer Hatza'ir*, Jan. 25, 1928.
45 Yaari, "Principles," *Hashomer Hatza'ir*, Jan. 1, 1929.
46 Ibid.

his concern about the response of the citrus-growers in Palestine, who were an important source of employment. He saw that the recently arrived Shomrim's support for the class struggle led them to detest those who could provide them with jobs—and that the feeling was mutual.[47]

His assessment was that the Shomrim who received their movement indoctrination in Europe, especially Galicia, where they were called on to demonstrate fuller identification with the line of historical materialism, were more susceptible to the allures of Po'alei Ziyyon Left and the Communists. The economic depression in Palestine at the start of the 1930s exacerbated this danger. With a sensitive pen and a heavy heart, Yaari described the situation in early 1931 in a commune of recent olim from Galicia, then based in Haifa:

> The strong winds and rains have come and the commune has no roof over its head, and its so-called dining hall, ... is about to collapse. All around are sadness, gloom, neglect, and a sense of orphanhood. The glass has never been installed in many of the windows in the dining hall, so the wind howls back and forth through the room. At mealtime, people huddle in the corners, chilled, eating hastily and without appetite. ... Sometimes the door opens when they are holding a meeting and there appears, as if someone had invited him, an emissary of the [Communist] faction, who tosses some leaflets on the tables and disappears. In this climate, it is no wonder that in the course of two months the leftist camp has doubled in size and is still on the prowl for new recruits.[48]

This encounter of young adults brimming with lofty ideas and hope for change with a grey and stagnant reality must have reminded him of his own early days in Palestine. Now, having been taught by experience, Yaari wanted to prevent them from soaring into the stratosphere and losing contact with the solid ground of reality, as had happened with

---

47 Yaari, letter dated July 17, 1930, in Margalit, *Ha-shomer Ha-ẓa'ir*, 187.
48 Yaari to E. Pra'i, Jan. 17, 1931, quoted by Margalit, *Ha-shomer Ha-ẓa'ir*, 188.

Bitaniyya and *Qehilliyatenu,* or falling off the left edge of Zionism, the fate of Gedud Ha'avodah. Aware of the peril that leftism posed for the movement's future, both in Palestine and abroad, he argued furiously with its proponents. His perseverance in the struggle was also related to the intergenerational aspect of the conflict and the attempt to prevent the rise of a young guard that would depose the older leaders.

The leftward slide at the margins of the Hashomer camp in Palestine occurred at a time when the Jewish economy in Palestine was about to emerge from the depression. In the early 1930s, graduates of Hashomer Hatza'ir who arrived in the country with the Leftist ideological baggage they had picked up in Europe went straight to the smallholders' colonies in search of work, and found themselves competing with the cheaper Arab laborers, more skilled and not unionized, for whom the orchards were not the sole source of income but only seasonal employment to supplement their family's income. Weighed down by their revolutionary concepts, the Shomrim encountered the real world of Palestine and experienced the conflict between the lofty ideas of class solidarity and the reality of a struggle for survival and labor-market competition. The situation forced Yaari to revise Kibbutz Artzi's position on relations between the workers of the two peoples.

The Kibbutz Artzi platform of 1927 proposed the gradual creation of a binational workers' organization ("a joint organization"), founded on mutual acceptance of the national values of each group. But the word "Arabs" was never mentioned. The joint organization was more of a slogan than a fact; from the outset, it had only a limited number of potential members and restricted scope of activity. All the same, Yaari made extensive use of it to highlight the difference between Hashomer Hatza'ir and Mapai.

When it came to actual relations between Jewish and Arab workers, the practical meaning of the "joint organization" was modest. It was much less genuine activity on the ground than a narrow path that Yaari could trace between the right and left wings of the labor movement and between the extremes within Hashomer Hatza'ir. In the early 1930s, Mapai advocated 100% Jewish labor while Po'alei Ziyyon Left championed 100% organized labor, with no distinction between

Jews and Arabs. This meant that the Histadrut would admit any Arab worker who wished to join it. Playing off against both extremes, Yaari arrived at the synthesis of "maximum Jewish labor," which would enable continued Jewish immigration and settlement. The "tempo of the [development of the] joint organization must be tailored to [the needs of] settlement and new olim; otherwise, the Arab element will overwhelm us," he said in 1931.[49]

The chief goal of the "joint organization," as envisioned by Hashomer Hatza'ir, was to protect Jewish laborers, and thus, among other things, to make it possible for members of Kibbutz Artzi to find jobs before their group's turn to found a settlement arrived. Parity in the wages of Jewish and Arab workers, as required by the concept of the "joint organization," would have had the not-so-incidental effect of neutralizing the economic advantage of employing the latter. The aim of Hashomer Hatza'ir's call for a binational organization was modest. In 1931, Yaari estimated that there were only about 3,000 Arabs eligible for membership in the joint organization and insisted that efforts should be made to prevent the entry of additional Arab workers; if not, Jews would be totally pushed out of the citrus groves.[50]

The changing circumstance of the mid-1930s shifted the focus of Yaari and his movement from relations between the workers of the two peoples and the idea of a "joint organization" to the political domain and the idea of binationalism. The section on the "Ultimate Prospect," left out of the original Kibbutz Artzi platform in 1927, was approved verbatim in 1933 and became an integral part of the movement's doctrine:

> The Ultimate Prospect: Taking account of the maximal aliyah of the Jewish masses to Palestine, which will lead to the concentration of a majority of Jews in Palestine and its environs, and, on the other hand, the existence of masses of Arab residents in Palestine, the development of social life after the period of national liberation will

---

49 Yaari at the Kibbutz Artzi Council 1931, in Margalit, *Ha-shomer Ha-ẓa'ir*, 206.
50 Ibid.

lead, by means of the socialist revolution and the abolition of classes, to the creation of a binational socialist society.⁵¹

Yaari was the father and author of this paragraph. His use of "society" rather than "state" derived from his Marxist orientation and the notion that the state would be succeeded by a classless society.

In general, the idea of a parity regime that ignored the demographic balance of the two peoples in Palestine was revived in Zionist circles in times of weakness—when aliyah was at a low point and during economic downturns. It faded from view at times of demographic optimism and a booming economy. Yet Hashomer Hatza'ir embraced binationalism in 1933, when aliyah was on the rise and every other Zionist faction that formerly supported the idea had discarded it.⁵²

The demographic situation in Palestine changed drastically between 1933 and 1936. The worldwide depression, triggered by the Wall Street crash of 1929, increased the number of Jews facing destitution. Until then, only in Eastern Europe were there Jews in economic destitution; but in the early 1930s, so were Jews in the United States, Germany, and elsewhere. Somewhat paradoxically, the depression stimulated the transfer of private capital to Palestine, whether in the pockets of immigrants of means or through investments by Jews who continued to live abroad but saw Palestine as an island of economic stability in the turbulent sea of the global financial crisis. The sentiment in the Yishuv was that Palestine had somehow managed to escape the storm.

The economic surge in Palestine began in mid-1932 and accelerated after Hitler came to power in Germany. Between 1933 and 1935, the Yishuv prospered and blossomed. Even though the quotas for working-class immigrants were increased, and many clandestine immigrants also found their way to Palestine, until the fall of 1935 the Jewish economy was beset by a shortage of working hands and immigration could not keep pace with the demands of the job market. During these boom times, it was only natural that the campaign for "Hebrew

---

51   Margalit, *Ha-shomer Ha-ẓa'ir*, 203.
52   See Halamish, "Bi-Nationalism in Mandatory Palestine."

labor" (meaning that Jews should hire only Jews) was dropped from the agenda and Hashomer Hatza'ir lost interest in a joint organization of Jewish and Arab workers. The "Ultimate Prospect" became a purely theoretical matter until the partition debate blazed up.

In April 1936, the Arabs of Palestine declared a general strike in support of three demands: an end to Jewish immigration to Palestine, a ban on the transfer of Arab-owned land to Jews, and the establishment of a national government responsible to a representative council. The first stage of the Arab Revolt lasted for about six months, until mid-October. During that time, 80 Jews were killed and more than 300 were injured. After the strike ended, a Royal Commission of Inquiry, headed by Lord Peel, was sent to Palestine to investigate the factors that had caused the disturbances, to hear each side's complaints, and to submit recommendations to address the situation and avert a renewal of the violence. The Peel Commission exceeded its brief and recommended going to the root of the problem by terminating the Mandate and partitioning Palestine between the two peoples. A Jewish state would be established in roughly one-fifth of the territory of Palestine west of the Jordan; the rest would be annexed to Transjordan and come under the authority of the Emir Abdullah. Jerusalem, Bethlehem, and a corridor linking them to Jaffa would remain under British control. These recommendations, published on July 7, 1937, sparked a fierce controversy within the Yishuv and the Zionist movement. The 20th Zionist Congress, which convened that summer, rejected partition as envisioned by the Peel Commission, but authorized the Jewish Agency Executive to conduct negotiations with Britain aimed at obtaining an improved proposal for a Jewish state in Palestine.[53] In other words, a majority of the Zionist Organization accepted the *principle* of partition, but shared the minority's rejection of the Peel Commission's map and hoped to persuade the British to revise it.

Hashomer Hatza'ir was not a party to the maneuvers related to the Peel Commission. When the recommendations, including the idea of partition, became known, it was already equipped with the "Ultimate

---

53   *20th Zionist Congress*, 359-360.

Prospect" as its preferred political solution for Palestine. From then until the late 1940s, Hashomer Hatza'ir was conspicuous for its opposition to partition and support for a binational state.

About two months after the Peel Commission published its report, the Arab Revolt flared up again. Bands of insurgents and ruffians seized control of rural and urban areas, disrupted transportation, sabotaged military and government installations, and attacked Jews and their property. A total of 415 Jews were killed between October 1937 and September 1939. The British adopted a heavy hand against the Arabs and cultivated cooperation with the Yishuv. This included an increase in the authorized level of the auxiliary police force and establishment of the Special Night Squads, in which British soldiers served alongside Jewish policemen under the command of British officers; the most famous of the latter was the originator of the new concept—Maj. Charles Orde Wingate. In a letter to Yaari, who was then convalescing in Europe, Hazan wrote that Wingate's Night Squads focused on protecting the oil pipeline (from Iraq to Haifa) and restoring quiet to the eastern Jezreel Valley and the Beit She'an Valley.[54]

Yaari did not need to be told about these units. He had already expressed his displeasure with their "pleasure jaunts" in Arab villages.[55] His statements seem to have been based on rumors about the Night Squads' forays into Arab localities. Stories spread about the havoc they wrought in Beit She'an, the assumed home base of those responsible for the death of Chaim Sturman of Kibbutz Ein Ḥarod. That operation produced extensive damage to property and several persons were injured, some of them critically. Then, fifteen Arabs were killed in the Wingate-led reprisal raid against the village of Dabburiyya, in early October 1938, immediately after Arabs murdered 19 Jews in Tiberias, including 11 children, who were burned to death in their beds.[56] One rumor had it that Wingate would enter a suspicious Arab village, line

---

54 Hazan to Yaari, Oct. 18, 1938, HHA, *heh*-3.27(1).
55 The discussion is based on Hazan's letter to Yaari, cited in the previous note, and a handwritten letter from Yaari to Hazan, KMA, MYF, 1(2). Although the letter is undated, the content makes it clear that it was a reply to the Hazan's letter to Yaari of Oct. 18, HHA, *heh*-3.27(1). Yaari's letter is unsigned and may in fact never have been posted. The content and style are significant nevertheless.
56 Michael B. Oren, "Orde Wingate: Friend under Fire," *Azure* 10 (Winter 5761/2001).

up the men in a row, and shoot every tenth one.[57] It was no secret that he was "not meticulous about the legality of his weapons and activities of his men," in the words of the head of the Jewish Agency Political Department, Moshe Shertok (later Sharett), in July 1938.[58] Shertok added that the behavior of the Special Night Squads had triggered "sharp internal reservations by some of our best men, who said that activities of this nature are not appropriate for us, and that they will inevitably destroy our relations with the neighboring Arab villages. Such operations, they hold, should be carried out only by the army, and not by our settlements."[59]

So Hazan's letter to Yaari was not intended to provide information about the squads' operations, but to express the writer's favorable attitude and appreciation of their achievements and to warn against the moral danger to the movement of Yaari's criticism of the "pleasure jaunts" in Arab villages. Hazan was asking Yaari whether he thought KA members should be part of the Night Squads. Hazan wanted them to continue their involvement, but thought that everything must be done to protect them against the risks this might produce. Kibbutz Artzi had to be vigilant and do everything possible to maintain the squads' morality and their defensive nature and to protect the comrades who belonged to them against insoluble dilemmas, of the sort that Yaari's view might spawn. Hazan was troubled by a situation in which KA members participated in the Night Squads' operations, while its leaders were writing contemptuously about "pleasure jaunts" in Arab villages. "Our members will not be able to bear this duality for long. Either they will become cynics who scoff at our ideology, or they will be consistent and not want to join the squads. That would be the outcome of this tragic new contradiction."[60]

Yaari was offended by the charge that he was creating a "tragic contradiction," an expression that he himself assailed fiercely when it was applied to the ostensible incompatibility of Zionism and socialism.

---

57 Shapira, *Land and Power*, 251; idem, *Yigal Allon*, 96.
58 Sharett, *Yoman medini*, III, 202.
59 Ibid.
60 Hazan to Yaari, Oct. 18, 1938, HHA, *heh*-3.27(1).

He supported an active defensive posture, which meant the tactic, just adopted by the Haganah, of "going past the fence" to repel attacks—but no further. As for collaboration between Haganah units and British troops, this should be continued, but only if accompanied by efforts in the appropriate institutions to modify the nature of the Night Squads' operations or at least to express reservations about the nature of their activities. This would be similar to what many pacifist socialists had done when they joined their country's armed forces during the First World War but continued to express their doubts about its causes. His remark about "pleasure jaunts" fell into this category, Yaari countered, drawing on an example from the wider world to legitimize his position. An alternative, which he seems to have attributed to Hazan, would be for Shomrim to continue to belong to the Night Squads and to give their operations a moral sanction, so as to avoid duality—effectively providing them with a fig leaf. This alternative would not put an end to the cynicism, but it would lead people to say that "when the test comes, we [Hashomer Hatza'ir] do the same thing as Mapai and invent an ideological justification of our own."[61]

The implications of this exchange transcend the specific issue at hand. From that time on, there was a sort of division of labor between the two leaders of Hashomer Hatza'ir: Hazan dealt with security matters and Yaari waved the flag of peace and Jewish-Arab coexistence. Yaari frequently expressed his concern about the moral ramifications of the national struggle; his statements were frequently of an educational and ethical nature, rather than political and practical.

In 1931, there was a changing of the guard in the Yishuv and Zionist leadership. In the elections for the Third Assembly of Representatives, held in January, Mapai emerged as the dominant force in the Yishuv. It won more than 40% of the votes, and the labor bloc as a whole polled more than half the votes (although it received less than a majority of the delegates). In second place came the Revisionists, headed by Zeev Jabotinsky, with 16%. Then, in advance of the elections for the 17th Zionist Congress, Yaari held discussions with members of the Mapai secretariat about

---

61 Yaari to Hazan (above, n. 55).

a joint list. Mapai agreed, on condition that the two parties run on a single platform, and "on condition that all of the list's delegates compose a single faction with internal discipline." Mapai acquiesced to Yaari's proposal that when it came to the Arab question and the ultimate goal of Zionism, "the faction will accord members of Hashomer Hatza'ir the possibility and freedom to express their special opinion."[62] In Palestine, the combined bloc increased its strength to 62% of the vote, while the Revisionists improved only slightly on their previous result (16.8%). But in the overall vote tally for the Congress, in both Palestine and Diaspora, the Labor bloc won 29% and the Revisionists 21%.

The rivalry between the Labor movement and the Revisionists intensified after the 17th Zionist Congress. It boiled over with the assassination of Chaim Arlosoroff, the head of the Jewish Agency Political Department, in June 1933, for which the Revisionists were blamed. His murder cast a pall on the elections for the 18th Congress, whose results indicated a significant change in the balance of forces: the Labor parties, again running as a joint list, increased their strength to 44%, while the Revisionists shrank to 14%. Yaari, who was in Poland during the campaign, called the Labor bloc's victory "brilliant and unexpected"; he told the members of his kibbutz that Arlosoroff's murder had probably attracted voters to "our side—and I added a few of my own."[63] Although this may sound like the fly seeking to share credit with the bull for plowing the field, we must remember that Hashomer Hatza'ir was much stronger in the Diaspora than in Palestine—56,450 members abroad, as against the 2,000 members of Kibbutz Artzi. Hashomer Hatza'ir returned 18 delegates to the 18th Zionist Congress; in 1935, when its membership had increased to around 60,000, it had 24 delegates at the 19th Congress.[64]

One of the foundations of the cooperation between Mapai and Hashomer Hatza'ir in the Zionist Organization in the early 1930s was the existence of a common adversary: the Revisionists. In Yaari's view, they were the archenemy, the devil incarnate. He had no doubt that

---

62 Yaari to Hazan, May 7, 1931, HHA, 95-7.7(6); Mapai Central Committee to the Kibbutz Artzi Executive Committee, May 6, 1931, HHA, *heh*-3.49(4).
63 Yaari to the Kibbutz [Merḥavia], Aug. 7, 1933, KMA, MYF, 1(2).
64 Margalit, *Ha-shomer Ha-ẓa'ir*, 197.

they had murdered Arlosoroff and that their fist was raised against the labor movement and Zionism.⁶⁵ When he spoke at the memorial service to mark 30 days after Arlosoroff's death, shortly before the elections for the Zionist Congress, he gave his tongue free rein. It didn't matter whose finger had been on the trigger and whether he would be apprehended and punished; no, the real culprit was "the force that inspired his murderous fury. That force may not proclaim its innocence."⁶⁶ The operative conclusion was that "at the upcoming Zionist Congress, the labor movement should declare merciless war on the impure zealots and the evil front, because Zionism and Revisionist fascism cannot coexist. The lesson of the great calamity is that we must deal a stinging defeat to the faction of the impure zealots, which must be eliminated from Palestine so that the Third Temple can be built and laboring Palestine will flourish."⁶⁷

During the campaign for the Zionist Congress in 1933, Ben-Gurion also denounced the Revisionists with the intemperance and militancy typical of electioneering.⁶⁸ But after the Congress, as a member of the Jewish Agency Executive, he acted with caution and responsibility. During the campaign, he was the leader of a party fighting to win power. But when the squabble over immigration certificates erupted between the Revisionists and the Agency Executive, in October 1933, he adopted a nonpartisan position and remained above the fray. Facing the imminent threat of a split in the Zionist movement and descent into civil war, Ben-Gurion was willing to buy an agreement with the Revisionists in the coin of certificates.⁶⁹ His negotiations with Jabotinsky in October and November 1934 led to a three-part agreement: a nonaggression pact between the labor movement and the Revisionists, an agreement on employment matters between the Histadrut and the Revisionist-led National Workers' Organization, and an agreement between the

---

65 Yaari, "After the Disaster," *Hashomer Hatza'ir* 2(4) (1933).
66 Ibid.
67 Ibid.
68 Ben-Gurion, *Zikhronot*, I, 645.
69 Halamish, "The Struggle for Certificates."

Zionist Organization and the Revisionist movement to abide by the will of the majority.

When the employment agreement was submitted to the full membership of the Histadrut for ratification, Yaari announced that his movement was unanimous in its opposition to it.[70] He threatened that its approval would force Hashomer Hatza'ir to draw far-reaching conclusions—a code for setting up its own political party. In the end, the Histadrut rejected the agreement, with 16,000 members against and 11,000 in favor.[71] The campaign to scuttle the employment agreement—and the fight against the Revisionists in general—marked Hashomer Hatza'ir's first appearance as an independent actor in the Labor movement. Its success increased the movement's sense of its unity and vocation.

From the start of the decade, the Nazis had cast a dark shadow over Europe. When Hitler became chancellor at the end of January 1933, Yaari—like many others—sensed that a world war would break out sooner or later. He said so explicitly in 1935, noting its scope, nature, and the anticipated dangers for Palestine—but nothing about its possible impact on the Jews in Europe.[72] In this, he was no different from other Zionist leaders, for whom the impending war lit up a red light only with regard to Palestine. What concerned them was the situation in Palestine, which required massive and swift Jewish immigration, so that when the moment of decision arrived the country would have a large Jewish population, and preferably a majority. At the time, the leaders of Hashomer Hatza'ir were optimistic about their movement's future, thanks to the numerical strength and high caliber of the youth movement in Europe, especially Poland, which Yaari saw as the "reserve force of Kibbutz Artzi."[73] When he returned to Palestine in September 1939, after the early adjournment of the 21st Zionist Congress, he left behind in Europe about 70,000 members of the movement.

---

70 Ben-Gurion at the meeting of the Histadrut Executive Committee, Dec. 27, 1934, LA.
71 Zait, Ḥaluẓim, 53.
72 Yaari, "The Hashomer Hatza'ir Movement," *Byulitin mazkirut ha-va'ad ha-po'el shel ha-Qibbutz ha-Artzi*, 120: 1–3 (1935).
73 Yaari, "Response to the Manifesto," May 15, 1938, HHA, 95-7.8(11).

The presidium table at the fourth World Convention of Hashomer Hatza'ir in Popard, Czechoslovakia, September 1935. From left to right: Aharon Cohen, Mordechai Orenstein (Oren), Zvi Lurie, Meir Yaari (standing), Yaakov Hazan, {?}.
Courtesy of Hashomer Hatza'ir Archive, Givat Haviva.

CHAPTER 7
Facing the Catastrophe

On August 23, the delegates and others attending the 21st Zionist Congress in Geneva were shocked by the announcement that Germany and the Soviet Union had signed a ten-year non-aggression agreement (the Molotov-Ribbentrop Pact). Like the rest of the world, they were unaware of the secret annex to the document, in which the two powers divided the territories between them into spheres of control: Germany would grab Lithuania and western Poland; the Soviet Union was allowed Finland, Estonia, Latvia, and eastern Poland. War clouds had been gathering over Europe for the past year; now it was clear the start of the hostilities was imminent. Panic and anxiety seized the Congress, which decided to adjourn ahead of schedule. At the closing plenary session, Chaim Weizmann—the president of the Zionist Organization—bid Godspeed to those present in a choking voice:

> Through the heavy clouds that are piling up over the future, it is with a heavy heart that I say goodbye to my friends of the rightwing, leftwing, and center parties. I have only one wish, that they live to see one other again, and if so, that they continue the work, and light will again shine from the darkness. [...] My heart is overflowing. I can say only this: our people is eternal and our country is eternal. We will work, fight, and live, until this nightmare passes. May we meet again in peace![1]

When he finished his statement, he embraced David Ben Gurion and other leaders before he slowly made his way from the hall, to a standing

---
1 Ben-Gurion, *Zikhronot*, 6: 526–527.

ovation. Many of those present wept.² The delegates bid one another farewell, with hugs and tears, and dispersed for their journeys home.

On September 1, 1939, while Yaari was making his way back to Palestine aboard the *City of Cairo*, Germany invaded Poland. Soviet forces crossed into the country about two and a half weeks later. More than three million Jews lived in Poland at the time, about 10% of the population. In the cities, they accounted for a third or more of the residents. Warsaw, for example, was home to 380,000 Jews. At the end of September, when the invaders partitioned the country, about 61% of Polish Jews found themselves in the territories held by Germany, with 39% in the territories that had come under Soviet control.

From Yaari's perspective as a member of the Jewish community in Palestine, the war was conducted in three arenas. The first was in Europe. There, after the months of the "Phony War," a German Blitzkrieg overran the Low Countries and northern France in the spring of 1940, after which the French sued for an armistice and dropped out of the war. A year later, on June 22, 1941, the Germans invaded the Soviet Union. The second front took place in the neighborhood of Palestine, although the unfolding situation was influenced by events far away. After the French capitulation in June 1940, the French mandate of Syria and Lebanon came under the control of the Vichy regime, which was allied with Germany. British troops defeated them in July 1941. After Italy entered the war in June 1940, Palestine became a target of the Italian Air Force. Haifa and Tel Aviv were bombed in July. On September 9, 1940, 117 persons were killed and about 400 wounded in an Italian air-raid on the center of Tel Aviv. In early 1941, the Germans renewed their offensive in North Africa, under the command of Field Marshal Erwin Rommel. For long months the Yishuv was panic-stricken that the Nazis would break through and reach Palestine, exposing it to the same fate as the Jews of occupied Europe—mass murder. This was the third arena of the war—the Holocaust. From time to time these three arenas overlapped to some extent, but they were generally considered separate. When the Afrika Korps was pushing east, the members of the

---

2 Ibid.

Yishuv were blissfully unaware of the catastrophe that had overtaken the Jews of Europe. It was not until November 1942, shortly after they had breathed a sigh of relief at the news that the British had halted Rommel's advance at El Alamein (west of Alexandria) and were looking forward to good news from Stalingrad, where a Soviet counterattack had begun, that they began hearing reliable reports of the systematic extermination of the Jews in the European territories under German control.

At the beginning of the war, Yaari divided the countries of Europe into two categories: those under occupation and those that bordered them. In the occupied countries, the task was to prepare for life in the underground and to save as many Shomrim as possible; in other words—to find a way to get them out.[3] To achieve this, it was decided to send special emissaries to the adjacent countries, to serve as counselors, assume public roles, take part in rescue activities, and develop contacts with the occupied countries.[4] A letter from a movement emissary in Lithuania, who asked to return to Palestine, which Yaari received in early December 1939, required him to deal for the first time on the practical level with the issues this raised. The desperate emissary recounted his personal hardship and the pain of being cut off from his girlfriend, whom he had been with for a few days at the Zionist Congress before they had to go their separate ways. He was miserable and depressed. In his letter to Yaari, which was private and included a request that the matter "stay between us," he asked, indeed begged him to come home.[5]

Yaari was personally acquainted with all of the movement's emissaries abroad. He was frequently the one who had recruited them for their missions. In an almost fixed ritual, the future emissary would make the pilgrimage to Merḥavia before leaving for Europe, meet with Yaari, and receive the wayfarer's blessing. Yaari was the person to whom the emissaries submitted their reports and complained of their personal problems from far away. But he phrased his formal response to the emissary in Lithuania in early 1940 in the first-person plural, in the name of the

---

[3] Yaari to Kibbutz Sha'ar Ha'amaqim, Oct. 16, 1939, HHA, 95-7.8(12).
[4] Ibid.; Also Yaari to the members of the central office of Hashomer Hatza'ir in Poland in Vilna, Jan. 10, 1940, HHA, 95-7.9(2).
[5] Levi Dror to Yaari, Dec. 7, 1939, ibid.

movement: "We require that you stay there another year and complete your two-year mission like every other emissary."[6] Later in the letter, adopting a more personal tone, he confessed that no one could know what was going to happen and expressed his confidence in the young man, who would find his way home when the time came. At the end he switched to the first-person singular, in a truly personal style, only to conclude with a collective *we*: "your conduct thus far has taught us to value your ability to restrain yourself and we believe that you will overcome your separation pangs."[7]

Yaari was very critical of the behavior of the Zionist leadership in the occupied districts. He had received reports from the territory under Soviet control of "Zionist leaders hiding in holes."[8] As time passed, he developed a "bad feeling [...] that we have abandoned the nameless millions in the Diaspora," and noted the flight of local activists.[9] When the time comes, "they will ask us: whom did you leave us to when we fell into the Nazis' clutches?"[10] Somewhat later he remarked that "only counselors who were members of the senior leadership of Hashomer Hatza'ir, Heḥalutz, and other pioneer youth movements remained with the young people trapped in the Ghetto."[11] In general, his public statements during the war combined deep concern for the Jews in the occupied territories with a lack of understanding and empathy, plus a large dose of judgmentalism, for those who were in a very different place than he was.

The situation in Vilna was a chapter unto itself. Between the wars, the city was part of Poland; in September 1939 it was occupied by the Soviets, who ceded it to Lithuania on October 10. In June 1940, it was annexed by the Soviet Union, along with the rest of the country. A year later it fell to the Germans. In the early months of the war, Vilna was a magnet for members of Hashomer Hatza'ir and other Zionist youth movements who had escaped from the Nazi-

---

6   Yaari to Levi Dror, Jan. 1, 1940, ibid.
7   Ibid.
8   Yaari to the members of the central office of Hashomer Hatza'ir in Poland in Vilna, Jan. 10, 1940, ibid.
9   Yaari at a meeting of the Histadrut Executive Committee, July 17, 1941 (110-111), LA.
10 Ibid.
11 Yaari, *Be-fetaḥ tequfah*, 128.

occupied areas. Yaari was proud of the Shomrim who flocked to Vilna, their extensive activities, and their behavior.[12] But a letter from members of the movement gathered in Vilna cooled his enthusiasm. They reported a series of decisions taken at meetings of the leadership there, including a merger of the executives of Hashomer Hatza'ir and Heḥalutz, that several senior leaders had been released from their duties and decamped to Palestine, and that two members has been tapped to return to the occupied territory and organize the escape from there. Yaari, who was assailed by doubts about the way they had chosen to keep the movement alive in the occupied areas, did not allow the Shomrim on the ground a free hand to act according to their best understanding of the situation in which they were working. In a letter dated January 10, 1940, he employed the first-person plural and ordered them not to liquidate the movement, no matter the cost. He explained, from his safe distance, that "going underground is not a game and it demands taking risks and dedication."[13] Another directive that he sent from Merḥavia to Vilna barred any merger of the leaderships of Hashomer Hatza'ir and Hakibbutz Hame'uḥad. He made clear to them that such a move was not within their authority, adding an unequivocal limitation on cooperation among the pioneer organizations in the occupied areas: there must be "strict maintenance of our independence in all respects."[14]

He forbade the higher-ups in Vilna to leave their posts without his explicit permission. "*In this emergency situation, every member of the leadership is considered to be an emissary* and in the absence of a world headquarters in the Diaspora, the only headquarters is here," in Merḥavia.[15] A few months later he instructed the Shomrim in Vilna to be cautious about readmitting members who had previously dropped out, for fear they were government agents trying to infiltrate the underground.[16]

---

12 Yaari to the central office of Hashomer Hatza'ir in Vilna, Jan. 10, 1940, HHA, 95-7.9(2).
13 Ibid.
14 Ibid.
15 Ibid. [emphasis in original].
16 Yaari to the head office in Vilna, May 28, 1940 HHA, 95-7.9(2).

His directives, as we see, were not restricted to movement issues, in which he made it quite clear that he was the boss. From the green fields of Merḥavia he also dispatched instructions to the members in Vilna about how they should conduct themselves under the occupation.

Shomrim in Vilna wrote their friends in Palestine that Yaari's criticism pained them, and their complaints came to his attention. They also wrote to him directly that they were astonished and hurt by his letter, particularly by the attitude towards them that emerged between the lines and the misunderstandings based on the insufficient knowledge of events in Eastern Europe possessed by those in Palestine.[17] He replied in late May 1940, explaining his position in detail, but without apology, and candidly excused his style and rhetoric: "Over the decades I have become accustomed to speaking with the movement in an explicit and sometimes abrasive manner."[18] In self-justification, he relied on the experience of other movements around the world: "In every Marxist and revolutionary movement, directives have been issued frankly and sometimes in a rather cruel manner, and this criticism was like a refreshing breeze."[19] This letter was written after he had remained silent for more than four months, and he seems to have had pangs of conscience about the long delay: "I faced mental blocks—this is already the third time I have sat down to write this letter, [...]. The reason may lie in my guilty feelings towards you. [...] One day chases another, and caught up in the maelstrom of developments I never find the time required for mental concentration so that I can convey to you our innermost feelings about the Vilna camp."[20]

There was a substantial difference between his friendly and open attitude towards the movement emissaries from Palestine, members of KA, with whom he corresponded directly and on a regular basis, and that towards the European Shomrim and leadership. He hinted to the people in Vilna that they should feel honored that he himself

---

17   Porat, *Me'ever la-gashmi*, 49–50 [omitted from the English translation, *The Fall of a Sparrow: The Life and Times of Abba Kovner*. Trans. and ed. Elizabeth Yuval. Stanford: Stanford University Press, 2009].
18   Yaari to the head office in Vilna, May 28, 1940, HHA, 95-7.9(2).
19   Ibid.
20   Ibid.

was writing to them.[21] They must understand that he, Yaari, the head of a political organization, was busy with more important matters. So they must not expect letters from him and should resign themselves to the fact that their contact person was Avraham Lipsker (Abramek).[22] Nonetheless, during the war, Yaari maintained a correspondence, with various degrees of frequency and intimacy, with movement emissaries and activists in Switzerland, Romania, Belgium, Poland, Slovakia, Bohemia, Moravia, Bulgaria, Hungary, and Yugoslavia.[23]

Within a few days of the start of the war, Ben-Gurion, as chairman of the Jewish Agency Executive, formulated the Zionists' wartime line: we must assist the British in their war against Hitler as if there were no White Paper, and we must fight the White Paper as if there were no war.[24] This was a fine slogan, rather like trying to square the circle; as long as the fighting continued the Yishuv stuck to the first clause and deferred the campaign against the White Paper until after victory over Hitler. The Zionist movement, which, during the First World War, had obtained the Balfour Declaration in favor of a national home for the Jewish people in Palestine, now hoped that the new world order established at the end of the Second World War would include a Jewish state in Palestine. Having learned from the experience of 1914-1918, the Zionist leadership endeavored to include the Yishuv in the war effort at the side of Britain, guided by the thought that an alliance with the victors would earn it a seat at the peace conference when the shooting was over. From the beginning of the war, the leadership sought the establishment of military units from the Yishuv, similar to the Jewish Legion of the First World War. These efforts did not bear fruit until September 1944, when the Jewish Brigade was established. Until then, alongside the campaign for the formation of all-Jewish units with the various national distinctive marks—a flag, badges, and so forth—the Zionist leadership maintained

---

21 Yaari to the members of the central office of Hashomer Hatza'ir in Poland in Vilna, Jan. 10, 1940, ibid.
22 Yaari to the head office in Vilna, May 28, 1940, ibid.
23 The correspondence is preserved in HHA, *heb*-3.
24 Ben-Gurion said this on various occasions and in various formulations. The version here reflects the general tenor of his thought.

a policy of cooperation with the British and made do with the enlistment of the young adults of the Yishuv into regular units of the British Army.

On September 10, 1939, the Yishuv launched an operation to identify potential military recruits. Young men and women were called on to volunteer for one or more of three tasks: (1) reinforcing the Hebrew economy in Palestine, (2) defending the Yishuv, and (3) helping the British Army when the time came.[25] The mobilization drive provoked a number of questions. The first was the dilemma associated with the very idea of serving in the British Army. The second was where the soldiers from Palestine would be sent. The third was how the burden of military service would be divided among the various sectors of the Yishuv. The fourth was how to balance military enlistment with satisfying the Yishuv's economic needs.

From the beginning of the war, KA, under Yaari's leadership, favored enlisting in the defense of the Yishuv but opposed the formation of armed units that would cooperate with the British. Cooperation with His Majesty's forces in Palestine could be countenanced only in the face of the threat of invasion by a foreign power or a neighboring country. At the time, the question was how to respond if Italy declared war on the Allies. But as long as Italy remained neutral and there was no danger of an invasion of Palestine, Yaari saw the formation of Jewish units within the British Army as diverting the Yishuv's limited manpower to other fronts. If we do not stress the defense of the Yishuv and Palestine, the British will ship these units elsewhere to defend the empire, Yaari warned. He did, however, support the establishment of Jewish combat units whose soldiers carried weapons (as opposed to unarmed or lightly armed support units).[26] But the British were adamantly opposed to that idea at the time.

In the early stages of the war, Yaari was anxious about the Yishuv's fate. Poland, with 30 million people, had been overrun within 30 days.

---

25 *Davar*, Sept. 10, 1939.
26 Yaari to Mordechai [Bentov], Sept. 27, 1939, HHA, 5-3.27(1); Yaari to Nehama Genussow, Oct. 1, 1939; *Yedi'ot penimiyot* 91, Oct. 11, 1939; Yaari at a meeting of the Histadrut Executive Committee, May 23, 1940, LA; circular 50 of the Kibbutz Artzi secretariat, June 10, 1940, HHA, 5-20.2a(2); Yaari at a meeting of the Histadrut Executive Committee, July 4, 1940, LA.

It would require a miracle for Palestine, with its half a million Jews, to come out of the war safely.[27] This was during the "Phony War," when the Eastern front was quiet and there was nothing new in the West. Then, a few days before Italy declared war on Britain and France (June 10, 1940), Yaari shared with the Kibbutz Artzi council his dread of a future catastrophe in the Mediterranean basin and Palestine. He intoned Bialik's lines—"The sun rose, the acacia blossomed, and the butcher slaughtered"—and mused aloud: "Who can know whether tomorrow, or the day after, the storm will rage here in Palestine as well."[28]

What message was he trying to convey to his audience? Given his senior position in the movement, his words were not taken as idle thoughts, but as a statement by the leadership. Here, between the lines, he was sowing fear, using words that were only just short of despair. Yaari frequently adorned his speeches with rhetorical flourishes borrowed from the Jewish classics and poetry, the fruit of his rich intellectual world and broad knowledge. Still, one could feel how the words and sentences were woven together in his mind as he spoke, in twisting spirals and associative links, as if he had not thought through the potential impact of his remarks on listeners. Yaari could voice frank and somber statements like this to his flock because he had no executive responsibilities for the Yishuv as a whole.

It was clear to every Jew, to every Zionist, to every member of the Yishuv, and to every Shomer that Nazi Germany was the embodiment of absolute evil and must be fought to the death. In June 1940, Fascist Italy joined that camp of evil. Yaari and other Yishuv and Zionist leaders had mixed feelings about Britain. Britain was the mandatory power. In 1939 they had published the White Paper, which formally renounced the goal of a Jewish national home, outlawed the sale of land to Jews in most of Palestine, and barred Jews who had escaped the conflagration in Europe by the skin of their teeth from entering Palestine. But the same Britain bore the torch—and, for an entire year after June 1940, almost single-handedly—of the resistance to the most vicious enemy

---

27 Yaari at the meeting of the Kibbutz Artzi Executive Committee, Mar. 11, 1940, HHA, 5-10.2(5).
28 Yaari at the 18th Council of Kibbutz Artzi, June 4-5, 1940, HHA, 5-20.2a(2).

that had ever assailed the Jewish people. Britain was Zionism's only ally in this most difficult hour, the only force shielding the Yishuv and that would protect it if the evil reached Palestine. Nonetheless, for Yaari, Britain remained what it had been in the 1930s—an imperialistic power with which Zionism had no more than a "confluence of interests." A partnership with it was and remained an "alliance of circumstance," a temporary and tactical cooperation whose goal was the creation of an armed Jewish force to defend the Yishuv in Palestine.[29]

After Italy entered the war in the summer of 1940 and sent its air force to bomb targets in Palestine, including the heart of Tel Aviv, the argument about enlistment took on a somewhat different emphasis. Serving in the British armed forces became increasingly logical. Yaari, having resigned himself to the new reality, dug in his heels and insisted that the only acceptable goal of military service was to defend Palestine. At first, Hashomer Hatza'ir rejected the idea of enlistment except in the transport unit, which was to be based in Palestine and thus could be seen as guarding the home front. When that unit was posted to Egypt, Kibbutz Artzi submitted a protest to the Political Department of the Jewish Agency, reminding it, in early 1941, that the Agency's position was that enlistment was meant chiefly to defend Palestine, that members of the Yishuv would sign up only for combat units in which they would bear arms, and that the Agency was opposed to the idea of support units (sappers) and demanded the establishment of a Jewish brigade. The letter called the reassignment of the Jewish drivers from the transport unit to the sappers as "an affront to our national and human honor, which absolutely must not be borne."[30] In the outline (or theses) that Yaari wrote during 1941 in preparation for the sixth General Council of Kibbutz Artzi, he stated his principled opposition to the idea of obtaining a Jewish state in return for military service by young Jews from the Yishuv and the Diaspora on various fronts, far from Palestine, and warned against the "danger of exploiting the blood of thousands of young Jews for political goals on fronts that are not our

---

29 In advance of the 20th Council of Kibbutz Artzi, September 1940, HHA, 5-20.2a(3).
30 To the Political Department of the Jewish Agency [unsigned], Feb. 20, 1941, HHA, 5-3.40(1).

own."[31] The first reports of the extermination of the Jews in Europe, which reached Palestine in late 1942, caused him to reverse course and favor service in the British armed forces in pursuit of political gains.[32]

When enlistment quotas were imposed for different sectors of the Yishuv, Yaari feared—and with good reason—that the main burden would fall on the kibbutzim. His complaint was that because the Jewish Agency had no power to force compliance by all sectors in the Yishuv, there were relatively few volunteers from the veteran settlements (moshavot), and the moshavim, too, did not meet their quotas. The kibbutz movements, by contrast, were disciplined and could be given orders. He was afraid that the kibbutzim, called on to send off more and more of their young men when they were already plagued by a shortage of working hands, would suffer economically. Still, the bottom line was that "we are asked to provide such and such a percentage—and we will strain ourselves to do so."[33]

After years when there had not been enough jobs in the towns and farming communities of the Yishuv, there was suddenly a labor shortage. Late 1939 saw the first offers of work in British military bases, and the number of such positions increased throughout the next year. The British military began placing orders with local manufacturers and relied upon various services provided by the Yishuv. This led to increased employment on the kibbutzim, at a time when the channels of immigration were blocked and the human reservoir of the youth movements in the Diaspora were being destroyed. The departure of young men and women to join the British forces dealt a serious blow to the kibbutz economy.

The establishment of the Palmach (the Hebrew acronym for "strike forces," the elite commando unit of the Haganah) in the spring of 1941 posed the dilemma of whether to enlist in the British forces or join the new organization. The latter option was more in keeping with KA's preference for defending the home front and serving without a British uniform. It immediately decided to require every kibbutz to send two or

---

31 Yaari, Be-fetaḥ tequfah, 10–11.
32 Yaari at the Histadrut council, Dec. 3, 1942, LA.
33 Meeting of the Histadrut Executive Committee, Aug. 14, 1941, LA.

three members to the Palmach, and they complied.[34] Between 60 and 70 of the 460 recruits to the Palmach in October 1941 came from the KA settlements.[35] In the spring of 1942, the KA Executive Committee decided that another 149 members would join the Palmach, 113 the British armed forces, and 133 the supernumerary police force.[36] Between 1941 and 1948, 29% of all Palmach members from kibbutzim came from KA.[37]

In this time of trial, the members of Hashomer Hatza'ir reported for duty on other fronts as well. They enlisted in various units of the British armed forces (including the Jewish Brigade when it was established in 1944), and were among the agents parachuted into Europe. Two of the three young women in the group, and one of the seven who did not survive, were members of KA. When he said goodbye to Haviva Reik of Kibbutz Ma'anit, who would not return, and Shalom Finzi, of Kibbutz Gat, who did, Yaari knew—as did they—that their farewells were more likely an *adieu* than an *au revoir*. Nonetheless, Yaari did not oppose their mission, which he saw as one to rescue Jews in Europe.[38]

Slowly but surely, and from various sources, reports trickled into Palestine about what was going on in Nazi-occupied Europe. Like many others, Yaari refused to believe what he had heard and read. He was strongly affected by the account included in a letter that Tosia Altman, a leader of the movement in Poland, sent to a friend in Palestine on April 7, 1942. Choosing her words carefully and writing in a sort of code, so as to evade the censor, she wrote that "the disease afflicting Israel and me ... has now been diagnosed as quite incurable. [...] *Peraotski* [Heb. *pera'ot* = pogroms] and *Shehitah* ['slaughter'] are living with me and Israel. ... Israel is dying slowly in front of my eyes, and I am wringing my hands and can do nothing to help."[39]

In a reconstruction of Yaari's actions and statements during the war, as in the entire field of research into the Yishuv and the Holocaust,

---

34 Bauer, *From Diplomacy to Resistance*, 167.
35 Zait, *Ḥaluẓim*, 161.
36 Meeting of the Kibbutz Artzi Executive Committee, May 1942, HHA, 5.10.3(1).
37 Zait, *Ḥaluẓim*, 161.
38 Yaari at a meeting of the Histadrut Executive Committee, Aug. 5, 1954, LA.
39 *Sefer Ha-shomer Ha-ẓa'ir*, 1:523.

the end of November 1942, when the first authenticated reports about the systematic annihilation of European Jewry were received, is a decisive juncture. This was when the unprecedented nature of the Nazi war against the Jews became clear, and when people, including Yaari, began to realize that this was not simply another episode of pogroms or massacres, like so many in the past, but a catastrophe far exceeding anything that had ever been known in the history of the Jewish people and of the entire human race. Like other Zionist leaders, Yaari had sometimes employed the Hebrew word *shoah* before then.[40] But just as the use of that word before the autumn of 1942 does not connote some prophetic power, neither does its use in the first years afterwards reflect a real internalization of the magnitude of the Holocaust and its uniqueness in Jewish and world history.

When the reports were received, the Yishuv leadership had to consider a number of issues: how to respond, what forms of rescue might be possible and how to organize them, and where and how to mobilize the financial resources to fund such operations. First came the organized public response, intended to sound "an alarm, a protest, and a cry"; its main practical manifestations were rituals of mourning and fasting.[41] A few months later, Yaari observed that "there are those who are looking for consolation in prayer and fasting."[42] From this we can infer a note of demurral, as well as the pain that he and the members of his movement were emotionally unable to take part in the traditional Jewish expressions of mourning, with their essentially religious nature—given that such rituals, although devoid of practical ramifications, could provide a measure of catharsis. In retrospect, the public manifestations of grief can be seen as a sort of excuse that the Yishuv could invoke to counter the claim that it was indifferent to the Holocaust.[43]

Yaari was candid in his sober portrayal to his flock of the Yishuv's powerlessness to do anything about the catastrophe that had overtaken

---

40   See Halamish, "Meir Yaari's Attitude toward Rescue and Aliyah."
41   Porat, *Hanhagah be-milkud*, 74–78 [omitted from the English translation: *The Blue and the Yellow Stars of David: The Zionist Leadership in Palestine and the Holocaust, 1939–1945*, Cambridge, MA: 1990].
42   Yaari, "Facing the Disaster," *Be-derekh arukah*, 261.
43   See Halamish, "The Yishuv and the Holocaust."

the Jews in Europe: "What can we do? We shout and make demands. Is there anyone we can address the demands to?" he asked in the winter of 1942/43.[44] He was painfully frank: the Yishuv could do very little to hasten the Germans' defeat and there was no escape from the sense of helplessness. At the time, his thoughts were still focused on Palestine and he prayed that the Germans would be defeated before they reached it.[45]

During the war, the Yishuv was involved in five different types of rescue and assistance operations: the major effort to extricate Jews from territories controlled by the Nazis or their satellites, the more modest attempts to send assistance to the Jews in those regions, the dispatch of emissaries to the occupied territories, the efforts to get the Allies to bomb rail lines and death camps in order to obstruct the extermination process, and enlistment in the British armed forces. Yaari, as the head of a relatively small organization within the Yishuv and Zionist movement and with no executive responsibility at the national level, was not racked by some of the hesitations that afflicted those who did bear such responsibility. He had no opportunity to play a significant role in either large-scale or modest rescue campaigns or on the diplomatic front, and was limited to expressing an opinion. When he spoke to his movement as its leader, he portrayed rescue as the political mission of Zionism in this hour, but did not offer operational proposals.[46] But speaking as a rank-and-file delegate in a wider forum (the Histadrut Executive Committee), shortly after the Warsaw Ghetto Uprising, he asked: "Can we save anyone? To what extent can our assistance be useful? Can we get there? Can we reach them? Sometimes we have the feeling that we are trying to put out a terrible conflagration, an impure fire, an inferno that has spread to the entire world, with small pails of water. Aren't we just pouring a few small buckets onto an all-consuming fire?"[47]

The period from the first authenticated reports of the Nazi extermination operations until after the Warsaw Ghetto uprising—late 1942 through mid-1943—was the "shock stage" of Yaari's coping with

---

44 Yaari, "Facing the Disaster," *Be-derekh arukah*, 261.
45 Ibid.
46 Ibid., 259-261.
47 Yaari at a meeting of the Histadrut Executive Committee, May 5-7, 1943. LA.

the Holocaust in Europe. During that time, he gave public expression, in the first-person plural, to the process he was going through:

> We are standing next to the open grave of the Jewish masses. The catastrophe has not yet penetrated us through and through! We are in mourning, along with the entire Yishuv. We are in mourning—but we are not capable of fully understanding the news of the Holocaust. [...] Comrades, what I have said and will say will be only a pathetic expression of the horrible truth. Only on sleepless nights does the naked truth show itself fully. Then this black certainly feeds on us like a vampire. When day returns—every morning—we are still harnessed to our cart and ply our route between Merhavia and Tel Aviv and back again. We still do not understand the implications of the fact that the towns of our parents and our childhood have become cities of slaughter.[48]

Here we see the elements of the shock stage, when the mind is still incapable of digesting and comprehending what the ears are hearing and the eyes are seeing: "And how is it possible for such a city, for entire cities, to be forced into sealed freight cars, to be burned in crematoria, to be exterminated by electricity within a few hours?! Can our mind conceive of such a thing? Can our soul bear it? Will our hearts ever know peace?"[49] Overcome by a burst of nostalgia for the town of his youth, Reisha, and his father's home, he returned to his childhood roots:

> How many historical layers met in the life of such a city! The remnants of the ghetto, the controversy between Hassidism and its opponents, the last stage of the Enlightenment, the early stirrings of Zionism, political emancipation, Zionism's struggle against assimilation and the Bund. The distinctions within Zionism, with its various parties and class-oriented and socialist proclivities. And Hashomer Hatza'ir itself—didn't it extend its taproots into those layers of our people's lives in the last century? Wasn't it nurtured by Hassidism, its

---

48 Yaari, "Facing the Disaster," *Sefer Ha-shomer Ha-ẓa'ir*, 1:520.
49 Yaari, "Facing the Disaster," *Be-derekh arukah*, 260–261.

opponents, and the Enlightenment? Didn't we fill our packs there with provisions for the journey when we immigrated to Palestine?[50]

The Warsaw Ghetto Uprising, in the spring of 1943, was a more significant watershed in Yaari's thinking about the Holocaust and its ramifications than the initial reports in autumn 1942 had been. The Uprising made the Holocaust closer and more tangible for at least two reasons. First, it stood out from the rest of a situation in which the Jews seemed to be passive victims. Second, members of Hashomer Hatza'ir were prominent in the leadership of the Uprising and were conspicuously represented among both the fighters and the slain. The Warsaw Ghetto Uprising forced Yaari to wrestle with the message of fighting to the last, fighting not in order to win—that was hopeless—but on behalf of human dignity and national honor. Yaari tried to juxtapose this message, whose core was death, with the mandate of living heroism. In addition, the Uprising turned "Warsaw"—as a metaphor for the movement's activities in Europe during the war—into a focus of identification and an example for the Shomrim in Palestine. Yaari feared that "Warsaw" would be linked with Masada and serve as the inspiration for heroic death, overshadowing what he saw as the proper source of inspiration, which could be termed—again metaphorically—"Merhavia," though he never spoke its name explicitly.

The Warsaw Ghetto Uprising is an essential prism for understanding Yaari's ideas about heroism and how they changed as the war progressed and under the influence of the Holocaust.[51] At the start of the war, he lectured the movement activists assembled in Vilna about the need for a "heroic war," even if it was likely to end tragically.[52] Three and a half years later, he called on the few survivors of the Warsaw Uprising to save themselves and bow out of the armed struggle, so as to preserve the movement's leadership and leave voices to recount its members'

---

50 Ibid., 260.
51 See Halamish, "The Attitude of Hashomer Hatzair's Leadership toward the Heroism" and the references listed there.
52 Yaari to the members of the central office of Hashomer Hatza'ir in Poland in Vilna, Jan. 10, 1940, HHA, 95-7.9(2).

heroism.⁵³ Hashomer Hatza'ir began highlighting the heroism of Tosia Altman. At first this was in tandem with veneration of Zivia Lubetkin, a member of Dror. The initial reports were that both had perished, but due to a mistake in the cable the news of their deaths was delayed for a week. Only after the final confirmation (which was in fact mistaken: Lubetkin survived the war and passed away in 1978) were their deaths made public. Yaari saw the transmission of Altman's legacy as the well-known practice of a people who weave their own myths. "The two young women, their letters, their actions, became a legend while they were still alive. The emotional tremor was shared by all." ⁵⁴ To buttress the veneration of Altman, Yaari drew on an example that he invoked more and more frequently in those days: the Soviet Union under Stalin's leadership. In this case, it was a Soviet propaganda pamphlet that happened his way, with the story of the young woman named Tanya, a member of the Komsomol, who fought with the partisans and died a heroic death, and "the entire Red Army now sings the song of Tanya. … After her death, Stalin named her a 'hero of the Soviet Union.' [...] Tosia is our Tanya."⁵⁵ Here he was awarding a member of his movement the highest decoration for valor at his disposal in those days.

In addition to sending instructions to the members of the movement "over there" about how they should conduct themselves, Yaari also dealt with the impact of the Warsaw Ghetto Uprising on his own flock in Palestine. He took great pride in the Shomrim who had led and taken part in the uprising, but the educational lessons of their heroism were complex. Their efforts to organize, their revolt, and the fight they put up conveyed strength and determination, but, in his view, they also had a negative potential. In particular, he was afraid of the consequences of the message of "fighting to the death." Starting in mid-1943, he frequently quoted the Psalmist's motif of "I will not die, but live," while emphasizing the heroism of life as preferable to

---

53 Porat, *Hanhagah be-milkud*, 441–442; Stauber, *The Holocaust in Israeli Public Debate*, 86.
54 Yaari to Halina Smadar, June 20, 1943, HHA, 5-3.43(b1).
55 Ibid.

a courageous death. Shortly after the uprising, Yaari addressed the problematic nature of the ethical messages it conveyed, head on and in public. Between the lines we can read the lesson that eventually came to be labeled "from Holocaust to rebirth" and was fostered in subsequent years by the Zionist movement and the State of Israel:

> The thousands of years of Jewish martyrdom have left us a charge: not to lay down our weapons until the last Jew; [but] we are not fighting the war of Masada in Warsaw. Masada was the last flame, the last gasp of Jewish independence before we began thousands of years in exile. For us, [...] these days are a period of annihilation there and of the beginning of Jewish independence here, which is being and will be established! [...]
>
> This charge that has been handed on to us forbids us to hold to Masada thinking and the Masada line. We are not fighting the last battle. We will not choose ourselves a fine death, not even a fine heroic death. We will not die, but live![56]

The background to these remarks was the events in Europe as well as other people's reactions to them. They echo, for example, the report conveyed two months earlier by Eliezer Kaplan of Mapai about the Jewish resistance in Sosnowiec: "When rumors spread about deportations, a number of comrades decided to defend themselves—or, it would be more accurate to say, to choose an honorable death."[57] A few days before that (in mid-March), Ben-Gurion told those assembled at the memorial service by the grave of Josef Trumpeldor and his comrades that the resisters in Warsaw (he was referring to the four days of fighting in mid-January, led by the ZOB [the Jewish Fighting Organization]) "had learned the new doctrine of death that the defenders of Tel Hai and Sejera bequeathed us—a heroic death."[58] At the meeting where Yaari made the statements quoted above, Eliyahu

---

56 Yaari at a meeting of the Histadrut Executive Committee, May 6, 1943, LA.
57 Meeting of the secretariat of Histadrut Executive Committee, Mar. 31, 1943, LA.
58 Yechiam Weitz, "Heibetim," 76.

Golomb told of Jews who "rose up not to defend their lives, but their honor," and Zalman Rubashov (Shazar) spoke about the fact that the "flag of Tel Hai was raised" in the cities of Europe.[59]

Yaari endeavored to take some of the shine off the ghetto fighters' heroic ends and to exalt life over death. He told those gathered at a movement event (the remarks were then published in its bulletin) that "sometimes it seems to be easier for a Jew in these times to die heroically than to live heroically—to live and to follow the thorny path that leads to redemption." And, he added: "Those who must live and go on will have to display greater courage than [those who sacrifice themselves in battle ...]. Any solution or political orientation must face the issue of restoring the belief in life to the generation that emerges from the Nazi inferno."[60] Yaari rejected Warsaw and Masada as a symbol and example, while fostering the legacy of Tel Hai. Stalingrad, too, began to be emphasized as worthy of admiration and emulation.[61]

Historians have devoted much attention to how the news of the Holocaust was processed and internalized by the Yishuv. Several main stages are usually identified: The reception of the reports was followed by digestion of the information and by its mental and emotional processing into awareness and action. To what extent, and when, did the information about the Holocaust penetrate Yaari's consciousness? For most people, the Holocaust did not produce any real change in worldview, religious belief, or ideology, and Yaari was no different. An exception must be made for the period between late 1942 and mid-1943, when, still in the shock stage, he went through both emotional and ideological trauma. In those months he spoke about "rescue," not only in its sense during the Holocaust, but also as it was defined in the Zionist discourse as the polar antithesis of "redemption"— "rescue" in the sense of a solution to the Jews' existential crisis. In

---

59 Meeting of the Histadrut Executive Committee, May 6, 1943, LA.
60 Yaari, remarks at the opening of the branch of the Hashomer Hatza'ir youth movement in Tel Aviv, HHA, 95-7.3a(1).
61 See Halamish, "The Attitude of Hashomer Hatzair's Leadership toward the Heroism."

1943, immediately after the Warsaw Ghetto Uprising, Yaari sang a different tune than he had previously, or than he would at a later date as well. He spoke about unity for the sake of rescue: "In every disagreement, we must never forget the rule that is certain for all of us: 'walk alone, but fight together!' There is no alternative and sometimes we must walk alone, but—to rescue, to create, to fight—for these we must be together!" And going beyond fighting as one, he added: "We must now make every effort to restore in the Diaspora the maximum of Jewish unity for the sake of Palestine and the rescue enterprise! [...] Let us give over quarreling about divisive goals."[62] These and similar sentiments, to which he gave vent during the shock stage, were exceptional for Yaari, who strove consistently to preserve the distinctiveness and autonomy of Hashomer Hatza'ir—before the war, during most of it, and afterwards as well.

Yaari's statements during the "shock stage" about his hometown expressed not only nostalgia but also compassion for the Diaspora, for its Jews of all classes—an emotion that coexisted with his negation of the exile. Relatively early in the war, he published a defense of the Diaspora, in the sense of the Jewish masses.[63] In the fall of 1941, he put it explicitly: "Negation of 'the eternal exile' is good, but it is not good to be detached from the Diaspora."[64] The Holocaust reinforced both sides of this dictum: negation of the exile as a condition and as a way of life, alongside sympathy for the Diaspora, meaning the Jews still living "there." But this attitude did not inspire him with any real empathy for the survivors and did not lead him to renounce the principle of selective immigration after the war.

---

62 Yaari at a meeting of the Histadrut Executive Committee, May 6, 1943, LA.
63 Yaari, "My Reply," *Davar,* Jan. 29, 1940.
64 From the theses drawn up in advance of the session of the General Council, Sept. 21, 1941, KMA, MYF, 7(2). [Note that in Hebrew this is almost a play on words—*galut* "exile" and *golah* "Diaspora."]

CHAPTER 8
Facing the Forces of Tomorrow

During the war years, as before, Yaari's schedule was overflowing with conferences, meetings, tours, and writing. He divided the week among Merḥavia, Tel Aviv, and Haifa, and sometimes traveled to Jerusalem. He even put in a few hours on Saturdays. In the family domain Yaari experienced intergenerational changes. On September 27, 1941, when he was 44, his youngest child was born. The baby was named for Meir's father, Chaim, who had died in 1924, and for Menachem Ussishkin, who died (on October 2) between the boy's birth and his circumcision. About a year later, Yaari's daughter, Rachel, married Lushek Groll, a member of a group of Hashomer Hatza'ir graduates that had joined Merḥavia.

In March 1941, Yaari asked to be released from his executive duties so that he could write his "theses" in advance of the next Kibbutz Artzi council.[1] But yielding to his comrades' pressure, he continued to serve as the general secretary of KA and also found time to write the essay that was published early the next year as a short book, *At the Doors of an Epoch*. This was after the Soviet Union had entered the war alongside the Allies, before the decisive battle at El Alamein that blocked the Wehrmacht's eastward drive to the Suez Canal and beyond, and before the systematic annihilation of European Jews became known. It was Yaari's literary debut and he proudly sent copies

---

[1] Yaari to the secretariat of the Kibbutz Artzi Executive Committee, Mar. 17, 1941, HHA, 95-7.9(4).

to people outside the movement.² At the very outset he proclaimed his strict loyalty to Marxist doctrine, but—as had been the case until then, and would remain so in the future—this loyalty neither cast a shadow on the fundamental tenets of Zionism nor challenged them. The book is less of a roadmap for the future than a commentary. Extensive sections read like an educational manual in the format of a youth movement discussion session, explaining and interpreting the past in order to corroborate the author's prophecies of future developments. Given its date of publication, a substantial part of the book was devoted to an analysis and explanation of a past that was already (or would soon be) irrelevant. It proposed programs that were soon revealed to be meaningless for a future that was shrouded in fog and did not reflect what was actually taking place during those very days. This problem is evident in the preface that Yaari added at the last minute: "I submitted the section that deals with international problems for discussion by the movement institutions even before Soviet Russia entered the war, and I note with great satisfaction that I had to make only slight modifications [...] and change the tense from future to present."³ This means that what had been in the past remained the case in the present so far as his positions were concerned; the upheavals of the past year had not budged him from his opinion.

At the Doors of an Epoch was published in advance of the Sixth General Council of Kibbutz Artzi, which met in Mishmar Ha'emeq in April 1942. The Mishmar Ha'emeq council went down in the annals of the movement as the "Council of the Three Flags," referring to the three demands that Yaari advanced in his book and presented at the council: a pro-Soviet orientation, a binational state, and laying the groundwork for the establishment of a political party. A month afterwards, an "Extraordinary Zionist Conference" convened at the Biltmore Hotel in New York, with the participation of the leaders of the Zionist movement, notably Weizmann and Ben-Gurion, and drafted a political platform for the postwar era. The main thrust of the

---

2 Yaari to Berl [Katznelson], Apr. 7, 1942, HHA, 5.3-36(2c), where he also wrote about reactions he had already received.
3 Yaari, *Be-fetaḥ tequfah*, 6.

"Biltmore Program" was the demand to open the gates of Palestine to Jewish immigration, the transfer of responsibility for immigration to the Jewish Agency, and the constitution of postwar Palestine as a Jewish commonwealth integrated into the new democratic world order. The program was approved unanimously; the representative of Hashomer Hatza'ir cast the sole abstention. In November 1942, the Biltmore Plan (henceforth, at least officially, the "Jerusalem Plan") was adopted by the Inner Zionist General Council in Jerusalem, over the opposition of two representatives of Hashomer Hatza'ir and the representative of the centrist Aliyah Ḥadashah, replacing the 1897 Basel Program as the operational platform of the Zionist movement.

The deliberations of the Inner Zionist General Council in Jerusalem took place shortly before the first reliable reports of the Nazi's extermination campaign in Europe had reached Palestine. At its first session (in mid-October), Hazan submitted Hashomer Hatza'ir's proposal, whose chief divergence from the Biltmore Program was that instead of a Jewish commonwealth (in plain terms, a Jewish state) covering all of Palestine, it was willing to make do with a political entity under international supervision, with a binational state as the long-term goal.[4] On November 10, 1942, when the Inner Zionist General Council met again in Jerusalem, Yaari made only one small amendment to Hazan's proposal of four weeks earlier. He rephrased the demand that the Jewish Agency be granted all the rights needed to develop and build the country, including settlement on all "state land" and uninhabited districts, in a way that would promote dense Jewish settlement without marginalizing the economic interests of the Arab sectors, in positive terms: "Giving the Jewish Agency the necessary authority to develop and build the country, including the settlement on all state lands and uninhabited districts, according to a program that aimed to benefit both peoples, which would promote dense Jewish settlement and development of the Arab peasant economy."[5]

---

4 Hazan at a meeting of the Inner Zionist General Council, Oct. 15, 1942, in Yaari and Hazan, *Neged ha-zerem*, 11–12.

5 Yaari at a meeting of the Inner Zionist General Council, Nov. 10, 1942, Ibid., 14.

Yaari also observed that it would be impossible to "realize grand plans peacefully without working towards an agreement with the Arabs," although "we will continue the Zionist enterprise even without an agreement with the Arabs."[6] He rejected the Biltmore Program because it meant that one people would rule over the other; avoiding this situation required political parity between the two peoples.[7] However, both in his speech to the Inner Zionist General Council and in all his statements during that period about the appropriate arrangement in Palestine, Yaari emphasized that the paramount question in everyone's mind was finding the most effective way for the Jews to stop being the minority group in Palestine.[8] In his contacts with those who advocated a binational state, including Judah L. Magnes, he stuck to the call for a Jewish majority in Palestine.[9]

When presenting the establishment of a binational state as the ultimate goal of Zionism, he focused on the rate of Jewish immigration, where his stand was essentially the same as it had always been, with a minor adjustment:

> It is clear to me that after this war we will not be able to make do with immigration exclusively in accordance with the [country's] economic absorption power. We will have to demand more than that. This is why, in our political declarations, we have not been content with the economic absorption capacity, but demanded that immigration after the war be in accordance with the full absorption capacity, taking account of the distress in the Diaspora. [...] For years after the war we will have [...] to bring over many Jews, many more than are permitted by the concept of economic absorption capacity.[10]

There was nothing new in the insistence on immigration "in accordance with the full absorption capacity"; that had been the line taken by the

---

6 Ibid., 23.
7 Ibid., 24.
8 Ibid., 25.
9 Halamish, "Bi-Nationalism in Mandatory Palestine," 109,113.
10 Yaari at a meeting of the Inner Zionist General Council, Nov. 10, 1942, in Yaari and Hazan, *Neged ha-zerem*, 21.

Zionist Organization during the interwar period. The last part of the statement, referring to the distressed state of the Diaspora and the need to bring more Jews to Palestine than could be supported by its economic capacity, may hint at a change in Yaari's position in light of the harrowing times. But when he stated his position in a more explicit form—as noted, before the full dimensions of the extermination were known—his difference with Ben-Gurion stands out. Ben-Gurion called for the immediate admission of two million Jews to Palestine, while Yaari spoke about two million immigrants over the course of a decade. In his opinion, talk about an influx of two million in two years endangered Diaspora Jewry. He opposed a "general flight from the Diaspora after the terrible pogrom" and held fast to the idea of a more deliberate migration spread out over a fairly long period. Rapid mass immigration was liable to turn the country into "one big Tel Aviv" and repeat the failure of the Fourth Aliyah on much larger scale—"a catastrophe," in his words.[11]

Yaari countered Ben-Gurion's two million in two years, which he defined as a fantasy, with his own proposal to demand the return of the property that had been stolen from the Jews and the renewal of Jewish life in Poland. "Why should we bring them here broken and shattered and indigent?" he asked. "Those who wish to and are able should return to their homes. Then these millions will immigrate in an organized way over the course of ten years."[12] The first to immigrate would be those with no homes to return to; immediately after the war, children and able-bodied adults would be brought to Palestine. The first stage would be a rescue aliyah, followed by an organized and planned immigration.[13]

These ideas encountered angry responses at once. When he said, "I do not advocate a general flight from the Diaspora after this horrific pogrom. No power in the world could organize such a flight by the broken and shattered masses," a loud voice from the floor interrupted

---

11 Ibid., 19.
12 Ibid., 17, 20–21. For the full record, see the meeting of the Inner Zionist General Council, Nov. 10, 1942, CZA, S25/294.
13 Ibid.

him: "And what will we do with these Jews?"[14] Katznelson accused Yaari of feeling contempt for the broken Jews and closing the gates of Palestine to them.[15] These statements provided ammunition for an assault on Yaari and his movement that went on for quite some time.[16]

About two weeks after the meeting of the Inner General Council at which Yaari had made these remarks, the Jewish Agency released an official communiqué about the systematic annihilation of the Jews of Europe. Somewhat later, Yaari recanted and told his associates in the movement leadership that he regretted some of what he had said. He admitted that, in retrospect, he would not have challenged the immigration plank of the Biltmore Program; now the dispute should be forgotten and the focus placed on immigration and rescue. "I don't see the incitement against us as important right now. [...] Biltmore, too, was merely an episode. Only the tragedy in the Diaspora is not an episode."[17] Another ten days went by and he told the members of the KA executive: "We wanted it to be clear to everyone that even in light of the catastrophe, there is no reason for us to review our ideas and principles. [...] No one disputes the premise that every Jew has the right to make aliyah and not just to dream about it. But is this sufficient reason for us to drop the idea of building Palestine in accordance with a plan and not in an anarchic fashion?" He went on: "Even if the gates of Palestine are opened wide, we will not stop calling for a planned and constructive absorption of immigrants, we will not renounce the primacy of agriculture, and we will not renounce the line of Zionist construction that has accompanied us thus far."[18]

In the last stages of his work on *At the Doors of an Epoch*, Yaari was under the dazzling influence of his movement's achievement in the Histadrut elections, which had seen its share of the vote balloon from

---

14 Yaari at a meeting of the Inner Zionist General Council, Nov. 10, 1942, in Yaari and Hazan, *Neged ha-zerem*, 21.
15 Yaari at a meeting of the Kibbutz Artzi Executive Committee, Dec. 15, 1942, in Yaari and Hazan, *Neged ha-zerem*, 41.
16 Zait, *Ḥaluzim*, 150.
17 Yaari to the Kibbutz Artzi Secretariat, Dec. 6, 1942, HHA, 3.5(4d).
18 Yaari at a meeting of the Kibbutz Artzi Executive Committee, Dec. 15, 1942, in Yaari and Hazan, *Neged ha-zerem*, 40–41.

8% in 1932 to 19.2% in 1941. The KA council for which the book was a preparation was supposed to decide on its future political structure—it being clear that merger with Mapai was not feasible, certainly not in the short term.

With his sights set on the establishment of an independent party, it was only natural that Yaari emphasized what distinguished Hashomer Hatza'ir from Mapai. He wrote in his book that there was no hope for a merger with Mapai, because, despite what the latter had in common with Hashomer Hatza'ir with regard to aliyah, defense, and developing the Histadrut, there was no possibility at present of a meeting of minds on the two fundamental issues: the Arab question and the attitude towards the Soviet Union.[19] And because he saw these two points as an obstacle dividing Hashomer Hatza'ir from Mapai, Yaari endeavored to amplify their importance. The chapter on the Arab question is the longest in his book, and Yaari's treatment of the issue there is more extensive than in his past attention to the subject.

One of the items on the agenda of the Mishmar Ha'emeq council was the definition, for the first time, of a comprehensive political program concerning the Arab question. The joint organization idea of the 1930s had faded away during the economic boom and given up the ghost during the Arab Revolt of 1936–1939. The ultimate goal of a "binational socialist society," added to Kibbutz Artzi platform in 1933, was in any case a vision for the distant future. Then, in 1941 and 1942, when he had to crystallize in his mind, put in writing, and disseminate Hashomer Hatza'ir's thinking on the Arab question, which would clearly set it apart from the other political players in the Yishuv, Yaari drew on a document popularly known as the "Bentov Book" after its principal author, Mordechai Bentov of Kibbutz Mishmar Ha'emeq.[20]

The Bentov Book—officially the report of the Committee on Constitutional Development in Palestine, published in English in 1941 (a Hebrew version came out later)—proposed a solution of the Palestine

---

19 Yaari, *Be-fetaḥ tequfah*, 202.
20 *Committee on Constitutional Development in Palestine: Report* (Jerusalem, 1941). On the "Bentov Book" and the discussion here, see Halamish, "Bi-Nationalism in Mandatory Palestine."

question that would give expression to the aspirations of the two peoples living there. It was the fruit of the labors of a committee convened by the League for Jewish-Arab Rapprochement and Cooperation, founded in October 1939. It brought together former members of Brith Shalom as well as members of Po'alei Ziyyon Left, Mapai, and other political parties. Even though Hashomer Hatza'ir initially sent only observers to the League, Bentov chaired the committee on Constitutional Development in Palestine, and its report came to be identified not only with him but also with his movement, Hashomer Hatza'ir. In fact, however, although Yaari approved Bentov's role on the committee, he did not keep close tabs on its work and the KA institutions never discussed the matter before the report was written.

The Bentov Book concluded that, in the current situation of minority and majority populations in Palestine, constitutional guarantees were essential to keep either people from dominating the other. The report's authors adopted a model of a Jewish-Arab state with governmental parity of the two peoples, linked in a federation with the neighboring Arab countries. Yaari was taken unawares by this conclusion and did not see the proposal in a favorable light. He feared that his movement would be accused of supporting the partition of Palestine into cantons and that the majority of the Zionist movement would react strongly against Hashomer Hatza'ir.[21] But in the absence of any other plan, Yaari was willing—in fact compelled—to adopt the Bentov Plan, with certain reservations—of which the first was an explicit rejection of the principle of numerical parity between Jews and Arabs. He emphasized that the minimum plan that could win possible allies must not renounce the full Zionist aspirations: the Jews must not accept permanent minority status or even agree to a freeze on the national home (namely, on Jewish immigration to the country) after numerical parity was achieved.[22]

Yaari recognized that there was no group on the Arab side that could be a party to a sustainable agreement between the two peoples. He assigned some of the responsibility, and even blame, for this

---

21 Yaari to the movement's emissary in the United States, Moshe Furmansky, Aug. 19, 1942, quoted by Zait, Ḥaluẓim, 108.
22 Yaari, Be-fetaḥ tequfah, 153.

situation to the Zionist leadership. Had it unwaveringly striven for such an agreement, a new and progressive force would have slowly consolidated among the Arabs, gaining strength and displacing the *effendis*—the rich landowners—as the dominant force in Arab society.[23] The use of this term for the Arab leadership, prevalent in the 1920s and 1930s, reflected a view of the Jewish-Arab question as mainly a class problem. By 1942, in the aftermath of the Arab Revolt, it was largely outdated. Today, it would certainly be castigated as "orientalist."

The comprehensive political plan that Yaari presented in *At the Doors of an Epoch* as the basis for a workable agreement with the Arabs of Palestine was Zionist through and through. It included the demand that the Arabs agree to continued Jewish immigration in accordance with the country's absorptive capacity, on a scale that would eventually see millions of Jews living in Palestine and its neighbors, that they relinquish their status as the majority in the country and accept political parity divorced from actual population figures, and that they consent to political independence for Palestine.[24] He sought to prove that the binational solution was preferable to partition, on the grounds that the latter would leave too small a territory for Jewish settlement; whereas his binational solution, including an eventual federation of Palestine and the neighboring countries, would leave all of Palestine, as well as its neighbors, open to Jewish settlement.[25]

A fierce debate erupted at the Mishmar Ha'emeq Council about Yaari's proposal on the Arab question. In the first ballot, 63 delegates voted to table it and reconsider the section on a federation, 55 voted in favor, and 21 abstained. The original proposal was then amended by inserting "prospect": the motion, including "with the long-term perspective of establishing a federation," was then adopted.[26] As usual, it was easier to agree about the long term. The resolution as passed accordingly spoke of a binational state in Palestine, with a Jewish majority and a government based on parity between the two

---

23 Ibid., 142.
24 Ibid., 148.
25 Ibid., 117.
26 Zait, *Ḥaluzim*, 109.

peoples; a country in which Jews would be the main element and where Jews from all over the world could settle. Eventually, this country would become part of a federation with its Arab neighbors. This line was the basis of Hashomer Hatza'ir's political program for the rest of the war period, lasting until 1947.

At various opportunities, Yaari framed his vision of a binational state in class terms. At a meeting with visiting Soviet diplomats in the summer of 1942 (see below), he admitted that the fate of Zionism was bound up with that of the toiling masses of the Arab people and emphasized that the Yishuv could not prosper if its Arab neighbors were mired in poverty and subject to a feudal regime. The country had sufficient untilled land to sustain newcomers without harming the existing inhabitants, and was large enough for the full national and social liberation of both the Jewish people and the Arab people. He even noted that the demographic increase of the Arab population of Palestine was a result of the prosperity generated by the Jewish sector.[27]

In support of the binational idea, in the early 1940s, he collected statements in favor of parity made by Arlosoroff, Ben-Gurion, and Katznelson in bygone years, ignoring the passage of time—as if subsequent developments were meaningless and what had been true in 1931 and 1935, or in Ben-Gurion's testimony to the Peel Commission in 1936 and his statements at the Zionist Congress in 1937, remained equally relevant in late 1942.[28]

In his forecast for the day after the war, Yaari expected that the Capitalist and Socialist forces would work together to resolve the Jewish problem; he knew that the Zionists would have to address the world's conscience and court international public opinion. An appeal to those forces, who were the natural allies of Zionism, would have to offer them a portrait of a Zionism of Socialism and the brotherhood of nations.[29] When Hashomer Hatza'ir launched a daily in 1943, *Mishmar*,

---

27 Yaari, *Be-derekh arukah*, 258; Yaari at a meeting of Histadrut Executive Committee, Feb. 23-24, 1944, LA.
28 Yaari at a meeting of the Inner Zionist General Council, November 1942, in Yaari and Hazan, *Neged ha-zerem*, 16.
29 Yaari at a meeting of Histadrut Executive Committee, May 5-7, 1943, LA.

the motto that appeared over its masthead every day was "for Zionism, for socialism, for the brotherhood of nations."

Even before the bitter fate of European Jewry became known, Yaari gave thought to the Jewish communities around the world. In the summer of 1942, he tried to persuade the Soviet diplomats visiting Palestine that their country should allow Jews living in Soviet refugee camps and straining its resources to emigrate to Palestine, where they would join the camp of builders and fighters. He was referring to refugees who had escaped to the Soviet Union during the war, not to Soviet citizens. To convince the visitors that this strategy would pay off, he added that after their arrival in Palestine the refugees would join the anti-Fascist front in the Near East.[30]

Yaari felt that American Jewry would be Zionism's great hope after the war and anticipated that it would produce a large pioneering immigration, immigrants by choice and not fleeing persecution.[31] The Zionist movement should woo this community. There were also the Jews in Muslim countries—about 700,000 he estimated, in early 1942.[32] For him, as for other Zionist leaders, this group became more important when the news of the Holocaust emerged. In 1943, he proclaimed his confidence that all Jews, wherever they lived—including those of Syria, Iraq, Iran, and North Africa—were capable of rising to the challenge, just as a young woman from a remote village in Poland (he meant Tosia Altman) had known what to do.[33] And when it became clear that the fate of the Jews of Poland and the other occupied countries had been sealed, he asserted that Zionism must turn to the Jews in North Africa and the refugees in the Soviet Union—a million all told, including those in the Middle Eastern countries. There were also the Jews of Romania, Hungary, and Bulgaria, and still cracks through which other Jews could be saved.[34] But this expansion of the geographic range of potential immigrants was not accompanied by a change in his ideas about their

---

30 Yaari, *Be-derekh arukah*, 258.
31 Yaari, *Be-fetaḥ tequfah*, 96.
32 Ibid., 85.
33 Yaari, "A Ring of Fighting Brotherhood," *Sefer Ha-shomer Ha-ẓa'ir*, 1: 588.
34 Yaari, "Facing the Catastrophe," *Sefer Ha-shomer Ha-ẓa'ir*, 1: 522.

preferred character and the pace of their arrival. As we have seen, even after the news of the Holocaust reached Palestine, and then when the war was over (as we will see below), Yaari derived the scope and pace of immigration from the needs and resources of Palestine and cited figures that would produce a Jewish majority in the country.[35]

In early 1943, while the Yishuv was agonizing about what was happening in Europe, a group of 1,230 Jews arrived from Egypt by rail. They had escaped Poland and made their way through the Soviet Union, Iran, and India. Among them were 860 youngsters known as the "Tehran Children," of whom 719 arrived without their parents. The group's odyssey was a source of great excitement in the Yishuv from the moment they left Tehran. Even though they had not come from the territories under Nazi occupation, they were first group of survivors to reach Palestine since the start of the hostilities. Crowds gathered along the tracks as the train made its way to Atlit, giving the newcomers a warm and passionate reception. After their initial processing in the British internment camp in Atlit, the children were sent to transit camps to recuperate from their travails.

The arrival of the Tehran Children ignited a stormy and prolonged argument between the religious and the Ultraorthodox, on the one hand, and the Histadrut and the agricultural settlements, on the other hand, over which educational system the children would be sent to. In the end, it was decided that screening committees would assign them to the stream appropriate for each of them: 298 children were sent to secular schools, mostly on kibbutzim and moshavim, 36 to secular schools with which Youth Aliyah was already working, 288 to schools run by the religious Mizraḥi party, and 38 to schools associated with the Ultraorthodox Agudath Israel. The rest, about 200 who were already 14 or older, were allowed to select their own institution. The

---

35 In late 1942 he spoke of immigration by two million Jews in the space of ten years (meeting of the Inner Zionist General Council, Nov. 10, 1942, CZA, S25/294). In early 1944 he spoke about another 600,000 or 700,000 Jews, who would arrive in Palestine at an annual rate of 200,000 over the next three or four years, so that the Jews would soon cease to be a minority in the country (meeting of the Histadrut Executive Committee, Feb. 23-24, 1944, LA).

84 counselors that Youth Aliyah assigned to the transit camps were also selected according to an ideological key.[36]

After the Tehran children arrived in Palestine, some newspapers launched a campaign denouncing the counselors from Hashomer Hatza'ir, asserting that they were persecuting the religious children, would not let them pray, and forcing them to remove their caps and go around bareheaded. In this charged atmosphere, a letter from the chief rabbis, Yitzhak Isaac Halevy Herzog and Ben-Zion Meir Hai Ouziel, landed on Yaari's desk in the fall of 1943: "We are no longer able to bear the shame and disgrace when we read in the newspapers about the very strange and reprehensible phenomenon of shared showers for boys and girls on all the moshavim and kibbutzim under your patronage and administration."[37] Because they had not heard a denial of this by Hashomer Hatza'ir, they saw themselves as compelled to sound the alarm against this shameful iniquity. After rebukes along the lines of "have we become like animals, who are naked and not embarrassed," they demanded that the addressees cleanse themselves and the entire Yishuv of "this shameful stain and disgrace" and totally abandon the practice of shared showers and sleeping quarters for boys and girls.[38]

Yaari sharpened his quill and launched a counterattack. He defined the rabbis' letter as slander "wrapped in rabbinic rhetoric" and set out to teach them a lesson in polite behavior. Would Rabbi Herzog, when he served as rabbi in Ireland, "have had the audacity to break into the private domain of a socialist of his own religion without knocking on the door—for example, Harold Laski?"[39] He, Yaari, was proud of his movement's schools and their graduates, the purity of their actions, and of their behavior. In conclusion: "Your honors the Chief Rabbis! You have indeed set yourselves on a slippery path. We allow ourselves

---

36 Porat, "Tehran Children."
37 Y. I. Halevi Herzog and Ben-Zion Meir Hai Ouziel to the board of the Hashomer Hatza'ir Organization, 7 Elul 5703 [Sept. 7, 1943], HHA, 5-3.43(1b).
38 Ibid.
39 Yaari on behalf of the Secretariat to the Presidents of the Chief Rabbinate, Rabbi Herzog and Rabbi Ouziel, Nov. 8, 1943, ibid.

to warn you that it will not be to your credit. You ought to understand that it is possible to put a spoke in the wheels, but the wheel cannot be turned back."[40]

The rabbis sent out another letter, inasmuch as the answer they had received evaded a response to the facts that had led to their first letter. They expected a clear reply: yes or no.[41] Yaari was not deterred: "You wrongly assert that we dodged giving an unambiguous answer. It is perfectly clear and its content is: *We reject the Chief Rabbinate's right to intervene in our domestic and public lives. We refuse on principle to rely on your counsels and instructions on matters of morality and education.*"[42] He again gave them a lesson in the aesthetics and ethics of public speech and made it plain that although it was possible that this kind of invective was of a family nature, "we—as you know—do not belong to the family of believers."[43] He gave them back as good as he got, repelling their attack on his movement by mentioning that some elements saw the tragedy that had struck the Jewish people as an opportunity to restore the lost glory of the crown of clericalism, and he could not release the chief rabbis of their indirect responsibility for the spirit of intolerance and incitement that was spreading in the streets. He concluded by presenting his sober and principled stand in favor of the separation of religious and state, while treating believers with respect and recognizing the need to provide for their religious needs.[44]

The attitude towards religion and its place in individual and public life engaged Yaari on several occasions and in various contexts. At one of the Zionist congresses in the 1930s, the question of Sabbath observance was on the agenda. Yaari explained to the Mizraḥi delegates why Hashomer Hatza'ir had absolutely no interest in a religious war in

---

40 Ibid.
41 The Presidents of the Chief Rabbinate to Hashomer Hatza'ir, 21 Marheshvan 5704 [Nov. 19, 1943], Archives of Religious Zionism, Mossad Harav Kook, Mizraḥi 5704 file.
42 Yaari on behalf of the Secretariat to the Chief Rabbinate, Dec. 20, 1943, HHA, 5-3.43(1b); *Be-derekh arukah*, 265–266 [emphasis in original].
43 Ibid.
44 Ibid.

Palestine and in fact had a high regard for the weekly day of rest.⁴⁵ In the late 1930s, it was hard for him to see his old friend, Berl Stock (Dov Sadan), "going back to yesterday." In his view, "your neo-religiosity and that of other intellectuals in the ranks of the labor movement are a demonstration of a lack of faith in socialism as the driving force of the Jewish rebirth," he wrote to him.⁴⁶

During the war, Yaari's pro-Soviet orientation, already a central element of his worldview, grew stronger. During the 1930s, it should be remembered, the Soviet Union seemed to be a success story, in contrast to the string of crises of Capitalism. Before that, in the early 1920s, many circles in the Yishuv were united in their sympathy for the country of the revolution. Arthur Ruppin, a member of the bourgeois General Zionist party, summed up the year 1921 in his diary: "If I were not a captive of Zionism, I could not imagine a higher aim in life than to be working in Russia now on a peaceful reorganization of that country."⁴⁷ Ben-Gurion, who visited the Soviet Union in 1923, came back enthusiastic about its achievements and aspirations, but also full of criticism of what was being done there and consumed with doubts about its future.⁴⁸ But by the time that Yaari became captivated by the magic of the Soviet Union and gave it his heart, many of that country's admirers in the Yishuv had already turned their backs on it.

Various factors pushed Yaari towards an increasingly pro-Soviet orientation. One was his Marxism, which was deepening and taking on a more Leninist coloration after he worked through his hesitations about which socialist stream to choose. It was also fed by the prevailing mood of the movement abroad and in Palestine and by his desire to comply with it so as to avoid losing members and his status; all this, of course, while staunchly insisting on the primacy of Zionism. His pro-Soviet orientation also derived from his assessment of the Soviet Union's anticipated future role and increasing involvement in the Middle East. He wanted Hashomer Hatza'ir

---

45 Yaari, *Be-meri vikkuaḥ*, 9.
46 Yaari to Berl [Stock (Dov Sadan)], July 31, 1939, HHA, 95-7.8(6).
47 Arthur Ruppin, *Memoirs, Diaries, Letters*, entry for Dec. 31, 1921, p. 195.
48 Ben-Gurion, *Zikhronot* 1: 267–268, entry for Dec. 16, 1923.

to be the organization in the Yishuv and Zionism with which the Soviet Union would forge ties in the future. Another factor was the desire to follow a different path than the rest of the labor movement. Sympathy for the Soviet Union and the adoption of the Marxist lexicon increasingly served as important points in the debate that precluded merger with Mapai.

During the 1920s, members of Hashomer Hatza'ir criticized the Soviet Union's negative attitude towards the pioneer movement, its persecution of Zionism and the Hebrew language, its deportation of Zionists to Siberia, and its terror tactics against socialists.[49] Starting in late 1934, reports appeared in the Palestinian press about mass executions in various parts of the Soviet Union.[50] Later in the decade, there was a rash of reports on the purges, show trials, and executions. In its proclamation to mark May Day 1938, Hashomer Hatza'ir criticized the Soviet Union because, even though it was "the only workers' country in the world," it "had not set itself as a revolutionary force at the head of the workers' movement in the world; and, what is more, the bloody trials based on deception and humiliation are sowing disappointment and distrust in the workers' camp."[51] Yaari himself was less firm about the Moscow Trials. In the early 1940s, he confessed that the trials and the debate about the Popular Front in Europe had raised doubts about Hashomer Hatza'ir's positive attitude towards the socialist enterprise in the Soviet Union.[52] But he justified what was happening there, indirectly and almost directly. What he wrote at the beginning of the Second World War is quoted here at length in order to give an impression of the content, argumentation, phrasing, firmness, and quantity of energy he invested in the matter. This is when his attachment to the Soviet Union seems to have overpowered his sober senses, starting him and his movement on a path that not only turned out to be mistaken in retrospect, but whose dangers were already apparent to some back then.

---

49 E.g., Gotthelf's remarks at the convention of Hashomer Hatza'ir in Warsaw, October 1927, Zait, *Ha-Utopia ha-shomrit*, 248.
50 E.g., *Palestine Post*, Dec. 24, 1934.
51 Patish, *Ha-siḥrur ve-ha-ivvaron*, 85.
52 Yaari, *Be-fetaḥ tequfah*, 31.

> I have always rebelled against the failure to acknowledge that the Soviet Union has been immersed in a state of war from the October Revolution to the present. [...] Throughout that time, it has defended itself against the danger of the Fifth Column and against all the perils that materialize in wartime. [...] Had more normal conditions prevailed rather than a state of siege for decades, it would not have been necessary for socialism in Russia to be built under the ever-more-stringent oversight of the secret police.[53]

After he surveyed the espionage, provocations, and betrayals that had infected all the parties in every country and were among the factors contributing to their defeat by Hitler, he asked, in what we can hardly avoid calling a blatant whitewash: "Should we not assume, in light of these facts, that there was a basis for the trials of the terrorists in Russia and that Hitler's espionage in the Soviet Union had managed to lead the weaker elements in the Communist Party astray, that provocateurs were able to forge documents, cast suspicion, and stir up public hysteria?"[54] Citing examples of the Fifth Column in France and referring to Charles Lindbergh (the legendary American pilot who admired the Luftwaffe and accepted a medal from Herman Goering in 1938), he asked, in a paragraph that began, "and now to the Moscow Trials":

> Is it so fantastical to assume that treason has permeated the ranks of the Soviet Army and that it was only thanks to the advantages of proletarian dictatorship that the traitors' plots were unraveled in time? Is it really impossible to assume that provocation from the outside and treason from the inside joined forces and permeated not only the ranks of the armed forces but also of the Party? [...] Is it impossible that Nazi provocateurs played a major role in these trials?[55]

---

53 Ibid., 48–49.
54 Ibid., 49.
55 Ibid., 49–50.

When the war broke out, Yaari made his peace with Moscow's actions and even defended them. Even before it had joined the Allies, Yaari did not vacillate in his stand *vis-à-vis* the Soviet Union and was concerned only about how to explain his favorable attitude towards that country to both his flock and to the broader public. Yaari felt a need or obligation to crystallize and express a position on every issue related to it. Just as he defended the show trials of the 1930s, the purges of the Soviet Communist Party and Red Army, and Stalin's dictatorial regime, he justified the Molotov-Ribbentrop agreement, which he always described, both in conversation and in writing, as a "neutrality pact." That label may have been appropriate when it was first signed and its secret annexes were still confidential, but Yaari stuck to this designation even when the facts on the ground—the dissection of Poland as the spoils of war between Germany and the Soviet Union, the Soviet attack on Finland, and seizure of some of its territory—had revealed its true nature. Yaari's assumption was that the Soviet Union was neutral in the war between Nazi Germany and the Capitalists; but should there be an alliance between Communism and Fascism, he said about two months after the war broke out, he would feel that his world had grown dark.[56]

These statements were made at the meeting of the Kibbutz Artzi Executive Committee on November 7, 1939, the first time a broad movement forum was discussing the Molotov-Ribbentrop Pact, and precisely on the anniversary of the Bolshevik Revolution. Yaari was not eager to engage in a discussion about the Soviet Union after the signing of the pact; had it been up to him the debate would have been shelved. But it did take place and he could not avoid taking part. He analyzed the Soviets' actions in detail, defending some and cautiously criticizing others; his bottom line was clear—the agreement was justified. Even Lenin, he reminded his listeners—assuming they would understand that he was referring to the Treaty of Brest-Litovsk between Russia and the Central Powers, in March 1918—had signed agreements with Imperialists. Another excuse for the present agreement was simply that

---

56 Meeting of the Kibbutz Artzi Executive Committee, Nov. 7, 1939, HHA, 5-10.2(5).

Hitler would have gone to war even without it. After all the merits he claimed for the pact, it was time to acknowledge the other side: the agreement had dealt an ethical blow to the workers of the world, and he was opposed to the attack on Finland. Then, as if placing himself in Stalin's boots, he said that he would not have signed a pact with Hitler, because it would not prevent the German invasion of the Soviet Union, which was inevitable.[57]

It was not easy to explain Soviet actions between August 1939 and June 1941. Yaari tried to transmit his favorable attitude towards the Soviet Union to the movement activists who had fled to Vilna when the war started. He hastened to rebuke them when they spoke about that country in a way that troubled him. The incident took place after some of the leadership group in Vilna sent greetings via the pages of *Davar* to Kibbutz Amir when it broke ground at its new permanent location.[58] In their message, they describe developments in both the Soviet and German zones of occupation in similar language. Yaari warned them: "You must not deviate from the line we have taken all these years and will also take in the future. Despite all the tribulations of life underground, do not be tempted by the vulgar thinking that does not distinguish between the two occupied zones."[59] He also instructed them to rid themselves of all bitterness and antagonism with regard to the Soviet Union.[60]

Many of those who sympathized with the Soviet Union and had been trapped in deep perplexity since August 1939 let out a sigh of relief when Germany attacked it on June 22, 1941. Yaari did not. If he did feel some measure of relief, it was mainly because the new situation resolved a dilemma that troubled others, not him. Now a source of friction and misunderstanding between him and some members of the movement was no longer relevant. In any case, it was more comfortable to be aligned with the Soviet Union in the fight against the Nazis.

---

57 Ibid.
58 Levi Dror to Meir [Yaari], Feb. 14, 1940, HHA, 95-7.9(2).
59 Yaari to the senior leadership of Hashomer Hatza'ir in Poland, Jan. 10, 1940, HHA, 95-7.9(2).
60 Ibid.

When it joined the Allies in their difficult, courageous, and arduous battle against Germany, Yaari—like so many other good people—felt a surge of sympathy for the Soviet Union, and even adoration, especially during the Battle of Stalingrad and afterwards. Another point to the Soviet Union's credit was that it had become a place of refuge for hundreds of thousands of Jews who fled to the depths of Asiatic Russia. "Soviet Russia," observed Yaari at the height of the war, "is the only country that saved hundreds of thousands of Jewish refugees and gave each one of them 400 grams of bread [a day]—a patent miracle!"[61]

A Soviet delegation visited Palestine in the summer of 1942. Sympathy for the Soviet Union, which was spilling its blood in the war against the Nazis, was at its peak, and the delegation was received with spontaneous enthusiasm everywhere it went. "The heart of the Yishuv yearned for you. We waited for you for so long, as for a relative arriving from a great distance after a long period of isolation and separation," Yaari said with great emotion when he told the visitors goodbye.[62] Comrade Mikhailov, the first secretary of the Soviet legation in Ankara, and Comrade Petrenko, the legation's press attaché, visited two kibbutzim of Hashomer Hatza'ir—Merḥavia and Ma'abarot. Before they left Palestine, Yaari sent them a brief general survey of the Hashomer Hatza'ir movement and its urban arm—the Socialist League—for their own and their superiors' benefit. The survey, which reads as if it were a report on the achievements of a Soviet Five-Year Plan, provides interesting information about the situation of Kibbutz Artzi and Hashomer Hatza'ir in the summer of 1942, even if some of its details should be treated with caution:

> Hashomer Hatza'ir comprises 40 autarkic and wage-earning communes in towns and villages all over Palestine. Most of Hashomer Hatza'ir's economic production is from agriculture. Our harvests last year were as follows: 2,000 tonnes of wheat, 200 tonnes of barley, 1,000 tonnes of corn, 2,000 tonnes of potatoes, 2,500 tonnes

---

61 Yaari at a meeting of Histadrut Executive Committee, May 5–7, 1943, LA.
62 Yaari, "The Bridge will be Erected," *Be-derekh arukah*, 257.

of vegetables, about 1,000 tonnes of bananas, about 1,000 tonnes of grapes and fruits, about 2,500 tonnes of hay, 20,000 tonnes of animal fodder from irrigated fields, 4 million liters of milk, 3½ million eggs, 250,000 liters of sheep's milk. We also have a serious collective industry that produces agricultural machinery, bricks, asphalt, paint, glucose for medical uses, and more.[63]

Yaari also informed them that Hashomer Hatza'ir and the Socialist League were the second largest bloc in the Histadrut and the main force in the left wing of the labor movement in Palestine. It had sent 30 delegates to the last Zionist Congress before the war. The Hashomer Hatza'ir youth movement was the largest in the Jewish world; before the war it had enrolled some 80,000 young people in 30 countries. The weekly *Hashomer Hatza'ir*, distributed in 5,000 copies, was the most widely read in Palestine; the Hashomer Hatza'ir publishing house—Sifriyat Po'alim (the Workers' Library)—was the largest publisher in Palestine and the only Marxist one in Palestine and the Near East. He added a partial list of the titles it had printed to date: *Selected Writings* of Marx and Engels, Engels' *The Origin of the Family, Private Property, and the State*, Franz Mehring's *Karl Marx*, Karl Kautsky's *The Agrarian Question*, Otto Bauer's *The Question of Nationalities and Social Democracy*, Paul Frölich's *Rosa Luxemburg*, and others. He also reported proudly that Lenin's works would appear in Hebrew for the first time later that year. The list of translations from Soviet literature was also distinguished: Makarenko's *Pedagogical Poem*, Valentin Katayev's *A White Sail Gleams*, a selection of new Russian poetry, Vodopyanov's *Polar Fliers*, and Kolbach's *The Zalmans*. A special anthology on the Soviet Union had also been published. In a separate section, he wrote about the movement's Arab Department, which strove to create solidarity among Jewish and Arab laborers, published in Arabic, and stayed in contact with Arab groups.

Yaari acquainted the Soviet guests with "the main points of Hashomer Hatza'ir's political program." Some of them were familiar

---

63 Yaari (on behalf of Hashomer Hatza'ir and the Socialist League) to Comrade Mikhailov and Comrade Petrenko, undated [summer 1942], HHA, 5.3(2).

from days gone by, some were also known from the past but now presented with greater emphasis, and some of them were new; but they were all phrased in a manner calculated to speak to the hearts of the Soviet readers.

He expounded on Hashomer Hatza'ir's attitude towards the Soviet Union in a separate section, beginning with the statement that "Hashomer Hatza'ir is an immovable fortress of solidarity with the USSR in all possible circumstances."[64]

In conclusion, he presented "our requests of the government of the Soviet Union." In the draft copy, this is the only section with his handwritten corrections made to the typescript before the document was ready for translation into Russian: "(1) support for the territorial concentration of the Jewish masses in Palestine—for their immigration to and settlement in their renewed homeland, (2) creation of contacts between the collectivist, cultural, Marxist, and educational movement in the Soviet Union and our movement," and maintaining contact by means of a "Soviet collectivist delegation to Palestine, which we will host, [...] and our reciprocal delegation to the USSR."[65] It is almost certain that he saw himself as a member of such a mission, which never took place. Even earlier, shortly after the German invasion of the Soviet Union, he had proposed that the Histadrut express solidarity with the Soviet Union's struggle and organize a medical assistance mission that would also convey information about the labor movement in Palestine.[66]

In his farewell speech to the Soviet delegation, Yaari spoke less dryly: "We have only one wish to express—and it is that you pass on to your superiors what you discovered here. After all, you cannot have failed to sense that there is an active national and social liberation movement here in Palestine, which is a natural ally of the tremendous enterprise that you have produced over more than one-sixth of the globe."[67] He expressed confidence that they were capable of

---

64 Ibid.
65 Ibid.
66 Yaari at a meeting of Histadrut Executive Committee, July 17, 1941, LA.
67 Yaari, "The Bridge will be Erected," *Be-derekh arukah*, 256.

understanding the unique character of KA, which integrated farming with education, literature, and a labor organization, and took its place at the forefront of a fighting political movement, "because we, like you, are a movement that both builds and fights. [...] We are flesh of your flesh."[68]

The formal excuse for the arrival of the Soviet delegation was the first conference of the V League for Friendship with the Soviet Union. The activities on behalf of the Soviet Union and cultivation of ties with it began after the German invasion of its territories. In October 1941, the Histadrut Executive Committee announced an urgent fund drive as an expression of solidarity with the Soviet Union; with the funds collected from Jewish laborers in Palestine, two sterilizers were purchased and delivered to the Soviet ambassador in London. In October 1941, at the initiative of Martin Buber, the Public Committee for Aid to the Soviet Union in its Anti-Fascist War was formed, and various circles in the Yishuv coalesced around it. On May 2, 1942, the committee met in Haifa and approved the "Buber Platform," an action plan whose crux was increasing the Yishuv's participation in the assistance that the democracies were providing to Soviet Russia. The committee was a nonpartisan organization that accepted anyone who agreed with its goals and was willing to help its work. There was no requirement of hewing to any particular position towards the Soviet regime.[69] The representatives of Hashomer Hatza'ir, and others from the labor movement, called for the platform to include an article stating that the committee aspired to achieve mutual understanding between the Soviet Union and the Jewish and Arab communities in Palestine, and another clause to the effect that the committee would endeavor to win Soviet support for the Zionist enterprise in Palestine. When these were approved, Hashomer Hatza'ir joined the Public Committee, and it was decided to erect on the new platform the V League, to assist Soviet Russia and strengthen ties with it. The League held its first

---

68 Ibid., 257.
69 Chizik, *Yaḥaso shel Ha-shomer Ha-ẓa'ir*, 167. The discussion here is based on Ibid., 166–178, on Zait, *Ḥaluẓim*, 205–206 and on Patish, *Ha-siḥrur ve-ha-ivvaron*, 98–102.

convention on August 25–26, 1942, and, as noted, an official Soviet delegation attended. Its membership came from diverse groups in the Yishuv, including some from Mapai, as well as prominent Arabs. The funds it collected were used to buy ambulances that were handed over to the Red Army in Tehran in May 1943. Another League delegation went to Tehran in December 1943 and a third in November 1944. All of them included a member of KA.

During the war, Yaari fought the Soviet issue on two fronts, against those who denounced its conduct and against those who went too far in worshiping it. At the start of the war, while he was criticizing movement members in Europe for their similar attitudes to the Soviet and German zones of occupation, he was also concerned about "Red Assimilation" in the districts under Soviet control. In Palestine, too, he battled the tendency, on the margins of his camp, to slide leftward, while also opposing members who had carried their disgust with the Molotov-Ribbentrop Pact so far as an unqualified denunciation of the Soviet Union.

Going back to the days of the leftward drift by Gedud Ha'avodah, which had ended with some of its members leaving Palestine for the Soviet Union, and continuing with the growing leftist orientation in Eastern Europe in the late 1920s and the leftist agitation of the early 1930s in the movement's communes in Nes Ziyyona and Binyamina, Yaari's concern about his exposed left flank always exceeded his worries about his right flank and Mapai, and his reaction to the former was more vigorous. In the late 1930s, he ignored the establishment of a Mapai cell on Kibbutz Ein Haḥoresh. On the other hand, in the early 1940s, Yaari had threatened the members of Kibbutz Hama'apil that if its internal deliberations did not conclude with a vote of approval for Hashomer Hatza'ir's Zionist socialist path, it would be necessary to reconsider the future of their kibbutz.

There were two absolute limits to his sympathy and admiration for the Soviet Union. One was its treatment of Zionists and Jews, which he condemned in scathing terms. His second scruple was that in no case and in no situation should the Soviet Union be seen as a substitute for Zionism as the solution to the Jewish problem, neither on the national nor on the socioeconomic plane. It was precisely in the Soviet Union, he argued, that the Jews were abandoning the village and farm for the city, and he noted as well the failure of the Birobidjan project. He observed that the total number of the Jews living on *kolkhozes* in the Soviet Union was only a third of the number of the people affiliated with the kibbutz movement in Palestine. This great admirer of the Soviet Union concluded unequivocally that "Zionism is potentially just as good for the Jews of Russia as for the Jews of a capitalist country."[70]

Yaari found arguments to justify his pro-Soviet orientation and applied them to all his reference domains: Palestine, the Middle East, Soviet Jewry, and European Jews after the war. His assumption was that the war would be followed by a period of international revolution, when waves of revolution would sweep country after country—"a permanent revolution" and not a one-time revolutionary event or transient revolutionary crest. Because it would be impossible to ride the revolutionary wave in Palestine without help from the Soviet Union, "our faces will certainly be turned towards humankind's forces of tomorrow." But, he added, "the social revolution will not march forward at the bayonet points of the Red Army if it is not welcomed by the independent revolutionary vanguard in every country."[71] And in Palestine, the role of the revolutionary vanguard fell to Hashomer Hatza'ir. As the war continued, his faith that when it was over the Soviet Union would look for leftist socialist forces to collaborate with intensified; and when they looked for such progressive forces in Palestine, they would find Hashomer Hatza'ir. The movement's role then would be to win the support of the revolutionary proletariat all over the world for mass and orderly Jewish immigration to Palestine, as part of a political agreement with the Arabs.[72]

His pro-Soviet orientation was deepened not only by his assessment of what the future held in store for the region, but also by his forecast about the fates of the countries in which (he assumed) Jews would live after the war. He foresaw common Zionist and

---

70 Yaari to Kibbutz Hama'apil, 16.2.1941, HHA, 95-7.9(4).
71 Ibid.
72 Yaari, *Be-fetaḥ tequfah*, 120.

Soviet interests not only in the Middle East, but also in Russia and in Europe, and expected that almost all European Jews would be living under Communist regimes. This would provide an opportunity for cooperation between the Soviet Union and the Jewish people. The relocation of millions of Jews to Palestine could help to solve one of the gravest problems that the Soviets would face at the end of the war. If the Zionist movement did not take a hostile stance *vis-à-vis* the Soviet Union, it stood to reason that the Soviet leadership could be persuaded that accelerating the Jews' concentration in Palestine coincided with its own interests and would facilitate its reconstruction when peace returned.[73] Throughout the war years, and even more so afterwards, Yaari defined the Soviet Union as "the forces of tomorrow" and expressed his strong desire to be part of that legion. He saw the Soviets as the pillar on which Zionism should rely on after the war, and steered his movement accordingly.[74]

Yaari's position on the Soviet Union was also influenced by developments in Palestine and was fed by his desire to stay in harmony with public opinion. During the 1930s, sympathy for the Soviet Union was not widespread. After June 1941, however, it burgeoned to the point of adulation, nurtured by stories about the valiant Soviet resistance to the Nazi invader, the siege of Leningrad, the battles around Moscow, and, most of all, the battle for Stalingrad. That saga included everything: stubborn defense of the homeland, brave resistance to the enemy, the war of the few against the many, the victory of the beleaguered over the aggressor, the triumph of the good and moral over the forces of evil. The sympathy for the Soviet Union that Yaari had cultivated and the positive attitude towards the Soviet Union that prevailed in those days nourished each other. Yaari's ideas fell on fertile soil where they could sprout and grow; and the existence of such a positive atmosphere was one reason for the development and cultivation of his approach.

The first rays of light in the protracted war reached Palestine from the Soviet Union in early 1943, when the German forces capitulated

---

73 Ibid., 90–91.
74 Yaari at a meeting of the Histadrut Executive Committee, May 5–7, 1943, LA.

to the Red Army in Stalingrad. It was the first great defeat for Hitler's armies and came soon after Montgomery stopped Rommel at El Alamein. It marked the end of the almost continuous string of successes by the Axis powers and the start of their expulsion from the territories they had occupied. Until then, although the newsreels shown in the cinemas of Palestine depicted the heroism of the British—the people, the pilots, and the soldiers—along with the fortitude of the Muscovites and horrible siege of Leningrad, the screens had been dominated by German victories and conquests. In early 1943, this gave way to the steady stream of German defeats, and morale improved. The Soviet Union was the hero of the war with a capital H. The Soviet troops' battle cry, *Za rodinu! Za Stalina*—"For our motherland! For Stalin"—was echoed by every mouth. The heroism of Stalingrad purged Stalin of his crimes, as it were, and silenced criticism of him. The terrible hemorrhaging of the Russian people and the casualties suffered by the Red Army fed renewed suspicions that there was a Western conspiracy to weaken and exhaust the Soviet Union. As long as the opening of the second front in the west was delayed, these suspicions grew and served those who wanted to define the war as a struggle pitting the Socialist world against the Capitalists and Imperialists.

With these events and sentiments in the background, Hashomer Hatza'ir fell into an almost blind worship of the Soviet Union. Its youthful charges and kibbutz members heard Yaari's speeches and read his pronouncements, which most of them accepted as gospel truth. His positions on every issue, and with regard to the Soviet Union in particular, sparked no demurrals. Some 60 years later, the poet Nathan Yonathan (1923–2004), a long-time member of the movement who had written Hebrew lyrics to be sung to Russian folk tunes, explained the adulation for the Soviet Union as based on the belief that the Soviet revolution would build a new and better world. That was why "we forgave them their worst injustices" for so long. "Today that absolution amazes me. But back then, we were in such need of an alternative to capitalism that we looked for something grand and meaningful that the whole world could seize on. For years, we lived with an emotional and intellectual faith that was based on analyses, comparisons, and debates, some of which were mistaken and some of which turned out to be lies."[75]

After Stalingrad, veneration of the Soviet Union was not limited to marginal groups, people on the fringes, movements at the farthest Left of the political map of the Yishuv, movements who felt that the future belonged to them and that the Soviet Union was an integral part of it; pro-Soviet adulation also extended to broad circles of the moderate Left and even the center. It was manifested not only in the ideological and political arena, but also in cultural life. There was a "Soviet" cultural influence, distinct from the Russian culture that had formed the members of the Second Aliyah and those of Third Aliyah who came from Russia. Most of those who admired the Soviet Union, including Yaari, did not know Russian; neither did the young people who enthusiastically danced the krakowiak and kalinka, captivated by the Russian melodies given Hebrew words and imbued with Soviet patriotism. The Soviet influence and admiration for the Soviet Union were expressed in both high and popular culture, in the general atmosphere that prevailed in the Yishuv, and even in its slang. The Palmach fighters referred to themselves as "partisans," avidly read Alexander Bek's *Volokolamsk Highway* (a novel celebrating the defenders of Moscow in 1941)—excerpts were translated and published in the Palmach bulletin—and drank vodka from tin mugs.[76]

In this climate, it is no wonder that Yaari felt that his stand on the Soviet Union had the potential to attract young people to his movement. The Soviet Union offered a response to Yaari's intellectual and emotional needs, providing him with inspiration for his leadership. It occupied a larger place in his thoughts than it did in the general *milieu* of his movement, providing him with a cultural and terminological reference point and dominating his universe of concepts and metaphors. This found expression both explicitly and implicitly, directly and indirectly, and sometimes in off-the-cuff statements and innocent remarks. In September 1940, while talking to young members of Hashomer Hatza'ir,

---

75 Aviva Lurie, "Sometimes Life is Longing for a Prize," *Ha'aretz Weekend Magazine*, Mar. 14, 2003 [Hebrew].
76 Gouri and Hefer, *Mishpaḥat ha-Palmaḥ*, 58.

Yaari dropped an offhand comparison between himself and Lenin, assuming that his audience shared his universe of associations: "When I left for the Diaspora as an emissary on behalf of the JNF, my intention was to give a push to the establishment of the world movement, to issue a call for the renewal of immigration. [...]. This is how movements with potential renew themselves. You travel by train to [*sic!*] Switzerland and then build socialism in one-sixth of the globe. You travel to the Diaspora [...] and press forward towards construction."[77]

He recruited the Soviet Union, in an indirect and allusive fashion, to justify the principle of ideological collectivism.[78] Events and processes in that country served as his point of reference, source of inspiration, spiritual conscience, model for emulation, and example to prove his arguments. For example:

> I hereby inform you, Ben-Gurion, that we will go to Syria, to Egypt, to educate the youth. We will even educate Yemenite youth! Why aren't we allowed to dare think that young people in Syria and Egypt can join Hashomer Hatza'ir? Is this idea so strange, after a Georgian, a student at a teacher's seminary who came from the robbers' nests of the Caucasus, rose to be the socialist leader of one-sixth of the world?[79]

Yaari did not have direct experience of the October Revolution and it was a not a formative event for him. At the start of his career in the movement and in Palestine, Russia lay far beyond the horizon and did not serve him as a frame of reference. It did not assume this role until roughly a decade after the revolution; but then its grip on him intensified with the passage of time, to the point that the world of Soviet concepts, with all its special codes, assumed almost the status of religious faith for him. He developed a special attitude towards Stalin and was careful not to minimize him in Lenin's shadow. During a debate about the Molotov-Ribbentrop Pact, when a speaker averred that one should favor the socialist construction project, but not Stalin, who should be overthrown, Yaari told the

---

77 Yaari, "Stages," in Shadmi, *Meqorot*, No. 4, 21.
78 Yaari, *Be-fetaḥ tequfah*, 32–33.
79 Yaari at the conference of Hakibbutz Hame'uḥad, *Mishmar*, Jan. 19, 1944.

participants that "today, overthrowing Stalin would mean a horrible civil war in Russia. [...] If you want to replace Stalin, it would have to be done with arms. That's what Trotsky wanted to do. Here we have to draw all the necessary conclusions. That is why I explicitly oppose these remarks"— as if Stalin's fate depended on a resolution passed by the Kibbutz Artzi Executive Committee.[80] For Yaari, the positive attitude towards Stalin and the justification of the dictatorship that he ran in the Soviet Union were bound up together. Yaari linked his admiration for Stalin with his defense of Stalin's dictatorial regime. He saw that regime as warranted, because Russia was a backward and weak country surrounded by enemies, a country where socialism was being built. Given the country's appalling economic and cultural backwardness, there was no way to make progress without a dictatorship. Led by the inspiration of Yaari, who said that it was not the time for settling accounts with the Soviet people, who were heroically defending their country, the Sixth Kibbutz Artzi Conference affirmed the justice of "Stalin's proletarian dictatorship" in May 1942.[81]

With regard to Stalin's cult of personality, too, Yaari took a clear stance: "I have never seen a political movement that did not venerate its leaders. Every political movement has an emblematic figure who is worshiped by the masses."[82] When he bid the Soviet delegation farewell in 1942, he allowed himself to voice a secret wish he had left out of his letter—to meet with Stalin, "the great builder and warrior of our time, [...] the head of the Soviet state, [...] the leader of the revolution."[83]

---

80 Yaari at a meeting of the Kibbutz Artzi Executive Committee, Nov. 7, 1939, HHA, 5-10.2(5).
81 Resolution of the Sixth Kibbutz Artzi Convention, Apr. 10-17, 1942, Chizik, *Yaḥaso shel Ha-shomer Ha-ẓa'ir*, 139.
82 Yaari at a meeting of the Kibbutz Artzi Executive Committee, Nov. 7, 1939, HHA, 5-10.2(5).
83 Yaari, *Be-derekh arukah*, 258-259.

CHAPTER 9
A Gaping Abyss

Ruzka Korczak, a member of Hashomer Hatza'ir from the city of Plock, northwest of Warsaw, had been among the leaders of Hashomer Hatza'ir in Poland who streamed to Vilna at the outset of the war. When the ghetto was liquidated, she escaped to join the partisans, along with other Shomrim, including Abba Kovner and Vitka Kempner (later Kovner). In July 1944, she returned to liberated Vilna, and then, in accordance with the decision of the local secretariat of the movement, proceeded to Romania and thence to Palestine. She was the first Shomer to arrive from "over there," and what she told the movement institutions and leaders—speaking in Yiddish, because her Hebrew was weak—made a strong impression on them. Of particular note was her appearance at the Histadrut Convention on February 1, 1945, after which Ben-Gurion admitted his positive reaction to her remarks, even though she had spoken in a "foreign and grating language."[1] On a wintry day in December 1944, soon after her arrival in Palestine, as she sat alone in a room at Kibbutz Artzi's headquarters in Merḥavia, a man who until that moment had been only a symbol and a dream for her entered the room and introduced himself in Yiddish: "I'm Meir Yaari." He offered her a bashful and almost unwilling hand.

This is how Korczak described her first meeting with Yaari, in a note she sent to Anda and Meir 33 years later, thanking them for attending her daughter's wedding: "When you hugged and congratulated me, Meir, I recalled our first meeting in Merḥavia—in the movement offices. [...] The memory of that meeting, and many others, is stored in my heart. And the man I met, in whose presence I had the privilege to spend time

---

1 *Ha'aretz*, Feb. 2, 1945.

(even if not so much!) is greater than the symbol and far more human."² It is no wonder that Yaari's eyes filled with tears when he read the letter, in 1977. It further intensified the friendship and esteem he had felt for Korczak ever since their first meeting.³ On another occasion, in 1983, Korczak recalled that the first sentence she heard Yaari say was, "did you receive the telegram that Tabenkin and I sent, not to stage an uprising?"⁴ But the overall impression is that the feelings the two expressed in their 1977 exchange of letters indeed reflected their relationship, going back to the very beginning. Even in the 1940s, Yaari saw Ruzka as the most congenial and wonderful of all the partisans.⁵ He felt a special affection for her, and his relationship with her was much closer than that with the other comrades from "over there."

After that meeting with Korczak, Yaari received reports about Abba Kovner's ideas about the Jewish unity that had been forged during the Holocaust, a unity encompassing every Jew, no matter how he or she had survived the war, a unity that ignored political opinions and made no distinction between Right and Left within the Jewish people. He also heard rumors that Kovner, who was still in Europe, was trying to establish a "Brigade of the Survivors from Eastern Europe," which would cut across the old lines of organizational affiliation. Yaari, by contrast, whose position on the political balance of power in Zionism and the Yishuv had not been affected in the slightest by the Holocaust, continued to focus on maintaining the unity and distinctive character of Hashomer Hatza'ir. In what seems to be the first letter he sent to the Shomrim in Europe after the war, he emphasized that although Hashomer Hatza'ir did aspire to cooperation, solidarity, and unity among the constructive forces in Zionism and the labor movement, it would continue to follow its independent course. He warned them against those who opposed holding on to the movement's separate existence and favored an inclusive organization of all movements.⁶

---

2 Ruzka to Anda and Meir, Oct. 5, 1977, KMA, MYF, 4(3).
3 Yaari to Ruzka Korczak, Oct. 16, 1977, Ibid.
4 Porat, *Hanhagah be-milkud*, 442 and 565 n 11. The reference is to a telegram, which may never have been sent, from Yaari and Tabenkin to the members of their movements in Poland, *after* the Warsaw Ghetto uprising.
5 Yaari to Rivka [Gurfein], Mar. 6, 1947, HHA, 95-7.10(9).
6 Yaari to "Dear Comrades," July 2, 1945, HHA, 95-7.9(10).

He was even more explicit in the letters he sent to movement members serving in the Jewish Brigade who had met with Kovner and been impressed by him. Yes, Kovner was a "charming person, with a glorious partisan past, and strong powers of suggestion."[7] But when it came to his ideas, Yaari wrote from his heart, "fate has laughed at us and the devil has hatched us a Revisionist version of Hashomer Hatza'ir."[8] Relying on what Ruzka Korczak had told him—as he understood or interpreted her—he wrote about Kovner and his colleagues: "Despite the purity of their hearts and intentions [...] they have adopted ideas that are almost fascist."[9]

Weighed down by these concerns about development in the movement in Europe, and still not fully aware of the efforts being made in postwar Poland to unify the pioneer youth movements, Yaari traveled to London to attend the Zionist gathering in August 1945. The first Zionist forum after the war, it was intended to draw up a general balance sheet of the Zionist movement and its political prospects after the Holocaust. It was also the first time since the hasty adjournment of the 21st Congress in August 1939 that Zionist and Yishuv leaders from Palestine met those from Europe. Yaari felt strong emotions in anticipation of the arrival of the movement's delegate from Poland, Chaika Grossman, who had been one of the leaders of the uprising in the Bialystok ghetto. She arrived in Warsaw in May 1945 and joined the commune of the survivors of the pioneer movements. In the best pioneer tradition for coping with the housing shortage, she was the third person in the room of Zivia Lubetkin and Yitzhak (Antek) Zuckerman, leaders of the Dror movement and of the Warsaw Ghetto Uprising.[10] She was party to Zuckerman's initiative to merge Hashomer Hatza'ir and Dror, but Yaari was not yet aware of this when she arrived in London several days after him. As described by Yaari, theirs was an emotional meeting. He and Hazan hugged her in plain view and went all out to display their affection for her. She, too, was moved and somewhat bewildered.

When the three of them sat together in the hotel, Grossman opened up, and Yaari and Hazan were treated to a "terrifying picture."

---

7 Yaari to Yehuda [Tubin], July 24, 1945, HHA, 95-7.*bet*-2(5).
8 Ibid.
9 Ibid.
10 Barzel, *Ad kelot u-mineged*, 200.

By this, Yaari did not mean her stories about the Holocaust. Of everything Grossman recounted about the war itself in their long talks in London, Yaari forwarded to Palestine only her assessment that the Warsaw branch of the movement, led by Mordechai Anielewicz and Shmuel Breslaw, had tilted Leftwards, and her confidence that had Breslaw survived he would not have remained in the movement. Yaari was also strongly impressed by the information that Grossman conveyed about the Shomrim assembled in Vilna, who, despite their wartime cooperation with the Communist partisans, made a 180 degree turn after liberation and turned their backs on Socialism, were full of suppressed hatred for the Soviet Union, and favored the creation of a pan-Jewish movement that would even include the Revisionists. The "terrifying" (as he defined it) picture that emerged for him was that "Zuckerman in Warsaw managed to ensnare her and the other survivors of our movement with the same sweetness typical of some of the lads from the Kibbutz Me'uḥad."[11] He was terrified that Hashomer Hatza'ir might lose its Polish branch.

By the time Grossman reached Warsaw after the war, Kovner was already in Italy, but the impact of his ideas about the creation of a united Jewish organization remained strong in Warsaw. The tiny band of Shomrim who were in the city was soon joined by others who had returned from Central Asia—known as the "repatriates" or "Asiatics"—who were fiercely anti-Soviet. He inferred from Grossman's remarks that a majority of the Shomrim in Poland did not want to follow Kovner's path, but they also had reservations about Hashomer Hatza'ir's pro-Soviet orientation and preference for a binational state in Palestine. To counter Kovner's vision of wall-to-wall unity, Grossman and Zuckerman decided to establish a united leftwing organization, "Dror Hashomer," whose members would call for a merger between Hashomer Hatza'ir and the Kibbutz Me'uḥad in Palestine.

Yaari and Hazan sat with Grossman for an entire night, peppering her with questions about the proposed merger and pressing her to abandon the idea. They worked hard to persuade her this was not the

---

11 Letter from London, signed by Meir Yaari, Aug. 21, 1945, HHA, 95-7.9(10) ["the purloined letter"].

way to go. Their impression was that she was "a smart and courageous comrade, but naïve."[12] Yaari felt that the survivors were committing movement suicide and believed that this meeting in London had saved Hashomer Hatza'ir in Poland, and perhaps not only there. Before they parted, Grossman promised that she would convey the call to revive the movement to the Shomrim in Poland; but, she told them, emissaries from Palestine would be necessary to achieve this.[13]

This account of the meeting in London is based primarily on a letter written by Yaari, which has gone down in the movement's history as the "purloined letter."[14] In transit from London to Palestine, the letter was filched by some Mapai sympathizer who worked in the postal service, and, within a few days, thousands of copies were circulating in the DP camps in Europe. Its contents were printed in the Revisionist daily *Hamashkif* and in *Ha'aretz* (but not in *Davar*). Yaari wrote to the editors of *Ha'aretz* to protest: he had written a private letter, "full of melancholia," to an intimate friend, in which he had allowed himself to express heavy thoughts and harsh remarks about people and events. The damage to Chaika Grossman was more painful than the insult to himself.[15] He apologized to her for wounding her unintentionally—having in mind his description of her as "naïve."[16] And to one member of the movement he wrote: "In political life, there is a sphere of intimate expressions, which are like conversations between husband and wife," and those who distributed the letter "were stealing secrets from the bedroom."[17] The style of the "purloined letter" and the candid confessions in it were nothing new for members of Hashomer Hatza'ir, who were used to Yaari's manner of expressing himself. The difference was that this time his remarks had been exposed for all to see. His apology related less to the content and style of what he had written and more to their having become public property.

12 Ibid.
13 Yaari to Chaika [Grossman], June 11, 1946, HHA, *heh*-3. 60(1); Yaari to Kibbutz Merhavia, Aug. 14, 1945, KMA, MYF, 1(3)
14 See above, n. 11.
15 Yaari to M. Medzini of *Ha'aretz*, Jan. 22, 1946, HHA, 95-7.9(5).
16 Yaari to Chaika [Grossman], June 11, 1946, HHA, *heh*-3.60(1).
17 Yaari to Yehuda [Tubin], Jan. 15, 1946, HHA, 95-7.9(10).

Yaari summarized his position on the role of Hashomer Hatza'ir in postwar Europe with a two-part slogan: "We must be the compass for those who flee and the anchor for those who stay."[18] Sometimes he replaced "those who flee" with "those who leave" and also said explicitly that the slogan should be "departure" rather than "flight."[19] In those days, "flight" (Hebrew beriḥah) had a double sense: both the westward escape from Eastern Europe and the organized movement of groups of Jews out of Eastern Europe en route to Palestine. To avoid the word "fleeing," Hashomer Hatza'ir members sometimes used "a compass for the wanderers."[20] Even before the war was over, Yaari declared that the movement in the Diaspora had to be resurrected and sent instructions in that vein to the Shomrim in Europe.[21] In this he continued the line he had sketched before the news of the Jews' extermination reached him; namely, that after the war Hashomer Hatza'ir would strive to rebuild the ruins of the Diaspora.[22] In the August 1945 meeting with Chaika Grossman in London, he instructed her "to begin by reestablishing Hashomer Hatza'ir. That is our victims' last will and testament!"[23] He told the movement emissaries who left for Poland after the war to revive the movement in Europe with all its old content, symbols, and demands: "The movement in Poland must be reborn as an educational movement built from the foundations to the rafters. [...] Among the surviving remnant, our movement must take the lead as the dominant youth movement on the Jewish street."[24]

Right after the end of the war, Yaari's statements were general and had the nature of slogans. But when he was confronted by what he saw as concrete dangers to the independent existence of Hashomer Hatza'ir, such as the ideas floated by Mapai to establish the "United

---

18 Yaari, *Be-derekh arukah*, 288.
19 Barzel, *Ad kelot u-mineged*, 96–97.
20 *Sefer Ha-shomer Ha-ẓa'ir*, 1:15.
21 Yaari at the 25th Kibbutz Artzi Council, Apr. 10, 1945, HHA, 5-20.4(3); Yaari to "Dear Comrades," July 2, 1945, HHA, 95-7.9(10).
22 Yaari to Yudeks [Meir Talmi], Feb. 26, 1942, HHA, *heh*-3.36(*gimel*-2).
23 Joint meeting of Hashomer Hatza'ir and Po'alei Ẓiyyon, Dec. 26, 1945, HHA, 90.9(3).
24 Yaari to Arthur [Ben-Israel], Nov. 13, 1945, HHA, 95-7.9(8).

Pioneer" (a single organization encompassing all the pioneer youth movements), he made it very clear that essential contrasts must not be blurred; Hashomer Hatza'ir would cooperate with the other pioneer forces but must continue to function as an independent group.[25]

After Grossman returned to Poland from London, she made vigorous efforts to rebuild the movement. She proved so successful at this that Yaari felt a need to defend his own part in this feat. He was not willing for the movement's revival in Poland to be attributed exclusively to Grossman's influence and the visits there by Avraham Lipsker (Abramek). He too deserved some of the credit. The same applied to Abba Kovner's return to the strait and narrow (as he put it).[26] Looking back, Grossman justified Yaari's opposition to unification of the camp and stated that the concept of a united pioneer movement in postwar Europe failed to withstand the test of reality not because of Yaari's instructions, but because of the inclinations of the survivors themselves. "Those who had not been able to unite in the ghetto—how could they have coalesced afterwards, when all their desires were oriented towards aliyah?" she wondered.[27] She explained that her disagreement with Yaari in London in 1945 had to do with the extent of cooperation with the members of Kibbutz Me'uḥad, and not about a merger with that organization.

Yaari had a very high estimation of Grossman's abilities and sent her to the United States to spread the movement's message and raise funds. He was glad to make use of her talents but was afraid that she would become a professional politician. One has the sense that he began to see her, and some of her circle, as potential rivals to the current leadership. He wrote to tell her that when she returned from America she must come on aliyah, along with all the movement veterans in Poland, while ensuring the movement's future.[28] For reasons that seem to have been personal, Grossman did not make aliyah until two years later. Immediately after her arrival, in May 1948, she launched a political career that continued for many years, during which her relationship with Yaari saw ups but mostly downs.

---

25 Yaari to "Dear Comrades," July 2, 1945, HHA, 95-7.9(10).
26 Yaari to Yehuda [Tubin], Dec. 10, 1945, Ibid.
27 "Chaika Grossman vs. Anita Shapira," *Koteret Rashit,* Nov. 6, 1985.
28 Yaari to Chaika [Grossman], June 11, 1946, HHA, 95-7.10(1).

Yaari's relationship with Ruzka Korczak was very different, and, as we have seen, always warm. He never perceived her as a threat, and she followed the path he expected of the comrades who arrived after the war—finding her place on the kibbutz. In contrast to his enthusiastic support for Grossman's mission from Poland to the United States, he did not want Korczak to follow suit. He argued that although her presence would have provided American Jews with another experience, it would have made it more difficult for her to assimilate in Palestine. If she failed to settle down on a kibbutz, she would only have her past and her book, *Flames in the Ashes*, published in 1946, and her future would be shrouded in fog.[29]

His first encounter with Abba Kovner was on September 17, 1945. The two of them came to the meeting full of emotions and ideas based on what they had heard about each other in the preceding months. Yaari was aware of Kovner's influence over the survivors in Europe and was leery about his leadership potential. Even before the two men met face to face, Yaari told Korczak that he was willing to accept Kovner and his colleagues with open arms—"if they report for duty as comrades." But, he warned, "if they turn their backs on us from the start and try to establish their own organization and their own kibbutz, then, naturally, we will have no choice but to bury them."[30] The first conversation between Yaari and Kovner, on September 17, 1945 (which was Yom Kippur), went on for 11 hours. As soon as their meeting was over, Kovner wrote: "I listened carefully to what he had to say. He revealed himself as having the principles of a great leader and a preeminent Jew. However, Meir listened closely to what I had to say and learned from it (that is his strength!)"[31]

The first meeting between Yaari and Kovner and their entire relationship seems to have made a stronger impression on Kovner than it did on Yaari. This conclusion derives not only from the fact that what was written about their first postwar encounter was mainly from the younger man's perspective, but also and mainly from the reality

---

29 Yaari to Rivka [Gurfein], Mar. 6, 1947, HHA, 95-7.10(9).
30 Porat, *The Fall of a Sparrow*, 207–208.
31 Kovner to Pinhas Groner, Sept. 17, 1945, quoted by Porat, *The Fall of a Sparrow*, 221.

that Yaari played a more central and meaningful role in Kovner's life than the other way around.[32]

In December 1945, Kovner left for Europe to pursue the *Nakam* ("revenge") campaign against the Germans, but was betrayed and arrested, and spent some two month in British jails in Egypt and Palestine. In early 1946, while in a deep depression, he wrote his first long poem, in which he enumerated his differences with Yaari and recounted the miracle of their friendship that evolved after the meeting. Here is his description of Yaari: "Meir Yaari is a man of faith. One of the great believers. One of the few. He is a sort of distant and pure reincarnation of a great patriarch, like the Baal Shem Tov or Marx. [...] Meir believes. He is not naïve. His eyes are not blinded. They see clouds, and behind them they see light."[33] For Kovner, Yaari was a paternal figure, a master and a guide, and Kovner did not challenge his leadership even when their beliefs differed.[34] This was the secret of the special relationship between them, as far as Yaari was concerned. The Brigade of the Survivors from Eastern Europe, which he had feared, fell apart after only three months, in July 1945. Not only did Kovner make no effort to establish a separate organization, he did not aspire to achieve a leadership position or pose a threat to the veteran leaders. This made him "kosher" in Yaari's eye, even when they disagreed about almost every issue.

After his first conversation with Yaari, Kovner expected that Hashomer Hatza'ir would modify its path to suit the Jewish people's new situation, while maintaining its core identity and values.[35] Korczak, who was present for most of the conversation, came away with a different impression. Drawing on her almost yearlong acquaintance with Yaari, she concluded that he had not yet internalized the facts presented by Kovner and that his worldview would not be affected by a single conversation.[36] Looking back, Chaika Grossman found an

---

32 Porat, *The Fall of a Sparrow*; Barzel, *Ad kelot u-mineged*, and especially the chapter "The Confrontation between Abba Kovner and Meir Yaari," 85–103.
33 On Kovner's arrest and imprisonment and the writing of *Ad Lo Or,* see Porat, *Me'ever la-gashmi,* 244–246 (quotation is on 246). [This passage was edited out of the English translation.]
34 Porat, *The Fall of a Sparrow,* 265.
35 Kovner to Pinhas Groner, Sept. 17, 1945, quoted by Porat, *The Fall of a Sparrow,* 221.
36 Porat, "Meir Yaari and Abba Kovner," 343.

explanation for the ideological and emotional tension between Kovner and Yaari. For Kovner, the war had not ended with the fall of Hitler's bunker; "for Meir Yaari, by contrast, it never took place in its true essence and significance."[37] Kovner and Yaari typify the difference between those who experienced the war in Europe and those who were in Palestine at the time. For Kovner, the Holocaust was the ultimate trauma and totally remade his universe, including his ideology and organizational affiliation. For Yaari, by contrast, the world continued in its old course even after the Holocaust.

In February 1945, when the end of the war was on the horizon, Yaari addressed the Kibbutz Artzi Secretariat about the call by the German-born Yehuda Brieger (later Ben Ḥorin) to establish a band of "avengers" who would travel around the world and hunt down the murderers of the Jewish people. Yaari was much taken with the idea and thought that Brieger and his associates should constitute the core of the group. He opposed forgiving the Germans, but did not advocate blind vengeance against the German people. Instead, he supported attacks on senior Nazis and members of the S.S.—what was designated "Plan B." In the meantime, Kovner arrived in Palestine with his thoughts of total revenge and what was called "Plan A"—poisoning the drinking water of four large German cities.[38] Did Yaari know about this plan? Dina Porat, Kovner's biographer, believes that he did discuss Plan A with Yaari, but this cannot be corroborated from Yaari's papers and published materials about him. There may be an echo of the matter in a letter he wrote in 1947, in which he expressed his sense that Kovner's gang "was haunted by the feeling that their revenge had not been sufficient, and this issue is becoming an obsession that destroys every constructive fabric."[39] In any case, Yaari conveyed to Kovner and Brieger his consent to "Plan B" only, with the explicit conditions that only undoubted Nazis be targeted, that the assistance to the survivors not be impaired, and that the plan be implemented in coordination with Brieger.

---

37 Ibid., 355.
38 The discussion that follows is based mainly on Porat, *The Fall of a Sparrow*, 222–236.
39 Yaari to Rivka [Gurfein], Mar. 6, 1947, HHA, 95-7.10(9).

The twilight interlude—or perhaps the morning mist— between war and peace evoked Yaari's memories of his military service during the First World War and the chaotic period that followed. Those years were formative experiences for him; he returned to them over and over and drew lessons from them, including insights about the Holocaust survivors after the Second World War. In remarks to partisan fighters who had recently arrived in Palestine, in late 1945, he described himself as "an old soldier," a man who had fought in the trenches and knew that very few come out of the bunkers and trenches toughened and annealed, like the Bolsheviks and pioneers of the Third Aliyah. The majority "carry inside themselves the risk of turning peace into a continuation of war." These are people for whom "death was such a routine phenomenon that they have come to see all human beings as corpses."[40] He was afraid that the pogroms, riots, and barbarism would infect those who had so recently escaped the horrors of war and that, God forbid, they would find their outlet in fascist and terrorist methods. But he was also concerned by the possibility that they would fall prey to a feeling that they were sated with war and suffering and that now it was time to settle down in a quiet corner, where they could find some respite for their tired bodies. Certainly no one deserved time off as much as they did; nonetheless, they must harness themselves to the movement's struggle to save the entire nation, and not merely save themselves. What is more, he lectured the people from "over there" so as to inculcate the ideal of heroism he had fostered during the war as an educational message for the young people settled in Palestine. He emphasized the acute difference between the heroism of those who had fought and died "over there," whose hour, he insisted, had passed, and the valor of those who toiled and lived "here," which should predominate in the future. And, he summed up for the recently arrived partisans, "perhaps it is easier to die a heroic death once than to live a heroic life for the long stretch. [...] How to die a heroes' death—that we can learn from you; but how to live a heroic life—please let us teach you that lesson."[41]

---

40 Yaari, *Be-derekh arukah*, 142.
41 Ibid.

Is it ever permitted for a biographer to intrude an opinion? "To argue" with her subject? If such license is given only once, then this is the place where I shall invoke it. The passage just quoted is painful to read and hard to digest. It radiates emotional obtuseness and seeks to minimize the heroism of his audience, all of them returnees from the inferno, while preaching the virtue of obedience to the veteran leaders, i.e., to himself. These remarks were not a slip of the tongue or a flight of oratorical passion. Yaari repeated these main points on other occasions, and made sure to circulate the speech to the Diaspora—in Yiddish, so all would understand it—under the title "After the Years of Agony," inquiring "whether it has been used and distributed en masse."[42] He approved its inclusion, under the title "Not Road-Weary, but Trailblazers" (the original title in Hebrew was "We Shall Avenge Sevenfold") in the collection of his speeches and writings, *On a Long Road*, that was published about a year and a half later.[43]

Yaari also lectured the partisans that the tragic fate of the Jewish people had no precedent and was unparalleled; "nevertheless, we must not forget that it was not only our people that trod the Via Dolorosa in this war. Let us remember the heroic nation, which had its fill of great anguish and suffering throughout this war—the Russian people."[44] Following this line, he equated the Battle of Stalingrad with the Warsaw Ghetto uprising. These two indices of wartime heroism were linked for him, in what seems like an attempt to diminish the heroism of those of his own people and movement who resisted "over there" and to provide a solid foundation for his pro-Soviet orientation. He challenged the credibility of those who associated violent deeds, corruption, and antisemitism with Russia and even the Red Army. The comrades who came from Russia and slandered it, he said, were failing to perceive the forest and seeing only the occasional blighted trees.

---

42 Yaari to Yehuda [Tubin], Jan. 15, 1946, HHA, 95-7.9(10).
43 Yaari to Yehuda [Tubin], Dec. 10, 1945, HHA, 95-7.9(10); Meir Yaari, *Noch di martirer yor'n: An address to immigrant partisans at Evron 1945*, published by the Supreme Headquarters, Merḥavia [Hebrew]; "We Shall Avenge Sevenfold," *Kibbutz Artzi News*, January 1946; Yaari, *Be-derekh arukah*, 140–146.
44 Yaari, *Be-derekh arukah*, 145.

And then, as was his wont, he segued into a sweeping denunciation: "They were unable to explain the sources from which Stalingrad drew its heroism. Festering in their heart was a rejection of socialism and everything created in the divine image"—followed by scattershot, sweeping, and cutting accusations, which led, inter alia, to the conclusion that "these comrades must be reeducated."[45]

His speech to the partisans was marked by the same arrogance and stratification of prestige that he, as a member of the Third Aliyah, had protested in Berl Katznelson and the members of the Second Aliyah. When they build their first hut, he told the comrades so recently arrived from the Diaspora, they should see "before their eyes the beginnings of a new Mishmar Ha'emeq, a new Merhavia."[46] He was opposed to the establishment of a new Hashomer Hatza'ir kibbutz composed exclusively of ghetto fighters and partisans, on the model of Lohamei Hagetta'ot and Nezer Sereni, affiliated with Kibbutz Me'uhad. He directed them to go as cadres to reinforce the existing kibbutzim, from Dan in the north to Gevulot in the Negev.[47]

After the war, Yaari, the movement's paramount leader and almost 50 years old, came into contact with people who were much younger: Kovner was 27 in 1945, Grossman 26, and Korczak 24. They were separated by a full generation, like a father and his children. The children, who had gone through the agony of the Holocaust and gained experience as public leaders at a time of a supreme test, encountered a father who was still vigorous and saw them as potential rivals. The ideas and opinions they brought with them, and the inclinations of the Shomrim who had survived the war, posed an organizational and even existential threat to the movement. Clearly Yaari, after two decades as the unchallenged leader of Hashomer Hatza'ir, was wary of the prestige and authority that the youngsters from "over there" had acquired in the war years.

Yaari's encounter with movement leaders who reached Palestine after the war necessarily brings to mind the episode of his relationship with the Shomrim who flocked to Vilna at the start of the war. During the

---

45 Ibid., 141.
46 Ibid., 146.
47 Ibid.

intervening six years, the members trapped in Europe had demonstrated their ability to run things on their own and even lead large groups. But when it came to the source of authority and discipline, Yaari's outlook was unchanged. This rigidity was reinforced by the fear of the emotional load of resentment and disappointment that the "Europeans" had accumulated during the war years. Their "where were you?" resounded in the air. Yaari had heard about Kovner's complaint that the movement leadership in Palestine had not stayed in touch with the European members during the war. And whereas there were objective reason for this breakdown of communications while the fighting raged, Yaari found it more difficult to answer the charge that the leaders, including himself, had not come over to the regions of Eastern Europe that were gradually liberated from Nazi occupation, and all the more so after VE Day. The KA emissaries in Europe made it plain to him, in late 1945, that he and Hazan were making a mistake by not visiting Europe, when other leaders were making the effort to do so.[48] And how did Yaari respond? He scolded those emissaries for not responding appropriately to the locals' claims that the movement leadership was guilty of "criminal neglect" and was "utterly unqualified." He saw these accusations as casting aspersions on the leadership and demanded that the emissaries defend the honor of the comrades "who have been with the movement from the start to the present day, who fostered it and developed it"—meaning principally himself.[49]

Woe to anyone who dared criticize him, directly or indirectly. The comrade who wrote him in late 1945 about the emissaries' harsh disappointment with the leaders in Palestine and their abandonment of the movement in Europe was severely chastised. Yaari defined the letter as an uncomradely act and denounced its content as totally unfounded. And the comrade should know that this was not the opinion of Yaari and Hazan only, but of others as well.[50] It is no wonder that after such scathing attacks, which spilled over into the realm of the personal, members hesitated to criticize him and rarely did so.

---

48 Porat, *The Fall of a Sparrow*, 207–208.
49 Yaari to Yehuda [Tubin], Dec. 10, 1945, HHA, 95-7.9(10); Yaari to Yehuda in Warsaw and Shaike Weinberg, Jan. 1, 1946, HHA, 95-7.10(1).
50 Yaari to Yehuda [Tubin], Dec. 10, 1945, HHA, 95-7.9(10).

To those who advised him and Hazan to go to Europe, Yaari explained that such a trip would take at least two months and that he did not have that much time to spare, because in these difficult times he needed to be at the helm—in Palestine—and could not allow himself a European tour.[51] In the event, more than a year passed before he traveled to western Europe, and it was even longer before he visited the east, following the 22nd Zionist Congress in Basel in December 1946—nineteen months after VE Day. There was great excitement before his visit to the Fernwald DP Camp in the American Zone, to which representatives of Shomer communes near and far made their way, sporting the movement's uniform. On September 12, 1946, 1,200 Shomrim assembled at Fernwald, decked out in their uniforms, and marched in review, waving their banners. Yaari could not believe what he saw. After the parade, the comrades filed into a large auditorium to hear him speak. He addressed them in Hebrew and emphasized the movement's resurgence from the ashes of the ghetto.[52]

In his report on his trip to Europe, Yaari wrote that he had found Jews from the small towns of Poland and Galicia among the DPs, as well as close and more distant relatives. "When I saw them, homeless and helpless, I could scarcely control myself," he wrote.[53] But then he went on to report on what seems to have really disturbed him: the slogans in support of the Biltmore Plan that were painted on the walls.[54] His impression from his time in Germany is quoted here at length because of the information it conveys, the insights it includes, the spirit it exudes, the associations it reveals, and the concern for the future expressed in it.

> Our movement has risen again in Germany and already numbers thousands of members; communes have formed that recall the communes in Poland and Galicia of the good old days. When they reach

---

51 Ibid.
52 Letter dated Sept. 21, 1946, HHA, 90.117(3). The page is torn and the author's identity is unclear.
53 Yaari, *Be-derekh arukah*, 286.
54 Ibid.

Palestine we will have to give them back what they lost during the six years of the Nazi occupation; our young people in Palestine are superior to them in their education, their health, and their joie de vivre. On the other hand, they are endowed with one special quality, of unparalleled importance. They do not leave themselves many choices. They have not come to us of their own free will and they will not turn their back on us on a mere whim or caprice. [...] There is no more voluntarism in the Diaspora. Free will survives in the movement only in America or in Palestine: their members can book passage on a ship to go back to America, or buy a bus ticket home. The people in Bavaria have no such option. They have no free choice. [...] This is how they were rescued, assembled, and bonded together into a single ideological family, which makes aliyah on trackless paths and aboard rickety ships through Cyprus to Palestine. There is necessity here, but no servitude. [...] After they have experienced our educational climate for a year or two in the orphanages of the movement, the movement becomes their father and a mother. They do not just come to the clubhouse a few times a week for a lecture, but are together day and night.[55]

So Yaari understood that what drew the young people to the kibbutzim and the movement was not the ideology he emphasized and insisted upon, but their emotional bond to the social framework. He was also well aware that what had made it possible for them to rise up in revolt against the Germans was their education and character, strongly influenced by the movement—but not its ideology. Even before he saw with his own eyes that these people were not bound together by that, but by the solidarity forged by their shared experiences in the past, soldiers of the Jewish Brigade, the first Palestinians to encounter the survivors, had hinted as much to him. It was very important, they told him, that he write letters to Kovner, to Vitka, and to Shlomo Klass, expressing comradely, amicable, and serious feelings for them. The Shomrim in Europe "need social assistance first of all, and not an ideological debate."[56] Yaari knew

---

55 Ibid., 288–289.
56 Porat, *The Fall of a Sparrow*, 207–208.

that the survivors' link to the movement was social and emotional, but insisted on speaking about them as "an ideological family." He knew that the ideological common denominator was national—Jewish and Zionist—but he persisted in digging up associations from the Socialist world, as if he could not avoid mixing in the Marxist element. Still, it is evident that he himself felt the internal tension, almost a paradox, which his obstinacy had created. As he put it in October 1946: "One could say that we are Marxists nursed on Hassidic sources. The ideas, methods, and goals have changed, but the same devotion remains, the same passion has been preserved."[57]

Even though Yaari emphasized that Hashomer Hatza'ir derived its power from its ideological collectivism and its historical continuity, what actually kept the survivors in the movement and prevented a rift between them and the leadership was not ideological collectivism but the sense of social solidarity, the legacy of the youth movement, and the desire to continue living together in the future as well—on a kibbutz. The survivors may have disagreed with Yaari's line in all the ideological and political matters on the agenda at the time, but these disputes collapsed under the weight of the communal framework, which took them in, was a natural continuation of their education in the movement, and gave them a home and almost a family.

The first ideological disagreement between Yaari and the Shomrim who had been in Europe (or the depths of Soviet Asia) during the war involved the organizational framework. He focused on buttressing Hashomer Hatza'ir's separate identity and strictly preserving its unique character and unity. They moved between merger with Dror and Kibbutz Me'uḥad and Kovner's notion of the Brigade of the Survivors from Eastern Europe. The second issue was the attitude towards the Soviet Union. Whereas Yaari and the movement in Palestine worshiped it, the survivors' sympathy for the country where Socialism was being realized stood in inverse proportion to their awareness of what actually went on there. There was also a vast gulf between Yaari and the survivors about the goal of Zionism and the political future of Palestine.

---

57 Yaari, *Be-derekh arukah*, 283.

Until November 1947, Yaari adhered to the binational model, viewing the establishment of a state—which would be binational—as a long-term goal. The survivors wanted an independent and sovereign Jewish state, and soon. This became clear to him as early as the summer of 1945, during the Zionist gathering in London.[58] In September, Yaari heard Kovner tell the Kibbutz Artzi Executive Committee that "for the masses, the Jewish state is not a political category. [...] That state is the ship the people want to scramble aboard in order to be saved."[59] Yaari also knew that when the news reached Poland that the Hashomer Hatza'ir delegates in London had voted against "a Jewish state without delay," they had run into outright hostility. On the eve of the 22nd Zionist Congress Yaari was well aware that the survivors had rejected the idea of a binational state.

A fourth area where the survivors did not see eye to eye with him was the pace and scale of aliyah. The Europeans wanted immediate mass aliyah, while Yaari supported selective and gradual immigration. He stuck firmly to his position even after the Kielce pogrom of July 4, 1946, when local Poles slaughtered more than 40 Jews—an event that set off a tidal wave of Jews leaving Poland for the DP camps in Germany. Even reports from the Shomrim in Poland that the Jewish masses wanted out, and soon, rejecting the idea of a gradual and organized departure, did not budge him.

In early 1947 Yaari traveled to Poland, to honor the memory of the dead and visit the survivors, especially the members of the movement. His foremost goal was to organize the political party and strengthen its ties with the new Communist regime in that country, led—as he put it—by "the forces of liberation and democracy."[60] During this visit, Yaari found widespread support for Hashomer Hatza'ir among non-Jews as well. Anielewicz was a holy figure there, and Hashomer Hatza'ir was viewed as a movement of heroes. He sensed that all doors were open to the movement in Poland (and in Romania as well), and

---

58 Yaari to the members of the kibbutz, Aug. 14, [1945], KMA, MYF, 1(3).
59 Kovner, at the Kibbutz Artzi Executive Committee, Sept. 22, 1945, HHA, 5-10.5(6).
60 Yaari to Kibbutz Merḥavia [no date], KMA, MYF, 1(3).

that the regime related to Hashomer Hatza'ir as a Zionist movement that could be trusted. The government included former members of the movement; some of them even knew Hebrew. It was clear to everyone in Poland, Yaari believed, that Hashomer Hatza'ir was destined to serve as a bridge between Zionism and the forces of tomorrow. He himself felt a wave of sympathy all around him and sensed that the movement's hour had arrived.[61]

Yaari cited two reasons for the esteem in which the movement was held by the political leaders in Poland: the role of its members in the ghetto uprisings and its position as a bridge between the Jewish people's nationalist and socialist war of liberation and the liberation forces in Poland and the other countries under Soviet control. His conclusion was that the survivors should remain in Poland and that Hashomer Hatza'ir would play a key role there.[62]

And here we have an explanation, even if only partial, for his attitude towards the Beriḥah enterprise, the rehabilitation of Jewish life in Poland, and the importance of the "anchor for those who stay behind." We can make the point sharper: his opposition to a rapid Jewish exodus from postwar Europe crystallized before the immensity of the tragedy was known; but it was reinforced by the situation he discovered in Poland a year and a half after the end of the war. The drastic change in the Jews' situation had a complex impact on his thoughts. Yaari did not change his mind about the appropriate pace and composition of aliyah, but the new situation in Eastern Europe, where a Socialist regime evinced a positive attitude towards his movement, bolstered his preference for a gradual exodus and the rehabilitation of Jewish life there in the meantime. Even under the best conditions, he expected that the process of bringing the survivors to Palestine would go on for many years; in the meantime, the main concern should be directing the Jews into productive occupations and forging solidarity and cooperation with the local and (as it was called then) democratic regime.[63]

---

61 Yaari at a meeting of the Central Committee of the Hashomer Hatza'ir Party, Jan. 29, 1947, HHA, 90.117(3).
62 Yaari, *Be-derekh arukah*, 296–297.
63 Ibid., 297.

Yaari with members of Hasomer Hatza'ir youth movement at the Fernwald DP Camp in the American Zone of Germany, September 12, 1946. 1,200 Shomrim assembled at Fernwald, decked out in their uniforms, and marched in review, waving their banners.
Courtesy of Hashomer Hatza'ir Archive, Givat Haviva.

CHAPTER 10

Against the Current

In analyzing the history of Hashomer Hatza'ir we must not omit the junctions and intersections at which the movement chose the wrong path and took inappropriate actions. And Yaari played a major role in shaping the movement's decisions and actions—both those that history has smiled upon and those that seem to have been mistaken, not only in retrospect but even in light of the information at his disposal at the time. In earlier chapters we noted or hinted at a number of instances in which Yaari swam against the tide—the tide of history, the preferences of his flock, and the path taken by other groups within Zionism and the Labor movement. Two prime examples are the attitude towards the Soviet Union and support for the "forces of tomorrow," and the position on the political future of Palestine, marked by opposition to partition, adherence to the binational idea, and the long and stubborn fight against the Biltmore Program.[1] Another example is his position on the pace and composition of aliyah from Europe after the Second World War. All these seem to fall into the category of positions whose errors should have been obvious at the time.

In those years, 1945 to 1947, Yaari was aware that his stand ran counter to the "spirit of the age" and was not accepted by the Zionist movement or even his own movement. From a broad and critical perspective, not only were his positions on the Jews' future in Europe and the appropriate political solution for Palestine swimming against the tide, they were riddled with internal contradictions and did not

---

[1] The title of this chapter is borrowed from that of a pamphlet published by Kibbutz Artzi in 1942 to defend itself against the attacks on its rejection of the Biltmore Program.

propose a valid plan or a realistic solution to problems of which he was fully aware.

Of course, we should consider the possibility that Yaari adhered to his antediluvian ideas because he did not fully intuit the new situation that had emerged or failed to understand its full implications. But it could also be that he understood the new circumstances and their ramifications all too well and wanted to avert their negative impact on Hashomer Hatza'ir's future.

On the first day of 1946, he declared: "As long as the slogan of the *Beriḥah* enjoys untrammeled domination, the Jewish masses will be prey to reaction and false messianism. They will be taught to believe that all the nations are hangmen and every country a gallows." [2] The association with the line in Bialik's poem "On the Slaughter," written after the Kishinev pogrom in 1903, is inescapable: "The whole world is a gallows for me."[3] Did Yaari hear it too? And what about this 1942 line by Nathan Alterman: "When our children cry in the shadow of the gallows"?[4] Was Yaari's metaphor simply a matter of rhetoric, or were the allusions deliberate? If so, to what purpose? Both Bialik and Alterman had written against the background of extreme manifestations of antisemitism. Did Yaari believe that the bloody era in the history of the Jewish people was over, at least under the Communist regimes in Eastern Europe? The continuation of his speech is of no help in answering this. He was afraid of a precedent: if the Jews fled Poland, the Jews of Slovakia would be the next to run away from antisemitism, and after them the Jews of Romania and Hungary, and "with our own hands we will turn Europe into a barren wasteland for Jews."[5]

But why should Yaari think it wrong to leave the countries of the Diaspora a barren wasteland without Jews? Moreover, the official position of Hashomer Hatza'ir in those years was somewhat at variance

---

2 Yaari, during the discussions about the establishment of the Hashomer Hatza'ir party, 1946, HHA, 95-7.28(8).
3 https://www.theparisreview.org/blog/2014/07/31/on-the-slaughter.
4 Nathan Alterman, "Among All Peoples," in Michael Walzer, Menachem Lorberbaum, Noam J. Zohar (eds.), *The Jewish Political Tradition*, vol. II: New Haven and London: Yale University Press, 2003, 80–82.
5 See above, n. 2.

with his. In October 1945, the Kibbutz Artzi Council decided that "the Jews who survived the Nazi murder in Europe should be told: you have no viable alternative to aliyah. [...] We will not be silent and we will not rest until the last of the survivors of the Jews of Europe, who are seeking to join us, set foot in the homeland."[6]

We have seen that he did not change his mind even after the pogrom in Kielce (July 1946). On the contrary, in October 1946, in the run-up to the 22nd Zionist Congress, after his visit to Western Europe and to Bratislava, he held to a different line than the Zionist policy of the time. The national watchword then was the demand that 100,000 DPs be admitted to Palestine without delay. The plans for clandestine immigration were motivated in part by the fear that the rapidly descending Iron Curtain would seal off the Jews' exit path from Eastern Europe. In internal discussions and secret contacts, a new Zionist consensus took shape, motivated in part by the need to solve the problem of the DPs: accepting partition of Palestine so as to permit the establishment of a Jewish state without delay. And Yaari? Given the slow pace of the Zionist solution, he preferred for the Jews to remain in Eastern Europe rather than escape to the West.

> ... what will happen to the Jews in the meantime? What a satanic joke it is that Munich—Hitler's capital—is becoming a sort of Jerusalem of Bavaria. The uprooting continues and the disappointment leaves its mark. Jews are already looking for visas to America and hunting for places of refuge. They are even beginning to disperse in Bavaria itself. There have already been mixed marriages between refugees and German women and we can see signs of a degenerative acclimation. Was it worth it to uproot Jews by the hundreds of thousands from the eastern democracies, for this?[7]

His words are a mirror image of official Zionist policy at the time, which was a race against time, haunted by a sense of "now or never."

---

6 Political manifesto issued by the 26th Kibbutz Artzi Council, Oct. 19-22, 1945, HHA, 5-20.34(1).

7 Yaari, *Be-derekh arukah*, 286-287 [October 1946].

On the other hand, Yaari, the champion of "when the time is ripe," was not prepared or able to deal with the imperative of rapid and immediate decisions. In fact, the title of the collection of his articles, letters, and speeches, published in 1947 when he turned 50, was *On a Long Road*.

Yaari was optimistic about the policy of the governments in Eastern Europe and made light of the dangers of the "Iron Curtain." He expected that the Soviet Union would soon recover from the wounds inflicted by the war and that the regimes in its client states would stabilize. There was no reason to assume that an iron curtain would really descend and that those countries' governments would change their favorable view of aliyah. He believed that cultivating the Jews' sense of solidarity with the new democratic regimes was the best way to ensure these governments' sympathetic view of aliyah and of the Jewish national home in Palestine.[8]

When Yaari visited Poland in early 1947, he came away with the impression that the situation there was not as bad as people were trying to portray it. It was not true that most of the Polish people were waiting for the moment they could cast off the democratic regime and get rid of the Jews. Polish democracy had a promising future. The Polish government, which viewed the war against antisemitism as a test of its strength, would stamp out the pogromists sooner or later and the Jews would once again be able to live in security. So even then—a few months after the pogrom in Kielce—he wanted to see an end to the Jewish exodus from Poland.[9] Before the Jews come to Palestine, he wrote, we must "make them partners in the war of social liberation of the nations among which they are living."[10]

In those months, Yaari scrutinized the problems of the Jewish people through the lens of Hashomer Hatza'ir and outlined the appropriate course of action for Zionism in the light of his movement's own needs and possibilities. Before the war, his optimism was nursed by the movement's numbers and strength in the Diaspora. After the war, he relied on its resurgence there as a reservoir for the future

---

8 Ibid., 287.
9 Ibid., 294.
10 Ibid., 287.

development of KA. He was troubled by the demographic situation of KA: the aging of its members made an infusion of new blood a matter of survival. Taking in 3,000 young people was one way for it to grow.[11] Looking out both for the young people and for the movement, Yaari called on the kibbutzim to take the lead in absorbing the young survivors and opposed sending them to transit camps. It was not only that the kibbutzim had a proven educational record and were performing real miracles with the children they were bringing from the Diaspora, but also that the kibbutzim could absorb young people more cheaply than the camps could.[12]

The numbers both excited and worried him. Yaari expected that in addition to 3,000 children and teenagers, some 7,000 Shomrim from the Diaspora would join the KA settlements—almost doubling their population at the time. The numbers were important, too, because he was thinking not only of the kibbutz movement and the social vanguard, but also of the political party. And because this numerical increase meant giving up the principle of selection, ideological collectivism would have to be reinforced.[13]

Seeking to expand the movement, Yaari looked for new human resources to replace those destroyed in the war. He saw France as a potential source of growth; the United States, too, was a very important reservoir in the post-Holocaust world. Hoping that many young people would join the pioneer movement after their discharge from military service, he dispatched emissaries there.[14]

But if Yaari pinned great hopes on American Jewry, he had a sour attitude towards the United States.[15] He saw the country as

---

[11] Yaari at the meeting of the Kibbutz Artzi Executive Committee, Mar. 15, 1945, HHA, 5-20.4(3).
[12] Yaari at the meeting of the Histadrut Executive Committee, Nov. 12, 1947, LA.
[13] Yaari at the meeting of the Kibbutz Artzi Executive Committee, Mar. 15, 1945, HHA, 5-20.4(3); Yaari, *Be-derekh arukah*, 288–289 [October 1946].
[14] Yaari at the meeting of the Histadrut Executive Committee, June 20, 1945; Yaari, *Be-derekh arukah*, 279 [October 1946]; Yaari to members of the Kibbutz Artzi Executive Committee, Aug. 10, 1946, HHA, *heb*-3.60(1).
[15] Yaari at the Central Committee of the Hashomer Hatza'ir party, June 6, 1946, HHA, 90.117(1).

warmongering and provoking a third World War—the antithesis of the Soviet Union, which was "the bastion of peace and Socialism and even of democracy, in the true sense of the word—rule by the people."[16] In America, freedom and democracy meant the freedom to practice social discrimination against Jews and segregation against Negroes, and to engage in wild incitement against the Soviet Union. What were Yaari's sources of information about the United States? On what basis did he arrive at his attitude towards the country? His command of English at the time was not good enough for him to read texts in the original and follow events there on his own. We can assume that he read books in translation—perhaps Upton Sinclair and John Steinbeck (*100%* was published in Hebrew in 1932; *The Grapes of Wrath*, in 1941)—that painted a bleak picture of poverty and the injustices of Capitalism in the United States.

While he was searching the Diaspora for new recruits for the kibbutzim, Yaari was also aware of the sagging commitment to kibbutz life among members of the youth movement in Palestine. He experienced a bitter disappointment when the young author Moshe Shamir (b. 1921) left Kibbutz Mishmar Ha'emeq. Shamir, who had been a youth movement member and counselor in Tel Aviv, announced his departure to Yaari in a personal letter: "Meir, I am fully aware of the magnitude of the injustice I have committed by this action," he confessed, and left the door open for a possible return to the kibbutz someday.[17] Yaari replied without delay. Shamir's departure from the kibbutz had been a blow to him, he wrote. He rebuked the young comrade and presented a clear scale of values based on what he had picked up from two of his teachers: the Polish poet Adam Mickiewicz, from whom he had learned that it is more difficult to live honestly through one day than to write a book; and Karl Marx, who taught him the difference between those who interpret the world and those who change it. Yaari, as an old pioneer, was not capable of showing understanding regarding Shamir's

---

16 Yaari to Yonah [Yannai, the emissary of Hashomer Hatza'ir to the United States], July 18, 1946, HHA, 95-7.9(7).

17 Moshe [Shamir] to Yaari, July 2, 1947, HHA, 95-7.11(1). On his copy of the letter, Yaari underscored the words "fully aware of the magnitude of the injustice."

departure and the motives behind it: "When we were young we burned all our boats and bridges that might suggest retreat. We placed the path of labor, the kibbutz, and the movement above our parents, above personal affairs."[18] Whereas Shamir was being seduced by easy successes and going after his weakness. In the wake of his departure, Yaari informed Shamir, the movement publishing house, Sifriyat Po'alim, would not release his book about kibbutz life (the novel *He Walked through the Fields* was published the following year, after the great success of the play on which it was based).[19]

Yaari's passion for kibbutz life did not diminish even after Hashomer Hatza'ir reconstituted itself as a political party in early 1946. Kibbutz Artzi was assigned a cardinal role in the party and was meant to set its tone and provide for the people to fill its major positions.[20] By the late 1930s it had been clear that Hashomer Hatza'ir could not be a substantial political force in the Yishuv unless it formed a partnership with the urban working class. The results of the elections to Yishuv institutions in the thirties and early forties demonstrated that such an alliance did amplify KA's political power and could help it to safeguard its own interests. But Yaari repeatedly rejected the idea of transforming the movement into a political party. In the mid-1930s, several town dwellers had contacted KA to propose the establishment of an urban political group—even if not an official party—linked to it; the Socialist League was established in June 1936, a year after KA responded in the affirmative.[21] But Yaari was loath to cooperate with kibbutz dropouts and preferred to work exclusively with members of the urban proletariat who had never belonged to a kibbutz.[22] One reason for Hashomer Hatza'ir's longstanding aversion to the establishment of the party was the potential damage to KA, mainly moral, of offering a warm home to those who had left the kibbutz—denounced by the regnant ideology as traitors unworthy of sharing a political tent with the pioneers who

---

18 Yaari to Moshe Shamir, July 8, 1947, ibid.
19 Ibid.
20 Meeting of the Kibbutz Artzi Executive Committee, Apr. 9, 1947, HHA, 5-10.5(12).
21 Zait, *Ḥaluẓim*, 31–32; Margalit, *Ha-shomer Ha-ẓa'ir*, 286.
22 "A Reply to the Manifesto," *Hashomer Hatza'ir*, May 15, 1938, p. 10.

were realizing the dream. But the decision to establish a party became inevitable after the dimensions of the Holocaust and the decimation of the youth movement in Europe became apparent. Thus, in 1946, when it was clear that there was no longer a significant movement abroad that could provide a large number of recruits and develop into a significant electoral force in the Zionist movement, and that KA needed to look for allies elsewhere, Hashomer Hatza'ir became a political party as well.

In 1943, the daily *Mishmar* had been launched as a step towards the establishment of this party. Yaari found it difficult to adjust to the requirements of daily publication, with its professional demands and tight deadlines. He frequently complained that its reporters and editors did as they pleased with his words. Once, after presenting one of many examples of how he thought his statements were being distorted, he asked: "Am I really speaking such nonsense?" [23] Time and again he asked the editors not to publish his remarks without verifying them with him. The response he received from his old friend and fellow member of Merḥavia—Elazar Pra'i (Peri), is no less instructive than the complaint. The problem of publishing Yaari's remarks in *Mishmar* was not new and had already left the editorial board in total despair, wrote Pra'i. Yaari had disqualified every correspondent assigned to cover him, to the point that the journalists and editors were unwilling to report his statements, because they could not be sure they would manage to satisfy him. In the past, they had tried to get him to submit a summary of his remarks before he spoke, but he had declined to do so. The reason for this refusal (and here the biographer intrudes on Pra'i) is that he was not in the habit of speaking from a written text or outline. At most, he scribbled down his main points and developed them from the podium on the fly. Pra'i continued: Yaari's demand that he be allowed to edit his remarks *post factum* was unfeasible. If his speech ran on until ten or eleven at night, and then he sat down to edit the transcript, nothing would appear in the newspaper the following day. There had already been cases when he begged off touching up his statements at such a late

---

23 Yaari to the editors of *Mishmar*, July 1, 1947, HHA, 95-7.11(1).

hour, out of fatigue or for some other reason.[24] Given Yaari's oratorical style and the difficulty of understanding his statements on first hearing and transcribing them, as well as our knowledge of the massive editing he performed on his lectures and speeches in various forums before they were recorded in the official minutes, we can only sympathize with the reporters who tried to do this while meeting the deadlines of a morning newspaper.

Yaari cultivated trappings of leadership that bordered on a cult of personality. Many kibbutzim were in the habit of sending him presents. Not only did he make no attempt to put an end to this adulation, he even encouraged it: "Every year, around Tu Bishvat, your crate [of oranges] shows up in my room at the Secretariat. It is not the only crate," after which he launched into the praises of the fruit from Ein Shemer: "I have never in my life tasted such fruit as this. The fragrances, the rind, and the pulp—everything joins together in a delight that almost leaves the physical behind and transcends mere culinary pleasure." He added his hope that in the future, too, "you will not forget me and I will continue to receive crates and you—blessings."[25] As the years passed, Yaari's birthdays were turned into movement celebrations. In 1947, when he turned 50, Sifriyat Po'alim published *Be-Derekh Arukah* (*On a Long Road*) in a deluxe cloth-covered edition on fancy paper, the front cover decorated with a red border, with the title and author's name printed on the spine in gold letters against a red background.

For Yaari and Hashomer Hatza'ir, the Yishuv's fight against the British from 1945 to 1947 posed dilemmas about the methods appropriate for such a struggle. Clandestine immigration was renewed about three months after VE Day. Yaari supported it throughout those years because he saw it as a refusal to accept the White Paper rather than a tool or launching pad for the founding of an independent state.[26] As the Zionist struggle increasingly turned to other methods, Yaari reiterated his positive attitude towards clandestine immigration

---

24 Pra'i to Yaari, July 10, 1947, ibid.
25 Yaari to Kibbutz Ein Shemer, Feb. 5, 1947, ibid.
26 Yaari to Arthur [Ben-Israel], Nov. 13, 1945, HHA, 95-7.9(8).

and the need to redouble the effort.[27] He did not advocate limiting the campaign to passive resistance; the methods of Mahatma Gandhi, which were suited to India with its 400 million people, were not appropriate to the small Yishuv under the British Mandate. He favored active resistance, but only with regard to the defense of settlements, aliyah, and stockpiling arms. The day after the Palmach raid on the Atlit detention camp to free the clandestine immigrants held there (October 9/10, 1945), Yaari explained that he would not have ordered it, but supported it after the fact.[28] The establishment of the United Resistance Movement *(Tenu'at ha-Meri ha-Ivri)* in the fall of 1945, in which the Haganah, Etzel, and Lehi were partners, posed new dilemmas for him. Yaari vehemently rejected cooperation between the Haganah and the two dissident organizations. He was furious that they were not called on to disband and were invited to coordinate their actions with the Haganah. Yaari compared the Etzel's recourse to terrorism with the methods employed by the Arab gangs.[29] His revulsion at the cooperation with the Revisionists was so great that he equated it with violation of religious precepts: just as an Orthodox Jew was simply incapable of eating on Yom Kippur, so large segments of the working class could not "swallow" such a partner.

Addressing Parliament on November 13, 1945, the British Foreign Secretary, Ernest Bevin, announced a policy that severed the link between Palestine and the fate of the Jewish people, and especially that of the Holocaust survivors in Europe. Palestine alone could not solve the distress of the Jews of Europe, he asserted. Referring to Britain's willingness to permit some Jewish immigration to Palestine, he made it clear that a distinction must be drawn between the humanitarian aspect of the Jews' distress and the political aspect of the Zionists' demands. He went on to tie the future of Palestine and of the Jews living there with the prevailing mood in the Arab and Muslim world, including an explicit mention

---

27 Yaari at the meeting of the Histadrut Executive Committee, Nov. 14-16, 1945, LA.
28 Yaari at the meeting of the Kibbutz Artzi Executive Committee, Oct. 11, 1945, HHA, 5-10.5(8).
29 Yaari at the meeting of the Histadrut Executive Committee, Nov. 14-16, 1945, LA.

of the 90 million Muslims of India.³⁰ The Yishuv's angry response to this speech spilled over into violence. Six persons were killed and dozens injured in riots that erupted in Tel Aviv. These developments troubled Yaari, who could not stomach some of the methods employed by the United Resistance Movement. Terrorism would not win over world public opinion, which could not be mobilized with filthy weapons and partnership with the Revisionists. The focus should be on diplomatic efforts that highlighted the justice of the persecuted Jewish people's case, and all other operations should be toned down.³¹

Several days after the violent demonstrations in Tel Aviv, one of the first manifestations of nonviolent public protest about the draconian restrictions on Jewish immigration took place in the Hefer Valley. It came after Palmach squads blew up police stations in Givat Olga and Sidni Ali—an operation that fell within Yaari's rules, because the targets were involved in thwarting clandestine immigration. After the attacks, large British forces surrounded Kibbutz Givat Chaim, in pursuit of the assailants. Hundreds of people who lived nearby—kibbutz members and residents of Hadera and Pardes Hanna—made their way there, unarmed, to surround the soldiers. The troops opened fire, killing eight people. This protest was led by a member of Kibbutz Ein Shemer. Yaari was proud that members of Hashomer Hatza'ir had been at the forefront of the Givat Chaim protest and had participated in the raids in Givat Olga and Sidni Ali. He made it clear that Kibbutz Artzi was a full partner in the campaign for aliyah and settlement.³²

As the United Resistance Movement continued its operations, Hashomer Hatza'ir members continued to be involved, despite the movement's unhappiness with some of the methods employed. For example, on February 22, 1946, the Palmach attacked British targets in Sarona (today the Kirya in Tel Aviv), losing four men. Members of Hashomer Hatza'ir took part in the operation, but *Mishmar*

---

30 Hansard, *Parliamentary Debates*, 415 H.C. DEB. 5 s., 1927-1931.
31 Yaari at the meeting of the Histadrut Executive Committee, Nov. 14-16, 1945, LA.
32 Yaari at a joint meeting with Po'alei Ziyyon Left, Dec. 26, 1945, HHA, 90.9(3).

denounced it in an editorial. The movement's message to its members was complex: criticism of some operations, while encouraging the comrades who took part in them and demanding obedience to the decisions of the national institutions and the Haganah command. Yaari was anxious for the souls of the young people, but also feared the result of forcing them to choose between moral principles and their orders. This is exemplified in a speech he delivered at a meeting of the Histadrut Executive Committee after the riots in Tel Aviv in November 1945. He expressed the dilemma he faced as leader of Hashomer Hatza'ir in light of the cooperation with the Revisionists and the methods being employed: "It is well known that we too had a hand in everything that was done. Nor are we usually in favor of sitting on our hands and doing nothing. But if we are to speak in terms of politics, in terms of the Histadrut, in terms of the Yishuv, emotionally, educationally—this is not the way. This is the road to suicide and will lead to our annihilation."[33]

He sketched out the line that Hashomer Hatza'ir followed consistently and faithfully: political opposition to the goal and to some of the means employed to reach it, accompanied nonetheless by discipline and a share in the execution. As in previous cases, and later after independence, Hashomer Hatza'ir was more active and loyal on the ground than might be inferred from Yaari's statements. In his speeches and articles he tended to emphasize his uncertainties, the arguments pro and con, to stretch points in order to combat his opponents, and was frequently more ambiguous than his own bottom line. In the same November 1945 speech, after expressing his strong displeasure with the new model of action, he added: "I am afraid of the steep and narrow path that remains to us, and on this path, too, we will have to walk together. We certainly know that we are all in the same boat!"[34]

And because Yaari was anxious about the impact that verbal and not only practical extremism was liable to have on the soul of the younger

---

33 Yaari at the meeting of the Histadrut Executive Committee, Nov. 14-16, 1945, LA.
34 Ibid.

generation, he warned against unbridled language. Young people were liable to take radical statements seriously and jump to the other camp, that is, to join Etzel and Lehi.[35] And they were indeed eager for battle. Yaari identified and stated the problem with clarity, but does not seem to have been sufficiently aware of the conflict in which members of the movement found themselves, which he himself made worse: the tension between disagreement with the nature of the campaign (or, at least, reservations about it), and, in effect, its goal as well, on one side, and the imperative of obedience to the decisions of the elected institutions and the orders of the executive arm, on the other.

In the political arena, Hashomer Hatza'ir was often groping in the dark. It was not part of the ruling coalition in the Zionist Organization and had no representatives on the Jewish Agency Executive. In anticipation of the arrival of the Anglo-American Committee of Inquiry, in late 1945, Yaari announced that he would not express an opinion on the matter before he heard what Ben-Gurion and Shertok had to say, but they did not include him in the preparations for the committee's visit.[36] Moreover, the Zionist Executive forbade separate testimony by the various Zionist factions, so Hashomer Hatza'ir had to make do with submitting a memorandum, entitled "The Case for a Bi-National Palestine."[37] Historians generally believe that this document affected the Committee's conclusions, whose core was a vague recommendation that Palestine be "neither Arab nor Jewish" and that progress towards binational independence be a protracted process associated, among other things, with an improvement in the Arabs' social and economic situation.

That Yaari and Hashomer Hatza'ir were cut off from the decision-making centers was especially conspicuous at a conference in Paris, held in August 1946, to discuss the strategic objectives of Zionist policy and the tactics for achieving them, and the events that had both preceded and followed it. After a dialogue with Ben-Gurion and unproductive correspondence with the Agency Executive about the nature of his participation in the conference, Yaari did not attend. Even the letter

---

35 Ibid.
36 Ibid.
37 *The Case for a Bi-National Palestine.*

in which he stated his position on the appropriate political solution and methods to be employed in the struggle was filed away and not brought up for discussion by the Executive. He was astounded to hear from some of those present that Ben-Gurion had presented a distorted version of his (Yaari's) position, based on an earlier conversation between the two.[38] Yaari had no real information about the deliberations of the Paris conference and about the dramatic change of direction decided on there. At the tactical level, the conference decided to modify the character of the campaign against the British, suspending the across-the-board and continual military operations against British targets and conducting only operations whose time and place were determined mainly by the needs of clandestine immigration and settlement. It was also resolved to switch the focus of the Zionist efforts to the political and diplomatic arena. At the strategic level, the Zionist goal was redefined: no longer the Biltmore Program that envisioned all of Palestine as a Jewish commonwealth, but rather acceptance of the establishment of "a viable Jewish state in an adequate area of Palestine."[39]

Yaari understood that his blackest predictions were coming true and that the Biltmore Program had indeed led to partition, as he had always maintained. At the same time, in the summer of 1946, Yaari's expectation that external forces, meaning the Great Powers, would devise a plan to his liking began to dissipate. Weizmann and the moderate elements in the Zionist Organization had come around to support partition, leaving Hashomer Hatza'ir isolated in its opposition and with only one potential partner: Aḥdut Ha'avodah. The two parties, Aḥdut Ha'avodah–Po'alei Ziyyon Left and Hashomer Hatza'ir, along with their respective kibbutz movements, Kibbutz Me'uḥad and Kibbutz Artzi, may have been on the same side of the fence in rejecting partition, but the former was holding out for a Jewish state in all of Palestine, while the latter aspired to a binational solution.

With this array of positions in the Zionist camp, the 22nd Congress convened in Basel in December 1946. It was the first

---

38 Yaari to Ben-Gurion, Zurich, Aug. 19, 1946, HHA, 90.19(1a).
39 Resolutions of the Jewish Agency Executive, [Paris], Aug. 5, 1946, CZA, S25/7161.

Congress in which Hashomer Hatza'ir appeared as an independent faction and had real weight. Yaari reported joyfully to his comrades in Palestine—following a warning at the start to "be careful about publication!"—that "we are considered to be *the* Opposition. [...] We are not one of the largest parties at the Congress, but we are among the most prominent."[40] The Hashomer Hatza'ir faction had 25 out of the 585 delegates. The Congress agenda included various topics, and the lines between supporters or opponents of a certain position on one issue did not necessarily hold for another. Hashomer Hatza'ir disagreed with both Weizmann and Ben-Gurion about the goal of Zionism. Regarding Weizmann's continuation as president of the Zionist Organization, Hashomer Hatza'ir, which had long been partial to Weizmann and held a position similar to his on the methods to be employed in the struggle, found itself torn. As things then stood, support for Weizmann meant support of partition. A third issue was whether Zionist representatives should take part in the proposed London talks. Unofficial talks between representatives of the Jewish Agency and the British government had been held that autumn and proved fruitless. Now the latter announced its intention to renew talks in London, with the participation of British, Arab, and Jewish representatives, in January 1947. Weizmann believed that the Agency should take part. But Ben-Gurion was opposed and treated the matter as a vote of confidence in his leadership. Should the Congress decide to go to London, he would resign as Agency chairman.

In the political dynamic that emerged, the key vote was not about the Zionist goal or Weizmann's reelection, but about participation in the London talks. The vote on that issue also tilted the balance with regard to Weizmann. A motion to boycott the London talks "in the current circumstances" passed by 171 to 154. The 25 delegates from Hashomer Hatza'ir abstained. Another 235 delegates did not take part in the vote at all. After the Congress, it was asserted that Hashomer Hatza'ir's abstention had enabled the victory of the anti-Weizmann coalition, which was led by Ben-Gurion and Abba

---

40 Yaari to "dear comrades," Dec. 14, 1946, HHA, 90.21(4).

Hillel Silver.⁴¹ Historians have cautiously tended to blame Hashomer Hatza'ir for Weizmann's failure to carry the day.⁴² Hazan's biographer, Zeev Tzahor, saw it this way: "Most ironically, it was the Hashomer Hatza'ir movement that brought about Weizmann's ouster at the 22nd Zionist Congress. [...] The Hashomer Hatza'ir movement tipped the balance of history, which henceforth designated Ben-Gurion as the man chosen to lead it in the direction that Hashomer Hatza'ir opposed so loudly."⁴³ According to Tzahor, it was during the all-night closing session that Yaari and Hazan decided not to support Weizmann. Why? He conjectures "that the two of them took future developments into account and planned one more step ahead": that is, Hashomer Hatza'ir's contribution to Weizmann's defeat was conscious and deliberate. This assumption, Tzahor believes, "passes the test of the steps taken by the movement during the year after the Congress. The historical leadership looked ahead and steered itself towards support for of the idea of partition as advocated by Ben-Gurion."⁴⁴

The biographer accepted his subject's retrospective interpretation in full and without change. From the distance of almost 40 years, Hazan marked his party's vote at the 22nd Zionist Congress as the decisive moment when Hashomer Hatza'ir assumed a historical role in the annals of the State of Israel, given that it led to Weizmann's resignation and allowed Ben-Gurion to lead the Yishuv towards independence. Looking back, Hazan viewed this in a positive light, as if his movement had thereby provided the necessary, though not sufficient, condition for the establishment of the state.⁴⁵ But consideration of the issue from another, more objective perspective produces a different picture. There were 585 delegates accredited to the Congress, but only 350 took part in the decisive vote. After the fact, Hashomer Hatza'ir's failure to cast its 25 votes in support of Weizmann's position was decisive. But how could

---
41 Central Committee of the Hashomer Hatza'ir party, Jan. 30, 1947, HHA, 90.24(5).
42 Gorni, *Shutafut u-ma'avaq*, 193 and 197; Shaltiel, *Tamid be-meri*, 356.
43 Tzahor, *Hazan*, 175–176.
44 Ibid.
45 Ibid., 176 and 188, according to a letter from Hazan to Yisrael Ring, dated Jan. 8, 1984.

Hazan and Yaari have known in advance that 235 delegates would not vote at all? Did they have time to regroup when it turned out that the vote on the London conference would come before the election of the new Zionist Organization president? It seems that the outcome of the Congress was not so much a result of Hashomer Hatza'ir's naiveté, as some have asserted, or of a deliberate calculation by Hazan and Yaari, as others maintain, as it was of Ben-Gurion's political and parliamentary skills. These skills allowed Ben-Gurion to steer Zionist policy in the direction he wished, emerging without Weizmann breathing down his neck, without having to attend the London talks, and with the freedom to advance towards partition by diplomatic methods, all the while loudly proclaiming his loyalty to the Biltmore Program.

As to the question of whether Hashomer Hatza'ir's abstention regarding the vote on participation in the London conference actually led to Weizmann's ousting, the fact remains that the Congress decided not to elect a president for the organization and to refer the issue to the Zionist General Council. That body decided, by a vote of 47 to 32, that the Zionist Organization could manage without a president.[46] Hashomer Hatza'ir played no role in this decision. Nonetheless, Yaari felt remorse over how events had unfolded at the Congress and sent Weizmann a letter in which he expressed his strong desire "to maintain, especially after the Congress, the friendly relations that developed between us and grew stronger over the years. Please take us as we are: undeterred and utterly loyal to the voice of conscience."[47]

In the tangle of issues debated by the 22nd Congress and which dominated the Zionist agenda between the end of the Second World War and the passage of the UN partition resolution on November 29, 1947, Yaari and his movement advocated a position supported by no other Zionist leader or political group—not Weizmann, not Ben-Gurion, not Tabenkin, and not the rising force Abba Hillel Silver, the leader of American Zionism. Even within the ranks of Hashomer Hatza'ir, their

---

46 Shaltiel, *Tamid be-meri*, 358–359.
47 Yaari to Weizmann, Feb. 4, 1947, HHA, 95-7.*bet*-2(5).

position attracted criticism and opposition. At some point, however, Yaari and Hashomer Hatza'ir abandoned binationalism. When? In early 1947, Britain referred the Palestine question to the UN, which meant that the future of the country depended not only on Britain but also on the other member states, and especially the two superpowers, the United States and the Soviet Union. Even though Yaari did not have great hopes of Soviet support for the Zionist position after the war, when the Palestine question landed with the UN he seems to have piled up a mountain of assumptions and conclusions as to the Soviet Union's position, despite his total lack of information of which direction it would take. Here he was in for a surprise, although it took time to emerge. Its essence was a pleasant surprise—Soviet support for the Zionist demand; but as time passed he discovered that the Soviets supported partition, and this forced him to rethink his own position. It was not that he had to toe the Soviet line, no matter what, but that the Russian support for partition created a new international climate to which Yaari had to adapt.

On May 14, 1947, when a special session of the United Nations General Assembly to discuss the Palestine question decided to establish the United Nations Special Committee on Palestine (UNSCOP), the Soviet representative, Andrei Gromyko, loosed a bombshell:

> During the last war, the Jewish people underwent exceptional sorrow and suffering. Without any exaggeration, this sorrow and suffering are indescribable. [...] It would be unjustifiable to deny this right to the Jewish people [to establish their own State], particularly in view of all it has undergone during the Second World War.[48]

In his speech, Gromyko presented two alternatives. The first, the establishment of a unitary state with equal rights for Jews and Arabs, was the preferred solution, he said. But should it turn out that the deterioration in the relations between the Jews and the Arabs had made it impossible to carry out this plan, and were it demonstrated that the

---

48 United Nations General Assembly, 27th Plenary Meeting, 14 May 1947 (at-http://www.zionism-israel.com/zionism__ungromyko.htm).

relations between the Jewish and Arab populations of Palestine were so bad that they could not be reconciled and guarantee peaceful coexistence between them, then and only then it would be necessary to consider the second plan of partitioning Palestine into two independent autonomous states, one Jewish and one Arab. Yaari saw Gromyko's declaration as a "historic date," which was Hashomer Hatza'ir's "reward for the long period of isolation and swimming against the current."[49] Six days after Gromyko's speech, Yaari was still certain about the outcome: "There is no doubt that the Americans will not help get the British out of Palestine. So neither is partition into two independent states possible."[50] On the basis of this assumption that two independent states would not emerge, but neither would the solution be a binational state, Yaari concluded as follows: "We must henceforth fight for an international trusteeship, which will lead through the growth of the national home to binational independence, and present it as a contrast to partition."[51] Partition, in his opinion, would necessarily lead to enslavement to reactionary trends at home and imperialist trends abroad. Hence, Hashomer Hatza'ir must work to persuade the Soviet Union to accept the idea of international control, with its active participation.[52]

In the months between the establishment of UNSCOP in mid-May 1947 and the publication of its conclusions in late summer, Yaari supported the conversion of the British mandate into an international trusteeship, administered on behalf of the UN by the USSR, the United States, and Great Britain, for a protracted period that would end only after the consolidation of a Jewish majority in Palestine, after which a binational regime would be established. As at the time of the Anglo-American Committee, representatives of parties that were not part of the Jewish Agency coalition were not allowed to appear before UNSCOP, so once again Hashomer Hatza'ir had to make do with submitting a memorandum, "The Road to Binational Independence for

---

49 Yaari to Nathan Friedel, June 9, 1947, HHA, 95-7.9(7).
50 Yaari to Levy, May 20, 1947, HHA, 95-7.10(3).
51 Ibid.
52 Ibid.

Palestine," which was also published for the general public.⁵³ In his own testimony to UNSCOP, Ben-Gurion offered a fair description of Hashomer Hatza'ir's plan: it was a Zionist plan, but its realization would require another quarter century of international administration of Palestine.⁵⁴

The watershed in Yaari's support for a binational state came on August 31, 1947, the day that UNSCOP published its report, whose majority recommendation was for the establishment of separate Jewish and Arab states in Palestine, linked by an economic union. From Zurich, where he was attending a session of the Zionist General Council, Yaari dispatched a series of letters to his fellow kibbutz members, to the movement, and to its leadership, all with the following motif: "It is possible that the situation will force us to give a brave answer and that we will not be able to sabotage the facts."⁵⁵ He presented a pragmatic position: "The facts must not strike us in the face, so that one fine day we find ourselves right, but abandoned by everyone else. [...] We have to take reality as a starting point."⁵⁶ It is impossible for us to stick to our old position, he wrote, after the publication of the UNSCOP report, and a fortiori after the majority recommendation is approved by the General Assembly. The establishment of a binational regime, which Yaari had championed until then, would require a protracted transition period, and Zionism could not allow itself that luxury. He expressly emphasized that he had modified his position for pragmatic and not ideological reasons, because of his fear that Hashomer Hatza'ir would become a sect divorced from the real world.⁵⁷

Yaari anticipated his movement's institutions in turning away from a binational vision and accepting partition. While he was still in Europe, and before his instructions and explanations reached it, the Kibbutz Artzi Executive Committee announced its opposition to

---

53 *The Road to Bi-National Independence for Palestine.*
54 Zait, *Ḥaluẓim*, 233.
55 Yaari to Kibbutz Merḥavia, Sept. 4, 1947, KMA, MYF, 1 (3).
56 Yaari to Bernard and Barzilai, Sept. 14, 1947, quoted by Zait, *Ḥaluẓim*, 238.
57 Yaari to Party and Kibbutz Artzi Secretariat, September 1947, HHA, 90.19(1).

partition as a matter of principle and defined the UNSCOP recommendations published a few days earlier as a terrible division of the country with impossible borders.[58] Inertia locked the movement in its old position, which it did not allow itself to modify drastically as long as Yaari and the other senior leaders were abroad. Events from early September 1947 and onwards demonstrate Yaari's vast power to steer the movement as he wished. From the moment he understood that the old position was untenable and made this plain to the movement, it fell in step and adopted his line without delay.

The tension between ideology and pragmatism about the future of Palestine became evident to Yaari only after the publication of the UNSCOP recommendations. His statements during the interim between early September and the General Assembly vote on partition, in late November 1947, can be interpreted either as personal indecision or as steering an intelligent course between his political role, on the one hand, and his educational role, on the other, or between realpolitik and ideology. In mid-October, he still insisted that partition was not inevitable and asserted that this solution stemmed first of all from the Zionist movement's political mistakes, including its failure to demand a transition period during which the Yishuv would grow and develop closer relations with the Arabs, and the Soviet Union would be involved in deciding the future of Palestine.[59] During those eventful days, Yaari expended more energy on analyzing past mistakes by others than on sketching out his party's future course. With regard to the latter, he was clearly ambiguous and flitting between the dream he had not yet abandoned and the new situation that was still not totally clear.

During these weeks, Yaari repeatedly made it clear that his new stance was a pragmatic adaptation to the current reality. It would be wonderful if the situation on the ground developed in the direction of a binational state; and if did not, it was important to amend the Partition Plan to the maximum feasible extent. Even though Yaari had reached

---

58 Kibbutz Artzi Executive Committee, Sept. 4, 1947, HHA, 90.19(3).
59 Yaari at a meeting of the Central Committee of the Hashomer Hatza'ir party, Oct. 16, 1947, HHA, 90.117(3).

a decision and altered course, he seems to have found it difficult to reconcile himself to the new tack. Although he preceded the movement in revising the goal, he then found it more difficult to abandon the old line than the movement did. Hashomer Hatza'ir dismissed the binational idea without many tears. "Matters developed very quickly for us," recalled Bentov, one of the originators of the idea, many years later. "In the Hashomer Hatza'ir party, they reached the conclusion that a historical opportunity for Zionism had emerged. It also turned out that there was no desire on either side—the Jews or the Arabs—to proceed together. The conclusion: there is no alternative to partitioning Palestine. And this position was accepted almost without pain or 'sacrifice.'"[60]

The ease of the conversion from the vision of a binational society in all of Palestine to acceptance of a Jewish state in part of the country may indicate that binationalism never struck deep roots in the soil of Hashomer Hatza'ir. Not only was no arm-twisting required for it to drop one plan and adopt the other; in fact, the Jewish state satisfied desires long entertained by the members. Yaari, who swam against the current for years, including that within his movement, came to his senses; when the hour of decision came, he elected to go with the direction in which Zionist history was flowing. A few days after the General Assembly voted for partition and the establishment of a Jewish state, he said: "This date, when the Jewish people were given independence in half of the homeland, is a date that fills us with joy. [...] Bittersweet joy. We are happy for our independence—but we mourn the fact of partition."[61] He reiterated his movement's aspiration "for independence for all of the Jewish people and in all of Palestine" and promised to work with all his might "to turn partition into a transitional phase on the road to the recovery of the entire country as a place where our people can assemble, as the scene for the ingathering of our exiles."[62] In the edited text of the minutes of the session of the Histadrut Executive Committee, which he himself

---

60 Bentov, *Yamim mesapperim*, 91.
61 Yaari at the meeting of the Histadrut Executive Committee, Dec. 3, 1947, LA.
62 Ibid.

approved, he added emphasis only to the following few words of all his lengthy remarks: *"We are prepared to be among the founders, builders, and defenders of this Hebrew state,"* namely the Jewish and not binational state, and in part of Palestine only, not all of it.[63] When the fateful hour came, he and his movement did precisely this, with all their forces and total discipline, in the war that was beginning as he made that statement.

---

63 Ibid.

CHAPTER 11
From Military Glory to Marking Time in the Opposition

It was standing room only in the auditorium of Beit Ha'am in Tel Aviv on Friday night, January 23, 1948. Outside, the wind was shrieking and the rain pelted down. Inside the hall, the 500 delegates and many guests were packed together for the Unity Convention to consecrate the merger of the Aḥdut Ha'avodah–Po'alei Ziyyon Party and the Hashomer Hatza'ir Workers' Party. The walls were adorned with placards reading: "We will continue to bring in the Holocaust survivors" and "for the brotherhood of nations." The table for the presidium was surrounded by an inscription in giant letters: "Workers of all countries unite!" High above the platform hung a banner: "May the hands of our protectors be strong" (playing on the first line of the labor Zionist anthem "Teḥezaqna"). A bloody war was raging in the country and there had already been many casualties.[1]

Everything had been meticulously and carefully planned. The dais was draped with both red flags and blue-and-white flags. On their lapels, the participants wore the convention badge, featuring a blue-and-white flag (two parallel stripes, but with no Star of David between them) and a red flag: the blue-and-white banner was above the red one, but slightly behind it. Flag-bearers from both the parties' affiliated youth movements, Hashomer Hatza'ir and Hamaḥanot Ha'olim, entered the auditorium. The blue-and-white banner led the way, followed by a

---
[1] The description that follows is based on the opening pages of the booklet containing the convention's proceedings and published by the party (*Ve'idat ha-iḥud*). The participants' remarks, too, are taken from there. The pamphlet also contained photographs of the convention.

line of red flags. The evening began with boisterous renditions of the "Internationale" and "Teḥezaqna." The assembly stood for a moment of silence in memory of those who had fallen in battle. At the end of the evening, they sang "Hatikvah." All three anthems were sung when the convention adjourned the next day.

Meir Yaari, with his flowing grey locks and black mustache, sat at the center of the presidium table, a grim look on his face. On either side of him sat the representatives of the two parties; a keen eye could make out one woman, at the very end of the table. There were also few women in the audience. The published convention booklet includes the remarks of 23 speakers, of whom only one was female. During the speeches, Yaari sat there with a serious and attentive mien.

The first to mount the podium was Yaakov Zerubavel of Po'alei Ziyyon, followed immediately by Yaari. After greetings by the representative of the Histadrut and the chairman of the Va'ad Le'ummi (the National Council of the Yishuv), it was Yitzhak Tabenkin's turn. Serious thought had been given not only to the sequence of speakers, but also to the captions in the convention booklet, where the arrangement of the photographs reflected the participants' relative standing. The speakers on the first night, Zerubavel, Yaari, and Tabenkin—the leaders of the three groups that had merged to form the new party—each received his own page. Yaakov Hazan, Yaari's long-time partner at the head of Hashomer Hatza'ir, shared a page with Shlomo Kaplansky. Yaari was of equal status with the leaders of the other two parties in terms of his placement on the platform and other external marks of honor. In the (former) Hashomer Hatza'ir party, however, he was number one, with Hazan slightly below him.

Mapam—the United Workers' Party—was established in relatively short order, certainly when compared with the long period that had elapsed between the establishment of Kibbutz Artzi (1927) and the inauguration of Hashomer Hatza'ir Party almost two decades later, when Kibbutz Artzi merged with its urban arm, the Socialist League. What was nowhere on the horizon in August 1947 had become a *fait accompli* within less than five months. Since the split in Mapai, in 1944, Hashomer Hatza'ir, with Yaari at its head, had been interested in merging with Aḥdut Ha'avodah; but the latter preferred a three-party fusion. Only after it became clear that there was no possibility of a merger with Mapai—at least for now—was Aḥdut Ha'avodah amenable to union with Hashomer Hatza'ir. The story of the merger, Mapam's years as a united party, and its subsequent fission is often told using expressions of the sort generally employed for romantic relationships. In this spirit, Aḥdut Ha'avodah originally pictured the merger with Hashomer Hatza'ir as a temporary liaison and kept batting its eyelashes at the preferred bridegroom Mapai, with Moshe Sneh playing the role of marriage broker.

The merger had been kick-started start during the meeting of the Zionist General Council in Zurich, in the late summer of 1947, immediately after the publication of UNSCOP's recommendations for the future of Palestine. It was the UNSCOP report, with a majority in favor of partition, which had brought the two left-wing Zionist parties together. Until then, the political future of Palestine had been a matter of dispute between them and an obstacle to their rapprochement. One of them favored a Jewish state in all of Palestine; the other envisioned a binational state. The UNSCOP report eliminated the main issue dividing them. When their contradictory goals became a matter of faith, to be realized only at "the end of days," they were no longer an obstacle to union. Moreover, the question of how to conduct the struggle against the British and whether to use force against the Mandatory power, on which Hashomer Hatza'ir and Aḥdut Ha'avodah had disagreed since the end of the Second World War, also dropped from the agenda in late 1947. Another unifying factor was their shared and growing sympathy for the Soviet Union.

In the new circumstances of the second half of 1947, as he understood them, Yaari was keen to merge with Aḥdut Ha'avodah. In Zurich, he told Tabenkin that the merger could be implemented within a matter of days.[2] As the moment of decision drew near, he taunted the opponents of merger within his movement and described them as "that same perpetual groom who remains a bachelor because only his mother

---

2 Kanary, *Tabenkin*, 585.

is good enough for him."³ He made it clear to the members of Aḥdut Ha'avodah that—in the interests of unity—Hashomer Hatza'ir would not be dogmatic, expressing a willingness to rewrite its program. After all, this was the hour of destiny and they had to strike while the iron was hot. They must pursue negotiations energetically and implement the merger promptly.⁴

How certain was Yaari that the merger was the right thing to do? Did he believe it would endure? In public, he expressed the belief that despite the trials that the new party would face, it would stride firmly ahead after the merger. But there is no way to know whether he truly believed this or was merely regaling his comrades with his hopes in order to persuade them. About a week before the fateful vote at the United Nations (November 29, 1947), he took as an encouraging sign that "it is the members of the Palmach who are so avid for a merger"; perhaps he himself needed them in order to persuade himself.⁵ Even though no one said it in so many words, it was obvious that the expedited merger was motivated to a large extent by the two parties' apprehensions about the future of their kibbutz movements and the status of the kibbutz in the state that was about to be born.

At the start of the Unity Convention, Yaari asserted in his speech that the two parties had had much in common from their inceptions. Both of them had always emblazoned pioneering Zionism and revolutionary socialism on their flags. The present extreme circumstances had catalyzed their merger so that together they could fight for Zionist-Socialist hegemony and the progressive image of the nascent Jewish state, keep it from adopting a one-sided (meaning pro-Western) orientation, and enable it to maintain its independence and serve as a "bridge and address for the forces of socialism and democracy throughout the world."⁶ Yaari referred frequently to the past and drew on it for galvanizing slogans for the future path, slogans that were

---

3 Yaari to Simha Flapan, Dec. 30, 1947, HHA, 3.60(1).
4 Zait, *Ḥaluẓim*, 249.
5 Hashomer Hatza'ir Central Committee, Nov. 21, 1947, HHA, 90.117(3).
6 *Ve'idat ha-iḥud*, 10.

dominated by an unambiguous commitment to bearing the burden of the war and to Zionism.

In the speech, which addressed many topics—some practical and others theoretical—Yaari never breathed a word about a merger of the two kibbutz movements, the keystones of the united party. The platform, too, was silent about this. The separate existence of the two kibbutz movements was a sort of ticking bomb: leaving them untouched and separate in the first act was a sure recipe for an explosion before the final curtain. Several problems festered beneath the surface of the new party; everyone ignored them for the moment, but sooner or later they would emerge into the light. The prevalent view is that the seeds of the schism were sown on the united party's first day and that the merger process papered over more than it resolved. The unresolved disagreements and the separate organizational traditions that the original parties had brought with them left their mark on Mapam's structure and operating methods. The damage inflicted by these phenomena was even more severe because no single, charismatic, and authoritative leader ever emerged who could bridge the various contradictions within it. In the larger party, the internal dynamic of leadership was not the same as that of the old Hashomer Hatza'ir. Not only did a leadership *troika*, similar to the collaboration of Yaari and Hazan, fail to develop; the new situation actually produced cracks in what the outside world perceived as their harmonious partnership.

When Yaari turned 50 in early 1947, about a year after the establishment of the Hashomer Hatza'ir Party, Hazan spoke nostalgically about what had once been, the intimacy that had formerly been a hallmark of the relations among the comrades, and the changes that accompanied the establishment of the party:

> We began as a very small family. Everything was 'togetherness.' [...] It was a movement that was effectively a family. There was ideology, there was the path, there was a war about the path, but mostly there were the personal bonds. [...] Today we have become a movement, where it is not individual friendship that matters but the connection to the movement. We have matured. Our relationships have

become more objective. What counts is the path, the partnership on the path, walking together, the common war.[7]

This was even more the case after the establishment of Mapam, a year later.

Did Yaari's leadership style make the transformation required by the new organizational arrangement? At the start of his speech at the Unity Convention, he proclaimed that his remarks would be political in nature, not programmatic—a departure from his custom. In the speech itself, however, there is no indication of such a change. On the contrary, what stands out is a repetition of his ingrained tendency to explain past events and demonstrate how we were right and our opponents were wrong, rather than outline a path for future action. The speech was a fabric of heartfelt desires. The gap—almost a contradiction—between Yaari's selective approach, which included a measure of elitism, and his position at the head of the party that was trying to attract as many voters as possible, is unmistakable.

Mapam was founded at the height of the war.[8] About a week before the Unity Convention, 35 young fighters, *en route* to reinforce the Etzion Bloc south of Jerusalem, fell. The day before the convention opened, seven members of the Haganah were killed near Yazur (today Azor). These incidents, and the war as a whole, echoed in all the speeches; they cast a pall on the convention and were reflected in its program. In his speech, Yaari emphasized that security had to take precedence over everything else and addressed the educational dilemmas posed by the war. To the question that hovered in the air—"are we fated to having to maintain our independence at bayonet point?"—he answered: "As long as we have no choice, we are duty-bound in all conditions to defend the borders of the land and the territory of the Jewish state."[9] The resort to arms was a cruel necessity; there was no way to avoid casualties among the Arabs. But we were also under an obligation to maintain our humanity and not lose hope for a better future: "While we grip a

---

7 Kibbutz Artzi Council, Apr. 10, 1947, HHA, 5-20.5(1).
8 See Halamish, "Mapam in the War of Independence."
9 *Ve'idat ha-iḥud*, 16.

weapon with one hand, with the other we must raise high the banner of brotherhood and solidarity."[10] It is possible, of course, to dismiss such statements as bleeding-heart apologetics. But we must not minimize the educational importance of such messages, which derive from the movement's deep-seated humanism and Yaari's conception of his role as its leader—first and foremost an educator and guide.

Late February and March 1948 were one of the grimmest periods the Yishuv had ever known. On March 11, a dozen people were killed when a car bomb exploded in the courtyard of the National Institutions in Jerusalem; three weeks earlier, a truck full of explosives had blown up on Ben Yehuda Street in the center of town, killing some 50 persons. The Jews also suffered serious defeats in the war to keep the roads open. Within a single week at the end of March, the Negev was cut off, convoys to Neve Yaakov, the Etzion Bloc, and Kibbutz Yeḥiam were attacked, near the Arab village of Hulda, in the Judean foothills, a convoy to Jerusalem was intercepted and turned back. In the north, the situation went from bad to worse, as foreign volunteers continued to stream into the country in the uniform of the Arab Liberation Army commanded by Fawzi al-Qawuqji. At the same time, a new front was opened in the diplomatic arena. The Jews' desperate military situation had triggered doubts about their ability to hold out, especially when the war expanded after the departure of the British and the Arab regular armies could be expected to invade the country. The United States backtracked on its support for the Partition Plan and proposed a temporary UN trusteeship regime for Palestine.

During those dark days, Yaari found some glimmers of light in the complex situation that had emerged—possibilities that he would welcome and for which Mapam should fight. One such was an international trusteeship arrangement that included the Soviet Union. In that case, the residents of Palestine would not be solely under the thumb of the West and it might be possible to install a government with parity between the two peoples, admit 100,000 Jewish immigrants, and repeal the draconian Lands Law (of 1940) that effectively made it illegal

---

10 Ibid., 17.

for Jews to purchase land in most of Palestine—aspirations cast in the terms of an earlier time that was no longer relevant.[11] In those months right before the establishment of the state, Yaari clearly vacillated between his fundamental and pragmatic loyalty to the decisions that had been made, on the one hand, and his strong desire for things to develop in a different direction, on the other; between the political obligation to defend the Partition Resolution and the hope that the UN might rethink the matter in the next few weeks.

In the meantime, the Yishuv institutions made ready to declare independence. The five Mapam delegates to the 37-member People's Assembly, the provisional parliament established in April, did not include the party's senior leaders. Because he was not a member of the Assembly, Yaari could not participate in the deliberations about the text of the Proclamation of Independence. In an internal party debate held on the morning of May 14, he stated his view that "the phrase 'the Rock of Israel' [a biblical term for God] has no place in the declaration" and instructed the Mapam representatives on the drafting committee to act accordingly.[12] But if they were not able to have it removed, at least they should see to the deletion of the word "faith" (in the Rock of Israel).[13] The final version of the proclamation, as read out by David Ben-Gurion that afternoon (May 14, 1948), has "*trust* in the Rock of Israel."

Two of the thirteen members of the People's Administration, which became the Provisional Government of the new state on May 14, represented Mapam—one from Hashomer Hatza'ir and the other from Aḥdut Ha'avodah. But they were second-tier figures in the party, setting a precedent for the future: Mapam's top leaders did not serve as cabinet ministers.

A new stage in the war began the next day, when the regular Arab armies invaded the newly declared state. Many kibbutzim found themselves on the front lines. Some repelled the attackers and held

---

11 Mapam Political Committee, Mar. 22, 1948, HHA, 90.66(1); Yaari to [Ya'akov] Majus and Levi Greenblatt, Apr. 15, 1948, HHA, 95-7.11(3).
12 Mapam Political Committee, May 14, 1948, HHA, 90.66(1).
13 Ibid.

their positions after heavy losses in life and property. At a few, the defenders withdrew (temporarily) after fierce fighting. A handful of kibbutzim were abandoned without a battle, and one was overrun by the enemy and surrendered. On June 10—the night before the first cease-fire went into effect, after four weeks of fighting—Yaari drew up a sort of situation report. "It is easier to boast of our victories"— evidently referring to Nirim and Negba, two kibbutzim in the south that had withstood the Egyptian onslaught and became heroic myths and the emblems of stubborn resistance.[14] Particularly indelible was the banner that had been hung in the Nirim dining hall for May Day and continued to fly there even after everything around it had been destroyed: "It is not the tank that will win—but man."[15] Negba became the symbol of the resistance of the few against many.

But Yaari also had to relate to two kibbutzim that were not tales of victory: Sha'ar Hagolan and Yad Mordechai. The latter, whose fighters had pulled back on May 24, after six days of fierce fighting and many losses, is remembered mainly for having checked the advance of an entire Egyptian brigade, making a mockery of the enemy's plan to conquer it within three hours, and providing a respite during which the Israeli forces acquired arms and ammunition, organized, and then blocked the Egyptian army's northward advance. The decision to withdraw was taken after 26 members of the kibbutz and Palmach fighters had been killed, many were wounded, and their ammunition was almost exhausted.[16]

Everyone was proud of Yad Mordechai, Yaari said, but, he added, the defenders had withdrawn contrary to their orders. The minutes of that discussion about "the resistance by the kibbutzim" are fragmentary and not always clear, but he seems to have believed that Yad Mordechai should have held out to the bitter end.[17] Nevertheless, in conversation with members of Yad Mordechai, a few days later, he quoted the slogan that had hung on the wall of the conference room: "We held out as

---

14 Kibbutz Artzi Executive Committee, June 10, 1948, HHA, 5-10.5(12).
15 http://www.nirim.co.il/viewStaticPage.aspx?pageID=26
16 Rappel, "U-mi yizkor et ha-zokherim," 1.
17 Kibbutz Artzi Executive Committee, June 10, 1948, HHA, 5-10.5(12).

long as was humanly possible." He made it clear that he saw nothing apologetic in this and that he found meaning in the deaths of "the heroes of Yad Mordechai, who fell to prevent the invader from getting past."[18] Yaari believed that Yad Mordechai belonged in the pantheon of national heroism: "There is no difference between Yad Mordechai and Negba."[19]

Kibbutz Sha'ar Hagolan was a different story. On May 18, 1948, at the height of the Syrian military offensive in the north, the members of Sha'ar Hagolan and Massada, which were located east of the Jordan Valley road, abandoned their settlements and found temporary shelter at Beit Zera and Afiqim, west of the road. Six days later they returned home, to discover that their kibbutzim had been looted, set on fire, and razed to the ground. The Palmach bulletin was quick to pounce on the members of the two kibbutzim: "Those who were entrusted with the portal to the Golan [Hebrew: *Sha'ar ha-Golan*] should have stood in the gate; those who bore the name of 'Masada' were not loyal to the symbol emblazoned on their flag."[20] The two kibbutzim were branded with the mark of Cain.

Precisely during the week of Sha'ar Hagolan's exile, Yaari expressed the view that children, childcare workers, and all others who could make no contribution to resisting the enemy should be evacuated from the frontline settlements, but the others must stay: teenagers from the ages of 13 or 14, adults, and the elderly. As a matter of principle, he held that they must fight "to the last man" and opposed the abandonment of the settlements because "we have nowhere to go and no Volga [River to retreat behind]."[21] Just before the first cease-fire went into effect, as we have seen, he had voiced veiled criticism of the withdrawal from Yad Mordechai.[22]

---

18 Yaari, "At Kibbutz Yad Mordechai," [May/June 1948], in *Be-ma'avaq le-amal meshuḥrar*, 301–303.
19 Yaari, "At the Victory Rally at Negba, 1949," ibid., 300.
20 Agin, "Sha'ar Hagolan and Massada in the War of Independence," 205–271.
21 Mapam Political Committee, May 20, 1948, HHA, 90.6(1). See also Cohen-Levinovsky, "The Evacuation of the Noncombatant Population in the 1948 War."
22 Kibbutz Artzi Executive Committee, June 10, 1948, HHA, 5-10.5(12).

Notwithstanding the direct and implicit criticism of Sha'ar Hagolan and Yad Mordechai, the reigning tone of Yaari's remarks at that June 10 meeting were sympathetic and friendly. Despite all that Sha'ar Hagolan had gone through, its members are "flesh of our flesh" and we must identify with them. He was angry that one of those castigating Sha'ar Hagolan was his partner at the head of Mapam, Tabenkin. "Sha'ar Hagolan stands innocent before every court," he told the latter, and concluded his remarks on an inspirational note: "We will not be quiet and we will not rest until, when the battle is over, all the kibbutzim have been reestablished"; now we must visit every kibbutz and encourage its members.[23] In times of trial and distress, he knew how to comfort and show sympathy.

During the war, most of the debates in Mapam and Kibbutz Artzi were conducted in a heavy fog, if not indeed a total news blackout. A modicum of information on battlefield developments reached Yaari from soldiers on leave. All his statements about the military and diplomatic conduct of the war leave the sense that he was groping in the darkness, full of whys and what ifs. In conversation with the comrades, he frequently vented about phenomena that kept him awake at night, expressing his opinions and asking questions. What follows here is based on what he said at meetings of movement, party, and Histadrut institutions, frequently relying on information that was unreliable and inaccurate. The test to be applied to these statements is not whether the events described took place, or took place as he described them; their importance is that they reflect what he knew and how he responded to the information that reached him (some of it in the form of rumors). On several occasions he admitted that he did not investigate everything, that he was not willing to put his signature to everything he said, and that he would be very happy were some of it proven incorrect.[24]

Much has been written about the Deir Yassin affair. For our purpose, it is important that, soon after the events, it was public

---

23 Ibid.
24 Histadrut Executive Committee, June 16/17, 1948, 41-43, LA.

knowledge that this Arab village, located on the outskirts of Jerusalem, had been attacked and destroyed by a joint Etzel and Lehi force on April 9, 1948, and that many of those killed were women and children. Rumors spread of a massacre, of houses deliberately blown up with their inhabitants inside, of women raped and corpses desecrated. The Jewish Agency dispatched a condolence telegram to King Abdullah of Transjordan, in which it "vehemently condemned the Deir Yassin incident, which was carried out by Jewish dissident organizations," as "a brutal and barbaric act that is incompatible with the spirit of the Jewish people and its cultural tradition and heritage."[25] Writing in *Al Hamishmar* in the last week of April, Yaari asserted that at Deir Yassin, "they murdered Arab women and children so that all the Pontius Pilates could wring their hands and say, 'the Jews, too, are capable of carrying out a Lidice.'"[26] He was skeptical that the residents of Deir Yassin had chosen to run away and demanded a real answer: if they had fled, who told them to do so? He assumed that they had done so because they were afraid, but suspected that they had also been expelled by the English as well as the Jews—a statement that he did not mean to limit to Deir Yassin.[27]

Yaari saw the fighting that took place immediately after the establishment of the state and the invasion by the Arab armies as a war of the few against the many, of "Sten guns against cannons," a war in which the Palmach fighters were "mown down as if by a scythe."[28] In those days he evinced an understanding of the harsh treatment of the Arabs and even their expulsion, but later in the war he saw things in a different light.[29] It was not only the expulsion that he saw as one of the sick consequences of the war, but also the looting, blockades, and starvation. He spoke about these phenomena with pain and anger.

---

25 *Davar*, Apr. 13, 1948.
26 Yaari, "Dir Yassin or Mishmar Ha'emeq," *Al Hamishmar*, Apr. 23, 1948. Lidice was a village near Prague, which was destroyed by the Germans in June 1942. All men over 15 were shot; the women and children were deported to concentration camps.
27 Political Committee, May 27, 1948, HHA, 90.66(1).
28 27th Council of Kibbutz Artzi, Dec. 12, 1948, HHA, 95-7.29(3).
29 Ibid.

In his *j'accuse* he called attention to the fact that not only the army engaged in plunder and looting, but also members of all the agricultural settlements, including kibbutzim of his own movement.[30] By the end of 1948 he saw this as an epidemic and not a matter of one or two weak links.[31]

The expulsion of Arabs from their homes to which Yaari later applied the term *transfer* (construed as a Hebrew word), worried him for its own sake, and all the more so because members of his party were involved.[32] As he saw it, the eviction of the Arabs from Ramle was the nadir, chiefly because of the involvement of Yigal Allon (the Mapam member with the most-senior position in the IDF), and also because the commanders carried it out even though they knew they were acting counter to the party's opinion. He may have gone so far as to demand that they be summoned to a hearing in front of the party's institutions and to call for Allon's expulsion from Mapam.[33]

Within two weeks after independence Yaari was sunk in melancholy because of the events of the war.[34] One reason was his concern about the loss of humanity in the storm of the battle. "How easy it is for them to say that it is possible and permitted to take women, children, and old people and fill the roads with them, because this is what strategy calls for," and even after the town had surrendered.[35] Two things in particular enraged him. First, that the phrase "fill the roads" was attributed to Yigal Allon, who had come up with the idea of the expulsion so that the Arab Legion would be forced to provide for those banished from Lod and Ramle, thereby burdening its supply lines and making it less mobile. Second, that the same idea had been taken up by members of Hashomer Hatza'ir, who should remember who had used it against their own people during the world war.

---

30 Histadrut Executive Committee, June 16/17, 1948, LA.
31 27th Council of Kibbutz Artzi, Dec. 12, 1948, HHA, 95-7.29(3).
32 Ibid.
33 Yaari's remarks at the meeting of the Kibbutz Artzi Executive Committee, Nov. 4, 1948, HHA, 5-10.5(12); 27th Council of Kibbutz Artzi, Dec. 12, 1948, HHA, 95-7.29(3); meeting of Mapam security officers, July 25–26, 1948, HHA, 90.206(2).
34 Political Committee, May 27, 1948, HHA, 90.66(1).
35 27th Council of Kibbutz Artzi, Dec. 12, 1948, HHA, 95-7. 29(3).

The reports from the battle zone led Yaari to infer that there was a fixed policy to remove the Arabs from the country and that the order had come from the highest echelons.[36] He was tormented by the suspicion that the leaders of Mapai were taking advantage of the rising wave of chauvinism and now said aloud what yesterday they had not dared hint at even in secret. Some had started suggesting that the Arab refugees should not be allowed back.[37] By the last week of July, addressing a closed Mapam forum, he spoke with even greater conviction about "the notion of transfer" and asserted that it was being orchestrated from above. He went on to say, in a way that makes it impossible to know whether he was expressing his own opinion or was mocking other people's idea, "we will steal the Arabs' property and livelihoods so they leave"; in exchange, "they will give us the Jews of the Arab countries" after they had been stripped of their property.[38]

Despite his growing concern about the expulsions, Yaari was also opposed to allowing the refugees to return home, and certainly not as long as the fighting continued. He saw the Arabs' ejection from Palestine as a great tragedy; on the other hand, Arabs whom Israel had turned into its enemies could not be allowed to return, lest they serve as a fifth column.[39] On various occasions he repeated his opposition to the refugees' return while the war was in progress, but raised the possibility that Israel would pay them compensation. Yaari saw a possible model in the arrangement that had been worked out between Greece and Turkey in the 1920s—"a village for a village, possessions for possessions."[40] He looked for a way to promote Jewish settlement without forcing the Arabs out; perhaps the latter could be given land elsewhere in exchange for what had been taken from them. As the head of a settlement movement, he made it clear: "Our party must not dispossess small landowners. We have to do something for them."[41]

---

36 Histadrut Executive Committee, June 16-17, 1948, LA.
37 Yaari to [Ya'akov] Majus and Levi [Greenblatt], June 21, 1948, HHA, 95-7.11(3).
38 Meeting of Mapam security officers, July 25-26, 1948, HHA, 90.206(2).
39 Histadrut Executive Committee, June 16/17, 1948, LA.
40 Meeting of Mapam security officers, July 25-26, 1948, HHA, 90.206(2); Mapam Central Committee, Sept. 16, 1948, HHA, 90.66(1).
41 Political Committee, Nov. 25, 1948, HHA, 90.66(1).

Within Mapam, opinions about appropriate wartime conduct were divided more or less according to party affiliation before the merger. Yaari's main opponent in the debate on the war in general and the soldiers' treatment of Arab civilians in particular was Tabenkin, whose motto was "à *la guerre comme* à *la guerre*." For Yaari, by contrast, war was the continuation of diplomacy by other means: "There cannot be a different political line in peacetime than in wartime. There cannot be one worldview for peacetime and one for wartime. You cannot be a Communist in peacetime and a Fascist in wartime. No one can be a humanist in peacetime and a chauvinist in wartime."[42] This debate was just one manifestation of the many almost genetic differences between the two leaders and between the components of the party, and an expression of the chasm between the educational approaches of Hashomer Hatza'ir and of Tabenkin and Aḥdut Ha'avodah. From the outset, Yaari saw the "brotherhood of nations" and the treatment of the Arabs as a test of the movement's humanity and an indication of the party's future course; Hashomer Hatza'ir's and Aḥdut Ha'avodah's different attitudes towards these issues led him to wonder whether "perhaps we were wrong about each other." He even said explicitly that they might have to part company and go their own ways because of these topics, which he saw as Zionism's most precious asset. The merged party's breakup was in the air before it was a year old.[43]

During the war, Yaari continued to call for peace between Jews and Arabs and frequently expressed his anxiety about the fighters' moral decline. Concern about the distortion of the intrinsic humanity of the Zionist enterprise festered in his heart. He called for the respectful treatment of the noncombatant Arab population that remained in the territory of Israel and for care to avoid damaging enemy property, lest such actions mar the fighters' souls and warp Israel's international image. Alongside these misgivings and breast-beating, which originated in the principles of moral combat and humane values, Yaari did not ignore military and strategic considerations, which, he allowed, were the true

---

42 Meeting of Mapam security officers, July 25–26, 1948, HHA, 90.206(2).
43 Political Committee, May 27, 1948, HHA, 90.66(1).

determinants of behavior during a do-or-die war. One can dismiss his statements about war and morality as based on naiveté and an inability to comprehend the situation; they can also be seen as a deliberate and cynical process of wrapping pragmatic considerations in multiple layers of moral and ethical principles. The question is whether, during the war, he continued to be chiefly a guide and educator who, directed by moral considerations, conveyed educational messages, interspersed with more earthly considerations that spoke to his audience in order to get their attention and have them treat his words seriously. Or, on the contrary, perhaps he was a pragmatic leader who bedecked himself with moral and humanistic arguments.

As an educator and counselor who saw himself as responsible for shaping the character and image of his flock, Yaari was worried about the long-term impact of the war and its terrors on soldiers. You know who a soldier is when he leaves for war, but not when he returns. The experience of combat can cleanse the soul and rectify flaws; but it can also enslave a person to impulses that divert him from the moral path. Some return from war wielding a hatchet, while others have been refined and purified. The latter are the national liberators, those who work the great revolutions.[44] He had said something similar three years earlier, when addressing a group of partisans who had arrived in Palestine after the Second World War. In 1945, he was afraid that those who had only recently emerged from the trenches of the Second World War would be contaminated by the pogroms, riots, and barbarism they had experienced so recently and would, perish the thought, look for an escape through "fascist and terrorist recidivism."[45] In 1948, he was afraid of the war's negative impact on movement members who had returned from the front. Fraught memories of his own time as a soldier during and after the First World War caused him to be concerned about the appearance of a new Freikorps, a private militia of disgruntled veterans (like those in Germany, Poland, and the Baltic States in the years after 1918, most of which had a Rightwing orientation).[46]

---

44 Meeting of Mapam security officers, July 25–26, 1948, HHA, 90.206(2).
45 Yaari, *Be-derekh arukah*, 145.
46 Meeting of Mapam security officers, July 25–26, 1948, HHA, 90.206(2).

Mapam members commanded eight of the twelve brigades that composed the Israeli fighting forces at independence. When the army was reorganized by front, three of the four theaters were directed by party members. Many Mapam members served on the General Staff and commanded combat units.[47] In July 1948, Ben-Gurion suspected a Mapam plot to seize control of the armed forces and overthrow him. In September, he estimated that 90% of all command positions were held by Mapam members; in October, by his count, only two of the 64 Palmach commanders belonged to other parties.[48] In other units, too, many officers were inclined towards Mapam and some of them had joined it. Everyone knew that Ben-Gurion preferred officers who were veterans of the British army; the Palmach fighters who were card-carrying members of Mapam were afraid that he was trying to kick them out. His intention to disband the Palmach had long been public knowledge. When the order was finally issued, on November 7, 1948, there was a great uproar among party members and a bitter public controversy.

Yaari took a complex and cautious attitude towards the future of the Palmach after independence. He saw its abolition as one of the many manifestations of the declining luster of the pioneering ethos. The disbanding of the Palmach and what he called the purge of Mapam commanders—the very people who had brought about Israel's victory—was the beginning of the end of the covenant between the Labor-Zionist parties and the harbinger of a new alliance between Mapai and the "bourgeois and clerical reactionaries." He made these statements about a month and a half before the elections to the Constituent Assembly and long before the start of the coalition negotiations whose course and outcome confirmed this prediction.[49]

Yaari was well aware of the threat that the Palmach's dissolution posed for his party and of the injustice of Yisrael Galili's dismissal as head of the National Military Command. It was clear to him that

---

47 Eilat, "Security Party," p. 101.
48 Ben-Gurion, *Yoman milḥamah*, entry for July 4, 1948, p. 574; entry for Sept. 7, 1948, p. 674; Ben-Gurion at a meeting of the Histadrut Executive Committee, Oct. 14, 1948, LA.
49 27th Council of Kibbutz Artzi, 10-12 Dec., 1948, HHA, 5-20.5(4).

Ben-Gurion "was cleaning out the high command by party key."[50] Despite his anger and frustration, Yaari moved cautiously on the Palmach issue. He did not think it wise to use that as an excuse to call for Ben-Gurion's resignation, because that would cause Mapai to close ranks around him. At the same time, he was looking for ways to keep Ben-Gurion from being the sole authority in military matters.[51]

In general, Hashomer Hatza'ir reacted more mildly to the military appointments and to the dismantling of the Palmach than did Aḥdut Ha'avodah. The latter was unhappy with Yaari's cautious response to Galili's sacking.[52] This was exacerbated by the controversy over the resignations that some Mapam officers submitted to protest Ben-Gurion's new appointments. Yaari was opposed to such action as long as the fighting continued. He believed they should accept the government's authority and serve loyally. Their resignations would lead to accusations of mutiny and open an internal political front while they were still engaged with the external enemy. Yaari was also aware of political considerations, notably the impending elections. In his opinion, the party should object to Ben-Gurion's hostility towards the Palmach but bow to the government's authority and postpone the struggle against the Prime Minister and Defense Minister until the war was over. In the meantime, they should find the golden mean between acceptance of the government's authority and presentation of the party's positions to the public. By a vote of 17 in favor, with eight abstentions, Mapam's Political Committee resolved in early July 1948 that "our comrades in the army will continue to operate under its authority."[53]

Thirty-one years after this act, Yaari declared in public: "I stood behind Ben-Gurion when he took the unambiguous decision to dismantle the Palmach and maintain a single organizational framework

---

50 Mapam Political Committee, July 1, 1948, HHA, 90.66(1).
51 Ibid.
52 See, for example, Liebschutz to Bar-Yehuda, July 7, 1948, quoted by Tzur, *Nofei ha-ashlayah*, 86.
53 Mapam Political Committee, July 3, 1948, HHA, 90.66(1).

for the IDF. Ben-Gurion did not forget my loyalty to him all his life."⁵⁴ It is likely that his support for the disbanding of the Palmach was motivated in part by his perception of that militia as "Tabenkin's Red Army" and a potential source of political power for Tabenkin within the party as well.

Mapam's members and leaders found it difficult to internalize the change that took place on May 14, 1948, with the transition from a voluntary society to a sovereign state, and to adjust to the new rules of the game. Yaari believed that in the new situation, too, Mapam members' primary allegiance should be to the party.⁵⁵ For example, he expected that Abba Kovner would provide the secretariat of Kibbutz Artzi with the battle sheets he wrote as the Giv'ati Brigade's propaganda, culture, and education officer, even if only at a later date and only to be kept on file. He reproached Kovner for having forgotten, in the excitement of his army service, that he was a member of the Kibbutz Artzi Executive and the Mapam Central Committee and duty-bound to maintain close contact with their institutions.⁵⁶ According to a document sent by the Kibbutz Artzi Security Department to the Mapam Central Committee and the Kibbutz Artzi Executive, about a year and a half after the establishment of the state, one of the party's primary roles was to infuse the IDF with the movement's ideological values and political principles. To achieve this, it should establish circles comprising both officers and enlisted men that would support vibrant mutual relations among party members and guide them in all fields of endeavor.⁵⁷

At that time, several kibbutzim were amassing weapons and munitions in hidden caches. Was this a clandestine operation that bordered on subversion and a threat to national security, as has frequently been claimed? Does the charge that the weapons were stashed away for a future link-up with the Red Army when it landed in the

---

54 *Bamesheq* (Kibbutz Merhavia newsletter), May 1, 1979.
55 Meeting of Mapam security officers, July 25–26, 1948, HHA, 90.206(2).
56 Yaari to Abba Kovner, Dec. 29, 1948, HHA, 95-7.11(4).
57 Kibbutz Artzi Security Department to the Mapam Central Committee and the Kibbutz Artzi Executive Committee, Nov. 9, 1949, HHA, 95-7.12(1); Kibbutz Artzi Executive Committee, Dec. 12, 1949, HHA, 5-10.5(15).

region hold water? Or perhaps it was simply a matter of guaranteeing the means for the kibbutzim to defend themselves against some future attack without having to depend on the IDF, which might be late in showing up on the scene. This interpretation is based in part on an item in the same Security Department document of November 1949: "In light of the army's condition and the unsettled security situation on the borders, we see an urgent necessity to bolster our settlements' defensive capacity and ability to hold out, making fullest use of our members who have been discharged from the Israel Defense Forces."[58] This interpretation also draws on the similarity between the initiative to stockpile weapons on kibbutzim in the early days of the State and the underground arms caches (hidden not only from the British but also from the Haganah and everyone else) established at Kibbutz Kfar Gil'adi after the Galilee Panhandle incidents in the winter of 1920, when the four isolated settlements there, including Tel Hai, were left to their own devices and did not receive reinforcements from the center of the country.

Either way, the arms caches were soon history. Under Yaari's leadership, Hashomer Hatza'ir continued to obey the elected institutions of the State of Israel, whether Mapam was part of the government coalition or on the opposition benches.

The election campaign for the Constituent Assembly (which soon transformed itself into the First Knesset) began in early January 1949, right after the end of Operation Horev—the last major Israeli offensive during the War of Independence. In this operation, the IDF attacked and battered the Egyptian expeditionary force in the Negev and eastern Sinai. On December 29, 1948, the UN Security Council ordered an immediate cease-fire and the withdrawal of forces to the positions that the sides had held before the operation began. Great Britain and the United States presented Israel with an ultimatum to pull back to the international boundary, accompanied by a stern warning from President Truman. The massive international pressure achieved

---

58 Kibbutz Artzi Security Department to the Mapam Central Committee and the Kibbutz Artzi Executive Committee, Nov. 9, 1949, HHA, 95-7.12(1).

its end and Ben-Gurion ordered the IDF to withdraw. Yigal Allon, who as OC Southern Command directed the operation, flew to Tel Aviv in an attempt to convince the Prime Minister to cancel the order, but to no avail. All the IDF forces left Sinai by the morning of January 2, 1949; Operation Ḥorev ended without fully achieving its objective of expelling all Egyptian forces from the territory of mandatory Palestine.

It was only then (about two months before the IDF reached Um Rash Rash/Eilat and the war came to a *de facto* end) that the campaign for the Constituent Assembly, scheduled for January 25, effectively began.[59] In the intensive three-week campaign, twenty-one lists competed for the favor of roughly half a million voters. City streets and rural roadsides were festooned with signs displaying the various parties' ballot-slip symbols—notably *aleph* for Mapai and *mem* for Mapam. Mass rallies were the most common form of direct communication between the candidates and the electorate. At these events Mapam, like its principal rival Mapai, filled the stage with senior officers who were still on active service. For Mapam, these included generals Yitzhak Sadeh and Yigal Allon; for Mapai, colonels Moshe Dayan and Asaf Simḥoni. Mapam rallies were also addressed by the leading poets and writers of the "1948 generation." But the heroic officers, leading Palmach and Haganah commanders, and other well-known personalities who enjoyed strong public recognition were not placed in realistic slots on the Mapam list, which was based on a meticulous interweaving of representatives of its three components. The first nineteen names (that is, those who made it into the Constituent Assembly after the votes were counted) included nine from Hashomer Hatza'ir (of whom eight were kibbutz members); the other ten were split between representatives of Aḥdut Ha'avodah and Po'alei Ẓiyyon, including Moshe Sneh. None of the military heroes was given a slot higher than 56.[60]

The two Zionist workers' parties—Mapai and Mapam—were the main contenders and the friction between them played a central role in the campaign. The main question before voters was whether to continue

---

59 On the elections, their outcome, and the coalition negotiations that ensued, see Halamish, "Mapam in the War of Independence" and references there.
60 *Al Hamishmar*, Jan. 14, 1949.

the war or to push for an end to the fighting and the signing of agreements that would freeze the boundaries along the current cease-fire lines. Mapam called for continuing the offensive and occupying the entire territory of Mandatory Palestine. Mapai favored peace accords based on the territory occupied to date (although Ben-Gurion hinted in his speeches that "we are not done yet"). So voters had to choose between continuing the war, as Mapam demanded, or ending it at the price of territorial concessions—more precisely, bidding farewell to some territorial dreams—as Mapai advocated. Looming over this question was the two parties' rivalry over which of them had contributed more to the founding of the state.

Mapam launched its campaign with high expectations. A year earlier, when the united party was created, it felt more or less on a par with Mapai in terms of electoral appeal; now it was confident that "they won't be able to manage without us."[61] On the surface, there were strong grounds for this optimism. Some 40% of the members of the Histadrut identified with Mapam's component factions. The day before the election, Ben-Gurion estimated that the relative strengths of Mapai and Mapam were 60/40.[62] Mapam was very attractive to much of the population. "During the War of Independence, Mapam exerted a pull on many," wrote Uri Avneri almost 40 years after he, like many of his fellow soldiers, cast a ballot marked with the letter *mem*.[63]

> It was almost taken for granted. Mapam back then—the united Mapam—was the party of the fighters, the party of the 'gang,' the party of the Palmach and the other combat brigades. From it there wafted the aroma of a genuine and deep sense of belonging to the Land of Israel. It spoke about peace and brotherhood of nations, and in the late stages of a long and cruel war that was a message we wanted to hear. All of those we esteemed and admired during the war—from Yitzhak Sadeh and Yigal Allon to Shimon Avidan ('Giv'ati')—were Mapam people.[64]

---

61 *Ve'idat ha-iḥud*, 88.
62 Zait, *Ḥaluẓim*, 258; Tzahor, "The Establishment of the First Government," 386–387.
63 Uri Avneri, "Foreword," [June 1, 1988], in Yossi Amitay, *Aḥvat amim be-mivḥan*, 9.
64 Ibid.

But this Mapam, which was a magnet for the young elite, was out of touch with other sectors of Israeli society, whose numbers were growing larger as waves of new immigrants arrived. From May 15 to the end of 1948, more than 100,000 immigrants entered the country, increasing the Jewish population by almost 17%. But even after tens of thousands of new voters had been added to the rolls, Mapam continued to convey the same old messages, which did not speak to the newcomers. It sanctified the organizations and values of the past, and its universe revolved around the kibbutz.

Only 12 of 21 lists that contested the election passed the electoral threshold. As expected, Mapam emerged as the second-largest party, but its performance was far less than expected. Its 64,018 valid votes (14.7%) gave it 19 seats in the Knesset, a distant second to Mapai's 46.[65] Ben-Gurion's predicted ratio between Mapai and Mapam was too optimistic for the later; the actual result was 70/30. Yaari's deep disappointment was proportional to his high expectations. Since the formation of Mapam he had consistently and publicly expressed the aspiration to be part of the government of the new state. Because of his familiarity with his comrades from Hashomer Hatza'ir and his memory of the controversies about joining the People's Administration, he had prepared himself for potential opposition within the party to sitting in the government by laying the groundwork and preparing public opinion for a change in the party's outlook. All over the world, the Left was trying to be on the inside, part of the government, he argued in the party's Central Committee, and Mapam could not slough off its share of responsibility for the destiny of the Jewish people.[66] About a month and a half before the elections, he publicly expressed his intense desire to be part of a "progressive coalition, headed by the united front of the Socialist parties in the Histadrut."[67]

During the year that intervened between the establishment of Mapam and the coalition negotiations with Mapai, the central thread in Yaari's speeches was his strong desire that the party be included in

---

65 https://knesset.gov.il/description/eng/eng_mimshal_res1.htm.
66 Mapam Central Committee, Sept. 16, 1948, HHA, 90.66(1).
67 27th Council of Kibbutz Artzi, December 10-12, 1948, HHA, 5-20.5(a).

the circle of decision-makers and among the pilots of the state, along with the suspicion that Ben-Gurion and Mapai had other ideas. He was gripped with anxiety that Mapai was sidling towards an alliance with the "reactionaries," as he called the General Zionists, the Progressives, and Mizraḥi, and not even ruling out cooperation with Ḥerut.[68] His fear that Mapam would be left high and dry was so great that six months before the elections he imagined an extreme scenario in which Mapai invited the Communists and Ḥerut to join the government after the elections in order to stifle Mapam's revolutionary and pioneer forces.[69]

Even before President Chaim Weizmann asked Ben-Gurion to form a Government, a full month after the election (February 24, 1949), Mapam submitted its coalition proposal to Mapai. Its starting point was that the Government should be based on foreign and domestic policy lines agreed to by Mapai and Mapam, who together held a majority in the Constituent Assembly (65 of the 120 seats). On the basis of this program, other factions of a democratic and progressive nature would be invited to join the coalition in order to expand its parliamentary base and bolster its stability.[70] In the way of the world, the first approach dealt with matters of substance and did not mention the portfolios the party wanted to receive. But was the issue of ministries what ultimately left Mapam outside the government?

Although Mapam expected the first agreement to be signed between itself and Mapai, after which other parties that might want to join and met certain criteria would be invited in, what actually happened was just the opposite. The main player in the negotiations was Ben-Gurion. He held the cards, and he frequently held them very close to his chest. He broadcast contradictory messages that sowed confusion among those seated across the negotiating table and have left historians debating the strength of his desire to have Mapam in the Government and the reasons for the failure of the negotiations between the two parties. All agree that it is impossible to explain the

---

68 *Ve'idat ha-iḥud*, pp. 13, 15–16.
69 Yaari to [Ya'akov] Majus and Levi [Greenblatt], June 21, 1948, HHA, 95-7.11(3).
70 To the Central Committee of the Eretz Israel Workers' Party [Mapai; no signature], Feb. 16, 1949, HHA, 95-7.29(6).

conduct of the negotiations, and especially their outcome, on purely logical grounds.

In a radio broadcast a few days after the election (January 29, 1949), Ben-Gurion proclaimed his desire to form a Government with a majority drawn from the two workers' parties. He opened the door for Mapam to join the coalition, on condition that it accept collective responsibility and stop attacking the government in which it was then sitting (the Provisional Government).[71] During the negotiations, he repeated that he preferred a government with Mapai and Mapam at its center and wanted to base the country on socialist foundations. But at the same time, he signaled clearly that he did not attach great importance to Mapam's participation in the Government and left the impression that he had resolved to leave it in the opposition. He conducted the negotiations with a certain brutality that created a harsh atmosphere, and it was clear that he wanted to strip Mapam of its legitimacy.[72] Mapam's negotiators felt that they were running into a brick wall.[73]

The discussion of the portfolios that Mapam would receive began only after Ben-Gurion had assigned ministries to the Progressives and to the religious parties. The controversy between Mapai and Mapam was not over the number of portfolios it would receive (three), but over which ones. Ben-Gurion offered Agriculture, Housing, and Health, while Mapam demanded three of five key portfolios—Agriculture, Education, Labor, Interior, and Defense—with a director general from the party in the two ministries that it did not receive. But the disagreement was not only about portfolios and extended to matters of foreign policy, the military, and coalition discipline.[74]

The discussion that follows, with its focus on Yaari's role in the negotiations and how he perceived them, offers another interpretation for Mapam's banishment to the sidelines. Of course, like all historians,

---

71 Tzahor, "The Establishment of the First Government," 387.
72 Tzur, *Nofei ha-ashlayah*, 95; Anita Shapira, "Lineaments of the leftward drift," 217.
73 Yaari, "Enemy-of-the-People: The Synthesis," *Al Hamishmar*, Mar. 20, 1953.
74 "Meeting on Tuesday, Mar. 1 [1949] at 3:15 PM," HHA, 90.41(4).

the present author can rely only on the written and accessible record and has no ability to probe the hearts and minds of the main actors. The documents do seem to indicate that Ben-Gurion was not interested in including Mapam in his government, and certainly not with the senior status appropriate to its weight as the second-largest faction in the Knesset. He did not trust its loyalty or the way it was run and disagreed with it on substantive issues. Yaari, by contrast, was almost desperate for Mapam to be on the inside. His statements ranged from "yes" in principle to "but" on substantive matters, and altered as time passed. At first, he demonstrated great flexibility on material issues; in the end, when it was clear that the negotiations had failed, he clung stubbornly to principles.

On February 28, 1949, Yaari defined the possibility that Mapam might not enter the government as a "catastrophe," because a coalition between Mapai and the right meant that Mapam would be relegated to the opposition along with Ḥerut. But he did not want Mapam to join the Government on humiliating terms. His conclusion from Ben-Gurion's proposal was that the party should give up the idea of sitting at the cabinet table.[75] It was very important for the public to know that Mapai was to blame for Mapam's relegation to the opposition. Furthermore, were the negotiations to fail, Yaari wanted it to be for a reason that the public would understand. This made it preferable to blow up the negotiations over a policy issue rather than the distribution of portfolios. And a final tactical point: he would prefer to enter the Government and then quit it for persuasive political reasons rather than not join it at the outset.[76]

On March 1, Yaari participated in the talks with the Mapai negotiators, including Ben-Gurion, and again expressed his interest in joining the Government. It would be a tragedy if his party, with all its accomplishments in the fields of defense and settlement, was not part of the Government. All the same, "we will not enter this Government humiliated.... But neither do we pursue [sitting in] the opposition for

---

75 Mapam Political Committee, Feb. 28, 1949, HHA, 90.66(1).
76 Mapam Political Committee, Mar. 1, 1949, Mar. 2, 1949, Ibid.

its own sake."⁷⁷ In the end, despite his strong desire for his party to join the government, Yaari insisted on defending its honor. The next day's meeting doomed the negotiations to failure. Yaari was there, but the last word was spoken by his colleague Yitzhak Ben-Aharon: "The division of portfolios you are proposing," Ben-Aharon told the Mapai team, "is incompatible with the principle of partnership, comradeship, and influence that Ben-Gurion, too, sees as conditions for our presence in the Government. Keeping us out of the Government is the worst thing you have ever done in the history of our mutual relations. It must come between us. Goodbye."⁷⁸

That same day, the Mapam Council discussed the situation of the coalition talks. Yaari and Hazan were present but did not ask for the floor, until, finally, Nehemiah Rabin proposed "adjourning now and continuing tomorrow." Hazan did not agree: "We will keep arguing until three in the morning and then we'll decide." Yaari disagreed: "It isn't democratic to vote like corpses. I move to end the debate." The resolution on the floor, "we will not enter the Government on the terms offered," passed by a vote of 150 to 33.⁷⁹ The next day, a laconic letter was sent to Ben-Gurion, over the signatures of Yitzhak Ben-Aharon and Ya'akov Riftin: "The Council of the United Workers' Party has decided not to enter the Government on the terms offered."⁸⁰

Various hypotheses can be floated to explain the failure of the negotiations. It was because of Ben-Gurion's calculated preference for an alliance with the religious parties. It was rooted in Mapam's pro-Soviet orientation, and Ben-Gurion, who had decided from the outset to leave it out of the coalition, for considerations of foreign policy, conducted the negotiations only for the sake of the record. Perhaps it was simply the dynamics of the coalition talks, marked by misunderstandings and failures of communication. Or was it Ben-Gurion's impatience—another 24 hours and the parties would have found the middle ground? And perhaps the answer is there in Yaari's

---

77 "Meeting on Tuesday, Mar. 1 [1949] at 3.15 PM," HHA, 90.41(4).
78 "Meeting on Wednesday, Mar. 2 [1949]," ibid.
79 Mapam Council, Mar. 2, 1949, HHA, 90.66(1*aleph*).
80 HHA, 90.59(3).

gloomy prediction, in early 1948, that Mapai was headed for an alliance with the "reactionaries"—not knowing just how right he would prove to be. The conclusion proposed here is that the negotiations between Mapai and Mapam were foredoomed to failure because a Government dominated by the two workers' parties ran counter to the path of "from a class to a nation," which Ben-Gurion had pursued since the early 1930s, as the leader of Mapai and the Histadrut, and which culminated in his doctrine of *mamlakhtiyut*—placing the state above partisan, ideological, sectoral, and tribal considerations. Another reason for leaving Mapam out of the government was to catalyze its decline by unplugging it from the source of power and action.[81]

In addition to these reasons, the consensus among historians is that Mapam's positions, demands, and conduct of the talks, were affected by its feelings of frustration, anger, humiliation, and bitterness, as well as by considerations of self-esteem. Several more points should be made about its negotiating method. Firstly, Mapam was a young party based on maintaining the delicate equilibrium between its factions, roiled by internal distrust, and had no formal processes for making fateful decisions of the magnitude it faced in late February and early March 1949. Second, whereas Mapai's negotiators were canny veterans, Mapam's representatives were much less experienced. To lock horns with Ben-Gurion, Ziama Aharonowitz (Zalman Aranne) and Pinhas Lubianiker (Lavon), Mapam sent Ben-Aaron and Riftin, who were not of comparable rank in their own party. Yaari attended only a few of the meetings. Where was he the rest of the time? Where were Hazan and Tabenkin? Had the party prepared itself for this important hour? Perhaps its leaders, chiefly Yaari, who were used to negotiations within the movement, based on persuasion and decisions reached by consensus, were not sufficiently skilled in the political haggling required to assemble a coalition.

The first elected Government of Israel was composed of Mapai, the United Religious Front, and the Progressives. Mapam was left on the sidelines—and "the rest is history." Even though historians prefer not to amuse themselves with hypothetical scenarios—and some steer

---

81 Miron, *Ḥaluqqah meḥudeshet shel ha-zirah ha-politit*, 8, 80, 417–420.

totally clear of them—it is hard to avoid wondering what sort of country Israel would have become had Mapam served in the first Government, which would have been socialist through and through. Whether it was a conscious and deliberate decision by Ben-Gurion, made in advance, or whether it was the Mapam Council, in a fit of pique, that closed off the possibility, all agree that the make-up of the first Government effectively shaped the country for years to come.

To remain in the realm of the hypothetical: Based on the precedent of the Provisional Government and the arrangement instituted by Mapam after it finally joined the coalition in 1955, Yaari would not have been a cabinet minister even had it sat in the Government in 1949. The change in his status after the 1949 elections was limited to his becoming a rank-and-file member of the Knesset. Even though he served in the house for 25 years, he was never a real "parliamentarian" and the Knesset was not his finest arena. He spoke infrequently in the plenum and knew that Hazan—recognized as one of the most brilliant orators there—far surpassed him. In fact, Yaari never delivered a memorable speech in the Knesset and was not known for his interruptions from the floor.[82] Although he acknowledged the serious responsibilities of his parliamentary membership, he tried to avoid serving on committees and was not assigned to any of the important committees in the first two Knessets.[83]

The Knesset's move from Tel Aviv to Jerusalem in late 1949 forced him to reorganize his life. He lived in three apartments—in Merḥavia, in Tel Aviv, and in Jerusalem—dividing his time among his roles in Kibbutz Artzi, the party, and the Knesset. His visits to the cafeteria—the beating heart of the Knesset—were infrequent and he rarely ate there. Instead, he made do with a cheese sandwich (eschewing meat to keep his expenses down). He used the money he saved to furnish his apartment in Tel Aviv.[84] Just as he made a minimal impact on the Knesset, his tenure as a backbencher was marginal in the overall scheme of his public activities and was not a key element in his career.

---

82 Yaari, "Memoirs," 47, KMA, MYF, 8 (3).
83 Yaari to Mordechai [Oren], Mar. 20, 1949, HHA, 95-7.11(3); Yaari to Yehuda Tubin, Jan. 15, 1950, HHA, 95-7.12(2).
84 Yaari to Dov Peleg, Mar. 12, 1984, HHA, 95-7.23(7).

A few days after the coalition negotiations ended, while Mapam was still licking its wounds, MK Meir Yaari made a few sharp observations in the Knesset plenum, in a painful settling of accounts. He castigated Mapai that its pact with the center and rightwing parties "violated the trust of those who, with their bodies and without proper equipment, managed to block the Egyptian invader's assault on Tel Aviv at Negba and Yad Mordechai, at Revivim and Nirim, along with units of the Palmach and the Israel Defense Forces that were under the command of our comrades." He added: "This is a Government that has betrayed the commanders of the ghetto uprisings and the *Exodus 1947*, those who piloted the clandestine immigrant ships and those suppressed the *Altalena* insurrection."[85] The speech oozes with the accumulated humiliation of the failed coalition negotiations, the chagrin of the man who had confidently predicted "they won't be able to manage without us," of the head of a party that had marched out with the feeling that it was the essential vanguard but was now totally helpless, reduced so quickly to a fifth wheel in the emerging Israel. The next day, Hazan delivered his "second homeland" speech in the Knesset, remembered for its support and adulation of the Soviet Union.[86] What role Mapam's pro-Soviet line played in its exclusion from the Government remains an unsettled question, but all agree that its relegation to the opposition made its pro-Soviet orientation more extreme.

---

85 Yaari, *Al Hamishmar*, Mar. 9, 1949. In June 1948, there was a clash on the Tel Aviv waterfront between the *Altalena*, a ship belonging to the Irgun (Etzel), loaded with weapons and fighters, and the IDF. After the commanders of the *Altalena* refused to surrender and hand over the cargo, the IDF shelled and sank it. The incident is considered a milestone in the consolidation of the unified army of the new state, operating under the sole authority of the democratically elected civilian institutions.
86 Tzahor, *Hazan*, p. 192; and see further in the next chapter.

Yaari with his partner to the "historic leadership" of Hasomer Hatza'ir, Yaakov Hazan.
Courtesy of Hashomer Hatza'ir Archive, Givat Haviva.

CHAPTER 12

Unrequited Love

In the first years of Israeli independence, Yaari had to steer his course between the shoals of ideological and theoretical topics, on the one hand, and existential issues, on the other. At the same time he needed to maneuver cautiously among ideas, individuals, and groups, while constantly on the *qui vive* to defend his status as the leader of the recently established enlarged party and of his longtime movement, with Aḥdut Ha'avodah on the right flank and the Leftists on the other. Multiple crises occurred, at the same time and in succession. While he was still fighting on one front, a new one opened, sometimes internally and sometimes against the outside world—sometimes on both simultaneously. In December 1949, Yaari shared his feeling of the burden on his shoulders with a movement emissary abroad. "You must understand," he wrote, "that in addition to Kibbutz Artzi, the party, the Knesset, the Youth Movement, and the Peace Committee, I have to show many people due consideration, notice, and even attention."[1]

A leader with his finger in every pie, Yaari saw himself as responsible for all facets of the movement's activity and for much of what its members did. Many of them, in turn, expected him to provide them with guidance on every matter. Some listened to his words with bated breath, ready to follow him with their eyes shut; others complained that "his logic is lame; he is as full of prejudices as a pomegranate is of seeds; he does not distinguish between law and legend; he is drowning in a sea of illusions."[2] In addition to abundant leadership skills, he had to demonstrate intellectual prowess as well, an area in which he was

---

1 Yaari to Yehuda [?], Dec. 5, 1949, HHA, 95-7.10(11).
2 Eliyahu Porat, "Profile of Meir Yaari," *Yedioth Aḥronoth*, Feb. 18, 1954.

surrounded by many brilliant comrades, blessed with fine minds and oratorical powers, some as writers, some as speakers, and some in both domains. He devoted much thought to ideological issues but never expounded ideology for its own sake in his writing. His words were intended to curb what he considered to be the negative influences of the ideologies preached by others and an attempt to keep such ideas and their advocates from pulling the movement in inappropriate directions. He endeavored to crystallize an ideology suited to the spirit of the age, one that could serve as a unifying myth, interpret and explain current events, reconcile contradictions, and provide the comrades with answers to their questions and to the arguments hurled at Mapam from the outside. He employed devious Marxist formulations to counter the Leftists with their own ammunition and show them that he was no lightweight in their own field. Deep in his heart he hoped to be recognized as a serious thinker and was hurt when Tabenkin made it clear that he was not all that impressed by his ideological prowess.[3]

In those years, Yaari was one of the leaders of a political party that found itself excluded from the circles of government responsibility, even though its members and kibbutzim had withstood the supreme test during the War of Independence and Yaari fervently believed that it should share the burden in peacetime as well. The magnitude of their hopes and expectations was in direct proportion to the depths of their disappointment and frustration, and broke through in Hazan's statement in the Knesset, soon after the new government had been presented in March 1949. "For us," he said, "the Soviet Union is the stronghold of world socialism. It is our second, socialist homeland."[4] Yaari reacted by putting his head in his hands. "Why did he have to say that?" he mumbled (in Yiddish).[5] After March 1949, expressions of support for the Soviet Union by the two leaders helped to console both the rank-and-file and leadership for the pain of relegation to the opposition benches.

---

3 Letter to Tabenkin [1954?] with no complimentary close or signature and which may never have been sent, HHA, 95-7.30(6).
4 Tzahor, *Hazan*, 92.
5 Ibid.

The attitude towards the Soviet Union had been an important catalyst for the rapprochement and merger between Hashomer Hatza'ir and Aḥdut Ha'avodah. In fact, however, they never really saw eye to eye on this matter and the gulf between them only widened as time passed. The members of Hakibbutz Hame'uḥad and Aḥdut Ha'avodah had an essentially emotional attachment to the Soviet Union. They were captivated by its revolutionary romanticism and swooned at the triumphs of the Red Army; they took the country as a source of inspiration but not as a model for imitation. By contrast, the members of KA and the former Hashomer Hatza'ir party assigned great importance to both the ideological element and the way in which the Soviet Union was implementing Marxism. Some also thought of it as the high command of the world revolution, whose orders must be followed, and believed that Mapam should have a centralized structure, as would be appropriate for a revolutionary Communist party.

The Soviet Union's role in the annals of the merged Mapam played out on multiple levels. Internally, it began as a unifying element that over time turned into a destructive factor. For the outside world, the Leftward drift attached a stigma to the entire party. Yaari wanted to reinforce the positive aspects of the bond to the Soviet Union and curtail its negative influences. He frequently expressed his admiration for that country and its accomplishments and held it up as a model, to the point of sometimes being carried away in his praise and adulation.

The special affinity for the Soviet Union was Mapam's distinguishing feature during the first years of the state, just as it had been for Hashomer Hatza'ir during the Mandate. Now, as then, Yaari and others presented it as an obstacle to merger with Mapai, especially to divert the wind blowing in that direction in the Aḥdut Ha'avodah faction of the merged party. Yaari cultivated the attachment to the Soviet Union (and this applies especially to the Hashomer faction of Mapam) as a way to compensate for or cover up the deferral of the transition to the revolutionary phase, which, according to a possible interpretation of the theory of stages or *étapes* incorporated into the Kibbutz Artzi platform in 1927, was supposed to have begun with the establishment of the state. Identification with the worldwide revolution was intended to serve as a substitute for the delay in the transition from the national/pioneering stage of Socialist Zionism to the Socialist revolutionary stage and to immunize the party against those who were forcing matters in their hurry to reach the world of tomorrow. Promoting a positive attitude towards the Soviet Union was also a way to entrench his status as leader.

The transition from Yishuv to independent state altered the bond to the Soviet Union. Before 1948, the Soviet Union served as a symbol, a role model, and the object of inchoate desires. After 1948, however, the pro-Soviet posture took on political implications as well, inasmuch as it was now an issue in Israeli foreign relations and domestic politics. An opposition party that was looking for a banner issue found it convenient to cast the country's international orientation in that role, because it did not require any real action on its part. As is the way of politics, however, things did not develop as intended or expected, and Mapam's allegiance to the Soviet Union harmed its prospects of inclusion in the government, fostering a certain internal radicalization. Yaari's stand on the Soviet Union coalesced as a result of processes within the movement more than as a response to developments in that country or its attitude towards Israel and Zionism.

When Mapam was formed, in early 1948, its identification with the Soviet Union made good sense. The Soviet Union had many fine points, from both the international and Zionist perspectives: the refuge it had provided to hundreds of thousands of Jews who fled the Nazi occupation during the Second World War, the valor displayed at Stalingrad, its role in the victory over Germany, its liberation of the concentration and death camps in Eastern Europe, its decisive contribution to the passage of the partition resolution by the United Nations, and its contribution to Israel's victory in the War of Independence through the weapons provided by Czechoslovakia (with Soviet consent, of course). In a broader perspective, the territorial spread of Communism after the Second World War painted the Soviet Union and the Communist bloc it headed as the rising and victorious force in the postwar era. Political logic required supporting it in the emerging East-West conflict and the Cold War, which was becoming more acute just then. In those circumstances, Yaari made political hay out of the sterling qualities of the Soviet Union to boost his party's fortunes, standing vigilant lest Mapam be deprived of its rightful credit (in his eyes) for that country's support for Zionism, the product of Hashomer Hatza'ir's many years of sympathy for the country of emerging socialism. It was not the Biltmore Program of 1942, which Hashomer Hatza'ir had opposed, or Mapai's efforts to win statehood by means of an alliance with Churchill that had brought Israel into being, declared Yaari in late 1948; the state had been achieved thanks to the alliance with Stalin.[6] In the brief period when the Soviet Union took a friendly position towards Zionism and Israel and it seemed to be a given that Israel would adopt a pro-Soviet orientation, Yaari endeavored to ensure Mapam's role as the bridge between the two countries. Here the great rival was Maki, the Israel Communist Party, which he had in his sights when declaring in no uncertain terms that *"we are the address [for contacts with the Soviet Union] and we will lead the revolution."*[7]

In Mapam's first year, the Soviet Union was the friendliest of the world powers towards the emergent and newborn state, at a time when the Western powers' attitude towards independence for the Jews varied from British hostility to American hesitation. By the time Mapam found itself in the opposition and took the pro-Soviet line as its trademark, the Kremlin's attitude towards Israel was already tepid if not actually chilly. The relations between the two countries took a further turn for the worse in October 1950, when Israel—abandoning its official neutrality—aligned itself with the United States in the Korean War. Yaari wavered between justification of the increasing Soviet hostility towards Israel and blaming it on the one-sided Israeli policy orchestrated by Mapai, on the one hand, and criticism of the Soviet Union's cold attitude towards Israel in general and Mapam in particular.

Yaari remained steadfast in his admiration for the Soviet Union despite the deterioration in its attitude towards Israel. He and other

---

6 27th Kibbutz Artzi Council Dec. 12, 1948, HHA, 95-7.29(3).
7 Political Committee, Mar. 25, 1948, HHA, 90.66(1).

members of the party were certain that a Third World War was just around the corner and that the Soviet Union would come out on top, becoming the dominant power in the Middle East. With such expectations, it was a short way towards a stronger pro-Soviet line and the hope of being an integral part of the revolutionary forces. Some members of Mapam truly and sincerely believed that the Soviet Union and Zionism had common interests and acted in the clear knowledge and deep conviction that Zionism's future depended on its finding its place in the revolutionary world. They were gripped by Moshe Sneh's prediction that Israel's inclusion in the Soviet bloc "is not a matter for the messianic age"; rather, "there will be a war and the Soviet Army will advance to the outskirts of Israel. And then [we, the leaders of Mapam] will send them a cable that we are here."[8] According to Sneh, "finding our place in the revolutionary camp that is marching towards victory" was the only way to save Zionism and the State of Israel.[9] In order to fulfill its historic vocation, Mapam must be ready and prepared for that world war and for the worldwide revolution in whose course it, Mapam, in concert with the victorious Red Army, would install a new regime in Israel.

In their mind's eye, members of KA who shared this line envisioned that when the revolutionary army reached the borders of Israel it would hand over control of the country to a revolutionary party with deep roots among its people—both Jews and Arabs—and this would be Mapam (not Maki). In 1949, Aharon Cohen, considered to be an expert on the Arab world, prophesied that within three years there would be revolutions in the neighboring countries and the Red Army would be stationed on Israel's borders.[10] A story made the rounds that, in reaction to such predictions, some members of Mapam applied to join kibbutzim in northern Israel so they would be among the first to greet the Red Army when it entered the country.[11] They imagined the joy of hosting Comrade Stalin on their kibbutz, taking him on a tour

---

8 Sneh to the Mapam Council, November 27-29, 1949, UKA, 13/*yod*/2.
9 Ibid.
10 Yaari to Yosef Waschitz, Dec. 4, 1955; Yaari to Aharon Cohen, Dec. 16, 1955, HHA, 95-7.14(1).
11 Shapira, "Lineaments of the leftward drift," 224.

of its agricultural branches, and sitting around him in the evening on the grass and hearing him say that the kibbutz was a more successful realization of Marxism than anything in the Soviet Union.[12]

The sympathy for and even worship of the Soviet Union, which came very close to indoctrination and went as far as hanging pictures of Stalin on the walls of the children's houses (or is this too only a myth?) surged in Hakibbutz Hame'uḥad too and was one of the reasons it split in 1951. "If they wake me up at two in the morning I say, 'an inseparable part of the revolutionary world, with the Soviet Union at its head,'" confessed a young man from Kibbutz Beit Hashitah (affiliated with Hakibbutz Hame'uḥad).[13] Yaari's emphasis on close ties with the Soviet Union was not just a way to shape the minds of party members, but also a response to what many of them desired.

In those years, the Soviet Union and related topics tripped off of Yaari's tongue almost automatically, as if they were a natural and obvious part of his public's universe of associations. In May 1948, for instance, he observed that the movement's kibbutzim then under Arab attack "are little Stalingrads."[14] When an author complained that his kibbutz was demanding that he make himself available for the work roster, Yaari replied: "It seems to me that in the Soviet Union and other countries writers, too, are sometimes conscripted to provide assistance to the rural sector."[15] In 1949, China became another source of inspiration; as an advocate of the "long road," Yaari took the example of that country to support his demand for patience and not trying to rush the revolution. That was the lesson to be learned from the Long March of the Chinese Communist Army, led by Mao Zedong, which lasted for decades before reaching its destined hour of triumph.[16]

But there were limits to the adulation of the Soviet Union. Despite all the tributes and praise for it, and the hopes for a change in its attitude

---

12 Tzahor, *Hazan*, 214.
13 Tzur, *Nofei ha-ashlayah*, 211.
14 Histadrut Executive Committee, May 27, 1948, LA.
15 Yaari to Zvi Arad, Dec. 20, 1953, HHA, 95-7.13(6).
16 Yaari at the anniversary council of Kibbutz Artzi, Oct. 3-5, 1952, HHA, 5-20. aleph-6(1).

towards Israel and Mapam, Yaari never took leave of his senses or gave way to uncritical worship. He never stopped deploring its unfavorable attitude towards Zionism and the Jewish aspect of the national question. In early 1953 he was sufficiently clear-sighted to call attention to a spate of anti-Zionist articles in the Soviet press and other manifestations of anti-Zionism, all of which predated Israel's abandonment of official neutrality.[17] What is more, he uncompromisingly defended Mapam's ideological independence and was adamant that it must not become a Soviet puppet. Even during the honeymoon between the Soviet Union and Zionism he reiterated that "we are Zionists first of all and it is in a Zionist context that we will implement Communism."[18] Mapam, he said unambiguously, could not accept dictates from the outside. His opponents' quip, "when it rains in Moscow they open umbrellas in Merhavia," was not fair to Yaari's attitude about the Soviet Union.

The love affair between Hashomer Hatza'ir and the Soviet Union was a one-way romance. It was not even a case of disappointed love; there have to be two partners for that. In 1949 Yaari lamented, "we proclaim our identification with the forces of tomorrow, but those forces refuse to identify with us."[19] Five years later he expressed his disappointment that the revolutionary world "does not recognize us"—a double disappointment, both with the Soviet Union's attitude towards the State of Israel and with its refusal to see Mapam as its correspondent party in the country.[20] And in 1956 he painfully confessed that "the revolutionary forces have not pampered us."[21]

Both Yaari and Hazan fostered the bond with the Soviet Union primarily as a means to consolidate ranks within the movement and to create a united front against external political forces. But like a genie, once out of the bottle this tie posed an ideological peril and, still worse, an organizational danger, threatening Yaari and Hazan's authority and

---

17 Yaari, *Al Hamishmar*, Jan. 9, 1953.
18 Political Committee, Mar. 25, 1948; July 20, 1948, HHA, 90.66(1).
19 Yaari to [Ya'akov] Majus, Mar. 15, 1949, HHA, 95-7.11(3).
20 Kibbutz Artzi Executive Committee, Jan. 27, 1954, HHA, 5-10.6(11).
21 Joint session of the Kibbutz Artzi Executive Committee and the Mapam Central Committee at Mizra, May 17, 1956, to mark Mordecai Oren's release from prison in Prague, HHA, 5-10.6 (4).

position at the head of the movement. Yaari had to maneuver between the advantages of using the Soviet Union as a myth to rally his troops and the threat of overblown adulation and extreme leftism, which might end with abandoning the Zionist camp and blackening Mapam's name. Originally, mainly in 1948, the Soviet support for Zionism and Israel had produced sympathy for it; but the later manifestations of hostility towards Zionism, Israel, and Mapam forced Yaari to engage in acrobatics of political and educational guidance.

Then, on April 30, 1950, "Communism and Us," by Yaakov Riftin, resounded like a thunder clap on a clear day. The article, published in the festive May Day edition of the party newspaper *Al Hamishmar*, was strewn end to end with potential landmines, doctrinal and ideological as well as practical and organizational. To begin with, its very publication without the leadership's approval or advance knowledge generated serious friction within the party. It was clear to Yaari that no one in the other factions of Mapam believed that it had gone to press behind the backs of the leaders of Hashomer Hatza'ir. His fury at Riftin was redoubled because, despite the explicit prohibition against washing dirty linen in public, the article trumpeted the existence of internal disputes within Mapam on three issues: its structure, the admission of Arab members, and the attitude towards the Communist camp.[22]

The article caused Yaari a major headache not only because of what it said but also and no less because of what it did not say. On the first front, he was troubled by Riftin's assertion that Marxism-Leninism must be "the firm foundation of all of our educational and information activities and an inalienable possession of all our activists."[23] On the second front, there was not a single reference to Zionism. This combination added up, even if only implicitly, to assigning primacy to Marxism-Leninism and relegating Zionism to the margins. Riftin's total neglect of the national aspect, his focus on Marxism-Leninism, and his declaration that the time had come for the revolutionary phase—each point by itself, and certainly all of them together, threatened to nullify

---

22 Yaari to Zvi [Lurie], July 8, 1950, HHA, 95-7.12(2).
23 Riftin, *Al Hamishmar*, Apr. 30, 1950.

the substance and purpose of the doctrine of stages as formulated by Yaari. According to Riftin, the national stage had been completed and the revolutionary phase had arrived; consequently, Mapam had to be a revolutionary party, unified, selective, and centralized. And, he added, "the revolutionary party *must* from time to time purge its ranks, without showing mercy to regular members and their leaders, if this is essential for carrying out the revolutionary mission."[24] The threat to the leaders was there for all to see.

Riftin's statements did not fit in with how Hashomer Hatza'ir was supposed to operate. Ever since its birth, KA had been beset by the friction between the tradition of humanistic socialism that was the core of the Hashomer Hatza'ir youth movement—which emphasized the social group, and education—and the revolutionary Marxism that Yaari infused into the KA ideology. Revolutionary Marxism always harbored a latent danger of radicalization and of the adoption of a conceptual universe alien to the humanism of Hashomer Hatza'ir. Along came Riftin's article, with its call for a purge of members and leaders, and made this danger only too tangible.

The threat to Yaari's position implied by the article, and by Riftin's activities in general, was plain. Riftin had already informed Yaari that the era of the veteran two-man leadership was over and that he (Riftin) deserved to be elevated to a senior position, perhaps even outranking Hazan; he went so far as to propose a new leadership quartet of Yaari, Hazan, Riftin, and Sneh.[25] Yaari was terrified by this direct challenge to his status and by the fact he and Hazan were no longer masters in their own house. He feared that, in Mapai's perception of Mapam, there was only Riftin and Sneh at one extreme and Tabenkin and Galili at the other, while he and Hazan had become invisible.[26] Thus he was geometrically in his favorite situation, between Left and Right, only now that was a sort of vacuum. In addition, on more than one occasion he found himself in an unaccustomed place, the minority, while his

---

24 Emphasis in the original. Ibid.
25 Hazan to Yaari, Nov. 14, 1965, HHA, 95-7.20(1).
26 Yaari to Zvi [Lurie], July 8, 1950, HHA, 95-7.12(2).

rivals—Riftin, Sneh, and others—attracted more votes for their stands on various issues.

In the early 1950s Yaari suffered from various ailments, medical problems, and general poor health, augmenting the emotional stress to which he was prey in any case and making him even more sensitive about his status, authority, and treatment by his flock. During his long sojourns in hospitals, rest homes, sanatoria, and spas, both in Israel and abroad, he endeavored to remain in contact with his comrades and to pull strings from a distance. In early 1951 he was hospitalized for complications from pneumonia. After that he spent time in a sanatorium on Mount Carmel, and then traveled to Geneva for treatment of his eyes, which were getting worse.[27] The heavy medical expenses forced him to request financial assistance from his kibbutz. The outlays were even greater because Yaari's wife accompanied him when he went abroad. Requesting additional funds so that Anda could join him made Yaari uneasy, but he realized that he could not take care of himself and required her presence.[28] In letters to various correspondents he spared few details about his ailments and the tests he underwent, linking the deterioration of his health to his exhausting efforts on behalf of the movement. He also hinted, alleging his doctors' advice, that people should be more sensitive about his condition and not aggravate him.[29]

Particularly difficult was an ophthalmologic condition that caused him to be "literally half-blind."[30] His physicians forbade him to read and write. When the situation worsened, he and Anda returned to Switzerland in August 1953 to consult with Professor Goldman, a well-known expert.[31] Yaari's ailments frightened him to death. In early 1952 he felt that he was "on his deathbed"; because his parents had died at around the age he was then, Yaari sometimes entertained the feeling

---

27 Yaari to Kibbutz Gat, Mar. 22, 1951, HHA, 95-7.12(6); Yaari to Kibbutz Artzi Secretariat, Oct. 24, 1951, HHA, heh-3.66(1).
28 Meir to "Dear Comrades" [Kibbutz Merhavia], Oct. 23, 1951, KMA, MYF, 1(3).
29 Yaari to Kibbutz Artzi Secretariat, Oct. 24, 1951, HHA, heh-3.66(1); Yaari to Bunim [Shamir], Apr. 19, 1953, HHA, 95-7.13(2); Yaari to Rafi Cohen, Apr. 20, 1963, HHA, 95-7.1(5).
30 Anda and Meir to "Dear Comrades," Sept. 9 [1953], KMA, MYF, 2(1).
31 Ibid.

that "my life is sort of a windfall, a sort of free ride."[32] In the summer of 1954, a journalist described him as "suffering an eye ailment that almost prevents him from reading, but he is still marked by a young voice and a very strong power to act."[33]

Meanwhile, despite the expectations that the Unity Convention (January 1948) would resolve all the issues in dispute and the separate factions within Mapam would be dissolved, what happened was just the opposite: the factions grew stronger and threatened to paralyze the party. Mapam was established on the basis of parity between its main components, Aḥdut Ha'avodah and Hashomer Hatza'ir, with lesser representation for the junior partner, Po'alei Ẓiyyon Left. In practice, it was more like a federation of five groups, the three parties (or two and a half parties) plus the two kibbutz movements. This was a structure whose very nature doomed it to failure. The formal parity within Mapam institutions did not reflect the situation on the ground. In mid-1949 it had 27,000 card-carrying members, 16,000 of them affiliated with the Hashomer Hatza'ir faction.[34] But this numerical advantage did not give KA and the former Hashomer Hatza'ir party a leg up in internal votes. The mismatch between the formal parity and the actual balance of forces threw a spoke into Mapam's wheels. In late 1950, trying to overcome the problem, members of the Hashomer Hatza'ir faction, mainly from the left wing of KA, established the "Party Unity Front." Yaari and Hazan, too, were involved in the initiative, whose goal was to allow the Hashomer Hatza'ir faction, and chiefly KA, to assert control over the party by abolishing the veto that the parity arrangement gave Aḥdut Ha'avodah. But the monster soon turned on its creator; within a short time the historical leadership of Hashomer Hatza'ir found itself facing a Leftist rebellion spearheaded by the Unity Front, which had joined forces with Moshe Sneh.

With this intricate and contentious balance of internal forces, the second Mapam convention opened at the Amphitheater movie house

---

32　Meir to Bunim Shamir, Feb. 4, 1952; Yaari to Bunim [Shamir], May 4, 1952, HHA, 95-7.13(2).
33　"Why is Mapam Splitting?" *Ha'olam Hazeh*, July 15, 1954.
34　Tzur, *Nofei ha-ashlayah*, 109.

in Haifa on May 30, 1951. That was where the Hashomer Hatza'ir party had been founded five years earlier—but what a difference there was! There may have been some symbolism in the fact that unlike the two founding conventions, first of the Hashomer Hatza'ir party and then of Mapam, both of which opened on a Friday evening—a time whose very nature added a festive element to the gathering—this one convened on a weeknight. The high spirits of 1946 and 1948 gave way to interruptions from the floor and heckling of the speakers. Outside the movie house, Hakibbutz Hame'uḥad was on the verge of a split, and Israeli society was experiencing vast changes, mainly as the result of the mass immigration that had almost doubled the country's Jewish population since May 1948. In addition, the country was in a black mood following the clash with Syrian forces at Tel Muteila, north of the Sea of Galilee, in which, over the course of several days in early May, 41 soldiers were killed and more than 70 wounded. In the outside world, American prestige was on the rise as the tide of battle in Korea turned in its favor. A Soviet victory in a third World War no longer seemed to be guaranteed, and the worldwide revolution was farther away than ever. For more than a month it had been known that the Knesset elections would be held almost two years early, in July; to outside observers its seems that the party convention was taking place in a fantasy-world bubble. The delegates discussed internal party matters and ways to realize international socialism, utterly detached from what was actually happening in the country, the processes that were shaping Israeli society, and the issues that had led to the early elections: the education of immigrant children in the transit camps and the conscription of women to the IDF.[35]

After losing a Knesset vote about education policy in February, the Government had resigned and called for new elections. Looming in the background were the results of the municipal elections from the previous November, in which Mapai suffered a stunning defeat and the General Zionists almost matched its countrywide vote tally.

---

[35] The discussion here of the Second Mapam Convention is largely based on Ibid., 117–150.

But even though the Knesset elections were imminent, Mapam found itself embroiled in internal disputes and preparing for its convention. By the time the convention adjourned, on June 6, less than two months remained until election day. Unlike the situation two years earlier, Mapam was not Mapai's main challenger. This time it was the General Zionists who offered themselves as an alternative to the governing party. Domestic issues stood at the center of the campaign, notably the economic austerity policy, which the General Zionists attacked with the catchy slogan, "let the people live in this country."

All those aged 18 or over and residents of Israel as of March 1, 1951, were eligible to cast their ballot. Mainly due to the mass immigration, there were 924,885 names on the voter rolls, a huge increase from the 506,567 in 1949.[36] The altered composition of the population did not deprive Mapai of its plurality; but Mapam, which received 86,095 votes (up from 64,018 in 1949), won only 12.5% of the vote (down from 14.7%) and lost four Knesset seats (falling from 19 to 15). It was no longer the second-largest party in the Knesset, an honor taken by the General Zionists. Even though the latter, too, had contested the election from the opposition benches, they almost tripled their strength and won 20 Knesset seats (and, with their affiliated Sephardi and Yemenite lists, 23 seats).[37] In Yaari's analysis, Mapam's electoral failure could be attributed to the new immigrants, Arabs, and Tel Aviv; in the same breath he commended how the kibbutzim had rallied to the campaign.[38] But their actual contribution to Mapam's vote total was much less than that of urban voters and totally out of proportion to their representation on the Knesset list.

The coalition negotiations dragged on for more than two months. It was not until October 7, 1951, that Ben-Gurion presented his new government, based on the support of 65 Knesset members. Like the first government, its core consisted of Mapai and the religious parties, but

---

36 Israel Central Bureau of Statistics, *Statistical Abstract of Israel*, 2009, online at http://www1.cbs.gov.il/shnaton60/st10_01.pdf.
37 For details and results of Knesset elections (years, total votes, percentages), see http://www.knesset.gov.il/deSCRIPTion/eng/eng_mimshal_res.htm.
38 Kibbutz Artzi Executive Committee, Aug. 6–7, 1951, HHA, 5-10.5(15).

this time without the Progressives. Once again Mapam was excluded, its negotiations with Mapai having merely repeated those of two years before. Even though Yaari now occupied the first slot on the Knesset list (Tabenkin had renounced parliamentary activity during the term of the First Knesset), his involvement in the negotiations and his ability to influence their direction and outcome were even less than in 1949. He himself would have preferred for Mapam to join the coalition and play a role in the national mission of the ingathering of the exiles.[39] But Yaari had to maneuver between Tabenkin, who wanted to enter the Government at any cost, and the Leftwing of the party, which held uncompromisingly to the platform, adopted at the Haifa convention, which emphasized pioneering Zionism, Borochovism, and Marxism-Leninism, and brandished it to make it joining the Government impossible. As the summer passed it became clear that the Left was pulling the party in the direction it wanted and that Yaari could not reverse its course.

The full cost of this Leftward drift became apparent a year later, when, on December 23, 1952, Ben-Gurion presented a new Government, now incorporating the General Zionists (Agudat Yisrael having pulled out of the coalition), following negotiations to which, for the first time, Mapam was not even invited. In other words, by the end of 1952 Mapam was no longer deemed a potential candidate for seats at the Government table. Its hard Leftism, orchestrated by Riftin and Sneh, had relegated it to the status of permanent opposition, with no ability to exert real influence on the power centers and national decision-making process. As noted earlier, it cannot be stated categorically that the party's pro-Soviet orientation was the decisive factor in Mapam's failure to be included in the Government in 1949. It is certain, however, that the Leftward bent, which grew stronger while it sat on the opposition benches, tarnished Mapam and disqualified it for membership in the coalition in 1952.

How did Yaari conceive of Mapam's role and status in running the country? Did he see his party as an alternative to Mapai, a claimant to

---

39 Political Committee, Sept. 19, 1951, HHA, 90.66-*aleph*(1).

power, the leading candidate to replace it? Or did he see it as a corrective force, sitting in the Government alongside the larger workers' party and influencing its course in the right direction? Perhaps we should not understand things in their plain sense but follow the lead of Yaari, who distinguished between an alternative *path* and an alternative *force*, meaning that Mapam was an ideological alternative to Mapai but not an alternative ruling party.[40] Even those who believe that Mapam originally saw itself as a serious candidate to run the country agree that after the results of the first general elections in 1949, and especially after the voting patterns of the new immigrants emerged, the dream that Mapam could ever challenge Mapai for primacy vanished, even for those who had first toyed with the idea.

As for Yaari, it is doubtful that he ever succumbed to the dream of Mapam as an alternative, even during the short period between the party's formation in January 1948 and the publication of the election tallies a year later, because that option was essentially incompatible with his notion of the nature of his party and of himself as its leader. He never sought to be the leader of the entire nation and, more precisely, never presented himself as such. His statements and consistent desire to join a Government headed by Mapai lead to the conclusion that he saw Mapam as a corrective. The essence of his position over the years was that Mapam was neither an alternative ruling party nor an opposition on principle, but was willing, hoping, and even eager to sit alongside Mapai at the cabinet table (in a coalition based on a minimum negotiated program and the standard slogans, of course).[41]

In the meantime, while Mapam found itself treading water in the parliamentary opposition, the internal friction and debates intensified, putting Yaari's leadership and partnership with Hazan in jeopardy. Sneh's impact was so great that the public at large saw him as the leader of the Unity Front; even within the party the impression was that Yaari and Hazan's people were a minority in the party bureaucracy, which was controlled by those aligned with Riftin and Sneh. Feeling uncertain

---

40 Yaari, *Be-siman aḥdut ve-azma'ut*, 124–125; Yaacov Hurwitz, *Meir Yaari*, 65–96; Tzur, *Nofei ha-ashlayah*, 39.
41 Yaari, *Qibbuẓ galuyot*, 74–75.

about his ability to shape party decisions, Yaari began submitting issues for deliberation and decision by KA before they were referred to the party institutions. To guarantee the effectiveness of this majoritarian method, he tightened the screws of ideological collectivism in KA and represented it as the source of the movement's strength.[42]

In June 1952, the weekly *Ha'olam Hazeh* featured Yaari in its "Man of the Month" column, under the headline, "A Man Who Didn't Want a Political Party." The article reveals how those outside Mapam perceived him at the time. It was illustrated by a photograph of the dais at a large gathering of the Hashomer Hatza'ir youth movement—a scene that recalls the Kremlin balcony during a May Day or November 7 parade—with the caption, "A row of men stood on the dais. Prominent in the center was a short and stooped man, with a somewhat sickly appearance, an untrimmed mustache, and short bristly hair."[43] The article reviewed his biography since his Vienna days and proposed an explanation for the secret of his power: "Meir Yaari's special talent is somewhat like Joseph Stalin's—the ability to be moderate among the extremists and extreme among the moderates."[44]

When the article was published, it was already known that Mordechai Oren of Kibbutz Mizra, a prominent member of the Leftist clique in Mapam, had been arrested in Prague. Oren had attended the Congress of Labor Unions in East Berlin in December 1951. On December 24, while making his way back to Israel, he was arrested in Czechoslovakia and disappeared as if the Earth had swallowed him up. Only in early February 1952 did the Israeli press publicize the fact of his disappearance. *Al Hamishmar* did not refer to his arrest until March 24, after weeks of rumors, unconfirmed by any reliable source, that he was in jail in Prague.[45] Mapam officials were rebuffed when

---

42 Yaari at the Kibbutz Artzi 25th anniversary council, Oct. 3–5, 1952, HHA, 5-20. *aleph*-6(1).
43 "The Man of the Month: A Man who Didn't Want a Political Party,"*Ha'olam Hazeh*, June 5, 1952.
44 Ibid.
45 Yishai, "The vision and its lesson," 77. Also arrested with Oren was Shimon Orenstein, a businessman who had been the Israeli commercial attaché in Prague and was involved in the shipments of Czech arms to Israel during the War of Independence.

they made inquiries about his fate with the Czechoslovak legation in Tel Aviv.[46] During those weeks, the Prague authorities were preparing a show trial of the general secretary of the Czechoslovak Communist Party, Rudolph Slánský (who gave his name to the entire affair) and other government figures. They were charged with subversion against the regime, in a move that was part of the Soviet campaign against local leaders who Moscow feared might follow the example of Tito in Yugoslavia, that is, prefer their own country's interests over those of the Soviet Union and try to escape its orbit. Oren's chance presence in Czechoslovakia was a windfall for the case against the Slánský group. The prosecution's initial idea was to use him as a witness against them. Later, in a process that associated Zionism with other opponents of the regime in Czechoslovakia, Oren was accused of being an agent in a Zionist spy ring. Oren admitted to his involvement in espionage and sedition against Czechoslovakia, though it was clear that the confession had been extorted by means of psychological and physical pressure.

The members of the Slánský group were denounced as "traitors," "Trotskyites," "Titoists," "Zionists," "bourgeois" and as enemies of the Czechoslovak people, the popular democratic regime, and Socialism. They were accused of espionage, of planning to undermine the foundations of the regime, sabotage the development of the Socialist society, weaken the unity of the people, rupture the friendly relations between Czechoslovakia and the Soviet Union, restore Capitalism, and so on. In this context, the Zionist movement as a whole was accused of operating as a spy network in the service of Western Imperialism. The Czechoslovak Communist party daily highlighted the Jewish origins of 11 of the 14 defendants. An acrid odor of antisemitism permeated the entire affair. The trial began on November 20, 1952. It lasted for a week and had all the trappings of a show trial. The most important defendants, including Slánský and Foreign Minister Vladimir Clementis, were sentenced to death and hanged. Oren received a 15-year prison term.[47]

---

46 Patish, *Ha-siḥrur ve-ha-ivvaron*, 150.
47 Cotic, *The Prague Trial*.

Oren's trial in Prague dragged Mapam into the vortex of the conflict that swirled about its identification with the revolutionary world, Zionist faith, and loyalty to comrades. Sneh led the line of total identification with the revolutionary world, justifying every aspect of the Prague trial, even if this meant repudiating Zionism. Yaari took a firm stand against him and held unwaveringly to the primacy of Zionism. Sneh saw the Prague trial as just and the charges as true, whereas Yaari perceived it as another instance of classic antisemitism. Sneh expressed his full confidence in Communist justice, which he saw as outweighing Zionism, while Yaari viewed the trial as an attack on the Jewish people and their right to self-determination and on Zionism as a legitimate movement of national liberation. Having to choose between national solidarity and international solidarity, Yaari opted for the first and Sneh for the second.[48] Yaari denounced the case against Oren as blatant antisemitism but did not abandon his two-part affirmation that "we must take a stand of total loyalty with the socialist world and also defend Zionism faithfully."[49]

In this delicate situation, Yaari had to employ convoluted phrases that distinguished the absolute justice of Socialism, which he did not challenge, and its implementation in the specific case of Zionism, Mapam, and Mordechai Oren, which he rejected. The resolution he submitted to the party council was an enthusiastic vindication of Socialist justice until it touched home. He painted the Prague trial as marking a serious deterioration in the Communist bloc's attitude towards Zionism, but was certain that it was a passing crisis. His defense of Oren was total. But the bottom line was that "the United Workers' Party [Mapam] sees itself as an inseparable part of the revolutionary camp in the world, which is led by the Union of Soviet Socialist Republics."[50] Yaari walked a fine line between uncompromising defense of Zionism and the need to avoid an attack on Czechoslovak justice as long as Mordechai Oren remained in its clutches.

---

48 Mapam Political Committee, Nov. 19, 1952, HHA, 90.120(1).
49 Ibid.
50 "Proposal by Yaari," submitted to Eighth Mapam Council, Dec. 24–25, 1952, HHA, 95-7.12(10).

For Yaari, the decisive element in determining the party's stand on the Prague trial was the treatment of Mordechai Oren, and here he felt that Sneh had crossed a red line. Sneh sought a public acknowledgement that Oren had engaged in reprehensible activities; Yaari demanded total support for their colleague and put loyalty to comrades above all: "The world will stand or fall on our loyalty to a comrade who has served with us for many years. The comrade is in a situation of to be or not to be."[51] It can be alleged, of course, in light of the intense conflict then raging within Mapam, that Yaari's vigorous defense of Oren was intended as a way to attack Sneh and stake out a different position. It is almost certain that such considerations were not far from his mind, but they do not detract from the decisive weight of loyalty to a comrade. Yaari and Oren had not been on the best of terms since the latter's Leftist activity in Galicia in the late 1920s. Yaari even allowed himself to complain in public, while Oren was being held in Prague, that Oren "had more than once made himself out as more consistent, more radical, and further left than we are, not to mention more clever."[52] But when the test came, Yaari's defense of Oren was firm and unambiguous.

While the Prague trial tore Mapam apart, Oren was rotting in his jail cell in Czechoslovakia. Then, unexpectedly, he was released in May 1956. His wife, Rega, Menachem Bader of his own kibbutz, and Hazan met him in Zurich.[53] Yaari waited for him at Lod airport and spoke at the public reception there on May 15, referring to Oren's ordeal as "a second Dreyfus trial" and proclaiming that Mapam would not rest or be silent until Oren's name had been totally cleared.[54] Two days later Yaari addressed a joint session of the Mapam Central Committee and KA executive committee, which had convened in Mizra to celebrate Oren's return. Once again Yaari pledged to continue the struggle until Oren's full exoneration and proposed that the Mapam Central Committee and the KA Executive Committee restore Oren to all the party and movement institutions of which he had been a member before his arrest; the

---

51 Mapam Political Committee, Nov. 19, 1952, HHA, 90.120(1).
52 Yaari, *Al Hamishmar*, Mar. 27, 1953.
53 Oren, *Reshimot asir Prag*, 364.
54 For the full text, see Ibid., 365–366.

motion carried with loud cheers. To Oren himself he counseled a week or two of rest.⁵⁵ But his remarks to the Mapam Secretariat about two weeks later were already rather chilly and accompanied by a demand that Oren give up the campaign to clear his name. It was time to drop the matter, Yaari said, given that Mapam had paid for it in the 1955 elections and in the public arena. He again advised Oren to take time off, work quietly, and leave it to the movement to do what it could to clear him.⁵⁶

Oren did not take this advice. Two years after his release he revived the campaign to win full exoneration. Yaari feared the anti-Soviet ramifications of such efforts. When Oren asked him about arranging a translation of his book, *Notes of a Political Prisoner in Prague*, so that it could be published in America, Yaari made crystal clear his reluctance to embark on a crusade in the capitalist countries against the socialist countries. In any case, such a campaign of condemnation, especially if carried out in collaboration with circles that were not friendly towards the Socialist countries, would not further the prospects of obtaining permission for Soviet Jews to make aliyah.⁵⁷

In a letter that a member of Kibbutz Mizra sent Yaari in the summer of 1955, complaining about the movement's handling of Oren's case, he added that "Mordechai's case saved the movement from utter destruction, because Mordechai's arrest sounded the alarm for us to stop the penetration of our body by the Sneh-ist cancer while there was still time—and in this way we came out of the battle hale and alive."⁵⁸ There is much truth to this. The campaign against Sneh's supporters in KA had begun in 1952, before Oren's trial. At first it was orchestrated by Hazan, because Yaari was in Switzerland for a rest cure. After Yaari's return to Israel, in late 1952, he joined it energetically.⁵⁹ Yaari had always been wary and even suspicious of Sneh, who was renowned as a brilliant orator and sharp-penned publicist. In 1948, speaking

---

55 HHA, 5-10.6 (4); Yaari, *Al Hamishmar*, May 18, 1956.
56 Mapam Secretariat, June 4, 1956, HHA, 90.63(3).
57 Yaari to Mordechai Oren, Apr. 17, 1958, HHA, 95-7.15(6).
58 Avraham Amarant to Yaari, Aug. 29, 1955, Kibbutz Mizra Archives, Avraham Amarant papers, bin 20.
59 On Hazan's role, see Tzahor, *Hazan*, 205–221.

about Sneh's trip to America, Yaari warned that the man "is not careful about what he says" and expressed fear of his appearance there as "a meteor."[60] As another proof of Sneh's lack of discretion (one of many), Yaari cited his appearance at the convention of the Israel Communist Party, ostensibly representing Mapam. His presence there was noted in the American press (including the *New York Times*), after which the family of the movement's emissary in the United States had been asked to leave the country—at least that was how the emissary understood or represented the case.[61] Whether or not there really was a connection between the two, these were the years when the "Red Scare" was running amok in the United States and people were terrified of Senator Joseph McCarthy. Sneh's action, without taking counsel with others, played, however unwittingly and unintentionally, not only into the hands of his domestic rivals, but perhaps also into those of the "Commie hunters" in the United States.

Sneh came to Mapam from Ahdut Ha'avodah. During the debate about the party's joining the Government in early 1949, Sneh moved closer to the Hashomer Hatza'ir faction. But this development did not alleviate Yaari's fears of him. On the contrary, it intensified his concern about the new recruit's influence within the party, in the Hashomer faction, and especially in KA. The peril became more substantial when Sneh and Riftin joined forces. The threat that Sneh, and even more so Sneh and Riftin together, posed to Yaari, to Mapam, and to KA was organizational, ideological, and educational, and also a matter of leadership. Yaari was afraid that Sneh would not bond with the entire Hashomer Hatza'ir faction but only with some of its elements and might set up his own faction, thereby undermining the unity of the party and of KA.[62] After Sneh and Riftin formed their alliance, the two came to be surrounded by key officials in the party bureaucracy, constituting a relatively small group, cohesive and almost conspiratorial, that controlled the party apparatus and its daily newspaper. Facing this very real organizational threat, Yaari geared up for battle against the rival power center. Riftin the kibbutznik was in some

---

60 Political Committee, Mar. 25, 1948, HHA, 90.66(1).
61 Zvi Lurie to Yaari, June 7, 1952, HHA, 95-7.13(2).
62 Yaari to Zvi [Lurie], July 8, 1950, HHA, 95-7.12(2).

senses the more dangerous of the two opponents, and Yaari had to find a way to repulse him without causing a split in KA.

Even though the crux of the threat from Sneh and Riftin was in the organizational dimension, the other challenges that Sneh posed must not be dismissed lightly. The man stressed foreign affairs and focused on matters of cosmic import, while giving short shrift to the grey routine of everyday duties and showing no commitment to the class struggle. This approach, which Sneh wanted to instill in the movement's left wing, posed a special danger for the kibbutz, because it made it legitimate to evade the daily grind so as to concentrate on global topics, in the expectation that the social revolution would arrive from the outside, as the result of international developments. Such a deterministic approach could lead to passive acceptance of the socioeconomic status quo. What is more, Sneh's picture of the impending revolution, already at the gates, just around the corner, was incompatible with Yaari's educational approach and attitude towards the Soviet Union. Yaari, the advocate of the "long road" and "eventually," mobilized Ber Borochov, his ideological inspiration at the time, for the assault on Sneh and his followers: "Borochov's doctrine describes a protracted historical process, but they intend to cut it short and bring it to a quick conclusion, no matter what."[63] Sneh, with his powerful intellect, expounded Marxism-Leninism in a clear, persuasive, and immensely logical fashion, speaking to the mind while not making any practical demands on individuals with regard to their daily personal commitment. Yaari, by contrast, fostered the belief in "the world of tomorrow" in order to give some sense to the demands of the present, to encourage the comrades who were toiling in the fields and orchards and at other exhausting jobs, providing a vision that allowed them to straighten their backs at the end of the grueling workday and look past the seemingly endless furrows towards the horizon, seeing in the distance the meaning of the great mission of the kibbutz, which they carried forward on their sweat-drenched shoulders.

In December 1952, *Ha'olam Hazeh* explained the nature of the threat that Sneh posed to the party's veteran leadership, and chiefly Yaari, to its readers, who were not expert in the nuances of the debates within Mapam:

---

63 Yaari, *Al Hamishmar*, Apr. 17, 1953.

Before the founding of the state, the status of Meir Yaari, Yaakov Hazan, and a handful of their comrades was unchallenged. But now the star of a new man has risen in the party, a man who did not follow the tortuous path that runs from road-building to the fields of Merhavia, someone who comes straight from the city, from the party offices and meeting hall.

What Moshe Sneh said is quite similar to what Meir Yaari said, and they were allies in the internal struggle within the party. But the two men's approaches were totally different. Sneh placed the emphasis on the political war only and created an ideological group in which there was no longer any real need for personal and pioneering fulfillment. A man can be an authentic revolutionary in the Sneh mold without having to follow the more difficult and less attractive path of living in a ramshackle hut in the isolated southern Negev.[64]

The Prague trial exposed Sneh's strength within the organization and the danger posed by the Riftin-Sneh axis. Yaari had to defend his views and status not only within the party, against the members of Ahdut Ha'avodah, but also within his own home base, against the Leftists of the Unity Front. It was clear to all that organizational issues stood at the center of the debates and conflict in Mapam, so Yaari's main concern was to bolster the party's clout over members and keep it from degenerating into a loose federation of rival factions.[65] The party and movement periodicals were a main front in the conflict, because they were the key arena for the ideological debates and clashes within the party and against other parties. A familiar syndrome of Zionist history made yet another appearance in the episode of Mapam's Leftward tilt: the views and ideas of the faction blessed with the more talented speakers and writers, who had easier access to the various public forums, resounded more loudly at the time and left a more lasting imprint on the historical record. We know much less about what the rank and file, the largely silent majority, thought and felt. During his years in Mapam, Sneh—an inspired writer—published hundreds of articles in *Al Hamishmar*, including dozens of editorials. In December 1952, when he

---

64 *Ha'olam Hazeh*, June 5, 1952.
65 Yaari at the Eighth Mapam Council, Dec. 24, 1952, HHA, 90.69(1).

wanted to publish an article about the Prague trial, Yaari informed him that the decision to do so exceeded the competence of the newspaper's editors and that publication would have to be delayed pending a discussion by the party Central Committee. Sneh was unwilling to wait and published the article in *Hador* (the Mapai evening paper).[66] The fierce inner debate in Mapam spilled out into the open and the leadership lost control of what was going on.

The Prague trial gave Yaari the opening he needed to settle accounts with Sneh and to eject him and his circle from the party. Hazan and Yaari went from party branch to branch, from kibbutz to kibbutz, and forced party members to declare whether they supported or rejected the guilty verdict against Oren. Yaari estimated that around 200 members of Kibbutz Artzi fell into line behind Sneh and his circle and were expelled.[67] Yaari felt great relief after the purge of Sneh and his followers, but had to work hard to persuade his flock that he had acted appropriately and to prevent other members of Kibbutz Artzi from seceding to join Sneh. Kibbutz Artzi was Yaari's life's work and project; he was aggrieved that a Johnny-come-lately had tried to steal the fledglings from his nest; that the youngsters he had brought up would fall prey to a man who proposed a brilliant and even pragmatic analysis, but rather bloodless, of what could be expected to occur, along with a (supposedly) foolproof scheme for Israel, and especially its leftists, to join the victorious camp. The ferocity of his statements against Sneh—in public forums, in the press, and in private conversations—was proportional to his frustration and anger. The bulk of these attacks came after Sneh had been expelled from the party and was menacing it from the outside. Yaari's pen depicted Sneh as a "cancerous growth," "an arch-traitor," "a liquidator," "erratic," "two-faced," and "treacherous."[68]

---

66 Yaari to Sneh, Dec. 24, 1952, HHA, 90.*bet*-32 (5); Moshe Sneh, "Some Thoughts from those Days," *Hador*, Dec. 8, 1952. A summary of the article was published in *Kol Ha'am* [the Israeli Communist Party daily], Dec. 25, 1952.
67 Yaari at the Sixth Mapam Convention, Dec. 26, 1972, HHA, 90.70(1). Elsewhere he referred to 250 members who were expelled for supporting Sneh: interview with Yaari by Rafael Bashan, IDF Radio, Oct. 10, 1977, KMA, MYF, 6(5).
68 Yaari to Peretz Merhav, Mar. 10, 1953, HHA, 95-7.13(3); Yaari to Peri, Aug. 25, 1953, Ibid.; Yaari to Bunim [Shamir], Apr. 19, 1953, HHA, 95-7.13(2); Yaari, *Al*

Yaari was determined to eradicate Sneh-ism, in cooperation with Hazan. As a rule, Hazan orchestrated the purges in Kibbutz Artzi, while Yaari concentrated his efforts on the movement press. They worked with stubborn determination because the war against the Leftists and their threat threatened the survival of Kibbutz Artzi. As Yaari put it,

> for others, outside our party, it may be an academic debate. Even within our party, in the urban branches, there are upstanding comrades who thundered against leftism in the past but are now sidestepping this episode because it is more comfortable to do so. For us, though, as members of Kibbutz Artzi, this episode is a matter of destiny, a life-or-death battle.[69]

Several lines characterized Yaari's positions and actions in the liquidation of Leftism in Kibbutz Artzi. The first is that his attacks on the Leftists were more restrained than Hazan's. The overall impression is that Yaari debated and Hazan expelled. It was usually Hazan who traveled to kibbutzim that had a wayward minority and steered its general assembly towards a decision to oust the Leftists.[70] Second, Yaari was stern in his treatment of the rank and file, to the point of expelling them from their kibbutzim, but showed a milder disposition towards the leaders of the Leftist deviation. Those banished from Kibbutz Artzi during these purges included members of cadres originally from Egypt (at Ein Shemer and Mesillot) and France (at Karmiya), as well as graduates of the Hashomer Hatza'ir youth movement in Israel on young kibbutzim. Most of them did not have an extensive social network or deep roots in the movement. The procedure was the mirror image of the comradely allegiance displayed in the Oren affair. Just as Yaari and Hazan had fiercely defended their veteran comrade, so now they showed no mercy for the young members who were not "flesh of our flesh." And again, as with Oren, the principle of comradeship outweighed everything else. The iron broom did not sweep out "our

---

 Hamishmar, May 18, 1956; Yaari, *Qibbuz galuyot*, 80–81, 94.
69 Yaari at the 32nd Kibbutz Artzi Council, Mar. 29–31, 1956 (p. 25), HHA, 5-20.8(1).
70 Tzahor, *Hazan*, 205–215.

people," towards whom they followed the principle that "a Jew, even if he has sinned, remains a Jew."

This approach was most conspicuous in Yaari's treatment of Riftin. In the wake of his article "Communism and Us," Riftin had attracted a large following that identified with his Leftist positions. He was a potential and in fact real threat to the exclusive status of the historical leadership, disposed of organizational power within the movement, and made life miserable for the movement and the leaders. Yaari reacted with torrents of verbal abuse in both public and private correspondence. He demanded that Riftin break off all contact with the diplomatic representatives of the Communist Bloc in Israel, stop debating those outside the party, and curtail his public activity.[71] But even though his positions and activities were giving Mapam a bad name, Riftin was treated with indulgence. In advance of the general elections in 1951, after the publication of "Communism and Us," he was moved up to number four on the party's Knesset list (from eight in 1949).

Yaari displayed this lenience towards Riftin because he was worried about the repercussions of treating him harshly. The comrades often determined their stand on the internal movement and party disputes not (or at least not only) on the basis of deep ideological conviction, but out of personal identification with the advocates of a certain position. This rule, which explains the members' continued loyalty to the historic leadership, also applied to the attitude towards the leading Leftists. Yaari was afraid that crushing Riftin would trigger a chain reaction among his supporters and weaken his own standing in the Hashomer Hatza'ir faction of Mapam. This was why Riftin and other leading Leftists were not expelled by their kibbutzim. However, they were asked to repent their deviation if they wanted to hold official posts in the movement and have their articles published in *Al Hamishmar*. All those who acknowledged their errors and returned to the true path would be forgiven, but only after a full and public confession.[72]

---

71 Tzur, *Nofei ha-ashlayah*, 305; see also 228.
72 Yaari to the editors of *Al Hamishmar*, Sept. 15, 1954, HHA, 95-7.13(7).

CHAPTER 13

In the Shadow of Big Brother

The first months of 1953 were particularly difficult for Yaari. The battle with Sneh and his followers was not the only front with which he had to contend. From late January to mid-March, every Friday saw the publication in *Davar* of an article signed "S. Sh. Yariv" (which everyone knew meant *sabba shel Yariv* or "Yariv's grandfather," i.e., David Ben-Gurion), under the running headline, "On the Communism and Zionism of Hashomer Hatza'ir"; each of them was a vicious attack on Mapam.[1] Yaari responded to these eight articles in four long pieces that were published at intervals between late February and mid-April in the Friday issues of *Al Hamishmar*, under the headline, "Their Enemy: The Synthesis of Pioneering Zionism and Revolutionary Socialism."[2] People on the Mapam kibbutzim waited for these articles with bated breath. They needed a leader who would guide them.

In his articles, whose direct instigation was the Prague trial, Ben-Gurion launched a brutal attack on Yaari and Mapam that sometimes descended to genuine malice. Towards Yaari Ben-Gurion showed some clemency, because he saw his remarks not as ideology or political doctrine but rather as educational messages. At the same time, and precisely for that reason, Ben-Gurion criticized them as confused and confusing. The essays

---

1 The articles signed S. Sh. Yariv were published in the Friday issues of *Davar* on January 23 and 30, Feb. 6, 13, 20 and 27, and March 6 and 13, 1953, and later collected in book form, *Al ha-qomunism ve-ha-ziyyonut shel ha-shomer ha-za'ir*, to which references are made.
2 Yaari's articles were published in *Al Hamishmar* on Feb. 27, Mar. 20 and 27, and Apr. 17, 1953.

that made up this exchange were published in two different papers—the attacks in *Davar* and the rebuttals in *Al Hamishmar*. Not everyone who was exposed to one side of the debate read the other. In fact, many members of Mapam in the town and kibbutzim drank in Yaari's articles but never bothered with Ben-Gurion's. But this did not interfere with their understanding of what was going on; not only because Yaari quoted Ben-Gurion at length in his replies, but chiefly because he did not really relate to what his adversary had written and rebut his arguments.

Ben-Gurion focused his assault on the distinction that Hashomer Hatza'ir had drawn between universal Socialist justice and its specific application in the case of Mordechai Oren. He lambasted the liberty that the movement took to exempt Zionism and itself from the universalism mandated by Marxism in its Marxist-Leninist version. With regard to the Prague trial, Ben-Gurion pounded hard on Mapam's weak point: "When does Mapam allow itself to deviate from Maki and the Cominform? When the casualty is a member of Mapam or Mapam's interests."[3] Ideological collectivism, or "collective ideologism," as he called it, was Ben-Gurion's preferred target. He saw it as a "fiction," given that there will always be profound disagreements among the members when it comes to fundamental problems. What united Hashomer Hatza'ir was "the collective family nature of the kibbutz," as Ben-Gurion aptly described the social dynamic within Kibbutz Artzi.[4]

Ben-Gurion exposed the internal contradictions of Yaari's ideology and of Mapam's practice with a few sharp statements. As he saw it, the source of the ideological crisis in Hashomer Hatza'ir was the contradiction between Zionism and Socialism, despite what Yaari asserted about the redeeming synthesis between them. As for practice, Hashomer Hatza'ir had been able to adhere to the formula of a synthesis between Zionism and Socialism because to date "it had never once been called on to implement its sham synthesis, which is in fact a contradiction, and has never faced the need and the possibility of guiding the Zionist movement and the State of Israel according to its program, which is riddled with

---

3 S. Sh. Yariv, *Al ha-qomunism*, 8.
4 Ibid., 32.

contradictions."⁵ And to exemplify Hashomer Hatza'ir's divorce of theory from practice, Ben-Gurion added, "it cooks and eats the same kneidlach as the rest of us in the 'reformist world' [Yaari's term for Mapai], but it reads the Haggadah of the revolutionary world."⁶

As already mentioned, Yaari did not offer any real refutation of Ben-Gurion's arguments—and this was deliberate. His articles were more in the nature of an educational series for internal consumption, a solidarity sermon for Mapam in the wake of the expulsion of Sneh and his followers. They were composed with Yaari's finest journalistic skills, which he exploited fully when debating opponents. His writing employed rich and incisive language, playing on motifs that spoke to the hearts of his readers and sounded notes that were sweet and familiar to their ears. In those days his doctors had forbidden him to read or write, so Yaari had to dictate to his secretary; the result reads as if the author had been addressing a live audience. This is one of the secrets of their charm. They are juicy, replete with bitter and ironic humor, linked together by associative thinking and have something of a stream of consciousness structure.

Yaari understood Ben-Gurion's remarks in the *Davar* articles as expressing doubt about the loyalty of members of Hashomer Hatza'ir as soldiers, should they find themselves confronting the Red Army. Ben-Gurion stated this with hypothetical indirectness; Yaari responded in his own circuitous fashion. Despite the rhetoric, both men made their meaning clear. Ben-Gurion was unsure about the allegiance of members of Hashomer Hatza'ir, and Yaari had no doubt that they would pass the test of loyalty to the homeland.⁷ One goal of his articles was to expose Ben-Gurion's scheme "to paint Kibbutz Artzi as a fifth column in Israel and the frontier kibbutzim of Hashomer Hatza'ir as potential allies of Arab invaders" and to demonstrate that his movement's devotion to Israeli security, and, in earlier years, that of the Yishuv, was faultless.⁸

The baseless charge that Ben-Gurion leveled against the movement, whose loyalty to the state was immaculate, was behind the approval

---

5 Ibid.
6 Ibid.
7 Yaari, *Al Hamishmar*, Apr. 17, 1953.
8 Yaari, *Al Hamishmar*, Mar. 20, 1953.

he seems to have given to plant a listening device in Yaari's office in Tel Aviv. "Wireless Listening Device Discovered in the Room of MK Meir Yaari," screamed the main headline of *Al Hamishmar* on January 30, 1953. After workers at the Kibbutz Artzi building in Tel Aviv discovered the device by chance, they set an ambush and caught two men coming to service it. One of them said that he had been sent by Mapai "to explore, to look around, and if there was anything, also to take."[9] The newspaper provided readers with a detailed description of the ambush and how the two men had been caught red-handed, giving prominent play to the fact that the device that had been concealed under Yaari's desk was American-made.[10] At *Al Hamishmar* they saw the use of technical devices provided by the FBI as another link in the infiltration of Israel by negative elements, products of the United States, which had been preceded by "the pornographic American literature that poisons the minds of our youth" and the attempt to import Coca Cola to Israel.[11] Referring to the listening device affair, Yaari attacked Ben-Gurion and the United States in the same breath and, in a sort of counterblow to the criticism of the despotic Soviet regime, denounced the Western superpower as rotten with McCarthyism.

The distrust of Yaari as a potential security risk affected his son, Aviezer, as well. In 1952, while serving as the intelligence officer of a reserve battalion, Aviezer requested a transfer to the Intelligence Corps, citing his very high grades in the course for intelligence officers and his experience in the position. The response, to his astonishment and disappointment, was that he was deemed unsuitable for the Intelligence Corps. Only later did he learn that, tarred with his father's "sin," he had been disqualified at the explicit instruction of Isser Harel, the head of the *Shin-Bet* (security service). The ban remained in effect for 15 years, even after Mapam joined the government. It was not until 1967 that Aviezer Yaari received the posting he had sought; ultimately, he reached a senior position in the Intelligence Corps and retired from the IDF as a major general.[12]

---

9   *Al Hamishmar*, Jan. 30, 1953.
10 Ibid.
11 *Al Hamishmar*, Feb. 1, 1953.
12 A. Yaari, *Ha-derekh mi-merḥavya*, 60–61.

At the height of the verbal sparring between Ben-Gurion and Yaari, *Al Hamishmar* published an extra on the morning of Friday, March 6, 1953, reporting the death of Stalin. A huge picture of him in military uniform occupied a prominent place on the front page. Red flags and Israeli flags, with black ribbons tied to their staffs, were hung on Mapam institutions and the *Al Hamishmar* building in Tel Aviv. A Mapam rally to express solidarity between urban laborers and the rural sector, already planned for that evening, was turned into a memorial convocation. The speakers' table was draped in black, a picture of Stalin in a black frame was hung at the center of the stage, and the Red and Israeli flags—with black ribbons attached—stood at either side. On Sunday, March 8, another photo of Stalin dominated *Al Hamishmar*'s front page, alongside the text of the cable of participation in the Soviet nation's grief that Mapam had sent to the Communist Party Central Committee in Moscow, over the signatures of Meir Yaari, Yaakov Hazan, and Yitzhak Ben Aharon, to mourn "the passing of the great leader and heroic commander, [...] the great revolutionary warrior, architect of socialist construction, and helmsman of the movement for world peace."[13] Yaari extolled Stalin as "the giant of the revolution," "who had worked what is perhaps the greatest change in the history of humankind," and as a great fighter for peace.[14] Critical and indeed sarcastic reports about those days regularly mentioned that Mapam and its leaders had reacted to the death of Stalin as "the setting of the sun of the peoples." In fact, none of the movement's publications used that expression in those days and it is not to be found anywhere in Yaari's oral or written statements, even though he had esteemed Stalin for many years and viewed the Soviet leader's doctrine as "a true teaching from which nothing must be subtracted."[15]

Yaari was proud that he had aligned himself with Stalinism long before the Leftist wing of the party had come up with its interpretation of Marxism-Leninism.[16] Nevertheless, he was deeply troubled by Stalin's rejection of Jewish nationhood. He tried to find arguments to excuse

---

13 *Al Hamishmar*, Mar. 8, 1953.
14 *Al Hamishmar*, Mar. 20, 1953.
15 Yaari to Peretz Merhav, Apr. 29, 1953, HHA, 95-7.13(3).
16 Yaari to Peretz [Merhav], Jan. 7, 1952, HHA, 95-7.12(10).

this blind spot: notably, that Stalin was not consistent in his negative attitude about Jewish nationalism, as demonstrated by his support for the establishment of Israel. Yaari had never accepted the definition of nation advanced by Stalin in his 1913 book, *Marxism and the National Question*, because it excluded the Jewish people, who had no territory of their own, from the roster of nations entitled to independence. He devoted great effort to resolving the contradiction between his admiration for Stalin and what he saw as the man's refusal to recognize the global character of Jewish nationalism.[17] His devotion to Stalin, despite the dark corners in the Soviet leader's career, survived for many years.

In the meantime, major internal problems continued to roil Mapam, even after the Leftists had been thrown out and the leadership had emerged on top in the confrontation within KA. The seeds of the split that had existed within the party since the day it was founded began to germinate. Tabenkin saw the root of the evil in the nature of Hashomer Hatza'ir, which "cannot connect with anyone except itself," and was bound together by its common origins.[18] Yaari was disturbed by Tabenkin's attitude towards Hashomer Hatza'ir and Kibbutz Artzi. In his complaints, we hear the irritation of a younger brother with his older sibling, which is the thread linking all his remarks about the members of the Second Aliyah and his disputes with its leaders—Katznelson, Ben-Gurion, and Tabenkin. Yaari also disagreed with Tabenkin's portrayal of the members of Hashomer Hatza'ir as "Hassidim," ruled by emotion, whereas the members of Kibbutz Me'uḥad were rationalist *mitnagdim*.[19] Yaari's criticism of Tabenkin intensified when he realized the latter was about to split the party, even though he was well aware that the divorce was inevitable and it was common knowledge among the public at large. In the summer of 1954, *Ha'olam Hazeh* took up the challenge of trying to explain to readers why Mapam was breaking up:

> The rival camps within Mapam are very far apart in their political outlooks. The majority are moderate on the national question, rad-

---

17 Yaari, *Al Hamishmar*, Apr. 17, 1953.
18 Yaari to the Kibbutz Artzi executive committee, May 9, 1954, HHA, 5-10.6(11); Yaari to Zvi [Lurie], July 8, 1950, HHA, 95-7.12(2).
19 Letter to Tabenkin [1954?], HHA, 95-7.30(6) (probably never sent).

ical on the socialist question. The minority are extreme nationalists but moderate socialists.

But it was not the political differences, which kept widening, that triggered the split. They were only like the tip of the iceberg above the water. Mapam could have remained united for a long time even with such conflicts.

The causes of the split, hidden below the surface, were much more practical: the old problem of the relationship between majority and minority; and the problem, just as old, of coalition or opposition.

These were the true problems that led to the split between the two large kibbutz movements affiliated with Mapam, and between the two groups of leaders who had left their indelible mark on the construction project that was the establishment of the state.[20]

It is hard to know just how much the incompatibility and conflict between Tabenkin and Yaari as leaders contributed to the failure of the merged Mapam, or, to put it another way, to its dissolution. There were also many other factors and causes, ideological, political, organizational, and psychological, that ended with Aḥdut Ha'avodah's secession from Mapam in mid-August 1954. Once again, as in the episode with Sneh, the straw that broke the camel's back was an organizational matter related to the party newspaper. Yaari assigned extreme importance to the movement's publications and wanted them to serve as a forum for a careful and guided debate and a tool for imposing the views of the leadership on the party rank and file. For himself, Yaari demanded and received free access to the pages of *Al Hamishmar*, with no review, censorship, or editing, but from time to time denied this privilege to his opponents. The editorial staff of *Al Hamishmar*, dominated by Hashomer Hatza'ir, frequently censored articles by party members, especially those from Aḥdut Ha'avodah, and occasionally rejected them. Even Tabenkin was subject to the censor's scissors and outright rejection of some of his submissions. The Aḥdut Ha'avodah wing took steps to put out its own newspaper; the first issue of the fortnightly *Lamerḥav* appeared on June 2, 1954. This made it public knowledge that Aḥdut Ha'avodah felt it was being stifled and not

---

20 "Why is Mapam Splitting?" *Ha'olam Hazeh*, July 15, 1954.

receiving its due access to the columns of Mapam's official organ.[21] Taking it for granted that he had the power to impose the principle of ideological collectivism that ruled KA on the entire party, Yaari demanded a forceful condemnation of *Lamerḥav*, its closure, and disciplinary measures against those involved in its publication. At the same time he called for opening *Al Hamishmar* to a debate of the questions related to its editors' authority to "guide the newspaper."[22]

Did Yaari want Mapam to break up, or would he have preferred for it to remain intact? The impression conveyed by his statements in this period is that he wanted the party to stay united. On the very eve of the split, when he realized that the decisive hour was at hand and he suspected that his erstwhile partners had already made their choice, Yaari considered it crucial to make sure the public was aware that the other side was responsible for the split. His final maneuvers in August 1954 were intended to clear the Hashomer faction of Mapam of any blame in the matter.[23] From Yaari's perspective, the continued existence of the united party had both advantages and disadvantages. The advantage was that he was more comfortable leading a party with two factions—Aḥdut Ha'avodah on the Right balanced by the moderate Leftists, with him at the equilibrium point of this parallelogram of forces. It is true that after the purge of the radical Leftists in 1953, it was no longer so important to have Aḥdut Ha'avodah pulling to the Right, but he still needed it as a political and ideological counterweight to the Unity Front. Among the disadvantages was that he was not the undisputed leader of the united party and had no deep emotional attachment to it.

The status of the two kibbutz movements also played a role in shaping Yaari's position on the continued existence of the united party. It was clear to him that a true merger of the parties was impossible without a merger of the kibbutz movements as well.[24] The political logic was that a single kibbutz movement was essential, but the tribal

---

21 Tzarfati, "*Lamerḥav*."
22 Political Committee, June 2, 1954, HHA, 90. 121(1).
23 Kibbutz Artzi Executive Committee, Aug. 8, 1954, HHA, 5.10.6(11).
24 Yaari to Zvi Lurie, July 8, 1950, HHA, 95-7.12(2); Yaari to the Kibbutz [Merḥavia], Dec. 10, 1951, KMA, MYF, 1(3).

inclinations dictated preservation of the status quo, and Yaari went along. He was not willing to jeopardize or sacrifice Kibbutz Artzi's independence in the name of full unity and a stronger party. What is more, he felt that KA was his home; in the years he was fighting on multiple fronts—against the Unity Front inside the party and against opponents on the outside, especially Ben-Gurion—Yaari's status in his own kibbutz movement remained unassailable.

In those years Yaari was a lecturer in great demand and an honored guest at countless movement events. The members wanted to meet the leader and he enjoyed the live contact with them. He was on the program of every seminar at Givat Haviva (the educational institution of Hashomer Hatza'ir)—a course on management of the kibbutz economy, a seminar for female members, a seminar for twelfth-grade pupils. In general, he accepted all such invitations, except when prior commitments made this impossible. When he met with members of the youth movement their questions were submitted in advance.[25] In the late 1940s and early 1950s he was invited to almost every movement event. Kibbutz Revadim postponed its party in honor of the return of members from Jordanian captivity in early 1949 so that Yaari could attend and, at the specific request by the released POWs, asked him to speak at the event.[26] In 1951 he was invited to the groundbreaking ceremony of the new settlement of Gevulot, to the first anniversary of the groundbreaking for Kibbutz Naḥshon, and to the fifth anniversary of Kibbutz Nirim. Kibbutz Shoval invited him to its fifth anniversary celebrations and Kibbutz Nir David asked him to attend its fifteenth anniversary party, because

> in every stage of our development, in times of crisis and days of progress, starting from our first camp in the cemetery near Tel Aviv and continuing through the temporary camps in advance of groundbreaking, and in the towns of Poland where the first cadres of our kibbutz began to form and operate, we were deeply moved when we heard you speak and had direct contact with you.[27]

---

25 The material is collected in HHA, 95-7.13(5).
26 Kibbutz Revadim to Yaari, Mar. 20, 1949, HHA, 95-7.12(1).
27 Kibbutz Nir David / Tel Amal to Yaari, Jan. 10, 1951, HHA, 95-7.12(6).

The stream of invitations continued unabated in subsequent years: from Mishmar Ha'emeq, from Beit Qama, from Megiddo, from Magen and from Amir, as well as requests to take part in the first fruits ceremony at Gan Shmuel, the fifth-anniversary parties of Sasa and Givat Oz, and a private party at Shamir to mark ten years since its groundbreaking.[28] There were so many invitations that during a reception at Kibbutz Hama'apil he calculated that, based on the number he was receiving, "if I had to be a good father and be fair to all the kibbutzim and take part in every anniversary and every dedication of a new dining hall ... I could feed myself for the whole year!"[29]

People developed strong feelings of veneration for him, with sentiments normally reserved for family members. After Hannah Shadmi of Kibbutz Ma'abarot passed away, her husband Menachem wrote to tell Yaari that she had loved him like a father. The couple had had many conversations with him at their center.[30] Zvi Ben-Avraham had only one request on his deathbed: "I don't want anything to drink, I don't want anything to eat. I want to see Meir Yaari."[31] "At the most trying times, in moments of disappointment and confusion," Simha Ben-Or of Gan Shmuel would always tell his wife, "Leah, Meir will not disappoint us. [...] Like a hassid who stays close to his rebbe, he believed in you and was loyal to you."[32] Author Naomi Fraenkel's daughter, just discharged from military service, told her parents that she was so grateful to Yaari that she dreamt about him at night.[33] There were also public expressions of adulation, verging on a cult of personality. Seven pages of the weekly KA review were devoted to the full text of his speech at the organization's eighth conference, in 1954, accompanied by praise for what he had said, "which was read and studied by thousands. [...] The words are clear and precise, with nothing vague. [...] Silence and taut attention. [...] Even the outside guests listened attentively."[34]

---

28   HHA, 95-7.13(1); HHA, 95-7.13(8); HHA, 95-7.13(6).
29   Yaari, at a reception at Kibbutz Hama'apil, Nov. 1, 1960, KMA, MYF, 6(2).
30   Menachem [Shadmi] to Yaari, 1954 [undated], HHA, 95-7.13(8).
31   Sonia Ben-Avraham to Yaari, Jan. 19, 1962, HHA, 95-7.18(1).
32   Leah and Esther Ben-Or to Yaari, May 9, 1964, HHA, 95-7.19(5).
33   Naomi Fraenkel to Yaari, Aug. 26, 1958, HHA, 95-7.15(6).
34   *Ha-shavu'a ba-Kibbutz ha-Artzi*, HHA, 5-20.7(1).

The members of the movement felt a need for live, direct, and unmediated contact with the leader, whether in face-to-face meetings or in letters—and he needed it as well. He was in the habit of writing back to all correspondents. His letters were candid. He praised but also censured; he offered friendly advice but could also offend. When he complimented an author on an article it was clear that he had actually read it. Not everyone worshiped him. Some saw him as an ill-tempered demagogue who harbored suspicions of people who had done nothing wrong. When he met with this attitude himself Yaari responded in kind, and in spades: "I never imagined that you were so prone to become entangled in egocentric accounts. It is true I knew how easily you take offense, but I did not know that it had reached such fantastic dimensions." [35] But even the rebuking and cutting letters ended with an expression of his desire to maintain proper working relations.

Yaari cultivated his ties with writers and poets. His longest and deepest relationship was with Avraham Shlonsky, going back to when they were neighbors in the tent camp in Tel Aviv in the 1920s. When he read a new volume of Shlonsky's poems about 30 years later (in 1954), he felt that he was breathing in chapters of his own autobiography.[36] Shlonsky was involved in the cultural activities of the Hashomer Hatza'ir party and its Mapam successor in various ways, and was the founder and living spirit of the Center for Progressive Culture, whose establishment was announced at a conference of leading authors and poets, held in Kibbutz Merḥavia in 1946.[37]

Until 1955, when it inaugurated the Tzavta Club in a modest space on the ground floor of an apartment block at 214 Dizengoff Street in Tel Aviv, the Center for Progressive Culture was just a bohemian clique comprising Shlonsky's urban admirers and kibbutz members who happened to find themselves in the big city. They would gather around Shlonsky in a coffee house or in a small room at 48 Naḥalat Binyamin Street. Hazan, who was close to Shlonsky, joined the group

---

35 Yaari to Levi [Greenblatt], Oct. 26, 1952, HHA, 95-7.13(1).
36 Yaari to Shlonsky, July 4, 1954, HHA, 95-7.13(7).
37 Elmaliach, *Ẓavta*, 11; Yaari to Avraham Shlonsky, Feb. 4, 1947, HHA, 95-7. 9(5); Shaham, *Shalom ḥaverim*, 222; Tzahor, *Hazan*, 231-233; Halperin, *Ha-ma'estro*, 483-486.

from time to time.³⁸ Yaari's connection with Shlonsky was more formal, consisting mainly of cordial letters and mutual verbal compliments on the stages of festive events and for each other's birthdays. On Shlonsky's seventieth birthday, Yaari placed him in the same rank as Nathan Alterman and referred to them as the two poets of the pioneer generation. He attached great merit to Shlonsky's linkage of poetry and ideology, and found another virtue in such an urban poet: his daughter was a longtime member of Kibbutz Sha'ar Hagolan.³⁹

Some friction developed between the two men in 1962, triggered by Shlonsky's behavior at an evening to mark the publication of *The Father's Death (Mot ha-Av)*, the second volume of Naomi Fraenkel's *Saul and Johanna* trilogy. The event was held at the Tzavta Club in Tel Aviv, with Shlonsky in the chair, and Yaari and the literary scholar Baruch Kurzweil as the main speakers. Shlonsky, Yaari felt, deliberately focused the spotlight on Kurzweil, as if he were the evening's star attraction, and made sure to "encourage applause for him." Things went too far when the evening's honoree spoke. Fraenkel, who had implored Yaari to attend, referred repeatedly to Kurzweil as if Yaari didn't exist. He finally left the hall in a rage and remained in a funk for several days, almost to the point of a decision to drop all involvement with Fraenkel's book and to boycott the planned reception at her home kibbutz of Beit Alfa. Deeply wounded, he wrote to Shlonsky: "I am not just anyone and will not play second fiddle to Kurzweil."⁴⁰ Ultimately Shlonsky persuaded him to change his mind.⁴¹

Yaari's disappointment with Fraenkel was all the greater because of his close relationship at the time with her and her then-husband, Yisrael Rosenzweig. Their daughter, Yehudit, saw Yaari as a sort of surrogate grandfather, and Naomi enjoyed a warm and even familial relationship with Meir and Anda.⁴² Fraenkel kept him informed of the

---

38 Tzahor, *Hazan*, 231–233.
39 Yaari, *Be-ma'avaq*, 244; Yaari to Shlonsky, July 4, 1954, HHA, 95-7.13(7).
40 Yaari to Shlonsky, Jan. 25, 1962, HHA, 95-7.18(1).
41 Yaari to Shlonsky, Feb. 7, 1962, Ibid.
42 Yaari, memoirs, Oct. 25, 1983, Dec. 21, 1983, KMA, MYF, 8(2).

state of her work in progress.⁴³ At the book launch in Tel Aviv, Yaari said that he remembered Naomi from their first meeting, when, as he recalled, she was 13, newly arrived in the country with her group of immigrant youngsters from Germany. "I looked into her eyes then and was sure that this girl had spirit." Nor had he been disappointed. He was happy that he had always believed in "Naomi's star" and declared that "*Saul and Johanna* is worthy of being numbered among the outstanding prose works of our age."⁴⁴ Later, however, she caused him bitter disappointment by moving to Hebron. He could not accept that "she was capable of descending so far as to identify with Gush Emunim and Kahanist anti-Arab racism."⁴⁵ He did not believe that she could spit into the well from which she had drunk—Hashomer Hatza'ir and its principles

He had a very different relationship with another author from Kibbutz Beit Alfa—Nathan Shaham. There was a candid and painful exchange of letters between the two in 1958. Shaham charged that when Yaari spoke at Beit Alfa about his novel, *Even al pi ha-be'er* (*A Stone on the Mouth of the Well*), he had been guilty of Zhdanovism, abusing his position to insist that Kibbutz Artzi writers hew to the party line in their works: "The right that a man like you, who wields such great authority in so many areas of life, arrogates to himself to crush the intellectual labors of another in public, with a single stamp of your foot, even if you do not agree with it, is a grave matter."⁴⁶ Shaham's accusation reflects Yaari's great influence on the members of Kibbutz Artzi, and not only in political matters: "Meir Yaari is a byword for the people who heard your comments. And your opinion will always be worth more in their eyes than their own opinion about literature and its quality. So your negativity dealt a death blow to my book."⁴⁷

---

43 Naomi Fraenkel and Yisrael Rosenzweig to Yaari, Sept. 15, 1960, HHA, 95-7.15(6); Naomi Fraenkel to Yaari, Aug. 21, 1961, HHA, 95-7.17(4).
44 Yaari, *Al Hamishmar*, Feb. 2, 1962; Yaari to Shlonsky, Jan. 25, 1962, HHA, 95-7.18(1).
45 Yaari [memoirs], Oct. 25, 1983, Dec. 21, 1983, KMA, MYF, 8(2).
46 Nathan Shaham to Yaari, Aug. 30, 1958, HHA, 95-7.15(6).
47 Ibid.

In a profile that appeared in *Maariv* in 1954, Yaari was described as having a strong emotional attachment to music, poetry, and literature.[48] He read constantly, either by himself or listening to someone else. He devoured the writings of Marx and loved Adam Mickiewicz's *Pan Tadeusz*. When he visited Vienna in 1928 he purchased 30 volumes by Gorky, Balzac, Kipling, Shaw, Gogol, Edgar Allan Poe, Turgenev, and Chekhov, and hoped to add many more to the list.[49] In both his oral and written remarks he frequently mentioned authors and literary works: *Hamlet*, *The Sorrows of Young Werther*, S. J. Agnon, the writings of Rosa Luxemburg, Lenin's conversations with Clara Zetkin, and Ernst Toller's *Letters from Prison*.[50] In his letters to Anda in the 1920s he mentioned that he was reading novels in German and recommended that she find Polish translations and read them herself.[51] He added that he had been reading works by Tolstoy, Gorky, Anatole France, Romain Roland, the Dane Martin Andersen Nexø, Joseph Opatoshu, Max Brod, Thomas Mann (*The Magic Mountain*), and many others. Over the years, he read original Hebrew works in addition to translated literature. Even when he was overloaded by party and Kibbutz Artzi matters he found time for poetry and novels and for correspondence with writers and poets.

There was an element of reciprocity in his relations with authors. They sent him their books, with a personal dedication, and waited for his reaction; for his part, he expected them to send him their works.[52] He saw that as recognition not only of his leadership, but also of his status as an intellectual. He always wrote back to thank writers who had sent him their works, trying to do so within a reasonable delay, and usually adding a comment—encouraging or critical—on the content and style. Even when his reply was brief, it was sympathetic.

---

48 "D. Dyukanai" ["profiler"], "Meir Yaari," *Maariv*, Apr. 9, 1954.
49 Meir to the Kibbutz, Aug. 14, 1928, KMA, MYF, 1(1); Fifth Kibbutz Artzi Council, July 12–17 1935, HHA, 5-20.2(1)
50 Yaari, in Shadmi, *Meqorot*, no. 4, p. 8 [September 1940]; Yaari, *Be-derekh arukah*, 111 [1937].
51 Meir to Anda, Haifa, June 18, 1928, KMA, MYF, 5(2).
52 As shown by his remarks to Shaham: "You are the only one of our authors who doesn't send me his books" (Yaari to Nathan Shaham, Aug. 27, 1958, HHA, 95-7.15(6)).

When Nathan Yonathan sent him a volume of his poems, in 1957, Yaari replied that Yonathan was a poet after his own heart and offered some practical advice: "I would suggest, in my great innocence, that you join forces with a sensitive and intelligent composer, because your poems seem to have been written to be played on a violin and harp."[53] In fact, nearly 200 of Yonathan's poems were set to music over the years, some of them by more than one composer.

Yaari relished his connections with intellectuals, authors, and poets. "Dear Leah," he wrote to Leah Goldberg in 1959, "your book is pure perfume."[54] She used to make him a gift of her books, and he replied that he was among the fans of her poetry, even though

> [you] sometimes cultivate the image of a person who, behind his penetrating sense, piercing vision, and sensitive thought, has hidden reservations about a definite public and political struggle. But I submit and accept you as you are. I have come to realize that these reservations have never carried you to the side of reaction and retreat and that when matters come to a head you have always been on the right side in the battle. The genuine humanism that sparkles in every line of your poetry is evidently what has come to your aid in these times of trial.[55]

With his great sympathy and interest in authors and their works, Yaari did not always avoid crossing the line to active intervention. In 1956, he spent several days reading the novel *Yemei Nisan* (*Spring Days*) by Zvi Arad of Kibbutz Ein Shemer. He thought it "the most mature and penetrating story ever written about a kibbutz," a full depiction of the essence and singularity of life on Hashomer Hatza'ir communes.[56] But it also stirred up gloomy thoughts about the passing of the main tenets of socialist belief and the neglect of the precept of the brotherhood of all nations. In the novel, political matters were thrust far into

---

53 Yaari to Nathan Yonathan, May 28, 1957, HHA, 95-7.15(3).
54 Yaari to Leah Goldberg, Sept. 30, 1959, HHA, 95-7.16(5).
55 Yaari to Leah Goldberg, June 24, 1955, HHA, 95-7.14(1).
56 Yaari to Zvi Arad, Dec. 7, 1956, HHA, 95-7.14 (8).

the background. In short, he castigated Arad, "you have obscured everything that constitutes our mission, everything that united us as an ideological collective and defined our place within the people and proletariat."[57]

In 1960 he criticized poets,

> most of whose verses are a stylized flight from the struggles of life into a sort of speculative symbolism or formalism. This generally involves turning their back on the battle for a better tomorrow for society. They denounce everything that gives off a whiff of partiality as 'socialist realism' or Zhdanovism, and whatever involves a political struggle as vulgar and conventional.

He also criticized authors who were eager to declare their divorce from Marxism "and express their contempt of the political parties whose waters they drank and on whose lap they were raised."[58]

Even though he enjoyed poetry and prose and related to style as well as content, Yaari found it impossible to sever works of art from real life, from the tasks incumbent on the generation, from politics and ideology. In the early days of the state, he expected the young writers of his movement to dedicate their literary works to the service of the public and believed that "the cadence of our poetry and literature must match the cadence of this generation's march towards national and social liberation."[59] His model, in 1949 was the "socialist realism" that had helped pave the way for the revolution in Russia; and, by analogy: "our young literature [...] was born in the War of Independence; it is the child of the pioneer 'regime' and the kibbutz movement."[60] As such, he demanded that it be imbued with revolutionary fervor. That same year saw the publication by Sifriyat Po'alim of a Hebrew translation of Andrei Zhdanov's *On Culture and Society*, and it is hard to escape the feeling that Yaari was indeed tainted by Zhdanovism.

---

57 Ibid.
58 Yaari, *Al Hamishmar*, June 10, 1960.
59 Yaari, *Al Hamishmar*, Dec. 30, 1949.
60 Ibid.

He attacked the growing strength of cheap urbanization, as manifested in the movies, "worn with age," that were screened on the kibbutzim,[61] and criticized the fact that "modern poetry is forbidden to speak about feelings and is a speculative intellectual game, hollow and dry like the depths of the wilderness."[62]

His literary correspondence crossed the ocean as well. In 1952 he was deeply moved when Howard Fast sent him a copy of his historical novel *Spartacus*. In his reply, Yaari wrote that Israeli readers had drawn great inspiration from Fast's *My Glorious Brothers*, about the Maccabees. "In it you managed to bring alive, as with a magic wand, one of the most glorious periods in the history of our people. With deep intuition and the feeling of true artist you wandered the Judean Hills as if you had been born there, as though it was your childhood landscape."[63] He invited Fast to visit Israel and told him that a Hebrew translation of *Spartacus* was in the works. After the 20th Party Congress in the Soviet Union (1956), Fast published *The Naked God*, about his disenchantment with Communism. Unlike the historical novels, its Hebrew translation was not published by Sifriyat Po'alim.

His movement and party duties frequently required Yaari to travel all over the country. In the spring of 1947 he started the bureaucratic wheels moving to purchase a new and better vehicle to replace the old Ford he had been using. In an attempt to jump the queue for an import license, the movement tried to get sympathizers in the United States to make him a gift of a Plymouth, Mercury, or Chrysler.[64] Months passed, the War of Independence was raging in the country, but there was still no new car.[65] He wrote to the movement's emissary in the United States again, asking him to expedite the shipping of the vehicle; "and if you don't forget the radio, that would be wonderful."[66] In the spring of

---

61 Yaari to Yosef Shamir, Aug. 22, 1949, HHA, 95-7.12(1).
62 Yaari to Nathan Yonathan, May 28, 1957, HHA, 95-7.15(3).
63 Yaari to Howard Fast, Mar. 22, 1952 (and Fast to Yaari, July 10, 1952), *Al Hamishmar*, Sept. 19, 1952.
64 Yaari to Bar-niv, Apr. 6, 1947, HHA, 95-7.11(1); the Supervisor of Road Transport (in English), Mar. 18, 1947, HHA, 95-7.10(10).
65 Yaari to Nathan [Peled] and Yehuda [Tubin], Feb. 3, 1948, HHA, 95-7.10(11).
66 Yaari to Holish, Feb. 20, 1950, HHA, 95-7.12(2).

1950 the movement's American office informed him that it had decided to send him a car as a token of esteem for his efforts on behalf of the State of Israel, in the Knesset and Histadrut.[67] Yaari's American car, a Chrysler, became a byword in the movement and sparked no little criticism. At the Kibbutz Artzi conference in 1956 he vented himself in emotional and angry words about all the backbiting on the subject and complained that such a wonderful movement was being nagged about an issue of this sort.[68] When one member accused the leadership of becoming estranged from the rank and file, Yaari replied angrily. At which point Daniel Ben-Nahum of Beit Zera got up and regaled the Kibbutz Artzi executive committee with a Hassidic tale:

> Why will the messiah arrive riding on a donkey and not on a white horse, as would be appropriate for such a distinguished Jew? [...] Because were the messiah to come riding a noble stallion, people would look at the horse and not at the messiah. And the analogy: that horse is like the flashy car Meir Yaari travels in. When a person demands that the people make do with a pittance while he travels in an American sedan, we may well fear that the people will look at the car and not at him.[69]

Years passed, and Yaari needed a new car again. This time, too, circles close to the movement in the United States decided to make him a present. After he consulted with those in the know he proposed that this time they send him a Dodge, with a powerful engine; adding, as a show of expertise, "perhaps with eight cylinders."[70] The reason for this requirement was his frequent ascents to Jerusalem. He paid close attention to every detail and asked for double springs, a radio, a heater and cooling fan, a tinted and if possible shatterproof windshield, with a sun-visor for the driver, and leather upholstery. And the car itself should be steel grey.[71]

---

67 Yehoshua Porter (New York) to Yaari, Apr. 21, 1950, Ibid.
68 Yaari at the 32nd Kibbutz Artzi Council, Oct. 31, 1956, HHA, 5-20. 8(1).
69 Shaham, *Shalom ḥaverim*, 220.
70 Yaari to Avraham Shenker (New York), Feb. 25, 1957, HHA, 95-7.13(4).
71 Ibid.

Yaari at his office, 1950s.
Courtesy of Hashomer Hatza'ir Archive, Givat Haviva.

CHAPTER 14

The Kibbutz during the Transition from Yishuv to State

While Mapam and its affiliated kibbutz movements were embroiled in internal power struggles and fighting to survive, not to mention trying to figure out where they fit into the global revolution, vast changes were taking place in Israel, with major implications for the health and status of the kibbutzim. Some 700,000 new immigrants arrived in the country between Independence and the end of 1951, doubling its Jewish population. In that same interval, the kibbutz population grew by only 25%. In early 1948, the kibbutzim had reached their high-water mark of 7.5% of the Jewish population. By 1952 they were down to 5%.

Many problems beset the kibbutzim in those years, because so many of the functions they had played in the voluntary Yishuv society were now the province of the state. Now, unlike in the past, the kibbutzim were only a minor partner in what had become the most important venture of Israeli society—absorbing the mass immigration. The main reason was demographic. When the tidal wave of immigration began after Independence, all the kibbutzim in the country had a total population of less than 50,000; they simply lacked the capacity to absorb hundreds of thousands of newcomers.[1] In addition, the two groups—the immigrants and the kibbutzim—were not on the same wavelength and were not a good match for each other. Most of the immigrants were

---

1 At independence, the total kibbutz population was around 45,000 persons, including 21,500 members. Kibbutz Artzi was the second-largest movement, after Hakibbutz Hame'uḥad, with about 6,500 members and a total population of 14,000.

repelled by the kibbutz way of life, which ran counter to their values and aspirations. Few if any had a background that prepared them for communal living and they were not attracted by farming and rural life. Their primary value was the family and they wanted to cultivate close family settings. Most of the immigrants from Muslim countries were religiously observant, to varying degrees, and were put off by the blatant secularism of the kibbutzim. (The religious kibbutz movement was tiny and many of its settlements were immersed in reconstruction after the havoc wreaked by the War of Independence.) The Holocaust survivors from Eastern Europe were repelled by what they saw as a local version of the Soviet *kolkhoz*, a social format that was too rigid for their taste. In general, material conditions on the kibbutzim were inferior to those elsewhere in the country; and after many years of hardship and wandering, what the Holocaust survivors wanted to do, more than anything else, was rebuild their own homes.

From the other side, the kibbutzim were not falling over themselves to take in people they saw as foreign and alien.[2] Integrating immigrants into a kibbutz is very different from absorbing them in other forms of settlement and rather like admitting strangers into the family. In the past, the kibbutzim had absorbed olim with prior training and socialization in Europe; there was a strong bond and sense of solidarity between the kibbutz members and the young adults of their movements in the Diaspora even before the latter arrived in the country. During the post-Independence era of mass immigration, however, the newcomers were older, arrived with families, and had no preparation for kibbutz life. As far as the kibbutzim were concerned, identification with the cardinal principles of communal living was a prerequisite for joining them, and this was not possible for those without a prior ideological and occupational education. Kibbutz Artzi, under Yaari's leadership, was the most inflexible of all the kibbutz movements on this matter.

In fact, all the kibbutz movements found it difficult to absorb newcomers, to offer them appropriate living conditions, and teach them Hebrew. Many kibbutzim had been severely damaged during the War of

---

[2] Yablonka, *Survivors of the Holocaust*, 199–207, 221–230.

Independence. Almost all of them were in economic straits, they did not receive the full absorption budgets allocated them on paper, and living accommodations were at a premium. The daily reality on the kibbutzim was backbreaking toil and scant physical comfort. In 1954, some 40% of their members were still living in temporary structures; only 30% lived in apartments with attached sanitary facilities.[3] The members worked very hard, received only six to eight days of vacation a year, and their annual individual budget (for items not provided by the kibbutz) was 30 Israel pounds (equivalent to four days' salary of an industrial worker at that time).[4] The two kibbutz movements affiliated with Mapam, which had once been in the forefront of immigrant absorption, were now attached to a party that was languishing in parliamentary opposition, far from the circles of power and the budgetary tap. They were up to their necks with the problem of members' leftward drift and veneration of the Soviet Union, which, in fact, soon led to a bitter split in Hakibbutz Hame'uḥad.

The kibbutz, previously the most important form of agricultural settlement, had now been relegated to second place; it was the moshavim that absorbed most of the new immigrants in the rural sector. During the War of Independence, and even more so afterward, vast new territories became available for Jewish settlement, but the kibbutz movements lacked the capacity to exploit this opportunity. Their pool of human resources was sparse: their youth movements in Europe had been annihilated and they had few new settlement cadres abroad or in Israel. To make matters worse, many members, both veterans and newcomers, were abandoning the kibbutzim for the cities. This demoralizing phenomenon was exacerbated by the decline in the social and ideological prestige of the kibbutz. In brief, the establishment of the state, the districts freshly available for settlement, and the mass immigration—all of which should have presented the kibbutzim with new opportunities for growth and activity—actually confronted them with highly complex problems and a sense that they had missed the boat.

---

3 Shlomo Rosen in *Hedim* 49 (1956)
4 Yisrael Pinhasi in *Ha-shav'ua*, Mar. 2, 1956, 3.

In KA, there were two main lines of thought about the future path. Some believed that everything should be done to maintain the pioneering tension of the past; others held that the time had come to develop the kibbutz as a home and raise the members' standard of living. The first approach was championed mainly by the leadership echelons, the second, by the rank and file.[5] The tension between the two was a modern version of the fundamental dilemma that had been with the kibbutz since its inception—the contrast between the kibbutz as a means for realizing national and social goals, on the one hand, and the kibbutz as a commune, a unique human and social milieu with value in its own right, a way of life whose very existence was a goal to be pursued, on the other. Yaari's position was clear: in the current stage (the early years of the state) the kibbutz was not an end, but a means, "a national social-class instrument serving as the avant-garde in settlement, in the class war, and in the ingathering of the exiles."[6] He accordingly called on the comrades to make concessions today in the name of tomorrow's achievements. This can be put in a slightly different formulation, in which the dilemma that had always troubled KA reverberates clearly: in the first years after Independence, Yaari saw the kibbutz as the vanguard, the pioneers marching before the camp and leading the country towards the social revolution, rather than as a model or prototype of the future society.

However, many members were inclined to see the kibbutz as a goal and wanted to build their own home, not society at large. After so many years of effort for the collective, they were less willing to sacrifice in the name of national goals, if it came at the cost of their own standard of living. Rank-and-file members and their representatives at movement gatherings vehemently demanded that it think about ways to satisfy the members' desire for some reward after their years of toil. Remarks in this spirit were heard as early as the Kibbutz Artzi Council in December 1948. The official topic on the agenda was ideological collectivism, but the delegates deflected the debate to the internal

---

5 The discussion that follows is based largely on Pauker, "Utopia."
6 Yaari, *Qibbuz galuyot*, 8.

situation of kibbutz society. Within about six months, grassroots pressure forced the convening of a council to address domestic kibbutz affairs. This gathering has gone down in the folklore of Kibbutz Artzi as the "electric kettle council," because it ended with a decision to allow members to have radio sets and electric kettles in their own rooms.[7]

The "electric kettle council" was not Yaari's initiative. Quite the contrary. He could not fathom why there was a need for a formal consideration of problems linked to the standard of living on the kibbutzim. Even before the council met he knew which way the wind was blowing in Kibbutz Artzi; as it proceeded he heard very clear statements that were antithetical to his own position. For example, a member of the host kibbutz, Nir David, said: "For us, the kibbutz is not just a means to achieve national and socialist goals; the kibbutz is also a goal in its own right, to benefit our people and see them happy."[8] Yaari's response to these and similar statements was: "Work twice as hard! That is the remedy. And fight against all the self-indulgence and public fatigue."[9]

All appeals to Yaari and the demands that he take steps to change and improve the situation are evidence of his lofty status in the movement and of the members' high expectations of him. They assumed that the situation would get better if he did something. But his responses make it clear that even though he knew which way the members were leaning, he did not grasp or internalize their wishes and was effectively out of touch with developments on the ground and estranged from the sentiments of the rank and file. The gulf between the leadership's position and what the members wanted was obvious and a topic of public discussion; but the leadership continued to ignore the voices that called for improved living conditions on the kibbutz.

"Why this hue and cry?" Yaari demanded of the critics. "Were things better 20 years ago?"[10] In 1949 he made it plain that he took

---

7 Minutes of the 28th Kibbutz Artzi Council (June 1949), HHA, 6.20-5(1)
8 Sala Altman at the Kibbutz Artzi Council in Nir David, June 1949, *Yedi'ot ha-Kibbutz ha-Artzi*, August 1949, 29.
9 Yaari at the 28th Kibbutz Artzi Council (June 1949), HHA, 6.20-5(1).
10 The criticism was voiced in the debates of the Kibbutz Artzi executive committee held in advance of the council at Nir David. See Pauker, "Utopia," 403–404.

a dim view of the construction of two-room suites for members. For him, that was bursting the dam of the planned socialist economy. He was also opposed to increasing the "provisions" budget (the quota for outlays on items that made life slightly more pleasant). Yaari knew that his positions were causing the members to grumble, but he stuck to his somewhat Spartan line on the standard of living. His promise for 1954 was: "We will see to a fair standard of living for the kibbutz member, which should be more or less equal to the standard of living of a skilled worker, and no more."[11]

Given Yaari's deafness to the members' wishes, it is hard to avoid the criticism that he did not exactly practice what he preached. He was not really living the kibbutz way of life and sharing the members' daily hardships. He spent most of his time away from Merhavia, mainly in Tel Aviv. Members carped about his apartment, his car, his driver, his office, his telephone, and his private secretary. He dismissed the criticism as petty and represented all these perks as tools that were essential for his job. As we have seen, he traveled abroad frequently for medical care. Some wondered whether every kibbutz member, or even every ordinary citizen of the young state who had health problems like his, could keep flying off to Europe for treatment, as he did.[12]

In the deliberations and debates about the standard of living and building the kibbutz as a home, the rank-and-file members were arrayed against the leaders—both of the movement as a whole, at the various levels, and of each individual kibbutz. The intermediate leadership echelons amounted to a sort of coalition of interested parties, who held or could aspire to relatively cushy jobs in the city and even abroad. Such positions were accompanied by a fair amount of emotional gratification, compelled (or allowed) them to spend the week away from the kibbutz, and exempted them at least temporarily

---

11 Yaari, *Qibbuz galuyot*, 182–183.
12 In late 1971, Yair Kotler published a series of articles on the kibbutz in the *Ha'aretz Weekend Magazine*, in which he referred to Yaari's standard of living, including his trips to Switzerland for ophthalmologic care. Yaari replied in a letter to Gershom Schocken, the newspaper's owner and editor, in which he explained why these trips were necessary (letter dated Dec. 15, 1971, HHA, 95-7.22(4)).

from the daily grind there, with all of its problems and frustrations. Yaari had a major say in who got these jobs; the need or desire to please him, combined with the urge to escape daily life on the kibbutz, left these "apparatchiks" somewhat estranged from the yearnings of the ordinary members. These differences and conflicts of interest amounted to class gulf; members of the second and third rank of the movement and party bureaucracy generally supported the leader, in part to promote their own interests, and turned their backs on the needs and desires of the comrades on the kibbutz whom they were supposed to represent.

The intermediate leadership echelons shielded Yaari from most of his flock and left him oblivious to what the latter were thinking. It is only a slight exaggeration to say that Yaari was cushioned by the sycophancy of the local and intermediate-level officials, who fell into step with him, defended his positions, and agreed with everything he said. There was a widespread feeling in the movement that he cultivated a clique of yes-men, people who bent to satisfy the leader's needs and whims instead of criticizing them.[13] This pattern was not really to his benefit, because it shielded him from the criticism and left him in the dark about the sentiments of most members of KA.[14]

As in the past, one of the methods employed to secure the historical leadership's power and control was ideological collectivism. As a rule, the members recognized its importance for keeping the movement intact and avoiding a split, but had two strong criticisms of the principle: the content of decisions and how they were reached. Members complained that, as implemented in KA, ideological collectivism entailed dictates from on high rather than an expression of the members' opinions, and was thus in fact a species of "guided democracy." As for content, they were irked by the emphasis on political matters and expressed their fear that, in its current guise, ideological collectivism was turning KA into a

---

13 Yigal Wilfand to Yaari, 1976, *Yedi'ot ha-kibbutz*, Dec. 4, 2009, 32.
14 Interview with Betta Reuveni, who was Yaari's secretary in 1969–1974, HHA, 95-7.3(9); Menachem Gerson to Yaari, Feb. 7, 1955, HHA, 95-7.14(1); Avraham Benshalom, 25th anniversary council of Kibbutz Artzi, October 1952, HHA, 5-20.6.

political party only and failing to represent the meaning of the kibbutz as a social and economic entity as well.[15]

It did not escape the members that ideological collectivism was effectively a device to safeguard the leadership's position; it was hinted that the latter's heavy-handed interpretation of ideological collectivism was intended to protect its own standing and did not have the movement's best interests in view. Some even asserted that the leaders were fanning the hysteria about the threat that ideological debate posed for the movement in order to justify the need to crush the leftists who deviated from the official line. Yaari was the main target of the various shafts directed at the leadership, whose essence was that ideological collectivism achieved only a superficial ideological uniformity, when, in fact, the movement lacked a collective ideology with deep roots. What is more, the leadership was not responsive to the members' expectations and was not steering the movement where the members wished to go.[16] But these criticisms, and others, did not budge Yaari from his habitual methods, and everything went on as before.

This isolation from or indifference to what the members wanted was reflected in the condescending treatment that Yaari and the other leaders meted out to the movement's settlement cadres from Israel and abroad. For example, the Latin American cadre that established Kibbutz Ga'ash in the Sharon had wanted to settle in the Negev rather than the center of the country, but the Kibbutz Artzi institutions decided otherwise without consulting them.[17] Representatives of another cadre, from Argentina, told Yaari that they and their comrades hoped to set up their own kibbutz in the Negev. "You will not tell me what the movement needs," he replied. "I know what to do," and the cadre was sent to the Lower Galilee (Gazit).[18] Such contacts with the leadership left the enthusiastic youngsters with a bitter taste in their mouth. The

---

15 Theodor Holdheim at the 29th Kibbutz Artzi Council (June 1950), *Yedi'ot ha-Kibbutz ha-Artzi*, August 1950, p. 63; Avraham (Buma) Yas'ur at the 25th anniversary council of Kibbutz Artzi, October 1952, HHA, 5-20.6.
16 Pauker, "Utopia," 210-214.
17 Bar-Gil, *Be-reshit hayah halom*, 77.
18 Ibid., 86, 89, 141; Yaari at the Kibbutz Artzi Executive Committee, Aug. 28, 1950, HHA, 5-10.5(15).

immigrants from Latin America felt that Yaari, Hazan, and Tabenkin were arrogant and disdainful. It was an encounter between young immigrants who esteemed and even worshiped the senior leaders, and leaders who saw the cadres as raw material to be worked as they wished and expected total obedience to their orders.

The comrades' true desires and the hardship that made their lives so difficult did not trouble Yaari nearly as much as the social status of the kibbutz in the young state. He gave less thought to the conflict between improving the members' standard of living and continuing to pursue the mission of the kibbutz than to the disparity between the opportunities for new settlements offered by the territorial situation after the War of Independence and the sorry state of the kibbutzim and shortage of prospective recruits. It was essential to decide which took precedence—assuring the stability of existing kibbutzim or establishing new ones. The grass roots insisted that new cadres be sent to reinforce existing kibbutzim, much to the displeasure of Yaari, who had to give in on this occasion.[19]

As a result of the kibbutzim's pleas for new members and the dwindling pool of potential new settlers, the establishment of new settlements was all but frozen. The existing kibbutzim, both older and newer, were groaning under the burden of the economic austerity and a shortage of working hands, and Yaari was well aware of this. Kibbutzim did not just invite him to their anniversary celebrations; they also complained to him and the movement institutions about the unbearable situation and submitted repeated requests for an infusion of new blood. On Kibbutz Gat in the summer of 1950, the teenagers were putting in full workdays instead of attending school, because there was no one to pick the fruit, the straw was lying uncollected in the fields, and only 1,500 of its 2,500 acres for field crops had been plowed. The kibbutz secretariat anticipated what the movement leadership's response would be and forestalled it: "We have already been living on hope for six months."[20] As expected, Yaari's reply was that the kibbutz

---

19 Yaari at the 29th KA Council, *Yedi'ot ha-Kibbutz ha-Artzi*, August 1950, 96.
20 Meeting of the Kibbutz Artzi secretariat, Aug. 13, 1950, quoted by Pauker, "Utopia" 156.

should just hold out; there was no immediate solution, because at least a third of the movement's kibbutzim were in a similar situation.

The manpower shortage could have been alleviated to some extent by using hired workers, a solution that would also have helped absorb new immigrants. But reliance on wage labor was anathema for Yaari and he would hear nothing of it. "Hired labor would consume the kibbutz movement like cancer or gangrene," he thundered.[21] Any leniency in the matter would write *finis* to the movement and the kibbutz would no longer be a kibbutz. He had no shortage of ethical and moral arguments against using hired labor and turning the kibbutz into a "commune of exploiters," but he never really related to the practical implications of his stand for the movement or appreciated how it was understood by those on the outside.[22] He was not alone in his opposition to hired labor: all the kibbutz movements believed that it would jeopardize the communal kibbutz way of life and saw it as a danger to their essence and unique socioeconomic model.

The refusal to employ hired workers drew down a critical barrage, orchestrated by Prime Minister Ben-Gurion, that the kibbutzim were not doing their part to help absorb new immigrants. Ben-Gurion's stand and actions made it even harder for the kibbutz movements to meet the challenges raised by the establishment of the state. Ben-Gurion, who held firmly to his concept of *mamlakhtiyut*, which meant placing the state above all partisan, ideological, sectoral, and tribal considerations, expected every element of society, including the kibbutzim, to accept the rules of the game as he defined them. He called on the kibbutzim to place themselves at the service of the mass immigration and the Jewish people, but was disappointed. This spurred his attack on them during the election campaign in January 1949: "It is unthinkable," he said, "that the Chinese wall erected around our various forms and varieties of settlements will now serve to exclude the new immigrants."[23] A year later, in the Knesset, he assailed the kibbutzim for their failure to help

---

21 Kibbutz Artzi Executive Committee, Jan. 12, 1949, Aug. 28, 1950, HHA, 5-10.5(15).
22 Yaari to Yehoshua Mano'ah, 1950, HHA, 5-20.6(5).
23 David Ben-Gurion, "What the Future Holds, remarks at the Mapai council, Jan. 12, 1949," *Ḥazon ve-derekh*, 1: 19.

absorb the immigrants: "Over the past two years I have been embarrassed and ashamed by the sight of the pioneering movement's failures. The greatest event in our history has come to pass, the exodus from Egypt has begun, the ingathering of the exiles is in progress—but what have our pioneers done? Have the kibbutzim rallied to this cause?"[24] Yaari was the only member of Knesset who heckled the speaker from the floor. The catchphrase "embarrassed and ashamed" became part of Israeli political folklore, with two very different meanings attached to it: for the public at large, it stood for the kibbutz movements' failure to help absorb the immigrants; for the kibbutz movements, it symbolized Ben-Gurion's crusade against them.

The "embarrassed and ashamed" speech was only the visible tip of the disagreements that pitted Ben-Gurion against the kibbutzim on a broad spectrum of issues. At the root of the dispute was the nonpartisanship that he championed and the new and additional meaning he wanted to assign to the concept of pioneering. Ben-Gurion expanded this concept and the definition of "pioneers" to the point of negating the traditional essence of the pioneering identity, which he replaced with an array of moral qualities, character traits, and tasks that drew on willpower, while depriving the kibbutz of its exclusivity and even its primacy in implementing this mission. Ben-Gurion expected the kibbutzim to dance to his tune: he, Ben-Gurion, would define the content and objectives of pioneering, which the kibbutzim would obediently realize. "In the past, all of the immigrants and indeed the entire Jewish people were a sort of reserve for Degania and Mishmar Ha'emeq and Ein Ḥarod and Nahalal," said Ben-Gurion during the 1949 election campaign. "There may have been a psychological, but not a moral, justification for this approach once. But now it is dangerous. Now we have to go about things the opposite way."[25] Again and again he attacked Hakibbutz Hame'uḥad and Kibbutz Artzi—his political rivals—for failing to shoulder their responsibility to the country and asserted that their refusal to join his government and do their share

---

24 *Divrei Haknesset*, III, 106th session, Jan. 16, 1950, 536.
25 Ben-Gurion, "What the Future Holds," p. 19.

in immigrant absorption severely detracted from their pioneering nature, which he denounced as "limited liability pioneering." But he distinguished between the pioneering ethos of individuals on the kibbutzim, which remained as it had been, and their movements' "isolationist and truncated pioneering." Ben-Gurion had no quarrel with the rank-and-file kibbutznik; his criticism was directed at the leaders. In part, due to his actions and statements, the public no longer viewed kibbutz membership per se as helping to realize the objectives of the national collective. This undermined the movement's pioneering self-image and contributed to the decline in its luster.[26]

Yaari, like other kibbutz movement leaders and members, saw Ben-Gurion's actions as an attempt to rob the kibbutz of one of its main pillars, an idea that had been unchallenged in the Yishuv before independence: that the kibbutz was the ultimate embodiment of the pioneering ethos. Yaari fought back, citing the achievements of the past and noting it was the kibbutzim that had determined the borders of the state.[27] He also accused Mapai of leaving the kibbutz movement out of the immigrant absorption process.[28] Nevertheless, he was aware of the movements' paltry contribution to immigrant absorption; only a week before the "embarrassed and ashamed" speech he himself had expressed his sense that the kibbutzim had failed on this front and had proven unable to make a significant contribution to immigrant absorption.[29]

In the first years of statehood, when Mapam sat in the parliamentary opposition, Yaari attacked the state for allowing clerical forces free rein, for undermining the IDF's status as a people's army, and for obstructing the growth of the kibbutz movement, and warned about the dangers of a police state.[30] In combination with his tendency to concentrate on international matters on the one hand and the domestic affairs of his

---

26 Horowitz and Lissak, *Trouble in Utopia*, 111-113.
27 Yaari, *Be-ma'avaq le-amal meshuḥrar*, 303.
28 Yaari, *Qibbuẓ galuyot*, 9-10.
29 Mapam Central Committee Secretariat, Jan. 9, 1950, HHA, 90.62(2).
30 Mapam Political Committee, Sept. 19, 1951, HHA, 90.60-*alef*(1); Yaari to the Kibbutz [Merḥavia], Dec. 10, 1951, KMA, MYF, 1(3).

party and the kibbutz movement, on the other, we might conclude that Yaari was estranged from the state. I would suggest, however, that his remarks were prompted by his sense of exclusion and frustration and were intended to strengthen the camp within while marking the outside forces that threatened it—but, without drawing a sufficiently clear line between Mapai, the ruling party, and the state. All the same, just as he was consistent in assigning Zionism primacy over Socialism, so too here, in the tension between partisanship and nonpartisanship, and despite his criticisms and the disaffection he felt and demonstrated, Yaari's loyalty to the state never waned and he never reached the point of challenging the principles of democracy or working against them. Thus he combined opposition to Ben-Gurion's doctrine of the state above all with a fierce loyalty to the State of Israel.

In his eyes, the state posed two potential threats. The first was that it was arrogating to itself the roles previously played by the kibbutz and thus, as the sole instrument for realizing national missions, rendering the kibbutz unnecessary. The second was that statehood might be viewed as the final realization of Zionism and tantamount to the end of the national stage as sketched out in his theory of stages of 1927. Either might lead to the conclusion that the kibbutz had outlived its historical role and that its pioneering mission was over. For Yaari, the interpretation that hovered in the background, namely, that establishment of the state meant that the national phase was over and the socialist and revolutionary phase had begun, had catastrophic implications. He enlisted the full measure of his intellectual powers and persuasive abilities to convey his own reading of the map to the members of his movement and the public at large: the constructive and national stage was still in progress and the revolutionary and socialist stage had not yet arrived.[31]

His repeated efforts to reconcile the establishment of the independent state with the Theory of Stages and prove that the first stage had not ended with the achievement of statehood derived first and foremost from his deep concern about the status of the kibbutzim

---

31 Yaari, *Qibbuz galuyot*, 62–67.

in Israeli society and their economic future. One function of the original Theory of Stages had been to permit Hashomer Hatza'ir to cooperate with the bourgeoisie and receive money from the Zionist Organization. The end of the first stage and transition to the second stage, the revolutionary, would require terminating this collaboration, with all this implied. Yaari certainly wanted the kibbutzim to continue to receive their share of the funds contributed by overseas Jews of all classes, and for Mapam to join a parliamentary coalition with non-proletarian parties. For him, the pioneering stage would not be over as long as Israel required the financial assistance of world Jewry so that it could absorb immigrants. In the first years of statehood he drew on Borochovist terminology and declared that as long as the Jews were an ex-territorial people and still in the process of reuniting in their own country, an abnormal people scattered all over the world and aspiring to normal existence in its homeland, Mapam would collaborate with the bourgeois parties that dealt with the ingathering of the exiles. In short, the first stage, the pioneering and national stage, would be over only when the Israeli economy and Israeli society could stand on their own two feet, both financially and politically. Until then, cooperation with all socioeconomic classes remained essential, and Diaspora Jews' philanthropic support of Israel, including the kibbutzim, must continue.[32] His fears for the kibbutzim's economic stability had always guided his path. If they moved too far Left, he feared, the result would be near-excommunication of the movement and an economic boycott of its kibbutzim.[33] In fact, Mapam's Leftist tendencies did threaten the allocation of land to its affiliated kibbutzim and budgets for its Naḥal cadres and its border settlements.[34]

Statements and appraisals of this sort, along with the fact that Yaari made the kibbutz his top priority, so that all his actions were measured by how they affected its prestige and material wellbeing, may lead us to wonder whether perhaps the kibbutz was a hindrance, rather than a springboard, to the development of a genuine Socialist

---

32 Ibid., 11, 62, and 63; Yaari, *Al Hamishmar*, Apr. 17, 1953.
33 Kibbutz Artzi Executive Committee, Sept. 24, 1950, HHA, 5.10-5 (15).
34 Yishai, "The vision and its lesson," 88.

Left in Israel (just as Marx asserted that a property-owning proletariat would be hesitant about mounting the barricades of the class struggle). Mapam was in fact a kibbutz political party that relied on its urban voters to produce a parliamentary bloc of sufficient strength to defend the interests of the kibbutzim. The other side of this coin is that the nature of KA as a settlement agency with material interests prevented it from wandering outside the Zionist tent.

In 1954, Yaari produced a systematic and focused exposition of how he saw the processes and changes that had taken place since independence in a small-format book of some 200 pages, *The Ingathering of Exiles in the Mirror of our Day*. Although it was conceived as an outline for discussion in advance of the Eighth Kibbutz Artzi convention, it dealt almost entirely with political issues and all but ignored internal kibbutz matters. At the opening session of the convention, in April 1954, he spoke in lofty terms about the Zionist, settlement, and class objectives of the kibbutz, but said not a word about the kibbutz itself.[35]

Yaari invested much effort in the book. He solicited his comrades' reactions to the early drafts, often replying in the vein of "I have noted some of your comments" or "the final version was modified in the spirit of your comments." To what extent did he really pay attention to readers' remarks? "I gave consideration to every idea that had the potential to add, correct, and improve, if it was compatible with my views and stylistic preferences."[36] When the task was complete he was very proud of the book he had written and sent copies to many people. Shlonsky responded with flattery: "We have very few leaders among us who are equipped with a full intellectual quiver, so that they can employ appropriate weapons in their political battles, too. It is truly a shame your many tribulations—at home and abroad—allow you to write so infrequently."[37] President Itzhak Ben-Zvi returned the favor by sending Yaari his own book about the Second Aliyah, with a friendly inscription. From distant Sede Boqer, the recently retired Ben-Gurion wrote him a candid and cordial letter. But there was no response from

---

35 Eighth Kibbutz Artzi Convention, Apr. 2, 1954, HHA, 5-20.7(2).
36 The correspondence is filed together in HHA, 95-7.13(7).
37 Shlonsky to Yaari, Mar. 25, 1954, HHA, 95-7.13(7).

Prime Minister Moshe Sharett, other than from his private secretary, which—as we learn from the complaint that Yaari addressed to Sharett—"was sent, by chance or not, in a used envelope."[38] In the meantime, he encountered Sharett in the Knesset building three or four times and persuaded himself that the Prime Minister had decided to ignore his greetings. Yaari wondered whether he was the party at fault and remembered that he had never had an appropriate opportunity to congratulate Sharett in person when he became Prime Minister, because ill health had kept him away from the Knesset just then. In the letter in which he expressed his grievance, Yaari complimented Sharett for "cultivating relations that are cordial, if not more so, with the representatives of the various parties, even Agudat Yisrael," and added, feeling wounded, that "there is no justification for you to deviate from your habit in my case and intentionally refrain from the same degree of cordiality and friendship that you show the representatives of all the parties in Israel."[39]

Sharett, astonished by this letter, replied to Yaari in two densely typed pages that make it clear how other people saw the recipient. "Good God!" wrote Sharett, "do you really imagine that I maintain such detailed ledgers in my memory of who congratulated me and who did not and draw precise conclusions from this distinction?" He would avoid "suggesting psychoanalytic reasons" for why Yaari thought him so cool to him. And he added, after explaining just how overworked he was, "nevertheless I will make an effort, because the danger that extraneous intentions may be assigned to my conduct, as reflected in your letter, is truly appalling." Below his signature he added a handwritten postscript: "One small detail. There is a standing regulation in government offices to reuse envelopes whenever possible. I was delighted to learn from your letter that there are clerks who are at pains to follow this rule. I am astonished that you saw this economy measure, which should be praised, as a mark of condescension and even intentional condescension."[40]

---

38 Yaari to Moshe Sharett, July 26, 1954, HHA, 95-7.13(7).
39 Ibid.
40 Sharett to Yaari, marked "personal," Aug. 8, 1954, HHA, 95-7.13(7).

The phrase "ingathering of the exiles" that features in the title of Yaari's book replaced "the process of the territorial concentration of the Jewish people," a phrase taken from Borochov and the original title of the manuscript. Yaari used both expressions in the text itself. *The Ingathering of Exiles in the Mirror of our Day* is a manifesto that draws on Borochov's thought as the guiding ideology of Kibbutz Artzi and uses it to ground and defend Yaari's interpretation of the Theory of Stages and keep the movement focused on its pioneering mission in the national stage, without trying to speed up the clock of history and hasten the start of the revolutionary stage. It is another example of Yaari's instrumental application of ideology to buttress his leadership and defend the organization he headed. He had adopted Marxism in 1924, making it the second pillar, alongside Zionism, of Hashomer Hatza'ir's ideology; now he turned to Borochov's doctrine to extract a contemporary ideology, relevant to the present, which served as a sort of enhancement, a Zionist supplement, to Marxism-Leninism.

After Yaari adopted Borochovism, loyalty to this doctrine became the acid ideological test for members of KA. According to the principles of ideological collectivism, a person who rejected Borochovism could not be part of the movement. This meant that, in Yaari's eyes, a Marxist who did not accept Borochov could not be a Zionist; one of his charges against Sneh was that he rejected Borochov's theoretical explanation for the historical phenomenon of a dispersed people that had survived for thousands of years even though it did not satisfy Stalin's definition of a nation.[41] Only after Yaari, followed by Mapam, endorsed Borochov's doctrine did the KA publishing house, Sifriyat Po'alim, begin issuing his works.[42] Borochov's elevated status after Yaari took him as his master is indicated by the Mapam Central Committee's decision, in 1952, that

---

41 Yaari to Peretz Merhav, Mar. 10, 1953, HHA, 95-7.13(3).
42 Three thick volumes of Borochov's writings appeared between 1955 and 1966, in a copublication by Sifriyat Po'alim and the Hakibbutz Hame'uḥad publishing house. Each volume had two editors, one affiliated with KA and the other with Hakibbutz Hame'uḥad.

his picture would be carried in the May Day parade alongside the long-traditional quartet of Marx, Engels, Lenin, and Stalin.[43]

Now, more than on previous occasions when he had adopted some doctrine and made it part of the ideology of Hashomer Hatza'ir, Yaari saw himself as the heir of the original author and wanted to adapt it to the present situation and be its authorized interpreter to the movement and the public at large.[44] He aspired to play the role, *vis-à-vis* Borochov's thought, that Stalin had assumed in promoting Leninism, and explicitly saw his part as analogous to that of Mao Zedong.[45]

The Ingathering of Exiles in the Mirror of our Day concludes with what amounts to the abandonment of the old definition of the final objective of Mapam and KA as "finding their place in the global revolution" and the announcement of a new objective: "the triumph of socialism in our country."[46] In this formula, Yaari perpetuated and in fact emphasized the primacy of Zionism over socialism. The third component of the party's slogan was "the brotherhood of nations." The order in which the three elements are stated reflected the priorities of Yaari and his party. In the coming years he would have to deal with the challenges raised by each component and the practical difficulty of pursuing all of them at the same time. Doing so would require different proportions than in the past of ideology and practice, of ideas and action. Over time, the weight of ideology would diminish and the dictates of realpolitik would be allowed an ever greater weight.

---

43 Mapam Coordinating Committee, Apr. 8, 1952, HHA, 90.64(2).
44 Yaari to Peretz [Merhav], Jan. 7, 1952, HHA, 95-7.12(10).
45 Yaari, *Qibbuz galuyot*, 64–65; Ibid., 111.
46 Ibid., 184.

Meir and Anda with members of their Kibbutz, in the old dining room of Merḥavia.
Courtesy of Nadav Man, Bitmuna Collection, Kibbutz Merḥavia.

CHAPTER 15

For Zionism, for Socialism, for the Brotherhood of the Nations—and in That Order

The split with Aḥdut Ha'avodah in 1954 made it possible for Mapam, reduced to its Hashomer Hatza'ir core, to open its ranks to Arab members, a step that its erstwhile partner had rejected out of hand. In the jargon of those days, the two factions of the United Mapam differed as to whether it should be a "territorial party," accepting all prospective members who were citizens of Israel, both Jews and Arabs; or a "national party," exclusively Jewish, linked in some fashion to a sister Arab party. There is no consensus as to whether the disagreement about welcoming Arabs into the party was the real reason for the breakup of Mapam, or whether it was just an excuse and the true causes must be sought elsewhere. In any case, both factions' sensitivity on this matter and the knowledge that it could trigger a split led Yaari to be doubly careful. As long as the united party survived he was cautious in his words and moderate in his demand that Arabs be allowed to join it; in retrospect, he attributed the split to this issue.[1]

Within the united Mapam, Yaari offered various arguments in favor of opening its ranks to Arabs. Some of them were pragmatic: the field should not be left solely to Maki; an independent Arab party might take a stand against Jewish immigration. Some of his arguments were in the spirit of the slogan, "without a vision of a militant brotherhood of nations in the party we have no future as a revolutionary party."[2] Still others

---

1 Yisrael Zamir, interview with Yaari, Folder 1, p. 20; Shaul Paz, interview with Yaari, Jan. 28, 1983, HHA, 95-7.3(7)
2 Third Mapam Council, Nov. 27, 1949, HHA, 90.69(1).

presented the attitude towards Arabs not as a favor to them but as a step that would benefit the Jews: a lack of solidarity with the Arabs would harm Zionism and keep it from continuing to advance towards realization of its goals. Yaari believed that a majority in the party wanted to admit Arabs; he was frustrated that his hands were tied by the need to preserve party unity. He did not conceal his unwillingness to trigger a divorce on these grounds,[3] and was candid with Arabs who wanted to join Mapam, letting them know the true situation: Mapam's conversion into a binational party would not take place overnight and they must be patient.[4]

But after Aḥdut Ha'avodah walked out there was no longer any need for patience and deliberation. At the very first session of the Central Committee of the truncated Mapam, Yaari announced that the party would accept Arabs as full members.[5] A month after the split, the party council ratified new bylaws welcoming Arabs into its ranks, making Mapam the first Zionist party to admit them on an equal footing with Jews. Even without Arab members, the Mapam faction had included an Arab since the Second Knesset and the party had insisted on placing an Arab in a realistic slot on its list.

Yaari saw the Arab citizens of Israel as a small minority, less than 15% of the country's population (in 1954) and subject to severe discrimination, and who should be granted full civic equality. He was opposed, however, to allowing them the right of national self-determination within Israel, because, after partition, self-determination was available to the Jews in Israel and to Palestinian Arabs in Jordan (including the West Bank).[6] He rejected the existence of an Arab Palestinian people inside Israel, linked to their brothers and sisters living in the refugee camps. Even before the Six Day War he was opposed to the idea of a "Palestinian entity," which would pose the threat of irredentism and the creation of a fifth column, thus endangering Israel's sovereign existence.[7]

3 Mapam Coordinating Committee, Dec. 29, 1952, HHA, 90.64(2); Mapam Political Committee, Aug. 18, 1949, HHA, 90.66(1).
4 Mapam Coordinating Committee, Dec. 15, 1952, HHA, 90.64(2).
5 *Al Hamishmar*, Aug. 20, 1954.
6 Yaari, *Qibbuẓ galuyot*, 69; idem, *Al Hamishmar*, June 23, 1954; Yaari to Yossi Amitay, May 16, 1961, HHA, 95-7.17(7).
7 Yaari to Aliza Dror, May 7, 1967, HHA, 95-7. 21(1); Yaari to Yossi Amitay, Dec. 24, 1963, HHA, 95-7.18(6); Yaari, *Mivḥanei dorenu*, 116–117.

To the Arab minority, Yaari assigned the role of a bridge for peace with the Arab world.[8] He believed that an intelligent policy could win the hearts of the Arabs as loyal Israeli citizens—even patriots— and enable them to play the role of natural mediator in the efforts to achieve peace with the neighboring countries. To his disappointment, however, the tensions between Israel and the Arab masses, both in Israel and around it, continued to increase, with some of the blame resting on activist groups in Israel. "The dominant line in the country has done everything to turn the Arab minority from a loyal sector to a fifth column," he wrote bluntly at a time when Mapam was a member of the Government.[9]

Yaari's position on the Arabs' status in Israel was a corollary of his acceptance of partition and the consequent establishment of a Jewish state in only part of Palestine. He found it difficult to abandon the idea of Jewish sovereignty in all the territory between the Jordan and the sea; over the years he vacillated between admitting, accepting, and understanding that it was a lost cause, on the one hand, and obsessively holding fast to slogans and dreams. It is possible that in the first years of statehood the concept of the "whole Land of Israel" served him as compensation for abandonment of the binational ideal, as well as post-factum rationalization of his support for that idea. On the eve of the first general elections, in January 1949, Yaari said that instead of bowing to the Great Powers and withdrawing from the Sinai Peninsula, Israel should have occupied Rafiah, and added his fear that Ben-Gurion's approach meant that Israel would not extend to the Jordan River.[10] After the war, he spoke about reuniting the land by means of the brotherhood of the nations and not by military aggression.[11] On this issue, the Shomer faction of Mapam found itself at odds with the former Aḥdut Ha'avodah. Yigal Allon, for example, stated openly that Israel should annex all of Mandatory Palestine up to the Jordan River

---

8 Yaari, *Mivḥanei dorenu*, 126 et passim.
9 Ibid., 119, 124.
10 Mapam Political Committee, Jan. 13, 1949, HHA, 90.66(1).
11 Mapam Political Committee, Apr. 16, 1949, Ibid.; and in retrospect, Yaari, *Mivḥanei dorenu*, 71.

by force of arms.¹² Perhaps we should understand Yaari's statements in favor of Israeli expansion in the first years after independence as a response to the aspirations of Ahdut Ha'avodah or as lip service to keep Mapam united.

But Yaari continued to speak in favor of the "whole Land of Israel" even after the split in 1954 while still rejecting the use of force to achieve that goal. He was still following this line on the eve of the Sinai Campaign in the autumn of 1956. Did his position change after that? In 1957, it was clear to him that Israeli sovereignty from the Jordan to the sea was not on the horizon. The lesson he had learned from the Sinai Campaign and the subsequent Israeli withdrawal from the Gaza District was that achieving that dream by force was a hopeless delusion and merely made peace more distant. But he had not yet totally given up on the idea and repeated it time and again, in various formulations.¹³ It was only in the early 1960s that he totally abandoned the idea of "greater Israel" itself and not just its realization by force.

The clinching argument behind his long support for an expanded Israel was demographic rather than sentimental. Until the United Nations voted for partition, Yaari believed that the entire territory of mandatory Palestine would be needed to absorb and settle the Jewish masses from abroad. Ten years later, after the withdrawal from the Sinai Peninsula, he had realized that it was possible to double and even triple the current population within Israel's 1949 borders.¹⁴ A decade after the UN partition resolution, having finally accepted it, he could assign a new meaning to the concept of "territorial integrity": no longer that of the Land of Israel, but that of "the State of Israel in its current borders."¹⁵

For many years Yaari was troubled by the plight of the refugees created during and after the War of Independence. In 1949 he expressed his concern about what he called the murder of infiltrators: "Arabs are

---

12   Allon was addressing an election rally in Haifa in 1951, where Yaari also spoke; Yaari to Elazar Peri, May 11, 1961, HHA, 95-7.17(7).
13   Yaari, *Mivhanei dorenu*, 71, 124, 151.
14   Ibid., 71.
15   Ibid., 124.

murdered in large numbers as infiltrators. We mustn't murder people who are starving. ... These are people who have been living here for two thousand years. What is necessary is a program for dealing with the refugees and not one leading to genocide."[16] From then on he held a clear position on the refugees, shaped by several principles. The first was that refugees could not be allowed back in Israel before there was peace. Admitting refugees before peace was established would be tantamount to opening the gates to a fifth column. The second principle was that when peace did come, Israel would play its part in solving the refugee question, but the vast majority would be rehabilitated in the countries where they were currently living, especially Jordan, on the basis of development programs funded by the United Nations, Israel, and the neighboring countries. That is, even then the refugees would not be given the option of returning to Israel or accepting compensation, because if every Arab had the right to return to Israel when peace arrived, as a matter of principle, a million Arabs would be added to its population. Nevertheless, Israel would do its part and accept some of the refugees. After the Sinai Campaign he was willing to absorb 250,000 refugees, as part of a deal to annex the Gaza District in order to guarantee peace on the borders.[17]

The basic line that guided Yaari on this question, as on so many others, was that Israel was the state of the Jews and not a binational state. There was only one sovereign people; the Arabs had the right of self-determination in the other part of the land.[18] The difference between the two parts of the land was that Israel had an Arab minority, but there was no corresponding Jewish minority in the Arab-controlled districts. In a broader perspective, he suggested dealing with the refugees in the Middle East based on the principle of population transfer, such as had taken place between India and Pakistan and between Greece and Turkey; he balanced the one million Jewish refugees who had fled to Israel from Arab countries and the death camps of Europe against the Arab refugees.[19]

---

16 Mapam Political Committee, Apr. 16, 1949, HHA, 90.66(1).
17 Mapam Political Committee, Feb. 24, 1960, HHA, 90.121(1); Yaari to Yossi Amitay, May 16, 1961, HHA, 95-7.17(7).
18 Mapam Secretariat, June 28, 1961, HHA, 90.65(1).
19 Yaari to Yossi Amitay, May 16, 1961, HHA, 95-7.17(7).

His position was clear and rested on three pillars: Israel as the homeland of the Jewish people, opposition to an Arab right of self-determination in the State of Israel, and an Israeli obligation to contribute to a solution of the refugee problem when peace came, mainly by helping fund their rehabilitation in the Arab states. Yaari had an opportunity to discuss these ideas with Jean-Paul Sartre and Simone de Beauvoir when the two visited Israel shortly before the Six Day War. He was among those who greeted the couple at the airport, and they came to visit him in Merḥavia.[20] Less than a week before the war broke out, world public opinion was exposed to his views in an article published in a special issue of Sartre's periodical *Les Temps Modernes*, on the Arab-Israeli conflict.

He had been working on the article about the Mapam peace plan, which Sartre had commissioned, since 1966. Claude Lanzmann, the editor of the special issue of *Les Temps Modernes*, had visited Yaari early that year. Yaari, who found Lanzmann sympathetic and attentive, made it plain that before the article turned to the Mapam peace plan he would acquaint readers, candidly and unapologetically, with the Jewish people's unassailable historical right to reclaim its homeland, by right and not by favor. He would refute the claims "that we had stolen another people's homeland" and make it clear that "ever since the Bilu pioneers [of the late nineteenth century] our settlement and efforts here have [not] contained an iota of colonialism or been in the service of imperialism."[21] When the article was published, about a third of it was devoted to explaining the Zionist idea and the motives behind it, so as to counter the argument that Zionism was the direct heir of British Colonialism and Imperialism.[22]

---

20 Some complained that Sartre and de Beauvoir were "prisoners of Mapam" during their visit to Israel. See *Davar*, Apr. 14, 1967; see also the interview with Yaari in *Maariv*, May 5, 1967.
21 Yaari to Simha Flapan, Mar. 2, 1966, HHA, 95-7.20(2).
22 The issue, published on June 1, 1967, stretched to 994 pages. Lanzmann made sure that half of the contributors reflected the Israeli position and half the Arab position. Yaari's essay was 30 pages long: Meir Yaari, "Vers la coexistence pacifique et progressiste entre l'Etat d'Israël et les pays arabes," *Les Temps Modernes* 253 bis,

The elections to the Third Knesset (1955) were the first time that the Hashomer Hatza'ir version of Mapam ran independently. This time Yaari played the role of party leader in every respect and was involved in every detail: finances, personnel, lists of names, kibbutzim that enlisted in the campaign and those that sat on their hands. He insisted that "the style of the platform does not have to be all that intelligent but should be on a level that all can understand."[23] He defined the main points of the party platform in a series of objectives and slogans, including independence and security, the hegemony of the workers' parties, patriotism, the hope for peace with the Arabs, and flying the banner of the brotherhood of the nations. No less important is what was missing from this list: there is no mention of the Soviet Union.

In the elections, on July 26, Mapam won nine Knesset seats, which made it only the sixth-largest faction in the Knesset.[24] What worried Yaari more than anything else was the sharp gain of Herut, headed by Menachem Begin, which almost doubled its electoral strength and won 15 seats. Until this achievement, he said, we had thought of Begin as a circus clown. But during the campaign one could see that "people were bused to Ben-Gurion's rallies; to Begin's they came spontaneously."[25] Yaari denigrated Begin, directly or by allusion, as a demagogue and a fascist. About a year before the Likud came to power in 1977 he expressed his belief that its leader had not changed since the days his followers had thrown rocks at the Knesset (during the debate about accepting reparations from Germany), and that this was what might still be expected of him.[26] After Begin's electoral triumph, Yaari depicted the new prime minister as the disciple of Jabotinsky, intent on hauling

---

1967: Le Conflit israélo-arabe, pp. 661–690. See also Denis Charbit, "Un numéro des *Temps modernes* revisité," *La Règle du jeu* 34 (May 2007): 82–145.
23 Yaari at a meeting of the Kibbutz Artzi Executive Committee, Feb. 20, 1955, May 22, 1955, HHA, 5.10.6(11).
24 For the results of the elections to the Third Knesset, see: http://knesset.gov.il/description/eng/eng_mimshal_res3.htm.
25 Kibbutz Artzi Executive Committee, Aug. 21, 1955, HHA, 5-10.6(1).
26 Yaari to Yigael Yadin, June 20, 1976, HHA, 95-7.23(2).

down the red flag and building a chauvinistic Israel.[27] On the personal plane he resented Begin for having described him as "a stuttering old man about to keel over."[28] Nevertheless their relations were always correct and they exchanged birthday greetings, compliments, and expressions of mutual esteem.[29] Once Yaari even gave Begin credit for having belonged to Hashomer Hatza'ir in his youth.[30]

In 1955 Yaari exaggerated the threat posed by Herut's rise as a stratagem to ease his party's way into the Government. Nevertheless, he guarded against running to join the coalition without conditions. His working assumption during the coalition talks was that Aḥdut Ha'avodah would certainly be in the government; he and Hazan were afraid that Mapam might be left on the outside, with (perish the thought), the "speculators [General Zionists], the enemies of Zion [Maki], and the fascists [Herut]."[31] The climate of the negotiations between Mapam and Mapai was different than in the past, because both sides arrived with the intention of bringing them to a successful conclusion. We have seen that in the failed rounds of previous years, Yaari's position was clear: he wanted his party to have a share of power. The experience of 1949 to 1955 taught him how dangerous it was for his party and movement to sit in the opposition. The danger lay not only in being kept away from the trough, but also in the idleness imposed by the situation and the alternatives to productive activity—pointless debates and useless disagreements.

This time Ben-Gurion sought to conclude coalition agreements with the two workers' parties, Aḥdut Ha'avodah and Mapam, and only then to dicker with the other potential partners, the Progressives and Mizraḥi.[32] Yaari and Hazan chose to conduct the negotiations

---

27 Raphael Bashan, interview with Meir Yaari, Oct. 10, 1977 [IDF Radio], KMA, MYF, 6(5).
28 Mapam Central Committee, Aug. 31, 1959, HHA, 90.68(1).
29 Begin to Yaari, Sept. 3, 1963, HHA, 95-7.18(4) (thanking Yaari for the congratulatory telegram sent for his fiftieth birthday); Begin to Yaari, Nov. 15, 1965; Yaari to Begin, Nov. 21, 1965, HHA, 95-7.19(6).
30 Interview with Yaari, *Maariv*, May 5, 1967.
31 Mapam Political Committee, Aug. 25, 1955, HHA, 90.121(1).
32 Yaari at the Mapam Council, Sept. 25, 1959, HHA, 90.69(3).

themselves. Yaari was interested in a smaller coalition limited to the three workers' parties, which was mathematically possible, if the five seats of Mapai's Arab satellite parties were added to its 40 (which, with Aḥdut Ha'avodah's ten and Mapam's nine, made a total of 64 in the 120-member Knesset). But Ben-Gurion wanted a broader coalition and got what he wanted: the new Government consisted of Mapai, Mizraḥi, Aḥdut Ha'avodah, Mapam, and the Progressives.

For Mapam, the main obstacle to joining the coalition was Ben-Gurion's insistence on a military pact with the United States. Ben-Gurion made it clear that if Mapam's opposition to a treaty with the United States was by way of an ultimatum, "we will not sit together."[33] Both sides looked for a way out and found it; the negotiations, which had been on the verge of breaking down, reached a successful conclusion after this obstacle was overcome. When it came time to allocate ministerial portfolios, it was demonstrated that where there is an overwhelming desire to sit at the Government table, the distribution of the spoils is no obstacle. Even though Mapam had demanded the ministries of Agriculture and Labor, and had to make do with Development and Health, it did not blow up the negotiations on this account.

There were some matters on which Yaari and his party did not agree with the policies of the Government in which they sat; security issues were one of the first that came to the fore. Yaari consistently and adamantly held to the principle that security needs must take precedence over everything else, but also demanded that a line be drawn between national security and aggressive militarism and insisted on meticulous adherence to the purity of arms.[34] A strong inner tension between peace and security marked his ideas. Even when he called for holding to ethical values and wielding moral arguments, Yaari never challenged the primacy of security considerations. The complex and extremely tense Israeli situation produced a dissonance between the values he wished to inculcate in the youngsters of his movement and

---

[33] Political Committee, Aug. 25, 1955, HHA, 90.121(1); Yaari to Ben-Gurion, Jan. 16, 1957, HHA, 95-7.15(2).

[34] Raphael Bashan, "This Week's Interview, with Meir Yaari," *Maariv*, Oct. 14, 1960; Kibbutz Artzi Executive Committee, Mar. 17, 1961, HHA, 5-10.7(5).

the security outlook that many of them held. The almost irreconcilable tension between the dream of the brotherhood of nations and the insistence on the primacy of security needs spawned an anecdote that spread through Kibbutz Artzi: "How do you view the Arab problem?" Yaari supposedly asked a native-born kibbutznik. To which the young man responded, "Through my gunsight!"[35] Nevertheless, although his sermons on behalf of peace and the brotherhood of nations might come to be heard as a droning mantra, they had educational significance, even if not all his listeners absorbed the message and did not always express it in practice.

During the coalition negotiations in 1955 and in the years that followed, when Mapam was part of the Government, Yaari employed the defense card to justify the party's joining and remaining in the coalition. When Israeli reprisal raids became frequent and escalated in 1956, he asserted that Mapam's role was to stand vigil in the government and prevent automatic and disproportionate reactions that would turn world public opinion against Israel, when "for every three or five Jews we kill 50 [Arabs]."[36] The winds of war, which had been blowing since 1955, and the calls for a preemptive strike, voiced not only by the usual suspects, Aḥdut Ha'avodah and Begin, but also by some in Mapai, worried him. He sounded a clear note against launching a war or staging provocations that might endanger Israel's survival. "In a war to defend our lives we can cope even with Stalingrad, but not if we are the aggressors," he said. He denounced a war of choice as "the greatest sin since the Second Temple was destroyed."[37]

During the preparations for the Sinai Campaign, which began on October 29, 1956, Mapam was left in the dark and ignorant of the facts.[38] Yaari suspected that one reason for the compartmentalization of party members who held key positions was that Mapam was a mixed Jewish

---

35 "The Man of the Month: A Man who Didn't Want a Political Party," *Ha'olam Hazeh*, June 5, 1952.
36 Political Committee, Oct. 4, 1956, HHA, 90.121(1).
37 Mapam Secretariat, Dec. 21, 1955 and the continuation of the debate on Dec. 26, 1955, HHA, 90.62(2); Mapam Central Committee, Jan. 18, 1956, HHA, 90.75(1) heh.
38 Mapam Secretariat, Nov. 19, 1956, HHA, 90.63(3).

and Arab party.³⁹ When the decision was brought to the Government for a final vote, the Mapam ministers cast the only nays. Along with Mapam's principled stand for peace and the need for caution in the use of force that was incumbent upon a small people, Yaari noted two other defects of the Sinai Campaign: that Israel had started it and that it was in cahoots with Great Britain and France.⁴⁰

His position on the Sinai Campaign had three main aspects. First, Mapam must and did bear its full share of the burden once hostilities were under way, despite its previous opposition to the war. Second, as the situation on the diplomatic front worsened, he could not resist saying "we told you so."⁴¹ Third, the war was no reason to quit the coalition and Mapam should continue fighting for its ideas from the inside.⁴² During the postmortem after the shooting stopped, Yaari stated that in his view the Sinai campaign had not been just a mistake but also a serious failure, but he was not willing to denounce it on moral grounds. Against the backdrop of the cheers and victory paeans following the war, he insisted that "a rickety peace is better than war."⁴³

How can we explain his position on the Sinai Campaign during and after the fighting? It rested mainly on his commitment to national security and sense of total responsibility in matters related to it. To this must be added that Mapam's membership in the coalition did not allow it the luxury of criticizing from the outside. Recall too that when the war began it enjoyed sweeping public support, so that acceptance of

---

39 This can be inferred from what Foreign Minister Golda Meir said at a meeting with members of Mapam: "Her answer was that we are a Jewish-Arab party, so we cannot be included in foreign missions." Political Committee, Oct. 30, 1956, HHA, 90.121(1).
40 Lahav, "A Small Nation Goes to War"; Mapam Secretariat, Jan. 23, 1957, HHA, 90.63(3). On Mapam's position on the Sinai Campaign, see Barzilai, *Demoqratiyah be-milḥamot*, 55–77.
41 Political resolution passed by the Central Committee on January 31, 1957, HHA, 90.41(2).
42 Kibbutz Artzi Executive Committee, Nov. 25, 1956, HHA, 5-10.6(7); Political Committee, Oct. 30, 1956, HHA, 90.121(1); Yaari, "Memoirs," KMA, MYF, 8(1).
43 He defined the decision to go to war as a mistake but not a crime: Political Committee, Nov. 22, 1956, HHA, 90.121(1); Mapam Secretariat, Nov. 19, 1956, HHA, 90.63(3).

the situation was also a response to the spirit of the time.⁴⁴ But just as Yaari had made clear that Mapam supported the war from the moment the die was cast, despite its reservations about it, he also insisted, in response to dissenting voices and in his best dialectic tradition, that support for the war did not mean an end to his misgivings about it.⁴⁵

When the issue of withdrawing from the Sinai Peninsula and Gaza District came up, Mapam and Yaari were again in the minority. The strength of Yaari's opposition to starting the war was matched by the vigor of his opposition to withdrawing afterwards. In the turbulence of the war he opposed a rapid IDF pullback from Sinai. In March 1957, the Mapam Central Committee voted to oppose the withdrawal agreement and to continue the campaign against withdrawal without adequate guarantees, but with the clear caveat that the coalition must remain intact.⁴⁶

As time passed, Yaari became increasingly critical of the war and of the policy that had led to it. But he also expressed hope for an eventual reconciliation between Israel and its neighbors, in part because Israel bore some of the responsibility for the tension and could take steps to improve the situation. The impression produced by the text he wrote in 1957 to serve as the official agenda for the party convention is that he had yet to fully internalize that he was the head of a party with representatives seated at the Government table. He accused the Government of an activist policy motivated by the assumption that force could solve all problems. The pilots of the state did not believe that reconciliation with the neighboring countries was possible and assigned no importance to mechanisms for peace and mediation. They preferred to continue the situation of no war and no peace, while continuing to ensure relative security along the borders by means of deterrence and intimidation.⁴⁷

---

44 Political Committee, Nov. 22, 1956, HHA, 90.121(1).
45 E.g., Mapam Secretariat, Nov. 19, 1956, HHA, 90.63(3).
46 Mapam Secretariat, Nov. 5, 1956, HHA, 90.63(3); Resolutions of the Mapam Central Committee, Mar. 3, 1957, HHA, 90.41(2).
47 Yaari, *Mivḥanei dorenu*, 117–118.

On October 29, 1956, the first day of the Sinai Campaign, a Border Police unit shot and killed 43 Arabs, including women and children, who were returning from their fields to the village of Kafr Qassem and were unaware that a curfew had been imposed. Four more residents who were killed that evening, another who died of a cerebral hemorrhage after learning of his son's death, and the fetus of a pregnant woman who was shot and killed raised the number of the victims to 49. At first the authorities tried to conceal the massacre by imposing censorship and blocking all access to the village. When Knesset members Tawfik Toubi and Meir Vilner of Maki informed the Knesset plenum of what had happened, their remarks were stricken from the record. But the story got around nevertheless. The first newspaper reports appeared in *Ha'aretz* on November 6 and in *Al Hamishmar* the following day. Even then the details were suppressed; in his weekly column in *Davar*, more than a month later, Nathan Alterman wrote about the "secret whispers" and "darkness" that enshrouded "that incident."[48]

Yaari learned of the massacre from a report sent to him (and to the minister of health, Yisrael Barzilai) by Latif Dori, the secretary of the Arab section of Mapam, who had interviewed wounded villagers at Beilinson Hospital in Petaḥ Tiqvah. Even before then, the day after the massacre, Yaari had told a meeting of the Mapam Political Committee that "the Arab minority in the country is at risk. We have seen our comrades' anxiety for their families and all the Arab members of Mapam. Our sacred task is to instruct the comrades to visit the Arabs and tell them that Mapam will protect them against the hooligan pogroms that have already taken place."[49] The Kafr Qassem massacre made him fear that the principle of the brotherhood of the nations would disintegrate. In retrospect he called it "an atrocity perpetrated by Jewish chauvinism" and mentioned it in the same breath as Deir Yassin.[50]

A year after the Sinai Campaign, about two years into the Knesset's term, Yaari summarized the advantages and disadvantages of sitting in

---

48 Nathan A[lterman], "In the Pale of the Triangle," *Davar*, Dec. 7, 1956.
49 Political Committee, Oct. 30, 1956, HHA, 90.121(1).
50 Yaari to Zvi Arad, Dec. 7, 1956, HHA, 95-7.14 (8); Yaari, *Mivḥanei dorenu*, 125.

the Government. It was desirable to stay in the coalition because of the material benefits, but it would be easier to contest an election from the opposition. Given that Mapam was in the Government, it would have to find a way to demonstrate, shortly before the elections, that it deserved the voters' trust, by taking a stand on matters of interest to the public that influenced its life. One of these was the "ethnic problem," meaning discrimination against Oriental Jews.[51] Mapam had been sorely disappointed in this arena, where there was a stark disparity between its awareness of the problems, candid admission of what was wrong, and presentation of ideas to redress the situation, and its inability to win the votes of Oriental Jews (Mizraḥim). Mapam always made sure to place a candidate of Mizraḥi origin in a realistic place on its Knesset list, but harvested only disappointment from the voting habits of the immigrants from Muslim countries. In 1949, it was their votes that made Mapam painfully aware that it had no chance of being an alternative to Mapai as the ruling party. In 1957, Yaari was aware that the vast majority of the immigrants who had not been absorbed properly were from the Oriental communities and that they were "prey to bitterness and despair and an easy target for the propaganda of Herut and Maki."[52] In the elections for the Fourth Knesset, in 1959, Mapam again failed to do well in concentrations of Mizraḥim in the towns and moshavim. In 1961, Yaari expressed his frustration that Mapam had still not found a path to the hearts of the residents of the development towns and slum neighborhoods, who were in thrall to Herut's slogans and materially dependent on Mapai.[53]

He saw the Wadi Salib riots that erupted in Haifa around the time of the elections to the Fourth Knesset as evidence of the social fissure and the failure to merge all the Diasporas into a single nation; or, in more universal terms, the failure of the melting pot.[54] The immigrants

---

51 Mapam Secretariat, Oct. 28, 1957, HHA, 90.63(3).
52 Yaari, *Mivḥanei dorenu*, 96.
53 Yaari to Avraham Sluck, Oct. 11, 1961, HHA, 95-7.16(6).
54 Mapam Central Committee, Aug. 31, 1959 HHA, 90.68(1). In July 1959, there were several days of violent street demonstrations in the Wadi Salib neighborhood of Haifa. The riots, ignited by the shooting of a Jew of Moroccan descent by police

came to Israel from countries at very different economic, social, and cultural levels. "The decisive question," Yaari thought, "is whether the different communities will amalgamate into a single people, with all the dross that had clung to them in their diaspora lives discarded and all their social and cultural advantages fused together."⁵⁵ Drawing on the conclusions of the Etzioni Commission that probed the Wadi Salib riots, he concluded that a change in the social policies of the government and the Histadrut was a precondition for speeding up the immigrants' assimilation and enumerated a series of steps to achieve this: reducing income disparities, raising the wages of the disadvantaged strata, improving housing conditions for large families, establishing factories in all the development towns, guaranteeing full employment, and enacting laws to ban ethnic discrimination and promote the integration of the different communities.⁵⁶

In his eyes, the discrimination was social and class-based in content and ethnic in form. He saw great danger in the relegation of Oriental Jews to unskilled occupations, while the Ashkenazim were rapidly establishing themselves as skilled tradesmen and liberal professionals. The Oriental Jews were being sent to border communities and disadvantaged neighborhoods, while the Ashkenazim were concentrated along the coastal plain and in the newer neighborhoods in the urban centers. Yaari had the demographic statistics showing the correlation between ethnic origins and socioeconomic status at his fingertips.

The situation in education was especially bleak. He denounced the Education Ministry's plan to assign "talented pupils" and "lagging pupils" to separate classrooms, because that would merely increase the ethnic discrimination. He also condemned as racist the idea that the Mizraḥi immigrants' deficit was congenital; the root of the problem, he maintained, was in primary education, which was set up in a way that deterred Mizraḥi teenagers from continuing on to high school and later

---

officers, protested the authorities' discrimination against immigrants from Muslim countries.
55 Yaari, "There can be no Ingathering of the Exiles without a Fusion of the Exiles," [1960], HHA, 95-7.31(6). This document is the basis of the discussion that follows.
56 Ibid.

to university. As proof that another way was possible Yaari cited the situation of the Mizraḥi immigrants on kibbutzim, where they received equal schooling and consequently acquired an education and employment skills and played a vital and honorable role in the kibbutz society and economy, like all other members.

Yaari believed that in order to create conditions that would make it possible for the children of immigrants from Asia and North Africa to reach university, their parents needed to be allocated housing of a size appropriate to the number of people in the family and an income that could provide a satisfactory level of nutrition and standard of living for the children. He was painfully aware of the ethnic problem and proposed ideas to solve it; policy guidelines to deal with it were always among the conditions Mapam set for joining the Mapai-led coalitions.[57] But as we have seen, Mapam never managed to find the way to the hearts of the Oriental Jews, who did not reward it in the polling booth. At least, though, despite the demographic changes in the country, Mapam emerged from the November 1959 elections with the same number of Knesset seats it had won four years earlier—nine.

After the elections, Yaari put the full force of his prestige behind Mapam's joining the coalition.[58] Mapam's fierce desire to be part of the coalition was no secret; the joke went that "not even a heavy bulldozer could budge the Mapam ministers from their seats."[59]

At the session of the party secretariat that was to nominate the party's representatives at the Government table, one member proposed that Yaari and Hazan be the Mapam ministers this time. Four years earlier the same member had proposed that one of them serve as a minister, and it was clear that he had meant Hazan. This time he moved that both men do so, and justified this with the idea that Mapam's status in the Government would be affected by its ministers' seniority and standing with the public and the party. Anyway, if Mapai sent its leading lights to the Government, why shouldn't Mapam do

---

57 Mapam Council, Sept. 25, 1959, HHA, 90.69(3).
58 Kibbutz Artzi Executive Committee, Nov. 23, 1959, HHA, 5-10.7(3); Mapam Central Committee, Dec. 16, 1959, HHA, 90.68(1).
59 Raphael Bashan, interview with Meir Yaari, *Maariv*, Oct. 14, 1960.

the same? Another committee member countered that the party could not afford to have Yaari or Hazan unavailable for movement business. He also hinted, however, that their membership in the Government could be considered if Mapam received more important portfolios than those currently offered to it (Development and Health). A third speaker, who, like the first two, came from the urban sector of the party, said, "I know that the comrades feel that one of the members of the government must be Hazan. The man's weight in the Government is what is decisive. I am expressing the voice of the public."[60] He did not mention Yaari. Still another committee member said that were the party offered a more important portfolio, such as defense, he might favor the proposal relating to Hazan. In his reply, Hazan spoke as if the motion was for both himself and Yaari to sit at the Government table; he rejected the idea not because of the portfolios, but because at the present stage Mapam could not do without Yaari or himself. Yaari did not relate directly to the proposal about the two leaders, but said that if Mapam retained the same portfolios as before the ministers should stay the same. And that is what happened: Mordechai Bentov continued to be minister of development and Yisrael Barzilai minister of health.[61]

About a year earlier, on October 19, 1958, Aharon ("Aharonchik") Cohen, a member of Kibbutz Sha'ar Ha'amaqim, has been arrested on suspicion of passing information to a foreign agent, after he had been seen fraternizing with a member of the Soviet diplomatic mission in Israel. In plain English, he was suspected of espionage. Cohen was a leading Arab affairs expert for Hashomer Hatza'ir and Mapam, who published a number of books about the Arab world, both before his arrest and after his release from prison. His contacts with the Soviet diplomats were evidently motivated by his desire to travel to Moscow to meet with Soviet scholars of Islamic and Arab history. Convicted in January 1961, he was sentenced to five years in prison; on appeal, the Supreme Court reduced the sentence to 2½ years.[62] His arrest and conviction set off a public storm. Mapam's political rivals accused the

---

60 Mapam Secretariat, Dec. 15, 1959, HHA, 90.65(1).
61 Ibid.
62 *Maariv*, Jan. 9, 1961.

party of disloyalty to the state; on the other hand, the heads of the security service were accused of plotting to blacken the party's name.[63]

The episode threatened Mapam's reputation as a party with a clean record in security-related matters and left Yaari, Mapam, and KA in the uncomfortable situation that loyal defense of a comrade would lead to being denounced for collaborating with the Soviets. In private correspondence Yaari did not shy away from criticizing Cohen for his "irresponsible" actions and for doing many "stupid things," but added that he was certain of his innocence. The movement took a clear stand: Cohen was not a spy.[64] Mapam and Kibbutz Artzi stood by him and did everything they could to win his acquittal. A special committee handled his defense and visited Cohen in jail; a member of the movement monitored the progress of the trial and reported back to Yaari. The presence of Mapam members in the courtroom was important not only for Cohen's morale but also as a demonstration to the public and the judges that the movement stood behind him. Mapam made efforts to amend the law that Cohen was accused of violating and also filed a request for clemency. The latter was somewhat tricky, because it implied an admission of guilt. In the end, Cohen's sentence was commuted by Zalman Shazar soon after he became president, following the death of Itzhak Ben-Zvi, and he was released from prison on June 15, 1963.[65]

In his efforts on Cohen's behalf, Yaari was guided by three principles. The first, which had already emerged at the time of the Oren affair, was to let bygones be bygones and to refuse to allow old accounts to interfere with helping a comrade who found himself in trouble. "We have a

---

63 See Wilfand, *Aharon Cohen*.
64 Yaari to Rivka Cohen, May 27, 1962, HHA, 95-7.18(1); Yaari to Yosef Talmi, Mar. 1, 1963; Yaari to Aharon Cohen, Mar. 1, 1963, July 10, 1963, HHA, 95-7.19(2).
65 Yaari to Aharon Cohen, May 16, 1961, HHA, 95-7.17(4); Yaari to Yosef Talmi, Mar. 1, 1963; Yaari to Aharon Cohen, July 10, 1963, HHA, 95-7.19(2); Mapam Secretariat, May 23, 1962, HHA, 90.65(1); Yaari to Baruch Rabinov, June 20, 1961, HHA, 95-7.17(4); Yaari to Rivka Cohen, May 27, 1962, HHA, 95-7.18(1). When the law was amended, in 1967, the new text stipulated that contact with a foreign agent, even if no confidential information was transmitted, was a criminal offense, unless it was demonstrated that there was no intention to harm national security—and the burden of proof rested on the defendant. So it is by no means certain that Cohen would have been acquitted under the revised law.

heavy account from the past," Yaari wrote to Cohen's wife Rivka, "but we have decided to file it away and act only through our comradeship."⁶⁶ Both sides had bitter memories of past spats. These had begun back in the 1930s, when Cohen was among the first to criticize Yaari's leadership and call for his replacement; Yaari could not forgive him for raising the need to replace him when he was sidelined by illness. Another source of friction dated to the early days of the Second World War. Yaari accused Cohen of abandoning his post as the movement's emissary in Romania and blamed him for untoward incidents (at least as Yaari saw them) in the kibbutzim settled by immigrants from Romania. In reaction, Cohen sent him a long and angry letter in October 1940, overflowing with bitter criticism of Yaari's direction of Hashomer Hatza'ir. In Cohen's view, the regime and tradition imposed on it placed a heavy weight on the movement's neck and impeded the optimum utilization of its vast potential. "A leadership has to know how to listen," Cohen wrote to Yaari, "to listen to itself and also to what is happening among the ranks." And, Cohen added, "does everyone have to think exactly what Meir Yaari thinks? Is it really forbidden for comrades to have their own thoughts and assessments, their own opinions, and to speak them aloud? Why is there such a sensitivity to any breath of criticism?"⁶⁷ The zenith of the bad blood between Yaari and Cohen, and here the entire movement was involved, was in the early 1950s, when Cohen was one of the leaders of the leftwing faction that threatened the unity of Kibbutz Artzi. Yaari saw Cohen as the most obdurate member of that group, even more so than Riftin.⁶⁸ But when the critical hour came he set all these past accounts aside.

The second principle that marked Yaari's conduct in the affair was expressing loyalty to a comrade in the movement and fulfilling his obligation as its leader to take action on Cohen's behalf, while avoiding friendly intercourse with him and his family. In April 1962, when Cohen was still in prison, his wife asked to meet with Yaari. The latter explained candidly that any contact between them "would create

---

66 Yaari to Rivka Cohen, May 27, 1962, HHA, 95-7.18(1).
67 Aharon Cohen to Yaari, Oct. 26, 1940, HHA, 95-10.4(6).
68 Yaari to Aharon Cohen, Dec. 16, 1955, HHA, 95-7.14(1).

unnecessary complications for me and for the two of you." There was no doubt of his engagement with the issue; "what will it add if family members spill their pains to me?"[69] Rivka Cohen came to visit him anyway, and Yaari warned her during the meeting not to snub Hazan.[70]

This was the third principle: he and Hazan were full partners, evincing strong loyalty to each other throughout the affair and coordinating their actions. The affair placed such a burden on the movement that they felt a need to divide up their tasks and responsibility.[71]

Yaari went to pay his respects to the widow after Cohen's death (he could not attend the funeral because of his health) and got into the habit of sending her Rosh Hashanah greetings every year.[72] Rivka Cohen had warm memories of his behavior during the affair. Years later she would open her letters to him with "dear and admired Meir Yaari," and noted to his credit the essential quality he preserved throughout his career: "loyal friendship despite disagreements that were sometimes extremely bitter."[73]

In the autumn of 1960, the Israeli public was given a rare opportunity to get to know Yaari in his house slippers, as it were, through an extensive interview published in *Maariv*.[74] The interview took place in his somewhat austere apartment in Tel Aviv. The interviewer, Raphael Bashan, described Yaari as a gracious host: "Would you like something to drink? Cold, hot, coffee? Perhaps some brandy? Just tell me! Don't be bashful! Maybe you would like a sandwich?" In his unique style, which had won him the name of a gifted interviewer, Bashan added color to the scene. Readers learned that the subject "kept on speaking, all agitated," "was angry, his hair bristling with fury," that "his clenched fist landed on the table," that Yaari "suddenly sank into hermetic silence," that he sometimes spoke "in a raging torrent" and sometimes "in rushing anger," sometimes "scornfully" and sometimes "with a bitter cry," sometimes "with a sigh" and sometimes "very

---

69 Yaari to Rivka Cohen, Apr. 27, 1962, HHA, 95-7.17(4).
70 Yaari to Rivka Cohen, May 27, 1962, HHA, 95-7.18(1).
71 See Tzahor, *Hazan*, 234; Yaari to Aharon Cohen, July 10, 1963, HHA, 95-7.19(2).
72 Wilfand, *Aharon Cohen*, 251–252.
73 Ibid., 196–198; Rivka Cohen to Yaari, Aug. 7, 1983, KMA, MYF, 3(5).
74 Raphael Bashan, interview with Meir Yaari, *Maariv*, Oct. 14, 1960.

softly, with the tiniest bit of emotion" or "excitedly" and even "in a voice trembling with anger." Once he mused for a minute or two, walking about the room, "and then the cannons begin to roar."

Bashan shared his general impression of Yaari with his readers: "He is one of those people that you don't agree with 90% of what they say, but are willing and able to listen to them reverently, out of esteem for the honest, candid, and idealistic personality that peers out through the curtain of words."[75] The interview lasted for six hours. Yaari dominated the conversation, to the point that Bashan found it hard to get a word in edgewise and ask questions. And when he tried to raise a point of interest, Yaari's response was, "we'll get to that later. But now I am in a 'trance' and you must not distract me from the main thing." At one point the two switched roles and Yaari prompted Bashan, "why don't you ask me about the threat of a dictatorship?"[76]

The interview was unusual as a clear, comprehensive, and systematic presentation of Yaari's thinking to those outside his movement. Yaari did not address the Knesset very often. When he did speak, listeners could not always fathom his meaning and his ideas were not conveyed to the public as he might have wished. We have seen that on more than one occasion Yaari chewed out the staff of *Al Hamishmar* for the version of his remarks they printed in the paper; he did not hesitate to write acid comments about journalists who interviewed him or covered his statements in other media outlets.[77] Time and again, an interview or report of his remarks generated a letter of complaint in which he clarified what he had said and corrected how it had been presented. He grumbled that his words were treated "like a head full of lice, which has to be combed and combed so you can go out in public."[78]

In March 1961 he was certain that early elections were on the horizon. He was eager to establish a front of the pioneering Leftwing

---

75 Ibid.
76 Ibid.
77 Yaari to Yeshayahu Ben-Porat, May 11, 1961, HHA, 95-7.16(6); Yaari to Mr. Meisels (*Maariv*), Nov. 11, 1962, HHA, 95-7.18(4); Yaari to Yoram Ronen, Feb. 27, 1966, HHA, 95-7.19(6).
78 Yaari to Y[a'akov] Amit, July 4, 1965, HHA, 95-7.20(1).

parties, Mapam and Aḥdut Ha'avodah, which would force Mapai to cooperate with them and forestall the takeover of the latter by Shimon Peres and his clique.[79] Yaari was prepared to do "everything" in order to form a joint list of two parties. In the wake of the establishment of the Liberal Party (through the merger of the General Zionists and the Progressives), Mapam proposed to Aḥdut Ha'avodah that they form a "parity bloc" for the Knesset elections; the negotiations advanced as far as discussing the allocation of slots on the joint list. Yaari's desire to contest the elections together was so strong that he was willing to allow Aḥdut Ha'avodah's Tabenkin the first place on the list, even though Mapam was the larger party.[80] But Aḥdut Ha'avodah had reservations about the idea, fearing that a joint list would not impress the public or increase the combined strength of its component. "It's like putting bread on bread," quipped Yisrael Galili of Aḥdut Ha'avodah.[81] So the partnership never came into being. But despite the negative residue of the failure, Mapam decided not to open a second front against Aḥdut Ha'avodah during the campaign and to focus its attacks on Mapai.[82]

Mapam held on to its nine Knesset seats in these elections, but was left out of the Government that was formed.[83] At the start of the coalition negotiations, it was a member of the "club of four" (along with Aḥdut Ha'avodah, the National Religious Party, and the Liberals), who together held 46 seats, the same number as Mapai (along with its satellite parties). Given this numerical parity, the four parties demanded equal representation with Mapai in the new government. But Mapai, and especially Levy Eshkol, its lead negotiator, managed to split the club apart. First Aḥdut Ha'avodah abandoned it, and then the National Religious Party. In the end these two parties joined the Government, while the other two were left

---

79 Mapam Secretariat, Feb. 1, Feb. 5, Feb. 8, 1961, HHA, 90.65(1); Kibbutz Artzi Executive Committee, Mar. 17, 1961, HHA, 5-10.7(5).
80 Kibbutz Artzi Executive Committee, Mar. 17, 1961, HHA, 5-10.7(5); Mapam Secretariat, Mar. 8, 1961, HHA, 90.65(1). Mapam had nine seats in the outgoing Knesset; Aḥdut Ha'avodah, only seven.
81 Mapam Secretariat, Mar. 15, 1961, HHA, 90.65(1).
82 Mapam Secretariat, May 17, 1961, June 8, 1961, Ibid.
83 For the results of the elections for the Fifth Knesset, see http://knesset.gov.il/description/eng/eng__mimshal__res5.htm.

out. During the negotiations, Yaari was frantic to cooperate with Aḥdut Ha'avodah so that Mapam would not remain isolated in the opposition.[84]

During the various rounds of coalition negotiations over the years, whether they concluded with Mapam on the inside or the outside, the military government imposed on Arab citizens of Israel since 1948 was always placed on the table. Mapam demanded that it be abolished, but never made that a do-or-die issue that would determine its willingness to join the Government. Ultimately, given Mapai's stubborn insistence that the military government must continue, the coalition negotiations focused less on the issue itself than on trying to find a way to allow Mapam to enter the Government while preserving its honor, even though it had failed on this important front.

During its four years in the opposition, from 1961 to 1965, Mapam worked harder for the abolition of the military government than it had during its six years in the Government. It exploited almost every possible opportunity to raise the issue for debate in the Knesset—"almost," because it contented itself with motions for the agenda and statements during debates on related matters and when the Government was presented to the Knesset for approval, but never went so far as to submit a motion of no-confidence over the issue. The high points were two Knesset debates, initiated by it and by other opposition parties precisely a year apart, in 1962 and 1963.[85] Yaari's direct involvement in the campaign to abolish the military government was not great, but he took a vigorous stand on the matter on many other occasions. Purely as a slogan, his words were short and to the point: the military government must be totally eliminated. But an unambiguous reservation was attached to this—national security must be guaranteed.[86] This was his own and his party's overt and consistent position, accompanied by the argument that the military government

---

84 Mapam Secretariat, Oct. 11, Oct. 18, Oct. 26, 1961, HHA, 90.65(1).
85 On Mapam's stand and activity related to the military government between 1955 and 1965, see Halamish-Goldstein, *Mapam and the Arab Minority in Israel*; Halamish, "Loyalties in Conflict."
86 Yaari, *Mivḥanei dorenu*, 125; Yaari at a meeting of the Mapam Secretariat, Dec. 12, 1955, HHA, 90.62(2).

made no contribution to security, and that Mapam would not oppose it if it believed that it was essential for national security.[87]

In the elections for the Sixth Knesset, in November 1965, Mapam lost one seat (from nine to eight). In the Histadrut elections, which took place at about the same time, it received some 15,000 more votes than in the Knesset elections, which may indicate that the public was more enamored of its socioeconomic positions than of its ideas on matters of defense and foreign affairs.[88] Once again, Yaari's preference, which he made no attempt to conceal, was to be included in the coalition.[89] After four frustrating years in the opposition, and the decline in Mapam's electoral strength, he saw this as more important than ever. He tried to persuade the comrades that the prospects for progress on the issues important to Mapam were better if it was in the coalition rather than in the opposition.[90] After the new Government, including Mapam, was sworn into office, he sought to avoid providing Mapai with an excuse for expelling it from the coalition. He opposed street protests against the high cost of living and preferred the quieter options of an editorial in *Al Hamishmar* and resolutions passed by the party secretariat.[91] Nevertheless, Yaari did present the cost-of-living wage increment as a red line: Mapam would not remain in the Government if that mechanism was canceled.[92]

In the years covered in this chapter, as in the past, Yaari was frequently outside Israel for medical treatment. His eyes continued to deteriorate. Glaucoma cost him the sight of one eye and threatened the other; in the early 1960s he developed cataracts as well. It became almost a standard routine: Yaari would travel to Switzerland, where

---

87 Yaari at the meeting of the Mapam Central Committee, Oct. 30, 1957, HHA, 90.68(1).
88 Mapam received 80,000 votes in the Knesset elections and 95,000 in the Histadrut balloting. Mapam Central Committee, Feb. 27, 1977, HHA, 90.140(1).
89 Political Committee, Dec. 2, 1965, Jan. 7, 1966, HHA, 90.121(2).
90 Political Committee, Dec. 2, 1965, Ibid.
91 Mapam Secretariat, Feb. 23, 1966, HHA, 90.65(2).
92 Interview with Yaari, *Maariv*, May 5, 1967. In the deliberations by the Mapam Secretariat in late 1966 and early 1967 he said that "we cannot give up the cost-of-living increment" (Mapam Secretariat, Jan. 26, 1967) and that "not for a single day will we agree to starving the workers" (Mapam Secretariat, Oct. 12, 1966), HHA, 90.65(2). But nothing was done about the cost of living.

Professor Goldman would admit him to the first-class unit in his hospital and then examine him in his private clinic in Berne. Yaari arranged his stays in Switzerland with the help of the movement's emissaries there. He would tell them to contact Professor Goldman, set up a schedule for the treatment, make all the required arrangements, and make hotel reservations for him and Anda. When Bashan asked him, in the 1960 interview, why he went alone for treatment abroad, Yaari answered, with a hint of astonishment at the question, that "his wife is part of the regular labor roster at Kibbutz Merḥavia, where there is a shortage of working hands."[93] He did not tell the interviewer that in fact, even though he had traveled alone on occasion, Anda did accompany him most of the time, going back to the 1930s.

The instructions he sent to the movement emissaries in Switzerland in advance of his arrival were precise, detailed, and exacting: the name and address of the hotel, a room with twin beds, and a request that the emissary find him an apartment just like the one they had lived in two years earlier. Once he requested the very best room in the Schweizerhaus hotel in Berne. On one trip, after the treatment was over, he continued on to the Peace Congress in Warsaw. Because he and Anda were planning to spend several days in Zurich-Berg after the congress, Yaari asked the emissary to reserve him a room in one of the hotels there.[94] About a year later, he came out strongly against what had become a common practice: every party member who was sent abroad for several days to attend some conference "forgets the way home." He saw protracted stays abroad, beyond what the mission required, as a breach of the public trust and a slackening of the movement's ethics. He called for reinstatement of the practice that trips be limited to the mission at hand, "and for that purpose only, with insistence on returning home when the mission is over."[95]

---

93 *Maariv*, Oct. 14, 1960.
94 Yaari to Ze'ev Taub, May 7, 1959; Yaari to Nathan Ginsburg, May 29, 1958; Yaari to Rafi Cohen, Jan. 21 and May 2, 1965, HHA, 95-7.1(5); Yaari to Avraham Heller, Sept. 25, 1967, Ibid.; Yaari to Ze'ev Taub, Oct. 11, 1961, HHA, 95-7.1(5); Yaari to Rafi Cohen, Apr. 20, 1963, HHA, 95-7.1(5).
95 Yaari to Ya'akov Majus, Mar. 4, 1964, HHA, 95-7.17(3).

Yaari and Arab members of Mapam at the movement headquarters in Merḥavia.
Courtesy of Nadav Man, Bitmuna Collection, Kibbutz Merḥavia.

CHAPTER 16
Fractured Beliefs

During the Second World War, the discourse of Hashomer Hatza'ir focused on two emblems of bravery: Stalingrad and Warsaw. Yaari ranked them in that order and had some reservations about Warsaw, because of his discomfort with the negative implications of "fighting to the death." During and immediately after the war he sought to dim the aura of the ghetto fighters' courage and to exalt the value of life over death. His recurrent motif was the psalmist's "I shall not die, but live," ranking the bravery of living over a heroic death.[1] During the War of Independence, while the Yishuv was fighting for its very survival, Yaari dropped this theme, but continued to insist on a hierarchy of forms of death. It was nobler to fall in and on behalf of one's own land than to die fighting in the ghetto.[2]

During the War of Independence Yaari linked the heroism of Hashomer Hatza'ir members during the Holocaust into the long chain of Jewish bravery over the generations.[3] He appropriated the courage shown "there," in Europe, to serve the movement "here," in Eretz Israel, and exploited what had happened "then" to bolster the status of Mapam and Kibbutz Artzi "now." This was the first stage in the creation of two categories of heroism, equal in value—"Anielewicz's people" and "the defenders of the frontiers of our land"—which gained momentum after the installation of the first elected Government, from which Mapam was excluded. Isolated in the wilderness of the political opposition,

---

1 Halamish, "The Attitude of Hashomer Hatza'ir's Leadership toward the Heroism of Movement Members."
2 Kibbutz Artzi Executive Committee, May 6, 1948, HHA, 5-10.5(12).
3 Ibid.

Yaari enlisted the Holocaust-era uprising to shore up Mapam *vis-à-vis* the outside world, to encourage the members, and to combat the Leftward drift. In the ceremony marking the tenth anniversary of the Warsaw Ghetto uprising, held at Yad Mordechai in 1953, Yaari declared that the movement must cherish the great truth of the Ghetto resisters as a holy testament with lessons for the present: "By the example of their lives and deaths, the ghetto fighters taught us that we will not save Jewish lives by capitulation to reactionism or by a leftist denial of our origins."[4] Now, unlike 1945, he saw the fighters "there" as a model not only for how to die but also for how to live and fight.

In 1955, the name of Uri Ilan of Kibbutz Gan Shmuel was added to the pantheon of Hashomer Hatza'ir heroes. On December 8, 1954, Ilan and four other Israeli soldiers were dispatched on an operation into Syrian territory. The five fell into a Syrian ambush, surrendered almost without a fight, and were imprisoned in separate cells in the Mezzeh prison in Damascus. His interrogators told Ilan that his comrades had broken under questioning, provided full information about their mission, and been executed. On the night of January 12/13, 1955, Ilan committed suicide. Before that, he used a sliver of wood to prick out his last statement on nine scraps of paper, some of which he hid in his clothing and one of which he stuck to his toe. Defense Minister Pinchas Lavon instructed the censor to ban publication of the contents of these notes. At Ilan's funeral, Chief of Staff Moshe Dayan mentioned only one phrase from them—"I did not betray"—and left out the continuation—"I committed suicide." Ilan's repeated call for "revenge" was suppressed.[5]

In a memorial service for Ilan, held in Tel Aviv on the thirtieth day after his death,[6] Yaari declared that Hashomer Hatza'ir brought up its sons to show total devotion to defending their people's lives and their country's security. A constant element of the education provided by

---

4 Remarks at the gathering to mark the tenth anniversary of the Warsaw Ghetto uprising, HHA, 95-7.30(2).
5 On Uri Ilan, his capture, and the attitude towards him after his death, see Baumel, "Uri Ilan's Testament."
6 Advertisement in *Davar*, Jan. 28, 1955.

the movement was "unreserved attachment to the Jewish masses when they face hardship and catastrophe strikes them, and defending their lives even at the price of self-sacrifice."[7] This was the path taken by Mordechai Anielewicz and his comrades, by the defenders of Negba and Nirim, and by the fighters of the Palmach; and also "Uri Ilan as a member of that same movement, as a kibbutznik, as a soldier. He was brought up on the knees of this extraordinary combination of self-sacrifice and radical self-fulfillment, and thus died in the Damascus prison."[8] Yaari's rejection of suicide is clear, as is the moral that one must keep fighting until a way out of the difficulty appears, as long as the tiniest bit of hope remains. Even though "none of us can truly know the situation Uri faced and the physical and emotional tortures he experienced until he decided to end his life, so as not to betray and to remain loyal to the end," we must nevertheless acknowledge that "this time, too, our heart mourns that our dear son, in his unremitting loyalty, was unable to fight for his life all the way."[9]

"This time too" alluded to the Warsaw ghetto. Yaari was deeply troubled by the choice between falling bravely in a desperate fight to the death and finding a way to survive even when there seems to be no hope, especially in light of the different fates of the leaders of the Warsaw ghetto uprising who were members of his movement and fell to the last man and woman, and of their comrades who were affiliated with Hakibbutz Hame'uḥad, led by Yitzhak (Antek) Zuckerman and Zivia Lubetkin, who survived and left their own and their movement's imprint on the historical memory of the uprising.

Yaari continued his remarks at the memorial service for Ilan:

> How the heart breaks at the knowledge that not one of the magnificent band that led the Warsaw Ghetto Uprising—Mordechai Anielewicz, Tosia Altman, and Yosef Kaplan—understood the wisdom of saving themselves for the sake of us, even after all hope was lost. How blessed we would be today, and how blessed the entire people, had

---

7 Yaari, *Al Hamishmar*, Feb. 11, 1955.
8 Ibid.
9 Ibid.

we merited that at least one of those sublime figures survived; that one of them would be with us today as a witness of our movement's epical heroism in the Warsaw Ghetto and to educate generations of fighters and defenders.[10]

Soon after the memorial service for Ilan, Yaari took the same line in his remarks after an IDF raid in the Gaza District (Operation Black Arrow) on the night of February 28/March 1, 1955. The Israeli soldiers killed in the operation included a young member of Kibbutz Merḥavia, Ehud Shahar. On this occasion, too, Yaari sought to convey both an educational and a political message. "We have taken an oath that Jewish blood will not be cheap and have told our sons when they go to serve in the IDF that their lives are a sacred trust to defend the borders of our land and people."[11] He wove the long chain of Shomer bravery into his eulogy—Mordechai Anielewicz, the defenders of Negba, Uri Ilan, and the precious sons who had just fallen in Gaza.

Between the lines of these remarks in early 1955 we can read an echo of the "debate of the two paths"—referring to the two forms of Jewish resistance during the Holocaust. The debate was triggered by a column by Nathan Alterman, "Memorial Day and the Ghetto Fighters," published on Holocaust Memorial day in late April 1954. Alterman, casting himself as the ghetto fighters' mouthpiece, lambasted the leaders of their movements:

> And on Memorial Day the fighters and resisters said:
> 'Do not place us on a pedestal, separate from the exiles, like a shining beacon.
> In this hour of memory we descend from the pedestal
> To rejoin the experiences of the Jewish masses in the darkness.'[12]

The united Mapam, from which Aḥdut Ha'avodah had not yet seceded when Alterman's column was published, and later its separate factions

---

10 Ibid.
11 Yaari [1955], HHA, 95-7.30(6).
12 *Davar*, Apr. 30, 1954.

after the split, was one of the most vocal proponents of distinguishing the resisters from the masses in Holocaust memorialization. They shone the spotlight on their members' role in the ghetto revolts, viewed as the only form of bravery worthy of official national commemoration. This was the spirit behind the Memorial Day for the Holocaust and Ghetto Uprisings Law enacted in 1951. The designation resulted from the efforts by the leaders of the united Mapam to assert their own movements' exclusive claim to Holocaust heroism, whose sole expression, as they saw it, was raising the standard of revolt, and to create a hierarchy of the several forms of deaths, elevating those who died fighting over all the other victims. Eight years later, despite fierce opposition by Mapam, the official name was changed to Holocaust and Heroism Remembrance Day. The word "heroism" was assigned an extended sense: not only armed resistance, but also the dignified maintenance of daily life, continued educational activities, efforts to preserve a human image, and to foster friendship, mutual aid, and community in the harsh conditions of the Holocaust years.[13]

On issues related to the Holocaust, its commemoration, and its implications for Israeli society, Yaari's voice was heard only infrequently. When he did speak out, it was the ghetto fighters and partisans he held up for admiration. He was scarcely involved in Kibbutz Artzi's protracted efforts to establish its own Holocaust museum. At the central observance of Holocaust Memorial Day, held each year in Kibbutz Yad Mordechai, it was always Hazan or some other senior figure who spoke for the movement (except in 1953, when Yaari did participate).

Yaari rarely expressed an opinion during the bitter argument about accepting reparations from West Germany (both to the state and to individuals) and preferred to dump the controversial topic in Hazan's lap. During the Knesset debate on the reparations agreement, members of Herut staged violent protests outside the building and hurled stones into the Knesset chamber (January 7, 1952). When the matter was brought to a vote the next day, Mapam opposed authorizing the Government to conduct negotiations with Germany. Its arguments

---

[13] See Roni Stauber, *The Holocaust in Israeli Public Debate*, 30–60, 66–77, 97–115.

against an agreement with Bonn rested on three main points: the agreement was a violation of the victims' dying charge and a betrayal of their memory, the establishment of economic relations with Germany would place Israel firmly in the Western camp, and the agreement would serve Capitalist interests.[14] Almost a year after the agreement was signed (on September 10, 1952), Yaari explained that Mapam was not opposed to the reparations themselves, and noted that back in the 1930s Hashomer Hatza'ir had supported the *ha'avarah* (funds transfer) agreement between the Zionist Organization and Nazi Germany. Its objections were to the channel, meaning the negotiations with West German Chancellor Konrad Adenauer. Yaari held that Israel should have negotiated via the United Nations; had it been possible to receive reparations and compensation from East Germany, too, he would have had a more favorable view of the matter.[15] In retrospect, he could find an argument in favor of accepting reparations from Germany: "Didn't the Soviet Union make use of foreign experts and goods?"[16] In this debate, as in others related to Germany, he focused on the present and future, not the past, and his position was determined mainly by Israel's current needs and by political considerations.[17]

In the late 1950s, Germany was the focus of a coalition crisis triggered by Mapam and Ahdut Ha'avodah. The actual spark was the sale of Uzi submachine guns to Germany. The fact that the issue surfaced shortly before the elections to the Fourth Knesset suggests that the entire exercise was a preparation for the campaign. Mapam (and Ahdut Ha'avodah) voted in the Knesset plenum against the Government decision to approve the sale (but the motion passed with the support of the General Zionists, who were in the opposition, so the Government did not fall). Ben-Gurion demanded that the two parties

---

14 Ofer Boord, *Kesef ha-shod*; Neima Barzel, "Honor, Hatred, and Memory."
15 Coordinating Committee, July 15, 1953, HHA, 90.64(2). According to the original agreement, two-thirds of the sum was to come from West Germany and the remaining third from East Germany, but the latter did not provide its share.
16 Coordinating Committee, July 15, 1953, HHA, 90.64(2).
17 When Ben-Gurion's efforts to purchase German arms were up for consideration, Yaari defined it as a security-related topic about which partisan concerns were inappropriate. Mapam secretariat, Mar. 23, 1960, HHA, 90.65(1).

leave the Government because of this violation of coalition discipline. When they refused to do so, he himself resigned (July 5, 1959), and the Government became a caretaker government.[18] In the coalition negotiations after the elections, Mapam demanded that it be allowed the freedom not to vote with the Government on matters related to Germany.[19] However, in response to Abba Kovner's emotional words against the pending coalition agreement, Yaari declared that relations with Germany could not be the sole factor determining whether the party joined the coalition.[20] In October 1960, after Ruzka Korczak, Yisrael Guttman, Chaika Grossman, Meir Talmi, and Abba Kovner announced their resignations from the party Central Committee because of the arms deal with Germany (in this case: buying weapons from Germany), Yaari asked them not to lose their sense of proportion and to focus on the real priorities. As long as Mapam had the ability to fight against an open alliance with Germany, thanks to its nine Knesset seats, it must do so from inside the coalition.[21] Even when he sat on the Opposition benches, Yaari stuck to the line that favored security ties with Germany.[22]

Yaari took a pragmatic position: buying arms from Germany was essential for Israel's security and thus acceptable, but diplomatic relations were another matter. He feared that if Israel rejected the German proposal, it would make a deal with Nasser and Israel would find itself isolated. But when it came to diplomatic relations he set conditions: the removal of German scientists from Egypt and Bonn's repeal of the statute of limitations on Nazi crimes. For now, in any case, the time was not yet ripe for diplomatic relations, so Yaari's position—quite typical for him—was that Mapam should vote against the idea, but not slam the door on it either.[23] For now, Mapam opposed

18 Zidon, *Knesset*, 313.
19 Coordinating Secretariat, Dec. 10, 1959, HHA, 90.64(2). For the relative weight of the German question (as compared with the military government) in Mapam's decisions, see Halamish, "Loyalties in Conflict."
20 Mapam Central Committee, Dec. 16, 1959, HHA, 90.68(1).
21 Mapam secretariat, Oct. 20, 1960, Ibid.
22 Yaari, *Bein ḥazon limẓi'ut*, 96–97.
23 Political Committee, Mar. 11, 1965, HHA, 90.121(2).

an exchange of ambassadors with Germany; because this was a matter of principle with symbolic value, it became a prominent element of the election campaign, and members of the Hashomer Hatza'ir youth movement were mobilized for protests all over the country.

Even after Israel and Germany established diplomatic relations, in 1965, Yaari did not believe there was "a different Germany." But there could be "different Germans," and those who wanted to visit Israel to learn how to be different should be welcomed. This approach would augment awareness of the Holocaust far more than an eternal boycott of Germany. In 1966, he sketched out a sort of golden mean with regard to Germany: no revenge, but not warm relations either; not "ties" with Germany, but "contacts" with students who came to visit, and trying to influence anti-Nazi and peace-loving Germans. As in the past, Yaari expressed a different and more positive attitude towards East Germany.[24] After the Six Day War he supported hosting groups of young Germans on KA settlements as a step to encourage German repentance, on condition that the Germans not just be a volunteer labor force but also be involved in serious discussions with their hosts.[25]

The core of the debate about Germany in Kibbutz Artzi and Mapam was the extent of the respect owed to the feelings of those who had been "there" during the Holocaust. Yaari supported subordinating the movement's preferences to those of "our comrades the partisans" as far as possible. The Eichmann trial in 1961 did not change his mind about the nature of relations with Germany and there are no traces of its impact on him, other than his appreciative remarks to Abba Kovner about the latter's testimony in the courtroom.[26]

The first cracks in the movement's sympathy for the Soviet Union had appeared several years earlier, when the Czech-Egyptian arms deal was announced in September 1955. Developments in 1956 expanded the breach. First came a speech in January by Stalin's successor as Soviet leader, Nikita Khrushchev, in which he declared that Israel

---

24 Mapam secretariat, Apr. 14, 1966, HHA, 90.65(2).
25 Kibbutz Artzi Secretariat, May 18, 1969, HHA, 5.16(5).
26 Kibbutz Artzi Secretariat, May 18, 1969, HHA, 5.16(5). Meir and Hazan to Abba Kovner, May 11, 1961, HHA, 95-7.17(4).

had been hostile towards its neighbors ever since its establishment.[27] This was followed in February by Khruschev's "secret" speech at the 20th Party Congress, the suppression of the anti-Communist uprising in Budapest in October and November, and the Sinai campaign, when the Egyptians used Soviet arms against Israeli soldiers.

At midnight of February 24/25, 1956, Khrushchev—the first secretary of the Soviet Communist Party—began his address to a closed session of the 20th Party Congress. Over the course of some four hours he castigated the cult of personality around Stalin and denounced the dead leader's brutality against those who had stood in his way. He recounted Stalin's crimes, including mass murder, the purges of the 1930s, the mass deportations of various national groups, and the "Doctors' Plot" of the early fifties. He even asserted that Stalin's role in the victory in the Great Patriotic War had been exaggerated. The main points of the speech leaked out by early March, and the full text was published in the West some months later. Yaari did not immediately absorb the magnitude of the disclosures and their implications from the initial scraps of information that became available; he was not the only one who failed to do so. His reaction was that one should not rush to draw conclusions. He noted the positive elements of Stalin's leadership and was not willing to totally smash the image of the man who had overseen the Red Army during the life-and-death struggle against the Nazi fiend. As usual, he trimmed: "We did not cultivate blind worship of Stalin (except for a small circle), but we must not allow him to be consigned to oblivion as one of the builders of Socialism."[28] Other statements he made during the first weeks after Khrushchev's speech indicate that life went on as before and Yaari continued to employ the same concepts and terminology.[29]

More than a month after the main points of the speech were known, Yaari still tried to avoid taking an explicit public position and waited to see what might develop.[30] In the meantime, he encountered

---

27 Mapam Central Committee, Jan. 18, 1956, HHA, 90.67(1).
28 Mapam secretariat, Mar. 7, 1956, HHA, 90.63(3).
29 32nd Kibbutz Artzi Council, Mar. 29-31, 1956, HHA, 5-20.8(1).
30 Mapam Secretariat, Apr. 9 and 17, 1956, HHA, 90.63(3).

diverse reactions from comrades, ranging from shock to entrenchment in previous positions. If in the past he had been worried by the leftists, now he was afraid of rightwing deviationists and came out in defense of the Soviet revolution using metaphors from the distant past: "During the French Revolution, too, the guillotine was active."[31] And further back in history: "An entire generation perished in the wilderness in order to save the tablets of the covenant."[32] He felt a strong need to emphasize that without "the harshness of dictatorship" the revolution could not have taken place and made itself secure at home and abroad.[33]

He saw one good point in the 20th Party Congress: "It sealed the fate of our leftists, with their errors and failures. Those who had not mustered the courage to acknowledge that the movement's decisions were correct were now defeated by the decisions that came from there."[34] Khrushchev's speech bolstered Yaari's standing, because it proved that he had been correct in his quarrel with the Leftists. He made sure that no one entertained any doubts about who was the victor and who the vanquished and demanded that the Leftists acknowledge that they had erred—when they defended the Prague trial and the charges against the physicians in Moscow, and when they stood behind Stalin's theory of nationalities that denied the Jews' claim to be a nation—and proclaim that the movement and its leaders had been correct.[35] He did not rely on the comrades' ability to work this out on their own and wanted the Leftists to make public confession. He demanded that Riftin and Peri go to Canossa and compelled them to stand up in the party Central Committee, review the annals of their debate with him and Hazan, and admit that the recent revelations conclusively demonstrated that they had been wrong and the movement right.[36] For Yaari, this was a

---

31 Mapam Central Committee, May 20, 1956, HHA, 90.67(1).
32 Ibid.
33 Ibid.
34 32nd Kibbutz Artzi Council, Mar. 29–31, 1956, HHA, 5-20.8(1); Mapam Political Committee Mar. 28, 1956, HHA, 90.121(1).
35 32nd Kibbutz Artzi Council, Mar. 29–31, 1956, HHA, 20-5.8(1).
36 "Statement by Riftin and Peri at the Central Committee Meeting, June 7, 1956," HHA, heh-3.78 (1).

golden opportunity to reinforce ideological collectivism and his own leadership.³⁷

In retrospect, one can discern how Yaari gradually changed his tune. After his initial denial, right after the main points of Khrushchev's speech became known, for a time Yaari joined the chorus of those who beat their breasts in atonement of their sins. After that, fearing that the disclosures from Moscow might push Mapam Rightward, Yaari returned to his former Leftist line. One reason for this may be his realization that too severe a reckoning about the past attitude towards the Soviet Union might also rebound against him. To ward off such a possibility in advance, Yaari launched a campaign to show that he had denounced Stalin's tyranny before Khrushchev did.³⁸ Still, he did not want to be painted as hostile towards the Soviet Union. As time passed he emphasized precisely his early condemnation of the Stalinist tyranny and buried every trace of his past understanding for it.³⁹

In 1956, after years of fighting the Leftward drift, Yaari found himself facing comrades who grumbled about the party's positive disposition towards the Soviet Union. Even earlier, in November 1955, he had been angry when some kibbutz had misgivings about celebrating November 7, the anniversary of the Bolshevik Revolution.⁴⁰ Now, after a year during which voices in the movement had expressed reservations about the Soviet Union, Yaari still had no second thoughts whatsoever about marking that day and believed that the very same sentiments expressed in the past should be proclaimed this year as well.⁴¹ He adhered to this position even after the Sinai Campaign.⁴²

That war, like Khrushchev's speech, did not produce a consistent change in Yaari's attitude towards the Soviet Union. About six months before the war, Yaari spoke about the difficulty of swearing allegiance to the revolutionary camp "at a time when MiGs from Czechoslovakia

---

37 "Meir Yaari's reply to the Statement by Riftin and Peri at the Central Committee Meeting, June 7, 1956," Ibid.
38 32nd Kibbutz Artzi Council, Mar. 29–31, 1956, HHA, 5-20.8(1).
39 Yaari, *Mivḥanei dorenu*, 60.
40 Kibbutz Artzi Executive Committee, Nov. 9, 1955, HHA, 5-10.6(11).
41 Mapam secretariat, Sept. 17, 1956, HHA, 90.63(3).
42 Political committee, Nov. 22, 1956, HHA, 90.121(1).

are stationed on our southern and northern borders, in the hands of the Egyptian and Syrian armed forces, ready for destructive sorties against us."[43] For a short period after the war, still in shock, he was even more critical of the Soviet Union and almost turned his back on it; but even when he criticized it he did not abandon the old distinction of rejecting its foreign policy while identifying with it as the builder of socialism. In light of the rightward slide in the party he warned against ideological revisionism.[44] In late November 1956, Yaari broke out in a song of praise for the October Revolution and proclaimed that there was no substitute for the dictatorship of the proletariat, even though by then he had already begun to have some conception of the true state of affairs.[45]

Yaari and Hazan were only too aware of the trend among the comrades to reassess the attitude towards the Soviet Union and knew that even though the grassroots did not speak out unanimously after the Sinai Campaign, the criticism grew more severe over time. A member of Kibbutz Merḥavia described the "insupportable shock" that they all felt when these blows fell on them one after another. "Is it any wonder that the faith of so many was shattered?"[46] The comrades expected that the leaders would acknowledge the error of their ways, but in vain. Some displayed an understanding of Yaari's inner conflict, recognized his inability to take criticism, and knew that he spoke in a Stalinist style as a means of self-defense.[47] With the passage of time, however, two seemingly contradictory phenomena emerged: as the comrades' criticism mounted, Yaari reverted to his old positions and entrenched himself in them; while the movement, despite the open criticism, fell into line behind him and passed resolutions that accorded with his positions.[48]

---

43 Joint session of Kibbutz Artzi Executive Committee and Mapam Central Committee, Kibbutz Mizra, May 17, 1956, HHA, 5-10.6(4).
44 Mapam Secretariat, Nov. 19, 1956, HHA, 90.63(3).
45 Political Committee, Nov. 21, 1956, HHA, 90.121(1); Yaari to Zvi Arad, Dec. 7, 1956, HHA, 95-7.14(8); Yaari to Ya'akov Greenwald, Jan. 2, 1957, HHA, 95-7.15(2).
46 Fishel, "On One Side in the Debate," Bamesheq (Kibbutz Merḥavia newsletter), Feb. 8, 1957.
47 Kibbutz Artzi Secretariat, Jan. 4, 1957, HHA, 5.6(4).
48 E.g., Kibbutz Artzi Executive Committee, Dec. 9, 1956, HHA, 5-10.6(8).

Yaari felt that it was his duty as a leader to stand as a bulwark against despair. In late 1956 and early 1957 he delivered 23 speeches on the integrated topic of the Sinai Campaign, the Hungarian Revolution, the United States, and the Soviet Union.[49] What was his message? The new formula went as follows: "We cannot say that we are an inseparable part of this world that rejects us. But we are bonded to it and must maintain our solidarity with it."[50] In fact, the Communist camp was somewhat more diverse and less monolithic than formerly: he saw Tito of Yugoslavia as an instructive model and Gomulka of Poland as a positive example. On the other hand, the Soviet Union's conduct merited censure because of the "Hungarian tragedy," its attitude towards Poland, its antisemitism, its Middle Eastern policy, and its treatment of small countries, especially Israel. But Yaari would not go further than this. Mapam should criticize the Soviet Union's assault on the independence of other countries, but it must also recognize the right of "the dictatorship of the proletariat to defend itself against enemies."[51] In sum, he rejected any fundamental revision of the attitude towards the Soviet Union and sought out an educational formula that would criticize that country without spilling over into an anti-revolutionary stand. Particularly dear to Yaari and Hazan in those days was the metaphor that you must not throw out the baby with the bath water. In short, neither the 20th Soviet Party Congress and the tide of events in 1956, nor the clear signs of anti-Soviet ferment in the movement effected a real change in Yaari's attitude towards the Soviet Union—and consequently, at least on the formal level and as perceived by the outside world, in the movement as a whole.

In 1957, Hashomer Hatza'ir sent a delegation to the Sixth World Festival of Youth and Students in Moscow. The visit to the Soviet Union and direct interaction with the Jews of Moscow made a strong impression, somewhat like the excitement that accompanied the newly appointed Israeli envoy Golda Meir's contact with the Jews outside the Moscow synagogue on Rosh Hashanah eve in 1948. Nathan

---

49 Yaari to Zvi Ra'anan, Mar. 10, 1957, HHA, 95-7.15(4).
50 Kibbutz Artzi Executive Committee, Nov. 25, 1956, HHA, 5-10.6(7).
51 Mapam secretariat, Nov. 19, 1956, HHA, 90.63(3).

Alterman devoted his weekly column, under the title "Rabbi Uzi," to the delegation's emotional encounter with Russian Jews, who were strongly moved by the young kibbutz members and especially by the bearded Palmach veteran Uzi, whom they took for a rabbi.[52] When the comrades returned from Moscow they were not singing paeans of praise to the country that was implementing socialism, as Yaari had expected. Instead, they recounted the hardships faced by the Jews there and spoke in the spirit of "let my people go." These reports were a source of concern for him. He worried that in Kibbutz Artzi they were avidly swallowing the stories of the atrocities wreaked on the Jews in the Soviet Union. He was particularly angry with one member of the delegation, a senior leader of Hashomer Hatza'ir, who "toured the kibbutzim in the Negev, holding his audience spellbound for five solid hours, stirring them up to a fever's pitch as he described our Jewish brothers' vast prison"—but said not a word about the bright spots and achievements of the Soviet Union.[53] He took the delegation's criticism of the Soviet Union personally; what angered him most was that "they are joking that in their surveys the delegation members are writing antitheses to Meir Yaari's theses."[54]

In 1957, as after the Second World War, Yaari endeavored to rebut the horror stories told by those who returned from the Soviet Union. He attacked the members of the delegation for going beyond a description of the attachment to Israel and yearning for it they had heard from the Jews they met by chance and actively hunting out, "under the ground," proof that "they were—ostensibly—subjected to an inquisitorial regime and living in what was tantamount to one huge concentration camp."[55] He reprimanded them for actions that damaged the movement and the party and for creating an atmosphere that endangered Israel, the future of Soviet Jews, and their prospects for Aliyah.

His old-new attitude towards the Soviet Union was expressed in the outline he drew up in mid-1957 for the third Mapam Convention, held

---

52 Nathan Alterman, "Rabbi Uzi," *Davar*, Aug. 30, 1957.
53 Yaari to Moshe Chizik [Kalif], Sept. 22, 1957, HHA, 95-7.15(2).
54 Yaari to Kalif, Oct. 6, 1957, Ibid.
55 Yaari to Moshe Chizik [Kalif], Sept. 22, 1957, Ibid.

in January 1958. Four main lines can be discerned in the flood of words and sections of *Mivḥanei dorenu (The Trials of our Generation)*, which was the final version of these theses. One was that despite all its blemishes and imperfections, throughout its forty-year history the socialist regime in the Soviet Union had proven its superiority to the capitalist system. The second was that the Soviet Union was not the only way to realize Socialism and that other and more democratic variants of the dictatorship of the proletariat had emerged, in China, Yugoslavia, and Poland. The third was that criticism of the Soviet Union must not be limited to the Jewish question, Israel, and Soviet foreign policy, but should also relate to development inside that country; for example, that even after Stalin's death terror continued to target citizens, workers, and Bolsheviks. The fourth, the only one on the domestic front, was the aspiration for the victory of socialism in Israel, with a Socialist regime established as the result of democratic choice.[56] The practical and operative conclusion was that a number of axioms that had not withstood the test had to be reexamined, but this "has nothing to do with the fundamental axioms of revolutionary Socialism *and does not require a general revision of the party platform.*"[57]

The term "Leninism" appears only rarely in these theses, and always appended to "Marxism." It was the last hurrah for the hyphen that had always linked these words in Yaari's writings and in movement publications. The convention was the scene of a heated debate about that hyphen. Moshe Shamir led the faction of younger members who insisted that it be kept. Others argued with equal vigor that it should be dropped and the term should henceforth be "Marxism Leninism." Yaari held that the time had come to advance to "Marxism and Leninism" and his view carried the day. The convention voted to drop the hyphen; henceforth Mapam was no longer a Marxist-Leninist party, but "Marxist and Leninist." In keeping with another section of his motion, it was decided that "Marxism-Leninism" would no longer be designated a "world view" but only an "ideological platform."[58]

---

56   Yaari, *Mivḥanei dorenu*, 66.
57   Ibid., 65 [emphasis added].
58   3rd Mapam Convention, January 1958, HHA, 95-7.31(9).

After the convention, Yaari seems to have feared that it might be perceived as a watershed and made efforts to curb what he felt were overly enthusiastic expressions of satisfaction with the change. He made it clear that he had not abandoned any battleground and did not support any fundamental revision. The deletion of the hyphen was merely tossing out a husk in order to preserve the core: "We are Marxists who support the well-known elements of Leninism and especially its main element, the dictatorship of the proletariat."[59] In the early 1960s he spoke in favor of the regimes in the Soviet Union, Poland, and Yugoslavia, because, he said, democratic socialism could not emerge without a transitional period of dictatorship.[60] A revision of Mapam's stand on the dictatorship of the proletariat "and rejection of anything that involves coercion and force to impose socialism" struck him as going too far.[61] If we continue along this line, he warned, "we will find that we have liquidated revolutionary socialism."[62]

By then, there was no longer any present danger from the Left; all the criticism was coming from the other direction. The party was sliding Rightward and the Left was growing weaker. Yaari was losing his traditional position between the two extremes and coming to be identified with the Left wing. The general public saw him as far Left. The press wrote that the Communist demon had reinfected Yaari and that Mapam was returning to Stalinism. The fuss was triggered by a Mapam Central Committee debate on whether Khrushchev had been right to blow up the Four Power Summit in Paris in mid-May 1960, following the downing, two weeks earlier, of an American spy plane over the Urals. According to the resolution passed at the end of the debate, "the summit conference failed even before it began, and the U-2 affair played a decisive role in muddying the waters."[63] In the interview published in *Maariv*, journalist Raphael Bashan asked Yaari

---

59 Yaari to Aharon Ephrat, Jan. 24, 1958, AHH, 95-7.16(20).
60 Yaari to Ephraim Reiner, Jan. 4, 1962, HHA, 95-7.18(3).
61 Yaari at a meeting of the Kibbutz Artzi Executive Committee, *Ha-shavu'a*, Mar. 22, 1963.
62 Ibid.
63 *Maariv*, Oct. 14, 1960.

why it was so important for the Mapam Central Committee "to probe, debate, discuss, and state with such fine precision why Khrushchev had left the summit conference? Is that the most burning problem facing Mapam in 1960?"[64]

Only about 30 of the 160 pages of *Between Vision and Reality*, the theses that Yaari wrote in preparation for the Fourth Party Convention in 1963, were devoted to the appropriate attitude towards the Soviet Union and the socialist camp; this chapter was preceded by the discussion of domestic Israeli affairs and the struggle to achieve the brotherhood of nations.[65] The proportions and sequence of topics can be seen as a response to the comrades' sentiments and the prevailing mood in Mapam and Kibbutz Artzi. Nevertheless, the content of these pages indicates the author's unwillingness to abandon his past positions and his firm adherence to the formulas of yesteryear.

Yaari was not yet a lonely voice in the wilderness in his adulation of the Soviet Union. A look at Kibbutz Artzi and Mapam publications of the 1960s reveals that despite all the traumas, the movement and party remained loyal to the revolutionary Socialism of the Soviet Union; the comrades still wrote effusive tributes for Bolshevik Revolution Day. After 1956, sticking to pro-Soviet positions was indeed holding on to the past, but Yaari's stance reflected the prevailing sentiment in KA and Mapam and he was not swimming against the tide there. What is more, until the Six Day War in 1967, Hazan was his full partner in taking the eastern bloc as the polestar.

---

64 Ibid.
65 Yaari stated explicitly that there was no intention to place the bond to the socialist camp at the center of the Convention's deliberations. See Yaari, *Bein ḥazon limẓi'ut*, 98.

Yaari with Jean-Paul Sartre and Simone de Beauvoir during their visit to Merḥavia, 24 March, 1967.
Photo: David Shiklovsky (Shiko), Merḥavia.
Courtesy of Nadav Man, Bitmuna Collection, Kibbutz Merḥavia.

CHAPTER 17

The Rebellion of the Sons

Over the course of some thirty years, Yaari and Hazan ran Kibbutz Artzi and Mapam almost without challenge. The two men were not even "first among equals" but higher still, exempt from the rules of election and rotation that applied to everyone else. They made all decisions, from ideology to organizational matters to the fate of kibbutzim, cadres, and individual members. Their exalted status as the "historical leadership" was taken for granted, an essential attribute of KA from its beginnings and then of Mapam. Conversations over coffee in members' rooms and in the dining halls sometimes included complaints, and there was sporadic grumbling about the excessive concentration of power in the two men's hands and about Yaari's style. On the few occasions when the criticism was voiced publicly, it had no serious impact. As long as the "historical leadership" defended the principles of KA and conducted an all-out war against Leftist deviationism, and as long as KA's unity and very existence, as well as the survival of the party, depended on these two, it was no time to voice strong criticism and challenge them aloud.

Things began to change in the mid-1950s. The Leftist peril had waned, Aḥdut Ha'avodah had seceded, Khrushchev's revelations about Stalin had shattered old beliefs, and the Sinai Campaign had spawned new dilemmas. That was precisely when the members born in the 1920s and early 1930s came to maturity: the first children of the kibbutzim, "externs" educated in the kibbutz schools, and graduates of the youth movement in Palestine/Israel and abroad. After military service and several years of labor on the kibbutz, they felt they deserved equal rights in the movement and party institutions and input to their decisions. Unlike the grumblers of the early 1950s, who were not that much younger than Yaari and Hazan and felt a generational bond and almost family commitment to them, these younger comrades had grown up in a different social and cultural milieu and belonged to a different generation in every respect. Their peers were forming interest groups in other political parties and there was a general feeling that if the time had not yet come for a full passing of the baton, then at least the younger generation should be allowed to participate in the political game alongside the old-timers.

Open criticism about the way the movement was run in general and about the leadership in particular first surfaced in 1956. The opening salvo was fired at the 32nd Council of Kibbutz Artzi, in March. Ephraim Reiner expressed his doubts about the utility of a council at which four or five topics were brought up for discussion, with "a series of speakers, and anyone knowledgeable in the matter knows what each of them will say."[1] This was no way to attract the younger stratum to the institutions of Kibbutz Artzi, he asserted. Yaari kept interrupting him from the floor.

Reiner, born in 1924, was a member of Kibbutz Gan Shmuel who had been an external pupil at the boarding school on Mishmar Ha'emeq. For more than a decade he was the standard-bearer of the younger generation's campaign against the historical leadership, Yaari's most prominent and articulate opponent among the rebels, and the first who dared to say openly that Yaari and Hazan were past their prime.[2] Reiner shouted from the rooftops what others were afraid to say or preferred to tell Yaari only in private, mainly through correspondence. They chose to do so in writing because that route was less awkward and more effective, because it was Yaari's preferred mode of communication, and also, as some acknowledged, because they found it easier to comment on his inappropriate behavior and leadership flaws in writing than directly to his face. Put simply, they were afraid of his reaction, whose substance and style could not be foreseen. Comrades who wanted to

---

1 32nd Kibbutz Artzi Council, Mar. 29-31, 1956, HHA, 5-20.8(1).
2 Yaari to Ephraim Reiner, Nov. 4, 1962, HHA, 95-7.18(3).

help him—not rivals or competitors, heaven forbid—screwed up their courage to hold up a mirror to his face, but he rejected, repressed, and denied what it showed, attacked the messenger, and tried to shatter the mirror.

Menachem Shadmi of Kibbutz Ma'abarot, who had once written Yaari that his late wife had loved him "like a father," felt close enough to tell him, in 1960, that people were grousing about him and whispering about a cult of personality, while the intimates surrounding him said only what they thought he wanted to hear or agreed with everything he said as a matter of course.[3] Shadmi told Yaari that he was writing polemic pieces for the party newspaper on issues of no importance, suffering from provincialism, and offending the urban comrades at meetings of the party secretariat. Yaari made it plain to his loyal friend, whose sole desire was to help him, that such "gossip" was of no interest to him. He was aware that over the years he had acquired not only loyal friends and allies, but also opponents, and he was willing to pay the full price for this.[4] This staunch conviction that his was the correct path and that he was destined for leadership was the source of his power; but the concomitant lack of any willingness to accept criticism or even listen to it, and an inability to discern the essence of the matter through the backbiting character it took, were also the source of his weakness. He did not look for the fire that was giving off the smoke and ignored the fact the comrades were talking behind his back because they were afraid of him and also because of the absence of formal channels of communication.

A discussion of ideological collectivism by the Kibbutz Artzi Executive Committee in late 1962 served Zvi Lavi as an opportunity to analyze the situation in KA and Mapam. Lavi, a veteran educator from Kibbutz Sarid who had held various positions in the movement but had no interest in displacing Yaari or inheriting his mantle, spoke sympathetically and to the point. In the past, he noted, the movement had had an informal organizational democracy based on deep and

---

3 Menachem [Shadmi] to Yaari, 1954 [no date], HHA, 95-7.13(8); Menachem Shadmi to Yaari, June 9, 1960, HHA, 95-7.16(6).
4 Yaari to Menachem Shadmi, June 26, 1960, HHA, 95-7.16(7).

exclusive emotional identification with it and on unreserved confidence in its leaders. Until recently, no one had ever thought of asking how those who were elected had been chosen, who had authorized the elected representatives to express this or that opinion, and other "irritating" questions. Today, though, quite a few were asking them. In the past, the comrades had felt that the opinions expressed by the leaders of the movement, both orally and in writing, were also their own opinions, which the leaders could formulate more skillfully. Over the years, the movement had coddled its leaders; this might be one of the reasons the leaders found it so hard to accept the changes. The patriarchal stage in the history of Kibbutz Artzi was over and could not be restored. Lavi also said, in words that reflected Yaari's habitual retorts to everyone, that anger and hurt feelings would not help anything and that the reaction to the new reality must be temperate. Yaari ignored this advice and erupted on the spot, without mincing words: "We were elected unanimously by a secret ballot and it is a lie that we were not elected."[5] Because he did not go into specifics we cannot know what electoral proceeding he was talking about and when it took place.

Yaari's reaction to Lavi's remarks was moderate and gentle in comparison with the sharp and cutting words he kept hurling at Reiner. As Yaari had viewed the matter in the past and would continue to in the future, he saw the crux of the danger not in the opinions themselves, but in the grassroots organization around them. Ideological challenges from the Left or Right did not pose a real menace as long as they were not accompanied by the coalescence of a faction. But not only was Reiner not afraid to speak up in movement institutions and even in outside forums, he had also gathered a circle of like-minded comrades around him. A veritable red flag for Yaari was the "Circle of Eleven," a group organized at Reiner's initiative in 1959, which met in private apartments in Tel Aviv and Kibbutz Shoval for several months. Yaari tried to ban it. Hazan found another way to deal with the challenge. With its members' consent, it was expanded and turned into a forum that operated with the movement's

---

[5] Kibbutz Artzi Executive Committee, December 7-8, 1962, HHA, 5-10.10(14).

blessing and under its supervision: the "Circle of Eleven" became the "Group of Seventeen" (Yaari wanted to increase the membership to 25). Four of the newcomers were selected by Hazan and Yaari and two by the original members. The Trojan horses admitted to the group shattered its ideological uniformity; the diversion of its activity towards ideological and theoretical debates effectively castrated it, eliminating its ability to offer a political alternative within the party and nudge Mapam towards an alliance with the other workers' parties, as its original members had wished to do.[6]

In the early 1960s, Reiner seemed to have his hand in every pot. Yaari, who had marked him as a dangerous rival, frequently reacted to his actions and statements. He often addressed Reiner in an admonishing and condescending style and threatened him: "If you are thinking about setting up your own party and your own kibbutz movement, that possibility is open. We do not live in a totalitarian regime. But within the movement, you will no longer be forgiven aberrant initiatives of this sort. I warn you that if things like this recur we will draw disciplinary conclusions."[7] Yaari does not seem to have taken into account that, unlike his rivals in the second echelon of the movement leadership (those born in the first and second decades of the twentieth century), Reiner could make up his own mind and was not totally subject to Yaari's wrath or mercies. And so it was: Reiner left the kibbutz in mid-1969.

Friends repeatedly warned Yaari about the style of his articles and letters and the form of his statements against Reiner and others of the younger generation. Even if we limit ourselves to what Yaari wrote, and set aside his oral remarks, which can be ascribed to momentary fits of rage, we must wonder: did he consult with any of his colleagues before he dispatched these texts that were overflowing with rebuke and censure? Wasn't there anyone who could tell him, before it was too late, before the letters were sent to their recipients and his articles to the press, what several of the comrades said or wrote after the fact?

---

6 Beilin, *Banim be-ẓel avotam*, 119–177.
7 Yaari to Ephraim Reiner, Nov. 4, 1962, HHA, 95-7.18(3); Yaari to Ephraim Reiner, June 8, 1961, HHA, 95-7.17(4); Yaari to Ephraim Reiner, Apr. 27, 1961, Ibid.; Yaari to Ephraim Reiner, Mar. 8, 1966, HHA, 95-7.20(1).

Among the veterans of KA there was no shortage of those with powerful intellects, autodidacts who in other situations would have become university professors or public intellectuals, but spent their lives on the kibbutz as manual laborers and devoted their best efforts to physical toil. For them, the ideological debates satisfied an emotional need. They never imagined leaving the kibbutz, or were unable to do so, even though it restricted their horizons, denied them the chance to acquire a formal education, and bound them in the chains of ideological collectivism. This was not the case for the younger generation, which had many more opportunities available, including, as time passed, attending university and finding a respectable job away from the kibbutz. The younger generation was more assertive and more willing to challenge the historical leaders and not always willing to be their faithful acolytes. Reiner was one of the trailblazers of this generation; some of them followed him out of the kibbutz, while others continued the battle from within.

Very few kibbutz members attended university in the 1950s and 1960s. For graduates of Kibbutz Artzi high schools, one barrier to doing so was the fact that they did not earn a matriculation certificate. Yaari, who was always suspicious of formal education, was one of the most zealous about perpetuating this situation. At the same time, he ascribed great importance to learning for its own sake, especially when it bordered on indoctrination. He proposed establishing a one-year institution for twelfth-grade pupils, "with the very best educational equipment, laboratories, and teaching personnel, a seminary that would ensure Kibbutz Artzi's ability to toughen its young guard so they will be faithful heirs of everything we have created and thought."[8] He was not pleased with the situation in the movement's educational institutions. Perhaps, he mused in writing, the educational method employed by the movement, overseen by Shmuel Golan with the support of Bertha and Yaakov Hazan, raises a mediocre generation lacking vision and a sense of mission. The situation was so serious that in 1956 Yaari sank into

---

8 Yaari, *Ha-shavu'a*, Jan. 27, 1956.

outright pessimism: "Our enterprise is certainly not assured. If things go on like this, we will take our mission with us to the grave."[9]

Since Independence, the sons and daughters of the kibbutzim had been inducted into the IDF after they finished twelfth grade; when they completed their military service, they came back home and were added to the kibbutz work roster. A small percentage of each cohort were sent to the towns and cities to serve as youth movement counselors, either after military service or when they graduated high school (thereby deferring their induction for a year). The latter path was taken by Yaari's younger son, Chaim. After graduation from the high school in Merḥavia in the summer of 1960, he became a counselor in Hashomer Hatza'ir's northern branch in Tel Aviv. He lived in his father's apartment in the city, because he found the shared accommodations allotted to the counselors from the kibbutzim "appalling" and too far away, on the outskirts of town.[10] To his father, who was abroad at the time, he reported: "The apartment is in fine shape. No thief or Security Service agent has broken in," alluding to the bugging of Yaari's office some years earlier.[11] The son wrote to his father about the situation on the kibbutz, shared his impressions of the big city and of what it was like to be a youth counselor, and also thoughts about political matters, such as the new levies that were effectively stealing the fruits of the battle for the cost-of-living increment. These remarks included a modicum of criticism regarding Mapam, whose position on the question was incomprehensible. He ended the letter with "kisses."[12] In a letter to his older brother Aviezer (Avik), who was then a movement emissary in England, Chaim expressed his dissatisfaction with the fact that "our family is becoming one of politruks. Father in the party, you in England, Lushek [their brother-in law, married to their sister Rachel] in [the movement's educational center in] Givat

---

9   Yaari to Bunim Shamir, June 28, 1956, HHA, 95-60.2(2).
10 Letter from Chaim [evidently to the family in England; no date, apparently late 1960], *Ḥayyim Yaari*, 35.
11 Ibid., 33 (no date).
12 Ibid., 33–34 (no date).

Haviva, and me in Tel Aviv."¹³ He thought this was unfortunate and was determined that after his military service he would never accept another mission like this one.

In the summer of 1961, Chaim Yaari was inducted into the IDF and assigned to the paratroopers. He sent letters home regularly, with paragraphs addressed to each member of the family. To his father, Chaim wrote that he hoped his eyes were better, and that even though he had no free time he had read something his father had written, "so you shouldn't think I am neglecting you."¹⁴ One of the letters voices a complaint: "This is already the second letter I have written you since my furlough, but I have yet to receive even one from you. Please note!"¹⁵ Chaim completed OCS with distinction and was commissioned a second lieutenant. While commanding a paratroop platoon, he injured his back in a training exercise. On March 18, 1964, after quarreling with his superior in the encampment of the Four-Day March (the precursor of today's annual Jerusalem March) near Kibbutz Hulda, he handed a letter to one of his soldiers, with instructions to give it to his friend the next morning. At eleven o'clock that night he left the camp in a pouring rain, with his gun, and disappeared into the darkness.¹⁶

In the letter that he left behind, addressed to his friend, he wrote:

> I am planning to disappear. Simply that. I have a feeling that the place to which I have been pushed by life is not one I want to be in, but also that I have no way to escape it.
>
> On the one side are the kibbutz, the movement, the party, the ideals. They do not strike me as wrong, but as out of date, impotent,

---

13 Chaim to the family in England, Oct. 5, 1960, Ibid., 34.
14 Chaim to the whole family [no date. at the end of five weeks of basic training], Ibid., 37.
15 Chaim to the whole family, Jan. 6, 1962, Ibid., 38. The Chaim Yaari file in the Kibbutz Merḥavia archives contains several letters from Meir Yaari, some without a full date (the year is omitted), but none seem to have been written while Chaim was serving in the IDF.
16 Information on Chaim Yaari's period of military service, his disappearance, the searches for him, the funeral and its aftermath, are based on A. Yaari, *Ha-derekh mi-merḥavya*, 101–112; Lurie, *Anda*, 71–95.

in constant retreat. Our socialist society has become filthy, or, more accurately, is suffering from incurable hardening of the arteries.

I myself was raised on all this. I cannot adapt and believe in something else—and I cannot go on this way.[17]

The note continued, mentioning the problems created by Chaim's own conduct, his romantic disappointments, his failures and mistakes. "The straw that broke the camel's back and brought all these traits to the light, by turning me into a failure, was my own broken back. Since then I have deteriorated rapidly." He lived with the feeling that he was being humiliated in the army. And the conclusion: "I ask that you not try to find me (I have not crossed the border—that is my 'last' promise). I simply am gone. I do not want to apologize, particularly not to the family. I know that what I am doing will shock many people. I suggest that they keep it quite and erase it and me as quickly as possible."[18]

The next day, when his disappearance became known, the letter was delivered to his parents. The search began at once. On Friday, March 20, the police published a statement that Chaim Yaari had gone missing.[19] At first the search was conducted by the IDF. Friends from Merḥavia and volunteers from other kibbutzim joined the effort as well, and continued looking for him after the military gave up. His brother Aviezer coordinated the operation for the family. After a while the mass searches were called off and the matter was left to the police. All sorts of theories were floated and checked out: he had gone off to Petra, he had taken a berth on a cargo ship, he had joined the Trappist Monastery (in Latrun, just over the border in Jordanian territory; some on the kibbutz gave credence to this rumor). The searchers went so far as to consult fortune-tellers and spared no effort to uncover Chaim's tracks.[20]

---

17 For the full letter, see A. Yaari, *Ha-derekh mi- merḥavya*, 102–104; Lurie, *Anda*, 72–73. The gist of the letter became public knowledge soon after Chaim's disappearance; e.g. "Chaim Yaari," *Davar*, Apr. 1, 1964.
18 Ibid.
19 *Al Hamishmar*, Mar. 22, 1964.
20 Lurie, *Anda*, entries for May 24, June 14, and June 25, 1964.

During the eight months between his son's disappearance and the discovery of his body, Meir Yaari mourned him and gave up all hope, but nevertheless clutched at any report or rumor that suggested he might still be alive.[21] Ten days after Chaim's disappearance, he sat down at his desk in the Mapam headquarters and tried to go back to work, but found he could not hold his head up. Many weeks passed during which nothing was published over his signature; he felt that he was not doing his job properly. Precisely because some small sliver of hope remained, the young man's disappearance continued to grip his parents and left them drained.[22] Yaari attended the National Council of Kibbutz Artzi, in the first half of April 1964, but did not speak. In a letter to the delegates he wrote that some of his friends had asked him to restrain his grief and take an active part in the deliberations. Their pressure made him realize that what he saw as a border he could not and must not cross in those days was not understood by the comrades, who were focused on the best interests of the council and the movement. So he felt obligated to explain that even though he was forcing himself to go to work every day, "standing up and speaking and debating in the Council would be tantamount to giving the signal to close the file, to extinguish the last glimmer of hope and shelve the matter."[23]

In the subsequent months he gradually returned to activity, but on more than one occasion he stayed away from party events and from time to time alluded to his difficulty.[24] During that period Hazan went on a mission to the United States, and Yaari felt bereft. "It is only rarely that I have felt myself so orphaned without you as I do now," he wrote to him.[25] Hazan hastened to reply that he could imagine "the tension you are living in. I would very much like to wind up my mission

---

21 Roman Frister, *Al Hamishmar*, Nov. 27, 1964.
22 Yaari to Y. Hertz, June 17, 1964, HHA, 95-7.18(2).
23 *Davar*, Apr. 14, 1964.
24 Eshel family (Kibbutz Hatzor) to Yaari, Apr. 23, 1965, KMA, MYF, 4(7); Yaari to Shimon Peres, July 11, 1977, KMA, MYF, 2(10); Yaari to Y[aakov] Nimri ["Kulik"], Sept. 22, 1964, HHA, 95-7.19(1). Many years later he said that after the disaster his activity had changed for "a certain period." See Mira Mintzer-Yaari (interviewer), the last interview with Meir Yaari, Oct. 2, 1985, KMA, MYF, 6(5).
25 Yaari to Hazan, Sept. 24, 1964, HHA, 95-7.19(3).

here so I could return and share your burden of troubles and worries." He ended the letter with a routine question: "How are you and how is Anda?"[26] The couple's friends did not know how to behave towards them. Some wanted to come visit but did not dare, and simply looked on in silence. Some found the courage to visit only after the bitter end became known. Others avoided a face-to-face meeting even then and sent their condolences in writing.[27]

The day before her son's disappearance, Anda Yaari began keeping a diary. In it, she almost never mentions her husband. She wrote when no one was around and he does not seem to have known of its existence. It was only after Anda, in the last year of her life, moved into the senior citizens' quarters on the kibbutz that the family became aware of it.[28] On November 21, 1964, Anda wrote there as follows:

> Chaim's secret has been discovered. Three days ago the first rains of the season started falling … and a Bedouin who went to see what had spooked his sheep found Chaim's body. … He found him in a military emplacement. The body had decayed and all that was left were his clothes, shoes, and weapon, and the identifying papers in the clothes. … He had lain down in the emplacement, covered his body with vegetation, and shot himself in the head. They say that death came instantly, so that he didn't suffer. … The emplacement is in very tall undergrowth, and because he covered his body with vegetation, they had not found him, even though they searched the area several times.[29]

Many questions troubled the bereaved mother's rest. "Why didn't he want us to bury him in our cemetery in Merḥavia?"[30] And: "Some say that [Yisrael] Galili's son committed suicide almost a year before you did, because they made his life hell in the army."[31] Many took note of the

---

26 Hazan to Yaari, Oct. 3, 1964, HHA, 95-7.19(3).
27 The correspondence is in KMA, MYF, 4(7).
28 Lurie, *Anda*, 73.
29 Ibid., 80 (entry for Nov. 21, 1964).
30 Ibid.
31 Ibid., 83 (entry for January 1965).

fact that two children of the kibbutz, both of them sons of leaders, had committed suicide during their military service, within a few months of each other. She wondered how much Chaim had been burdened by the fact that he was "the son of" and addressed him: "You no longer have to bear the destiny of the son of a leader. That too was complicated and sometimes difficult. You never spoke about it, Chaim. But your sister and brother told me a little bit about these difficulties."[32]

Lieut. Chaim Yaari was buried in the cemetery at Kibbutz Merhavia on November 23, 1964, in a full military ceremony attended by more than a thousand people. His mother thought that "many came because Chaim was the son of Meir Yaari, but even more came because the incident shocked everyone."[33] His father cried over the grave.[34] Moshe Yaari, Meir's older brother, recited the *Kaddish*.[35] During the *shiva*, the young woman with whom Chaim had been in love and who, he hinted in his farewell note, had rejected him, came to visit the family. Yaari was furious with her and took a dim view of her condolence call. He could not chase her away, but paid no attention to what she had to say and let her leave without uttering a single word to her.[36]

Many memorial notices were published in *Al Hamishmar*. Kibbutzim, party branches, and organizations all expressed their sympathy for Anda, Meir, the family, and Kibbutz Merhavia. When *shiva* was over, the Yaari family and Kibbutz Merhavia thanked "all those who helped us in various ways to look for our son Chaim of blessed memory and those who expressed their condolences in writing and orally."[37] On the day of the funeral, Yaari told the journalist Roman Frister that he and his wife had brought up their son to follow their path, "until the moment when reason and intelligence can overcome the impulses, until he could decide about the rest of his life for himself."[38]

---

32 Ibid., 87 (entry for Mar. 18, 1965).
33 Ibid., 80–81 (entry for Nov. 23, 1964).
34 A. Yaari, *Ha-derekh mi-merhavya*, 107–108.
35 *Al Hamishmar*, Nov. 24, 1964.
36 Mira Mintzer-Yaari, the last interview with Meir Yaari, Oct. 2, 1985, KMA, MYF, 6(5).
37 *Al Hamishmar*, Nov. 30, 1964, p. 1.
38 Roman Frister, "Flowers on the Grave of Chaim Yaari," *Al Hamishmar*, Nov. 27, 1964.

From cradle to conscription his father had never seen him in conflict with society, and throughout those years there had never been even the smallest crisis between father and son—"and with me, I confess, that is no easy thing."[39] From these private observations about his son and their relationship he turned to generalities:

> The way we think—myself, my older son [Aviezer] and Chaim— is different. I know that I am stricter. In everything. For me the debate may be free, but the effort to reach a common conclusion is more intense. And after the conclusion is reached there must be discipline in the execution. They say that this is ideological collectivism. Today I am willing to give up this term because of how it has been misused. But that is characteristic of any militant party. And *my generation* was educated in this spirit. The *second generation*, the sons, are more uncomfortable with a common conclusion. They search and winnow: maybe it is an order from on high, but maybe it's propaganda—and they don't like it. They sanctify freedom of opinion in particular; solidarity in the implementation comes only after the most meticulous examination. But they are loyal to the movement and its principles. And after them comes the third generation, which wants to reexamine everything. The generation that never had several intense experiences: the war in the ghettos and the Holocaust, the War of Independence. The generation that is afraid that someone created something for them. My son Chaim lived in that generation.[40]

There were 11 years between Yaari's older and younger sons. Only six years separated Yaari's younger son and his oldest grandchild, Rachel's son Yedidia. For Yaari, Chaim belonged to the third generation, that of the grandchildren.

The kibbutz published a memorial volume to mark the first anniversary of Chaim's death. Ben-Gurion read it from cover to

---

39 Ibid.
40 Emphasis in original. Ibid.

cover. He also read "what was not printed in the book, and perhaps not written at all—but the words are engraved in your hearts in the purest love and deepest grief. For there is indeed something to grieve about, and he deserves love. So do you. And from far away I clasp your hands in faithful comradeship—because I have no words of consolation in my mouth. Paula shares my sentiments and grief."[41] Yaari always remembered fondly that Ben-Gurion "was among the most moving and sincere participants in the tragedy that struck our family."[42] Anda preserved Ben-Gurion's letter almost as if it were a sacred relic.[43] The parents visited their son's grave in the Merḥavia cemetery every week, tended the plantings, and changed the flowers in the vases. Sometimes Anda went there alone.[44]

In the mid-1960s, Hazan came to realize that the period when he and Yaari were the sole pillars of the movement and determined its ideological, social, and political course was coming to an end, and that its structure and activities were changing too. How should they react? Hazan saw clearly that from now on the leadership would have to be broader and chosen by different methods. He believed that the young guard, who were no longer so young—they were all in their fifties or older—should be granted maximum independence. Hazan also recommended—and what is important for us is what the proposed change implied about the current situation—an end to the insistence on parity between the Left and Right. Instead, the comrades who had proven their loyalty should be promoted first (and preferred to the "penitents"). According to Hazan, the party structure that maintained a balance between Left and Right placed him and Yaari in the center, but "the concept of 'center' is a synonym for colorlessness, hesitancy,

---

41 Ben-Gurion to Anda and Meir Yaari, Apr. 15, 1965, quoted in A. Yaari, *Ha-derekh mi-merḥavya*, 108. Ben-Gurion had written earlier, in April 1964, soon after Chaim's disappearance became known.
42 Yaari to Y[aakov] Amit, July 4, 1965, HHA, 95-7.20(1).
43 Yaari to Shimon Peres, July 11, 1977, KMA, MYF, 2(10).
44 Lurie, *Anda*, 88–89 (April 1965); also 90–91 (Sept. 25, 1965) and 95 (Oct. 14, 1966).

and political pragmatism that are not deserving of respect."⁴⁵ Hazan, as others had, advised Yaari to listen to those who disagreed with him.

It was around this time that the first signs of a decline in Yaari's rhetorical powers became apparent, along with a lesser willingness by others to accept what he said. The mounting pressure from below, Hazan's cautious but firm criticism, and the feeling that the larger movement and party institutions were no longer his "home court" interfered with his concentration and frequently turned his public speeches, never known for their fluency, into an experience that did not increase listeners' respect and esteem for him. In October 1966, he delivered a confused and embarrassing speech to the Kibbutz Artzi Executive Committee. His remarks, cited verbatim in the official minutes, are full of ellipses to indicate an incomplete sentence or words that the person who kept the minutes or transcribed the recording could not make out. In one case, Yaari did not remember whether he had already said what he was about to say now; another time his train of thought was interrupted and he asked, "what was I saying?" And there was laughter in the hall when he mixed up Ephraim Reiner and Ephraim Reisner. He complained that he was being abandoned to attacks by his rivals and announced (six months early) that he would not agree to celebrations of his seventieth birthday but would stand for reelection as party general secretary. "I feel that it is forbidden for me to stand aside as long as I have my strength," he said.⁴⁶

By then he was largely out of touch with what was taking place on the kibbutzim. He received more and more hints that the sense of estrangement between the rank and file—even those who worked actively for the movement—and the leadership was getting stronger.⁴⁷ A narrow stratum of "professional activists" who spoke at KA and Mapam gatherings was coalescing, while daily life on the kibbutzim took place on a parallel and separate track. Yaari was aware of the ideological fatigue in the party, to the point that "in the kibbutzim and party branches ideological discussions attract a smaller audience than a

---

45 Hazan to Yaari, Dec. 10, 1965, HHA, 95-7.20(1).
46 Kibbutz Artzi Executive Committee, Oct. 20, 1966, HHA, 5-10.10(1).
47 Yaakov Nimri to Yaari, Nov. 7, 1960, HHA, 95-7.17(5).

mediocre suspense movie does."⁴⁸ His remarks about kibbutz matters no longer had the fervor that had characterized his part in the "electric kettle" debates of the 1950s.

His relations with party members from the urban branches were not as close and cordial as those with KA activists. This is evident in the tone of Yaari's letters to them and was reflected in the fact that he did not hesitate, for example, to ask someone from a town in central Israel to come see him in Merḥavia, because he himself had no time to meet him in Tel Aviv. In the late 1950s he expressed concern that the kibbutz members' influence in party institutions was waning, while that of the urbanites was growing stronger.⁴⁹ He took little interest in developments in the party's urban branches and was even willing to allow their secretariats to make their own decisions about joining local council coalitions.⁵⁰ But when he learned of an initiative to set up a party circle in Petaḥ Tiqvah he demanded that the organizer tell him who was invited and made it plain that "this is a classic underground. There will not be such a thing in Mapam. We have learned from experience."⁵¹

He zealously maintained the disproportionate representation of kibbutz members on the Mapam Knesset list. Anyone who dared criticize this was severely reprimanded.⁵² In 1959, kibbutz members occupied six of the nine spots the party expected to win (along with two city-dwellers and one Arab), even though most of Mapam's electorate was urban and the kibbutzim contributed only about 20% of its votes.⁵³ Although Yaari proclaimed that he and Hazan had been serving as a bridge between city and kibbutz for half a century, they never built a real link between the two wings of the party.⁵⁴ In the early 1970s, a veteran urban member complained about the disconnection between the city and the kibbutz: he had been a party member for decades and

---

48 Yaari, *Be-siman aḥdut ve-azma'ut*, 7.
49 Kibbutz Artzi Executive Committee, July 27, 1958, HHA, 5-10.7(3).
50 Mapam Secretariat, Mar. 5, 1958, HHA, 90.63(3).
51 Coordinating Committee, June 29, 1960, HHA, 90.64(2).
52 Mapam Secretariat, Aug. 26, 1959, HHA, 90.64(2).
53 Israel Central Bureau of Statistics, *Results of the Elections to the Fourth Knesset and the Local Authorities*, 60–63.
54 Yaari interview in *Maariv*, May 5, 1967.

served on the Mapam secretariat but had still "not managed" to visit Mishmar Ha'emeq, Merḥavia, and other kibbutzim.[55]

In the 1960s, there were signs of a desire for a rapprochement among the three kibbutz movements, felt chiefly by the younger generation. Yaari was panic-stricken by the idea and determined to frustrate it. Although an outright merger of the kibbutz movements was not on the official agenda or even practical then, the notion had become so prominent in kibbutz circles that Yaari felt obligated to pay it lip service at festive events, even as he exerted himself to raise the walls between the movements even higher. The fiftieth anniversary celebrations for Degania and Merḥavia, in 1960 and 1961 respectively, provided him with an opportunity to state his vague and convoluted position about the merger idea. His remarks on these topics moved in a circle that leave unresolved the question of what he thought should come first: a merger of the workers' parties or a merger of the kibbutz movements, whether merger of the kibbutz movements was a precondition for a political union, or vice versa, and whether he supported either option.[56]

In the meantime, the kibbutz movements were moving closer on two planes: regional cooperation between neighboring kibbutzim affiliated with different movements, and countrywide economic cooperation among the movements as part of the Federation of Kibbutz Movements. Yaari was opposed to regional cooperation, in part because it was a way to get around the ban on hired labor. He was also afraid that after the transfer of economic functions to a regional framework, social and cultural matters would follow as well. He was adamant that economic and social life must always remain under the control of the individual kibbutz and the movement.[57] On the other hand, he took a favorable attitude towards cooperation in the economic domain, because of its limited and partial nature and the fact that it had no pretensions about leading to a full union.[58] Yaari did everything he could to curb

---

55 L. Ternopoler, Mapam Secretariat, Nov. 3, 1971, HHA, 90.63(1).
56 Yaari, Be-ma'avaq le-amal meshuḥrar, 252 and 258–259.
57 Ha-shavu'a, Aug. 10, 1962.
58 Yaari, Be-ma'avaq le-amal meshuḥrar, 284–286; Al Hamishmar, Nov. 1, 1963.

initiatives that aimed at a merger of the kibbutz movements or even just bringing them closer together.

The first portents of the concept appeared in the periodical *Shedemot*, established in 1960. Under the direction of its founder and first editor, Avraham Shapira ("Patchi"), a member of Kibbutz Yizre'el, the periodical served as a forum for the misgivings of the younger generation of the kibbutzim and was an incubator for collaboration among those eager to lower or even eliminate the barriers between the kibbutz movements. Further impetus for rapprochement *en route* to a merger came from the Inter-Kibbutz Circle established at Givat Brenner in February 1966, which came to be known as the "Shedemot Circle." Its members, drawn from the three kibbutz movements, debated topics that *Shedemot* discussed on its pages, including the search for a generational common denominator that distinguished them from the founders. Another link in the chain of cooperation among kibbutzim was the establishment of a Tzavta club in the Hefer Valley, which held several events before the Six Day War (and then went on to spawn additional Tzavta clubs). Here too, the young kibbutzniks bonded over their strong desire for greater cooperation, the creation of their own generational identity, and elimination of the barriers separating the three movements.[59] The Six Day War accelerated the incubation process, thanks to the brotherhood of soldiers forged in combat, which transcended their movement affiliations. It was a sense of fraternity similar, *mutatis mutandis*, to the solidarity that produced Abba Kovner's Eastern European Survivors' Brigade at the end of the Second World War. In both cases, the initiators realized that those who returned from the battlefield, where they had fought shoulder to shoulder with no thought about movements or streams, desired unity and could not understand what prevented it.

About a month after the Six Day War, Yaari published an article in *Maariv* that exposed the generational conflict in Mapam for all to see. He wrote about "circles of a young and professional intelligentsia" who were loudly proclaiming that "their time has come, not to join their predecessors

---

59 Alon Gan, *"Hasiaḥ she-gava?"* 64; Elmaliach, *Tzavta*, 14–15.

but to take their place. They are swinging their elbows a bit too vigorously. They are signaling to those of their age in the other workers' parties that they should cooperate so that *biology* will defeat *ideology*."[60] Censuring these young people, Yaari noted that they were tossing Marxism on the scrap heap and decreeing the death of Socialism in general. In the background of his remarks was the argument then being made on the pages of the movement's periodicals and in oral statements; namely, that the Six Day War and the Soviets' alliance with Israel's enemies meant the time had come for Mapam to renounce its allegiance to Marxism and abandon its special feelings for the Soviet Union.[61] Young people who came back from the killing fields where they had faced Soviet weapons were disgusted and nauseated by the Soviet Union and the sympathy for it. Two weeks after the war, a speaker told a meeting of Mapam's political committee that "it is no happenstance that when our sons return from the front, their first question is 'what will be the party's position on the Soviet Union?' Of all the terrors of that awesome week, here lies, from the ideological and moral, the national and socialist perspectives, the greatest trauma of all."[62] In the conversations among soldiers who had fought in the war, eventually published as *Siaḥ Loḥamim*, a member of Kibbutz Ein Shemer spoke about the "terrible betrayal by the Soviet Union, a youthful creed that has became a *murderer*."[63] Another member of his kibbutz said:

> A serious problem has been created for people who believed in the Soviet Union and now see that that country knowingly assisted the possible annihilation of Israel. Several years have passed since the 20th Party Congress, but I still haven't digested this matter. There

---

60 Yaari, *Maariv*, July 16, 1967 [emphasis in original].
61 Many items in *Ha-shavu'a* called for an end to the link to revolutionary socialism, leading Yaari to appeal to the secretary of Kibbutz Artzi: "Have you stopped all oversight of what is going on in that publication?" Yaari to Meir Talmi, Aug. 18, 1967, HHA, *heh*-3.85(3*gimel*).
62 Chaim Shafir, Political Committee, June 22, 1967, HHA, 122.90(1).
63 Eli Alon, in Avraham Shapira, ed., *Siaḥ loḥamim*, 247 [emphasis in original] [This and the next quote are in a section that was omitted from the abridged English translation, *The Seventh Day*.]

are many more among us, who will not digest it overnight. This is a problem that struck many of us.[64]

Such remarks corroborate the conclusion, presented above, that the commitment to the Soviet Union did not wholly evaporate from Kibbutz Artzi and Mapam after 1956 and still had deep roots in 1967.

Immediately after the war it seemed that Yaari, too, had been traumatized to the point of changing his mind and turning his back on the Soviet Union. Echoing lines from Bialik's poem "On the Slaughter," he proclaimed: "If Soviet justice appears only after we have been exterminated—may Soviet justice be annihilated for ever!"[65] The spirit of those days, the experience of victory after a period of extreme tension and existential dread, along with the sudden relief felt by the kibbutzim in northern Israel after years of being threatened by Syrian artillery, seems to have affected him. Two or three days later, at a meeting of the Kibbutz Artzi Executive Committee, Yaari repeated his attack on the Soviet Union. This time the location—Kibbutz Lehavot Habashan, at the foot of the Golan Heights—may have played a part as well. He spoke of his pain and disappointment with the Soviet Union, which had incited war in the Middle East, of the revolutionary Russia that saw Israel as a tool of imperialism and that armed hostile nations against it. "We will no longer allow them to bombard our kibbutzim from these heights in peacetime," Yaari proclaimed.[66]

Nevertheless, his attachment to the Soviet Union had not vanished entirely. As November 7, the fiftieth anniversary of the Bolshevik Revolution, approached, he insisted that the party Central Committee hear a lecture about the revolution and publish a manifesto noting the milestone, despite all the criticism of the Soviet Union. But the majority voted him down; breaking with past tradition, Mapam would not hold a Central Committee meeting devoted to the October Revolution and would only publish a manifesto.[67] So even in late 1967, Yaari remained

64 Haggai, Ibid., 250.
65 Political Committee, June 29, 1967, HHA, 90.66*gimel*(1).
66 Kibbutz Artzi Executive Committee, July 1, 1967, HHA, 5-10.10(6).
67 Mapam Secretariat, Sept. 27, 1967, HHA, 90.65.(2).

faithful to the pro-Soviet line, on the grounds that the Soviet Union might yet do the unexpected, as it already had several times, and relations might improve. He noted that the Soviets had been permitting Jewish emigration to Israel before the Six Day War. Hence, rather than rupturing ties, an opening should be left "so they can still look for us" when the time came, when there was a change in the situation. A weak echo of the notion that Mapam should be the Soviets' political address in Israel, a familiar line of the early 1950s, can be heard in his remarks.[68]

Yaari was not the only one who believed that the party should continue to celebrate the Bolshevik Revolution. A broad range of opinions was expressed at the Mapam Political Committee in the fall of 1967, but there was a consensus—even at a meeting from which he was absent—that the event should be marked by a combination of a protest in the wake of the Six Day War with unswerving faith in Socialism, and reference to both the good and the bad in the Soviet Union. In November 1968, the Mapam Secretariat again voted to issue a public statement for Revolution Day, although this time not as the lead editorial in *Al Hamishmar*.[69] Yaari found the manifesto for November 7, 1967, worthy of inclusion as an appendix to the theses he drafted for the Mapam convention in 1968. And even though the main issue that year related to the negotiations with the Labor Party about setting up the Alignment (*HaMa'arakh*, an alliance of the Labor Party and Mapam), Yaari devoted extensive space in *Under the Sign of Unity and Independence* (about 40 out of its 150 pages) to a chapter on "Our Bond to the Countries of Developing Socialism." He acknowledged that nothing under this heading would have any influence on the political negotiations, but insisted that it could not be omitted. In late 1970 he carried on at length in his praises of the Soviet Union as it had been in the past and noted Israel's own contribution to the Soviet hostility towards it (the bomb that exploded in the courtyard of the Soviet Embassy in Tel Aviv in the early 1950s, the Government's adherence to the Eisenhower Doctrine). We must not allow the hatred

---

68 Political Committee, Nov. 22, 1967, HHA, 90.122(1).
69 Mapam Secretariat, Nov. 6, 1968, HHA, 90.65.(2).

to fill our hearts to the brim, he warned the comrades, because the day will come when Israel has to find its way back to the Soviet Union, and we must not leave Maki (the Communist Party of Israel) as the only player. Unlike the past, now he fiercely criticized the situation in the Soviet Union—the bureaucracy, the lack of democracy, and of course, as usual, the antisemitism. "Still, for heaven's sake, can we forget that [the Soviet] economy was built and twice totally destroyed by the Fascist enemies of socialism?"[70] He retailed statistics about the achievements of the Soviet economy and showed that they were impressive even when compared to the United States. He had also heard from people who visited there that the gap between workers on the one hand and teachers, engineers, and physicians on the other was diminishing, and that they were also striving to achieve equality between the sexes. "When you read about these immense enterprises, about the vast effort after two wars, such an effort of construction, can everything be rotten?"[71] He enthusiastically defended the people of the Soviet Union, those who had rebuilt the economy and fought in the Second World War, and reminded his audience that without the Soviet Union the Allies would not have emerged victorious. How is it possible to ignore "that heroic effort, banishing hunger from the world, giving bread to a third of mankind, and after that providing education and after that equality among nations, and giving this and that"—and then to argue "that this is not a basis for socialism"?[72]

In the early 1970s, it became increasingly apparent that Yaari and Hazan no longer maintained a united front about the Soviet Union; their disagreements on the subject produced no little friction and irritation. Whereas Yaari had entrenched himself in his sympathy for the Soviet Union, as part of his efforts to slow the headlong race to develop closer ties with the Labor party and form the Alignment, Hazan's inclination was just the opposite. He wanted to remove the Soviet Union from the party agenda not only in order to tighten the link with the Labor Party and Prime Minister Golda Meir, but also

---

70 Political Committee, Nov. 5, 1970, HHA, 90.121(2).
71 Ibid.
72 Ibid.

in order to save socialism as he understood it. In the early 1970s he sought to sever, once and for all, the awkward and harmful Gordian knot between socialism and the Soviet Union. Hazan believed that the Soviet regime was not socialist; for him, the main question was "how to save socialism in Mishmar Ha'emeq" and the movement as a whole.[73] For years he had felt a collegial and movement obligation to inform Yaari of every book he read about the Soviet Union and every interesting item he had found in the newspapers he received from that country, because he knew that Yaari's bad eyes made it difficult for him to read for any length of time (and in any case he could not read Russian). But Yaari kept complaining, "you bring me only the negative reports, only the stories from unfavorable books." To which Hazan would reply, "I keep searching diligently for a positive and favorable book, but I can't find any."[74]

What place did the question of the Soviet Union occupy in the relations between the two leaders? What was the cause and what the effect? Did the issue itself create the friction between the two, or did Yaari take an extreme pro-Soviet stand precisely in order to distinguish himself from Hazan and buttress his own position as the leader? If the second conjecture is correct, Yaari was riding the wrong horse, which came up lame and unpopular, and swimming against the current in his party and movement. His entrenchment in an obsolete attitude stemmed, in part, from his isolation from the mainstream of the movement and highlights the fact that Hazan was much more attuned to the grassroots than Yaari was.

The answer proposed here about cause and effect is that it was not Yaari's sympathy for the Soviet Union that caused the two men to grow apart; rather, this issue was a symptom of more complex processes. Hazan did not modify his ideas as a result of deep thought and analysis, but in response to the wishes of the rank and file and his realization that opposing Yaari on this matter would not endanger

---

[73] Mapam Inner Secretariat, May 2, 1971, HHA, 90.79(1); Ḥotam, Nov. 12, 1971; Al Hamishmar, Nov. 28, 1971.
[74] Hazan to Yaari, Dec. 12, 1971, HHA, 95-7.22(1); also meeting of the Kibbutz Artzi Secretariat, June 2, 1978, HHA, 5.17(2).

his own popularity. In later years, Hazan admitted that he and Yaari had had fierce arguments about the Soviet invasion of Hungary in 1956, Khrushchev's walkout from the summit conference in 1960, and relations with the Soviet Union in general, but in the end he (we may infer) closed ranks with Yaari.[75] When Yaari's standing in the party grew weaker, Hazan did not hesitate to speak more bluntly about the Soviet Union, knowing that he would find sympathetic hearers among the comrades. Yaari remained fixed in his old positions, in the hope that this would bolster his status; in practice, it did just the opposite. Just as Yaari exploited the Soviet issue to frustrate a merger with the Labor Party and distinguish himself from Hazan, so Hazan used it to draw a firm line between himself and Yaari.

The initial feelers about some form of alliance among the workers' parties took place in the late 1950s and early 1960s. But these sporadic contacts never led anywhere. Then, on January 11, 1963, an article by Yitzhak Ben-Aharon, one of the leaders of Aḥdut Ha'avodah, "The Courage to Make a Change before Disaster Strikes," was published simultaneously in *Davar* and *Lamerḥav*. In it he called on Mapai, Mapam, Aḥdut Ha'avodah, and their affiliated kibbutz movements to unite and establish a single organization of the working class, thereby reconstituting the Israeli Labor movement. He called on the three parties to overcome their ideological disagreements for the sake of unity. The article was the talk of the day in the kibbutzim, the three parties, and the public at large, and attained quasi-mythological status as the foundational document of the first Alignment of Mapai and Aḥdut Ha'avodah in 1965, their formal merger (along with Rafi) as the Labor Party in 1968, and the establishment of the second Alignment of the Labor Party and Mapam in 1969.

Yaari's considered response to the call for merger was incorporated into his theses in advance of the Fourth Mapam Convention in 1963. He saw Aḥdut Ha'avodah as a potential partner in the Knesset, the Zionist movement, the Histadrut, and the local councils—but

---

75 Mapam Secretariat, Dec. 13, 1978, HHA, 90.153(1).

not Mapai.[76] The latter was a reformist, Social Democratic party; Mapam, as a revolutionary faction, had nothing in common with its platform.[77] For Yaari, a comrade's position on cooperation with Mapai was the acid test of loyalty not only to the party, but to himself; he took a favorable attitude on the question as a personal affront. He systematically reined in every attempt and effort to establish a united workers' party. Everyone, inside and outside Mapam, knew what Yaari was doing and that all of his maneuvers and ideological positions focused on a single goal—preserving Mapam's independence. In the meantime, the party masses were taking small and quiet steps towards unity, including the establishment of ideological circles that supported an alliance among the parties. Yaari came out full force against these groups, but Hazan cooperated with them by closing his eyes or offering quiet encouragement.

As in many other domains, here too the Six Day War served as the catalyst. Not only did the experience reinforce its veterans' desire for unity, it also gave them the feeling that, having demonstrated their ability in wartime, they were competent to lead in peacetime as well and certainly had the right to express their opinions and make their voices heard. The war had intensified their desire to find common ground among the kibbutz movements. They emphasized the identity shared by members of the kibbutz-born generation of all the movements and demanded that the "silent generation" be allowed to make its mark in domains other than agriculture and the military.[78]

Soon after the end of the Six Day War, the Mapam Political Committee approved contacts with Mapai and Aḥdut Ha'avodah. This led to talks between Yaari and Hazan, on the one hand, and Prime Minister Levi Eshkol, Yisrael Galili, Yigal Allon, and Pinchas Sapir, on the other.[79] The Fifth Mapam Convention, whose agenda included a decision about the nature of the ties among the workers' parties, met on the evening of March 20, 1968, in Mann Auditorium in Tel Aviv.

---

76 Yaari, *Bein ḥazon li-mẓi'ut*, 144.
77 This was implied rather than stated outright. Ibid., 161.
78 Gan, "*Ha-siaḥ she-gava?*" 141.
79 Political Committee, June 19 and Sept. 6, 1967, HHA, 122.90(4).

When his turn came to speak, Yaari stood at the rostrum, facing the overflow crowd. Waving his hand towards the left, he dismissed the opinion of those opposed to any form of cooperation with the Labor Party; then, with a gesture towards the right, he rejected the opinion of those who favored full merger. Finally, he presented his own middle-ground position: both unity and independence, unity while maintaining independence.[80] The convention deliberations the next day took place under the shadow of the first major military operation after the Six Day War—the attack on Fatah headquarters in Karameh, Jordan. Around 30 Israeli soldiers were killed, many were wounded, and the IDF left armored equipment behind when it pulled back in the evening. The delegates followed developments tensely, listening to the news broadcasts on a transistor radio that was placed next to the microphone on the podium. The event affected the atmosphere and generated a desire for unity in a time of crisis. Some 64% of the delegates voted to begin negotiations with the Labor Party, with the results to be submitted to the next session of the convention for ratification; 35.5% were opposed.

The second session of the convention took place on November 22–23, 1968, again in Tel Aviv. This time the dark shadow was cast by the first large terrorist attack after the war, which killed 12 persons in the Maḥaneh Yehuda market in Jerusalem on the first anniversary of Security Council Resolution 242. The negotiating team recommended the establishment of an alignment with the Labor Party, while preserving Mapam's ideological and organizational independence. When it came time to vote, the leftist opponents of an alignment called for a secret ballot, to avert untoward "influence and pressure," but in vain. The vote was taken by show of hands and produced a result close to that of the first round. By a majority of 64.4% to 35.6%, the convention ratified the agreement to establish the Alignment.

After this, Yaari concentrated his efforts on a two-front war to keep the Alignment from developing into a full merger of the parties

---

80 Yaari at the opening of the Fifth Mapam Convention, Mar. 20, 1968, HHA, 90.60(2). The description is also based on my own recollections as a convention delegate representing Kibbutz Lahav [A.H.].

but also to prevent it from breaking up. At first sight, he was back in his preferred location, which was one of the secrets of his strength in the past: between those who had opposed the formation of the Alignment and those who wanted to move on to a single party. In practice, however, this midway position no longer gave him the power it had in the past, and for two reasons. First, Hazan was more strongly identified as a supporter of the Alignment than Yaari was and was considered to be the standard-bearer for cooperation with the Labor Party. Second, the balance of forces was inclined towards closer ties with the Labor Party rather than withdrawal from the Alignment, in part because the right wing of Mapam, which supported the Alignment, continued to express its views on the pages of party periodicals and at meetings of its institutions. But the left wing—which was in any case in the minority—splintered: some quit the party and found a new home elsewhere, leaving those who remained in Mapam with no real impact on its decisions.

One source of the younger generation's irritation and grumbling, shared by many of the old-timers, was the system of internal elections and methods used to fill key administrative positions in both the movement and the party, such as posts as emissaries in Israel and abroad, and slots on the party's Knesset list. Kibbutz Artzi and Mapam had never employed a process in which members presented their candidacy and competed against others. Such contests had always been foreign to the conceptual world of Hashomer Hatza'ir. Instead of democratic elections, the movement and party employed a two-stage process of "democratic ratification" of consensus nominations: first, a suitable candidate was identified in informal consultations, after which the party or movement institutions approved the sole candidate submitted for their consideration.[81] According to the movement folklore, a comrade "accepted the party's will." This procedure ceded authority, control, and power to the historical leadership, mainly Yaari, who until the late 1960s was more closely identified with personnel appointments than Hazan was.

---

81 Nathan Yannai, "Notes on the Leadership Type of Meir Yaari," HHA, 95-7.38(2).

How did the two men operate in this domain? Each had his own favorites whom he promoted and "black sheep" whom he blocked. Each wielded a veto. On more than one occasion, a member's fate depended on and reflected the balance of power between the two leaders.[82] Who received their nod? According to Yaari, "those who want to represent our movement's leadership cannot be further left than the two of us and cannot be further right than the two of us."[83] What this actually meant was not to the right of Hazan and not to the left of Yaari.

By the 1950s, some in the movement referred to Meir Yaari as "the dictator, who compiles, assembles, and dismantles lists to suit his fancy."[84] In the mid-1960s, Hazan said publicly that a young comrade had told him, "we will not allow Meir Yaari to continue to decide who is going to Argentina." Even though Hazan quickly labeled this as "just a story," the truth, as everyone knew, was that Yaari did indeed decide which members of Kibbutz Artzi would be posted to the city or abroad.[85] He would visit a kibbutz to persuade the members to release one of their number for party work, and it was difficult if not impossible for a kibbutz to reject such requests.[86] On the other hand, Yaari sometimes proposed cutting short a wayward emissary's posting and returning him to his home kibbutz ahead of schedule.[87] In short, he ruled over the emissaries and party bureaucracy with a high hand. Whether his decisions were based on germane considerations or personal pique, everyone knew that Yaari was the kingmaker, at whose will party functionaries rose and fell. This gave him great power in the years when such posts and trips abroad were almost the only way to escape the drudgery of the kibbutz, especially for the older generation, whose access to academic studies was almost totally blocked.

Putting together the Mapam Knesset list was the most sensitive and fraught task of all. Until 1961 (including that year), the list was

---

82 Yaari to Hazan, November [no day] 1965, HHA. 95-7.20(1).
83 Yaari to Hazan, Dec. 5, 1965, Ibid.
84 Yaari to Menachem Bader, July 2, 1951, HHA, 95-7.12(6).
85 Kibbutz Artzi Executive Committee, Oct. 20, 1966, HHA, 5-10.10(1).
86 Secretariat of Kibbutz Ha'ogen to Yaari, June 10, 1960, HHA, 95-7.16(7).
87 Hazan to Yaari, Nov. 22, 1965, HHA, 95-7.20(1).

drawn up by the Nominations Committee, which included Yaari, and then submitted to the Party Central Committee for an up-or-down vote. In the late 1950s, the party institutions began floating new ideas for assembling the Knesset list. Yaari rejected all of them. He was opposed to a secret ballot for each candidate and determined to keep full control of the composition of the list. He blocked a proposal to replace one-third of the list each Knesset term, deeming "rotation" a dirty word.[88] As for himself, Yaari said that he would be more than willing to leave the Knesset eventually, but not through rotation and only when he himself decided that the time had come.[89]

In 1961, Victor Shem-Tov was placed in a realistic spot on the Mapam Knesset list, because Yaari believed he could serve as a bridge between Mapam and the Oriental Jewish communities.[90] Shem-Tov, who had not expected to receive the nod, took the advice of an experienced comrade and went to call on Yaari and Hazan to thank them for choosing him. First he went to Merḥavia, where he found Yaari busily perusing documents. Without a word the host gestured his visitor to take a seat and left him waiting in silence for many long minutes. When Shem-Tov was finally able to express his gratitude for the honor of inclusion on the Knesset slate, Yaari replied, "it's not a matter of honor, Victor, it's a matter of trust."[91] Their conversation, in a cordial and earnest atmosphere, lasted for about an hour, with the focus on the party's political and ideological positions. The meeting with Hazan was friendlier, including a handshake that conveyed great warmth to Shem-Tov. "I am sure you'll succeed," Hazan told him with a smile. "I have confidence in you, in your talents and abilities."[92]

In advance of the next Knesset elections, in 1965, a new method for compiling the list was introduced.[93] The Nominations Committee drew

---

88 Inner Secretariat, Aug. 25, 1959, HHA, 90.64(2).
89 Mapam Central Committee, Sept. 1, 1959, HHA, 90.68(1).
90 Yaari to Avraham Sluck, Oct. 11, 1961, HHA, 95-7.16(6).
91 Shem-Tov, Eḥad me-hem, 32.
92 Ibid., 32–33.
93 On the changes in the method of assembling the list for the Sixth Knesset, see Mapam Secretariat, July 14, 1965, HHA, 90.65(2); Yaari to Mordechai Bentov, Aug. 31, 1965; Yaari to Yisrael Barzilai, Aug. 31, 1965; Yaari to Yusuf Khamis,

up a slate of 20 candidates for submission to the Central Committee, which added another seven names and then ranked all of them in a secret ballot. Or almost all of them, because the new system did not apply to Yaari and Hazan, whose placement in the first two slots was approved by a show of hands.[94] Yaari did not like the new system and believed that an appointments committee was the most democratic method.[95]

In 1965, Yaakov Riftin received the ninth slot on the Mapam Knesset list, thought to be realistic (as it had been in the last three elections). But this time Mapam won only eight seats. Riftin, left on the outside, was the subject of a lengthy and tense discussion between Yaari and Hazan, who batted around various ideas for his future role but agreed that it was unthinkable for him to go back to working on his kibbutz.[96] So there were privileged comrades who were not expected to return to manual labor in the fields and cowshed. The treatment of urban party activists was different and the party made no effort to help them even when their political work interfered with their livelihood. In 1961, Yitzhak Steinlauf, a Mapam activist in Acre, brought his own situation, which he believed was typical of many others, to the attention of "the revered comrade Meir Yaari."[97] Steinlauf had settled in Acre after arriving in the country in 1948. He and a few others established the Mapam branch in the town, with no guidance or assistance from on high. Steinlauf was employed by day as a construction worker, and devoted his evenings to party activity, on a volunteer basis. Urged on by his colleagues, he had agreed to represent the party on the local labor council (a paid position). After the 1959 elections, when Mapai decided to liquidate him publicly and economically, the Mapam representatives in the Histadrut institutions proved unable to protect him. Back in his

---

Aug. 31, 1965; Bentov to Yaari, Sept. 3, 1965; Yaari to Yisrael Barzilai, Sept. 5, 1965, HHA, 95-7.20(1); Yaari to Ephraim Sela, Feb. 27, 1966, HHA, 95-7.20(5).
94 Hazan to Yaari, Nov. 14, 1965, HHA, 95-7.20(1).
95 Yaari to Mordechai Bentov, Aug. 31, 1965; M. Yaari to Yisrael Barzilai, Aug. 31, 1965; M. Bentov to Yaari, Sept. 3, 1965, HHA, 95-7.20(1); Mapam Secretariat, Nov. 2, 1966, HHA, 90.65(2).
96 Mapam Secretariat, Nov. 2, 1966, HHA, 90.65(2); Yaari to Hazan, Dec. 5, 1965, HHA, 95-7.20(1).
97 Yitzhak Steinlauf to Yaari, May 8, 1961, HHA, 95-7.17(7).

old job as a construction worker, he served as the mouthpiece of the urban members who complained that the party spoke big words about workers' rights but did not defend its activists.[98]

As noted, even after a modicum of democracy for filling the party institutions and Knesset lists was introduced in the mid-sixties, Yaari and Hazan remained above it. Calls for rotation encountered fierce opposition from Yaari, for whom it was a make-or-break issue. He bolstered his stand with the examples of veteran leaders in other countries who had continued to hold high office when long past retirement age, but most of those he mentioned had been chosen in fully democratic processes.[99] Even after the Six Day War and Mapam's affiliation with the Alignment, the principles of rotation and a secret ballot did not apply to the historical leadership; Yaari and Hazan did not have to compete for their slots on the 1969 Knesset list.[100] They were equal with regard to this exemption, but in the voting for the rest of the list Hazan came out on top, as his preferred candidates regularly outpolled those favored by Yaari.[101]

The secret ballot was another *bête-noire* for Yaari. The intensity of his opposition and the nature of his arguments leads us to read between the lines and look for motives that he never stated explicitly. "Why should we have secrets among ourselves? Here we don't pay attention to who raised their hands," he said in late 1966.[102] Nevertheless, two years later, when Yaari was reelected Mapam general secretary, he did notice that, so far as he could tell, Eliezer Hacohen cast the only vote against him, while several of the Young Turks whom he had expected to oppose him did not.[103]

The party press played an extremely important role in guiding the members. Through the pages of the various movement publications

---

98   Ibid.
99   Yaari, *Maariv*, July 16, 1967.
100 Mapam Central Committee, Sept. 23, 1969, HHA, 90.68(1).
101 For example, after Barzilai's death, Yaari recommended that he be succeeded by Aharon Ephrat, but the choice fell on Nathan Peled, who was Hazan's candidate. Mapam Inner Secretariat, June 15, 1970, July 6, 1970, HHA, 90.79(1); Mapam Central Committee, July 15, 1970, HHA, 90.68(1).
102 Mapam Secretariat, Nov. 2, 1966, HHA, 90.65(2).
103 Yaari to Chaim Shoor, Apr. 29, 1968, HHA, *heh*-3.85(*3gimel*).

Yaari tried to dominate the discourse within the party, stifle opposition, disperse centers of resistance, and also allow a controlled release of steam. He succeeded at this for many years, while overruling journalistic considerations and frequently complaining about his treatment by correspondents and editors. He found fault with how his words were abridged in coverage of his speeches and public appearances and grumbled that others received more attention ("I got less than 50 lines. ... Galili got 70 lines").[104] But the day came when Yaari began to lose control of the movement periodicals. His involvement and influence on the selection of the editors waned and finally vanished, several publications broke free of his supervision, and he lost the power to censor articles that he viewed as expressing deviant positions. By the mid-1960s (and even less so after the Six Day War), the leader who had enjoyed veto power over submissions by others, who from time to time accompanied his complaints with warnings that "this is the last time," could no longer oversee *Al Hamishmar* and dictate its editors' conduct.[105]

This applied in spades to the weekly *Hotam*, which was the organ of the young guard of Kibbutz Artzi and Mapam until 1970, and then became a weekly supplement to *Al Hamishmar*. It irked Yaari from the very start; he complained to the secretary of KA that the youngsters were publishing a weekly "that had attained extreme ideological liberalization and even adorned its most recent issue with a picture of Peres (incidentally, for this alone it should be closed down)."[106] *Hotam*'s defining mark, as he saw it, was a nonconformism that suited chiefly those who had their eyes set on affiliation with the (first) Alignment.[107]

The Six Day War burst the dam that had blocked open expression of the members' dissatisfaction with the historical leadership's performance and of the desire to replace it. The initial shot in the public campaign took the form of an open letter published by Eitan Schreiber of Kibbutz Nir David, not long after the war, in which he called on "the historical leadership to agree voluntarily, without elections and councils, to vacate

---

104 Yaari to *Al Hamishmar* editorial board, Apr. 17, 1950, HHA, 95-7.12(1).
105 E.g., Yaari to [Yitzhak] Ronkin, Mar. 22, 1959, HHA, 95-7.16(3).
106 Yaari to Shlomo Rozen, Aug. 28, 1962, HHA, 95-7.18(1).
107 Yaari to Meir Talmi and Chaim Shoor, Feb. 5, 1967, HHA, *heh*-3.85(3*gimel*).

its seats for the good of the movement and themselves."[108] Schreiber expressed his esteem for Yaari and Hazan's vision and deeds, but advised them to stop entrenching themselves in their positions of authority and to accept the principle of rotation. He acquainted them with the feelings of the rank and file, inasmuch as "I feel, comrades, that you are not aware of the extent of the revulsion expressed in public and over coffee by most members of the kibbutz with regard to the concept of the historical leadership."[109] The movement's future, he promised them, did not depend on any particular individual, so they had no cause for apprehension on that front. After Schreiber broke the ice, an avalanche of similar pieces appeared on the pages of the Mapam and Kibbutz Artzi periodicals. The attacks against Yaari in the movement press became so fierce and frequent that in February 1971 the Mapam inner secretariat decided that *Al Hamishmar* would no longer publish articles attacking him.[110]

The second half of the 1960s saw a proliferation of movement forums that were open to the public at large. The pluralistic nature and freedom of open debate did not suit Yaari's leadership style. He felt out of place at the cultural evenings in the various Tzavta clubs, whether in Tel Aviv or the rest of the country. Tzavta was Hazan's home court, run for many years by his son-in-law, Nissim Ziyyon. It was no longer the Tzavta of Shlonsky, with high-brow literary and cultural evenings. Accustomed to being the keynote speaker at movement and party events, and with an unassailable right to the last word, Yaari was not able to share the spotlight with speakers who represented a broad spectrum of opinions, fluent orators blessed with the skills for addressing and swaying a heterogeneous audience.

He had always thought that he would make his own decision about retirement and hinted that only poor health would move him to resign his party functions. Even if now and then he intimated, noncommittally, that the party would have to find itself a new general secretary if some matter was not resolved the way he wanted, he never risked brandishing an actual threat of resignation. In fact, he did everything to keep from being displaced. "Nowhere in the world is there such a thing as rotation

---
108 Eitan Schreiber, "An Open Letter to Meir and Hazan," Ibid.
109 Ibid.
110 Mapam Inner Secretariat, Feb. 1, 1971, HHA, 90.79(1).

of the leadership," he said in late 1966. "There is no regime where there is rotation.... Should I feel that I no longer have the strength for this job, I will go home myself. Only in a case of treason do you switch the leadership. It's dangerous."[111] In the event, however, the scenario did not proceed according to his plans and wishes.

In the summer of 1971, the attacks on him in the party and movement organs reached a new pitch. Yaari was denounced as a dictator responsible for the movement's deteriorating situation. There were demands to introduce rotation in the senior positions in Mapam, there were calls to discard the party's outmoded doctrine, and there were even explicit calls for Yaari to resign or be replaced as general secretary of Mapam.[112] In a series of articles in *Hotam*, the journalist Binyamin (Benko) Adar asserted that Yaari had fashioned Mapam almost like a cult and that it held fast to Communist terminology such as "vanguard party," "dictatorship of the proletariat," and "democratic centralism." It had never managed to break through to the public at large, because it was held back by its antiquated image, tendency to entrench itself in the status quo, conservatism, and many more flaws and failures, for all of which Meir Yaari was responsible. Adar accused him of intentionally failing to cultivate successors to the historic leadership.

Yaari felt that his tolerance had reached the breaking point. When the party secretariat met on November 3, 1971, he astonished the members by reading out the following letter:

Comrades,

I have come to the conclusion that the time has come to inform the party and the public that I have decided not to present my candidacy for the position of general secretary at the coming party convention.

The circumstances and the facts that have emerged recently limit my ability to play my role as a bridge between viewpoints, between generations, between Kibbutz Artzi and the party. The venomous and

---

111 Mapam Secretariat, Nov. 2, 1966, HHA, 90.65(2).
112 Shimon Bein, *Ha-shavu'a*, June 4, 1971; Ezra Ben-Dor, Ibid., Aug. 27, 1971; Nahum Shoor, *Al Hamishmar*, July 28, 1971; Yaari's reply to Yoram Nimrod and Benko Adar, Ibid., Aug. 6, 1971.

unbridled campaign being conducted by a certain group on the pages of *Hotam* and the Kibbutz Artzi weekly against the 'historical leadership' and especially against me is only one of the symptoms of the deteriorating human and social relations that interfere with my ability to do my job as in the past. This campaign, more than it is directed against 'the historical leadership,' is directed against the historical path of our movement; but those comrades lack the courage to say outright what goal they have for Kibbutz Artzi and the party. I have specified this troubling phenomenon, but it is only one of the symptoms. The possibility I have been given to serve as a bridge between the generations and opinions, between the city and the rural sector, and the general identification with me over such a protracted period, have been my justification for an incumbency of decades in my post. This justification has recently been diminished to the point that I have suddenly remembered my age.

I have found it appropriate to move up this announcement to many months before the convention convenes in order to give the party an opportunity to gear up for the future. Until I am replaced I will endeavor to perform my job as I have in the past.[113]

It is possible that this announcement did not reflect Yaari's true intentions and was meant to serve only as a warning shot or alarm; but he totally lost control of the situation. Hazan moved that Yaari's letter not be taken as his resignation but as notice that he would not present his candidacy for another term. Shortly before the end of the meeting, Yaari took the floor again and made a statement he asked not to be published: "What has been happening recently is like the Saint Bartholomew's Eve that Dolek Horowitz sprang on me fifty years ago"—a line he would repeat in the future as well.[114]

Yaari explained the timing of his statement by his desire to allow the party to make preparations for his departure. The subliminal message was a sort of cry for help: please, stop the process. As the months passed this message became quite open. Every action he took was intended to thwart

---

113 Mapam Secretariat, Nov. 3, 1971, HHA, 90.63(1). This is also the source for the discussion that follows.
114 See, e.g.: Mapam Secretariat Oct. 25, 1972, HHA, 90.63(2); M. Yaari to Masha and Yitzhak Patish, Sept. 30, 1972, HHA, 95-7.22(5).

the process he had himself launched, part of a bitter reckoning with those who had accepted his resignation letter at face value. In his public and private statements he expressed his fear of banishment to the wilderness; as for life as a pensioner, he saw that as almost a death sentence.[115]

He made an agonized and touching appearance at the Mapam Political Committee about a year after the announcement of his resignation. His words were imbued with pain, saturated with regret, and full of hope that the wheel could be turned back. In his misery he almost lost control of himself: "There is one place in the world where they think you can replace the leadership like an old pair of gloves—Mapam and Hashomer Hatza'ir. It has become fashionable. So enjoy yourselves! I'll say it in so many words: It should make you healthy! I wish you only the best. May you succeed."[116] He tried to persuade them that he did not have to quit on account of his age or health: "Churchill accomplished his greatest deeds when he was past 70. So too Adenauer. Roosevelt was paralyzed and they didn't force rotation on him. Actually paralyzed.... Had Lenin lived, they would not have forced rotation on him. And if Ben-Gurion hadn't gone berserk against people ... would they ever have fired Ben-Gurion?"—and many more examples to show a leader's age was not the decisive factor.[117] Two weeks later he seemed to have accepted the situation. "A person is created from dust and returns to dust. I never imagined that this is how it would end. You mustn't argue against nature."[118] In his later memoirs, he recounted that the circumstances of the end of his tenure as Mapam general secretary, in which leading members betrayed him, were a crueler blow than the serious ailments he had suffered and the tragedies that had struck his family.[119]

Yaari left the post of Mapam general secretary in December 1972. Even before the convention at which he formally resigned, voices were heard against his inclusion on the party's Knesset list for the next elections. He should continue to be a member of all the party

---

115 Remarks by Moshe Chizik (Kalif), 1972, HHA, 90.116(1); joint session of the Mapam and Kibbutz Artzi secretariats, Feb. 24, 1972, HHA, 90.63(2); Yaari to Masha and Yitzhak Patish, Sept. 30, 1972, HHA, 95-7.22(5).
116 Mapam Political Committee, Oct. 9, 1972, HHA, 90.154(1).
117 Ibid.
118 Mapam Secretariat, Oct. 25, 1972, HHA, 90.63(2).
119 Yaari, [memoirs], July 25, 1980, KMA, MYF, 8(1).

institutions, but had to permit the emergence of a new leadership.[120] Yaari did not agree. "I am still essential to this movement," he said in the summer of 1973.[121] Two months later, when the inner secretariat convened to discuss the composition of the Knesset list in the general election scheduled for October 30 (and then postponed to December 31 because of the Yom Kippur War), the debate was placid. The new general secretary, Meir Talmi, proposed submitting the draft list of candidates, headed by Yaari and Hazan, to the Nominations Committee and Central Committee, with the final decision left to the Central Committee. After a short discussion of just how involved the Central Committee should be in choosing the candidates, of the ratio between the urban branches and the kibbutzim, and of the mechanisms for actually selecting the candidates, Hazan surprised all those present: "I have decided to leave the Knesset."[122] He had already had a long discussion about this with Meir, he said, but they had not come to a joint conclusion. Hazan reassured his comrades: there was nothing untoward behind his decision. He had decided to leave the Knesset after a quarter century, at age 74, because he wanted to quit when he still had the strength to do what interested him and remain active in Kibbutz Artzi and the party. He would continue to attend the Knesset faction meetings and serve on the Alignment executive committee.

"If Hazan resigns I have to go along with him and not enter the Knesset," Yaari announced.[123] He was not at peace with the *diktat* that Hazan had dropped on him and almost begged the comrades to free up two places on the list for them. "There cannot be a leadership without us," he said, adding, "in the outside world I still haven't been blotted out, but here they are blotting me out."[124] Hazan tried to save his partner's honor, to fix what Yaari had wrecked, to prevent him from slamming the door behind him, and to help him go home in dignity, free of bitterness. He saw it as important that the press know that the

---

120 Remarks by Moshe Chizik (Kalif), 1972, HHA, 90.116(1).
121 Mapam Inner Secretariat, July 9, 1973, HHA, 90.79(1).
122 Mapam Inner Secretariat, Sept. 10, 1973, HHA, 90.79(1). This is also the source for what follows.
123 Ibid.
124 Ibid.

two had decided not to stand for the Knesset, meaning that it was their own choice and not a palace coup.[125]

Yehuda Yudin candidly and sympathetically explained the situation to Yaari:

> Meir, don't build yourself a citadel of hatred or imbalance between yourself and Hazan. Both of you are important to the movement. Comrades who are anxious for your wellbeing see that some disparity has developed between you and Hazan with regard to your health. We are not talking about the leadership of the party. From the purely technical standpoint you cannot manage the daily grind of the faction's work [in the Knesset]. It is simply fate. I ask you to be realistic and accept things that do not depend on us.[126]

Even before the meeting at which Hazan announced that he would not be in the next Knesset, party secretary Talmi had explained to Yaari and Hazan that in the current situation he could not propose that they be selected by a different procedure than everyone else; that is, they could not have reserved places on the list and would have to submit to a secret ballot. It is hard to know just how much this influenced Hazan's decision to withdraw and how heavily it weighed in Yaari's decision to "go along" with him and not be subjected to a secret ballot on his own, without Hazan "on the same ticket." In any case, it is clear that he left the Knesset unwillingly. His resignation as general secretary had been the result of a miscalculation on his part and failure to think matters through, but now it was Hazan who made the decision for him.

A long chapter in the history of the party was over. Naftali Feder, the party political secretary, hit the nail on the head: "We are moving from a leadership to an executive."[127] Meir Talmi, who had succeeded Yaari as Mapam general secretary in 1973, was generous enough to refer to himself by that title, while still calling Yaari "the leader."[128]

---

125 Ibid.
126 Ibid.
127 Mapam Inner Secretariat, Oct. 10, 1972, HHA, 90.79(1).
128 Mapam Inner Secretariat, Sep. 10, 1973, HHA, 90.79(1).

The extended Yaari family, Merḥavia 1960. Standing, right to left: Tuvia (Yaari's younger brother) and his children Shlomit and Giora; Sonia (first wife of Yaari's son Avi'ezer), Avi'ezer Yaari, Yaari's daughter Rachel and her husband Lushek Groll. Seating: Zipora Yaari (Tuvia's wife), Meir and Anda; and to their feet: their son Chaim with Zohara (daughter of Avi'ezer and Sonia) and her sister Naomi; Vardit and Yedidya (Didi, children of Rachel and Lushek).
Courtesy of Nadav Man, Bitmuna Collection, Kibbutz Merḥavia.

CHAPTER 18

A Dove with Folded Wings

"We are making a fatal error by presenting our peace plan with folded wings. It is a sin of historic proportions."[1]

"I am a dove."[2]

"Several comrades ... decided to get rid of me [because] for them I was 'a rather dangerous dove."[3]

— Meir Yaari

Yaari's position on matters of peace and security was generally moderate—"dovish" in the terminology that emerged in Israel after the Six Day War. Until shortly before that war, he and Hazan had tended to see eye to eye in this domain. What differences there were between them tended to be matters of style rather than substance. But Yaari always saw Hazan as more "hawkish" than he was, an impression shared by others.[4]

The two men's remarks as the Mapam members of the Knesset Foreign Affairs and Defense Committee led Shimon Peres to conclude that the party supported, albeit implicitly, the "Dimona Project," the codename for Israel's development of nuclear weapons.[5] Reacting to reports that Egypt was developing ground-to-ground missiles, Yaari

---

1 Yaari in the Political Committee, June 29, 1967, HHA, 90.122(1).
2 Yaari in the Mapam Secretariat, May 15, 1974, HHA, 90.63(2).
3 Yaari to Nahum Mendel, Aug. 23, 1976, KMA, MYF, 3(5).
4 Yaari to Hazan, Dec. 5, 1965, HHA, 95-7.20(1).
5 Shimon Peres in the Mapai Secretariat, Sept. 14, 1962, quoted in Shalom, *Bein Dimona le-Vashington*, 132 [omitted from the English translation, *Behind the Scenes Diplomacy*].

believed it better for Israel to have "something" in hand and thought it should do the utmost to develop its arsenal, given its neighbors' arms build-up.[6] At the time, Mapam's official policy supported nuclear disarmament; the public at large viewed Yaari and his party as opposed to an Israeli bomb.[7] When the father of the Israeli nuclear project, Prof. Ernest David Bergman, retired as chairman of the Atomic Energy Committee in the summer of 1966, he contacted Yaari to offer his pessimistic forecast of nuclear proliferation in the world and the region and expressed his astonishment that Yaari was "willing to close his eyes and assume that the situation was just as we all wish it to be."[8] Two points stand out here. The first is that Bergman saw Yaari as one of those who shaped the country's defense policy. The second is that the public perception of Yaari and Mapam as being opposed to an Israeli nuclear option and in favor of a nuclear-free Middle East did not correspond with what was said behind closed doors.

On November 13, 1966, IDF forces attacked the village of Samu'a on the West Bank (then under Jordanian control), in response to a series of attacks launched from there. In this reprisal raid, the largest since the Sinai Campaign and the first in a decade conducted in the daytime and with air support, 26 Jordanian civilians and soldiers and one Israeli soldier were killed, and dozens of houses were blown up. Mapam opposed the operation. But because of the pressures on the Government at the time and Prime Minister Levi Eshkol's political weakness, Yaari did not want to take part in a campaign against him. "They are turning him into a limp dishrag."[9] He saw the operation as the use of heavy artillery against a sparrow and thought that such massive force should be employed only when there was absolutely no alternative, and not in the face of world opinion. "Our reprisals should not snowball into war," Yaari declared in December 1966.[10]

---

6 Political Committee, Apr. 13, 1965, HHA, 121.90(2).
7 *Al Hamishmar*, Sept. 2, 1962.
8 Segev, *The Seventh Million*, 370; Avner Cohen, *Israel and the Bomb*, 16.
9 Political Committee, Dec. 1, 1966, HHA, 90.122(1).
10 Ibid.

He held the same position six months later, during the waiting period before the Six Day War. It is impossible to know how much Yaari was influenced by a letter he had received from Mula Agin, a member of Kibbutz Shoval, writing from "somewhere," on May 24, 1967: "As a soldier currently serving in a combat unit, I am contacting you by virtue of your position and demanding that you take a political position *against the war* in a fashion that cannot be misunderstood."[11] Agin was killed in the war he so much wanted to prevent.

During the tense days of May and early June 1967, Yaari had to take account not only of the security threat and how Israel should respond to the external danger, but also of the political maneuvers at home, aimed at ousting Eshkol from the Defense Ministry and perhaps even from the premiership. Yaari believed that these schemes came close to an attempted putsch and was proud that it was Mapam that kept Rafi from pulling it off. On May 25, two days after Egyptian President Nasser announced the closure of the Straits of Tiran to Israeli vessels, Shimon Peres visited Yaari in his apartment in Tel Aviv and told him that, to judge by the information available to him, the IDF was not prepared for war and had no serious battle plans. The Israeli people had to be told that the country could not go to war now. The conflict was inevitable, Peres added, but it should be postponed, while taking advantage of the next six months to a year to hunker down and draft plans. And there was only one person who could state this truth to the people—David Ben-Gurion. Peres told Yaari that he assumed that Ben-Gurion was willing to accept this mission in tandem with Eshkol, putting an end to the bitter quarrel between the two men.

It was a private meeting; later that evening Hazan learned of the content from Yaari himself. In Yaari's presence, Hazan phoned Peres and verified the details of the conversation. The next day, with Peres's agreement, Hazan went alone to convey the information to Golda Meir, the secretary general of Mapai. He was quite agitated when he visited her offices on the morning of May 26, and was told, by Ben-Gurion's confidant Shaul Avigur, that everything Peres had told Yaari about the

---

11 Mula Agin to Yaari, May 24, 1967, HHA, 95-7.21(1) [emphasis in original].

situation and the IDF's lack of preparedness were his own views and not shared by Ben-Gurion. Hazan and Meir concluded that Peres had been trying to lure Mapam to establish a united front with Rafi against the Mapai leadership. Everyone implicated in this story had his own version of the details and sequence of events. Ultimately, however, Yaari and Hazan's response to the proposal to depose Eshkol and replace him with Ben-Gurion was an absolute and unequivocal "no."[12]

After Peres proved unable to recruit Mapam to join his campaign against Eshkol, Yaari was invited to a meeting with Ben-Gurion, who told him a story about some illegal affair that Eshkol was supposedly involved in. Yaari made it plain that notwithstanding his great respect for Ben-Gurion, he was sure that the latter was utterly mistaken and the charges against Eshkol were untrue. Yaari suspected that the matter Ben-Gurion alluded to involved Israeli intelligence, which had acted without Eshkol's knowledge. He had no idea, however, what that agency was supposed to have done, and the matter remained a mystery, both for Yaari then and for us today.[13] When Yaari recounted one of his versions of the whole affair, some 15 years later, Hazan retorted that Yaari was confusing several different incidents and had got his facts wrong. Hazan even scolded him for recording this unfortunate incident for posterity. The best guess is that it related to the disappearance and presumed murder of the Moroccan opposition leader Mehdi Ben Barka in Paris in October 1965, "an affair"—wrote Hazan—"that all those who knew anything kept mum about and still remain silent."[14] Hazan's skepticism about Yaari's description of the sequence of events on the eve of the Six Day War reached the point that he doubted whether the

---

12 On several occasions, and to various audiences, Yaari described the sequence of events and his part in the contacts that were taking place then. See: Political Committee, June 22, 1967, HHA, 90.122(1); Yaari, *Be-siman aḥdut ve-azma'ut*, 34; Mapam Convention, March 1968, HHA, 90.60(2); Political Committee, Oct. 18, 1972, HHA, 90.122(2); Yaari [memoirs], 1980, single sheet, KMA, MYF, 8(1); Yaari to Hazan, Feb. 25, 1982, HHA, 95-7.23(7); Hazan's version: Hazan to Yaari, Feb. 26, 1982, HHA, 95-7.23(7).
13 Yaari [memoirs], 1980, single sheet, KMA, MYF, 8(1); Yaari to Hazan, Feb. 25, 1982, HHA, 95-7.23(7).
14 Hazan to Yaari, Feb. 26, 1982, HHA, 95-7.23(7).

meeting with Ben-Gurion had even taken place.[15] In fact, Kibbutz Artzi and Mapam members who were involved with Israeli security tended to agree that sensitive defense-related matters should not be shared with Yaari, because of his tendency to run off at the mouth.[16]

However that may be, Yaari demonstrated national responsibility in the tense prewar atmosphere of late May and early June 1967. The day after the establishment of the National Unity Government, which included Moshe Dayan as defense minister, Yaari was quoted to the effect that he had risen above politics in the interest of national unity: "A time of emergency requires a heightened willingness for cooperation between different strata of the people. This is why it was not necessary to coerce us to reach the conclusion that, in view of the supreme tests facing us, Rafi and Gahal should be included in responsibility and added to the coalition."[17] He expressed the hope that this bold step would put an end to the prevailing climate of division and incitement. Even though Yaari's attitude towards Dayan in the past—and later as well—was critical and even hostile, Yaari declared that in recent years he had come to appreciate him not only as a military man but also as minister of agriculture (a post he held from 1959 to 1964), thanks to Dayan's talents and integrity in dealing with the affairs entrusted to him.[18] When the war was over, Yaari declared that Mapam had welcomed Dayan's entry into the government, reflecting the general feeling at the time that Dayan's appointment had helped raise national morale on the eve of the war.[19] But Dayan's interlude of grace was brief. About ten days after the end of the war Yaari was already criticizing him for the slogan he had floated—"with Herut and without Mapam"—and for his boastful statement that he alone deserved credit for the expansion of the Israeli battle plan.[20] The maneuvers that led to Eshkol's ouster as defense minister and replacement by Dayan left

---

15 Ibid.
16 Author's interview with Gidi Eilat, Beit Alfa, March 2006.
17 *Al Hamishmar*, June 2, 1967.
18 Ibid.
19 *Al Hamishmar*, June 11, 1967.
20 Political Committee, June 22, 1967, HHA, 90.122(1).

a bitter residue for Yaari. He had a warm spot in his heart for Golda Meir on account of her brave opposition to the maneuver.[21]

The three weeks from Independence Day, May 15, 1967, when large Egyptian forces entered the Sinai Peninsula, until the war began on the morning of June 5 were a fateful period. With Mapam and its ministers involved in the momentous decisions, the leadership found that the party's system of consultations no longer suited the circumstances. Yaari agreed with Hazan that matters of security must not be discussed in public and accordingly supported his proposal to expand the party's defense committee and submit its decisions for ratification by the secretariat. At his request, the latter authorized him to decide who would be added to the committee.[22]

In those weeks, the Government held some of its sessions in the Defense Ministry compound in Tel Aviv; the Knesset Foreign Affairs and Defense Committee convened nearby. The ad hoc Mapam forum designated the "expanded Defense Committee" or the "Situation Committee," whose 15 members included cabinet ministers Bentov and Barzilai, as well as Hazan and Yaari, who were the party's representatives on the Foreign Affairs and Defense Committee, met not far away, at Mapam headquarters. This group, which did not keep minutes, formulated the position that the Mapam ministers advocated in cabinet meetings: namely, to make the fullest use of diplomatic means to resolve the crisis.[23] On June 4, 1967, when the Government held its decisive vote to authorize the Prime Minister, the Defense Minister, and the Chief of Staff to decide on the timing of the Israeli operation, Bentov and Barzilai asked for time to consult with Hazan and Yaari before their position was entered into the minutes. Because even without them there was a majority for the motion, there was no need to wait for the outcome of that consultation and hold another vote. In fact, the Mapam ministers' formal vote on the motion was never recorded.[24]

---

21 Political Committee, Mar. 3, 1974, HHA, 90.154(3).
22 Shem-Tov, *Eḥad me-hem*, 36; Mapam Secretariat, May 26, 1967, HHA, 90.65(2).
23 Shem-Tov, *Eḥad me-hem*, 36–37.
24 Nakdimon, *Liqrat she'at ha-efes*, 278; Segev, *1967*, 358.

The outcome of the war created a new security and political situation, which required new thinking, and posed unprecedented dilemmas for Yaari. His positions after the war were more strongly colored than in the past by a security-first orientation; he arrived at them largely due to considerations rooted in Mapam's membership in the coalition and the fact that, after 1969, it was part of the Alignment. Yaari often called attention to actions that had proved to be in error and sometimes accurately predicted future developments. Two months after the war he came out against those who, drunk with victory, believed that Israel should hold on to all the territories it had occupied, denounced those who thought that a state of 2.5 million people could rule the West Bank with its 1.5 million residents, and estimated that within a decade the two populations would be equal.[25] At the end of 1968, Yaari identified Dayan's idea of employing workers from the West Bank and integrating the economies of Israel and the territories as a plot aimed at annexation, which Mapam must oppose.[26]

Despite this clear perception of the current situation and an accurate view of future developments, on more than one occasion Yaari's diagnosis was wrong and the path he prescribed mistaken. In general, he reacted to events and other people's ideas rather than taking the initiative. Apart for his uncompromising rejection of any form of partnership with those whom he saw as anti-Zionist or even just non-Zionist, in those years there was no topic or issue for which Yaari was willing to go to the wall. On all points, the decisive consideration was preserving the independence of Kibbutz Artzi and keeping Mapam in both the Alignment and the Government. Preserving his status as the head of the party and movement—a dominant factor in the past— no longer mattered after 1973, but Yaari's complex relationship with Hazan continued to impact on his positions about Israel's future and its borders, peace agreements, the fate of the Palestinians, and other vital issues.

---

25 Political Committee, Aug. 9, 1967, HHA, 90.122(1).
26 Mapam Secretariat, Nov. 13, 1968, HHA, 90.65(2).

In the first weeks after the Six Day War, when Yaari was still the undisputed number one in the party, he complained that Mapam remained silent when Begin spoke about the "greater Land of Israel" and insisted that Israel must not yield a single inch of the territory occupied in the war, when Dayan established facts on the ground in the West Bank, and Yigal Allon was already sending settlers to the Golan. "We are making a fatal error by presenting our peace plan with folded wings. It is a sin of historic proportions," he said.[27] Soon, though, it came out with a peace and security plan that assigned priority to an arrangement with Jordan, which would include the return of the West Bank, accompanied by border modifications deemed essential for Israeli security.[28] Yaari hoped for an alliance with Jordan, perhaps even a confederation; he attached great hopes to King Hussein, "and it doesn't bother me that he has a crown on his head."[29]

About three months after the war, Yaari assigned greater weight to security considerations than to peace. He saw negotiations as an opportunity to fix what had not been achieved in the War of Independence. All the same, the redrawing of the border should be limited to what was strictly essential for Israeli security; Yaari did not think these modifications would be all that great.[30] The West Bank and Sinai Peninsula should be demilitarized and returned to Jordan and Egypt, respectively, with border rectifications as required, the Gaza District and the Golan Heights should be annexed, and a united Jerusalem should remain the capital of Israel.[31] A return to the June 4 borders was quite out of the question.[32] In general Yaari believed that there was no point in sketching maps and no need for a precise definition of the secure borders Israel had in mind. In the interlude between the Six Day War and the Yom Kippur War, his preference for security over

---

27 Political Committee, June 29, 1967, HHA, 90.122(1).
28 "The Mapam Plan for Peace and Security," Aug. 24, 1967, Yaari, *Be-siman aḥdut ve-azma'ut*, 143–145.
29 Political Committee, June 29, 1967, HHA, 90.122(1).
30 Kibbutz Artzi Executive Committee, September 1967 [belated celebration of Yaari's 70th birthday], HHA, 5-10.10(3).
31 Yaari at the Mapam Convention, Nov. 22, 1968, HHA, 90.60(3).
32 Mapam Secretariat, Mar. 15, 1971, HHA, 90.79(1).

both peace and the return of territory was clear: "We never said that peace comes before territory. We said peace and security. And we said that to achieve security we need secure borders."[33]

Yaari was not interested in presenting Mapam's peace and security plan to the Prime Minister, for fear that it might lead to the dismantling of the Alignment. He repeatedly made it clear that Mapam would not break up the Alignment on this account. For him it was enough that the party had a plan.[34] Mapam institutions conducted countless debates about the future borders, the disposition of the territories occupied in the war and their residents, and matters of peace and security. For the most part these discussions were idle and pointless, with no practical goal and without operational conclusions. The minutes of these sessions frequently leave the impression that many of these protracted debates were quite unimportant and conducted chiefly as a matter of inertia and routine. At one session of the political committee Yaari acknowledged, "this discussion is useful, comrades are expressing their opinions, but ..."—and the rest went without saying.[35]

In his public remarks in the years between the Six Day War and the Yom Kippur War, the dominant motto was that there was no need for haste and that decisions could and should be deferred. As long as there was no peace, there were no borders.[36] The message that time was not pressing was especially prominent in what he said again and again in 1972: "Just now I have one thesis: not to decide now."[37] He held fast to the rule that haste was unnecessary, despite his awareness that Dayan was implementing plans that would effectively annex the territories and leave a million Arabs without political rights.[38]

After the Yom Kippur War Yaari gave freer rein to his dovish positions, because of the trauma that the war had wreaked on Israeli society and because he no longer bore the responsibility of a party leader. Even

---

33 "Al Hamishmar Editors Interview Yaari," *Al Hamishmar*, Mar. 20, 1972.
34 Mapam Inner Secretariat, Feb. 9, 1970, HHA, 90.79(1).
35 Political Committee, Jan. 12, 1972, HHA, 90.154(1).
36 Kibbutz Artzi Executive Committee, Dec. 31, 1967, HHA, 5-10.10(16).
37 Political Committee, Jan. 12, 1972, HHA, 90.154(1).
38 Political Committee, Oct. 18, 1972, HHA, 90.122(2).

after 1973, though, he continued to stand vigil over the unity of the Alignment and strove to keep Mapam in the coalition. After October 1973 he defined himself as a "dove" and sketched out his territorial red lines in more explicit terms: a united Jerusalem with autonomy for the Arabs, minor border rectifications, and the return of the territories.[39]

His stand on the West Bank was consistent, both before and after the Yom Kippur War. It should be given back—to Jordan. By no means should the Palestinians there be allowed an independent state.[40] After the Yom Kippur War Yaari again spoke about a major pullback from the West Bank, including the Jordan Rift Valley; the first step would be returning Jericho to Jordan.[41] His attitude towards the Gaza District, however, was different. Gaza should be incorporated into Israel, which would take steps to rehabilitate the refugees living there.[42] To him, the Gaza District was more important strategically than the West Bank and he wanted it to serve as a buffer between Israel and Egypt. Its residents would have to be given "human rights" and the problem of the refugees living there must be resolved; but not all of them could be resettled in Gaza. The bottom line was that Israel must not give up the Gaza Strip.[43]

He had a special relationship with the Golan Heights. At a meeting of the Kibbutz Artzi Executive Committee, held in Kibbutz Lehavot Habashan less than a month after the Six Day War, Yaari proclaimed that Israel could never permit Syria to return to the Golan. The Syrians must not be allowed the opportunity to renew their bombardment of the kibbutzim below the heights. He invited the comrades to tour the Golan and realize that "the Maginot Line is a dog compared to what's up there."[44] His remarks were greeted with applause. In late 1967, he reiterated that coming down from the Golan was inconceivable and that there could not be peace without Israeli control of the Golan. He rejected any

---

39 Mapam Secretariat, May 15, 1974, HHA, 90.63(2).
40 Political Committee, Jan. 12, 1972, HHA, 90.154(1).
41 Mapam Inner Secretariat, Apr. 27, 1976, HHA, 90.79(2).
42 Yaari, *Be-siman aḥdut ve-azma'ut*, 144.
43 Political Committee, Aug. 9, 1972, Aug. 16, 1972, HHA, 90.122(2).
44 Kibbutz Artzi Executive Committee, July 1, 1967, HHA, 5-10.10(6).

withdrawal that did not leave Israel in control of a strip as deep as the range of long-range artillery: "If we want to live, we will not come down from the Heights."[45] Even after the Yom Kippur War Yaari stuck to his position that the border must run through the Golan Heights and that Israel must remain there; that was also the dominant line in his party.[46] Prime Minister Yitzhak Rabin was more cautious. The problem with Syria is difficult, he told the members of the Mapam Inner Secretariat in 1974, and that was why he was careful not to say in public that "we will not come down from the Golan Heights. In an overall settlement I see the possibility of a certain withdrawal on the Heights as well."[47] But Yaari remained firm. "We do not agree to come down from the Golan"; "we will not accept that the Syrians will again be able to shell us from above."[48]

If Israel was going to retain the Golan, the question of settlement there became relevant. Yaari's position on the matter was based on three elements. First, the borders should be determined through negotiations, meaning that facts on the ground would not set them. Second, settlements could be founded there as long as they were not permanent. Third, in matters of national security, Kibbutz Artzi had never left the work to others. The decision to establish the first KA outpost there, in the Banias (Kibbutz Snir), was simple for him, because the area had been part of Israel before June 5, 1967.[49] As for the other KA settlements in the Golan, Geshur (founded 1971) and Natour (1980), it was agreed that they could be evacuated when peace came.

On Jerusalem, too, Yaari's stand was firm and unequivocal: "united Jerusalem as the capital of Israel."[50] The Yom Kippur War made no dent in this position. He opposed the idea of two capitals in Jerusalem: "They have a number of capitals. They have a religious capital—Mecca and Medina. Jordan has its own capital, Amman. We cannot and are not entitled to give them still another capital. We have only one historical

---

45 Kibbutz Artzi Executive Committee, Dec. 31, 1967, HHA, 5-10.10(16).
46 Mapam Inner Secretariat, May 6, 1974, Sept. 1, 1974, HHA, 90.79(2).
47 Mapam Inner Secretariat, Sept. 6, 1974, Ibid.
48 Political committee, Mar. 11, 1976, HHA, 90.156(1)*aleph*.
49 Kibbutz Artzi Executive Committee, Dec. 31, 1967, HHA, 5-10.10(16).
50 Mapam Secretariat, Apr. 22, 1970, HHA, 90.63(1).

capital, and that is Jerusalem." Could one imagine "Zionism without Jerusalem as the capital of Israel? Jerusalem has been the desire of all the Jewish generations."⁵¹ But he was opposed to building up Jewish settlement around Jerusalem, from Atarot in the north to Beit Jallah in the south to Ma'ale Adummim in the east. Jewish neighborhoods there would block the road to peace, and in any case the gain would be outweighed by the loss, since it would mean incorporating tens of thousands of Arabs into the city, thereby endangering its Jewish character.⁵²

Just as Yaari was resolute about the need to return the West Bank to Jordan and draw new borders there based on security considerations, he was equally opposed to Jewish settlement in the West Bank and the Jordan Valley. He saw the decision to permit a Jewish presence in Hebron as an act of political irresponsibility.⁵³ Before the 1973 elections he proposed that the Alignment's platform state that settlements are an obstacle to peace.⁵⁴ After the Yom Kippur War, when the momentum of settlement increased, Yaari's opposition became even more adamant, and he again declared that the settlements are "a provocation against peace," would lead to war, and, in brief, were a disaster.⁵⁵ But his position on settlement in the Rafiah Salient was more complex and evasive. After the forced evacuation of some 5,000 Bedouin to permit the establishment of settlements there, a meeting to protest the expulsion and demolition was held on Kibbutz Nir Oz in March 1972, under the slogan "we want neighbors, not enemies." The gathering, which attracted around 300 people from the 13 KA settlements in the Negev, won prominent headlines and triggered a fierce and protracted political debate. Yaari found himself on the horns of a dilemma. He was opposed to any settlement for which there was no security rationale and was certain that those planned for the Rafiah Salient, which were to be based on Arab laborers, would make no contribution to Israeli

---

51 Political committee, Mar. 11, 1976, HHA, 90.156(1)*aleph*.
52 Ibid.
53 *Al Hamishmar*, Apr. 24, 1970.
54 Mapam Inner Secretariat, Dec. 11, 1973, HHA, 90.79(1).
55 Mapam Inner Secretariat, Jan. 6, 1975, HHA, 90.79(2).

security. He was also afraid that if their residents were drawn mainly from persons affiliated with the Likud, they would threaten civil war when told to withdraw.[56] But he was also apprehensive that protests by members of KA would blow up the Alignment—and this was the decisive consideration in determining his position on the matter.[57]

Yaari was utterly against the establishment of a Palestinian state, opposed contacts with the PLO, and rejected out of hand any dealings with its chairman, Yasser Arafat. A Palestinian state would not be able to stand on its own two feet economically, would be unable to absorb the refugees, and would aspire to eliminate Israel.[58] Because he also opposed keeping the West Bank, with its million residents, under Israeli control, he favored the Jordanian option, both before and after the Yom Kippur War. To permit the establishment of a Palestinian-Jordanian state he was even willing to cede the Gaza District to Jordan—to Jordan, but never to the Palestinians.[59] As it became clear that the PLO was growing stronger in the West Bank, Yaari's adherence to the Jordanian option and rejection of the PLO and Arafat became even more adamant. Statements and declarations against the PLO became standard fare in his statements; in 1979 he was still waiting for Hussein to climb off the fence.[60]

Yaari's opposition to the PLO and its leader was so fierce that he saw any contact with Arafat as an anti-Zionist act.[61] His uncompromising rejection of recognition of the PLO and contacts with Arafat led him to statements that moved in a circle and verged on the illogical: There must be no negotiations with Arafat and meetings with the PLO should be banned as long as the organization did not recognize the State of

---

56 Mapam Inner Secretariat [no date, 1972], HHA, 90.79(1).
57 Mapam Secretariat, Aug. 16, 1971, HHA, 90.63(1); Mapam Inner Secretariat, June 26, 1972, HHA, 90.79(1); Mapam Secretariat, Mar. 15, 1972, HHA, 90.63(2).
58 Political Committee, Aug. 9, 1967, June 29, 1967, HHA, 90.122(1).
59 Mapam Convention, Dec. 28, 1972, HHA, 90.70(1); Political Committee, June 4, 1975, HHA, 90.155(2)*bet*; Mapam Inner Secretariat, Nov. 27, 1975, HHA, 90.79(2).
60 Mapam Inner Secretariat, July 15, 1974, July 22, 1974, Dec. 16, 1974, HHA, 90.79(2); Mapam Central Committee, May 17, 1979, HHA, 90.140(2).
61 Kibbutz Artzi Secretariat, July 8, 1973, HHA, 5.16(8).

Israel and renounce terrorism.⁶² At the same time, Yaari attacked the formula, devised by ministers Aharon Yariv (of Labor) and Victor Shem-Tov (of Mapam), that Israel should negotiate with any entity that recognized its existence and refrained from terrorism. He saw Hussein as the only counterparty, because he did recognize Israel, whereas the leaders of the PLO, to judge by their statements, were not potential negotiating partners.⁶³ Even after Mapam came around to a willingness to recognize a Palestinian right to self-determination, Yaari persisted in his steadfast opposition to negotiations with Arafat and offered a whole slew of reasons in support of his position.⁶⁴ Were a Palestinian state to be established on the West Bank, he prophesied blackly, "heavy missiles would begin to rain down on Tel Aviv and Ben-Gurion Airport."⁶⁵ His stand was clear and consistent and he stated it repeatedly, orally and in writing, but it had a very slight influence, if any. And he was very much aware of that.⁶⁶

It is well known that Golda Meir and Yaakov Hazan enjoyed close and friendly relations. Yaari, too, had warm feelings for her. It will be remembered that her opposition to the demand, on the eve of the Six Day War, that Dayan be appointed defense minister won her great favor in his eyes, and perhaps also the episode in her life, soon after her arrival in the country, when she lived at Merḥavia.⁶⁷ In the period before the Yom Kippur War he wrote and spoke about her on a number of occasions in glowing terms; for example, that he "could only be glad that this intelligent and brave woman is the head of our government."⁶⁸ And again, a few months after the war: "as long as

---

62 Political Committee, June 19, 1974, HHA, 90.155(1); Mapam Inner Secretariat, July 15, 1974 and June 5, 1975, HHA, 90.79(2).
63 Political Committee, Mar. 11, 1976, HHA, 90.156(1)*aleph*; Mapam Central Committee, May 17, 1979, HHA, 90.140(2).
64 Mapam Convention, June 10, 1976, HHA, 90.158(1); Mapam Secretariat, Apr. 22, 1979, HHA, 90.153(2).
65 Mapam Central Committee, May 17, 1979, HHA, 90.140(2).
66 Yaari in the Political Committee, Mar. 3, 1974, HHA, 90.154(3).
67 In 1976 he said that she was considered to be an honorary member of Merḥavia. Mapam Political Committee Mar. 11, 1976, HHA, 90.156(1)*aleph*).
68 Yaari to Pinchas Sapir, Mar. 17, 1971, HHA, 95-7.22(6).

this woman holds the tiller, we must support her."[69] Only later did he express his regret that "this wise woman ... was so rigid."[70] He praised her and lauded her efforts to achieve peace, even though she refused to allow Nahum Goldmann, the president of the World Jewish Congress, to travel to Egypt in the spring of 1970. At the peak of the War of Attrition, which had already cost hundreds of Israeli dead, there were feelers about a meeting between Goldmann and Egyptian President Nasser. Goldmann, who also held Israeli citizenship, contacted the Prime Minister and requested her permission to do so, and she turned him down. At a session of the Mapam secretariat, Naftali Ben Moshe charged that the government was capable only of waging war and not of bringing peace, and that Mapam was a negligible weight in it. These remarks infuriated Yaari, who warned against the mood they represented. Mapam must not break up the Alignment, he insisted, and consequently it must not support Goldmann's initiative.[71] In the public arena, the episode caused a major uproar and produced the "twelfth-graders' letter," whose signatories, including the son of the Mapam cabinet minister Shem-Tov, wrote that they would find it difficult to serve in the IDF as long as they were not convinced that the government was doing everything possible to bring peace closer.[72]

Yaari and Hazan took a dim view of the various groups that organized after the Six Day War and attracted members of KA and Mapam. Prominent among these was the Movement for Peace and Security, founded in 1969. Yaari was opposed, for various reasons, to Mapam members' joining it and to KA's formal participation in it, fearing that this might impair Mapam's membership in the Alignment, cause various people to abandon it, and lead to charges that it was two-faced. Another objection was that some members of the movement were insufficiently Zionist to Yaari's taste and he did not want to cooperate

---

69 Political Committee, Mar. 3, 1974, HHA, 90.154(3).
70 Political Committee, Mar. 11, 1976, HHA, 90.156(1)*aleph*.
71 Mapam Secretariat, Apr. 8, 1970, HHA, 90.63(1).
72 Photocopy of the letter at https://drive.google.com/file/d/0B__wZ8qKsEas2YUk3RWhYNExpWW8/edit

with those who favored a return to the 1967 borders. He was also afraid that the movement might compete with and overshadow Mapam.[73]

Even fiercer and more negative was his reaction to Mapam members who joined demonstrations against the Government's policy. This reached its zenith in 1970, in the demonstration against permitting a permanent Jewish settlement in Hebron. In Yaari's eyes, this protest skirted the edge of anti-Zionism. Hazan was more adamant and denounced it, with the War of Attrition in progress, as "a betrayal of the people who are under siege and in a state of war."[74] About a month later, Yaari went even further and defined the demonstration in question as a totally irresponsible action that was liable to endanger the very existence of Israel. The protest march, staged in "the occupied territory," during which the demonstrators "confronted a unit of the IDF, that same IDF that at the very same moment was on standing guard on the banks of the Suez Canal, in the Jordan Valley, and on the Lebanese border—I see this as a national betrayal."[75] Another reason the two leaders responded so sharply to the demonstration against Jewish settlement in Hebron was that the group behind it was Siaḥ (an acronym for "New Israeli Left"), a new Leftist movement that disturbed them greatly and awakened old demons from the 1950s. Even earlier, on the eve of the establishment of the Alignment, Yaari and Hazan were aware of the incipient cracks in the ideological collectivism. And after the Alignment was formed, Yaari remained haunted by the sense of spreading anarchy in KA with regard to "the ideological partnership"— the expression he now used instead of ideological collectivism. He saw the metamorphosis of the ideological partnership to pluralism as "suicide."[76]

Siaḥ continued to preoccupy Yaari (and KA) for a number of years. As usual, the peril lay not so much in the opinions it espoused as in

---

73 Mapam Secretariat, Apr. 13, 1970; July 22, 1970, Aug. 26, 1970, HHA, 90.63(1); Mapam Inner Secretariat, Mar. 15, 1971, HHA, 90.79(1).
74 Kibbutz Artzi Secretariat, Apr. 24, 1970, HHA, 5.16(6).
75 *Al Hamishmar*, May 22, 1970.
76 Mapam Secretariat, Aug. 28, 1968, HHA, 90.65(2); Kibbutz Artzi Secretariat, Aug. 10, 1969, HHA, 5.16(5); Kibbutz Artzi Secretariat, Apr. 24, 1970, HHA, 5.16(6).

its organizing to support them. Yaari was willing to allow freedom of thought only within the party, but not outside that limited arena. He insisted that those who joined Siaḥ be expelled from KA institutions and rejected the idea of accepting the group as an ideological circle.[77] "It's a cancer. It means abandoning Kibbutz Artzi and the movement. This is activity that is opposed to socialist Zionism."[78] Siaḥ continued to be a red flag for him for a number of years.[79]

Yaari and Hazan were more or less of the same mind regarding the Leftwing groups that attracted those who had quit Mapam; as in the 1950s, Hazan was the more extreme on this front. His remarks about Siaḥ in the summer of 1969 reflect his fanaticism on the subject, but also the change from the 1950s in the leadership's ability to impose sanctions on wayward comrades. "If they continue on this path," Hazan said, "I think that we will have to expel them from Kibbutz Artzi, from all the *institutions* of Kibbutz Artzi; the kibbutzim can do what they want."[80] This can be understood to mean that Hazan really wanted to oust them from KA. Bowing to reality, however, he was willing to make do with expelling them from its institutions and, throwing up his hands in despair or disgust, accepting that the individual kibbutzim would do what they wanted. Yaari was more cautious about expelling comrades from KA. He drew a red line—the rejection of Zionism. Anyone who crossed that limit must be ejected. In the spring of 1970, he said that if Siaḥ advocated a return to the June 4 borders, its members had no place in Mapam. He did not want persons who advocated full withdrawal involved in running the movement.[81]

The organizational response to the KA members who joined Siaḥ was different than that to the Leftwing deviationists of the 1950s, even though the ideological threat was similar—slipping outside the pale of Zionism.[82] In the 1950s, Yaari and Hazan stood guard over

---

77 Mapam Inner Secretariat, May 31, 1971, HHA, 90.79(1).
78 Kibbutz Artzi Secretariat, July 8, 1973, HHA, 5.16(8).
79 Yaari to Bunim Shamir, Oct. 1, 1972, HHA, 95-7.22(5).
80 Kibbutz Artzi Secretariat, July 13, 1969, HHA, 5.16(5) [emphasis added].
81 Mapam Inner Secretariat, Apr. 3, 1970, HHA, 90.79(1).
82 Kibbutz Artzi Secretariat, Apr. 24, 1970, HHA, 5.16(6).

Zionism against the Marxist-Leninist peril; after the Six Day War, they took their stand in defense of the primacy of Zionism against the call to recognize the Palestinians and their right of self-determination. Although this opposition was just as fierce as that of the 1950s, the difference in the responses and the sanctions meted out in the two decades are indicative of the changes that had transpired in the nature of ideological collectivism and the degree of control the movement exercised over its member kibbutzim.

In the period between the Six Day War and the Yom Kippur War, the right wing of Mapam, which aspired to a closer alliance with the Labor Party within the Alignment and perhaps even the formation of a single party, and was also interested in a merger of the kibbutz movements, was very active in the party and its institutions and maintained a prominent presence in the columns of its publications. This played a major role in Yaari's decision to step down as party general secretary. Hazan developed ties with those elements, who came to be identified with him and supported him. Yaari, by contrast, never developed any real links with those on the left, most of whom, by this time, belonged to the younger generation. This was a left wing in the distorted Israeli sense of the term, in which "left" does not refer to social and economic views but almost exclusively to a dovish attitude towards a resolution of the Middle East conflict in general and of the Israeli-Palestinian conflict in particular. The rightwing rebellion by the younger generation was triggered in part by anti-Soviet sentiments and a desire to dissolve the special tie to the Soviet Union; but this issue was of no interest whatsoever for the left of the late 1960s and early 1970s.

As a result, there was no mutual support between these Leftists and Yaari, whose views overlapped only slightly. He frequently scolded them for their political positions and conduct, while they did not see him as their faithful representative. Nor did they feel any collegial bond with him of the sort that existed between Hazan and the right wing of the party. Its tendency to throw over the traces, too, made the Mapam Left wing of the interwar years a broken reed for Yaari. Unlike the Right wing, which pursued its goals within the movement, some of the Leftists seceded from Mapam. Their status in KA was problematic and some were of doubtful allegiance to Zionism. The departure of the more extreme Leftists, along with the efforts by the party leadership, headed by Yaari and Hazan, to tighten the alliance with the Labor Party in the Alignment and to ensure Mapam's remaining in the coalition at almost any cost—all of this put paid to the existence of an effective leftwing Zionist opposition in Israel between 1967 and 1973, and after the Yom Kippur War as well.

The host of new dilemmas that troubled Mapam and Kibbutz Artzi after the Six Day War did not mean that Yaari could ignore the older problems. Some of them became more intense after 1967, while others were overshadowed by the new issues that required a different set of priorities. Over time, the changing situation began to influence Yaari's attitude towards the Arab citizens of Israel. In 1968, he supported the inclusion of Arabs comrades on party committees that dealt with matters of security and Israel's maneuvering *vis-à-vis* the UN mediator, Gunnar Jarring.[83] In May 1971, MK Abdul Aziz Zouabi was appointed deputy minister of health, making Mapam the first party in Israel to be represented by an Arab at that level. But a few years later, when MK Muhammad Watad complained that Mapam had ceased to be a binational party after Zouabi's death in February 1974 and demanded that an Arab be named to the party's political committee, Yaari replied: "Zouabi had a healthy instinct and whenever security matters came up would go out and leave the Jews alone."[84] Yaari accepted the need to include Arabs in party institutions, but not on its political committee, because that dealt with security issues.[85] About six month later, when the Arab section of the party protested that the Mapam inner secretariat did not include an Arab, Yaari said, "this is a national state with an Arab minority. There does not have to be an Arab member in every place, even in the party. In this institution there are security matters and 150% responsibility is required."[86] The appeal was rejected.

On a number of issues, Yaari's positions fell into step with the Labor Party. In 1972, he opposed revisiting the decision not to allow

---

83 Political Committee, July 24, 1968, HHA, 90.122(1).
84 Mapam Secretariat, Nov. 20, 1974, HHA, 90.63(2).
85 Ibid.
86 Mapam Inner Secretariat, May 5, 1975, HHA, 90.79(2).

the residents of the Galilee villages of Iqrit and Bir'im, displaced in 1948, to return to their homes, and rejected a campaign against the Government on those grounds (the Mapam ministers had voted to allow the villagers to return).[87] In the mid-1970s, he was no longer of two minds about the lands taken over by kibbutzim after 1948 and resolved that there was no need to pay compensation to their Arab former owners. One of his arguments was that there had been a sort of population transfer, by which he evidently meant (to judge by his previous statements) the Palestinian refugees who had left Israel and the Jews who had left Arab countries.[88] There was a clear difference between his position on the expropriation of the Bedouin of the Rafiah Salient, which he opposed, and his attitude against the allocation of land for Bedouin settlements in the Negev. In the later case, which involved land inside the Green Line, he called for a clear policy: "We will not throw away millions of dunams. There cannot be two opinions here—we are Zionists."[89]

His position on the events of Land Day, March 30, 1976, when protests by Arab citizens in the Galilee degenerated into violence and clashes with the security forces, and six demonstrators were killed by police and army gunfire, was complex. Yaari declared that Rakaḥ (the New Communist Party) and the PLO must not be allowed to turn the Galilee into another Lebanon. The Galilee must remain part of the State of Israel and there could be no compromise about this. He expressed his regret for what had happened and called for Arab-Jewish reconciliation, but opposed an inquiry by some ostensibly neutral party. He acknowledged that not enough had been done to achieve full equality for the Arabs of Israel; he saw the appointment of an Arab cabinet minister and an Arab Supreme Court justice as essential steps in this direction.[90]

---

87 Mapam Inner Secretariat, Jan. 31, 1972, HHA, 90.79(1).
88 Mapam Inner Secretariat, Nov. 27, 1975, HHA, 90.79(2). On this matter, see Yaari to Yossi Amitay, May 16, 1961, HHA, 95-7.17(7).
89 Mapam Inner Secretariat, Feb. 25, 1975, HHA, 90.79(2).
90 Mapam Inner Secretariat, July 15, 1976, HHA, 90.79(4), Mapam Inner Secretariat, Apr. 5, 1976, HHA, 90.79(2).

Yaari chastised Arab members of Mapam that even though their intellectual level was on a par with their Jewish comrades, in their private lives they continued to discriminate against women and left their wives "in a situation of *Kinder-Küche-Kirche*" (he himself used the alliterative German expression that means "children, kitchen, church").[91] The sad fact was that young Arab women had no path forward.

After the Six Day War, Yaari hoisted the political and security banner to the top of the flagpole, lowering and even (to some extent) folding the socioeconomic banner. He revived the theory of stages (originated in 1927) to justify the partnership with the Labor Party and defend his willingness to be flexible and compromise on socioeconomic issues in order to preserve the Alignment.[92]

Under Yaari's leadership, Mapam had always preferred considerations of national unity and security over those of class and economics. This inclination was even stronger when the party was constrained by its inclusion in the Alignment and membership in the coalition and had to carefully consider its steps in light of these two affiliations. For example, when legislation to limit labor actions and strikes was brought to the Knesset, Yaari focused on making the public aware that Mapam had opposed it fiercely until the last moment, but coalition discipline did not allow it to vote against the proposal; instead, he requested permission to abstain in the Knesset vote.[93] At the same time, Yaari continued to insist on celebrating May Day; in 1969 he called for a May Day demonstration in Nazareth so as not to abandon the street to the Communists. A year later he proposed celebrating May Day as a sign that "we are both good Zionists and good socialists" and asked that Kibbutz Artzi continue to make that day an official holiday.[94]

Yaari's anxiety about the growing strength of the right in Israel dated to 1967; by mid-1976 he foresaw Begin's impending victory.[95] On the eve of the 1977 elections he viewed a Begin-led government

---

91 Mapam Inner Secretariat, Dec. 2, 1974, HHA, 90.79(2).
92 Meir Yaari, *Hedim*, 98 (September 1972), 5–10.
93 Mapam Inner Secretariat, July 5, July 15, 1971, HHA, 90.79(1).
94 Mapam Secretariat, Mar. 20, 1969, Feb. 25, 1970, Mar. 25, 1970, HHA 90.65(2).
95 Mapam Convention, June 10, 1976, HHA, 90.158(1).

as a double threat: it would bring war closer and would impose mandatory arbitration of labor disputes, which could lead to fascism in social relations in Israel.[96] This gloomy prediction made him all the more apprehensive when Yigael Yadin threw his hat into the political ring. As the head of the newly formed Democratic Movement for Change (Dash), Yadin presented himself as a third force that could hold the balance between the two historic camps. Yaari called on him to back down, warning that the loss of the workers' hegemony could prove catastrophic. He attacked public figures who thought their self-proclaimed virtues made them qualified to lead the country and save the state, viewing this as a perilous phenomenon for Israeli democracy.[97] On May 17, 1977, the political earthquake he had foreseen and feared took place. Two years later, Yaari prophesied that despite Begin's great achievement of achieving peace with Egypt, he would ultimately lead the process to a dead end.[98]

---

96 Yaari at the Mapam Central Committee, Apr. 11, 1977, HHA, 90.140(1).
97 Yaari to Yigael Yadin, June 20, 1976, HHA, 95-7.23(2).
98 Mapam Central Committee, May 17, 1979, HHA, 90.140(2).

Meir Yaari with David Ben-Gurion (left), Yitzhak Tabenkin and Aharon Beker, December 22, 1970. Photo: Israel Sun. *Courtesy of Hashomer Hatza'ir Archive, Givat Haviva.*

CHAPTER 19
Twilight

Yaari was 80 when the Likud party came to power in 1977. In the subsequent years, the ninth and last decade of his life, he spent much more time on his own kibbutz than in the past. He sank into seclusion in his apartment in the old-timers' block at Merḥavia, at a time when Hazan was still in full vigor, playing an active role in movement and party institutions and engaged in the life of his own kibbutz, Mishmar Ha'emeq. These two kibbutzim were the Mecca and Medina of Kibbutz Artzi, the crown jewels of Hashomer Hatza'ir. Merḥavia was its official capital, the seat of the movement institutions, before they were gradually transferred to Tel Aviv and Givat Haviva. The latter, on a hill overlooking Mishmar Ha'emeq, was the first and best-known educational institution of Kibbutz Artzi. National gatherings of the movement and of Haganah and Palmach members took place in the adjacent Mishmar Ha'emeq Forest. This division of functions mirrored the status of the two historic leaders of Hashomer Hatza'ir, who were among the founders of these two elite kibbutzim. Yaari and Hazan were identified with Merḥavia and Mishmar Ha'emeq, respectively, and their kibbutzim with them.

For many years Yaari was number one in the movement and party, outranking Hazan, who acquiesced in the formal hierarchy between them, generally in silence but sometimes explicitly. Even after the balance of power had shifted in Hazan's favor, people in the movement always spoke of "Meir and Hazan" in that order and that way: Yaari, and by his first name, and only then Hazan, always by his surname.

It all began ... and already at this point there are two versions. Hazan used to tell how he first met Yaari around Passover of 1923, whereas Yaari remembered that it was six months later, at the assembly of Hashomer Hatza'ir graduates in Nahalal in the autumn of that same year.[1] Whatever the case, from that time on the two worked together to establish Kibbutz Artzi. They headed it from 1927, as well as the various avatars of Hashomer Hatza'ir's political party, well into the 1970s. This dual leadership by the two men, who pulled their movement's cart in tandem for so many years, aroused great curiosity at the time, and still does: How did this extraordinary collaboration work and what was the division of tasks between the two men? What force bound them together and prevented a rift, despite their differences of character, temperament, work methods, human relations, and so much more? They themselves were aware of the differences between them and certainly of their disagreements. More than once they engaged in mutual recriminations and launched harsh attacks at each other, causing the discomfort of those comrades who were involuntary witnesses to these exchanges of verbal blows. Some of their revealing letters to each other can only perplex latter-day readers.

Many scholars have looked at the differences between these two historical leaders of Hashomer Hatza'ir and tried to fathom the secret of their collaboration. Some cited the example of other well-known couples. They mentioned Marx and Engels, Lenin and Stalin, even that of the orchestra conductor and concertmaster.[2] Hazan's name and rhetorical skills suggest the rabbi and cantor (*hazan* in Hebrew) in the synagogue. Another favorite analogy is Moses and Aaron, where the resemblance between Yaari and Moses include the latter's speech impediment. Some have proceeded from this pair and, reversing the order, seen them as priest and prophet, alluding to Ahad Ha'am's famous essay of that title. When it comes to their personalities and behavior, "Meir Yaari was worshiped even by those who did not love him. Hazan was loved even by those who did not worship him."[3]

The extensive attention to the riddle of their dual leadership reflects the fact that theirs was an extraordinary symbiosis; the many

---

[1] For Hazan's version, see "Darki ba'aretz," 6.
[2] Tzahor, *Hazan*, 86–89; Shem-Tov, *Ehad me-hem*, 31–33.
[3] Cited from Shaham, *Shalom haverim*, 213.

potholes around which they steered in order to maintain their partnership increased the astonishment that it survived. Precisely the differences between them and the difficulty of preserving the team augment the appreciation of their ability to work together and pull the cart in the same direction, despite everything. The situation was not as idyllic as appeared from the outside. There was friction between them long before those around them were aware of it. Observers saw their partnership as closer than Yaari and Hazan saw it themselves. Their relationship was formal rather than open and friendly. They tended to write letters as a means to consult and exchange ideas even when they were both in Israel. In general, these letters were dry and to the point, with no warmth or other demonstrations of intimacy. One cannot really say that they were friends.

In their letters, it was always "Hazan" and "Meir," usually along with "(my) dear" in the salutation and "yours" in the closing, but sometimes in a colder vein: "Greetings, Meir" and "Greetings, Hazan." There were only occasional letters with a more personal tone. The Yaari children attended the boarding school in Mishmar Ha'emeq. When Yaari was abroad, Hazan wrote to him about Rachel with affection and enthusiasm. "I cannot mention her name without adding a few good words about her. I am happy that you have such a daughter. She will be a great comfort to you."[4] Rachel and Ruti, Bertha Hazan's daughter from her first marriage, were in the same class, and Hazan was delighted to tell Yaari about the friendship between the two girls. Bertha, who worked at the school, bonded with Yaari's son Aviezer and had good things to say about him. "He is really wonderful, that rascal," Hazan wrote to Yaari, as if sharing a secret of fatherly camaraderie.[5] When Bertha's due date approached, she relocated temporarily to Merḥavia (closer to the hospital in Afula) and stayed with Anda. But the two men did not attend social gatherings in each other's homes and their families did not spend time together.

---

4 Hazan to Meir, Oct. 18, 1938, KMA, MYF, 1(6).
5 Ibid.

Yaari and Hazan oversaw movement affairs in different ways and had different perceptions of the nature of the bond among its members. Yaari wanted to run the movement by means of assemblies of its various institutions, with political debates followed by decisions. Hazan thought that this was not enough and attached equal importance to the web of social life, the ties based on good fellowship and the desire to cultivate it. He could remember a time when Yaari, too, was direct and sociable, and was upset that Meir had changed and now (in 1965) saw any get-together of party members as a faction or plot. Even though he usually accepted Yaari's views in many matters, here Hazan was not willing to give way. He insisted that "good friendship that extends to multiple areas of life, in addition to politics, is the movement's lifeblood."[6] Hazan continued to foster such relationships even after Yaari stopped doing so, and tried to hand down this approach to the younger comrades.

In every couple, it is generally one member who makes the first move towards reconciliation after a quarrel, or launches a thorough investigation of why the relationship has gone off the track and looks for ways to mend it. In our twosome, this was always Hazan's role, and he invested greater efforts than Yaari in maintaining their "marriage." Why? It may be simply because he was more sensitive, or because Yaari took it for granted that he was number one; but chiefly it was because for many years Hazan needed the partnership more than Yaari did. To be more precise, until the second half of the 1960s the partnership was important for Yaari but it was essential or even imperative for Hazan. After the Six Day War, though, it became more difficult and finally impossible to preserve the partnership. Hazan no longer needed it, because his status was solid enough; nor was it as important for the movement as in the past. However, even though Yaari made things difficult for Hazan and the movement, Hazan, while acting independently on many fronts, continued to protect Yaari against those who attacked him or tried to undermine his primacy, in a way that

---

6 Exchange of letters between Hazan and Yaari, November 1965, HHA, (1)20.7-95. Quote from a letter from Hazan to Meir, Nov. 14, 1965, Ibid.

combined patronizing, pity, and benevolence.[7] Even when Hazan felt that the situation had gone beyond all limits and his patience was at an end, even then he did not argue with Yaari and did not react.[8] Although he never challenged the order in which they were placed at the top of the Mapam Knesset list and in the party and movement institutions, he made strenuous efforts to insist they were equals. In 1966 he referred to the historical leadership as a "duumvirate," and repeatedly demanded that Yaari respect the parity between them.[9]

Yaari was envious of Hazan. Sometimes he showed this openly, sometimes he kept it under wraps, and other times fiercely denied the envy in a way that attests to its existence.[10] The worst jealousy stemmed from the fact that Hazan was popular, esteemed, and even beloved at Mishmar Ha'emeq and involved in its members' lives, whereas Yaari's love for Merḥavia was more or less one-way and not reciprocated. People there were not fond of him; he seems to have aware of this and frequently felt estranged from his home kibbutz.[11] This situation prevailed even though he endeavored to maintain his link to the kibbutz when far away, was meticulous about reading the kibbutz newsletter even when abroad, expressed his opinions about economic and other affairs in his letters back home, and shared the details of his illnesses and impressions with the members. Over the years, however, Yaari's connection to Merḥavia frayed. The difference between them, he wrote to Hazan candidly just before he retired as Mapam general secretary, was that "you have both Kibbutz Artzi and a kibbutz, while I have neither a kibbutz nor Kibbutz Artzi."[12] Yaari was bothered by the fact that Hazan was *persona grata* throughout KA,

---

7   Mapam Inner Secretariat, Feb. 27, 1974, HHA, 90.79(1).
8   Mapam Secretariat, Dec. 14, 1978, HHA, 90.153(1).
9   Kibbutz Artzi Executive Committee, Oct. 20, 1966, HHA, 5-10.10(1); Mapam Secretariat, Dec. 14, 1978, HHA, 90.153(1).
10 Mapam Inner Secretariat, Sept. 10, 1973, HHA, 90.79(1); Yaari to Yudeks [Meir Talmi] Apr. 7, 1978, HHA, 95-7. 23(3); memoirs [no date], KMA, MYF, 8(3), bundle 17.
11 Tzahor, *Hazan*, 252–253; the author's informal conversations with members and formers members of Kibbutz Merḥavia.
12 Yaari to Hazan, Dec. 30, 1971, HHA, 95-7.22(1).

whereas he was no longer invited to visit its kibbutzim. Unlike Hazan, in his last years Yaari did not attend the meetings of his own kibbutz, because of his deteriorating sight and hearing, and made do with having the few members who were closer to him come with their reports and even ask his opinion.[13]

June 1976 was the first time he attended the Mapam convention not as the party's general secretary. Yaari was shown every honor. When his turn at the rostrum arrived, the chair, Zeev Zrizi, introduced him with "in a time of uncertainties, all of us want to hear what Meir Yaari has to say."[14] Unlike the members of KA, who always referred to him as just "Meir," Zrizi, who lived in Beersheva (where he served as mayor and deputy mayor), used his full name. Yaari's speech fills 18 pages of the convention record. By the time he was done, Zrizi had yielded the chair; his replacement thanked Yaari, wished him long life and good health, and requested "that he continue to keep us close to our sources and roots, as he does in his fruitful labors in writing and orally. All the best to him."[15] Officially and publicly, the party and movement treated him with great respect. For many years after Yaari left his official positions his name continued to come first in the list of the members of the KA secretariat, followed by Hazan. But the signs of respect and honor were accompanied by notes of criticism, themselves indications of the great weight that was still accorded to the views of the historical leaders. Even after his retirement, when his status was that of the tribal elder, Yaari was sensitive about the honor owed him and demanded that he be treated with due respect. When he resigned his post, he asked to be allowed to keep the apartment in Tel Aviv as long as he needed it, even if he was not a member of the Knesset; the incumbent secretary of KA, Shimon Avidan, saw this as a matter of course. Eleven years later, around his eighty-seventh birthday, he was wounded to the core when KA asked him to vacate the apartment and

---

13 Yaari to Yehuda Tubin, Jan. 15, 1950, HHA, 95-7.12(2); Yaari to Hazan, Mar. 26, 1982, KMA, MYF, 3(4).
14 Seventh Mapam Convention, June 9 and 10, 1976, HHA, 90.158(1).
15 Ibid.

request a driver from his own kibbutz. "Where is the justice here and minimum of decent behavior?" he cried.[16]

In the first years after he left his official positions, he did not really mean to retire. In 1976, he had second thoughts about his decision, even while realizing that he could not be as active and involved as he wished. It was getting hard for him to walk, his eyesight had worsened, and various physical ailments kept him at home. He would have liked to go from kibbutz to kibbutz and from comrade to comrade preaching his ideas, but this was more than he had the strength for. The isolation imposed by his physical limitations depressed him. From time to time, various comrades requested that he support their candidacy (for the Knesset list or a ministerial post) or provide a recommendation. But he did so infrequently, fearing that when he agreed to say a good word about someone, the recommendation might actually do more harm than good.[17]

As time passed, his active participation in party institutions waned. He missed meetings, and when present did not always speak. Aware that his contribution to the deliberations was modest, Yaari toyed with the thought of abandoning public activity completely and returning to ordinary life at home in Merḥavia. But he held back from this extreme step and was hurt that he was not always invited to important meetings. He realized that he was no longer at the helm and made his peace with the fact that it made no difference whatsoever whether or not he attended meetings, whether he spoke or kept silent.[18]

---

16 Yaari to Meir Talmi, Mar. 16, 1979, HHA, 90.200(4); Uri Pinkerfeld to Yaari, May 10, 1979, HHA, 5.27(3); Yaari to the secretaries of Kibbutz Artzi, Aliza Amir and Dov Peleg, Nov. 3, 1983, HHA, 5.27(3); meeting of the Mapam Inner Secretariat, Sept. 10, 1973, HHA, 90.79(1); Yaari to Dov Peleg, Mar. 12, 1984, HHA, 95-7.23(7); Shula Reinharz interviews Yaari, 1980, HHA, 95-7.3(13).

17 Seventh Mapam Convention, June 10, 1976, HHA, 90.158(1); Political Committee, Mar. 11, 1976, HHA, 90.156(1)*aleph*; Yaari to Danny Bloch, Dec. 11, 1978, KMA, MYF, 2(7); Yaari to Yosef Shamir, Oct. 21, 1979, HHA, 95-7.3(3); Yaari to Benko Adar, Dec. 9, 1980, HHA, 23.7-95(5); Yaari to Dov Peleg, Nov. 24, 1983, HHA, 5.27(3); Mira Mintzer-Yaari, the last interview with Meir Yaari Oct. 2, 1985, KMA, MYF, 6(5).

18 Yaari, [memoirs], July 29, 1980; Aug. 12, 1980, KMA, MYF, 8(1); Yaari, [memoirs], Aug. 12, 1980, Ibid.; Yaari, weekly diary, July 14, 1981, KMA, MYF, 8(2).

In those late years it clearly cost him supreme efforts to attend meetings and take an active part in them. "Meir, why are you doing this?" Hazan asked him. "Why suffer so much?" To which he answered, "this is my last contribution to our movement—for people to see that you must serve it until as long as strength holds out."[19] His close friends at Merḥavia and his family asked Anda to discourage him from traveling to meetings in Tel Aviv. His wife, who had always been impressed by his dignified appearance, was afraid that "now his friends see him in his poor condition, which might have a negative effect on his image."[20] Nevertheless she thought that he should keep making the trip as long as he wanted and was able to.

After leaving his official positions Yaari drew up his personal balance sheet, mainly in the pages of his memoirs and diary—which remained confidential as long as he lived—but also in private conversations and letters and in interviews conducted for the historical record. He tried to close various circles in his personal, family, and movement lives. One of these was the family—both as an institution and his own family. In the distant past he had been opposed to the institution. As a young man he had referred to marital passion as the enemy of the commune, rejected the family as a factor that destroyed young adults' potential for self-realization, and preached the cause of male fellowship. Later, the chief role he assigned to the family was procreation and perpetuating the movement. In his old age he took a dim view of the birth control pill, because it enabled couples to have sex without any biological result or stable bond between the partners. He was especially concerned by its implications for the younger generation of his own family.[21] And in his old age his family was the most important thing of all for him. It warmed his heart and served as his refuge in times of distress. He was proud of his descendants, especially the two who had illustrious careers in the Israel Defense Forces. He was overjoyed when his grandson Yedidia Groll (his daughter Rachel's son), needing to Hebraize his

---

19 "The Remarks by Yaakov Hazan over Meir Yaari's coffin at Kibbutz Merḥavia," Feb. 23, 1987, HHA, 95-7.38(1).
20 Lurie, *Anda*, 65.
21 Yaari, [memoirs], June 14, 1983, KMA, MYF, 8(2).

last name as was then standard practice for senior officers in the IDF, resumed his grandfather's name and became Yedidia Yaari.[22] But he was never able to bond with the youngest generation, his great-grandchildren. When they came to visit, he would sit in his chair, unable to play with them or tell them stories. The songs he had sung long ago, which had enthralled his children Rachel and Aviezer and their peers in the children's house in the 1920s and 1930s, were no longer familiar and no one sang them anymore.[23]

The tragedy of his younger son Chaim, to whom he had been particularly close, tormented him till his last days. Yaari was troubled by the sense that the young man had grown disappointed with his father, but did not know the cause of that disillusionment. Burdened with guilt that he had not been alert to his son's distress and could not help him escape his depression, Yaari reproached himself for this lack of sensitivity. Perhaps, after Chaim had injured his back, he should have tried to persuade his son to resign his commission and attend university.[24]

Yaari had great joy from his wife and their life together. He saw Anda as wiser than himself and considered himself very lucky in his choice of a spouse.[25] With the candor typical of his later interviews he told an interviewer that he had never "flirted with another woman," and indeed there is no evidence that he ever had any romantic attachments outside marriage.[26] This does not mean that he was oblivious to female charms. When he saw an attractive secretary he would ask endless questions about her and envy the man who had such a gorgeous secretary.[27] On one of his trips to Switzerland, after the

---

22 Yaari, [memoirs /diary], Jan. 29, 1982, Ibid. Yedidya Yaari concluded his military career as a rear admiral (*aluf*) and commander of the Israel Navy at the start of the twenty-first century.
23 Ibid.; Yaari, [memoirs], Dec. 21, 1983, KMA, MYF, 8(2).
24 Interview with Yaari, no date [apparently 1978] and unnamed interviewer, "Interviews File," HHA, 95-7.3(4); Mira Mintzer-Yaari, the last interview with Meir Yaari, Oct. 2, 1985, KMA, MYF, 6(5).
25 Ibid.
26 Shaul Paz interviews Meir Yaari, Jan. 28, 1983, HHA, 95-7.3(3).
27 Author's interview with Chaim Shoor, Tel Aviv, Nov. 8, 1998.

Second World War, he insisted on going back to a restaurant where he had eaten before the war in the hope of being served by the same pretty waitress he remembered from years before.[28] The poets of the pioneer generation disappointed him, because of the paucity of the erotic in their work (except for Tchernichowsky): "You can search their works with candles for poems about a flesh-and-blood woman."[29]

When asked, near the end of his ninth decade, "when you were young, Meir, did you allow yourself any pleasures?" he answered, "what do I know? Pleasures, pleasures, I have one main pleasure, but both of us are already old. What young people engage in we no longer engage in, but we are a good couple."[30] An erotic bond did not necessarily have to be sexual, "and such a bond can last until 120."[31] He rejected Freud and fiercely opposed psychoanalysis as a doctrine and educational method. Yaari's distaste for psychoanalysis even predated his adoption of Marxism, because he saw the former as worship of the impulses, fundamentally contrary "to the teachings of the prophets and the Jewish psychological wisdom, whose greatness always lay in subduing the impulses by means of the dictates of reason."[32] As in his youth and maturity, so too in old age Yaari had an opinion about everything under the sun. Nothing human was alien to him and he was ready to speak and express an opinion on (almost) any subject.

In the early 1980s Yaari turned to the subject of kibbutz education, as part of the debate about where the children of Merḥavia should spend the night. With him in the minority, the kibbutz voted to have the children sleep in their families' quarters and not in the children's house. This step led to sanctions by KA, which reduced Merḥavia to the status of an "adjunct kibbutz."[33] Yaari was deeply

---

28 Thus Matityahu Mintz to the author.
29 Yaari, *Be-ma'avaq le-amal meshuḥrar*, 243 [1970].
30 Mira Mintzer-Yaari, the last interview with Meir Yaari, Oct. 2, 1985, KMA, MYF, 6(5).
31 Ibid.
32 Yaari to Yosef Arnon (Yuzek), Nov. 20, 1975, HHA, 95-7.23(1).
33 "Excerpt from a meeting of the of the Executive Committee, date unknown, apparently 1983," HHA, 5-10.14(5); Yaari to Yaakov Horwitz, KMA, MYF, 2(6);

hurt by the bitter humiliation of the blow at Merḥavia, among whose founders he was numbered, and took it as tantamount to a personal attack. He had expected that the KA institutions would take his pride into account before taking such drastic action.[34] The crisis wounded the apple of his eye. In his diary he mused that if KA was going to expel Merḥavia, he would rather die first. He would be 86, the age at which Ben-Gurion passed away, and would go to his grave "full in years and full of anger."[35]

He took this opportunity for a final reckoning with the children's house concept and even more so with coed shower facilities, launching a direct attack on Mishmar Ha'emeq, where his daughter had gone to school since she was six, and its members, especially the educator Shmuel (Milek) Golan, who had introduced these forms of child-rearing. The shared showers, he argued, caused girls severe psychological problems and emotional scars. To his great joy, his daughter had overcome the trauma. Nevertheless, "to this very day she trembles when she remembers how the shared showers at the first school in Kibbutz Artzi wounded her soul."[36]

Of special significance was the tally he drew up about the Soviet Union and Socialism. In his later interviews he called the idea that the Soviet Union was the harbinger of the future a mistake and defined the period of worship for that country and Stalin as the most wretched episode in the movement's history. He fully acknowledged that he had been wrong about this and repented his sin. He claimed that his adulation of the Soviet Union had not been absolute, but acknowledged that he could not assert total innocence. By no stretch of the imagination would he have ever wanted to live there; please note that he had never visited the country. He repudiated Marxism-Leninism, with or without a hyphen, in full, and saw it as one of Hashomer Hatza'ir's major failures. In his farewell speech as party general secretary,

---

Aliza Amir-Zohar to Yaari, Mar. 13, 1983, KMA, MYF, 2(3).
34 Yaari to Aliza Zohar-Amir, Mar. 25, 1983, KMA, MYF, 2(3); Yaari to Zvi Shehori, Oct. 20, 1983, KMA, MYF, 2(3).
35 Yaari, diary, July 21, 1981, KMA, MYF, 8(2).
36 Yaari to Yaakov Horwitz, Mar. 15, 1983, KMA, MYF, 2(6).

delivered in the presence of the President and Prime Minister of Israel, he acknowledged that "it's the same thing, with or without a hyphen: the truth is that we were no less and no more than Marxist Zionists and we were never Marxist-Leninists."[37] By the mid-1980s he no longer had any truck with Leninism, in whatever version.[38]

The failure to integrate the younger generations into the movement was another issue he had to address. He had not cultivated a new crop of leaders; quite the contrary. Only after he retired did he start speaking of the need to co-opt younger comrades to senior positions. He had never delegated authority and did not pass on the baton in a timely and honorable fashion, leaving the second generation in the shadow of the historic leadership. Its successors came from the third generation. His own kibbutz did not produce political and social leaders. Talented members sought their outlet in other directions—the arts, the business world, academia, and the military.[39] Did Yaari's presence and behavior have anything to do with this?

He wanted to leave his imprint not only on history, by means of his actions and thought, but also on how that history was written—how he, his words, and deeds would be remembered by later generations. His extensive and well-organized personal archives were kept with those of Hashomer Hatza'ir at Merḥavia, and transferred with the latter to Givat Haviva in the 1970s.[40] In 1980, he asked the director of the Hashomer Hatza'ir archives to send all his personal files back

---

37 Yaari at the Sixth Mapam Convention, Dec. 26, 1972, HHA, 90.70(1).
38 Mira Mintzer-Yaari, the last interview with Meir Yaari, Oct. 2, 1985, KMA, MYF, 6(5); Israel Zamir interviews Meir Yaari, August 1978, Cluster I [deposited by I. Zamir], 8; Nathan Shaham interviews Meir Yaari [apparently 1983]; Yaari to the Movement for Progressive Judaism Scouts-the Association of Hebrew Scouts, the Movement for Progressive Judaism, May 24, 1985, KMA, MYF, 2(9).
39 He was proud that Merḥavia was home to a dozen or more poets, including some who had won prizes, like Tuvia Ribner. There were fifteen painters, some of whom exhibited in Israel and abroad, whose works fetched handsome prices that went straight into the kibbutz treasury. Merḥavia was home to seven university faculty members, who worked in the kitchen or factories or stood guard duty on their free days. Yaari to Danny Bloch, Dec. 11, 1978, KMA, MYF, 2(7).
40 His personal papers are still in the Kibbutz Merḥavia archives, with the papers of other members of the kibbutz.

to Merḥavia, for inclusion in the kibbutz archives. His hope, as can be inferred from the letter, was that this would reduce public access to his papers.[41] Ultimately, the material remained at Givat Haviva and he even agreed for it to be opened for study during his lifetime.

But his fear that his letters "are liable to serve as material for sensation revelations by clever journalists and graduate students" was soon realized.[42] The weekly *Koteret Rashit* published excerpts from the letter that Yaari had sent to the movement emissaries in Europe after he met Chaika Grossman in London in the summer of 1945— what had come to be known as "the purloined letter."[43] Not long after, the same magazine published two extensive articles based on Yaari's letters in his archives.[44] They were selective and left out the broader context—cherry-picking—and were not to his liking, to put it mildly. Through his daughter Rachel, he sent an angry reaction to the magazine's editors, along with a request that anyone who had been able to photocopy his private correspondence not publish any material without permission from the family. He directed the archives not to publish his letters and to seal his private papers for at least another 10 years.[45] He also left instructions, as a sort of last will, that his personal archives should be housed "in the Anda and Meir Yaari Culture Center, which will be established at Merḥavia after his death and serve the social, cultural, and intellectual life of the kibbutz and the movement."[46] About a month before his death, he and his family laid down that "access to Meir Yaari's personal archives should be

---

41 Yaari to Penina Doron, June 16, 1980, HHA, 5.27(3).
42 Ibid.
43 "Anita Shapira against Meir Yaari," *Koteret Rashit*, Oct. 23, 1985 [apparently written by Tom Segev, and based on Shapira's lecture at a Yad Vashem conference in the fall of 1985].
44 Tom Segev, "King Lear," *Koteret Rashit*, Jan. 29, 1986; idem, "The Man without a God," Ibid., Feb. 5, 1986. The caption "Yaari's Letters" and a portrait of Yaari by Eitan Kedmi appeared on the magazine's cover of the Jan. 29, 1986 issue.
45 "Yaari's Letters"; letter signed by Rachel (Yaari) Groll, *Koteret Rashit*, Feb. 5, 1986; Yaari to the director of the Givat Haviva archives, Jan. 31, 1986, KMA, MYF, 2 (3).
46 Document signed by Yaari, Nov. 10, 1985, HHA, 5-91(6).

permitted only to researchers with a recommendation from Givat Haviva and with the family's approval."[47]

As someone who kept an eagle eye on history, Yaari gave many retrospective interviews. He was furious when interviewers used a tape recorder and even video tape, and then (more than once) "evidently threw all the material in the wastebasket."[48] His fears were groundless, as the many source notes in the present work attest. In some cases the interviewers' goal was to collect material to be published only after his death, and he knew this.[49] Whether because he lacked confidence in the interviewers, or to compensate for the lack of a regular diary, he began writing his own memoirs; in June 1981 he replaced the memoir format with something like a diary, recording the day's or week's events. These too did not necessarily deal only with the present but also glanced back at the past. Writing the memoirs and diary were a sort of therapy for him. This does not mean that he wrote whatever came to mind. On the contrary, it was all based on deep thought. He would dictate to his secretary, who then read the text back to him; as part of the process the two made corrections and even deleted some of what he had said. He went back repeatedly to his childhood, adolescence, and early adulthood, and never got beyond the founding of KA, when he was 30. He himself attested to the limitations of his diaries and memoirs as a historical source when he acknowledged that it was hard to know what part of what he recorded there was true and what was only legend and imagination. The most reliable statement about the nature of his later testimonies is conveyed by his complaint to an interviewer in 1979: "Don't expect me to be responsible today, at a distance of more than 50 years, for all my uncertainties and contradictions when I was young!"[50]

---

47 Jan. 14, 1987, HHA, 5-91(6).
48 Yaari to Edna Sharir, June 10, 1980, HHA, 95-7.23(5).
49 Amiram Cohen, "Interview with Michael Shapira," Al Hamishmar, Feb. 27, 1987.
50 Yaari, [memoirs/diary], Apr. 17, 1981, KMA, MYF, 8(2); Yaari, [memoirs/diary], June 9, 1981, Ibid.; Yaari, [memoirs], Sept. 27, 1983, Ibid.; Yaari, [memoirs], no date, KMA, MYF, 8(3), bundle 17; Amiram Cohen, "Interview with Michael Shapira," Al Hamishmar, Feb. 27, 1987; Yaari [memoirs], July 29, 1980, KMA, MYF, 8(1); "Yariv Ben-Aharon Talks with Meir Yaari"; interview with Meir Yaari, interviewer: Y. Donitz, December 22, 1975, HHA, 95-7.3(3).

Yaari had always been sensitive about his dignity and never tried to evade honors and tributes, almost to the point of a cult of personality and even one step beyond.[51] His birthday parties were famous in the movement, mass gala celebrations; the older he got the more extravagant the festivities and the greater the praises heaped on him. Former prime ministers Golda Meir and Yitzhak Rabin attended his eightieth birthday party, as did the incumbent president, Ephraim Katzir, Shimon Peres, Histadrut secretary-general Yeruham Meshel, and many other dignitaries. The next year, the Meir Yaari Forest was planted on Givat Hamoreh, opposite Merḥavia. Every kibbutz was invited to participate in this project and plant at least 100 trees.[52]

Before his eightieth birthday, the heads of KA made efforts to get Tel Aviv University to award him an honorary doctorate. It was not easy to persuade Yaari that it was appropriate to accept this honor, and even after he consented he changed his mind.[53] The secretary of KA asked the writer and literary critic David Knaani, a member of Kibbutz Merḥavia, for assistance.[54] Quite by chance, Knaani was already aware of Yaari's demurral. To his great astonishment, over lunch in the kibbutz dining hall, in the hearing of other members, Yaari had told him that he was turning down the honorary degree. He added (a frequent comment) that he "could have been a doctor in another year and a quarter, even an agronomist, but I pushed it all aside … in order to be a pioneer … and so on and so forth."[55] In the end, however, Yaari gave in. In January 1978, he received an official letter that the university Senate and Board of Governors had decided to award him an honorary doctorate "in recognition of your work to

---

51 At the Seventh Mapam Convention, June 19, 1976, he said that he did not miss the cult of personality—which can be interpreted as his admission that one had existed in the past: HHA, 90.158(1)
52 Yaari to Aharon Ephrat [late 1986], KMA, MYF, 3(2); Nathan Peled to the secretariat of the [Kibbutz Artzi] kibbutzim, Sept. 18, 1977. The ceremony was held on Apr. 30, 1978, close to his eighty-first birthday. Other documents on this matter are filed in KMA, MYF, 4(5).
53 Note from Yaari to Nathan Peled, HHA, 5.27(3).
54 Nathan Peled to David Knaani, Feb. 8, 1977, HHA, 5.27(3).
55 David Knaani to Nathan Peled, Feb. 16, 1977, Ibid.

develop the pioneer movement in Eretz Israel and to established and promote Kibbutz Artzi, which is one of the outstanding enterprises in the State of Israel."[56] For Yaari, the most moving aspect of the episode was the fact that the president of the university who had granted him the degree, Prof. Chaim Ben-Shahar, had been a member of Hashomer Hatza'ir in his youth in north Tel Aviv and now stood before him like a pupil before his teacher. Ben-Shahar, too, was moved.[57]

This ceremony closed the circle of his ambivalent attitude towards formal higher education. Whereas Yaari respected, admired, and even venerated authors and poets, he always had his reservations about those in the academic world, both professors and students, and sometimes expressed his disdain for them. His fierce attacks on academia in the 1960s, intended to chill the eagerness of kibbutz members who had their eye on the ivory tower, were also part of the battle for status and standing in the Israeli social ethos. Research conducted then found that kibbutz members, both veterans and the younger generation, believed that military men and scientists were the most respected groups in Israeli society—a ranking that threatened the high status the kibbutz had always enjoyed.[58]

Yaari was always sensitive over how he was presented in radio interviews and the press. Late in life he lost the last shreds of his ability to control this arena, although he continued to try to do so. In early 1982, he responded favorably to the request by a member of Kibbutz Ein Shemer, Ron Edelist, to interview him for an article in the monthly *Monitin*. During the course of their conversation, Yaari realized where Edelist was headed, broke off the interview, and banned Edelist from using any of his remarks. When the article was published, it referred to him as "godfather," "pope," "rebbe," "old Terah," and "a spoiled and vulnerable lion"; there was also an unattractive description of his

---

56 Chaim Ben-Shahar to Yaari, Jan. 29, 1978, HHA, 5.27(3).
57 Yaari to Chaim Ben-Shahar, Feb. 6, 1978, KMA, MYF, 4(5); *Al Hamishmar*, June 7, 1978; *Ba-mesheq* (Kibbutz Merḥavia bulletin), June 16, 1978; Yaari to Aroch, June 16, 1978, HHA, 95-7.3(6).
58 Gan, "The 1960s," 344.

physical appearance.⁵⁹ More than he was hurt by the article in *Monitin* Yaari was furious that the weekly *Ḥotam* thought it appropriate to publish extensive excerpts from it. In an act of solidarity, the movement united ranks around the wounded leader. Journalist Israel Zamir of *Al Hamishmar* asked to interview Yaari, who agreed in order to amend the impression left by Edelist's piece.⁶⁰ A week after Zamir's article was published, another writer for the same paper, A.B. Yaffe, came to Yaari's defense, noting that many still paid close attention to whatever he had to say.⁶¹ About two months later, *Al Hamishmar* published a piece calling on both Yaari and Hazan to join forces with the members of the silent generation of KA and the party and enter the lists to battle for the future. The author, Yehuda Yudin, concluded with a half-statement, half-summons: "The veteran leadership has not yet completed its task!"⁶² But none of this brought Yaari back to center stage or stirred his desire to return there.

He spent most of the last decade of life at home in Merḥavia. His private secretary, Michael Shapira, would come to get him around six-thirty every morning, and together they walked slowly to the dining hall. For breakfast, Yaari generally ate semolina (he was particularly fond of cooked cereal) with a cup of milk. After the meal he walked very slowly, accompanied by Shapira, to his workroom, located one flight up, in what had formerly been the KA headquarters. It took him about 20 minutes to get there. He ended his workday around eleven o'clock. After a light lunch, the two went back to his one-and-a-half room apartment in the old-timers' block. The living room was furnished modestly, with a sofa, two armchairs, a record player, stuffed bookshelves, and a dining table covered with flowered oil cloth, surrounded by four chairs and always offering a bowl of fruit and a plate of homemade cookies.

---

59 The discussion here is based on the extensive excerpts from the article published in Shlomit Toib, "Meir Yaari: The Story of the Interview that was never Published," *Ḥotam*, Mar. 5, 1982.
60 Israel Zamir, "Spitting in the Well," *Al Hamishmar*, Mar. 12, 1982.
61 A. B. Yaffe, "The Man of Marble as seen by the Owner of the Flying Towers," *Al Hamishmar*, Mar. 19, 1982.
62 Yehuda Yudin, "Letter to Meir Yaari, Apr. 10, 1982," *Al Hamishmar*, May 27, 1982.

When his health deteriorated, Yaari was assigned a workroom on the ground floor of the dining hall building. Later, in the last two years of his life, he worked with his secretary in his own apartment, for no more than three hours a day and usually less. Even though he had many visitors—journalists, historians, researchers, professors, and authors—who made the pilgrimage in order to interview him and hear his accounts of his life and the history of the movement, as well as his opinions about matters past and present, and even though he endeavored to keep himself busy, he found to his distress that he had too much free time on his hands. He had his gloomy moods; most of all he was bothered by the fact that he could no longer read to himself.[63] Anda continued to make children's clothes in the kibbutz workshop. His daughter Rachel and son-in-law Lushek came over every afternoon. And once a week the couple visited the grave of their son.[64]

Age, the passage of time, and looming death preoccupied him.[65] "Extreme old age with its disabilities is no joy, even though it is no tragedy." He was "prepared to bear the 'troubles' for a few more years, as long as fate allows me."[66] He felt a strong desire to live, despite his physical ailments and emotional distress, and was not the suicidal type. He saw life as a one-time gift; "another year of life, even in these somewhat dismal conditions, is pure profit for me!"[67] Yaari remained lucid to his very last day, frustrated by the gulf between his intellectual acuity and his physical limitations.

Yaari admitted to himself that sometimes he had an instinctive feeling that he missed God, "but I cannot create him when he doesn't exist."[68] Such thoughts did not modify his attitude towards religion,

---

63 Yaari [memoirs], Jan. 3, 1984, KMA, MYF, 8(2).
64 Amiram Cohen, "'Interview with Michael Shapira," *Al Hamishmar*, Feb. 27, 1987; Mira Mintzer-Yaari, the last interview with Meir Yaari, Oct. 2, 1985, KMA, MYF, 6(5); Shula Reinharz interviews Yaari, 1980, HHA, 95-7.3(13); Yaari [memoirs], Jan. 18, 1983, KMA, MYF, 8(2).
65 The following depiction is based on: Yaari, [memoirs], Apr. 8, 1981, Apr. 17, 1981, KMA, MYF, 8(2); Yaari [memoirs], Feb. 3, 1984, Ibid.; Amiram Cohen, "Interview with Michael Shapira," *Al Hamishmar*, Feb. 27, 1987.
66 Ibid.
67 Ibid.
68 Ibid.

with its ceremonies and rituals: he was not one of those who are revolutionaries and rabidly anti-religious in their youth but become penitent at the end of their lives, making their peace with God and looking for Him. His love of Hassidic melodies, which he hummed to himself, had nothing to do with their religious content, but was simply a matter of culture and high spirits.

During the course of his public career, Yaari had had to define his position and set policy about many facets of the relations between religion and state, the role of religion in public life, and Mapam's political priorities. He had always tried to find a balance between his opposition to any interference with the lives of nonreligious individuals or collective with his acknowledgment that the nonreligious streams of the Zionist movement had to respect the religious sensibilities of others and refrain from public desecration of the Sabbath.[69] He consistently advocated the separation of religion and state, but the party he headed never fought the battle to achieve it.[70] As he explained in 1960, "out of consideration for the needs of building the land, we still hold back from a war against religion."[71] Just as the need to build up the land, the national aspect of his doctrine, was grounds for postponing the socialist phase, it also came before the separation of religion and state in Israel.

In 1965, public Sabbath observance was a key stumbling block in the coalition negotiations. Yaari declared that "we will not swallow the Sabbath Law" but made it plain that this was not a sacred reason to stay out of the government.[72] He favored allowing theaters to open on the Sabbath and thought it important for Mapam to be conspicuous in the fight against religious coercion.[73] He did not think the status of Reform Jews in Israel to be a matter worth leaving the Government

---

69 Kibbutz Artzi Executive Committee, Mar. 11, 1932, HHA, 5-10.1(6); Yaari and Elazar Pra'i to the Jewish Agency Executive, Apr. 18, 1932, HHA, 95-7.7(9).
70 Yaari to the Movement for Progressive Judaism Scouts, May 24, 1985, KMA, MYF, 2(9).
71 Yaari, *Al Hamishmar*, June 10, 1960.
72 Mapam Central Committee, Nov. 10, 1965, HHA, 90.68(1); Political Committee, Dec. 2, 1965, HHA, 90.121(2).
73 Mapam Secretariat, July 14, 1965, HHA, 90.65(2).

over (1974), even though he recognized the importance of the Reform movement abroad as a bulwark against assimilation.[74]

In general, Yaari did not believe that religion should serve as a *casus belli* and was not willing to fight for a whole series of related issues, such as raising pigs.[75] Nor did he see any reason to wage a battle on behalf of civil marriage.[76] As for another Jewish ritual, "circumcision is indeed a religious ceremony and causes the infant pain for a few seconds. But through it we enter the Covenant of Abraham and a covenant with 4,000 years of Jewish history. So though I am secular and not religious, I do not brandish the whip of militant anti-religiosity."[77] He saw no contradiction between his secular identity and his acknowledgment of the religious roots of the Jewish past and appreciation of their importance. He did not believe in God, but he thought that much could be learned from the Jewish wisdom of the ages and was opposed to reducing the time allotted to Bible study in the schools.[78] He never abstained from using phrases with religious associations. The movement's vision, whose birth he assigned to Bitaniyya Illit, was not the child of Marx and Engels, but rather the fruit of the enduring tradition, running back "from the hassidic feast to, perhaps, the Essenes' 'bread of poverty' on the shores of the Dead Sea."[79]

Yaari always maintained a warm spot in his heart for the Yiddish language.[80] He believed that Sifriyat Po'alim, the movement's publishing house, should bring out a series of monographs on the impressive literary and spiritual legacy of the classics of Yiddish literature. One of the few times he intervened in its affairs involved Nachman Meisel's study of J. L. Peretz and his generation (translated by Mordechai Halamish).[81]

---

74 Mapam Inner Secretariat, July 15, 1974, Sept. 23, 1974, HHA, 90.79(2).
75 Yaari to the secretariat of the Mapam branch on Kibbutz Maabarot, Sept. 20, 1957, HHA, 95-7.15(2); Mapam Inner Secretariat, Jan. 14, 1974, HHA, 90.79(1).
76 Mapam Secretariat, June 21, 1972, HHA, 90.63(2).
77 Yaari to Rachel Yogli, Sept. 21, 1975, HHA, 95-7.23(1).
78 Mapam Central Committee, Feb. 27, 1977, HHA, 90.140(1); Political Committee, Nov. 20, 1957, HHA, 90.121(1); Yaari, *Mivḥanei dorenu*, 95.
79 Yaari, *Be-ma'avaq le-amal meshuḥrar*, 262 [March 1, 1964].
80 Yaari to Yaakov Becker, Aug. 1, 1966, HHA, 95-7.20(5).
81 Yaari to Azriel Uchmani, Oct. 12, 1956, HHA, 95-7.14(8).

Yaari's love for Yiddish went hand in hand with his opposition to the negation of the Diaspora and to Canaanism. He saw Canaanism as nativist (sabra) arrogance and wholly inappropriate for a country of newly arrived immigrants; its tenets would lead to the neglect of the literature and culture of the Jews who had been annihilated by the Nazis.[82]

In a sort of last will and testament, Yaari expressed the wish that when his time came he would be buried in Merhavia with no religious rites and with no rabbis present.[83] When he learned of Communist leader Moshe Sneh's request that the Kaddish be recited for him, he snorted that it was a "kind of bankruptcy of the essence."[84] Yaari was curious about how many people would attend his funeral. "There was a time when I was certain that many people would attend my funeral. Today I am remote from the masses. They don't miss me. They can live without me and I without them," he said resignedly, about fifteen months before he died.[85]

As his ninetieth birthday approached he made preparations for a party. Not a gala like the one they had made for him when he turned 80; but to have nothing at all was simply impossible.[86] He never reached that milestone, however. On February 21, 1987, after rising at eight in the morning, as was his custom on Saturdays, he felt unwell. About half an hour later he passed away in his room, in the presence of Anda, "whom he loved at first sight until his last sight, ten minutes before he died."[87]

The next day, Sunday, Mapam published a mourning notice on the front page of *Al Hamishmar*:

> In profound sorrow, love, and pride, Mapam cherishes the unique and unmatched memory of the teacher, educator, and militant

---

82 Yaari, *Al Hamishmar*, Dec. 30, 1949; Yaari to Azriel Uchmani, Oct. 12, 1956, HHA, 95-7.14(8).
83 Yaari to Rivka Gurfein-Uchmani, Aug. 30, 1982, HHA, 95-7.23(7).
84 Amiram Cohen, "Interview with Michael Shapira," *Al Hamishmar*, Feb. 27, 1987; Yaari [memoirs], Feb. 3, 1984, KMA, MYF, 8(2).
85 Mira Mintzer-Yaari, the last interview with Meir Yaari, Oct. 2, 1985, KMA, MYF, 6(5).
86 Yaari to Aharon Ephrat [late 1986], KMA, MYF, 3(2).
87 "Daughter Rachel over the Open Grave," *Al Hamishmar*, Feb. 24, 1987.

leader, one of those who laid the foundations of socialist Zionism and shaped the path of pioneer realization in Israel—the innovative thinker and artist of the written word, who knew how to mold and crystallize a way of life for many generations.

Meir Yaari was one of those who fought for Jewish-Arab brotherhood and for a just and lasting peace between Israel and the Arab peoples.

For many days after that, the pages of *Al Hamishmar* were covered with mourning notices inserted by kibbutzim, institutions, party branches, and individuals. The sadness over his death was increased by the grief at the parting from one of the last of the titans and founders. On Monday, February 23, 1987, his coffin was placed in the plaza of the Histadrut Building in Tel Aviv. Young members of Hashomer Hatza'ir, in their blue shirts with a white ribbon, served as the honor guard. The secretary general of the Histadrut, Yisrael Kessar, and Mapam leader Victor Shem-Tov delivered eulogies to a crowd that numbered in the hundreds. From Tel Aviv the coffin was transported to the Jezreel Valley in a white minibus bearing the symbol of Hashomer Hatza'ir, at the head of a convoy that recalled days long past. Near Kibbutz Ein Shemer it passed by a group of its members, some of them in their work clothes, others in their Sabbath best, alongside teenagers wearing the Shomer uniform. Someone said, "this is the last funeral"—the last in this style.[88]

At Merḥavia the coffin was placed in the square outside the dining hall; crowds passed by to pay their respect, including President Chaim Herzog and Vice Premier and Foreign Minister Shimon Peres, who arrived by helicopter, as well as Deputy Prime Minister and Minister of Housing David Levy, from the nearby town of Beit She'an, along with other cabinet ministers, Knesset members, public figures, and rank-and-file members of kibbutzim, the movement, and the party. After Peres and a member of Merḥavia delivered eulogies, a long train of vehicles made its way to the cemetery at the foot of Givat Hamoreh.

---

88 *Al Hamishmar*, Feb. 24, 1987.

Al Hamishmar reported that thousands had come to Merḥavia to accompany Meir Yaari on his last journey. He was buried not far from his son, in a ceremony with no religious trappings. His daughter Rachel, a representative of Merḥavia, and Hazan delivered farewell addresses. Dozens of wreaths were piled on the fresh grave, on behalf of the Government, the Knesset, Mapam, Kibbutz Artzi, the United Kibbutz Movement, and many others.[89]

In the days after Yaari's death, many eulogies were published lauding his contribution and importance to the movement and the party, to the Jewish people and the country. Yaari was praised as a leader, as a man "of faith, thought, and action," as one of "the greatest Zionist thinkers after Theodor Herzl, and among the first to give a humanist and liberating sense to the socialist vision."[90] Even before he was buried in the soil of the Jezreel Valley, though, a note of criticism infiltrated the memorial tributes. Abba Kovner wrote that "the grandfatherly leader of Hashomer Hatza'ir" had "acute ideas that were not free of serious errors; he was sated with disappointments and failure."[91] Yitzhak Ben-Aharon's encomium was overflowing with praise and admiration for the man who "along with his disciples, adorned Eretz Israel with the magnificent kibbutzim"—but peeking between the lines were hints of criticism that "he was dangerously close to Stalin," of his inability to yield his primacy, and of "his egoism as head of the community and unchallenged hegemon."[92] Standing over the coffin, Victor Shem-Tov said that the members of the movement would remember the storm of battle, the demonstrations, and the endless long parades, but also "the debates, your stern-faced rebukes, and the praise with which you compensated us, a smile on your face."[93]

The family, the kibbutz, the movement, and the party took steps to memorialize Yaari in various ways. There were a number of events to

---

89 Ibid.; Amikam Rotman, "Yaari Has Gone: What's Left?" *Hadashot*, Feb. 27, 1987.
90 Editorial, *Al Hamishmar*, Feb. 22, 1987; Gadi Yatziv, "The Fundamental Principles," Ibid.
91 *Al Hamishmar*, Feb. 22, 1987.
92 Yitzhak Ben-Aharon, "A Zealous Father," *Davar*, Feb. 22, 1987.
93 *Al Hamishmar*, Feb. 24, 1987.

mark the first anniversary of his death, including a ceremony to name the Hashomer Hatza'ir documentation and research center at Givat Haviva "Yad Yaari." There was an architectural competition to plan the building for the Anda and Meir Yaari Culture and Social Center at Kibbutz Merḥavia, but it was never built. Yaari's workroom, on the second floor of the former Hashomer Hatza'ir headquarters building, was reconstructed not far away, in one of the structures that line the kibbutz central courtyard, in a building now known as "Yaari House." Senior members of Kibbutz Artzi conducted extensive correspondence with mayors and other local officials to request that streets and facilities be named for him; today there are Meir Yaari streets in Tel Aviv, Beersheva, Haifa, Petaḥ Tiqvah, and Rishon Lezion, and a Yaari Park in Ashdod.[94]

About two years after Yaari's death, an editorial board to publish his collected writings was established.[95] The fruits of its labors were modest. Five years after his passing, a volume on his first three decades came out, with a selection of his early writings and background notes.[96] Nothing more followed. There were discussions, of course, about a biography, an idea he himself had thought pleasant. Some suggested commissioning Yaakov Horwitz of Ein Haḥoresh to write a monograph on Meir Yaari—the man, his life, his ideas, and his achievements—out of a sense that "the movement owes itself first of all, as well as the chief of its founders, an ideological manual and expression of the historical experience of Hashomer Hatza'ir as anchored by the figure of Meir Yaari."[97] That volume was published in 1994.[98] But no full biography appeared until the Hebrew original of the present work came out (in two volumes, 2009, 2013).

---

94 The material is in HHA, 313.90(9).
95 Ezra Rabin to Yaakov Horwitz, Mar. 26, 1989, HHA, 5-91(6).
96 Zait and Shamir, *Meir Yaari*.
97 Adam Rand to Ezra Rabin and Elisha Shapira [the KA secretaries], June. 21, 1989, HHA, 5-91(6).
98 Horwitz, *Meir Yaari*.

Yaari's 80th birthday party at Merḥavia, 1977. From right to left: Yaakov Hazan, Golda Meir, Meir and Anda Yaari.
Courtesy of Hashomer Hatza'ir Archive, Givat Haviva.

CHAPTER 20
Epilogue

Meir Yaari was *the* leader of Hashomer Hatza'ir for nearly five decades. He was first recognized as such in the early 1920s, but without any formal title. His status was formalized in 1927; from then until the end of 1972 he was officially the head of the movement and the party. During that long period of incumbency his preeminence eroded, his power ebbed, and his authority weakened. This left a certain discrepancy and imbalance between his official position, which remained unchanged, and his declining prestige among the members and waning control of movement and party decisions and actions. On the other hand, even after Yaari "retired" he retained the aura of "the leader of Hashomer Hatza'ir," and this label continues to be attached to his name, many years after his death.

The present biography has tried to solve the riddle of Yaari's leadership. How did he become the movement's head? How can we explain his long tenure, despite his many mistakes—and not just the actions and stands that proved erroneous in hindsight, but the incidents and situations where the misstep was obvious in real time? What caused his eventual descent from the pinnacle? What were the milestones on his way down? Finally, why was he still seen as the leader of Hashomer Hatza'ir even in his twilight years, and how was his status as the mythological leader of the movement fixed for all time?

The riddle of Yaari's leadership touches on the eternal dilemma of "personality and history," the well-known issue of the person/leader and history. It requires us to consider the extent to which Yaari, as leader, shaped the movement's character and annals, and the extent to which it was the nature of the movement and circumstances of the time that facilitated his control in general and its nature and continuation in particular. We must identify the comrades' needs and aspirations that he satisfied and determine why they stuck by him as their leader and felt that there was an identity between the leader and the movement, to the point where he imagined that "the movement, *c'est moi*" and his flock believed that "the movement, *c'est lui*"—an identification accompanied by a measure of self-effacement in his presence and elements of a cult of personality.

There are three keys to our riddle: charisma, organization, and ideology. Each encompasses a broad range of qualities, aspects, phenomena, and processes. Each provides only a partial answer to the riddle. Taken together, in their synergy, they go a long way towards explaining—though still not fully—Yaari's ascent and long survival at the top, as well as his decline and departure and the perpetuation of his image.[1]

Yaari's primacy in Hashomer Hatza'ir was not self-evident from the outset. He was not among the founders of the youth movement, did not hold any senior post in its early days in Galicia, and was not part of its revival after the First World War. His ascent began only after he arrived in Mandatory Palestine and found his way to Bitaniyya Illit. It was there, in late 1920 and early 1921, that he emerged as a leader, thanks to his ability to satisfy the other member's spiritual and emotional needs, his intellectual powers, vast funds of knowledge, and broad education (most of it self-taught), his ability to listen to others, and the fact that he was slightly older than most of the group. In fact, his role there was reminiscent of a youth movement counselor. Contemporary testimonies indicate that he was recognized as endowed with the traits of a charismatic leader: personal charm, an ability to persuade, and good interpersonal communication skills. It was at Bitaniyya that his charismatic authority took shape; and this—in Weber's definition—is the kind of authority that does not derive from an official position.[2] He was able to employ these qualities to find a way to the hearts of others and to influence, persuade, inspire, and lead

---

[1] See Halamish, "The Historic Leadership."
[2] Weber, *The Theory of Economic and Social Organization*, 350.

them. The young men and women saw him as a guide expressing their individual and collective aspirations and showing them the way.

Yaari's leadership abilities, suited to the intimate format of the Bitaniyya Illit commune, ran aground several months after the group came down from the mountain and resettled at the Shomriya Camp. His comrades withdrew from him, rebelled against his ideas, had reservations about his leadership, and were turned off by his dictatorial tendencies. The first phase of his leadership ended when he left, was expelled, abandoned, was deposed, or quit the Shomriya Camp—each of these verbs has its own meaning and connotations with regard to the essence of that parting of the ways—and embarked on a period of nomadic meditation that lasted for about a year and a half. Then he returned to activity, stubbornly pursuing the goal of establishing a countrywide organization of the graduates of Hashomer Hatza'ir—under his leadership. By the time this process culminated in 1927, with the founding of Kibbutz Artzi, he was already recognized as the movement's leader, both by its members and by the outside world.

Yaari achieved his position as the unchallenged head of a countrywide movement after making the required transformation from counselor and guide of a small and intimate community to the leader of a large group scattered all over the country. He never lost the traits that had facilitated his early ascendancy; on the contrary, he refined them and added new layers. He continued to be in personal contact with the comrades, to hold intimate conversations in small groups or one on one, and to display the interest and attention that made his interlocutor trust him and feel that he could be relied on, to the point of emotional dependence. He continued to write and publish ideological pieces. He never stopped writing frank private letters that included material of significance for the public at large. He drafted ideological platforms. And he was involved in economic and organizational matters.

Yaari was a total leader, engaged with every sphere of the lives of the members of the movement he headed, from ideology to family matters, and involved in their lives to the point of intruding on their privacy. He was a polymath with impressive intellectual abilities, a faithful reader of everything published in the movement's periodicals, and never shy about expressing his opinion on any and every issue. He was a superb conversationalist face to face, and even better as a correspondent: exchanges of letters served him as a substitute for oral communications. He corresponded with dozens of comrades; it seems that no one ever wrote him without receiving a reply. His letters, even the official ones, generally included a personal reference to the recipient and his family. He persisted in this form of contact well past the age of 80. He never had any close advisors, a confidant with whom he discussed his ideas in total candor, or someone he consulted on a systematic basis. Yaari was never known as a hail-fellow-well-met, did not engage in idle chatter, did not spend time in coffeehouses, and rarely appeared in the Knesset cafeteria. For the most part he shut himself up in his office in the movement building in Merḥavia, in the Kibbutz Artzi offices and the Mapam headquarters in Tel Aviv, or in his apartment in that city, conducting business by letter or in small meetings set up in advance. He maintained a precise balance of intimacy and distance in his ties with other people, who felt that there was always a certain barrier between them. He had no close friends or soul mates.

Yaari's charisma and the status he achieved compensated for his shortcomings and made people ignore or forgive them. But they were no secret and were frequently noted. Everyone—including Yaari himself—knew that he was no great public speaker. His compositional skills covered up and compensated for his weakness as an orator. He was famous as a gifted writer and sharp-quilled antagonist, given to rich language and juicy phrases. As is the way with charisma, which is hard to define in precise scientific terms, Yaari's was in the eyes of the beholder. There is no doubt that he was a charismatic leader, as shown by how people related to him, and by the fact that members of the movement and others accounted him as such and enumerated various reasons for it. He himself was aware that he was seen as "a charismatic figure," and not only because people told him so explicitly. Those who met him for the first time discerned that he was marked by "the halo of a charismatic leader"; in hindsight, people said that he was "a person whose charisma, like that of a Hassidic rebbe, swept up an entire camp for more than half a century."[3]

---

[3] Interview with Betta Re'uveni (interviewer: Idit Amit), HHA, 95-7.3(9); Nathan Yannai, "Notes on the Character of Meir Yaari's Leadership", HHA, 95-7.38(2);

Leadership was the central motif of his life and a major element of his personality. From a young age he was imbued with the sense that he was destined to be a leader and pursued the goal of establishing an organization that he would head. He was a born shepherd in search of a flock, which he created in 1927 in the form of Kibbutz Artzi. From that time on, his leadership endured and grew stronger, largely thanks to his centralized control of the organization and by virtue of the dependence of the individual members and kibbutzim on the countrywide movement. A major source of this dependence was that, like almost everyone in the Yishuv during the Mandate, the founders and most members of Kibbutz Artzi were recent immigrants. Most had arrived as part of the immigration quota for laborers, as young people in search of employment, with no economic resources of their own. It was the movement that facilitated their aliyah and served as their agent of absorption in the country.

Yaari was one of those who shaped the dual dependence of members on their kibbutz and of the individual kibbutzim on the movement and worked strenuously to perpetuate it. He was able to do so thanks to his control of appointments to public positions and to movement and party functions. This power meant that comrades with political ambitions were at his mercy and flattered him; it forged a sort of alliance between him and the second echelon of the movement leadership and local kibbutz leaders—"you scratch my back and I'll scratch yours." They supported him and he protected their status, found them jobs, and promoted them on the movement ladder. In the movement they spoke openly of the yes-men, the lackeys who always did what the leadership wanted.

He was imbued with a sense of mission and leadership and had so strong a sense of "I was born to lead" that he felt himself above the masses and had no qualms about ignoring the principle of "practice what you preach" when it came to how he lived. This deviation was notorious; as for the comrades—some grumbled, while others ignored,

---

Yaari to Victor Shem-Tov, Aug. 19, 1984, KMA, MYF, 2(4); Gerti [Shem-Tov] to Yaari, Feb. 18, 1976, Ibid.; Ron Edelist to Yaari, [September 1981], HHA, 95-7.23(5).

forgave, or accepted it. In any case, his lifestyle, which was not marked by pious observance of the precepts of abstemious living on which the movement rested, never undermined his status.

Yaari ascended to the leadership summit of Hashomer Hatza'ir and remained there for so many years in part through a process of elimination. To some extent there were no serious alternatives to him: many of those who were prominent when Hashomer Hatza'ir was founded in Europe, including capable and charismatic counselors, never left the continent. Among those who did make aliyah, some soon returned to their families abroad, while others—the majority, in fact—left the kibbutz for town. Yaari encouraged this process of eliminating would-be rivals, directly and indirectly, thinning the ranks of potential challengers and leaving him to lead a group from which most of the "lions" had seceded. After his status as number-one was sealed, he systematically frustrated the emergence of rivals. He did battle against promising members of the next generation and blocked the promotion of comrades with leadership potential who might—in his eyes, threatened to—compete for the leadership and jeopardize his status.

And, of course, another factor behind his long years at the helm was his collaboration with Hazan. As long as they worked together and maintained a united front, with Hazan supporting him, Yaari's position was solid. Together they institutionalized the primacy of their duumvirate, exemption from rotation, and other rules that applied to the *hoi polloi*. For many years the two needed each other and supported each other even when they did not see eye to eye on some matters, manning the shared ramparts against the demand for greater democracy in the movement.

"Ideological collectivism," meaning freedom during the debate, reaching a consensus decision, and lockstep discipline in its execution, also played its part. Yaari was the founding father of ideological collectivism and worked tirelessly to apply it. In the phrase "ideological collectivism," the collective was more important than the ideology. It is not my contention to dismiss or contradict the importance of ideology for Yaari, but only to hint that its main purpose for him was to preserve the organization he headed and entrench his leadership. If this suggests a note of instrumental ideology, it is not only in the reader's ear. To put it another way, for Yaari ideology was a tool, a vessel whose content could be diluted or replaced as needed.

Similarly, the collective was no less important than the ideology in the two issues where Yaari led his movement to crystallize a dogma and political stance of its own—the Arab question and the attitude towards the Soviet Union. That is, the adoption of these concepts, and especially the great weight and importance attached to them, were intended to maintain Kibbutz Artzi's unity and separate identity and serve as an obstacle to merger with Mapai.

Yaari did not think that ideas incompatible with the position that he, the movement, and the party held were dangerous as long as they were not translated into a new or alternative bloc. Ideological challenges were perilous and required a reaction only when they threatened the organization by coalescing as a faction or, perish the thought, a new political group. He endeavored to preserve the united and monolithic party. As long as he retained the power, he never permitted the establishment of factions within the party. The sanctions he imposed, in concert with Hazan (and in practice under the latter's direction), on members who affiliated with other organizations went as far as expulsion from their home kibbutzim. The primacy of the collective over the ideology in the ideological collectivism was also manifested in the fact that it was enforced through organizational means. Kibbutz members toed the line more for economic and social reasons than because of intellectual conviction.

But we must not make light of the importance of ideology for Yaari when we try to decipher the secret of his leadership. A strong credo and solid doctrine informed his thoughts and motivated his actions. The humanistic Zionist core of his worldview shone through the Marxist wrapper; pragmatic considerations and the many ideological, political, and organizational fluctuations never overshadowed it. Throughout his career he remained loyal, in every form of expression, to the main tenets of his belief, and held consistently to that fundamental core and ideological bedrock, which was humanistic Socialist Zionism. It was always Zionism that had pride of place in his worldview.

As a Socialist Yaari believed that human beings could be perfected, despite the drive to competition and self-interest; education is important and people can change. For him, Socialism was first and foremost a faith in human beings, a belief in their ability to accomplish great deeds. His Socialist Zionist politics were "a war for a better tomorrow for humanity, for the working class, for the Jewish people, and for suffering human beings."[4] Many shared the Zionist, Socialist, and humanistic values that he championed and saw him as the authentic voice of their own ideas and desires. His ability to provide eloquent verbal expression to the thoughts, feelings, and yearnings of others was one of the secrets of his power as a leader.

There was something of the Hassidic rebbe in his leadership and his relations with his movement. Like a rebbe, Yaari was a charismatic leader who was "revealed" and achieved his status "naturally," whose followers stuck with him and accepted his authority—especially in the early stages of his leadership and again in its last chapter—voluntarily, and not because of his position. Like a rebbe, who, although his leadership relates first of all to the religious domain, does not ignore material and mundane matters, so too Yaari drew some of his power from the fact that he dealt not only with spiritual matters but also with earthly and physical issues; from his control of the distribution of honors and privileges, and from his involvement in almost every facet of the lives of the members of the community he led.[5]

To continue with this metaphor, we can add that every rebbe has his court. Yaari's was primarily KA, and to a lesser extent Mapam (lesser in two senses: a shorter time, because Mapam was established some two decades after KA, and the members' less intensive adulation of him, by virtue of the different natures of the two entities). Another key to the riddle of his leadership is his interaction with the movement, which accepted his elevated status and allowed him to hold it for so many

---

[4] Political Committee, Dec. 2, 1973, HHA, 90.154(2).
[5] Assaf, *The Regal Way*, 267–337.

years. After he resigned as general secretary, Yaakov Riftin compared his situation to that of a great artist. "Would anyone ever imagine asking Casals to stop playing, as long as he can do so? Or Chagall to stop painting as long as he has the strength to do so?"[6]

What was it in Yaari's "playing" that made such sweet music for the members of Hashomer Hatza'ir? What aspect of his "paintings" enthralled them? As we have seen, ever since Bitaniyya people felt that he expressed their thoughts and feelings better than they could do themselves. Some comrades assigned greater weight to his opinions than to their own, not only in matters of ideology and politics but also in literature. He responded to the needs and desires of the members who were looking for a father figure and was a guide to the perplexed for many. When they wrote to him with their requests, the comrades interjected expressions of their high regard for him; Yaari was only too ready to accept the compliments. On more than one occasion he employed the first person plural of royalty, and sometimes wrote about himself in the third person.

But along with the charisma there was also a demonic side. He was not cordial to everyone. Many feared him and his unpredictable reactions. He could be a bit coarse, using tactless phrases—"spitting boorishly," "plunging a knife in the back," "poisoning the wells," "fabrications," and so on. He hurt comrades' feelings, lost his temper with them, and insulted them. He was aware of these flaws, and just as he rebuked and humiliated people in public, he could also apologize and say he was sorry.

Those who witnessed his outbursts generally held their tongues; those hurt by them tended to restrain themselves. Why? Because they needed him, his ideas, his authority, his leadership. So despite all the sour notes in his behavior, he continued to be their counselor and the "responsible adult." As time passed and he gained the added weight of long tenure and status of founding father, his seniority lifted him above the host of mere mortals, immunized him against public criticism, and exempted him from the principle of rotation. His relationship with the

---

6 Nathan Yannai, "Notes on the Leadership Type of Meir Yaari," HHA, 95-7.38(2).

movement brings to mind the calf that wants to suckle at least as much as the cow wants to nurse it, though ultimately the calf expected more than the cow could provide. So we must look at both sides, the leader and the movement, if we would like to understand the riddle of his leadership.

The relations in Hashomer Hatza'ir, including those between the rank and file and the leaders, were familial in nature, with the voluntary loyalties typical of the family and little or none of the inhibitions and reserve that characterize other social frameworks. The movement veterans and leadership core were indeed like family for Yaari. He felt close to and committed to them, was always providing them with detailed reports on his health, and allowed himself to have tantrums in their presence. In times of trial he displayed bold and steadfast loyalty to comrades in distress, showing the devotion due to members of the family who, even if they have strayed, remain one's flesh and blood. In the last years of his life, when he no longer held any official position and his health had deteriorated, the family nature of the movement was expressed in its sensitivity to his needs and wishes.

For many years KA was shaped by Yaari's leadership. We have seen that his charisma functioned best in more intimate settings and that he preferred to be the total leader of a small and well-defined community than just the political leader of a larger group. It was thus in accordance with his leadership image and characteristics that Hashomer Hatza'ir—both the individual kibbutzim and the movement (Kibbutz Artzi)—was molded as a holistic social framework that embraced every sphere of its members' lives while remaining selective and exclusive.

The other side of the coin is that Yaari's doctrine and activities were not meant for the public at large. Unlike the leaders of the original Aḥdut Ha'avodah (and Mapai after 1930), David Ben-Gurion, Berl Katznelson, and others, who always saw themselves as responsible for the entire Jewish working class in Mandatory Palestine, and later for the entire Zionist movement, and finally for the entire Jewish people, and aspired to direct the Yishuv and run the country, Yaari was not interested in such authority. In terms taken from the family arena, Yaari's leadership and in fact the very existence of Hashomer Hatza'ir were made possible by the presence of the older brother, Mapai, which assumed responsibility for the entire clan. In his relations with Mapai and its leaders, especially those who arrived in the country as part of the Second Aliyah, one can detect signs of the younger-son syndrome that is the unifying thread of his entire life.

The familial nature of KA in its "Yaari format" was advantageous at certain points in its history, especially the early days; and there is no doubt that it was appropriate for the youth movement. But it was no longer suitable when KA grew and matured into an organization with multiple generations, and even less so for a political party, which is not an intimate group in which everyone knows everyone else.

Heading a large political party that aspires to come to power requires different qualities than those with which Yaari was blessed, which were better suited to a youth counselor, educator, preacher, ideologue, or pundit-prophet. For many years he opposed the establishment of a political party; after it came into being it was not his natural and best arena. He never accepted ministerial office, was not a member of the powerful and prestigious Knesset Foreign Affairs and Defense Committee until 1961, and never engaged in extensive parliamentary activity. In fact, politics interfered with his performance as a leader. There were different rules of the game in Mapam than in KA, and the establishment of the party weakened his connection with the latter. In retrospect, the transition from leader of a kibbutz movement to leader of a political party was not to his benefit.

His leadership began to ebb with the founding of Mapam and the establishment of the state, both of which took place within the span of a few months in 1948. From that time on Yaari was reduced to reacting to events, explaining, rationalizing, and justifying his own and the party's actions after the fact; he rarely initiated important processes in the movement or Israeli society. His leadership was channeled into preserving his status, frustrating initiatives by others, and blocking the trajectory of potential rivals. Unlike the 1920s, when he evolved from one type of leadership (Bitaniyya) to another (Kibbutz Artzi), after independence he remained stuck in the previous stage; despite the new circumstances, he continued to be essentially an educator.

As he approached 80 he said, relying on Marx: "The philosophers merely interpreted the world. Our duty as revolutionaries—and in this case, the Zionist-pioneer revolution—is to change the world; to change our reality, and not only among ourselves, but to again be the vanguard leading the camp."[7] But more than he endeavored to change the world, Yaari concentrated on explaining his and the party's positions in the present and interpreting the past, which included justifying grievous mistakes. He frequently spoke and wrote about what was beyond the horizon. He had impressive prescriptions for the distant future, for "one day," at the conclusion of the long journey; he had interpretations of the distant past and explanations of the present: but he had no good answers for next week.

The establishment of the party forced him to adapt to new modes of decision-making. In the youth movement and KA it was customary to rely on agreement and consensus, with a maximum effort to avoid formal votes and then bowing to the will of the majority. In the party, he had to get used to the dynamic of voting on resolutions, which requires assembling a majority and maneuvering among factions. As long as the game was one of debate and deliberation until a consensus was reached, Yaari's power of persuasion worked well. But he was not so skilled at getting his own way when decisions were made by show of hands or secret ballot after a tug of war between various factions, requiring the creation of alliances and coalitions behind the scenes—and this is why his control ebbed.

For many years he proved adept at maneuvering between the right and left wings of the party; this was one of the secrets of his leadership. He lashed out at both extremes, staking his claim to the middle ground between them. This practice justifies seeing ideology as the third key to the riddle of his leadership, after charisma and organization.

The conclusion that it was all downhill for Yaari's leadership after the founding of Mapam and the establishment of the state is 20/20 hindsight. The change was not felt at the time, certainly not before 1954 at the earliest. Until then, Yaari was engaged in a titanic battle to

---

7 Seventh Mapam Convention, June 10, 1976, HHA, 90.158(1).

keep Mapam, and even more so KA, intact—a life-or-death struggle. When the movement faced an existential peril the ranks closed around his leadership. As paradoxical as it may seem, the successful conclusion of the battle against the Left deviationists weakened his position: first, because there was no longer an "enemy" to unite against and second, because the balance of power within the party shifted towards the Right. The triumph over the Leftists was something of a pyrrhic victory for Yaari. Until then, part of his power derived from his position at the center of the party. After the Leftists were routed, however, Yaari was sucked into the vacuum that had been created and found that he himself was on the Left.

And then came the fateful year 1956. But none of that year's momentous events seriously affected his attitude towards the Soviet Union; despite the many voices of discontent, the movement's stand on the matter remained unchanged. Yaari made sure of this through his control of the decision-making apparatus, with Hazan's support. From that time on, his rigid adherence to the old positions undermined his standing as leader, but the organizational structure that he had forged prevented any impairment of his official status. Despite the open desire of many members to drop the pro-Soviet orientation, he continued to set the tone, without yet having to pay the price for the gulf that now yawned between his position and the views of the majority of his flock.

A similar gulf existed between the comrades' desire for closer ties among the three kibbutz movements, while Yaari and Hazan did everything they could to preserve the absolute independence of KA. It bears noting, however, that the attempt to unite the entire kibbutz movement and include KA in the merger of the other two movements was consistently thwarted for many years after the historical leadership had left the stage—twelve years after Yaari's death and seven after Hazan's. What is more, when the Kibbutz Movement (the *Takatz*) was finally established near the end of the twentieth century, through the consolidation of the United Kibbutz Movement (the *Takam*)—itself the product of the merger of Hakibbutz Hame'uḥad and Iḥud Hakevutzot Vehakibbutzim—with Kibbutz Artzi, for the first decade it had two general secretaries, one from each component. The protracted period required to achieve a full union between KA and the other movements, even after the historical leadership was no longer there to support or oppose the move, indicates that preserving its unique character and independence was part of KA's genetic code. Still, one can argue that the preference for going it alone was the fruit of the long-term education—or perhaps indoctrination—of its society and members, in which Yaari exerted significant influence. Whatever the case, the movement and its leaders shared a common interest in preserving the distinctive character and family framework of the movement, which was the core of KA from the birth of the Hashomer Hatza'ir youth movement, and was also one of the secrets behind the historical leadership's long staying power.

Some of the factors that had sustained Yaari's leadership began to dissipate in the late 1950s and early 1960s. The younger, native-born comrades were less dependent on the movement for social networking. They were also less dependent on Yaari for career advancement and had less reason to be in contact with him. His writing style and the nature of his bond to the older comrades did not speak to their hearts. Unlike the founding generation, the second generation scarcely engaged in private correspondence and direct exchanges of views with him, and he found it increasingly difficult to forge close ties with them. They treated him with respect, but there was none of the comradeship he had enjoyed with the second rank of the previous generation. What is more, the younger generation, better educated than its parents, or at least with greater access to information, did not need Meir Yaari to explain the world to them.

All these changes dulled the luster of his charisma, but did not yet diminish his official status or erode his power, thanks to the movement apparatus that he had helped establish and continued to control. He kept the younger generation out of the leadership echelon, did not try to foster an expanded collective leadership, concentrated the political and public functions in his and Hazan's hands, and tended to disqualify his critics from movement positions. This authoritarian behavior went on long after many of the comrades had become disgusted with it. Although Yaari knew about the rumblings of discontent from personal conversations, letters, and comments made openly in the movement's institutions and publications, he and Hazan blocked any change in the mode of election to movement institutions, assignment to jobs, and the decision-making processes.

But nothing lasts forever. The sum total of the changes—in ideology, the members' age, and other areas that elude precise definition—eventually affected the organization and finally impinged on Yaari's status. The process began in 1965, in the run-up to the elections for the Sixth Knesset, when, in response to voices calling for change, a new method for drawing up the candidate list was introduced. The Nominating Committee, which Yaari had always had under his thumb, lost its monopoly on assembling the slate and greater power was assigned to the party Central Committee.

From that time on, an increasing number of decisions were taken by secret ballot (and not by show of hands) and individual (and not bloc) voting. This gave individual members greater power; they allowed themselves to speak candidly and even vehemently to Yaari and against his views. Decisions were taken over his opposition, he found himself increasingly in the minority, and he no longer had the ability to neutralize internal groups of which he was not a member or to halt their activity, as he had in the past.

Yaari grew ever more distant from the grassroots until he lost contact with them. He was no longer the organization's guide and was no longer in tune with its members' inclinations. What stood out in this situation was the fact that he proposed no vision or path, that he reacted rather than initiated, and that he spoke *ad nauseam* about the past—but it was not clear what destination he had in mind, what ideas he wanted to promote, and what principles he would never compromise on. It was common knowledge that Mapam, under his leadership, desperately wanted to be part of the government coalition. Starting in 1955, and even more so after 1967, there was no issue he was willing to fight for to the bitter end. The only principles that still mattered to him were preserving the independence of KA and keeping Mapam part of the Alignment and in the Government.

In the late 1960s, the balance of power in the historic leadership tilted in Hazan's favor. On most matters, a majority of the members supported the latter whenever the two men were at odds, and this included the nature of the association with the Labor Party. Hazan felt strong enough to cut deals without Yaari, behind his back and even contrary to his position. With the passage of years, Yaari's status as number one continued to be eroded, while Hazan's qualities became more important. The time for ideological essays and opinion pieces that slaked the comrades' intellectual thirst and satisfied their need for explanations and guidance had passed; so had the era of intimate discussion groups and friendly correspondence, at which Yaari excelled. The weight of the spoken word in general and of speeches to larger audiences—where Hazan surpassed Yaari—rose. The periodical press, Yaari's *forte*, began to fade, yielding to a new rival for the comrades' time—television. The comrades stopped reading his wide-ranging, thoughtful, and long articles in the weekend edition of *Al Hamishmar*; they no longer waited on tenterhooks to find out "what Meir wrote." The surrender of his formal status as general secretary eroded one of his last advantages over Hazan, who was always closer to the members, in part because of the friendly relations he knew how to cultivate and preserve. Another reason Hazan overtook him was the growing importance of security affairs. And biology, too, played its part in the reversal of the hierarchy between them, as Yaari's health continued to decline and Hazan remained hale and hearty.

Historians are wary of hypotheticals and speculation and avoid them like the plague. But we can scarcely avoid considering one or two what-ifs here. What would have happened if, instead of setting up its own political party, Hashomer Hatza'ir had affiliated with Mapai in the 1930s or 1940s, while continuing to be an educational and settlement movement? For, as was evident time and again, the ideological and political distance between the two was not that great and there were no profound disagreements that separated them. How would this have affected Yaari's leadership and status? The united Mapam (1948–1954) did not suit his leadership style and required him to deal with intricate problems that damaged the movement and himself. But would this have been the case had there been a merger with Mapai? Perhaps leaving political affairs to others would have allowed Yaari to continue to shine as the leader of KA. In a broader perspective, what would have happened to Hashomer Hatza'ir–Kibbutz Artzi had it joined Mapai? Would this have prevented its relegation to the sidelines of Israeli society (whether it was pushed there or chose this station on its own) in the formative years of the state?

Yaari became a myth, a symbol, almost the movement personified. People identified the movement with him, and he represented it in their eyes. "We remembered your name in those terrible days" of the Holocaust, Yisrael Gutman wrote him in 1957. "For us, it symbolized the precious and fantastic dream: the land, the kibbutz enterprise."[8] The day after he died, Abba Kovner spoke of Yaari as someone who "had involuntarily become the object of veneration of tens of thousands of disciples."[9] Perhaps it was not really against his will, but it is true that his status became entrenched not only through his own activity but also to satisfy the needs of his flock.

Like the resolution of the riddle of his leadership and the secret of his charisma, the explanation of how he became the concrete symbol of the movement and a living myth is to be found not only in the man himself but also in the movement he led. People often look for concrete symbols to identify with, and Yaari filled that role for the members of Hashomer Hatza'ir. For many, he and the movement were one and the same. All those who came into contact with Hashomer Hatza'ir at any stage of their lives, whether briefly or for an extended period, had feelings about Yaari, which might be positive or negative, but were never indifferent. Even 13 years after he resigned as general secretary of the party, "the halo of adulation that crowns him is as bright as ever, as if he was still the all-powerful leader of his movement, as in the past. His image is precious to his followers, as is the man himself."[10] Here too the reason must be sought in the collective nature of the movement he led no less than in his leadership qualities.

---

8 Yisrael Gutman to Yaari, May 21, 1957, HHA, 95-7.15(3).
9 Abba Kovner, *Al Hamishmar*, Feb. 22, 1987.
10 "Anita Shapira vs. Meir Yaari," *Koteret Rashit*, Oct. 23, 1985.

Yaari continued to be sought after even in his old age. People liked to write him because they knew he would read their letters and reply. The author Yaakov Shabtai wrote him, about two months after Yaari announced his resignation (and several years after Shabtai himself had left Kibbutz Merḥavia), to confess that he sometimes felt a strong desire to meet him for a candid chat, even though he knew how difficult it was to speak openly with him and drill down to an investigation of the truth. Instead, he wrote "a plain personal letter" to let him know that his feelings for him were "a sort of combination of profound admiration, curiosity and astonishment, and fondness, and something like love that balances itself with a drop of mischief, a large dose of human sympathy, and sometimes also a note of sadness, perhaps pain, something like fear, sometimes with some sense of the tragic. Great interest. Don't exactly know."[11] Shabtai felt all this towards Yaari, despite his reservations about the latter's political path, without wanting or expecting to receive any perks from him, and in full awareness of the many weaknesses with which Yaari was "blessed," weaknesses about which one can say, "the greater the man, the greater are his drives." It would seem to require the talents of a gifted novelist like Shabtai to define the magic of Yaari's personality: "Precisely those weaknesses, in combination with everything else, are what made you such a complex and unique personality for me, with a strong and authentic character, something complicated and alive, someone with a true fire burning inside him, who inspires and illuminates his surroundings."[12] For Shabtai, Yaari's unique charm was so great that

> despite the great distance that separates us, a distance of age and time and place and outlooks and inclinations and lifestyles and life experience, for me you have remained that same special and fascinating personality, someone forged from the race of the great ones who, despite all their missteps, create movements and make history, good or bad, those who do not sell at retail, those who seek to wrestle with God

---

11 "Yaakov Shabtai to Yaari," *Koteret Rashit*, Feb. 5, 1986. The letter was written in 1972.
12 Ibid.

and with Satan, and even in their failures there is more beauty and greatness and importance and sense than in the successes of others.[13]

Because Yaari was the living symbol of his movement, it was often judged by his statements. In practice, however, there was a discrepancy between the leader's statements, which provoked criticism, and his movement's actions, which were viewed with respect. In the final reckoning, what the movement and Yaari himself achieved was more important than what he said or wrote—and his words cannot nullify the merits of the solid accomplishments. His controversial statements and actions do not overshadow his inspirational ideas, his constructive deeds, and his life's work. And, as is the way with myths, they are stronger than the fruits of the labors, however faithful, of historians and biographers with their critical skepticism.

Yaari was viewed as the leader of Hashomer Hatza'ir in its three forms—the youth movement, Kibbutz Artzi, and Mapam; and of Kibbutz Artzi most of all. He had scant involvement with the youth movement, nor was his renown in partisan political activity. More than anything else, what remains to his credit and compensates for his controversial views and misguided actions are the establishment of Kibbutz Artzi and his long years at its helm. The day after he died, this was put clearly by a comrade who had freuently disagreed with him, Abba Kovner:

> In 1927, still a young man, he was the one who stood up and pushed the establishment of Kibbutz Artzi. On that day he transformed a group of dreamers into a community of builders and fighters, liberated them from rootless symbols, and turned them into a movement that has left a lasting mark on the map of Eretz Israel, which is won by creative toil and pain.
>
> Even were this the only thing he did in a life so full of action, Meir Yaari would deserve to be inscribed among the most distinguished names in the Book of Life of the Jewish people over the generations.[14]

---

13 Ibid.
14 Abba Kovner, *Al Hamishmar*, Feb. 22, 1987.

Bibliography

Archives

LA = Labor Movement Archives, Lavon Institute, Tel Aviv
CZA = Central Zionist Archives, Jerusalem
KMA, MYF = Kibbutz Merḥavia Archives, Meir Yaari Files
HHA = Hashomer Hatza'ir Archives, Givat Haviva
UKA= Hakibbutz Hame'uḥad Archives, Ramat Ef'al

Agin, Asaf. "Netishah: Parashat amidatam u-nefilatam shel Sha'ar Hagolan u-Masada be-milḥemet ha'atzmaut, May 1948" ["Desertion: The Story of the Resistance and Fall of Sha'ar Hagolan and Masada in the War of Independence, May 1948"]. In *Ḥomat magen: Shemonim shanah le-irgun ha-haganah (alei zayit va-ḥerev, VI)* [*A Defensive Wall: Eighty Years of the Haganah (Olive Branch and a Sword*, vol. 6)]. Ed. Danny Hadari. 205-271. Jerusalem: Ministry of Defense, Israel, 2002.

Alterman, Nathan. "Among All Peoples," in *The Jewish Political Tradition*, vol. II. Michael Walzer, Menchem Lorberbaum, and Noam J. Zohar eds., 80-82. New Haven: Yale University Press, 2003.

Amitay, Yossi. *Aḥavat amim be-mivḥan—Mapam 1948-1954: Amadot be-sugiyat arviyei Erez Yisrael* [*The United Workers' Party (Mapam) 1948-1954: Attitudes on Palestinian-Arab Issues*]. Tel Aviv: Tcherikover Publishers LTD, 1988.

"Anita Shapira against Meir Yaari." *Koteret Rashit*, Oct. 23, 1985 [Hebrew; apparently written by Tom Segev, and based on Shapira's lecture at a Yad Vashem conference in the fall of 1985].

Assaf, David. *The Regal Way: The Life and Times of Rabbi Israel of Ruzhin*. Trans. David Louvish. Stanford: Stanford University Press, 2002.

Avneri, Uri. "Foreword" [June 1, 1988], in Yossi Amitay, *Aḥavat amim be-mivḥan—Mapam 1948-1954: Amadot be-sugiyat arviyei Erez Yisrael* [*The United Workers' Party (Mapam) 1948-1954: Attitudes on Palestinian-Arab Issues*]. Tel Aviv: Tcherikover Publishers LTD, 1988, 9-11.

Bar-Gil, Shlomo. *Be-reshit hayah halom: Bogrei tenu'ot ha-noar ha-haluziyot me-amerika ha-latinit ba-tenu'ah ha-qibbuzit, 1946–1967* [*In the Beginning Was the Dream: The Graduates of the Pioneering Youth Movements from Latin America in the Kibbutz Movement, 1946–1967*]. Jerusalem: The Ben-Gurion Research Institute, 2005.

Barzel, Neima. *Ad kelot u-mineged: Ha-mifgash bein manhigei mered ha-geta'ot le-vein ha-hevrah ha-yisre'elit* [*Until the End and Opposite: The Encounter Between the Leaders of the Ghetto Fighters and the Israeli Society*]. Jerusalem: The Bialik Institute and Publications, 1998.

———. "Dignity, Hatred and Memory—Reparations from Germany: The Debates in the 1950s." *Yad Vashem Studies* 24 (1994): 247–280.

Barzilai, Gad. *Demoqratiyah be-milhamot: Mahloqet ve-konsenzus be-Yisra'el* [*A Democracy in Wartime: Conflict and Consensus in Israel*]. Tel Aviv: Sifriyat Polaim, 1992.

Bauer, Yehuda. *From Diplomacy to Resistance: A History of Jewish Palestine, 1930–1945*. Trans. Alton M. Winters. Philadelphia: Jewish Publication Society of America, 1970.

Baumel, Judith. "Zava'ato shel Uri Ilan" ["Uri Ilan's Testament"]. *Iyyunim bi-tequmat yisra'el*, 15 (2005): 209–238.

Beilin, Yossi. *Banim be-zel avotam* [*Children in their Fathers' Shadow*]. Tel Aviv: Revivim, 1984.

Ben-Aharon, Yariv. "Mesohe'ah im Meir Yaari al ma'amaro 'semalim telushim'" ["Yariv Ben-Aharon Talks with Meir Yaari"]. *Shedemot* 72 (Tishrei 5740 [1979]): 20–30.

Ben-Gurion, David. "The National Vocation of the Working Class," *Kuntres* 210 [Mar. 20, 1925] [Hebrew].

———. *Hazon ve-derekh* I. Tel Aviv: Am Oved Publishers, 1951.

———. *Yoman milhamah* [War diary]. Eds. Gershon Rivlin and Elhanan Oren. Tel Aviv: Am Oved Publishers, 1982.

———. *Zikhronot* [Memoirs]. Vol. 1, Tel Aviv: Am Oved Publishers, 1973; Vol. 6, Tel Aviv: Am Oved Publishers, 1987.

Bentov, Mordechai. *Yamim mesapperim: Zikhronot me-ha-tequfah hamakhra'at* [*Stories of Past Days: Memoirs of the Crucial Period*]. Tel Aviv: Sifriyat Polaim, 1984.

Bistritzky, Nathan. *Yamim ve-leylot* [*Days and Nights*]. Jerusalem: Ha-Madpis, 1926.

Boord, Ofer. *Kesef ha-shod mi-ydei ha-horeg: Ha-tenu'ah ha-qibbuẓit ve-heskem ha-shillumim, ha-pizzuyim ha-ishiyyim, ve-hashavat ha-rekhush mi-Germaniya* [*Take the Stolen Money from the Hands of the Killer: The Kibbutz Movement and the Reparations Agreement, the Personal Compensation and the Restitution from Germany*]. Sede Boqer: The Ben-Gurion Research Institute, 2015.

The Case for a Bi-National Palestine. Prepared by the Executive Committee of the Hashomer Hatzair Workers' Party in Jerusalem. New York, May 1947 [first published in Tel Aviv, 1946].

Charbit, Denis, "Un numéro des *Temps modernes* revisité." *La Règle du jeu* 34 (May 2007): 82–145.

Chizik, Moshe. *Yaḥaso shel Ha-shomer Ha-ẓa'ir la-qomunizm u-le-verit ha-mo'aẓot* [*Hashomer Hatza'ir's Attitude Towards Communism and the Soviet Union*]. Tel Aviv: Sifriyat Poalim, 1991.

Cohen, Avner. *Israel and the Bomb*. New York: Columbia University Press, 1998.

Cohen-Levinovsky, Nurit. "The Evacuation of the Noncombatant Population in the 1948 War: Three Kibbutzim as a Case Study." *Journal of Israeli History* 27, no.1 (2007): 1–34.

Committee on Constitutional Development in Palestine. *Report*. Jerusalem, 1941.

Cotic, Meir. *The Prague Trial: The First Anti-Zionist Show Trial in the Communist Bloc*. New York: Herzl Press and Cornwall Books, 1987.

Eilat, Giddi. "A Security Party: Structure and Image." In *Lo yukhlu bil'adeinu: Emdot Mapam bishe'elot ḥuẓ u-vittaḥon 1948–1956* [*"Can't do Without Us": Mapam's Views on Security and Foreign Policy*]. Eli Tzur, ed. 91–174. Tel Aviv: Yad Yaari and Yad Tabenkin, 2000.

Elmaliach, Tal. "Ẓavta: Tarbut u-folitikah be-darko shel Ha-shomer Ha-ẓa'ir ba-shanim 1967–1973" [*"Tzavta: Culture and Politics in Hashomer Hatza'ir in 1967–1973"*]. M.A. thesis, University of Haifa, 2007.

Erikson, Erik. *Identity: Youth and Crisis*. New York: W.W. Norton Company, 1968.

Frankel, Jonathan. "The Yizkor Book of 1911 – a Note on the National Myths in the Second Aliya." In *Religion, Ideology and Nationalism in Europe and America*. Eds. Hedva Ben-Israel et. al. 355–84. Jerusalem: Zalman Shazar Center for Jewish History, 1986.

Gan, Alon. "Hasiaḥ she-gava? 'Tarbut ha-siḥim' ke-nissayon le-gibbush zehut meyaḥedet la-dor ha-sheni ba-qibbuẓim" ["The Discourse that Expired? The 'Discourse Culture' as an Attempt to Consolidate a Distinctive Identity for the Second Generation on the Kibbutzim"]. Ph.D. diss., Tel Aviv University, 2004.

———. "Shinuyim ḥevratiyim ba-tenu'ah ha-qibbuẓit bi-shnot ha-shishim" ["Social Changes in the Kibbutz Movement in the 1960s"]. *Iyyunim bi-tequmat yisra'el* 16 (2006): 343–372.

Giladi, Dan. *Ha-yishuv bi-tequfat ha-aliyah ha-revi'it, 1924–1929: Beḥinah kalkalit u-folitit* [*The Yishuv in the Period of the Fourth Aliyah*]. Tel Aviv: Am Oved, 1973.

Goldstein, Yossi. *Rabin: Biografia* [*Rabin: A Biography*]. Jerusalem: Schocken, 2006.

Gorni, Yosef. *Shutafut u-ma'avaq: Chaim Weizmann u-tenu'at ha-po'alim be-ereẓ yisra'el* [*Partnership and Conflict: Chaim Weizmann and the Labor Movement in Israel*]. Tel Aviv: Hakibbutz Hame'uḥad, 1976.

Gouri, Chaim, and Chaim Hefer. *Mishpaḥat ha-Palmaḥ: Yalqut alilot va-zemer* [*The Palmach Family*]. Jerusalem: Keter, 1973.

Hacohen, Dvora. *Immigrants in Turmoil: Mass Immigration to Israel and Its Repercussions in the 1950s and After*. Trans. Gila Brand. Syracuse, NY: Syracuse University Press, 2003.

Ḥayyim Ya'ari: Be-yom ha-shanah le-moto [*Chaim Yaari, on the First Anniversary of his Death*]. Merḥavia, 1965.

Halamish, Aviva. "The Attitude of Hashomer Hatzair's Leadership toward the Heroism of Movement Members during the Holocaust, 1939–1959." *Moreshet: Journal for the Study of the Holocaust and Antisemitism* 10 (2013): 211–247.

———. "Bi-Nationalism in Mandatory Palestine: The Case of ha-Shomer ha-Tza'ir." In *Nationalism and Binationalism: The Perils of Perfect Structures*, Vol. I. Anita Shapira, Yedidia Z. Stern, and Alexander Yakobson, eds. 89–120. Brighton: Sussex Academic Press and the Israel Democracy Institute, 2013.

———. "Ha-ma'avaq al ha-sertifikatim ke-mavo li-frishat ha-revizionistim me-ha-histadrut ha-ẓiyyonit" ["The Struggle for 'Certificates': Prelude to the Secession of the Revisionists from the World Zionist Organization,"]. *Yahadut zemanenu* 14 (2001): 165–181.

―――. "Hashpa'ato ha-dialektit shel A.D. Gordon al Ha-shomer Ha-ẓa'ir" ("The Dialectic Influence of A.D. Gordon on Hashomer Hatzair"). *Cathedra* 114 (Dec. 2004): 99-120.

―――. "Hayishuv ve-ha-sho'ah: Tor ha-sintezah" ("The Yishuv and the Holocaust: Time for Synthesis"). In Roni Stauber, Aviva Halamish, Esther Webman, eds., *Shoah ve-antishemiyut ba-meḥqar u-va-siaḥ ha-ẓibburi*. 95-117. Jerusalem: Yad Vashem, 2015.

―――. "Loyalties in Conflict: Mapam's Vacillating Stance on the Military Government, 1955-1966, Historical and Political Analysis." *Israel Studies Forum* 25(2) (2010): 26-53.

―――. "Mapam in the War of Independence: From the War Front to the Opposition Back Benches." *Journal of Israeli History* 33, no. 2 (2014): 145-168.

―――. "Meir Yaari's Attitude toward Rescue and Aliyah during the Holocaust." *Moreshet: Journal for the Study of the Holocaust and Antisemitism* 7 (Winter 2009): 83-120.

―――. "The Historic Leadership of Hakibbutz Ha'artzi: The Power of Charisma, Organization and Ideology." *Journal of Israeli History* 31, no. 1 (March 2012): 45-66.

Halamish-Goldstein, Aviva. "Mapam and the Arab Minority in Israel, 1957-1966." MA thesis, Columbia University in the City of New York, 1975.

Halperin, Hagit. *Ha-ma'estro: ḥayyav vi-yẓirato shel Avraham Shlonsky* [*The Maestro: The Life and Work of Avraham Shlonsky*]. Tel Aviv: Sifriyat Poalim & Hakibbitz Hame'uḥad, 2011.

Hansard, *Parliamentary Debates*, Commons, 5th Series (1945-46).

Hazan, Yaakov. "Darki ba'areẓ ve-ha-shutafut beini le-vein Meir Yaari" ["My Path in this Country and my Partnership with Meir Yaari"]. *Ya'ad: le-ḥeqer tenu'at ha-avodah ve-ha-ḥevrah ha-qibbuẓit* 10 (September 1992): 6-12.

Hazan, Yaakov, and Anita Shapira. *Berl ve-ha-shomer ha-ẓa'ir* [*Berl and Hashomer Hatza'ir*]. Haifa: University of Haifa, 1983.

Horowitz, Dan and Moshe Lissak, *Trouble in Utopia: The Overburdened Polity of Israel*. Albany: State University of New York Press, 1989.

Horowitz, David. *Ha'etmol sheli* [*My Yesterday*]. Jerusalem: Schocken, 1970.

Horwitz, Yaakov. *Meir Yaari: Pe'ulato be-derekh arukah* [*Meir Yaari: His Long Road of Activity*]. Keren Ḥavaẓelet: Kibbutz Dalia, 1994.

Israel Central Bureau of Statistics. *Results of the Elections to the Fourth Knesset and the Local Authorities 3.IX.1959*. Jerusalem, 1961. [Hebrew].

Kanary, Baruch. *Tabenkin be-ereẓ yisra'el [Tabenkin in Eretz Israel]*. Kfar Chabad: Yad Tabenkin & Ben-Gurion Research Institute, 2003

Katznelson, Berl. "It Hurts Even When I Laugh." *Kitvei Berl Katznelson* [Collected writing] 9. 195-238. Tel Aviv: Mifleget Po'alei Eretz Israel, 1948.

Lahav, Pnina. "A Small Nation Goes to War: Israel's Cabinet Authorization of the 1956 War." *Israel Studies* 15 no. 3 (2010): 61-86.

Lamm, Zvi. *Youth Takes the Lead: The Inception of Jewish Youth Movements in Europe*. Trans. Sionah Kronfeld-Honig. Tel Aviv: Yad Yaari, 2004.

Landshut, Siegfried. *Ha-qevuẓah: meḥqar soẓiologi al ha-yishuv ha-qibbuẓi be-ereẓ yisra'el [The Kevutzah: A Sociological Study of the Kibbutz Settlement in Eretz Israel]*. Jerusalem: Machon Le-Haskala Tziyonit, 1944.

Lurie, Shalom, ed. *Anda: pirqei ḥayyim shel ḥaluẓah [Anda: Chapters from the Life of a Pioneer]*. Merḥavia: Kibbutz Merḥavia, 1995.

Margalit, Elkana. *Ha-shomer Ha-ẓa'ir: me-adat ne'urim le-marksizm mahapkhani (1913-1936) [Hashomer Hatzair from Youth Community to Revolutionary Marxism (1913-1936)]*. Tel Aviv: Hakibbutz Hame'uḥad, 1971.

Meqorot le-ḥeqer toledot ha-shomer ha-ẓa'ir [Sources for Studying the History of Hashomer Hatza'ir]. Nos. 2-4, ed. Eli Shadmi. Givat Haviva: Yad Yaari, 1984, 1985, 1986; No. 5, ed. David Zait. Givat Haviva: Yad Yaari, 1987.

Mintz, Matityahu. *Ḥevlei ne'urim: Ha-tenu'ah ha-shomerit 1911-1921. [Pangs of youth: Hashomer Hazair 1911-1921]*. Jerusalem: Hasifriya Hatziyonit, 1995.

———. "Raq lo semalim mi-sham vi-yḥidei segullah mi-kan: iyyun be-ma'amaro shel Me'ir Ya'ari 'Semalim telushim'" ["A study of Yaari's 'Rootless Symbols'"]. *Iyyunim be-tequmat yisra'el* 13 (2003): 57-70.

Minutes of the Twentieth Zionist Congress, Zurich, August 3-21, 1937. Jerusalem: World Zionist Organization, n.d.

Miron, Leah. "Ḥaluqqah meḥudeshet shel ha-zirah ha-politit" ["A Redivision of the Political Arena: Coming Closer and Getting Farther in the Consolidation of the Identity of Mapai, Mapam, and Herut after the establishment of the State"]. Ph.D. dissertation, The Hebrew University of Jerusalem, 2009.

Nakdimon, Shlomo. *Liqrat she'at ha-efes* [*Before H-Hour*]. Tel Aviv: Ramdor, 1968.
Near, Henry. *The Kibbutz Movement: A History*, I-II. Oxford: Oxford University Press, 1992-1997.
Nur, Ofer. "Hashomer Hatzair Youth Movement 1918-1924 from Eastern Galicia and Vienna to Palestine: A Cultural History." Doctoral dissertation, University of California at Los Angeles, 2004.
Oppenheim, Yisrael. *Tenu'at he-ḥaluẓ be-folin (1917-1929)* [*The He-ḥalutz Movement in Poland*]. Jerusalem: Magnes Press, 1982.
Oren, Michael B. "Orde Wingate: Friend under Fire," *Azure* 10 (Winter 5761/2001): 33-49.
Oren, Mordechai. *Reshimot asir Prag* [*Notes of a Political Prisoner in Prague*]. 2nd ed. Merḥavia: Sifriyat Po'alim, 1958.
Patish, Yitzhak. *Ha-siḥrur ve-ha-ivvaron: Ha-shomer ha-ẓa'ir ve-ha-qomunizm* [*In the Blind Eye of the Maelstrom: Hashomer Hatza'ir and Communism*]. Tel Aviv: Yad Yaari, 2003.
Pauker, Alon. "Utopia bi-svakh ha-setirot: Hashva'ah bein ha-dimuyim ha'aẓmiyim shel ha-tenu'ot ha-qibbuẓiyot ha-shonot be-asor ha-rishon la-medinah" ("Utopia Entangled in Contradictions: a Comparison Between the Self-Images of the Different Kibbutz Movements in the First Decade of the State"). Ph.D. dissertation, Tel Aviv University, 2005.
Porat, Dina. *The Fall of a Sparrow: The Life and Times of Abba Kovner*. Trans. and ed. Elizabeth Yuval. Stanford: Stanford University Press, 2009.
_____. *Hanhagah be-milkud: Ha-yishuv nokhaḥ ha-Shoah, 1942-1945* [*Leadership in a Trap: The Yishuv Facing the Holocaust, 1942-1945*]. Tel Aviv: Am Oved, 1986.
_____. *Me'ever la-gashmi: Parashat Hayav shel Abba Kovner* [*Beyond the Reaches of Our Souls: The Life and Times of Abba Kovner*]. Tel Aviv: Am Oved, 2000.
_____. "Tehran Children." In *Encyclopedia of the Holocaust*. Ed. Robert Rozett and Shmuel Spector. 434. Jerusalem: The Jerusalem Publishing House and Yad Vashem, 2009.
Qehilliyatenu 5682: Hagut, levatim, u-ma'avayei ḥaluẓim [*Qehilliyatenu 1922*]. Introduced and annotated by Muki Tsur. Jerusalem: Yad Ben-Zvi, 1988.
Rappel, Hagit. "'U-mi yizkor et ha-zokherim?': Zikkaron kolektivi ve-zikkaron ishi be-kibbutz Yad Mordechai" ["'And Who Will Remember Those Who Remember?': Collective Memory and Personal Memory at

Kibbutz Yad Mordechai"]. Ph.D. dissertation, Ben-Gurion University of the Negev, 2004.

The Road to Bi-National Independence for Palestine: Memorandum of the Hashomer Hatza'ir Workers' Party of Palestine. Tel Aviv, 1947.

"Rudi" [Amnon Za'ir], *Vienna Gan Shmuel*, recorded and edited by Dalia Amotz-Vislib. Gan Shmuel: Kibbutz Gan Shmuel, 1980 [Hebrew].

Ruppin, Arthur. *Memoirs, Diaries, Letters*. Ed. Alex Bein. Trans. Karen Gershon. New York: Herzl Press, 1972.

S. Sh. Yariv [David Ben-Gurion]. *Al ha-Qomunism ve-ha-ziyyonut shel ha-shomer ha-za'ir* [*On the Communism and Zionism of Hashomer Hatza'ir*]. Tel Aviv: Mifleget Po'alei Eretz Israel, 1953.

Sadan, Dov. *Alufi u-meyuda'i: ishim be-ma'agal tenu'at ha'avodah* [*Leaders of the Labor Movement*]. Tel Aviv: Am Oved, 1972.

Sefer Ha-shomer Ha-za'ir [Hashomer Hatza'ir book]. Ed. Levi Dror and Yisrael Rosenzweig. Vol. 1. Merhavia: Sifriyat Po'alim, 1956.

Segev, Tom. "Ha-melekh Lir" ["King Lear"]. *Koteret Rashit*, Jan. 29, 1986.

———. "Ha-ish le-lo Elohim" ["The Man without a God"]. *Koteret rashit*, Feb. 5, 1986.

———. *1967: Israel, the War, and the Year That Transformed the Middle East*. Trans. Jessica Cohen. New York: Metropolitan Books, 2007.

———. *The Seventh Million: The Israelis and the Holocaust*. Trans. Chaim Watzman. New York: Hill and Wang, 1993.

Shaary, David. *Mi-stam ziyyonut le-ziyyonut kelalit* [*From Plain Zionism to General Zionism*]. Jerusalem: Rubin Mass, 1990.

Shaham, Natan. *Shalom haverim* [*Goodbye, Comrades*]. Tel Aviv: Devir, 2004.

Shalom, Zaki. *Bein Dimona le-Vashington: Ha-ma'avaq al pittuah ha-opziyah ha-gar'init shel Yisrael, 1960–1968* [*Between Dimona and Washington: The Struggle Over the Development of Israel's Nuclear Option*]. Jerusalem: Ben-Gurion Research Institute, 2004.

Shapira, Anita. *Berl: Biographia* [*Berl Katznelson: A Biography*], I–II. Tel Aviv: Am Oved, 1981.

———. *Land and Power: The Zionist Resort to Force, 1881–1948*. Trans. William Templer. Stanford: Stanford University Press, 1999.

———. "Me'afyenim shel tahalikhei hasmalah" ["Lineaments of the Leftward Drift"]. In *Ha-halikhah al kav ha-ofeq* [*Walking on the Horizon*]. 208–257. Tel Aviv: Am Oved, 1988.

———. *Yigal Allon, Native Son: A Biography*. Trans. Evelyn Abel. Philadelphia: University of Pennsylvania Press, 2008.

Shapira, Avraham, ed. *Siaḥ loḥamim* [*Warriors' Discourse*]. Tel Aviv: [A group of young Kibbutz members], 1968.

Sharett, Moshe. *Yoman medini* [*Political Diary*], vol. 3, 1938. Tel Aviv: Am Oved & Hasifriya Hatziyonit, 1972.

Shaltiel, Eli. *Tamid be-meri: Moshe Sneh* [*Moshe Sneh, Life*]. Tel Aviv: Am Oved, 2000.

Sheleg, Yair. "The Bitaniyya Myth." *Bamaḥaneh*. Sept. 22, 1988 [Hebrew].

Shem-Tov, Victor. *Eḥad me-hem* [*One of Them*]. Dalia: Ma'arekhet, 1997.

Sobol, Yehoshua. *The Night of the Twentieth*. Trans. Chanah Hoffman. Tel Aviv: Institute for the Translation of Hebrew Literature, 1978.

Stauber, Roni. *The Holocaust in Israeli Public Debate in the 1950s: Ideology and Memory*. Trans. Elizabeth Yuval. Portland, OR: Vallentine Mitchell, 2007.

Toib, Shlomit. "Meir Yaari: The Story of the Interview That Was Never Published." *Ḥotam*, Mar. 5, 1982.

Tzahor, Ze'ev. *Hazan, tenu'at ḥayyim: Ha-shomer ha-ẓa'ir, ha-qibbuẓ ha-arẓi, Mapam* [*Ya'kov Hazan–A Biography*]. Jerusalem: Yad Ben-Zvi, 1997.

———. "Mapai, Mapam, ve-haqamat memshelet yisrael ha-rishonah" ["Mapai, Mapam, and the Establishment of the First Israeli Government"]. *Iyyunim bi-tequmat yisra'el* 4 (1994): 378–399.

Tzarfati, Orly. "*Lamerḥav*: Gilgulo shel itton bein pillug le-iḥud" ["*Lamerḥav*: The Story of a Newspaper from Split to Unification"]. *Kesher* 35 (winter 2007): 118–131.

Tzur, Eli. *Nofei ha-ashlayah: Mapam 1948–1954* [*Landscapes of Illusion: Mapam 1948–1954*]. Beer Sheva: Ben-Gurion Research Institute, 2002.

———, ed. *Lo yukhlu bil'adeinu: Emdot Mapam bi-she'elot ḥuẓ u-vittaḥon 1948–1954* ["*Can't Do Without Us*": *Mapam's Views on Security and Foreign Policy*]. Tel Aviv: Yad Yaari and Yad Tabenkin, 2000.

Unity Convention of the Workers' Party Hashomer Hatzair in Eretz Israel and the Party Le'aḥdut Ha'avodah–Po'alei Ẓion. Tel Aviv, January 23–24, 1948. Tel Aviv: Mifleget Hapo'alim Hame'uḥedet, n.d. [Hebrew].

Weber, Max. *The Theory of Economic and Social Organization*. New York: Oxford University Press, 1947.

Weitz, Yechiam. "Heibettim be-yaḥas ha-yishuv ba-areẓ el sho'at yehudei eiropa" ["Aspects of the Yishuv's Attitude towards the Holocaust in

Europe"]. In *Nequdot tazpit: Tarbut ve-ḥevrah be-ereẓ yisra'el*. Ed. Nurit Gertz. 74–85. Tel Aviv: Open University Press, 1988.

Wilfand, Yigal, ed. *Aharon Cohen: Guf rishon, guf shelishi* [Aharon Cohen]. [n.p]: Hakibbutz Hartzi-Hashomer Hatzair, 1990.

Wrobel, Piotr. "The Jews of Galicia under Austrian-Polish Rule, 1867–1918." http://easteurotopo.org/articles/wrobel/wrobel.pdf [accessed Oct. 23, 2014].

Yaari, Aviezer. *Ba-derekh mi-merḥavya: Sippuro shel ish modi'in yisre'eli* [*The Road from Merḥavia: The Story of an Israeli Intelligence Officer*]. Or Yehuda: Kinneret, 2003.

Yaari, Meir. *Be-derekh arukah* [*On a Long Road*]. Merḥavia: Sifriyat Po'alim, 1947.

———. *Be-fetaḥ tequfah: Peraqim le-diyyun liqrat ha-mo'aẓah he-kelalit ha-shishit shel ha-qibbuẓ ha-arẓi–ha-shomer ha-ẓa'ir* [*At the Doors of an Epoch*]. Merḥavia: Hakibbutz Ha'artzi Hashomer Hatza'ir, 1942.

———. *Bein ḥazon limẓi'ut: Rashey peraqim la-ve'idah ha-revi'it* [*shel Mapam*] [*Between Vision and Reality*]. Merḥavia: Sifriyat Po'alim, 1963.

———. *Be-siman aḥdut ve-azma'ut: Rashey peraqim la-ve'idah ha-ḥamishit shel Mapam* [*Under the Sign of Unity and Independence*]. Tel Aviv: Sifriyat Po'alim, 1968.

———. *Be-meri vikkuaḥ* [*A Bitter Dispute*]. Merḥavia: Hakibbutz Ha'artzi Hashomer Hatza'ir, 1940.

———. *Be-ma'avaq le-amal meshuḥrar: Mivḥar devarim bi-she'elot ha-histadrut u-tenu'at ha-po'alim* [*In the Struggle for Liberated Labor*]. Tel Aviv: Am Oved, 1972.

———. *Mivḥanei dorenu* [*The Trials of our Generation: An Outline for the Third Convention of the United Workers' Party*]. Tel Aviv: United Workers' Party, 1957.

———. *Qibbuẓ galuyot be-aspaqlarya shel yameinu: Rashey peraqim le-diyyun liqrat ha-mo'aẓah he-kelalit ha-sheminit shel ha-qibbuẓ ha-arẓi–ha-shomer ha-ẓa'ir* [*The Ingathering of the Exiles in the Mirror of our Days*]. Merḥavia: Sifriyat Po'alim, 1954.

———. "Semalim telushim" ["Rootless Symbols"]. In *Hedim: qoveẓ le-sifrut*. Nissan 5683 [1923]: 93–106.

_____. "Vers la coexistence pacifique et progressiste entre l'Etat d'Israël et les pays arabes." *Les Temps Modernes* 253 bis, *1967: Le Conflit israélo-arabe*. 661–690.

_____. and Yaakov Hazan. *Neged ha-zerem* [*Against the Current*]. Merḥavia: Hakibbutz Ha'artzi Hashomer Hatza'ir, 1942.

Yaari, Yehuda. *When the Candle Was Burning*. Trans. Menahem Hurwitz. London: Victor Gollancz, 1947.

Yaari-Wald, Moshe, ed. *Qehillat Reyshe: Sefer zikkaron* [*Rzeszow Jews Memorial Book*]. Tel Aviv: Organizations of Reyshe Descendants in Israel and the United States, 1967.

Yablonka, Hanna. *Survivors of the Holocaust: Israel after the War*. Trans. Ora Cummings. New York: New York University Press, 1999.

Yishai, Yael. "He-ḥazon ve-liqḥo: Hashpa'at mishpat Prag al mifleget ha-po'alim ha-me'uḥedet" ["The Vision and Its Lesson: The Influence of the Prague Trial on the United Workers' Party"]. *Medinah, mimshal ve-yaḥasim beinle'ummiyim* 7 (1975): 76–94.

Zait, David. *Ha-ḥolem ve-ha-magshim: Pirqei ḥayyav shel Mordechai Shenhabi* [*Vision in Action: The Life story of Mordechai Shenhabi*]. Tel Aviv: Yad Yaari, 2005.

_____. *Ḥaluẓim ba-mavokh ha-politi: Ha-tenu'ah ha-qibbuẓit 1927–1948* [*Pioneers in the Maze of Politics: The Kibbutz Movement 1927–1948*]. Jerusalem: Yad Ben-Zvi, 1993.

_____. *Ha-utopia ha-shomerit: Ha-shomer ha-ẓa'ir be-folin, 1921–1931* [*The Shomer Dreams of Utopia: Ha-Shomer Ha-ẓa'ir Youth Movement in Poland, 1921–1931*]. Jerusalem: Ben-Gurion Research Center & Yad Yaari, 2002.

_____. "Iḥud ha-semol ha-ẓiyyoni-soẓialisti" ["The Unification of the Zionist-Socialist Left"]. In *Ha-semol ha-me'uḥad: Darkah ha-ḥevratit shel Mapam be-reshit ha-medina 1948–1954* [*The United Left of Israel: The Social Policies of Mapam during the Formative Years of the State, 1948–1954*]. Ed. Elkana Margalit. 25–70. Givat Haviva: Yad Yaari, 1991.

_____. *Ẓiyyonut be-darkhei shalom: Darko ha-ra'ayonit-politit shel Ha-shomer Ha-ẓa'ir, 1927–1947* [*Zionism and Peace: The Ideological and Political Course of Hashomer Hatzair, 1927–1947*]. Tel Aviv: Sifriyat Po'alim, 1985.

_____. and Yosef Shamir, eds. *Meir Yaari: Dyoqno shel manhig ke-adam za'ir* [*Meir Yaari: A Portrait of a Leader as a Young Man*]. Tel Aviv: Sifriyat Po'alim, 1992.

Zidon Asher, *Knesset: The Parliament of Israel*. Trans. Aryeh Rubinstein and Gertrude Hirschler. New York: Herzl Press, 1968.

Interviews

Gidi Eilat, Beit Alfa, Mar. 17, 2006.

Rachel Groll (Yaari), Merḥavia, Feb. 2, 2000.

Dagi Haboynik, Aug. 29–30, 2010 and Sept. 1, 2010. [by telephone and email]

Binyamin Yasour (Benjileh), Magen, Nov. 20, 2011.

Yair Tzaban, Tel Aviv, Feb. 1, 2011.

Chaim Shoor, Tel Aviv, Nov. 8, 1998.

Eitan Schreiber, Nir David, Nov. 22, 2010. [by telephone]

Index

A

Adar, Binyamin (Benko), 386
Adenauer, Konrad, 340
Agudath Israel, 151, 258, 305
Aḥdut Ha'avodah, 20, 27-29, 43, 66, 101, 106, 203, 213, 215-216, 220, 227, 230, 233, 244, 246, 255, 265, 267, 277-278, 310-312, 316-318, 330-331, 338, 340, 353, 376-377, 449
Agnon, S. J., 284
Al Hamishmar (daily newspaper), 252, 260, 270-272, 274-275, 277-278, 321, 329, 332, 364, 373, 384-385, 431, 435-437, 455 see also *Mishmar*
Alignment *(HaMa'arakh)*, 373, 376, 378-379, 383-384, 389, 398, 400-401, 403-404, 406-407, 409-410, 412, 454
Aliyah Ḥadashah, 142
Allon, Yigal, 225, 233-234, 311, 312n12, 377, 399
al-Qawuqji, Fawzi, 219
Alterman, Nathan, 191, 282, 321, 338, 348
Altman, Tosia, 131, 136, 150, 337
American Jewry, 150, 194
American Zionism, 206
Anglo-American Committee of Inquiry, 202
Anielewicz, Mordechai, 173, 187, 337, 338
Arab citizens of Israel, 309-310, 331, 410-411
Arab Revolt of 1936-1939, 112, 113, 146
Arad, Zvi, 285-286
Arafat, Yasser, 404-405
Arlosoroff, Chaim, 116-117, 149
Avidan, Shimon, 234, 420
Avigur, Shaul, 394
Avneri, Uri, 234

B

Balfour Declaration, 26, 60, 126
Barzilai, Yisrael, 325
Basel Program, 1897, 142
Bashan, Raphael, 328-329, 350-351
Bauer, Otto, 160
Bedouin settlements, 363, 403, 411
Ben-Aharon, Yitzhak, 376
Ben-Gurion, David, 120, 126, 137, 141, 144, 149, 154, 202-204, 206, 209, 220, 229-230, 234, 236-241, 257, 258, 271-272, 274, 299-301, 304, 315, 340, 365-366, 388, 394-396, 449
Ben Naftali, Moshe, 406
Ben-Nahum, Daniel, 288
Ben-Shahar, Chaim, 430
Bentov, Mordechai, 54, 146-147, 211, 325, 397
Ben-Zvi, Itzhak, 304, 326
Bergman, Ernest David, 393
Bernfeld, Siegfried, 16-17
Bethlehem, 112
Bevin, Ernest, 199
Biltmore (Extraordinary Zionist) Conference, 141
Biltmore Program, 142-143, 145, 184, 190, 203, 206, 248
binationalism, 96, 109-111, 113, 141-143, 148-149, 173, 187, 190, 202, 207-212, 215, 311, 313, 410
Binyamina, 31, 163
biography of a leader, x-xiii
Bistritzky, Nathan, 38-39
Bitaniyya Illit, 25-48, 71-72, 434, 441-442
Blüher, Hans, 17, 74-76, 104
Bolshevik Revolution, 13, 157, 345, 351, 372-373
Borochov, Ber, 266, 303, 306-307
Borochovism, 258, 306
Bratislava, 25, 192

Brenner, Joseph Ḥayyim, 28, 32
Brest-Litovsk, Treaty of, 157
Brieger, Yehuda, 179
Britain, 128–129
British military, 26, 130
Buber, Martin, 17, 75, 162

C

Canaanism, 435
Center for Progressive Culture (Tzavta), 281, 385
Chajes, Hirsch Perez, 16
Cohen, Aharon ("Aharonchik"), 249, 325–327, 326n65
Cohen, Rivka, 327–328
Communism, 57, 107, 157, 247, 251, 252, 270, 287

D

Dayan, Moshe, 233, 336, 396–400, 405
de Beauvoir, Simone, 314
Deir Yassin affair, 223–224
Democratic Movement for Change (Dash), 413
Diaspora, xiii, 27, 51, 65, 69, 77–78, 94–95, 106, 116, 123–124, 129–130, 139, 143–145, 168, 175, 181–182, 185, 191, 194–195, 291, 303, 323, 435
Dimona Project, 392–393
Doctors' Plot, 343
Dror, Binyamin, 33–34, 36, 42, 136, 172

E

Edelist, Ron, 430–431
Eichmann trial, 1961, 342
Elazari-Volcani, Yitzhak, 43
Elfenbein, Mina, 10, 14, 71
Elimelech of Lyzhansk, Rebbe, 4, 87
Eros, 35, 37, 74–75
erotic sharing, 35–36, 46, 67
Eshkol, Levy, 330, 377, 393–397
Etzioni Commission, 323
European Jewry, 150, 164, 192
Exodus 1947, 242

F

family relationships, 74, 80
Fascism, 105, 117, 157, 413
Fast, Howard, 287
Feder, Naftali, 390
Finzi, Shalom, 131

First Aliyah, 60
Fourth Aliyah, 58–60, 144
Fraenkel, Naomi, 280, 282–283
free love, 35–36, 79, 96

G

Galicia, xiii, 1–2, 13, 15–18, 32, 42, 51, 56–57, 71, 99, 108, 184, 263, 441
Hashomer groups in, 9
Russian invasion in, 11
Zionist youth groups in, 8
Galili, Yisrael, 330, 377
Gandhi, Mahatma, 199
Gedud Ha'avodah, 55–56, 62–63, 66, 68, 95, 109, 163
General Federation of Hebrew Workers in Palestine, see Histadrut
Germany, ix, 111, 120, 121, 157–159, 184, 187, 228, 247, 283, 315, 339–342
Givat Haviva, 279, 415, 426–428, 438
Golan, Shmuel, 358, 425
Golan Heights, 33, 372, 399, 401–402
Goldberg, Leah, 285
Goldmann, Nahum, 254, 333, 406
Golomb, Eliyahu, 137–138
Gordon, A.D., 31, 39–40, 44, 48, 57–58, 67
Gordon, Ben-Ami, 102
Gordonia youth movement, 58
Great War, 1914, 11, 19
Green Line, 411
Groll, Lushek, 140, 359, 432
Groll, Yedidia, *see* Yaari Yedidia
Gromyko, Andrei, 207–208
Grossman, Chaika, 172–178, 182, 341, 427
Guttman, Yisrael, 341, 456

H

Hacohen, Eliezer, 383
Haifa, 42–43, 53, 73, 82, 84, 108, 113, 121, 140, 162, 256, 258, 322, 438
Haifa-Jida road, 31–32, 38, 45
Ha'olam Hazeh, 260, 266, 276
Hapoel Hatza'ir, 20, 27–28, 43–44, 66, 101
Hapoel Hatza'ir, 36, 43–44
Hashomer Hatza'ir, 3, 9, 19, 20, 26, 27, 31, 35, 42–43, 49–50, 52, 55–58, 61–62, 66, 68, 95, 101–103, 106–107, 110–112, 116, 118, 123–

124, 136, 142, 146, 155, 159–160, 187–188, 201–202, 204–208, 216, 235, 248, 307, 316, 327, 335–336, 347, 349, 359, 379, 388, 415–416, 425–426, 438, 445, 449, 456, 458
aliyah, 27
attitude towards the Soviet Union, 161
communes, 35, 49–50, 52, 61–63, 285
cooperation between Mapai and, 116–117
in Palestine, 20–21
political program for, 149
role in postwar Europe, 175
youth movement, ix–xiii, 14, 160, 253, 260, 269, 342, 453
Hashomerim–Ẓe'irei Ẓiyyon, 15
Hazan, Bertha, 360
Hazan, Yaakov, 52, 113–114, 184, 205, 214, 217, 242, 251, 281, 324, 346–347, 356, 358, 362, 366–367, 374–376, 379–380, 383, 387, 389, 395, 397, 405, 415–422, 445–446, 452–455
Heḥalutz, 123–124
Herzliyya commune, 84–85 see also Kibbutz Merḥavia
Herzog, Yitzhak Isaac Halevy, Rabbi, 152
Histadrut, General Federation of Hebrew Workers in Palestine, 36, 42–43
Histadrut Convention, 170
Histadrut Executive Committee, 133, 162, 201, 211
Holocaust, 121, 131–132, 134–135, 138, 150–151, 173, 179, 182, 335, 339, 342
Holocaust and Ghetto Uprisings Law, 1951, 339
Holocaust and Heroism Remembrance Day, 339
Horowitz, David (Dolek), 22, 27, 32, 33–34, 41–42, 52, 55, 387
Ha-etmol sheli (My Yesterday), 22, 38–39
Horowitz, Shlomo, 13
Horwitz, Yaakov, 438
Ḥotam, 384, 386–387, 431
Ḥovevei Zion, 5
Hussein, King, 399

I
ideological collectivism, 63, 66, 94–118, 168, 186, 194, 260, 272, 278, 293, 296–297, 306, 345, 355, 358, 365, 407, 409, 445–446
adoption of Marxism, 100–101, 106–107
aim of, 101
principle of, 105
with totalitarianism, 96
Yaari's concept of, 96
IDF (Israel Defense Forces), 225, 231–233, 242, 256, 274, 301, 320, 338, 359–361, 378, 393–395, 406–407, 422, 423
Ilan, Uri, 336–338
Inner Zionist General Council in Jerusalem (1942), 142–143, 145
Iron Curtain, 192–193
Israeli Labor movement, 376

J
Jabotinsky, Zeev, 115
Jerusalem, 45, 54, 112, 140, 142, 192, 218–219, 224, 241, 288, 378, 399, 401–402
Jerusalem Plan. *see* Biltmore Program
Jewish Colonization Association (ICA), 33
Jewish immigration, 143, 198–199
Jewish National Fund, 20
Jewish state, partition and the establishment of, 203–212
joint organization, 109–110, 112, 146
Jordan, 33, 112, 222, 310–313, 361, 378, 399, 401–404, 407
Jugendkultur, 17, 51

K
Kafr Qassem, 321
Kaplan, Eliezer, 137
Kaplansky, Shlomo, 214
Karp, Anda (later Anda Yaari), 34, 49, 70–71, 333, 363, 417
arrival in Palestine, 72
health issues, 81–82
marriage with Yaari, 72–73
preparations for aliyah, 71
Karp, Sophia (Yaari's mother-in-law), 84
Katzir, Ephraim, 429
Katznelson, Berl, 57, 60, 95, 104–105, 145, 449

Kempner (later: Kovner), Vitka, 170
Khrushchev, Nikita, 342–345, 350–351, 353, 376
Kibbutz Artzi (KA), ix, xii, 52, 55, 61, 62, 64, 106, 140, 194, 203, 214, 223, 244, 268–269, 279, 283–284, 288, 291, 294, 297, 300, 306, 318, 327, 335, 342, 348, 351, 358, 372, 379, 396, 402, 415–416, 458
  adoption of Marxism, 100–101
  establishment of the Palmach, 130–131
  founding council of, 65, 67, 69, 146
  ideological axioms of, 66–67
  Katznelson's attacks on, 104
  platform, 65, 66, 67, 68, 69, 106, 109–110, 146, 246
Kibbutz Beit Alfa, 49, 53–56, 58, 62, 64, 79, 84, 282–283
Kibbutz Ein Ḥarod, 68, 86, 113, 300
Kibbutz Ein Haḥoresh, 163, 438
Kibbutz Ein Shemer, 64, 198, 200, 269, 285, 371, 430, 436
Kibbutz Ga'ash, 297
Kibbutz Gan Shmuel, 21, 280, 336, 354
Kibbutz Gat, 131, 298
Kibbutz Givat Chaim, 200
Kibbutz Hama'apil, 163, 280
Kibbutz Ḥulda, 219, 360
Kibbutz Kfar Gil'adi, 232
Kibbutz Lehavot Habashan, 372, 401
Kibbutz Ma'abarot, 64, 159, 280, 355
Kibbutz Massada, 222
Kibbutz Merḥavia, xii, xiv, 25n1, 64, 84–86, 92, 122, 124, 125, 134–135, 140, 159, 170, 174, 182, 197, 209, 241, 251, 267, 281, 295, 314, 333, 338, 346, 359, 360n15, 361, 363–364, 366, 368–369, 381, 405, 415, 417, 419 421, 422, 424–427, 429, 431, 435–438, 443, 457
Kibbutz Me'uḥad, see United Kibbutz Movement
Kibbutz Mishmar Ha'emeq, 64, 86, 141, 146, 148, 182, 195, 280, 300, 354, 369, 375, 415, 417, 419, 425
Kibbutz Nir David, 279, 294, 384
Kibbutz Nir Oz, 403
Kibbutz Revadim, 279
Kibbutz Sarid, 64, 355
Kibbutz Sha'ar Ha'amaqim, 325
Kibbutz Sha'ar Hagolan, 221–223, 282

Kibbutz Shoval, 279, 356, 394
Kibbutz Yad Mordechai, 221–223, 242, 336, 339
kibbutzim, 55, 61–62, 64, 66–68, 78–79, 81, 96–97, 99–102, 104, 130–131, 151–152, 159, 182, 185, 194–195, 198, 221–223, 225, 231–232, 245, 249–250, 257, 269–273, 280, 287, 290–291, 290–292, 294, 297–298, 298–304, 301, 315, 324, 327, 348, 353, 359, 361, 364, 367–370, 372, 376, 389, 401, 408, 409, 411, 415, 420, 436–437, 444, 446, 449, 452
Kielce pogrom, 1946, 187, 192, 193
Kinneret, 28
Kishinev pogrom, 1903, 191
Klass, Shlomo, 187
Kleiner, Rudy, 21
Knaani, David, 429
Knesset, 241–242, 244, 256, 257, 288, 300, 305, 310, 315, 321–322, 329, 331–332, 339–340, 376, 380–381, 383, 388–389, 420–421, 454
Korczak, Ruzka, 170–172, 177–178, 182, 341
Koteret Rashit, 427
Kovner, Abba, 170, 171–173, 177–179, 187, 231, 341, 370, 437, 456, 458
Krakow, 1, 6
Krause, Eliyahu, 50
Krongold, Chaim, 52, 54
Kurzweil, Baruch, 282

L

labor movement, ix, 38, 58, 59, 66, 101, 109, 116–118, 154–155, 160–162, 171, 190, 376
Lamerḥav, 277–278
Landauer, Gustav, 17
Lands Law of 1940, 219
Lanzmann, Claude, 314
Laski, Harold, 152
Lavi, Shlomo, 28
Lavi, Zvi, 355–356
Lavon, Pinchas, 336
leadership, x
League for Friendship with the Soviet Union, 162
League for Jewish-Arab Rapprochement and Cooperation, 147
Leivick, Halpern, 54
Les Temps Modernes, 314
Likud party, 315, 404, 415

Lipsker, Avraham (Abramek), 126, 176
Lubetkin, Zivia, 136, 172, 337
Lufban, Itzhak, 44
Luxemburg, Rosa, 284
Lwów (Lemberg or Lviv), 1, 19, 21–22, 27, 34, 71, 89

M
Magnes, Judah L., 143
mamlakhtiyut, 299
Mao Zedong, 250, 307
Mapai, 101–103, 106, 116, 146, 147, 163, 174, 175, 214, 215, 225, 233–234, 235–236, 237–241, 248, 257–258, 272, 302, 316, 317, 322, 324, 330–331, 376–377, 382, 446, 455–456
Mapam, x, xi, xiv, 214, 217–218, 220, 223, 225, 227, 229–231, 233–235, 237–241, 245, 247–249, 251, 255–272, 275, 291–292, 301, 303–304, 307, 309, 311–312, 315–316, 318–319, 322, 324–326, 330–332, 338–341, 345, 350–351, 353, 367, 368–372, 376–377, 379, 382, 385, 396–398, 400, 412, 433, 443, 447, 451–452, 455–456, 458
Mapam peace plan, 314
Marxism, 57
Marxism-Leninism, 349, 425–426
May Day celebrations, 412
McCarthy, Joseph, 265
Meir, Golda, 347, 374, 394, 397, 405, 429
Mickiewicz, Adam, 195
Mikveh Yisrael agricultural school, 50
Mishmar, 149, 197-198, 200
Mishmar Ha'emeq council, 1942, 141, 146, 148
Mizraḥi, 322-324
Mizrahi (party), 151, 153, 236, 316-317
Moscow Trials, 155–156

N
Nahalal gathering, 53
Nakam ("revenge") campaign, 178
Nasser, Abdel-, Gamal, 341, 394, 406
Nazi Germany, 128, 157, 340
Nes Ẓiyyona, 163
Nietzsche, Friedrich, 17
The Night of the Twentieth (Yehoshua Sobol), 39

Nominations Committee, 381–382, 389, 454

O
October Revolution, 156, 168, 346, 372
Operation Ḥorev, 232–233
Oppenheimer, Franz, 85
Oren (Orenstein), Mordechai, 107, 260–263, 272
Oren affair, 326 (see also Prague trial)
Oren, Rega, 263
Oriental Jews (Mizraḥim), 322–324
Ouziel, Ben-Ẓion Meir Ḥai, Rabbi 152

P
Palestine, 25–27, 42, 50–51, 60, 65–66, 109, 118, 131, 163-164, 179–180, 188, 195, 199
demographic situation in (1933–1936), 111
economic capacity, 26
economic surge of 1932, 111
Palestinian entity, 310
Palmach, 130–131, 167, 199–200, 216, 221–222, 224, 229–231, 233–234, 242, 337, 348, 415
Paris conference (1946), 203
Partition Resolution, 206, 220, 247, 312
Peel Commission, 112–113, 149
Peres, Shimon, 330, 392, 394–395, 429, 436
Peri (Pra'i, Wilder), Elazar, 197, 433n69
Petaḥ Tiqvah, 321, 368, 438
Po'alei Ẓiyyon Left, 28, 108, 147, 203, 213, 255
Poland, 175–176, 184, 187–188
Porat, Dina, 179
Potocki, Count, 6
Prague trial, 262–263, 267–268, 271–272, 344

Q
Qehilliyatenu (Our Community), 35, 39, 48–50, 109

R
Rabin, Yitzhak, 402, 429
Rafiah Salient, 403, 411
Rakaḥ (the New Communist Party), 411
Red Army, 136, 157, 163–164, 166, 181, 231, 246, 249, 273, 343
"Red Scare," 265
Reiner, Ephraim, 354, 356–358, 367

Reiss, Issachar, 12, 27
Remez, David, 102
Ribbentrop-Molotov Pact, 102, 120, 157, 163
Rieger, Eliezer, 27
Riftin, Yaakov, 252–254, 259, 266, 270, 344, 382, 448
Romania, 327
Rommel, Erwin, 121–122, 166
Rubashov (Shazar), Zalman, 28, 138 see also: Shazar, Zalman
Ruppin, Arthur, 59, 154
Rzeszów (Reisha), 1, 3, 6, 7

S
Sabbath Law, 433
Sadan (Stock), Dov (Berl), 57, 154
Samuel, Herbert, 26
San River, 1
Sapir, Pinchas, 377
Sartre, Jean-Paul, 314
Schreiber, Eitan, 384–385
Scouting for Boys (Robert Baden-Powell), 8
Second Aliyah, 60, 182, 304, 450
Security Council Resolution (242), 240, 378
Shabtai, Yaakov, 457
Shadmi, Hannah, 280
Shadmi, Menachem, 355
Shaham, Nathan, 283
Shahar, Ehud, 338
Shamir, Moshe, 195–196, 349
Shapira, Michael, 431
Shapira ("Patchi"), Avraham, 370
Sharett (formerly: Shertok), Moshe, 114, 202, 305
Shazar, Zalman, 326
Shedemot, 370
Shem-Tov, Victor, 381, 405, 406, 436–437
Shenhavi, Mordechai, 19, 27
Shertok, Moshe, see Sharett, Moshe
Shlonsky, Avraham, 50, 281–282, 385
Shomrim, 15, 32, 43–45, 51–57, 68, 71, 73, 107–109, 115, 122, 124–125, 135–136, 170–171, 173–175, 182, 184–187, 194
Shomriya Battalion, 38, 45–46, 73
Siaḥ Loḥamim, 371
Siaḥ ("New Israeli Left"), 407–408
Sifriyat Po'alim, 160, 196, 434
Silver, Abba Hillel, 204–206

Simḥoni, Asaf, 233
Sinai Campaign, 313, 318–321, 343, 345–347, 353, 393
Sinai Peninsula, 311, 312, 320, 397, 399
Six Day War, 310, 314, 342, 351, 370–371, 377–378, 383–384, 392, 394–396, 399–401, 405–406, 409–410, 412, 418
Slánský, Rudolph, 261
Sneh, Moshe, 215, 264–266, 271, 435
Socialist Zionism, 447
Soviet Union, x, 155–156, 159, 162, 163, 193, 207–208, 215, 219, 242, 245–252, 261, 266, 287, 292, 315, 340, 342, 345–351, 371–376, 409, 425, 446, 452
Special Night Squads, 113–114
Stalin, Joseph, 136, 157, 158, 166, 168, 169, 248, 249, 250, 260, 275, 276, 306, 307, 342, 343, 344, 345, 349, 353, 416, 425, 437
Stalingrad, 122, 138, 159, 165–167, 181, 182, 247, 250, 318, 335
Steinlauf, Yitzhak, 382
Sterner, Henrik (Zvi), 8
Stock, Berl, see: Sadan, Dov
Sturman, Chaim, 113
Szczupak, Alexander (Sasha), 52

T
Tabenkin, Yitzhak, 171, 206, 214–215, 223, 227, 231, 245, 253, 258, 276–277, 298, 330
Talmi, Meir, 341, 389–390
Tarnawa Wyżna convention, 15, 22
Teḥezaqna, 213–214
Tehran Children, 151
Tel Aviv, 49, 50, 81, 84, 91, 99, 121, 129, 134, 140, 144, 195, 200–201, 213, 233, 241–242, 257, 261, 274, 275, 281–283, 295, 328, 336, 356, 359–360, 368, 373, 377, 385, 394, 397, 405, 415, 420, 422, 430, 436, 438, 443
territorial integrity, 312
Third Aliyah, 25, 29–31, 52, 59, 77, 104–105, 167, 180, 182
Tiberias, 29
Torczyner, Harry, 16
Transjordan, 112, 224
Trumpeldor, Josef, 22, 137
Tzahor, Zeev, 205

Index

U
U-2 affair, 350
Umm al-Aleq, 31, 34, 72
United Kibbutz movement (Hakibbutz Hame'uḥad), 64, 68, 102, 124, 182, 203, 246, 250, 256, 290n1, 292, 300, 337, 452
United Nations Special Committee on Palestine (UNSCOP), 207-210, 215
United Resistance Movement *(Tenu'at ha-Meri ha-Ivri)*, 199-200
Ussishkin, Menachem, 140

V
Vienna, 10-23, 11, 28, 57, 71, 260, 284
Vilna, 123-124, 158

W
Wadi Salib riots, 322-323
Wald, Chaim (Yaari's father), 1, 4, 5, 7, 11, 140
Wald, Esther (Yaari's sister), 3, 11, 99
Wald, Frieda (Yaari's mother), 1, 4, 11
Wald, Moshe (Yaari's brother), 2, 11, 12, 15, 23, 99
Wald family home, 2, 4, 11
Warsaw, 52, 57, 61, 91, 95, 121, 136-138, 170, 172-173, 333, 335
Warsaw Ghetto uprising, 133-137, 139, 172, 181, 336-338
Watad, MK Muhammad, 410
Weininger, Otto, 17, 76
Weizmann, Chaim, 59, 120, 236
West Bank, 310, 393, 399, 401, 403-405
Wingate, Maj. Charles Orde, 113
Wisłok River, 1
Wissotzka, Ida, 91

Y
Yaari, Anda, see: Karp, Anda
Yaari, Aviezer ("Avik", Yaari's son), 83-84, 86-87, 359
Yaari, Chaim (Yaari's son), 359-362, 364-365, 423
Yaari, Meir, ix, 1, 24
 admiration for Stalin, 169
 article in *Hapoel Hatza'ir*, 36-37
 attachment to music, poetry, and literature, 284-287
 attitude towards Arabs, 309-310, 311, 317-318
 attitude towards female members of the kibbutz, 77-78
 binational vision, 209-211
 comparison with Hazan, 416-422
 cultural life in the kibbutz, 97-98
 distinction between a party and a community, 65-66
 early childhood, 3-5
 education, 6-10, 16
 encounter with Abba Kovner, 177-179
 on establishment of a Palestinian state, 404
 on establishment of new settlements, 290-307
 on family life, 78-80
 final years, 435-437
 health issues, 90-91, 332-333
 intergenerational changes, 140
 on kibbutz education, 424-425
 literary correspondence, 287
 male solidarity, 76
 and movement's emissaries abroad, 122-126
 personality and leadership abilities of, x-xi, 41, 440-444, 448-449
 perspectives on World War II, 121
 sympathy and admiration for the Soviet Union, 163-169, 247, 250-252
 ties with writers and poets, 281
 books:
  Be-fetaḥ tekufa (At the Doors of an Epoch), 105, 140-141, 145-146, 148
  Be-derekh arukah (On a Long Road), 22, 198
  Bein ḥazon limẓi'ut (Between Vision and Reality), 351
  Be-meri vikkuaḥ (A Bitter Dispute), 104
  Qibbuẓ galuyot be-aspaqlarya shel yameinu (The Ingathering of Exiles in the Mirror of our Day), 304, 306, 307
  Mivḥanei dorenu (The Trials of our Generation), 349
 "Rootless Symbols," (article), 50, 52, 67, 69
Yaari (later: Groll), Rachel (Yaari's daughter), 70, 81-83, 140, 427, 432

Yaari, Tuvia (Yaari's brother), 2, 5, 11, 12, 86, 92, 391
Yaari (Groll), Yedidia (Yaari's grandson), 365, 422–423
Yaari, Yehuda, 38
Yadin, Yigael, 413
Yaffe, A.B., 431
Yishuv, 126–127, 129–130, 132–133, 151–152, 154–155, 162–163, 171, 196, 198, 200–201, 205, 210, 219, 247
Yizkor book, 10
Yom Kippur War, 29, 177, 199, 389, 399–405, 409–410
Yonathan, Nathan, 285
Yudin, Yehuda, 390

Z

Zamir, Israel, 431
Ze'irei Ziyyon association, 7–8
  as an organization of high-school students, 10
  in Reisha, 10
  rivalry between Hashomer and, 9, 14
  in Vienna, 12
Zemah, 29

Zhdanov, Andrei, *On Culture and Society*, 286
Zhdanovism, 283
Zionism, 60, 66, 67, 107, 129, 133, 143, 149–150, 155, 164, 171, 186, 188, 190, 193, 216–217, 248–249, 252, 302, 307, 310, 314
Zionist Congress, 59–60, 82, 91, 93, 102, 115–118, 120, 122, 149, 153, 160, 184, 187, 192, 205
Zionist leadership, 58–59, 115, 123, 126–127, 148
Zionist movement, ix, xiii, 59, 69, 112, 117, 126, 133, 137, 141–142, 147, 150, 165, 172, 188, 190, 197, 261, 272, 376, 433, 449
Zionist Organization, 26, 44, 57–60, 112, 116, 118, 120, 144, 202–204, 206, 303, 340
Ziyyon, Nissim, 385
ZOB (the Jewish Fighting Organization), 137
Zouabi, MK Abdul Aziz, 410
Zrizi, Zeev, 420
Zuckerman, Yitzhak (Antek), 172, 337

www.ingramcontent.com/pod-product-compliance
Lightning Source LLC
Chambersburg PA
CBHW071354300426
44114CB00016B/2058